Cameos Featured on the Front Cover

from left to right

Old Forge at Totnes
Kingston House, Staverton
Lampen Mill, St. Neot
Sharksfin, Mevagissey
Lewtrenchard Manor, Lewdown
Pandora Inn, Mylor

Cameos Featured on the Back Cover

from left to right

Osborne Hotel, Torquay
Sampsons Farm, Preston
Ilsington Hotel, Ilsington

Stay and Eat

At the end of each chapter you will find a diverse selection of venues in which to stay and eat. Prices vary to provide you with choice, but each venue has been selected for the quality of service, ambience and value for money.

AUTHOR'S ACKNOWLEDGEMENTS

I would like to thank all who have helped with this guide, whether directly or indirectly, especially Maya Hussell, Janet Pryde, Ricky Baynes and Sue Craxton. Many people, notably Roddy and Marcia Willett, Sam Richards, Peter Moyle, Mick Bramich, The Rev. John Scott and Dr Todd Gray, have, at different times, provided ideas, insights and sometimes stimulating conversation, a little of which has, I hope, percolated into the text. Thanks also to Judith Tomline, editor of *South Devon Life*, in which the occasional passage has previously appeared. All errors are of course my own. Thanks, finally, to everyone at the Kingsley Company, for their patience and good humour.

Bob Mann

The Editor wishes to thank Paul Bugge, Sue Dymock, Anna Simpson, John Roberts and Ian Pethers for their help, enthusiasm and support. Without their invaluable assistance this book would not have been possible.

ISBN ..0 9526555 1 9

The Discerning Visitor *(A four seasons guide)*
Published by
Kingsley Media Ltd. - Plymouth

Origination and typesetting by Typestyle - Ivybridge, Devon
Printed and bound in the United Kingdom
by BPC Wheatons - Exeter, Devon

Concept by M Willcocks PHD Dom.Sc.

Edited by Nicola Miles

STAY FREE
(No charge for accommodation)

There are a number of superb hotels and inns that are happy to offer accommodation free of charge, please turn to page 503 for details.

When booking accommodation at any venue featured in this guide, please remember that you are entering into a legally binding contract. Quite inexpensive insurance cover against any claim arising through sickness or other unforseen circumstances , causing you to cancel your holiday, can be obtained and most insurance offices will be pleased to discuss premiums.

Accommodation can be booked via the internet:
E-Mail: kingsley@hotels.u-net.com
Internet: www.kingsley-hotels.com

The publishers accept no responsibility for errors or omissions, for price variations or alterations to services as published in this guide. All published material in this guide was believed to be correct at time of going to press. Please check for any price alterations when booking accommodation.

KINGSLEY MEDIA LTD
FREEPOST PY2100, THE HOE, PLYMOUTH, PL1 3BR

Dear Reader,

My Team and I hope you will enjoy the selection of venues and places featured in this guide as much as we have enjoyed researching and compiling them.

Please help to make the next edition even better with suggestions of new places and venues for possible inclusion.

In return I will be more than happy to send you a complimentary copy of any one of the other guides in this series, subject to availability.

I look forward to hearing from you.

Bon appetit!

Yours sincerely

Nicola Miles
Editor

For comments pages please turn to page 507

TAKE ADVANTAGE

of

Marketing Promotions

send for your

FREE

KING GOLD CARD

As a King Gold Card member you will
become part of an exclusive

Purchasers Club

As a Gold Club Member you will receive a Newsletter
at varying intervals, featuring promotions by the
participating businesses in the *Discerning Visitor Guide*
series, and additional information ie:
*Local events etc., plus discounts on a wide range of
services, attractions and amenities .*

**To obtain your personal *FREE* King Gold Card
please turn to page 511**

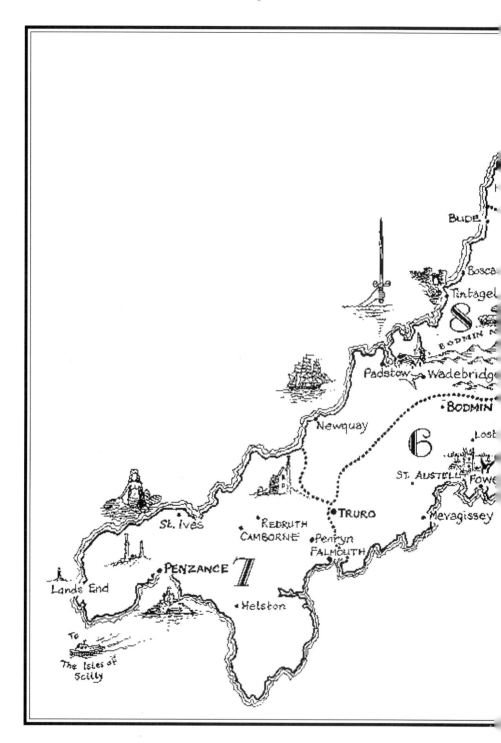

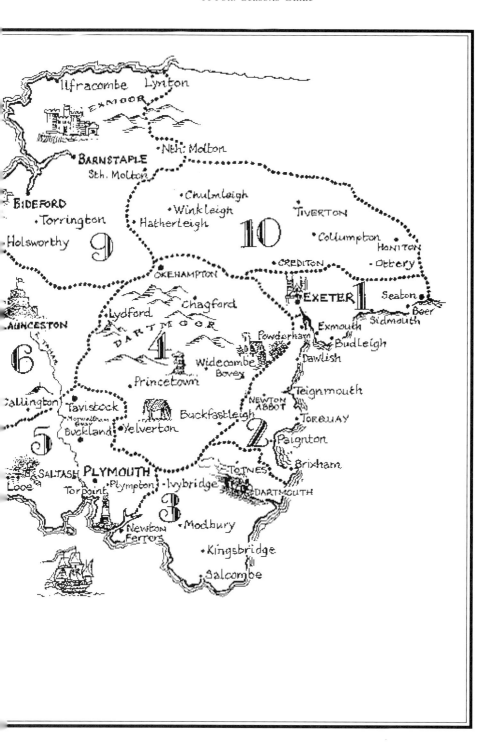

CONTENTS

"North Cornwall from Newquay to Bude"   **Page 377**
        Newquay, Padstow, Wadebridge,
        Bodmin Moor, Tintagel, Bude and Boscastle

Chapter Nine
"North Devon from Hartland to Lynton"   **Page 423**
        Hartland, Torrington, Bideford, Barnstaple,
        Ilfracombe, Lynton, North and Soutn Molton

Chapter Ten
"Mid and East Devon"   **Page 465**
        Hatherleigh, Winkleigh, Chulmleigh,
        Tiverton, Crediton, Cullompton, Ottery and Honiton

        Stay Free Section   **Page 503**
        Index   **Page 504**
        Readers Comments   **Page 507**
        King Gold Card Application   **Page 511**

INTRODUCTION

ABOUT THIS BOOK

The FOUR SEASONS GUIDE is a general introduction to the two counties of Devon and Cornwall. It also contains details of a wide range of hotels, restaurants, inns and guest houses to be found within them.

The book presents a tour of the region in a mainly clockwise direction, travelling from east to west along the south coast, and from west to east along the north. Each of its ten chapters covers a more or less well-defined and coherent area, followed by a selection of venues in that area where you can dine or stay. All the famous holiday centres and attractions are here, as well as some lesser-known places, and I hope it provides something of value and interest to all who are visiting this special part of Britain.

To facilitate easy reference, the names of places, when mentioned for the first time, are given in bold capitals (eg **EXETER**). Attractions are in capitals (eg PENDENNIS CASTLE) and telephone numbers are provided wherever possible. Opening times vary from season to season and from year to year, so it is always best to check before travelling miles to see something.

Although I have tried to proceed logically from one place to another within each area, you cannot see everything worth seeing in Devon and Cornwall without, at times, doubling back on yourself, taking minor roads instead of major ones and apparently going round in circles, so I have not attempted a mile-by-mile guide along any single route. Thus, the chapter on Torbay and the Teign Valley begins with its most famous town, Torquay, rather than with Dawlish, which is nearer to where the previous chapter ended at Exeter.

You will never discover the essential nature of the South West by sticking to main roads anyway, and there is no point in rushing. If you have the time, choose a part of the region you feel an affinity with, and try to explore it in detail, using the book as a general aid but creating your own route. Leave the car whenever you can, and use the local trains and buses, or seek out the networks of footpaths and cycle tracks. Don't disdain the famous tourist spots; they are rightly popular, and have the facilities and experience to cater for large numbers of people, but look as well for the quieter corners. Places of undiscovered beauty and interest can be found just a short journey away from the most gregarious visitor centres.

I have aimed to give an overview of what there is to see and do in the two counties, and to suggest something of the richness of their history, architecture, folklore and ecology. I hope I have been fair, and not imposed too many of my own preferences, but in a book of this type there is inevitably more to be said about Totnes or St Ives than about, say, Newton Abbot or St Austell. No guide can hope to contain everything, especially with the numbers of attractions changing all the time. If you should need more detailed information about a particular place, most towns now have a Tourist Information Centre - look for the distinctive *i* symbol - where the staff are usually helpful and well-informed (the telephone number of the TIC follows the first capitalised mention of the town).

Set out, then, to discover the romantic South West peninsula, a part of Britain which is almost unbelievably well-endowed with beauty, its landscapes ranging from wild moorland and rugged coastline to secure beaches and gentle farmland. Travel along smooth modern highways to elegant towns and cities, even the biggest of which remain human-scaled, then turn off onto winding lanes for ancient villages and lonely farmsteads.

The peninsula contains a wealth of castles, churches, mansions and a wide range of museums and heritage sites. There are gardens where tropical and sub-tropical plants, unknown elsewhere in Britain, prosper happily. You will always be able to sense, behind the new roads and buildings, a feeling of continuity with the past, often the very distant past, and creative or literary associations are to be found everywhere, adding an extra, imaginative dimension to your experience. Many parts of the region, particularly West Cornwall, South Devon and the towns and villages around the moors, have in this century attracted numbers of resident artists and craftspeople, whose work adorns the local galleries and studios.

Wherever you go in the peninsula you will enjoy the exhilaration of unpolluted air and a civilised pace of life and, at the day's end, you can settle down in the accommodation of your choice, whether sophisticated hotel, classic country inn or modest farmhouse, for the healing pleasures of good food, drink, convivial company and a comfortable bed.

THE PHYSICAL SETTING

Although this has to be an essentially practical guide, a brief look at the geographical and historical background of the area will help to set the scene. Devon and Cornwall occupy the extreme South West of England, a long, tapering peninsula which juts out into the Atlantic Ocean. It stretches for about a hundred and thirty miles from the Dorset-Devon border, and at its fattest, across the middle of Devon, is approximately seventy five miles wide from the north to south coasts. This narrows to twenty miles towards the end of Cornwall. It sounds like a small, easily-contained area, yet the figures are deceptive. When you are in it, the region seems vast, folding in upon itself endlessly. A lifetime would be too short in which to learn everything about just one of the two counties, with their myriad variations in geological structure and climate, and the effects of these differences on their history and culture.

The peninsula is an ancient land, created from a complicated diversity of rocks, many of them volcanic, all of them millions of years old. Through the middle runs a strong backbone of granite, exposed in the dramatic highlands of Dartmoor, Bodmin Moor and the moors of western Cornwall, which rise up in such contrast to the gentler terrain around them. The south coast is broken by numerous estuaries, drowned river valleys or 'rias', that reach far inland, and the climate is generally mild, giving the towns at the river mouths - Dartmouth, Salcombe, Fowey and Falmouth - a Mediterranean feel. The north coast is wilder, the Atlantic gales bending the trees into startling shapes many miles from the sea. The prevailing winds are westerly, warm and wet. The winters are mild, spring comes early and very often the autumn is almost as sunny as the high summer.

LAND AND PEOPLE

An important element of English popular culture, giving rise to endless jokes and prejudices, is the supposed division between North and South. Much more useful is the distinction made by geographers and historians between the Highland and Lowland Zones of Britain. This places Devon and Cornwall, with Wales and much of the North, together in the former, with the rest of the South and the Eastern Midlands in the latter. It is easier to understand the history and culture of the South West peninsula if its affinity with the other Highland regions is recognised: they are all areas of old rocks, of pastoralism, social insularity and stubborn survivals. They tend to have a strong non-conformist element. The connection can even be seen in the local taste, especially in Cornwall, for choral singing and brass bands. Although outwardly conservative, the people have a decidedly anarchic streak, which makes itself felt in the fierce independence of the region and the pride in its cultural traditions. Human beings have been living here from an early date, practising the timeless ways of making a living from land and sea - farming, fishing, quarrying, mining and basic crafts. Neolithic and Bronze Age remains litter the moors, and during the Iron Age, before and after the Roman period, the peninsula was home to the Celtic kingdom of the Dumnonnii, a loose tribal federation centred around hill-forts. Their name means 'the people of the land.' When the Romans left Britain and the Saxons started arriving from the east, a Dumnonian leader may have kept them at bay for a while, later entering European mythology as King Arthur.

The land east of the River Tamar was eventually penetrated by the Saxons and became the English county of Devon. The land to the west remained for a while obstinately Celtic, with its own language related to Welsh. Therefore, although they share many physical characteristics and have much in common, Devon and Cornwall are also very different, and appeal to different temperaments; people tend to love one and admire the other. They have had, for over a thousand years, separate histories and cultures, and like all neighbours, however close, they like to remind each other of this. Devon was always richer, full of substantial market towns, more connected withLondon and the great world.

Cornwall, although eventually drawn into the fold as an English county, remained a place apart, its people clinging to their Celtic identity. It is too simplistic to say, as some do, that Devon is Saxon and Cornwall Celtic; after so many centuries of interpenetration the people of both are as mixed a stock as people anywhere. But, in general, it is true that the further west you go, and the more mysterious and powerful the landscape becomes, so the more the Celtic past, like the granite beneath the soil, asserts itself. Throughout the 20th century the region's traditional activities have given way, in economic importance, to tourism, but today there is another significant trend. Increasing numbers of people are drawn to the Westcountry by the feeling that here, in towns and villages of manageable size, they can rediscover a sane, rooted way of life, where the closeness of the small community can be enjoyed without the narrowness and isolation that used to go with it. In terms of great historical changes, we are fortunate to have gone from the long agricultural age to the age of international communications without being too badly scarred by the intervening age of heavy industry. We therefore have no vast, decaying urban areas, but human-scaled settlements where, thanks to the fax and the Internet, one can live in a beautiful, peaceful environment whilst still being fully involved in the affairs of the world. The area thus has more to offer than just the loveliness of its landscapes - for many, it inspires a positive, civilised vision for the future as well. Devon and Cornwall are, undoubtedly, 'special'. They remain deeply in touch with their roots: multi-layered, resonant with history and legend. The present century has brought its share of unlovely roads and developments, but the essential qualities which make the region so unique, its position on the edge of the Atlantic, its rocks and soils, its moors and rivers, endure. Only a timescale much greater than ours can alter them.

The Discerning Visitor

CHAPTER ONE

Along The East Devon Coast To Exeter

"The County of red earth, ruddy apples,
rosy cheeks and honest men."
Sir Walter Raleigh

CHAPTER ONE

INTO DEVON: ALONG THE EAST COAST TO EXETER

Whether you enter Devon from the east or the west, you notice the difference almost immediately. The countryside really does become richer in foliage and deeper in colour, the lines and curves of the landscape are unmistakeably softer, and the hills have a decidedly rounder, fuller appearance, just as soon as you pass the signs that announce you to be within Devon's borders.

Although beautiful in the extreme, the scenery is usually less powerful or dramatic than that which can be found in Somerset, Dorset or Cornwall. Many have remarked that it is without, except on Dartmoor and parts of the coast, the element of mysteriousness which inspires and sometimes disturbs the visitor to those counties. Instead, Devon relaxes you, and draws you safely into its combes and along its sunken lanes, enfolding you within its myriad winding river valleys, so that you quickly feel at home and never want to leave. You begin to understand why so many generations of topographical writers have lost control of their prose styles once they have reached this large, fertile county whose name, as few poets have had the strength to resist pointing out, rhymes with heaven.

Devon is a county of great diversity, but there is somehow a unity as well, so that areas as different as the South Hams and the Tamar Valley, the foothills of Exmoor and the wide mid-Devon plateau north of Dartmoor, are all recognisably Devon landscapes, all equally typical in the vividness of their colours, as well as in the sense of security which is, undoubtedly, induced by such an abundance of beauty and gentleness of contour. Most of Devon's agricultural land was enclosed centuries before many other parts of England, so the fields, hedges and lanes, although man-made, appear more naturally part of the landscape, less imposed on it, than in some more eastern areas. Being a much older, deeper-rooted system of fields and hedges, it is fortunately also harder to destroy, so we don't have the endless prairies created in recent years in other parts of England by the demands of "agri-business". If you have the opportunity, go for a walk along a typical deep-sunken, high-hedged Devon lane, dense with ferns and flowers, taking you inexorably into the heart of the landscape.

Devon has always been, since the county was formed in Saxon times, an integral part of England, unlike Cornwall, but it is far enough from London and the great centres of culture and learning to be completely itself. In past centuries the roads were notoriously bad, and it took a long time to get here. Consequently Devon developed its own distinctive traditions, often markedly different from those further east. It had unique methods of farming, its own size of acre, its own breeds of cattle and sheep, as well as noticeable preferences in church architecture, house design and food.

In fact, it has often struck visitors as altogether too different. Early tourists in the Westcountry, during the 18th and 19th centuries, often complained that Devon, which they had expected to be a prettier version of the Home Counties, was inconveniently primitive, while Cornwall, which they hoped would be almost a foreign country, was a little too much like another English shire (they cannot have gone much further west than Truro).

The people of Devon have long been known for their almost complacent pride in coming from so rich and equable a place, and some observers have seen in this the source of the supreme confidence that the Devon heroes of the Elizabethan age displayed in their exploits. Sir Francis Drake's conviction that he could finish his game of bowls and beat the Armada is only the best known example of this tendency. Ronald Duncan, a 20th century poet and playwright who spent much of his life farming in North Devon, explained that it all came from the fact that you only need to put something in the ground in Devon and it will grow of its own accord.

It may be this powerful sense of confidence, nurtured by the great fertility of the land, which accounts for the seemingly paradoxical fact that, although Devon is such an inward-looking place, the most famous people to have come from the county have always been the most outward-going adventurers and explorers. From the Elizabethan "seadogs" to Scott of the Antarctic, from Sir

Francis Chichester to Ffyona Campbell, Devon has given birth to numerous restless spirits, who have journeyed to the ends of the earth, yet most of us who are born here find it a wrench to move out of the parish.

Of course, the affinity between Devon people and the sea is not difficult to understand, and throughout most of the county's history it was probably easier to communicate with the rest of the world by taking to the water than by any other means, so perhaps it is not such a mystery that so many Devonians have been compelled to set out from here on voyages of discovery.

The land of Devon is fertile in other ways. Innumerable writers and artists have found this a good place in which to find their roots, and have become unusually productive as a result, and many would agree with the founders of the Dartington Hall Trust, a wide-ranging experiment in rural regeneration in South Devon, that this was the right place for fulfilling their vision because "you can't stop things growing here."

A particularly rich and important time for Devon came at the end of the Middle Ages, and the period of the Tudors and early Stuarts. During the 15th and 16th centuries many fortunes were made from the cloth and tin-mining industries, and by extensive overseas trade and exploration (not to mention privateering). Much visual evidence remains of these years. During the 15th century a large number of Devon churches were rebuilt in the Perpendicular style, and are characterised by their elaborate roodscreens and their strong towers which, if not as ornate as the towers of Somerset, are remarkable combinations of architectural vision and engineering knowledge.

There is going to be less in this book about the minutiae of church architecture than you find in most guide books, but parish churches, quite apart from their religious function, can be wonderful repositories of history; their furnishings, monuments and atmosphere are often alive with stories and echoes from past ages. Visit them whenever you can find them open which, alas, is less often now than a few years ago.

As well as churches, Devon is rich in farmhouses and town dwellings rebuilt during the Elizabethan and Jacobean age. The county is not so well endowed with grand parks and big stately homes from later in the 17th and 18th centuries; more characteristic is the small manor or large farm house. This reflects the social history of Devon, in which great aristocratic landowners, although not entirely absent from the scene, were less significant than the more modest gentry, closely interrelated and regularly augmenting their numbers from upwardly mobile yeomen and merchants from the towns.

The south eastern part of the county, covered in this chapter, epitomises the quieter, most "English" qualities of the South West peninsula, but although it seems a long way from the wilder terrain beyond the Exe, from which geographers define the beginning of the Highland Zone, the countryside of **EAST DEVON** is very much part of the region. Its beauty provides a first, appetising taste of the show that is to come. Entering the county on the M5 or A30, you only skirt the area about to be described, but it deserves some attention before you follow the sun towards the west. You may even find it so congenial that you come back and stay for ever, as countless others have done before you.

The rocks of East Devon are mainly sandstone, giving it the famous soft, red soil, and the landscape is one of gentle hills and valleys, filled with orchards and quiet meadows. Thatched roofs, compact farmsteads, ancient trees and solid church towers rise above the fields, giving an impression of settled prosperity. This pastoral scene, watered by the East Devon rivers, the slow-moving and strangely named Axe, Yarty, Sid and Otter, can be a rich and sun-filled haven, a place for a relaxing holiday by the sea with unhurried explorations of the country villages nearby. Its visitor attractions reflect this gentleness: an electric tramway snaking slowly through the watermeadows, a world-famous donkey sanctuary. But the area is not without its livelier moments as well, as befits the birthplace of one of the greatest of Devon's visionary explorers, and a coastline that was once the haunt of notorious smugglers.

We shall finish our journey in the last chapter by looking at the inland towns of East Devon, but for now will follow the coast from the county border to the Exe estuary.

The enjoyable little town of **LYME REGIS** (Tourist Information 01297 442138) lies just outside the county boundary in Dorset, and thus has to wait for another volume in this series in order to be described. However, next to Lyme Regis, and within the borders of Devon, is a remarkable stretch of landscape, a long, slim corridor rich in every kind of wildlife and full of geological interest, which runs for about 6 miles along the coast towards Axmouth.

This is **DOWLAND'S LANDSLIP**, an area made famous as "the undercliff" in John Fowles' novel *The French Lieutenant's Woman*. A number of landslides, some of which happened centuries ago, but most of which occurred in the early Victorian period, have created what has been described as the least spoilt stretch of coast in southern England.

A series of deep chasms, filled to overflowing with trees and undergrowth as dense as a jungle, is hidden in a physically quite tiny area between the cultivated fields and the sea. In its luxuriance and undisturbed wildness there is nowhere else quite like it, and it has been a National Nature Reserve since 1955. The variety of trees, shrubs, flowers, birds and mammals that live here is extraordinary.

The local section of the SOUTH WEST COAST PATH runs through the slip, and those who wish to enjoy a fairly strenuous but rewarding walk through this magical place can join the Path at either end: look for signposts with an acorn on them, or the initials SWCP. Once you are in the landslip area, though, you have to complete the walk or go back, as there is no other way out. Have strong boots, protective clothing and be prepared to get muddy.

The **SOUTH WEST COAST PATH** is, at 613 miles, the longest footpath in Britain. It runs right around the peninsula, from Minehead in Somerset to Purbeck in Dorset, so whenever you are by the coast you will be on or near a section of it. Detailed information about the path, and the necessary maps, can be obtained at Tourist Information Centres. Anyone thinking of attempting the whole route will, obviously, need special equipment and some experience of long-distance walking, but short lengths of it are often easily manageable.

Each local section of the path tends, on signposts and in its publicity, to use its own name, so in South Devon you will see it referred to as the SOUTH DEVON COAST (or COASTAL) PATH, and in North Cornwall the NORTH CORNWALL COAST PATH. To add to the confusion it is also known as THE SOUTH WEST WAY. Very often the word "Heritage" is included somewhere in the title as well, but whatever it happens to be called, it is the same entity. Throughout this book it will be referred to by its full name as given above, but it won't be automatically mentioned every time we venture near the coast; just assume it is there!

As an alternative to the coast path, the EAST DEVON WAY, popularly known as "THE FOXGLOVE WAY", is a 40 mile inland walk through the countryside from LYME REGIS to EXMOUTH, and the newly created BUZZARD TRAIL, ideal, as its name suggests, for observing wildlife, covers 80 miles. Ask for leaflets about these and other paths at any TIC.

AXMOUTH, at the far end of the Landslip, is a quiet, one-streeted village above the water-meadows, with a stream running down the hill beside it. Though it is hard to believe now, Axmouth was once a busy port, possibly since Roman times when a major road, the Fosse Way from Lincoln, probably ended here. The 16th century antiquary John Leland called it "an old and big fisher town". The village is now about a mile from the sea, because the river has gradually silted up, leaving it literally high and dry for shipping, though it still has a peaceful little harbour and functions modestly as a FISHING and YACHTING centre. Nestling in the hills is a Norman church, expanded in the 13th century, dedicated to St Michael. There are some attractive thatched cottages, and WALKS in every direction take you into beautiful country. The woods of Pinhay, a house in the parish, are mentioned by Jane Austen in *Persuasion*. Nearby is the AXE CLIFF GOLF CLUB (01297 24371).

The Axe estuary is crossed near its mouth by the oldest surviving concrete bridge in Britain, built in 1877. On the other side of it is the pleasant little town of **SEATON** (Tourist Information 01297 21660). This is probably the first place on the East Devon coast which most visitors, other than walkers on the Path, will arrive at, by way of the A35 or A3052. With its mile long sandy BEACH and cliffs of varying colours, this small but popular resort, stretching along the shingle, is ideal for a restful holiday, and it has a good record for sunshine.

Although there is plenty of evidence that the Romans had a settlement here, when the Axe was a usable waterway, the town is mainly Victorian and later. It is generally rather genteel, as are most East Devon watering places, but a holiday park at one end gives it a youthful flavour as well. Black's Guide to Devon, published in 1867, described it as 'quiet without being dull and animated without being noisy', which stands up very well a hundred and thirty years later. There is plenty to do, in a mildly active sort of way, with bowling, tennis, swimming and putting facilities. The AXE YACHT CLUB can be found by the harbour. SEATON CARNIVAL, in August, is as colourful and varied as most such events in the Westcountry, while for quieter enjoyment, walks in the surrounding country will give you unforgettable coastal and inland scenery.

Colonel Percy Harrison Fawcett - "Exploration Fawcett" - the famous Devon adventurer who disappeared in the South American jungle in 1925, had a house in Seaton. Whilst in the area you should not miss a ride through the Axe Valley, past the silted river and its saltmarshes, on an open-topped, double-decker tram belonging to the SEATON AND DISTRICT ELECTRIC TRAMWAY (01297 21702). This is the country's last working narrow gauge electric tramway. Its pleasant route follows the line of a disused branch railway for about 4 miles, passing through Colyford to the terminus at **COLYTON.** Birdwatchers will particularly enjoy the journey's opportunities to see the wildlife of the estuary.

Colyton is a quiet old market town with narrow streets and an unusual church tower: it is a 'crossing tower' with an octagonal lantern at the top. It sits in a beautiful valley near the Blackdown Hills, and if you have a taste for wandering around old towns, looking at the houses and exploring the church and its monuments - here there is a restored 9th century Saxon cross - you will have an agreeable time. Many of the buildings date from the 16th, 17th and 18th centuries, including the old GRAMMAR SCHOOL. The shops are friendly, family-run establishments, and on Saturdays there is a lively "PETTICOAT LANE" MARKET. Other traditional pleasures to be found here are COLYTON FLOWER SHOW in July and the annual CARNIVAL in September: Colyton seems to possess all the wholesome ingredients of small-town life as many people dream of it. The countryside round about is full of old farms reached by deep lanes, as much archetypal lowland Devon as anywhere further west.

COLYFORD, now a tiny, out-of-the-way village by the low-lying meadows, is one of the county's numerous failed Medieval boroughs. Many Devon lords during the 12th and 13th centuries gave charters for small villages to hold markets and fairs, hoping they would turn into rich towns and repay the investment, but few made it and today they probably have no regrets about this. Sir Thomas Gates, an early Governor of Virginia from 1611-14, was born here. COLYFORD GOOSE FAIR in September is worth catching. A few miles from Colyton along the little river Coly is FARWAY COUNTRYSIDE PARK (01404 87224), occupying a hundred acres of grassy plateau and woodland. It features, amongst the usual SHOPS, CAFE and visitor facilities, an INDOOR TROPICAL GARDEN, BUTTERFLY FARM, PLAY AREA and MINIATURE GOLF. There is also an INTERPRETATION CENTRE for the natural history and ecology of the area.

Returning to Seaton, a mile along the coast is the famous old fishing village of **BEER**, the very name of which sets the mouth watering with anticipation. It is a beautiful spot, with the high white chalk cliffs of Beer Head, the most westerly chalk in England, contrasting strikingly with the more usual red Devon rocks. At low tide you can walk here from Seaton along the beach. Caves and quarries penetrate the cliffs and local fishing boats are still drawn up on the sands, while the attractive houses rise above and a stream runs down the street. It is the sort of place where you can happily idle away the time without any trouble at all, and is predictably popular with artists and craftspeople, who add their own colour to the scene. A lively REGATTA is held in August.

Beer's traditional associations are as markedly contrasting as its cliffs. It was once known equally for its lace and its smuggling. The lace for Queen Victoria's wedding dress was made here, not long after the most famous westcountry smuggler, Jack Rattenbury, a native of the village, published his autobiography. In it he openly described his adventurous, and sometimes desparate, activities. He is celebrated in an exhibition of smuggling at the museum in Budleigh Salterton, of which more later.

Just west of the village are the famous BEER QUARRY CAVES, in which regular GUIDED TOURS are given (01297 620986) and a MUSEUM display tells the story of the quarries. Near the base of the Beer chalk lies a white cretaceous limestone which was quarried extensively from the Roman period, and has been used for centuries to the most beautiful, uplifting effect, in Roman villas, cathedrals, churches and country houses both locally and further afield. Exeter's Cathedral and Guildhall, numerous screens and arcades in Devon churches and several local houses began here. It is always strangely poetic to find the very quarry out of which the stone for some loved or familiar building was dug, but this one in particular is awesomely full of ghosts and echoes. The great caverns extend for a quarter of a mile underground.

The PECORAMA PLEASURE GARDENS (01297 21542) are on the hills above Beer. A MINIATURE RAILWAY moves through the gardens, which give wonderful views of Lyme Bay. There are PICNIC PLACES, MINIATURE GOLF, a space for OPEN AIR PERFORMANCES and an indoor exhibition of MODEL RAILWAYS.

A few miles away is BLACKBURY CAMP, cared for by English Heritage. Now attractively covered with trees and foliage, this is an Iron Age Hillfort, defended by a bank and ditch. No charge is made for admission.

The next place along the cliffs, about 5 miles from Seaton, is **BRANSCOMBE**, lying in a cleft between the high rocks. It sometimes claims to be Britain's longest village, but is more an attractively winding, straggling series of hamlets, full of thatched cottages, ancient farms and mansions. THE OLD BAKERY (01297 680333), now owned by the National Trust, was, until 1987, the last traditional working bakery in Devon.

Branscombe church, dedicated to St Winfred, is particularly prized by connoisseurs of old churches for its peaceful atmosphere and sense of past ages. It has a Norman tower and an Elizabethan gallery, only reachable from outside, as well as box pews. BRANSCOMBE AIR SHOW is held in July, and the village APPLE PIE WEEK, full of lively events, takes place in September.

At BRANSCOMBE MOUTH is a fine shingle BEACH, with the cliffs rising on either side to hundreds of feet. In the Beer direction is HOOKEN CLIFF, the scene of another landslide in 1790 when nearly 10 acres dropped towards the sea. The result is a dramatic landscape of outcrops and pinnacles, often compared to castle ruins. Much of the coastal scenery here, on both sides of Branscombe, is protected by the National Trust.

The maverick archaeologist and writer T.C.Lethbridge retired from Cambridge to a 16th century house at Branscombe called Hole, where, during the 1960s, he experimented with pendulums and wrote speculative books on ghosts and other strange subjects. Two popular country writers of the early 20th century, W.H.Hudson and H.J.Massingham, were also very fond of the place, and it is not difficult to appreciate what drew them to it.

Inland, and a little to the west, is a much-loved and heartwarming attraction, not to be missed: THE DONKEY SANCTUARY (01395 578222) at the SLADE CENTRE, on the A3052 Sidmouth road. The sanctuary, founded in 1969 by Mrs Elizabeth Svendson MBE, has, over the years, given a home to nearly 7,000 donkeys and mules, many of which had been appallingly treated. Here they are guaranteed safety and care for the rest of their natural lives. It is probably the largest such establishment in the world, and the model for many others. When you see the joy and compassion the donkeys draw out of visitors of all ages, the greatest wonder is that such a place should be needed, but sadly it is.

Further on, about a mile from the sea, is the beautiful, unspoilt village of **SALCOMBE REGIS** (not to be confused with the other Salcombe, the famous port in the South Hams). Situated in a sheltered, south-facing combe, it has an attractive church and every year, in the spring, holds a lively COUNTRY FAIR.

Nearby is the NORMAN LOCKYER OBSERVATORY AND JAMES LOCKYER PLANETARIUM (01395 579941), an independent observatory dedicated to science education and the public appreciation of science. The famous Victorian astronomer Sir Norman Lockyer, who is buried in Salcombe Regis churchyard, is best remembered for his study of sunspots and for the discovery of helium. He founded the observatory just before the First World War, and its work was continued by his son, James. Lectures, demonstrations, guided tours and courses are held, and the public are welcome to walk and picnic in the grounds.

Another famous scientist lies in Salcombe Regis churchyard: Sir Ambrose Fleming, inventor of the helium valve.

At nearby **SIDBURY**, on the A375 from Honiton to Sidmouth, you can see well-preserved cottages, an interesting church with a Saxon crypt and Norman tower, and an old bridge over the river. There is also a remarkable Tudor house, surrounded by a four acre garden, which is still owned by the family who built it. SAND (01395 597230) came into the possession of the Huyshe family in 1560, and they rebuilt the mansion between 1592 and 1594. It is sometimes open in the spring and summer, but ring to check times before visiting. Another garden worth seeing, with the emphasis on old-fashioned, cottage-garden style and the preservation of wildlife, is at BUNDELS (01395 597312) - again, please ring in advance.

SIDMOUTH (Tourist Information 01395 596441) is invariably described as a genteel, old-fashioned watering place, which indeed it is, but there is more to it than this rather staid description suggests. Sheltered by dramatic, high, red cliffs, with wide sand and shingle BEACHES, plenty of sunshine and well cared for gardens and floral displays, it is a very attractive seaside town, and has a wealth of interesting architecture, containing hundreds of listed buildings. Sir John Betjeman thought the climate was almost tropical, and so palpable that you could reach out and grasp it. Sidmouth is also a lively social and cultural centre for the East Devon area, with always plenty going on.

Sidmouth began in the Middle Ages as a small but busy fishing town, which it remained for centuries. Then, in the late 18th century, the English middle and upper classes discovered the seaside, an environment they had previously recoiled from with a shudder. Now they decided it was beautiful and health-giving, and Sidmouth, being closer to London than anywhere further west, was one of the first resorts to develop.

The wealthy visitors built for themselves what they called 'cottages', many of which later became hotels. One of the best known, an excellent example of the style, is KNOWLE, now the headquarters of East Devon District Council. As well as these distinctive "cottage orne" buildings, many dignified regency terraces appeared along the front. Queen Victoria spent part of her childhood here, and the town quickly took on the refined, exclusive atmosphere which still comes to mind when its name is mentioned.

The traditional hard life of the fishing people continued, though, despite this overlay of gentlity. For a vivid impression of what it was like for the lower classes, seek out a book which has become a minor classic of social realism: Stephen Reynolds' novel *A Poor Man's House*, published in 1908, which describes the life of a Sidmouth fisherman's family in the early years of this century. It reminds us powerfully that Sidmouth was never all tea-parties and carriage drives.

Away from the sea front, with its big hotels and promenades, the town is pleasantly intimate, with winding streets, small friendly shops and lively pubs. The feeling is that of a real, if up-market, Devon town, and you will find plenty of places selling arts, crafts and antiques - SIDMOUTH ANTIQUES CENTRE, which includes the stock of three antiquarian booksellers, is well worth a browse. Wander around looking for the oval BLUE PLAQUES on the buildings, erected by the Sid Vale Association. These give a surprising amount of information, in a small space, on the history of the resort.

GUIDED WALKS around the town are organised from SIDMOUTH MUSEUM (01395 516139), which is housed in Hope Cottage, near the Parish Church. The museum was refurbished in 1995, and provides an excellent introduction to the area's local history and its personalities. These include the novelist R.F.Delderfield, a long-time resident of Sidmouth, whose books *Diana* and *A Horseman Riding By* entertained millions when they were serialised for television. Occasional demonstrations of traditional East Devon crafts are held at the museum. In FIELD'S DEPARTMENT STORE, in the Market Place, can be seen the VINTAGE TOY AND TRAIN MUSEUM, a fascinating collection of cars, trains and models from the 1920s to the 70s, and in the Old Fire Station in the High Street is MOTORING MEMORIES (no telephone number), an atmospheric display of motoring and garage memorabilia.

Sidmouth is rich in PARKS and GARDENS, the most popular being CONNAUGHT GARDENS, BLACKMORE GARDENS and THE BYES, where you can walk along by the River Sid.

Footpaths and cliff walks quickly take you out of the town into the beautiful countryside and along the coast, but there is plenty of recreation of all kinds available in Sidmouth. Visiting yachting enthusiasts are welcome to take temporary membership of SIDMOUTH SAILING CLUB (01395 512286), and fishermen are equally welcome to contact the SEA ANGLING CLUB (same number). There is a GOLF CLUB (01395 513451), while the SPORTS CENTRE (01395 577679) and SWIMMING POOL (01395 577075) have an excellent range of facilities.

For entertainment there is very often a show or a play going on at the MANOR PAVILION, and regular band concerts and exhibitions in the town are well advertised locally. Sidmouth has two annual CARNIVALS, the usual summer one in September and a CHRISTMAS CARNIVAL. The MIRROR NATIONAL DINGHY SAILING CHAMPIONSHIPS bring colour and excitement in May, whilst the REGATTA in August is not to be missed.

Sidmouth's greatest occasion of the year, however, has to be the world famous folk festival which occupies about ten days of every August. SIDMOUTH INTERNATIONAL FOLK ARTS FESTIVAL (Box Office: 01296 433669), to give the event its full name, is the largest in Europe, and one of the greatest of its kind anywhere. The festival is truly international. Singers, performers, dance groups, storytellers and musicians from every continent can be seen and heard at venues around the town, or mingling with the relaxed crowds walking between shows, and an increasingly important element of the festival is the ARTS AND CRAFTS FAIR. Away from the main entertainment areas and organised performances, you will always find a singing or 'jam' session going on in a pub.

West of Sidmouth is the pleasant village of **OTTERTON**, the main attraction of which is the restored OTTERTON MILL (01395 568521/567041). A mill at Otterton is mentioned in the Domesday Book, and the reference is probably to this one, as it has certainly been a working water mill for centuries. Wholemeal flour is made in the traditional way, and baked into bread which you can buy or eat in the RESTAURANT. There is an excellent MILL MUSEUM, a GALLERY showing fine arts and crafts, with exhibitions changing regularly, a number of CRAFT STUDIOS, SHOPS, and well laid out WALKS along by the river: enough to occupy the family for many hours.

Not far away is BICTON PARK (01395 568465). This is another good place for a day out, with more than enough to satisfy everyone's tastes. The house, once the seat of the Rolle family, is now an agricultural college, and not open. The famous GARDENS are often attributed to Le Notre, designer of the gardens at Versaille, but as he never came to England this is unlikely. Whoever masterminded them they are magnificent, covering 60 acres, and including Italian and American Gardens, lakes, a Palm House and Orangery, a Hermitage and many wonderful trees. Also at Bicton is a COUNTRYSIDE MUSEUM with a national collection of machinery and tools. There are CRAFT, GIFT and PLANT SHOPS, a CHILDREN'S PLAYGROUND, a MINIATURE RAILWAY and a CRAZY GOLF course.

A more modest garden, on a 4 acre smallholding with lovely views, 2000 varieties of plants and a wealth of animals and birds, can be visited at YONDER HILL, Combe Raleigh. Please telephone first: (01395 567541).

The pretty thatched village of **EAST BUDLEIGH** was, at one time, a market town and port, before the silting of the Otter made it unreachable by water. It is most famous as the birthplace of Sir Walter Raleigh, one of the greatest Devonians and the most versatile of England's many brilliant Renaissance figures; he was, amongst much else, a soldier, courtier, politician, seaman, explorer, poet, historian, philosopher, inventor and tragic hero. His personality has always fascinated, and his career, with its spectacular rise and fall, has taken on something of the pattern of myth. If we no longer make pilgrimages to his birthplace and revere him as one of the pioneers of the British Empire, he is still able to inspire and his story is endlessly retold. I shall not retell it here, but no one can visit this corner of East Devon without being reminded of him, and the other Devon adventurers of the Elizabethan age, most of them related to each other, who played such a prominent part in the history of that time.

Raleigh was born in about 1552 at a white, thatched, E-shaped farmhouse called Hayes Barton, which is not open to the public. Although he spent most of his full, tumultuous life away from Devon, he was obviously attached to his birthplace, as he later tried, unsuccessfully, to buy it. The Raleigh pew can be seen in the parish church.

BUDLEIGH SALTERTON (Tourist Information 01395 445275) is another quiet, old-fashioned resort, ideal for a peaceful holiday. Its popular image is that of a haven for retired people of comfortable means, and there is no doubt that this is true, but as with the other East Devon seaside towns, it does have its livelier moments as well, and as you walk through its quietly busy main street there probably won't be a bath-chair in sight. The town takes its name from the salt pans or salterns which used to be placed at the mouth of the Otter, and grew modestly as a watering place in Victorian times. The shops and cafes are small, locally run and good for personal service, and the place has an elegant, tranquil, very civilised air. A stream runs along beside the main street and there are lots of flowers.

For fine crafts, look for SHEILA AND JOHN STAFFORD in Stoneborough Lane. Please ring first: (01395 445443). Sheila Stafford produces beautiful etchings and silk paintings inspired by the local landscape, and her husband is a woodturner in British hardwoods. Budleigh has a pebbly beach with distinctive oval-shaped stones, familiar from the famous Millais painting

"The Boyhood of Raleigh", which so uplifted the hearts of earlier generations, and you can still locate the spot, against the sea wall, where the picture was set. It shows, as you will no doubt remember from the schoolroom, two boys listening to the tales of a grizzled seadog. The original is in the Tate Gallery in London.

There is, predictably, plenty about Raleigh in the FAIRLYNCH ARTS CENTRE AND MUSEUM (01395 442666) opposite the sea wall, as well as displays on smuggling, local geology and past industries. Lace-making demonstrations also happen here.

EAST DEVON GOLF CLUB (01395 443370) has a good reputation, as does the BUDLEIGH SALTERTON CROQUET CLUB (01395 442584) - croquet is just the sort of sedate, old-fashioned sport you would expect to be popular here.

SEA ANGLING and SAILING are available, and around the mouth of the Otter at the eastern end of the town is the 45 acre OTTER ESTUARY NATURE RESERVE, managed by the Devon Wildlife Trust. Footpaths on both sides of the river give access to the reserve, which is rich in flora and bird life.

At the other end of the town WEST DOWN BEACON, rising to 400 feet, gives spectacular views of the coast in both directions.

Budleigh Salterton's GALA WEEK takes place at the end of May, and, most appropriately for this little Victorian town, they have a GILBERT AND SULLIVAN OPERETTA in July, presented by Imperial College Operatic Society.

EXMOUTH (Tourist Information 01395 222299) is the largest and newest town we have yet come to on the Devon coast; in fact it is one of the biggest urban areas in the county. The word for it is spacious: Exmouth is spacious in its two-miles of broad, sandy beaches and in its sea-front with well-tended gardens, its large hotels and shopping centres, its streets of terraces and smart suburban houses. The climate is warm and sunny, while the white buildings of the town, and the palm trees in front of them, give a suggestion of the Riviera. Relax, and enjoy a leisurely exploration of its many attractions.

It is actually an old settlement, possibly a port and fishing centre from pre-Roman times, but you get little sense of this, as Exmouth only began to grow as a real town in the 18th century. Its development occurred because it was well placed to become a resort for the gentry of Exeter and beyond - it describes itself as Devon's oldest seaside town, and has a number of good Georgian houses. The presence of two well-known and long-suffering widows, Lady Byron and Lady Nelson, made it socially desirable in the 19th century. Since then it has expanded to embrace the nearby villages of Littleham and Withycombe Raleigh, although these retain an atmosphere of their own, and their churches are worth looking at. Unlike Sidmouth and Budleigh, and despite its origins in such class-conscious days, Exmouth has no predominant atmosphere of old world exclusivity; instead it is a friendly, family resort and has always been popular with a broad spectrum of society. The fact that the town contains part of the new and far-flung University of Plymouth, on the campus formerly known as Rolle College, helps to make its resident population an interesting and healthy social mixture. Indeed, the town once had a certain air of raffishness. A late 18th century American visitor carefully noted, in his journal, the large numbers of lascivious young women from Exeter who regularly descended on Exmouth, their "insufferable undress and ill-breeding" deeply offending his sensibilities. I have yet to encounter them.

The BEACHES at Exmouth provide everything that a beach should - miles of sand, rock pools, interesting rock formations, cliffs and plenty of room for everyone.

WATER SPORTS are well catered for, with the EXE SAILING CLUB (01395 264607), EXE POWER BOAT AND SKI CLUB (01395 278728), EXMOUTH SAILING SCHOOL (01395 222795) and EXMOUTH WINDSURFING CENTRE (01395 276599).

The town has excellent recreation facilities with an INDOOR POOL at the EXMOUTH SPORTS CENTRE (01395 266381), and a FUN POOL can be found on the sea front. SEA ANGLING and FISHING TRIPS along the Exe are also well advertised there. GOLF is at Phear Park (01395 277514).

One of the most popular attractions in Exmouth is THE WORLD OF COUNTRY LIFE at Sandy Bay (01395 274533). Ideal for family entertainment, with activities for all weathers and something to appeal to all ages, this 40 acre site contains a deer park, pets centre, falconry displays, a Victorian Street of gift shops, historic vehicles, working machinery, a craft studio, an adventure playground, bouncy castle and safari train rides. Animals include Fallow Deer, Llamas, Highland Cattle, Soay Sheep, Donkeys, Guinea Pigs and Goats. There is a RESTAURANT and PICNIC AREA.
On the sea front can be found the world's largest "00" GAUGE MODEL RAILWAY (01395 278383), 7,500 feet of it, weaving between miniature landscapes and around outdoor fishponds complete with Koi Carp.

EXMOUTH MUSEUM, in Sheppards Row (no telephone number), contains a Victorian kitchen, a 1930s dining room, railwayana and a clock mechanism. The best known historic feature of the town, however, is the unique house in Summer Lane known as A LA RONDE (01395 265514), now owned by the National Trust.

A La Ronde is a beautiful 16-sided house completed in about 1796. It was built for two spinster cousins, Jane and Mary Parminter, after their return from a tour of Europe, where they were inspired by the design of San Vitale's church in Ravenna. As well as its delightful form, the house contains a special collection of objects and artefacts brought back by the ladies, and is richly decorated with prints, pictures and needlepoint, some of it their own work. Of particular interest are a feather frieze and gallery encrusted with shells. Because of their delicacy these must now be viewed by closed circuit television. The garden has a ha-ha and some fine trees.

Further along Summer Lane is POINT OF VIEW, a chapel and almshouses for elderly women, also built by the Parminter ladies.

Modern Exmouth, away from the sea, is a busy urban centre, with everything you expect to find in a large town. It has a full range of shops, pubs and restaurants. The INDOOR MARKET (01395 264347), off The Strand, is worth browsing around, and in Albion Street can be found a number of ANTIQUE and JUNK shops. ANTIQUE FAIRS are also held every month at the PAVILION.

Events to look out for in the town include FLOWER SHOWS in the spring, summer and autumn, the CARNIVAL in July and the WINTER CARNIVAL in November. The Royal Marines Band from nearby Lympstone Barracks plays regularly in the town. Check in the TIC for other sporting and cultural activities throughout the year.

If one side of Exmouth faces the sea, another leads us inland along the broad, beautiful estuary of the River Exe, which we now follow towards Exeter. Despite its busy-ness it is a haven for wildlife, with regular BIRDWATCHING CRUISES leaving from the town. It is also popular with fishermen and sailors, not to mention those who just like to sit and watch the ever-changing tides and movements of the water.

Visitors of a literary bent will be reminded of the Victorian novelist George Gissing, who lived in Exeter during the 1890s and set his book *The Private Papers of Henry Ryecroft* in the countryside of the Exe. Its main character, a sensitive soul worn out by literary hack work, finds peace and healing by spending his days idling here by the river, and waiting for parcels of books from London. There is also the tantalising sight, across on the far bank, of such appealing places as Dawlish Warren, Starcross and Powderham Castle, all of which are covered in the next chapter.

On this side, above the estuary, is the pleasing expanse of WOODBURY COMMON, with splendid views of the estuary and an Iron Age hillfort. The village itself is beautifully situated amongst woodland. WOODBURY PARK GOLF CLUB (01395 233382) is nearby.

LYMPSTONE is an attractive village on the muddy bank of the Exe, with narrow streets, lovely cottages and good views. A striking building near the river is the PETERS' TOWER, built at the end of the last century as a memorial to Mary Anne Peters, who was generous to the local poor. Next to the village is the ROYAL MARINES COMMANDO TRAINING CENTRE.

A few miles further along, where the placid River Clyst joins the Exe, sits the little red and white town of **TOPSHAM** (pronounced "Tops-ham" or "Tops'am": there is no "sham" in Topsham, a statement which I offer, free, to the town's publicity committee). Most visitors find this ancient, decayed port completely restful and charming. Compact, full of interesting buildings, it is the sort of place in which to wander aimlessly around for a few hours, enjoying the strongly individual atmosphere. The great Devon historian W.G.Hoskins thought Topsham was the "most rewarding" small town in the county, and noted its "multitudinous cats". There is, perhaps, something almost feline about the place itself; you can visualise it as a large dozing cat, lazily stretching out a paw towards the river, while the yachts and fishing boats rock gently on the water and the wooded hills of Haldon on the far bank shimmer in the haze.

Not everyone has liked Topsham, though. The author of Black's 1867 Guide to Devon, who was so judicious in his opinion of Seaton, called it "one of the oddest of odd English towns, straggling along the river-bank for a mile or so, with a sort of restless, despairing motion as if it longed to get rid of itself". Most visitors, however, past and present, have taken nothing but pleasure in this old river town, where rich merchants once supervised the unloading of their ships by the spacious warehouses, and where you can now enjoy a drink in large, roomy pubs which echoed for centuries to the voices of sailors, fishermen and smugglers.

Topsham has one of the longest histories of any community in Devon. It is likely that a small Celtic trading settlement existed here, by the estuarine mudflats, before the Romans arrived. It was certainly, during the Roman period, a busy port, linked to the tribal capital of Exeter by a straight, four mile Roman road, which still connects the two places. It became a wealthy and important town during the Middle Ages, thanks to a tantrum by a very powerful and determined woman, which is still commemorated by the name of a nearby roundabout - not many road features have such historic resonance.

Isabella de Fortibus became Countess of Devon in the late 13th century. In 1284 she fell out with the city authorities of Exeter, and punished them very effectively by having a series of dams or weirs built across the Exe, preventing ships from getting near the city and thus ruining it as a port. Everything then had to be landed at Topsham and transported by road. Topsham became rich, and Exeter didn't recover until the Ship Canal, the first in England, was constructed in the 16th century, but even this never fully compensated for the damage. Isabella's action is remembered today in the name "Countess Wear".

Topsham's centuries of being the port for Exeter resulted in the variety of beautiful, distinctive merchants' houses which remain in the town, with their characteristic courtyards and sheltered walled gardens, of which you get the occasional seductive glimpse when walking about. The most famous of these are the so-called "Dutch Houses" in the Strand, built in the early 1700s. The local wool merchants traded extensively with Holland at that time, and they brought back as ballast quantities of Dutch bricks, using them in houses based on what they remembered seeing in the Dutch ports.

The best known house is TOPSHAM MUSEUM at 25 The Strand (01392 873244), which covers every aspect of the town's maritime history and the wildlife of the estuary; it also has a few surprises, like a tribute to the actress Vivien Leigh, whose first husband was a local man. The cliff-top Parish Church is generally agreed to be undistinguished, having been drastically restored by the Victorians, but is saved from being totally disappointing by its red sandstone tower and the spectacular views from the churchyard.

You are never far from the sight, sounds and smells of the river in Topsham, and it is satisfying to buy freshly caught fish from the Exe in the local fishmonger's shop, or dine on it in one of the riverside pubs. Most shops in the town are enjoyably old fashioned and individual. THE RESERVE GALLERY in Fore Street shows and sells the work of local artists and craftspeople, as does THE EXE GALLERY, while at JOEL SEGAL BOOKS the town has a second hand bookshop worthy of its atmosphere and sense of history.

The smaller of Topsham's two rivers, the Clyst, gives its name to no less than six interesting little villages on the eastern side of Exeter, lying in peaceful red-soil countryside. All are worth exploring. The nearest to Topsham, **CLYST**

ST GEORGE, has a modern church, built after the old one was gutted in 1940. The ancient farm of Marsh Barton, which now gives its name to a large industrial estate, was the home, for over six centuries, of a family with the distinctive name of "Sokespitch", sometimes rendered as the even more distinctive "Suckbitch". They were a dynasty who, it was said, never increased or decreased their holdings by so much as an acre in all that time; such is the complacency which this soft landscape can induce.

At **CLYST ST MARY** is the oldest recorded bridge in Devon, first mentioned in 1238. The history of the village reminds us that this countryside has not always been entirely peaceful - it saw the final defeat, in 1549, of the Prayer Book Rebellion. This celebrated protest came about because the people of Devon and Cornwall strongly objected to the imposition of an English form of service, in place of the familiar Latin; the Cornish, in particular, were against it, because, having their own language, many of them didn't even understand English. The rebels, mainly ordinary people armed with pitchforks, but including some gentry as well, were only put down when the government employed foreign mercenaries against them. The village was burnt during the final massacre.

Today, Clyst St Mary hosts the annual DEVON COUNTY SHOW each May at the WEST POINT CENTRE (01392 446000). One of the major events of its kind, the three-day show has something for everybody, and gives a vivid feel of Devon country life as it is in the 1990s. With show jumping, agricultural displays, trade exhibitions, entertainment of all kinds and plenty to eat and drink, it is a rich, satisfying mixture of the modern and the traditional. The centre is used at other times of the year for a variety of events, including ANTIQUES FAIRS and POINT TO POINT RACING.

To the north east, **BROADCLYST** is a large parish about seven miles from Exeter. Of its many ancient farms, the one called Churchill is worthy of mention, as it is where the great family of Sir Winston, and his illustrious ancestor the Duke of Marlborough, first enter recorded history; they named themselves after the farm, as so many families did, back in the 12th century.

Broadclyst is best known today for the presence of KILLERTON HOUSE (01392 881345), local headquarters of the National Trust. The present house was built in 1778 for the distinguished old Devon family the Aclands, who have owned the estate since the Civil War. It is a low, elegant, pleasingly-proportioned building of yellowish stone, backed by trees and with an intimate rather than an imposing air. It is furnished as a family home and includes the PAULISE DE BUSH COSTUME COLLECTION and a Victorian laundry. There is a RESTAURANT, TEA ROOM and SHOP selling books, gifts and plants. Occasional concerts are held here during the EXETER FESTIVAL in July.

The GARDENS and surrounding PARKLAND at Killerton are beautiful at all times of the year. Many rare trees, rhododendrons and other shrubs abound, and there is an ice-house and an early 19th century rustic summer house called the "Bear Hut". Well-laid outwalks in the woods have been prepared, and leaflets are available to help you find your way around.

If you particularly enjoy seeking out smaller, private gardens to look at, 1 FEEBERS COTTAGE (01404 822118) at Westwood, near Broadclyst should appeal to you. It is a modern cottage garden with a maze of paths, specialising in alpines and other plants which like heavy clay soil. Please ring, of course, before visiting.

EXETER (Tourist Information 01392 265700), the county town of Devon, has always been the regional capital for the Westcountry as a whole, since the days, nearly two thousand years ago, when it was the Roman city of Isca Dumnoniorum and the tribal peoples of Devon and Cornwall were ruled - insofar as they ever were - from here. For much of its history it has been as important to Cornwall as to Devon; the diocese of Exeter included both counties for many centuries, and there was never any town of comparable size or stature across the Tamar. Exeter has one of the greatest Medieval cathedrals in England. It contains national treasures like the unique *Exeter Book*, the 10th century collection of Anglo Saxon poetry which has been in the library of the cathedral for a thousand years. Although it suffered terrible damage during the Second World War and, according to some sensitive observers, it has suffered terrible damage from postwar planners, its historic shape as a compact walled city can still be traced easily, and many important buildings and features from past ages survive.

As well as being an administrative and ecclesiastical centre, Exeter is a university town and a focus for the artistic and intellectual life of the region. Its ambience is bright and warm, the old red sandstone buildings blending well with the newer red brick ones, and its streets are lively, full of young people, attractively kept and a pleasure to perambulate. There are parks, gardens and quiet oases of peace, very often next to a rose-red piece of city wall, "half as old as time", or a tiny Medieval church, where you can sit and meditate on the continuity with past ages which can be felt so vividly in an old place like this. Exeter seems to successfully combine a respect for a rich and colourful history with an awareness of the needs and energies of the present.

Above all, with a population of 105,000, it is just about the right size for a city - big enough to have everything that a city should properly provide, but small enough to be knowable, even intimate. You can stand at many points in its centre and see the fields of the surrounding countryside, just as the Medieval citizen, after his day's work, or the Georgian squire, up from the country to stay in his town house, could do.

The natural site of Exeter is superb. A steep sandstone ridge, rising a hundred feet above a bend in the River Exe, with long views in every direction, it is the archetypal situation for historic towns and cities all over Europe, an obvious place for people to settle for both defensive and commercial purposes. For the Romans it was the perfect frontier town from which to keep an eye on the highland region beyond the river, and walking down the steep hill of Fore Street, even now, you can get a sense of this function.

You reach Exeter today by way of the M5 motorway, which stops here and becomes the A38 to South Devon and Plymouth, and the A30 to Okehampton and Cornwall. By rail you can come from London and the rest of the country via Paddington or Waterloo. Or you can get here by AIR (01392 364816).

If you enjoy an organised but informal way of learning about the place you are in, the EXETER GUIDED TOURS, led by the distinctive, well-informed "REDCOAT GUIDES", are worth joining. Walks covering many aspects of the city's history, and one which covers its ghosts and legends, are available throughout the year - ask at the TIC for details. During the SUMMER MONTHS, SIGHTSEEING BUS TOURS leave from the BUS STATION in Paris Street and outside the CENTRAL RAILWAY STATION (for information on the tours ring 01392 233010).

Any appreciation of the charms of Exeter must, of course, begin with a visit to the CATHEDRAL OF ST PETER (Cathedral Office 01392 55573, Visitors' Officer 01392 214219).

Exeter has been a cathedral town since 1050, when Bishop Leofric moved the headquarters of the diocese from Crediton. Completed in its present form by the 14th century, the building still dominates the city skyline as it has for hundreds of years. It is unique amongst the cathedrals of England for its twin Norman towers, and inside it has the longest unbroken vaulted roof of any in the country, stretching for 300 feet. This roof is the result of the most perfect blend of religious and artistic inspiration, together with the practical, engineering ability to manifest that inspiration, which is characteristic of Medieval art.

The vaulting at Exeter is generally agreed to be one of the supreme masterpieces of English, and even of European, Gothic architecture. Ignore the rather obvious attempts to make the cathedral into a "heritage experience" which have sadly crept in since the 1980s, and instead find yourself a quiet seat, then look up.

Other special features of the building include the high Bishop's Throne and the Image Screen on the West Front, recently cleaned and restored to its bright colour. TheCATHEDRAL SHOP sells books in many languages, as well as gifts and souvenirs, and is particularly good for recordings of Early Music. The REFECTORY RESTAURANT serves light meals during the day. In the CATHEDRAL LIBRARY (01392 72894) can be seen early manuscripts and printed books, including of course the priceless *Exeter Book*.

Outside, the CATHEDRAL CLOSE is a pleasantly expansive but intimate green space, surrounded by interesting old buildings. The headquarters of worthy local bodies like the Exeter Institution and the Devonshire Association for the Advancement of Science, Literature and The Arts are to be found here, giving a feeling of Trollopian continuity such as one expects in an old cathedral town; scholarly looking men and women move quietly in and out of these placid houses as if all is well with the world.

The lawn is usually crowded with people, and if you enjoy people-watching you can sit on the wall or the grass and absorb the sights. Very often you will find a CRAFT FAIR or something of the sort going on here.

MOLL'S COFFEE HOUSE, an Elizabethan merchant's house, which is not actually a coffee house now, and the SHIP INN, have lots of historical resonance. The latter was popular with the great Devonians of the 16th century, meeting in Exeter to do the county's business; Sir Francis Drake is supposed to have stated that he prefered it to any ship except his own.

The ROYAL CLARENCE on the corner was the first English inn, during the 18th century, to describe itself by the French word 'hotel.' Why? Because the landlord happened to be a Frenchman.

In front of the cathedral is a dignified statue of the Elizabethan theologian Richard Hooker, a local man who, in his *Laws of Ecclesiastical Polity*, was largely responsible for setting the characteristically tolerant intellectual tone of the Church of England, a reminder that the great contribution to the nation by Devon people during the Tudor period was not confined to swashbuckling. Other famous Exonians include Nicholas Hilliard the painter, Sir Thomas Bodley, diplomat and founder of the Bodleian Library at Oxford, and Matthew Locke the composer.

Below the grass of the Close, unknown about until the 1970s, lie the remains of a Roman basilica and bath house, information about which can be found in the museum.

After the cathedral, the GUILDHALL (01392 265500) in High Street is probably the most interesting historic site in Exeter. Begun in 1330, with later additions, it is one of the oldest civic buildings in England. It is open to the public when not in use, and displays include the city silver and some interesting portraits.

TUCKER'S HALL (01392 436244) is another Medieval building, as is the 11th century ST NICHOLAS PRIORY (01392 265858), both in or just off Fore Street, and worth spending time looking at. The Priory contains a Norman undercroft and a 15th century guest hall and kitchen. The UNDERGROUND PASSAGES (01392 265887/265858) in High Street are a unique feature of the city. Probably created in the Middle Ages to provide water, they are extensive and very atmospheric. The City's GUIDED TOURS cover all these places (see above).

Near Fore Street is the little Medieval street of STEPCOTE HILL, at the bottom of which is the famous "HOUSE THAT MOVED", a 15th century dwelling that was jacked up and moved during the 1970s to allow for roadworks.

The area around the river is an important and very attractive part of old Exeter, and the QUAY HOUSE VISITOR CENTRE (01392 265213) provides an excellent introduction to this aspect of the city. Unfortunately, the world-famous Maritime Museum has closed, a victim of the recession.

The main museum in Exeter is the ROYAL ALBERT MEMORIAL MUSEUM AND ART GALLERY (01392 265858) in Queen Street. This contains collections of natural history, fine art, ceramics and glass which are of national significance, while the ethnographic material from Africa and the Pacific demonstrate local connections around the world. The local history and archaeology of Exeter and Devon are also extensively recorded, while exhibitions in the art gallery change regularly and are always of a very high standard. The museum has a SHOP and RESTAURANT.

The DEVONSHIRE REGIMENT MUSEUM can be found at Wyvern Barracks (01392 218178). The Regiment itself is now combined with the Dorset Regiment, and has its own chapel in the cathedral.

Exeter is a good city for the arts of today as well as the past. The DEVON AND EXETER ARTS CENTRE (01392 421111) is always busy, with exhibitions, performances, workshops, talks, information and, not least, a friendly bar and restaurant. The centre, in partnership with EAST DEVON DISTRICT COUNCIL, also organises a series of events and shows in the towns and villages of the District.

The SPACEX GALLERY (01392 431786) in Preston Street has a high reputation for the visual arts, while the NORTHCOTT THEATRE (01392 493493) has, since it was built in the 1960s, become one of Britain's leading regional theatres. Although situated on the campus of EXETER UNIVERSITY - a particularly beautiful one, as is appropriate for the county, with landscaped parks and gardens of great peace and rich colour - it is independent from the university. Performances also take place in the BARNFIELD THEATRE (01392 71808) and there is usually an event of some kind going on at ST GEORGE'S HALL (01392 265866). Many pubs and clubs feature live music and entertainment.

EXETER FESTIVAL (Box Office 01392 499123), in July, is one of the most enjoyable and wide-ranging regional cultural festivals in the country. A spectacular range of events, from concerts by leading orchestras and ensembles to flower shows and guided nature walks, takes place over two weeks, using every available venue from the cathedral and the university to churches, pubs, open spaces and country houses in the surrounding area. The festival seems to embrace the whole field of creativity and entertainment without anyone being troubled by questions of elitism or populism, highbrow or lowbrow; they just manage to provide something for everyone.

For sport and recreation there are a number of centres around the city, including theRIVERSIDE LEISURE CENTRE (01392 221771), the PYRAMIDS SWIMMING AND LEISURE CENTRE (01392 265898) and the CLIFTON HILL SPORTS CENTRE (01392 265888). EXETER GOLF AND COUNTRY CLUB (01392 876303) is on the way to Topsham.

LEAGUE FOOTBALL can be seen at EXETER CITY FC at their ground at St James' Park (01392 54073), and EXETER SPEEDWAY (01392 51479) has included amongst its members such international stars as Ivan Mauger.

Appropriately for a regional capital, Exeter has always been a shopping centre, and together with the major chains it contains a wealth of specialist and individual shops. The city does well for bookshops, both new and secondhand, imaginative clothes shops and craft centres. Look for DILLONS, EXETER RARE BOOKS, CHADNI CHOWK and THE GREAT BEAR as an example of each. There are also numerous outlets for gifts and antiques.

The pubs and wine bars of the city are equally enjoyable, with something for every taste. COOLINGS WINE BAR in Gandy Street, near the Arts Centre, is justly popular, as is the TURK'S HEAD, where Dickens is supposed to have seen the model for the "fat boy" in *Pickwick Papers*. One of the most atmospheric pubs I have been to anywhere is the DOUBLE LOCKS, out on its own beside the canal. The road to this wonderful pub leads nowhere else, and it is the sort of place you never wish to leave; local folklore, in fact, is rich in stories of people who disappeared from job or family, only to be found living here in happy obscurity. Seriously, its combination of waterside setting, choice of real ales and socially diverse clientele makes it a gem of a hostelry.

Whatever your particular interests or needs, you will find Exeter one of the most attractive small cities in Britain, and fully worthy of the county of which it is the ancient centre.

THE ROYAL GLEN HOTEL,
Glen Road,
Sidmouth, Devon EX10 8RW
Tel: 01395 513221 Fax: 01395 514922

AA/RAC Three Crowns.
ETB Four Crowns.

The same family have run this elegant, delightful hotel for over 100 years and today with Orson Crane at the helm it is outstanding. It stands a little set back from the seafront at the quiet end of Sidmouth and has an attractive secluded garden. Anyone who stays in Sidmouth or indeed who has read about this elegant little seaside town will no doubt be aware that Queen Victoria as a child lived here with her parents the Duke and Duchess of Kent in this very house and in one room there is a bullet hole in the window of the nursery she occupied, fired from an air pistol belonging to a small boy playing in the garden; it missed the Princess by inches and in so doing failed to alter the history of England. All this is interesting but it is only one small part of the charm of the Royal Glen.

Furnished throughout with taste and discernment and an eye for colour, every room has its own character. The Drawing Room is unique in its oval shape and has some splendid period furniture. The Kent Bar Lounge is quiet and relaxing and a great place in which to have a pre-dinner drink before going into the elegant and beautifully furnished Kent Dining Room to enjoy a meal that will be memorable both for the delicious food and the fine selection of wines. At night you may well find yourself sleeping in the Duchess of Kent's boudoir, the Duke of Kent's bedroom or even in the Princess Victoria's nursery. Where you will see a subtle blend of Royal heritage and modern luxury. All the bedrooms have private bath or shower facilities, colour TV, telephone and tea making facilities and each is furnished in accordance with the tradition of the hotel. The Royal Glen is open to non-residents for light lunches, bar snacks, afternoon teas and dinners. The hotel also specialises in small parties and functions.

Everywhere there is a sense of the past which is charming and perhaps the only real concession to modern times is the heated indoor Swimming Pool complex. Sidmouth is wonderful at anytime of the year and a stay at the Royal Glen will never be forgotten.

USEFUL INFORMATION

OPEN; February 1st-January 3rd
CHILDREN; Welcome

CREDIT CARDS; All cards
LICENSED; Yes. Fine wines
ACCOMMODATION; 33 ensuite rooms.
GARDEN; Secluded. Small putting area
RATES; High Season, from £49.50 D/B&B.
Low Season from £40 D/B&B.
Children sharing, meals only charged.
(All room charges vary according to category)
Winter 5 day breaks (Feb/March) £97/£140.
Three Day packages available all year.

DINING ROOM; Superb food in elegant
Surroundings. Open to non-residents
BAR FOOD; Snacks/ lunches, afternoon tea
VEGETARIAN; Always a choice
DISABLED ACCESS; Many steps all over
PETS; Dogs 3.00 per day

THE BARN AND PINN COTTAGE
Bowd Cross
Sidmouth
Devon EX10 0ND

Tel. (01395) 513613

The Barn and Pinn Cottage is a lovely, thatched and whitewashed 14th century listed building. Peacefully nestling between the hills in gentle East Devon countryside, between a mile and a half and two miles from Sidmouth, it is surrounded by its own two acres of beautifully tended grounds. These include gardens, an orchard and car parking. It is now a highly acclaimed and very attractive Licensed Restaurant and Tea Room, with luxurious Bed and Breakfast Accommodation.

Its owners, Dick and Jean Whittaker, have much experience of the catering business, having previously run a hotel in North Devon and a restaurant and tea room in the Cotswolds. Since coming to the Barn and Pinn Cottage they have totally refurbished the property to make it a very comfortable, relaxing venue for dining or staying.

The restaurant is a converted hay barn, with original oak beams an open fireplace where logs burn in the colder months. Old agricultural implements decorate the walls. There is a small bar where a wide range of alcoholic and soft drinks is available, including an extensive and high quality wine list. The food is good, traditional English fare, all home-cooked using fresh local produce, which includes game, when available, and locally caught fish. The menu changes daily, and always features red meat, fish and chicken dishes. Sunday roast lunches are very popular, comprising home-made soup, a choice of three meats or vegetarian substitute, and three or four desserts. Vegetarians and those on special diets can always be catered for with a little advance notice. All the food is cooked and prepared by Jean, except for the cakes and scones in the tea room, which are made by Dick.

Staying at The Barn and Pinn Cottage is a relaxing and restful experience, the atmosphere friendly and informal. All bedrooms have tea and coffee making facilities and clock radios and overlook the gardens. They have been tastefully decorated and furnished in cottage style. Guests have the use of a comfortable beamed lounge with colour television and access to the patio and garden, where in fine weather you can enjoy a drink before dinner or coffee afterwards.

The countryside surrounding the house is ideal for walking, birdwatching and quiet exploration. The lovely East Devon coast is very close, and all parts of Devon and Dorset are within easy reach.

USEFUL INFORMATION

OPEN All Year.
CHILDREN Welcome.
CREDIT CARDS No.
LICENCE Restaurant.
ACCOMMODATION 6 en suite beds.
PRICES B&B 1 night: Dble £21.50 p.p.,
Single £25, Child £11. Weekly rate: Dble £20,
Single £22.50.
GARDEN Beautiful. Patio with tables etc, over - looking extensive flower gardens.

RESTAURANT Traditional, mainly English food, including game in season. Sunday lunch. Residents' Dinner £11 (3 courses) with coffee.
VEGETARIAN As requested.
SMOKING In Residents' Lounge only.
DISABLED Access, 2 gnd flr rooms.
PETS Welcome on ground floor.
£1 per day.

THE DIGGERS REST INN,
Woodbury Salterton,
Nr Exeter, Devon EX5 1PQ

Tel/Fax: 01395 232375

Woodbury Salterton is a delightfully quiet village in which The Diggers Rest is an integral part. It is close to Nigel Mansell's Woodbury Park Golf Course and Country Park and Woodbury Common with views to Dartmoor and the English Channel. It is seven miles from Exeter and Exmouth, 3 miles from the M5 Junction 30, Sidmouth road. It is splendid walking countryside with walks commencing in the village to the coastal footpaths.

The Diggers Rest is a wonderful, 500 years old, cob and thatch building with the original oak beams and a friendly ghost or two. Once it was a Cider House selling cider made from local apples and remained so until it became a freehouse in 1955. It is furnished throughout with a nice mixture of antique and modern pieces. The pretty restaurant has 60 covers with a delicious a la carte menu and the friendly bar is always welcoming. Sally and Tony Pratt are the present members of the family to own and run it - forty years it has been in the family. Today they are assisted by their daughter Nicola who is the third generation to take part. Sally and Tony both look after the front of the house; their cheerful personalities soon put newcomers at ease as they sit alongside those who have been coming here for years. You will find no Juke boxes or Fruit Machines at The Diggers, just good, convivial conversation. The food is all home-cooked with an emphasis on traditional English fare. Fresh, local produce is used whenever possible and the end result is a delicious meal which will long be remembered. Try the 'Diggers' Specials, Peppered Steak and Roast Duckling. On Sundays there is a popular Roast Sunday Lunch.

USEFUL INFORMATION

OPEN; 11-2.30pm & 6.30-11pm	**RESTAURANT; Good traditional**
Sundays 12-2.30pm & 7-10.30pm	**BAR FOOD; Wide range**
CHILDREN;Well behaved	**VEGETARIAN; Always a choice**
CREDIT CARDS;All major cards except Amex	**DISABLED ACCESS; Yes**
LICENSED; Full On PETS; Only in public bar	**GARDEN; Yes**

WESTERN FIELDS GUEST HOUSE
Ebford
Topsham
Exeter
Devon EX3 0PA

Tel. (01392) 874780

This charming 20th century Guest House is set in 8 acres of its own grounds and has unsurpassed views of the Exe estuary. The emphasis is on peace, tranquility and relaxation, in an exquisite environment where you very quickly feel at home. Western Fields is run by Miss Sally Bunce and her fiance, Jason, who both work to the very highest standards, running the house as professionally as possible, but at the same time seeking to create an informal, homelike atmosphere in which every guest can feel individual and special. As well as her work, Sally enjoys horse riding - she keeps two horses on the premises - and Jason is a retired professional motor cycle racer (17th in the world) who is an enthusiast for motor sports and golf.

The house is beautifully furnished and laid out. All bedrooms are spacious, full of character and include en suite baths or showers. They enjoy wonderful views out over the estuary; their exclusive luxury suite boasts it's own elevated conservatory, making the most of this panorama. There are also two lounges available to guests. The sun lounge, where breakfast is eaten, takes full advantage of the magnificent situation the house enjoys, with large picture windows through which can be seen the wealth of bird life which is attracted to the garden. The snug lounge features an exposed fire place where there is a log burning stove, making this a perfect retreat in colder weather. Everything is done to bring out the best atmosphere from the house and its location, which is totally rural yet within quick reach of the attractive town of Topsham and its old fashioned shops.

Beakfast is generous and comprehensive. Guests are given a wide choice of cereals, full English or Continental style breakfast or vegetarian, or any combination which suits them. The gardens of Western Fields are a delight, and full of wildlife. The house is approached by its own private lane, and has ample, safe, security-lit parking. During the summer months, guests are encouraged to stroll or sit in the gardens, which are there solely for their enjoyment. Within easy reach of the house are many opportunities for recreation, sport, nature watching and visiting historic sites.

USEFUL INFORMATION

OPEN All Year.

CHILDREN Welcome.

CREDIT CARDS No

LICENCE No, but guests are more than welcome to provide their own sustenance.

SMOKING No.

ACCOMMODATION 4 spacious en suite rooms, double or twin or combinations.

PRICES B&B Low Season: £14 - £20 per person per night; High Season £15 - £21. Stay for 1 week, 7th night free

RESTAURANT Breakfast only. Great choice English, Continental or Vegetarian styles. Guests can be as choosy as they like

VEGETARIAN Breakfast by arrangement.

DISABLED 2 steps in, but 2 ground floor rooms

PETS Yes - under strict rules

GARDEN 1 acre of formal gardens with tables and chairs, pond, mixed fruit orchard, 7 more acres for strolling.

THE LORD HALDON,
Dunchideock,
Exeter EX6 7YF
Tel: 01392 832483 Fax: 01392 833765

This is an hotel that is different for several reasons. Firstly dating from the 1700's, its original design was used as the template for Buckingham Palace, secondly the extensive grounds were designed by the inimitable Capability Brown and thirdly there is a Robert Adam arch leading into the hotel. The whole is impressive and quite delightful. Today's hotel was the original stable block of the house built for the Lords of Haldon early in the 18th century by Sir George Chudleigh. Traditionally furnished with quiet elegance and with very much the feel of the 'old school' about it, there are 22 ensuite bedrooms, beautifully appointed and each with colour TV, and tea/coffee making facilities. Three of the bedrooms have four-posters.The Restaurant, which is open to non-residents, seats 80 people approximately in a room that is immaculately appointed with crisp tablecloths, silvery cutlery and sparkling glass. The Table d'hote menu is always interesting with choices at every course and prepared by chefs who delight in their task and have been at The Lord Haldon for sometime. Situated in a rural setting, the hotel is nonetheless very close to the cathedral city of Exeter, the coast at Exmouth, Sidmouth and other good beaches. Dartmoor is on the doorstep and one would never be bored staying here for whatever reason. Many business people use it rather than stay in the bustle of Exeter. The Lord Haldon also has facilities for small conferences.

USEFUL INFORMATION

OPEN; All year	RESTAURANT; Excellent Table d'hote menu
CHILDREN; Welcome	BAR FOOD; Traditional choice
CREDIT CARDS; All except Amex	VEGETARIAN; Always a choice
LICENSED; Full On	DISABLED ACCESS; Yes. Toilet facilities
ACCOMMODATION; 22 ensuite	GARDEN; Yes. Drinking & eating in courtyard
PETS; Yes. 3 pounds a day	

RATES:- All Year, from £64/50 to £74.50 per room per night.(Includes full breakfast)

HUNTERS MOON HOTEL
Sid Road,
Sidmouth, Devon EX10 9AA
Tel: 01395 513380
Fax: 01395 514270

This elegant Grade II early Georgian Residence stands in its own grounds of two acres adjoining Sidmouth's delightful 'Byes' (National Trust) and next to the River Sid, yet it is conveniently situated for the sea front and for Sidmouth's charming shopping centre with its narrow streets, some pedestrianised. The rooms are gracious and have been tastefully decorated and sympathetically modernised over the years, all have bathroom and toilet ensuite, colour television, direct dial telephone and tea making facilities.In the pretty dining room decorated in soft shades of apricot, with beautiful drapes and with well appointed tables, there is great emphasis and pride on the choice and balance of the Table d'hote menu, with a keen eye reserved for the presentation. The hotel has a Restaurant Licence so one can enjoy wine with your meal or a drink before dinner. In the mature wooded grounds with large lawns you can find peace and tranquillity in which to relax and unwind, read a book or plan a day out in one of the many natural beauty spots in Devon and Dorset. Julie and Martyn Fisher would like to welcome you to Sidmouth and the Hunters Moon, to a town and an Hotel with a style and elegance of times gone by.

USEFUL INFORMATION

OPEN; March-November	RESTAURANT; Excellent Table d'hote menu
CHILDREN; Welcome	BAR FOOD;Not applicable
CREDIT CARDS; major cards not Amex	VEGETARIAN; Catered for
LICENSED; Restaurant Licence	DISABLED ACCESS; Yes.Welcome
ACCOMMODATION;18 ensuite	GARDEN; Lovely grounds. Putting.& Bowls.
Two self-contained holiday bungalows open all year	
PETS; Yes	SMOKING; Bedrooms only

RATES: High Season DBB £39.50 pppn . Low Season DBB £30.00 pppn

AXE FARM
Axmouth,
Nr Seaton, Devon EX12 4BG
Tel: 01297 24707

For those who enjoy camping and caravanning this must be one of the most beautiful sites in Devon. It is a 12th century farm set on the Axe estuary with superb views and an abundance of bird life. For those who prefer the comfort of a bed under a roof, the thatched Axe Farm offers bed and breakfast accommodation which is homely and welcoming and has a simple rustic charm. The one large family room has its own bathroom and Roger and Jenny Webber will make sure you have a splendid farmhouse breakfast cooked on a Rayburn. The house is quite fascinating with wall to wall wooden panelling thought to be ship's timbers and doors that are either four foot six or five foot high, made for small people! There are flagstone floors and the original beams. The whole atmosphere of Axe Farm is one of relaxation. Whether you stay in the cottage or camp site you will find the Webber family very friendly and helpful. The whole family likes animals and dogs are very welcome on the site. The farm has been in the family for three generations and they are proud of the manner in which it is run which ensures everyone who comes here has an enjoyable stay. There are acres of fields to walk in, nearby there is a golf course and riding stables and an Undercliff walk. Closeby is a delightful 12th century inn which together with Axe Farm was one of the first settlements of which there is any record in the 12th century. A great place for an informal, relaxed holiday.

USEFUL INFORMATION

OPEN; All year	DINING ROOM; Farmhouse breakfast
CHILDREN; Welcome	VEGETARIAN; Catered for
CREDIT CARDS; None taken	DISABLED ACCESS; Not suitable
LICENSED; No GARDEN; Yes + fields, animals etc	
ACCOMMODATION: 1 fam room	PETS; Welcome
Camping and Caravans	

RATES: High season £20 pppn   Low season £18 pppn   Children half price

VENNEMILE
Tedburn St Mary
Exeter
Devon EX6 6EQ - Tel. (01647) 61242

Vennemile is a superb example of a late Medieval Devon thatched cottage, where Mrs Katherine Winch provides Bed and Breakfast Accommodation in an unforgettable, atmospheric setting. The listed building, which is featured in the 2nd edition of Pevsner's Devon volume of *The Buildings of England*, is situated in the quiet, peaceful village of Tedburn St Mary along the main Exeter to Okehampton road. The original thatch, and the survival of so much of the original structure unaltered gives the house great historic value. Surrounded by an acre of garden and quintessential Devon countryside, it makes a perfect rural retreat, as well as an excellent base for exploring the many delights of the area, including welcoming pubs, National Trust properties and golf clubs. Exeter is just seven miles away. The accommodation at Vennemile consists of three double bedrooms, all with their own individual characters. Breakfast, as you might expect in such a setting, is traditional and English, eaten around an oak table in a charming, relaxed family Dining Room. It consists of all the favourite ingredients: eggs, bacon, sausages, saute potatoes, mushrooms, tomatoes etc, complete with toast and home-made marmalade. If you thought chocolate box cottages only existed on chocolate boxes, you will be amazed at Vennemile to find the real thing, and in Mrs Winch you will find a hostess who gives careful attention to detail, ensuring that you have a relaxing and even therapeutic experience.

USEFUL INFORMATION

OPEN All Year	RESTAURANT Breakfast only.
CHILDREN No.	VEGETARIAN Catered for.
CREDIT CARDS No.	SMOKING Permitted.
LICENCE No.	DISABLED No special facilities.
ACCOMMODATION 3 double bedrooms.	PETS No.
PRICES B&B £22 per person.	GARDEN 1 acre.

DANSON HOUSE
Marsh Green
Exeter
Devon EX5 2ES

Tel. and Fax (01404) 823260

email dh2789@mail.eclipse.co.uk
Internet http://www.webscape.co.uk/danson/

ETB 2 Crowns, Highly Commended

Danson House is an exclusive English Country House in a secluded rural setting in Devon, offering Award-Winning Bed and Breakfast Accommodation and Evening Dinner. It is the family home of Dennis and Jenny Hobbs and their daughters, Caroline and Jessica, with their friendly Cocker Spaniel Oscar and Charlie the black horse. Situated on the edge of the tiny hamlet of Marsh Green and with its own private garden, Danson privates peace and comfort in carefully decorated, tasteful surroundings. It is within very easy reach of the city of Exeter, while the historic town of Ottery St Mary is only 4 miles away. The atmosphere at Danson House is extremely friendly and welcoming.

On arrival, guests are greeted with tea and home-made cakes, and in the sitting room is a wood-burning stove to provide warmth throughout the day. The traditional farmhouse kitchen has an aga, where all meals are home-cooked by Jenny, who loves meeting and catering for people. Dennis is always ready to help guests plan their day. All bedrooms have colour television, radio, tea tray, hairdryers, shoe-cleaning facilities and a complementary basket of toiletries. Dinner is provided in a beautiful oak-furnished dining room with 2 large chandeliers. Traditional, mainly English, food is served on Royal Doulton china, with silver plate cutlery and lead crystal glass. Breakfast consists of a selection of cereals, fresh fruit, grapefruit, yoghurt, juice, a traditional English cooked breakfast with toast and home-made preserves.

USEFUL INFORMATION

OPEN All Year.
CHILDREN By arrangement.
CREDIT CARDS Not Taken
LICENCE No.
ACCOMMODATION 2 large double/twin en suite rooms, 1 double with adjoining bathroom
PRICES B&B High Season: £19 - £22 per person per night, Double/twin £36 - £38; Low Season: £18 - £22 pppn, D/t £34 - £36. Children £8.

RESTAURANT 3 Course Dinner including coffee and mints £10.50. Table d'hote menu.
VEGETARIAN If required.
SMOKING Permitted.
DISABLED No special facilities.
PETS No.
GARDEN Very private garden, where guests can sit or join hosts in a barbecue.

FERNDALE,
92 Winslade Road,
Sidmouth, Devon EX10 9EZ

Tel: 01395 515495

ETB Two Crowns Highly Commended.

Sue Pink who owns and runs Ferndale describes herself as an extrovert chatterbox who likes people. This is to the advantage of everyone who stays in this substantial Edwardian terraced house in an elevated position facing south just three quarters of a mile from the sea front. You will find her genuinely welcoming and with a great desire to make sure you enjoy staying in her house and in Sidmouth. Sidmouth is a predominantly Regency town whose council and hoteliers association go to great lengths to maintain its character in an unspoiled manner. One cannot fail to admire the beauty of the floral displays both in gardens, hanging baskets and in the beautifully laid out public gardens which are so much a part of this nice town. The town has a quiet sophistication without being a noisy seaside resort. It is a pleasure to walk along the beautiful promenade, to explore the shops in the narrow streets and perhaps listen to a band concert in the Connaught Gardens.

People come to Sidmouth to relax away from the stress of modern times and certainly in the personalised service at Ferndale one could not be anything but relaxed. Ferndale has three charming bedrooms, furnished with style and an eye for colour. One double room has a private bathroom, a large, airy twin bedded room with a balcony facing south, has a shower ensuite and the other twin bedded room has a bathroom close to hand on the landing. All the guest rooms are on the first floor and each has Colour TV and Hostess Trays. The guest sitting room has plenty of reading material as well as colour TV. Sue enjoys cooking and serves a full English breakfast including Kippers, Haddock and Kedgeree.

USEFUL INFORMATION

OPEN; March-November   **DINING ROOM; Excellent breakfast**
CHILDREN; Over 9 years   **VEGETARIAN; Yes.**
CREDIT CARDS; None taken   **DISABLED ACCESS; Not suitable**
LICENSED; No   **PETS:No.**
ACCOMMODATION; One Double, Two Twin.
RATES; High Season,Single £26.pn. Double £44.per room. Children full price.
Low Season, Single £20. Pn. Double £36. Per room. Children £15.
All rates are for Bed & Breakfast.

HOPE COTTAGE
The Strand
Lympstone
Near Exmouth
Devon EX8 5JS
Tel. (01395) 268349

In the heart of the picturesque village of Lympstone, with its narrow streets leading down to the Exe and its lovely views across the estuary, Hope Cottage is everyone's dream of a Devon retreat. With thick cob walls, oak beams, a cobbled pathway and a hostess whose family has lived in it for 200 years, this 15th century cottage is full of character and individuality. Its owners, Margaret and Peter Clarke, will give you a warm welcome, and make you feel completely at ease in their home, which is furnished with family treasures and a wealth of pictures, books and a collection of teddy bears. Margaret is completely local, and has never lived outside Lympstone. Her husband has been around the world, courtesy of the Merchant Navy. All the rooms at Hope Cottage are very different. There are two twins, a single, a double en suite and a four poster room. Although there are no televisions in the bedrooms, the Clarkes have an old wind-up gramophone with a collection of 78s, and they often hear their guests having a quick foxtrot. Breakfast is a traditional full English one, with orange juice, cereals, egg, bacon, sausage, fried bread, mushrooms and tomatoes, with tea or coffee and toast with a fine selection of marmalades. If you can drag yourself away from such a lovely and atmospheric place, you will find that Hope Cottage is ideal for exploring the East Devon and Exeter areas and beyond.

USEFUL INFORMATION

OPEN All Year.	**RESTAURANT** B&B only. Full English breakfast.
CHILDREN Welcome.	**VEGETARIAN** Catered for.
CREDIT CARDS No.	**SMOKING** Permitted.
LICENCE No.	**DISABLED** Not really convenient for them.
ACCOMMODATION 5 rooms,	**PETS** No.
including 4 poster and double	**GARDEN** Guests welcome to stroll or sit.
en suite. Very individual.	**PRICES** B&B £14 - £16. Children half price.

REKA DOM
43 The Strand,
Topsham, Devon EX3 0AY
Tel: 01392 873385

This must be one of the most fascinating houses in Devon. It stands at the waters edge at the head of the Exe estuary. Its history is a charming mixture of fact and fiction and very difficult to decide which is which. Built in the 1600;s the original deeds described it as 'the cottage in the fields of seven limekilns. It was clearly a merchants house and warehouse in the 17th and 18th centuries and local legend says that it was leased by a Russian nobleman who called it Reka Dom, Russian for River House.. It is a house of many nooks and crannies and was added to in Victorian times when the then owner added a tower to store water - he did not want to drink the local water and had the liquid asset brought in from Exeter and stored in the Tower. It is a house that is full of light and exudes happiness which is probably why it is so popular with creative people; writers, musicians, artists, potters have all made Reka Dom their home. Richard and Marlene Gardner are the owners of Reka Dom. Richard is a piano maker and restorer - one of the top men in this country and Marlene is a superb needlewoman making and hand embroidering most of the linen as well as being an excellent cook. This is a lady of many talents who is also an actress and singer performing in cabaret, frequently with son Matthew who is a composer. All of this makes for the most wonderful atmosphere in the house where you will be extremely well cared for and fed perfectly.

USEFUL INFORMATION

OPEN; All year   **DINING ROOM;** Excellent Breakfast.
Special. Dinner on request
CHILDREN; Welcome   **BAR FOOD;** Not applicable
CREDIT CARDS; None taken   **VEGETARIAN;** Upon request
LICENSED; No   **DISABLED ACCESS;** Not suitable
ACCOMMODATION; Rooms with wonderful views   **PETS;** With advance notice
RATES:- High Season from £23 pppn B&B. In the Tower, from £28.50 pppn B&B. Low Season from £22. Pppn B&B In the Tower, from £27.pppn B&B.

JUBILEE COTTAGE
75 Chapel Street
Sidbury
Devon EX10 0RQ

Tel. (01395) 597295

'Staying Off The Beaten Track',
AA 3 Qs.

Jubilee Cottage is a lovely 16th century thatched cottage in the attractive East Devon village of Sidbury, where Bob and Marianne Coles offer Bed and Breakfast Accommodation and Evening Dinner in a setting of great atmosphere and peace. The cottage is formed out of two or perhaps three original dwellings, so has a feeling of spaciousness to it, although it is beautifully cosy and intimate as well, with inglenook fireplaces, oak beams and many nooks and crannies. The garden is secluded, with fine views of the Sid valley, and guests are welcome to sit and eat here when weather permits.

Bob Coles retired to his native Devon in 1992 after an army career. Marianne is German, and brings an international flavour to the cooking at Jubilee Cottage, providing a wide range of German, Italian and other recipes which she enjoys collecting on her travels. Their guests greatly appreciate her varied creations, especially the sweets and puddings, and the candlelit dinners, using silver and crystal, which are a feature of the Coles' hospitality. The bedrooms have excellent views of the surrounding countryside, and are tastefully decorated.

They all have televisions, radios and drinks making facilities. There is an honesty Fridge and Trolley in the Dining Room and Guest Lounge. The atmosphere at Jubilee Cottage is informal and flexible. Guests are given keys and are able to come and go as they wish, and breakfast is at any time, according to request.

USEFUL INFORMATION

OPEN All Year

CHILDREN Over 9 years

CREDIT CARDS Not Taken.

LICENCE Restaurant.

ACCOMMODATION 2 double rooms, 1 twin and 1 single. 2 bathrooms & separate shower room.

PRICES B&B £16 per person, £32 per room. Children half price if 2 sharing, age 9+.

RESTAURANT English and International Dinner Menu. Choice of beers and wines. Sandwiches as requested.

VEGETARIAN On request.

SMOKING No.

DISABLED No facilities.

PETS No.

GARDEN Yes. Guests welcome to sit.

POSTLAKE FARM
Clyst St Mary
Exeter
Devon EX5 1AP

Tel. and Fax (01395) 232298

In lovely Devon countryside, surrounded by wildlife, Postlake offers Farmhouse Bed and Breakfast Accommodation in an attractive 18th century stone building set within its own lands and with its own water supply.

Postlake is a mixed dairy, beef, sheep and arable farm run by Mr Pyne. Mrs Pyne, with help from a French student in the busy summer months, runs the bed and breakfast side of the business.

The spacious rooms of the house are individually decorated and tastefully furnished. All bedrooms have hot and cold drinks facilities, hairdryers, televisions and mending kits. There is a quiet sitting room for the use of guests.

A full English or Continental breakfast is provided, and vegetarian or other special diets are catered for, especially if requested in advance.

Postlake Farm makes an excellent base for exploring the many attractions of Exeter and East Devon, being within easy reach of the popular resort of Exmouth, the quiet old town of Topsham, the city of Exeter and the beautiful East Devon coast. Dartmoor, Torbay and the South Hams are also just a short journey away.

USEFUL INFORMATION

OPEN All Year except Christmas

CHILDREN Welcome.

CREDIT CARDS Not Taken.

LICENCE No.

ACCOMMODATION 3 double en suite rooms, 2 with an extra single bed

PRICES B&B £17 - £22 per person. Children depending on age.

RESTAURANT Breakfast only. Full English or Continental.

VEGETARIAN catered for on request.

SMOKING Not permitted.

DISABLED No facilities.

PETS No.

GARDEN Working farm.

MARIANNE POOL FARM,
Clyst St George,
Exeter, Devon EX3 0NZ

Tel: 01392 874939

Marianne Pool Farm is ideally placed for anyone wanting to explore the area, play golf either at Nigel Mansell's Woodbury Park or at Exeter Golf Club, seek out the coast at Exmouth or Budleigh Salterton, or for those who have business in Exeter or Honiton and prefer the peace and quiet of a farmhouse rather than the bustle of the city at the end of a days work. People also come here to stay when they want to visit Westpoint either for the Devon Agricultural Show or for the many concerts, exhibitions and antique fairs that are held there during the year. This thatched Devon Longhouse was built in the early 1600's and has undergone many changes but it has never lost its old world charm and still retains the original roofing timbers under the thatch. Thick cob walls keep it cool in summer and provide deep window recesses. You look out onto views of this mixed working farm of dairy and arable. Look closely and you can see the Dairy unit across the fields on the main road. Janet Bragg, whose home it is, welcomes guests with her daughter Lucy and husband Ivor, who are all Devonshire born and bred. There are two guest bedrooms - a family room ensuite and a twin bedded room with a wash hand basin and a bathroom with bath and shower close by. Each room has a hostess tray. Breakfast is a sumptuous feast with eggs from the hens in the garden and sausages and bacon from the local butcher. The large garden is there for guests use.

USEFUL INFORMATION

OPEN; March to November	DINING ROOM; True Farmhouse breakfast
CHILDREN; Welcome. Cot available	VEGETARIAN;Catered for/other diets
CREDIT CARDS; None taken	DISABLED ACCESS; Not suitable
LICENSED; No PETS; By arrangment. 2.00 charge	
ACCOMODATION; 1fam ensuite 1 tw	GARDEN; Large,
RATES; All Season, £16/£20 pppn B&B. Children £5/£10 Depending on age.	
Higher rates are for en-suite accommodation.	

THE GOLDEN LION INN
Tipton St John,
Sidmouth, Devon EX10 0AA
Tel: 01404 812881

Tipton St John is a picturesque, sleepy little village close to the Edwardian seaside resort of Sidmouth. In its midst is the Victorian village pub, the Golden Lion, which is a haunt of all the locals who enjoy its genuinely olde worlde atmosphere. The whole atmosphere of the inn is redolent of the past even down to its decor. Visitors are more than welcome here and rapidly find themselves involved in the friendly banter that goes on over the bar. Colin and Carolyn Radford are 'mine hosts' and their warm-hearted personalities have done much to make the Golden Lion so welcoming. The Golden Lion has had a lady chef for some twenty five years and her reputation for producing good old English country fare goes far beyond this part of Devon. You will find there are some tasty Daily Specials, a range of dishes on the menu that provides something that appeals to everybody and simple snacks such as freshly cut sandwiches and Ploughmans. The small restaurant has 28 covers and is strictly non-smoking and for those who would like to stay a night or two there are two guest bedrooms both with showers, television and a hostess tray.

USEFUL INFORMATION

OPEN; All year 11-3pm & 6-11pm	RESTAURANT; Traditional Old English
CHILDREN; Over 7 years, not after 7pm	BAR FOOD; Wide range
CREDIT CARDS; None taken	VEGETARIAN; Approx 3/4 dishes daily
LICENSED; Full On	DISABLED ACCESS; Yes + toilets
ACCOMMODATION; 2 ensuite rooms	GARDEN; Yes
PETS; No	RATES: £18.50 + VAT

NEWLANDS FARM
Broadclyst,
Exeter, Devon EX5 3BZ

Tel:01392 464887
Fax: 01392 462878

Newlands Farm is surrounded by National Trust Farms forming part of the 6,358 acre Killerton Estate given to the Trust by Sir Richard Acland, and to the North behind the farm by three fields is Ashcroft Forest, a haven for wild life, including Roe Deer, which can often, especially in Spring through to Autumn, be seen in the fields surrounding the farm. It is close to several Golf courses including Nigel Mansell's Championship course at Woodbury. Newlands also makes a great base from which to explore Dartmoor and Exmoor and the coast. The Grade II Listed house had been left empty for some years before Ian and Moley Anderson acquired it in 1987. They completely refurbished the house retaining the character and ambience resulting in the charming home they have today into which they welcome guests. Furnished with antiques and high class soft furnishings, Newlands Farm is centrally heated. The 3 double bedded-rooms are all en suite - one has a king size bed. Breakfast is served in the Dining Room which has period oak furniture. The food is excellent with a wide choice including Scrambled eggs with smoked salmon, plenty of toast and rolls with home-made preserves. It is a privilege to stay in such a delightful home.

USEFUL INFORMATION

OPEN; Closed Christmas & New Year & all Jan. **DINING ROOM; Superb breakfast**
Please book in advance **VEGETARIAN; Upon request**
CHILDREN; No **DISABLED ACCESS; No**
CREDIT CARDS;None taken **GARDEN;Yes**
LICENSED; No **PETS; Not in house but stabling can**
ACCOMMODATION;3 double rooms ensuite **be made available with notice**
RATES :- Single £53. Double £60/70 per room per night. All Year.

THE KETTLE RESTAURANT
15, Fore Street,
Seaton, Devon EX12 2LE

Tel: 01297 20428

Visitors delight in the quaintness of The Kettle Restaurant housed in a four hundred year old cottage in the centre of Seaton. They look with interest at the low beamed ceilings and comment on the pretty table's, but most of all they enjoy the friendly atmosphere and the excellent food cooked by Sue Thomas, who with her husband Ian, owns and runs The Kettle. They have owned the restaurant for eight years and in that time Sue has become renowned for food she serves from the a la carte menu. Everything she cooks is delicious but if one had to say she was famous for any one thing it would have to be her desserts which are irresistible.

Seaton is a charming place and if you would like to stay Sue and Ian have two charming guest bedrooms which are ensuite and furnished in a cottagey style.

USEFUL INFORMATION

OPEN; All year **RESTAURANT; Renowned for its good**
CHILDREN; Welcome **food especially desserts**
CREDIT CARDS; None taken **VEGETARIAN; At least 4 dishes daily**
LICENSED; Yes **DISABLED ACCESS; Not easy**
GARDEN; No **PETS; Yes, on a lead**
ACCOMMODATION; 2 ensuite rooms **RATES: £21 pppn (high season) £18.50 (low)**

Chapter One

CHAPTER TWO

Around Torbay And The Teign Valley

"For now I am in a holiday humour."
William Shakespeare

CHAPTER TWO

AROUND TORBAY AND THE TEIGN VALLEY

For countless numbers of people, over many generations, the words "a holiday in Devon" have immediately suggested a couple of sunny weeks spent in one or other of the famous seaside resorts around Tor Bay and the mouth of the River Teign, with occasional excursions onto Dartmoor and into the South Hams.

Between the estuaries of the Exe and the Dart are no fewer than four much-loved resorts, Dawlish, Teignmouth, Torquay and Paignton - each one somebody's favourite - with the old fishing town of Brixham at the southern end of the Bay, and many delightful villages in the rich country behind them. The climate is warm and the situation sheltered, while the surrounding landscape itself, lying upon a complicated mixture of limestone, slate and sandstone, is lush and beautiful; the softly rounded contours of the hills, the glowing red of the soil and the exuberance of vegetation, as well as the inspiring sight of Dartmoor away on the skyline, make it everyone's dream of rural Devon. In this chapter we shall make a circular tour of the area, beginning and ending at Torquay and going inland as far as Newton Abbot and the Haldon Hills.

TORQUAY (Tourist Information 01803 297428) is the biggest of the three towns around Tor Bay which make up the **BOROUGH OF TORBAY** (when referring to the geographical feature, the words "Tor" and "Bay" are separated, but when the administrative entity is meant, they are put together).

Despite being combined for local government purposes for about thirty years, each of the three retains its traditional difference in style and atmosphere: Torquay can still be thought of, quite accurately, as the upmarket watering place, Paignton remains the down-to-earth family playground and Brixham survives as a working fishing port. Torquay has always been the premier resort, not only of the Bay, but of South Devon as a whole.

Together, the three towns constitute a large and ever-expanding urban area, with a population of nearly 120,000 and barely a gap between them, but before the early 19th century the shores of Tor Bay were, compared with how they look now, in many ways virgin territory.

It must have been a wonderful place then, especially at the Torquay end, with its high, tree-covered limestone cliffs, deep gorges and an almost tropical growth of uninhibited vegetation. Only a few small human settlements, other than single farms, existed in the landscape, by the water or in the hills; most of them were safely away from the sea, out of sight of any invader. The beaches would have been avoided by all except fishermen and smugglers. The great Medieval abbey of Torre was there of course, surprisingly exposed in its position, but in general the human impact on the environment would have seemed minimal, especially along the shore.

There were two reasons for the sudden growth of Torquay, as for the other English seaside towns. One was the new fashion for sea bathing as a therapeutic practice, the other was the series of wars against Napoleon. These brought the British Navy to the Bay, and the families of the officers found it a delightful place in which to settle. The wars meant that the English upper classes were unable to travel in France, Italy and Germany, so they were forced to discover the more romantic and salubrious regions of their own country, often naming these after the foreign parts which they superficially resembled. Torquay thus became known as the "English Naples" and the nearby River Dart was christened the "English Rhine." (My favourite such title is the one given to Lynton and Lynmouth, on the wild North Devon coast. Someone decided they ought to be called the "English Switzerland", a country singularly lacking in just that feature...)

Torbay still advertises itself as the "English Riviera", and you can see the point of this. Torquay, in particular, with its sense of spaciousness, its warmth and clarity of light, the vivid colouring of sea and hill, the white glare of hotels and the gentle movement of sails, does offer a decidedly Mediterranean ambience.

The Victorians made the growing town one of the most fashionable resorts in the country. The once-separate settlements of St Marychurch and Babbacombe, to the north of the Bay, were joined up to it, as elegant crescents and mansions appeared on the hills and carriage drives wound amongst the cliffs. HESKETH CRESCENT is particularly noteworthy. Spacious churches of the local limestone appeared, and sloping gardens filled up with exotic plants from all over the world, although wealthy landowners carefully controlled all development to maintain the beauty and character of the surroundings.

Royalty and aristocracy from all over Europe came for the health-giving air and mild winters; in those days the winter, not the summer, was the time for going to the seaside. They were joined by politicians, writers and a significant number of scientists and naturalists, who marvelled at the geological diversity and richness of marine life, and made important contributions to the serious study of both. Amongst the famous residents of the town were Elizabeth Barrett Browning, Charles Kingsley and Isambard Kingdom Brunel. Torquay aquired a particular reputation for its healthy climate, and at one time it was so crowded with invalids that the authorities started to worry that this might, in fact, be counter-productive, so they quickly began promoting it amongst the healthy as well.

Torquay is no longer, of course, the exclusive haunt of the leisured classes that it was in the 19th and early 20th centuries, but a good deal of its genteel Victorian atmosphere remains. Some enjoy this aspect of the town, others have always been maddened by it. Rudyard Kipling, not a writer usually known for his revolutionary sympathies, said that the bourgeois complacency of the place made him want to run through it with nothing on but his glasses.

Most visitors, however, simply enjoy the spacious, relaxing air of Torquay, and take delight in its visual distinctiveness: the crowded thoroughfares following the bottoms of what were once steep-sided ravines, the exposed outcrops still sometimes visible behind the buildings, the intimate little paths of ROCK WALK, providing magnificent views over the Bay, the other beautifully kept parks and gardens. All this gives the town a slightly un-English feel, which can be very refreshing. If you are gregarious, and like to see crowds of people enjoying themselves, you can loiter in Torquay happily for hours, marvelling at the infinite variety of human face and form, and falling in love several times a minute.

Torquay covers a series of hills and valleys on a high rocky headland which thrusts itself out into the sea, creating the northern end of Tor Bay. Just off shore is the red stone THATCHER ROCK, on which nothing is found, apparently, except seabirds, red ants and a strange kind of cabbage. Around its edge, the town has no fewer than NINE BEACHES, some facing the Bay itself, others on the far side of the headland, looking towards the Teign estuary. All are safe, well cared for and perenially popular. TORRE ABBEY SANDS is the most accessible, but MEADFOOT, MAIDENCOMBE and BABBACOMBE are lovelier. ODDICOMBE, 240 feet below Babbacombe Downs, is reached by a ride in the little blue box-cars of the CLIFF RAILWAY (01803 328750), an experience in itself.

Around the busy HARBOUR you can book FISHING TRIPS and EXCURSIONS around the Bay and as far as the Dart estuary. SURFING, SAILING, MOTOR BOATING, WATERSKIING, PARASCENDING, WINDSURFING and DIVING are all available, and further details can be obtained from the TIC.

When you finally need a change from lying on the sands or sporting in the water, Torquay has many unique attractions, some of them famous for decades, others new and very contemporary. To start with the oldest and most dignified of these, TORRE ABBEY (01803 293593) is a peaceful and beautiful building, a sanctuary amidst the bustle of the modern town all around it, containing a MUSEUM and ART GALLERY with a wealth of history and a fascinating collection.

The Abbey was established just over 800 years ago in 1196, in what would have seemed wild and inhospitable terrain. It belonged to the Premonstratensian order, one of the less well known Medieval orders, at least in this country. They were rather austere, unlike the more worldly Benedictines, and favoured out of the way places. Despite their aloofness, Torre rose to be one of their wealthiest houses. After the Dissolution of the Monasteries it became a family home and passed through the hands of many different owners, including the Carys, until the 20th century, when the local council took it over.

Outside the large, ivy-covered building you can enjoy colourful gardens and the ruins of the original Abbey, with the gatehouse and the haunted Spanish Barn'. Prisoners from a captured Armada ship were kept here, and, according to legend, a young girl was amongst them, disguised as a boy so as to be near her lover. She died in the appalling conditions of the barn, but over the centuries her poignant ghost has been seen and heard by unsuspecting passers by.

The Abbey has an important collection of paintings and other artefacts, especially from the 19th century, including work by the Pre-Raphaelites. Its many rooms include one devoted to the "Queen of Crime-writing", Agatha Christie, Torquay's most celebrated daughter, of whom more in a moment. There is also a RESTAURANT and SHOP.

TORQUAY MUSEUM (01803 293975) is Devon's oldest, founded in the 19th century by Torquay Natural History Society, which still runs it. Its collections cover a wide range: archaeology, the history of Torbay, Devon folklife, Devon military history, local wildlife and much else.

There is more here about Agatha Christie and her work. Since 1990, the centenary of her birth, the world's bestselling writer has been made much of in her home town, and it somehow helps the reader to appreciate her world of tea parties, bridge games, deferrential servants and timeless villages, into which murder so dramatically intrudes, after wandering around the place where she grew up. The AGATHA CHRISTIE MILE is a specially designed trail to places associated with her, including a mystery for you to solve en route. At the TIC you can purchase leaflets and books devoted to her South Devon connections.

Another prolific 20th century writer who spent his childhood in Torquay, although not actually born here, was Beverley Nichols, and I cannot help feeling that his extravagant, over-ripe, somewhat camp style owes a lot to this early environment as well.

His neighbour, whilst growing up here, was the brilliant and eccentric scientist Oliver Heaviside, who pioneered wireless telegraphy and discovered the ionospheric band above the Earth which is now called the Heaviside Layer. Reclusive and hard of hearing, he indulged his individuality to the full, decorating his walls with unpaid bills and replacing his furniture with boulders from the beach. He died in 1925 and is buried in Paignton cemetery. Many compare him with Einstein for his mathematical ability and scientific genius.

Older than anything man-made in Torbay is KENTS CAVERN (general information 01803 215136, prices/out of hours hotline 01803 294059), Torquay's famous caves.

Some of the oldest human remains in Europe have been found here, reminding us that, though the towns are relatively young, human activity in this area is not. Kents Cavern is itself in the record books, for being the oldest Scheduled British Monument.

The caves are two million years old, and profoundly atmospheric. The rich colours of the rocks, the grottoes, the arrangements of stalactites, the so-called "organ chamber" all add up to a magical journey through time. The caves were first explored in the early 19th century by a Catholic priest, Father MacEnery, and later by William Pengelly, a self-taught Cornishman who made himself a leading intellectual figure of the Victorian westcountry. The William Pengelly Caves Studies Centre at Buckfastleigh commemorates him (see Chapter 4), and he was responsible for founding the Devonshire Association for the Advancement of Science Literature and the Arts, the annual 'Transactions' of which are indispensable for any serious student of the county.

Visiting Kents Cavern today is a well-organised and comfortable experience. An easy GUIDED TOUR on concrete paths is available, as well as special seasonal events, such as the dramatic GHOSTS OF CAVERN PAST evening tour during the summer; this uses loud sound effects and darkness, so is not recommended for very young children. A new exhibition for 1997 shows our cave-dwelling ancestors around their fire.

Not far from the caves, at BABBACOMBE, high above the sea with wonderful views from the Downs, is the world-renowned MODEL VILLAGE (01803 515315), set in 4 acres of landscaped grounds. Generations of children and adults have enjoyed a visit to the village, which is continually developing its facilities.

The Torquay area has a long tradition of making pottery, some of which is now very collectable. At BABBACOMBE POTTERY AND TEA GARDEN (01803 323322) you can see the tradition continue.

Babbacombe, with its rows of white hotels and expansive cliff walks, has an atmosphere of its own, away from the excitement down in the lower town. In the last century it was the home of Edmund Gosse, the literary critic, who wrote about his childhood here, with his naturalist father, in his well-known book *My Father and Myself.* Gosse senior was a troubled man, who spent his life trying to reconcile the existence of fossils with the Old Testament version of the Creation.

Gosse memorably described the state of the English coast as he first knew it, before it was discovered and developed: "No one", he wrote, "will see again on the shore of England what I saw in my early childhood." Over a century later you can still feel the heartache. Oscar Wilde spent a miserable weekend here with Bosie, and another Babbacombe name is that of the infamous John Lee, "the man they couldn't hang", of whom too much has been written already.

In neighbouring **ST MARYCHURCH**, which retains some of its independent atmosphere and has lots of interesting shops, can be found BYGONES (01803 326108), which features four very different attractions in one. First, there is a VICTORIAN STREET, with authentic, full-size shops, a pub and a forge, with period display rooms. A WALK-THROUGH TRENCH EXPERIENCE, complete with smells, sounds and bleeding bodies, is, says the leaflet, guaranteed to remind you of grandfather's tales of World War One, while upstairs is 'FANTASYLAND', magical and illuminated. Finally, a scenic miniature railway runs through a beautifully crafted model landscape.

FUN FACTORY (01803 201606), back in central Torquay, is an excellent indoor adventure centre for younger children. No visitor can see the visual delights of Torquay without taking in the ornate PAVILION by the sea front, which has long been a landmark of the resort. It opened in 1912 and served mainly as a concert hall - Sir Edward Elgar, Sir Henry Wood, Sir Thomas Beecham and Sir Adrian Boult all conducted here - before declining in the 1960s and 70s. Attempts to use it as a pop venue and skating rink failed and it was in danger of being demolished, but it is now an enjoyable shopping centre with a small INTERPRETATIVE EXHIBITION of the history and ecology of the Bay. I especially like the geological map fashioned out of coloured stone.

As a centre for SPORT and RECREATION, Torquay has many good facilities. The ENGLISH RIVIERA CENTRE (01803 299992), a large, glassy, 1980s prestige building, is a fully equipped conference, leisure and entertainment venue, with fun pool, fitness suite and squash courts. TORQUAY GOLF CLUB (01803 314591) has 18 holes in beautiful parkland.

At TORQUAY UNITED FC ground at Plainmoor, St Marychurch, you can see league football.

For SHOPPING, RESTAURANTS, PUBS and NIGHT LIFE Torquay has something for everyone, with live entertainment in many of its numerous clubs and bars. THE PRINCESS THEATRE (01803 290290) and BABBACOMBE THEATRE (01803 328385) offer traditional seaside summer shows and Christmas pantomimes.

Special events to look out for include TORBAY CARNIVAL in July and the TORBAY ROYAL REGATTA in late August. Consult the daily evening paper, the *Herald Express*, for the latest in entertainment and other activities.

Despite being such a built up area, with busy roads and its share of unlovely new structures, Torbay has a great deal of coast and inland countryside which is remarkably beautiful and unspoilt. The cliff walks, narrow, high-hedged lanes and woodland paths that are typical of rural South Devon are surprisingly close to the shopping centres and housing estates, if you know how to find them.

The TORBAY COUNTRYSIDE SERVICE (01803 607230/882619) has been set up to enable you to do just that. Its Rangers, in their distinctive uniforms and cowboy hats, actively look after and interpret the Bay's rural and ecological inheritance, with information points at COCKINGTON and BERRY HEAD. They organise an enjoyable series of WALKS and EVENTS throughout the year, for which you can pick up a programme from the TIC.

The most celebrated rural corner of the whole Bay area is, of course, the village of **COCKINGTON**, just a mile from the town along the pink and shady lanes, which are rich in the spring with primroses and bluebells.

Who is not familiar with the appearance of this lovely collection of thatched cottages beside the ancient forge, backed by mature trees? Probably nowhere in Devon, except possibly Widecombe and Clovelly, has been so endlessly photographed and marketed, so that even those who have never set foot here feel they have known it all their lives.

When you finally get to Cockington, as everybody does, you will not be disappointed. The beauty, when you see it in the flesh, is as real, and strangely touching, as it looks in the pictures. Millions of people dream of rural Devon when they see a postcard of this scene, and are uplifted by it, and it is good to mingle with them on a warm day and see the pleasure which is created by the reality of this gentle, well-ordered environment. Flower-bedecked cottages, cream teas, gifts and souvenirs, all with the famous image on them, and a well-run information point provide everything you will need.

You can walk around the village and through the park, or take a ride in a horse-drawn carriage to the CHURCH and the 17th century manor house of COCKINGTON COURT, where CRAFT DEMONSTRATIONS take place and you can buy REFRESHMENTS, including Devon farm cider. The expansive GARDENS of Cockington are very special, with carp lakes and a selection of rare bog plants. To walk through the gardens on a summer evening, with the rhododendrons and trees towering above, is a deeply memorable experience. THE DRUM INN is a 20th century building designed by Edwin Lutyens, and a perfect place to repair to after your walk.

At the centre of Tor Bay is the red-brick, red-cliff, red-soil seaside town of **PAIGNTON** (Tourist Information 01803 558383). Millions of people from the North, Midlands and London must have looked back with affection at their holidays in this unpretentious resort where the emphasis is very firmly on down-to-earth fun.

There is something enjoyably "ordinary" about Paignton, which, away from the big hotels and arcades at the front, is very much a working town, but the palm trees in the gardens of terraced houses, and the toylike harbour, remind you that its position on the 'English Riviera' is far from ordinary.

Although most of Paignton is 20th century, the settlement is old, dating from Saxon times. Around the dignified Parish Church you can see the shape of the original village, safely away from the sea. The Medieval Bishops of Exeter had a retreat here; the best known to stay in Paignton was Miles Coverdale, translator of the Bible. In those days it must have been a secretive place to get away to, with plentiful hunting of wild beasts.

Even in the mid 19th century there were still fields between the older part of the community and the area closer to the beach. Early pictures of the railway show it passing the huddle of old houses, with nothing except flat meadows and saltmarshes where now the hotels, guest houses, ice-cream parlours and gift shops line the streets towards the sea. Cabbages, for which Paignton had quite a reputation, were grown in these fields, and the surrounding area was rich in cider orchards. This historical fact explains why, so unusually for an English town, the railway comes right into the centre and almost through the streets, and why the pleasant ritual of stopping the traffic for the train to pass across the road punctuates the Paignton day.

It was the arrival of the railway in 1859 that spurred the growth of Paignton, and standardised the spelling of its name. For a while there was uncertainty as to whether it should be "Paignton" or "Paington", but finally the postmaster and the stationmaster, two new and representative figures of authority in those days, settled on the former.

The coming of the railway was celebrated by the production of the much-acclaimed "PAIGNTON PUDDING", a dish traditionally made twice in a century to mark major events. This one contained 500lbs of flour, 190 lbs of bread, 400lbs of raisins, 184 lbs of currants, 400lbs of suet, 96 lbs of sugar, 320 lemons, 150 nutmegs and 360 quarts of milk. Three thousand people were invited to partake of the pudding, but 18,000 others turned up as well, and in the ensuing fight very little of it actually got eaten.

Paignton's BEACHES are safe and sandy, with a pier and all the expected beach activities. The parks are bright and well-kept, and one of the most popular places to linger is on the green outside the FESTIVAL HALL AND THEATRE (01803 558383), where shows and concerts of all kinds, but tending towards the old-fashioned, take place. The pleasant little PALACE AVENUE THEATRE (01803 558367) also puts on interesting shows, and is set in a delightful street of arcaded shops with a carefully tended garden in the middle.

Paignton is not famous for being a hotbed for the arts. I have heard it stated that the town is the sort of place where "culture" is spelt with a "k", but this is not entirely fair. It has active and well respected choral and dramatic societies, and a Gilbert and Sullivan Society. This is singularly appropriate, as it was here that the world premier of *The Pirates of Penzance* took place in 1879, in a tiny theatre on the site of Woolworth's store in the town centre.

This unexpected venue for such an event was to establish the British copyright before the opera opened in New York. Gilbert and Sullivan had been cheated out of their royalties for their previous show, *HMS Pinafore*, when spies from America, planted at the London rehearsals, had copied down the words and music and set them back to the United States, enabling "pirate" productions to be put on. Hence the choice of a minute theatre in obscure Paignton for the first performance of their next masterpiece.

PAIGNTON REGATTA is in early August, and there are special events all through the year - see the TIC or a local paper for an idea of what's on. The town's foremost attraction for many years has been Paignton Zoo or, as it is now called, the ZOO AND ENVIRONMENT PARK (01803 527936), just outside on the way to Totnes. The zoo was founded in the 1920s by Herbert Whitley, a wealthy recluse whose main interest was his collection of animals. His home was at Primley, on the opposite side of the road leading into the town, protected by a long red sandstone wall. Whitley was taken to court in 1924 for not including an amount for Amusement Tax in his admission price. He insisted that the zoo was a serious educational service and 'amusement' had no part of it. The tax man won the case, and he was forced to close, but reopened in 1927. This time he swallowed the bullet and charged the unwelcome tax, but there is no doubt that he was right. The zoo has always been an educational and conservationist establishment, not a theme park.

The zoo site now covers 75 acres, and is developing in accordance with the latest thinking on the role of zoos in conservation. It has always sought to create the best environment for the animals, and is beautifully landscaped. People who are dubious of zoos in general have usually found this one acceptable. The collections of plants are spectacular, and as worth studying as the animals themselves.

Although Paignton has few historic buildings to see, it does have a couple. KIRKHAM HOUSE (01803 750700), owned by English Heritage, is an attractive 15th century stone house, built either for a merchant or an official of the Bishop's Palace. It gives a good impression of what it was like to live in a late Medieval building.

OLDWAY MANSION (01803 296244), now owned by Torbay Borough Council, is a remarkable 115 room pile, built in the style of a French chateau in the 1870s for Isaac Singer, the sewing machine millionaire, by his son Paris Singer. It was later remodelled and made to resemble a miniature Versaille. Isadora Duncan, Singer's mistress for a while, was a regular visitor. It has beautiful GARDENS, BOWLING GREENS, TENNIS COURTS and a CAFE.

A CENTURY OF PLAYTIME (01803 553850) is a collection of dolls, toys and playthings, with other childhood memoribilia. It is situated in WINNER STREET, towards the end of the town, away from the tourist trails, a special little shopping street where you get a strong sense of Paignton as a real Devon community.

For those who like to seek out the creative associations of a place, a good impression of the real Paignton can be gained from the work of the locally born author and artist Brian Carter, who still lives and works here. His autobiographical evocation of the town's working class community in the late 1940s, *Yesterday's Harvest* (1982), is as lyrical and vivid as *Cider With Rosie*, while in his novel about feral cats, *In the Long Dark* (1989) he charts the terrains and territories of his home town with the insight that only a native can possess. His many books of South Devon walks, usually leading to a pint of beer or farmhouse cider, and his daily column in the *Herald Express*, are essential reading for any visitor who wishes to see below the surface of the Torbay area and its hinterland.

In the middle of the town can be found the beginning of the popular PAIGNTON AND DARTMOUTH STEAM RAILWAY (01803 555872), a 7 mile journey of great beauty, which takes you quickly from the busy, red-brick heart of Paignton to the high wooded banks of the Dart and the lovely village of Kingswear (see next chapter for more information).

On its way the train passes GOODRINGTON SANDS, one of Torbay's most popular beaches, and the QUAYWEST BEACH RESORT (01803 555550), Britain's biggest and, it says, wettest and wildest waterpark, with rides, flumes, boats, go-karts, cafe and much more.

Also at Goodrington is the CLENNON VALLEY LEISURE CENTRE (01803 522240), with heated pool, fitness suite, sports hall, squash courts and sauna. The TORBAY GOLF CENTRE (01803 528728) is nearby.

Goodrington today is modern and fun-orientated, but the flat land around here was once marsh, and the beach was popular only with smugglers. They enjoyed a high reputation, and it is a fact that they were never caught, although they were known to be active.

A curiosity in Goodrington Park is the solitary granite headstone of a soldier, known as the "Major's Grave." Various stories exist to account for it, and there are said to be many other burials beneath the park, but there is nothing sad or sinister in this lively environment.

Moving towards Brixham, the next beach is at BROADSANDS, spacious as its name suggests, and from it you can take a very enjoyable cliff walk to ELBURY COVE.

After the busy-ness of Paignton, it is a relief to be approaching the countryside again; from Broadsands you can be quickly out of the built up area of modern Torbay and amongst fields, woodlands and pleasant footpaths. The villages of **CHURSTON FERRERS** and **GALMPTON** are worth exploring, the latter sitting by the River Dart at the end of Galmpton Creek and full of individual Devon architecture. The river here is only about half a mile from the sea at Broadsands, and apparently there was a scheme in the 19th century to link them by a canal, but we can only be glad it didn't happen.

Agatha Christie's home at Greenway is nearby, though not open to the public. It is best appreciated from the River Dart (see next Chapter). The poet Robert Graves was living at Galmpton during the 1940s, when he was writing his celebrated study of Celtic poetry and mysticism, *The White Goddess*, as well as working on his popular "Claudius" novels.

CHURSTON GOLF CLUB (01803 842894) is on the downs.

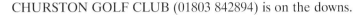

BRIXHAM (Tourist Information 01803 852861) is the last of the three Torbay towns, and the most historic. Its welcoming harbour, with the houses and church rising above, make a familiar picture, one that stays for ever in the mind, and the town is rich in memories and associations.

Here, William of Orange landed in 1688 to end the reign of the Stuarts and bring about the 'glorious, bloodless revolution.' Here a dying vicar, the Reverend Henry Francis Lyte, looking out across the Bay, was moved to write everybody's favourite hymn, "Abide With Me". Artists sit sketching by the quay, fishermen work on their boats, and locals and visitors alike move happily about the narrow, winding, flower-bedecked streets, or seek refreshment in old fashioned pubs with a genuine, unpretentious maritime flavour. The salt-sea smell and the cry of gulls is never far away.

Brixham has always been a fishing town, and for generations the men of the port have made a living from the sea. The town is known as the "Mother of the Deep Sea Fisheries", and it is perfectly true that the East Coast ports like

Hull and Grimsby were at one time way behind Brixham; indeed, it was only the fact that Brixham fishermen, journeying further afield, settled in these places, that caused the growth of the North Sea fishing industry.

In the 1850s Brixham was Britain's leading fishing port, but behind the prosperity was always a lot of poverty and hardship. The well-kept houses and cottages that are so desirable today, with geraniums outside the doors, were a different prospect in past centuries. BRIXHAM MUSEUM (01803 856267) tells the story of the town and its industries very thoroughly. By the harbourside is a replica of SIR FRANCIS DRAKE'S GOLDEN HIND, which visitors can board during the summer months.

Also on the Quay are THE DEEP (01803 858444), a nautical adventure centre which provides an imaginative experience for the whole family, and the MARINE AQUARIUM AND TRAWLING EXHIBITION (01803 882204).

Near the quay is the distinctively-shaped "COFFIN HOUSE". The story is that a disgruntled father built it for his daughter as a wedding present, an unsubtle way of saying that he disapproved of her choice of husband. If he hoped this would quickly lead them to their graves he was disappointed; they lived long and happily.

The once-popular novelist Francis Brett Young practised as a doctor in Brixham from 1907 to 1914, although he was a Midlander and most of his books are set there. The town itself is featured, rather unflatteringly, in a novel published in 1907 called *The Wingless Victory* by M.P.Willcocks, of whom there is more in the next chapter, but the best known literary connection of the town is with Henry Francis Lyte. He became vicar of Brixham in 1824, and amongst his famous hymns are "Praise My Soul The King of Heaven" and "Oh Worship the King". In 1847, at the early age of 55, knowing that he had very little time to live, he wrote "Abide With Me" whilst looking down over the town from Berry Head. He died in Nice a few weeks later.

Away from the harbourside area, with its wealth of gift shops, galleries, cafes and pubs, there is a surprising amount of Brixham which visitors never see. The traditional name for the upper part of the community is "Cowtown", while the lower, visitor-orientated area is called "Fishtown".

BRIXHAM HERITAGE FESTIVAL is in mid-May, while the REGATTA is in August. The former includes a race across the Bay for sailing trawlers.

Around Brixham are several small, quite intimate BEACHES which are worth seeking out, and at BERRY HEAD COUNTRY PARK is one of the most spectacular National Nature Reserves in the country. Berry Head is a prominent limestone eminence and forms the southern extremity of the Bay. It has a lighthouse, a fort built during the Napoleonic Wars, a network of footpaths and many rare species of plant, not to mention the seabirds. The LIGHTHOUSE is described as being simultaneously the highest, lowest and smallest in the South West: the highest because of being 200 feet above the sea, the lowest because of its mechanism, which is in an underground shaft, and the smallest because it is about the size of a newspaper kiosk. The Reserve is well looked after and explained by the Torbay Countryside Service, who have an Information Point here.

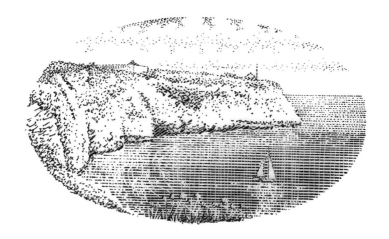

Moving inland from Brixham, the A3022 main road, becoming the A380, bypasses Paignton as it heads north towards Torquay. Two stretches of the road are named after Torbay's German and Dutch Twin Towns. The tribute to Hamelin, famous for its story of the Pied Piper, is easy to grasp; people have more trouble with Helevoetsluis Way. Locals have modified the pronunciation to "Helluva Way".

To your left, as you journey along the Ring Road, the rich countryside rolls off towards Totnes and the moors, and the vividness of the colours can be breathtaking: the brightness of blue sky and green foliage are only surpassed by the red of the ploughed fields, which glow as if lit from within.

Here, nestling in the hills, is **MARLDON**, a small village with a church and pub, surrounded by more recent estates of houses and bungalows. The village features as "Gentian Hill" in the much-loved novel of that name by Elizabeth Goudge, who lived here in the 1940s, and wrote gentle, mystical novels set in this countryside, which she described with exactly the right degree of visionary intensity.

Behind Marldon is the hamlet of **COMPTON**. The CASTLE (01803 872112), looked after by the National Trust, seems very un-warlike in this deep, peaceful setting, and in fact is less a defensive structure than a mildly fortified Medieval manor house. It was for many centuries the home of the Gilbert family, the most famous of whom was Sir Humphrey, half-brother to Sir Walter Raleigh, who was actually born at Greenway on the Dart (see next chapter). At the big junction at the bottom of the hill, turn left towards Newton Abbot, passing through **KINGSKERSWELL**, a large, mainly modern, roadside village. The road is new and fast, and as it leads you inexorably on from one big urban area to another, gives you little opportunity to appreciate the countryside. Beautiful villages, however, are actually not far away.

One such is **COFFINSWELL**, enfolded by the hills on the right, which was once the parish of the Reverend William Keble Martin, who achieved fame in his old age for his exquisite paintings in *The Concise British Flora*, published in 1970. Keble Martin was also responsible for the modern church of Milber, on the right as you enter the suburbs of Newton Abbot, and now closed for worship. The form of the church came to him in a dream, which was later realised by his architect brother.

NEWTON ABBOT (Tourist Information 01626 67494) is a town which is not, let us be honest, particularly compelling as a holiday centre. Instead it is a busy and useful market town, modern and spread out, a focus for commercial, administrative and industrial activity of all kinds. As the site of an important livestock market every Wednesday, it has always provided the people of rural South Devon, especially from the moorland farms and villages, with a refreshing and necessary burst of down-to-earth, urban liveliness once a week, and its many garrulous pubs include the famous OLD CIDER BAR in East Street. Some of the rough farm cider they serve here is definitely not for the faint-hearted or weak-stomached.

The town started in the Middle Ages as a couple of distinctive settlements, Newton Abbot and Newton Bushel, growing up around the confluence of the little River Lemon with the estuary of the Teign. It was the railway which brought about the joining together of these modest communities, and caused the spread of Newton Abbot's houses and terraces across the hills.

The place is not without its picturesque corners, and its parks and floral displays are well worth a look. Some old houses remain in Wolborough Street, which is dominated by the town's most famous landmark, ST LEONARD'S TOWER, "the tower without a church". It was here that Wllliam of Orange, after landing in Brixham in November 1688, promised to "maintain the liberties of England and the protestant religion" if he was accepted as king, which he duly was. The tower is opened to the public on Wednesdays.

Further along Wolborough Street, on the way out of town towards Totnes, is a row of attractive ALMSHOUSES, built in 1874, and soon afterwards you turn off to the right for BRADLEY MANOR (01626 54513), owned by the National Trust and occupied by the Woolner family.

Bradley is one of the most beautiful and well-preserved small Medieval manor houses in the country, surrounded by trees and fields, seemingly a million miles from the bustling town.

FORDE HOUSE (01626 61101) is an Elizabethan mansion with magnificent ceilings, now owned by Teignbridge District Council and usually open to the public.

NEWTON ABBOT MUSEUM (01626 334675) has good displays covering the history of the town and a lot of material on the Great Western Railway, which had such an effect on the community's growth.

Right next to the railway station is one of the most interesting of the more recent attractions in South Devon: TUCKERS MALTINGS (01626 334734). This is the only traditional working malthouse in England, and the malt for a great many famous real ales is made here. You can take a GUIDED TOUR of the factory and see the whole process, then buy the finished product from the BEER SHOP. You can also meet the malthouse cats, Edwin and Tucker, and enjoy a meal or a coffee in the CAFE. A BEER FESTIVAL is held in April.

Just outside Newton Abbot are to be found several gentle attractions which are a total delight to visit. The first of these, THE HEDGEHOG HOSPITAL AT PRICKLY BALL FARM (01626 62319) is ideal for young children, and a painless introduction for them to the ideas of conservation and respect for life.

On the way to Totnes, PLEASANT VIEW NURSERY AND GARDEN (01803 813388) is a 4 acre garden and arboretum with an international reputation for its shrubs, and a couple of miles further on, next to Dainton Golf Club, is FERMOYS GARDEN CENTRE (01803 813504) with a FARM SHOP, CHILDREN'S PLAY AREA, CAFE and much else.

On the other side of Newton, towards Bovey Tracey, THE ORCHID PARADISE (01626 52233) at Forches Cross is a rich and luxuriant indoor display of these rare and lovely plants, with an outdoor PICNIC AREA and NURSERY SHOP. Not far from here is STOVER COUNTRY PARK, in the grounds of Stover House, once a seat of the Dukes of Somerset and now a girls' school. Stover has beautiful GARDENS and WOODLAND WALKS around a lake.

For sport and recreation, Newton Abbot has a full range of facilities at the DYRONS CENTRE (01626 60426). GOLF can be enjoyed at STOVER (01626 52460) and DAINTON (01803 813812) courses, and at the HELE PARK GOLF CENTRE (01626 336060). NEWTON ABBOT RACE COURSE (01626 53235), between the town and Kingsteignton, features regular race meetings throughout the year.

The village of **KINGSTEIGNTON** is almost continuous now with Newton Abbot, but retains its own proud identity. It is a large, spread out, industrial and residential village, with an ancient centre around the church. Many of its houses are built of a distinctive yellowish brick. The land round about is flat, for Devon, but the area has its own appeal, with the small tussocky fields, and much visual evidence of the clay industry, past and present.

THE RIVER TEIGN, one of Devon's most beautiful streams, can be pronounced in no less than three different ways, according to the place it is linked with. On its own it is usually pronounced "Teen". At Kingsteignton and Bishopsteignton, however, it becomes "Tane", while at its mouth it is always "Tin" - "Tinmuff". Impress the locals by getting it right.

Before exploring the estuary we shall journey inland a little further to the area of the HALDON HILLS. Haldon and Telegraph Hills have to be traversed by anyone travelling between South Devon and Exeter, the former on the A38, the latter on the A380. The range of forested hills on either side of these main roads, rising to over 800 feet at the highest point, are becoming increasingly popular as an attraction in their own right.

There are some very enjoyable WOODLAND WALKS to be found, and look out for the deer which live in the forest. HALDON, with LITTLE HALDON to its right, are covered by a network of paths and trails which are well signposted from the main roads, so if you have time, stop and discover some of Devon's most individual hills. During the 1960s and 70s the area became well known for its number of resident tramps. The most often seen, Smokey Joe, was mourned by thousands of regular road users when he died in 1976.

The wide views from the Haldons are also magnificent, even if only seen from the highways, and can be quite dramatic in certain weather conditions. Very often the traveller from the west, crossing the rise and coming down towards Exeter, leaves rain and cloud for bright sunlight and clarity.

The eye-catching HALDON BELVEDERE is a tall, three-sided structure which has recently been restored and is occasionally open to the public (01392 833668). It is also known as LAWRENCE CASTLE, and was built in 1788 by Sir Robert Palk in memory of his friend and colleague in the East India service, General Stringer Lawrence.

A little further to the east is MAMHEAD PARK. Though not open to the public, Mamhead is a notable house, and, beside a tree in the grounds, James Boswell, biographer of Dr Johnson, swore never to drink again (he failed to live up to the vow). The OBELISK in the park can be seen for many miles across the countryside. LIDWELL CHAPEL, a ruined chapel in the woods near LITTLE HALDON, is reputed to be haunted by a monk who murdered travellers and threw their bodies down a well. Right on the brow of the hill next to the A38, HALDON RACECOURSE holds regular racing events, and is open every Sunday for a large CAR BOOT SALE.

The pleasant little town of **CHUDLEIGH**, nestling below the hills, has some interesting old houses and lanes, and a good choice of pubs, shops and cafes. Its character as an old town that grew up along the main road is still strong. The WHEEL CRAFT CENTRE (01626 852698) features the work of many fine makers, and has a SHOP and RESTAURANT.

CHUDLEIGH VINEYARD AND WINERY (01626 853258) is the only registered organic vineyard in Devon and Cornwall. From Easter to the end of October you can wander through the vineyard and enjoy a glass of wine afterwards as you admire the views of Dartmoor. The vineyard is open for sales throughout the year.

Imposing UGBROOKE PARK (01626 852179) is a late 17th century house designed by Robert Adam for one of the Lords Clifford of Chudleigh, whose descendants still live here. Its grounds were laid out by Capability Brown, and the poet John Dryden was a regular visitor. He dedicated his translation of Virgil's *Eclogues* and *Georgics* to the son of his host. The house has many interesting features and a collection of furniture, paintings, costumes and uniforms, while the gardens contain aviaries and ornamental wildfowl.

CANONTEIGN FALLS (01647 252434) is the highest waterfall in the country, and is now surrounded by imaginatively laid out LAKES and GARDENS, with all the usual visitor facilities. This relatively new attraction is being developed all the time, with a Victorian fern garden taking shape, and a WETLAND NATURE RESERVE already functioning.

CHUDLEIGH ROCK, a mile south of the town, is a large limestone outcrop looking a bit like a ruined castle, and has been a popular beauty spot since the last century.

The main railway line through South Devon traverses the southern side of the Exe estuary and along by the sea at Dawlish and Teignmouth. We shall end this chapter by following it, by road, to the Teign estuary and back to Torbay.

POWDERHAM CASTLE (01626 890243), in its peaceful deer park beside the Exe, is the historic family home of the Earls of Devon, as it has been for over six hundred years. The present Earl is a direct descendant of Sir Philip Courtenay, who built the original Castle between 1390 and 1420. It was damaged during the Civil War and extensively remodelled during the 18th and 19th centuries as a dignified country house.

Altogether, the Castle has a tranquil, very un-military atmosphere. Inside it is rich in furnishings and decoration; many portraits by, amongst others, the Devon artists Reynolds and Cosway, adorn the walls, and there is a fine 14 foot high clock by the 18th century Devon maker William Stumbels of Totnes, one of the best clockmakers of the time outside London. The late 18th century Music Room and the Grand Staircase are especially noteworthy.

The GARDENS at Powderham are informal and very attractive. The Rose Garden, with fine views of the Exe, is planted with sweetly scented, old fashioned varieties. Somewhere in the gardens you might encounter Timothy, the Powderham tortoise, who has been keeping the weeds down on the lawn for over 150 years.

STARCROSS is an attractive, long village beside the road and the railway line to Dawlish, looking over the wide estuary of the Exe, with the little harbour of **COCKWOOD** nearby. A regular FERRY makes the crossing to Exmouth during the summer months.

At the mouth of the river is the unique DAWLISH WARREN NATURE RESERVE. The WARREN itself is a spit of land, over a mile long, with a beach and sand dunes, extending almost to Exmouth. It is strange, rather haunting place, and quite possibly haunted as well. A fight between Dutch and English seamen once happened here, and all the Dutchmen were killed, being buried in unmarked graves. When the wind howls amongst the marram grasses and the waters crash onto the spit from both sides, they are supposed to rise from their sandy graves and howl for vengeance.

During the 1920s and 1930s a number of eccentric dwellings, some literally made of driftwood, were built at the far end of the Warren, and a diverse group of mainly wealthy but slightly bohemian people spent the summers in them. One of these was a young Devonian called Raymond B. Cattell, who later moved to America and went on to become one of the world's leading academic psychologists. He described his life here in a highly entertaining book, one of the most individual ever written about Devon: *Under Sail Through Red Devon* (1937), recording his adventures sailing around the coast and along the estuaries.

The Warren Nature Reserve covers 505 acres and is of international significance; the Jersey Lily is just one of the rare species which live here - the Warren is the only place on mainland Britain where you can find it. GUIDED WALKS are regularly organised through the reserve, which is jointly run by the Devon Wildlife Trust and Teignbridge District Council.

DAWLISH (Tourist Information 01626 863589) is an enjoyable, sunny, not too boisterous resort, mainly Regency and Victorian in style, but with an older core away from the sea front. Brunel's Great Western Railway audaciously runs right above the beach and through the red cliffs; legend has it that the great man designed the station on the back of an envelope.

Through the middle of the town extends THE LAWN, a beautifully laid out park which gives an expansiveness and brightness to the scene. DAWLISH WATER, a wide brook, is at its centre, and moving serenely on it can be seen the famous BLACK SWANS; generations of them have now lived here, after the originals were presented to the town from Australia. The swans are joined by ducks of various kinds, and it is all very restful and civilised. The author of Black's 1867 Guide to Devon obviously liked it here: "Through the bosom of the valley which here opens out upon the sea runs a crystal rivulet, spanned by numerous bridges, and lined on each side by a broad border of smooth greensward". He thought the climate had an "almost Italian geniality".

Dawlish is very much a friendly, family resort, with sandy beaches, some of them quite secluded, others wide and gregarious. Everyone is free to use them now, but at one time the authorities of the town were anxious that their lovely beaches should not be invaded by the lower classes from Exeter on cheap railway excursions.

They therefore arranged with the railway company that cheap tickets would only be issued to the servant girls and labourers of the city on the condition that they caught the earliest possible train back. This gave them exactly twenty minutes on the beach.

There is a large holiday park at the Warren end of the town, about which it is best not to wonder what the Victorian residents would think. Dawlish holds a varied ARTS FESTIVAL in June, and there is always plenty going on in the town to occupy all ages. DAWLISH MUSEUM (no telephone number) at the Knowle, Barton Terrace, has a local history collection including kitchen utensils, costumes, Victoriana and military items. At THE CRAWSHAW GALLERY you can look at - and buy - paintings by the internationally famous artist ALWYN CRAWSHAW and his family.

The highly esteemed Midlands folklorist Henry Possett, who retired to Dawlish in 1974, rediscovered the almost forgotten tradition of the DAWLISH GIANT, a huge effigy which used to be paraded through the backstreets on New Year's Eve with the aim of procuring liquor for the participants from the landlords of public houses. Possett was on the verge of reviving the custom just before his death, and though he did not live to see it done, he would be pleased to know that it was successfully achieved in the 1980s. Dawlish also has a FOLK FESTIVAL early in September.

The DAWLISH LEISURE CENTRE (01626 863873) provides a large swimming pool, a sports and exhibition hall, astro turf and grass sports pitches and a bar. Golf is available at DAWLISH WARREN GOLF CLUB (01626 862255). Boats for fishing or cruising can be hired along the front very easily.

A few miles along the coast, separated from Dawlish by the bright red cliffs, is **TEIGNMOUTH** (Tourist Information 01626 779769). Another favourite place for a traditional family seaside holiday, it is also a working fishing port and has a longer history than its mainly 20th century appearance suggests. It was razed to the ground twice by the French, in 1340 and 1690, and during World War Two it suffered more bomb damage than any other Devon town except Exeter and Plymouth.

This traumatic past is fortunately belied, today, by the cheerful and refreshing atmosphere of the place. There is also a pleasing contrast between the sights, smells and sounds of the seaside town at the front, and the estuarine fishing town just behind it.

The BEACHES at Teignmouth are particularly safe, and there are even some good old-fashioned DONKEY RIDES to be enjoyed. The PIER offers a variety of games and amusements and THE DEN, a beautifully kept park, is an ideal place to relax in the sun.

Between Teignmouth and Dawlish are two distinctive red sandstone rock formations known as THE PARSON AND THE CLERK. The story, which exists in numerous versions, one or other of which is repeated in every book ever written on the area, is basically that they were a real parson and his clerk, who were turned to stone after losing a bet with the Devil.

TEIGNMOUTH MUSEUM (no telephone number) contains a wealth of objects and information on the local history of the town, which has a place in the story of English literature because of the visit by John Keats in March 1818.

Keats came here with his brother, who was dying of tuberculosis. Their hope was that the seawater and the fresh air would help. Unfortunately, Keats didn't realise that he himself already had the disease as well. They stayed at what is now 35 The Strand, and the poet worked on the manuscript of his great work *Endymion*. He did not think much of Teignmouth, or of Devon as a whole:

"You may say what you will of Devonshire" he wrote, "the truth is, it is a splashy, rainy, misty, snowy, foggy, haily, floody, muddy, slipshod county." He went on to abuse the men of Devon for their weak, ineffectual, pusillanimous nature. Keats had little sense of history, and it had obviously slipped his mind that Drake, Raleigh, Hawkins, Grenville and the rest were men of Devon.

He cheered up a little when the sun came out, however, and wrote some charming lyrics about the surrounding landscapes, the villages and the pretty girls to be found in them; whenever I am on a train pulling out of Newton Abbot station, heading towards the marshes at the beginning of the estuary, I think of Keats watching the market girls dancing near here, on a spring evening, 180 years ago:

For there's Bishop's Teign
And King's Teign
And Coombe in the clear Teign head
Where close by the stream
You may have your cream
All spread upon barley bread
There is Newton Marsh
With its spear-grass harsh
A pleasant summer level
Where the maidens sweet
Of the Market Street
Do meet in the dusk to revel

TEIGNMOUTH GOLF CLUB (01626 774194) welcomes visitors, and there is a heated pool in the town. Imaginative ENTERTAINMENT is a strong point of this resort. Many outdoor shows and performances take place during the summer, and in November the town hosts a 3 day JAZZ FESTIVAL, one of the biggest in the South West. There is also a small THEATRE on the sea front where touring repertory shows take you painlessly back to the 1950s, and even beyond.

SHALDON (Tourist Information 01626 873723) sits across the estuary from Teignmouth. It is a beautiful, shapely village, gently climbing the wooded hills, and full of narrow streets, small shops and intimate pubs. You can reach it by FERRY or by the 1700 foot long bridge. Shaldon has a strong Georgian feel in its architecture, but there are some nice Victorian buildings as well, including the Parish Church. If you are in the village on a WEDNESDAY during the Summer you can see locals dressed in VICTORIAN costume. SHALDON WILDLIFE TRUST (01626 872234), which is sometimes described as a children's zoo, is actually a breeding centre for rare and small mammals, birds and reptiles, including some of the world's smallest monkeys.

Shaldon was not always so totally genteel. In 1773 the novelist Fanny Burney was at Teignmouth for her health, and she saw a rowing match between the fisherwomen of Shaldon, who were obviously aggressive and tough "Devon dumplings". They had to be, as their menfolk were, for much of the year, far away, catching Newfoundland cod. These women deeply impressed the novelist, as she described them as "robust and well made" with "striking teeth". Maybe it was in comparison with these Amazons that Keats thought the local men so pathetic.

THE NESS at Shaldon is a red, tree-covered cliff with lovely walks and views of the Teign estuary, which is wide, long and lake-like, surrounded by typical

South Devon fields and woods, with Dartmoor clearly seen in the distance. A "SMUGGLER'S TUNNEL", actually constructed in the late 18th or early 19th century to transport limestone to the kilns on the other side, takes you from the Ness to a beautiful beach on the other side of the headland.

From Shaldon you can take the A379 to Babbacombe and Torquay, which is only minutes' away, or you can journey along the river on either side and around to the Bay through Newton Abbot. On the way, if you have time, pay a visit to the pleasant village of **STOKEINTEIGNHEAD**, which has a famous pub.

Back on the Teignmouth side of the water, half way to Newton Abbot, is **BISHOPSTEIGNTON**, a large, mainly residential village. Near here is LINDRIDGE PARK, once the setting for the magnificent LINDRIDGE HOUSE, which was apparently destroyed by the careless removal of the "Lindridge Buddha". The Buddha was a statue brought back from the far east and placed on a terrace. It was predicted that if it was ever moved, disaster would follow. The years went by, country houses became harder to maintain and Lindridge went through many changes of ownership until, in the early 1960s, it was bought by a couple who set about restoring the house and gardens to their original state. They were all ready for the grand opening when somebody moved the Buddha from its place on the terrace... soon afterwards the house was totally destroyed by the worst fire in Devon for decades, and no cause was ever discovered.

Returning to the Shaldon bank, there is an enjoyable footpath which can be followed. This is part of the TEMPLER WAY (spelt correctly), a 15 mile walk from HAYTOR to TEIGNMOUTH, following the line of the HAYTOR GRANITE TRAMWAY and THE STOVER CANAL, both built to enable stone from Dartmoor to be taken to London and beyond for building purposes. More about this in the Dartmoor chapter.

About half way along the broad estuary is the large, prominent inn at COOMBE CELLARS, popular with sailors and fishermen, and with inevitable stories told of it concerning its use by smugglers. Local legend also has it that Nelson used to meet his mistress, Emma Hamilton, at the inn.

Hidden away in the hills near Newton Abbot, but a thousand miles away in atmosphere, is the beautiful little Medieval church of HACCOMBE. This sits below the large, and not especially beautiful, Haccombe House, built in 1830 for the Carews, an old Devon family who had lived in an earlier house here for centuries. When the owner, who had pulled down his out of date Elizabethan mansion and gone away to Europe whilst the new one was being constructed, saw the place for the first time, he said to the architect "Well, I believe that now I may take to myself the credit of possessing the very ugliest house in the country".

The house is not open to the public, but the church is, and is well worth visiting. By some curious church rule its priest was not subject to the Bishop of Exeter, but only to the Archbishop of Canterbury. It is full of Carew monuments, and is exceptional for its stained glass, its tombs, its brasses and its floor tiles. The brass for Thomas and Anne Carew, who died in 1676 within two days of each other, has the following verse below it (I have modernised the spelling):

Two bodies lie beneath this stone
Whom love and marriage long made one
One soil conjoined them by a force
Above the power of death's divorce
One flame of love their lives did burn
Even to ashes in their urn
They die, but not depart, who meet
In wedding and in winding sheet
Whom God hath knit so firm in one
Admit no separation
Therefore unto one marble tryst
We leave their now united dust
As root in earth embrace to rise
Most lovely flowers in paradise.

An old story is told of the rivalry between the Carews, who briefly held the title of Earls of Totnes, and the Chapernownes of Dartington and Modbury. A Carew wagered a Champernowne that he could ride his horse further into the sea at Tor Bay. Carew won, and saved the life of his opponent, later nailing two horse shoes to the porch door. One of them, and a small portion of the other, can still be seen.

From this peaceful corner it is but a short journey back to the busy roads and new buildings of Newton Abbot, and the highway which takes you quickly back to Torbay.

SAMPSONS FARM RESTAURANT
Preston
Newton Abbot
Devon TQ12 3PP

Tel. and Fax (01626) 54913

'A Thatched Restaurant With Rooms on the Banks of the Lower Teign'

Sampsons Farm is a unique Restaurant with Top Class Accommodation, situated in a small hamlet on the banks of the beautiful River Teign near Newton Abbot.

The Farm is set in its own peaceful grounds, and is a Medieval thatched Devon longhouse, with oak beams, panelling and inglenook fireplaces. It has been well restored and is maintained to a high standard, whilst retaining the unique atmosphere of such an ancient building, complete with creaky floors and a spiral staircase. Although it is so close to the bustling market town of Newton Abbot and main roads to Torbay, Exeter and Plymouth, it is wonderfully secluded and free of traffic noise. Chickens, ducks and geese occupy the paddock.

Sampsons Farm has a high reputation for the quality of its food and the friendly, caring approach of its owners and staff. Its proprietor is Nigel Bell, who has many years' experience behind him, and is fortunate in having dedicated and well-trained support from Kirstin Baker, Chris Holgate, the chefs and Nigel's mum,who specialise in providing delicious breakfasts for their guests.

The restaurant serves good, English and Continental cuisine, using fresh local ingredients as a matter of course. The house speciality is Half a Devonshire Duckling, served either with an orange or black cherry sauce; this dish requires 24 hours notice. All starters and sweets are made on the premises. The food is accompanied by a well-chosen selection of French and Californian wines, as well as English wines from the local vineyards at Bovey Tracey and Chudleigh.

All accommodation is comfortable, spacious and individual. Two rooms have four-poster beds, and all enjoy wonderful views of the South Devon countryside. Each has tea and coffee making facilities and colour television.

As a base for exploring Devon, and even Cornwall, Sampsons Farm is in an ideal position. Torbay and Dartmoor are about equally distant, while the historic city of Exeter and the fascinating old towns of Totnes, Dartmouth and Tavistock can all be reached within half an hour. There are excellent sports and fitness facilities in Newton Abbot, while for walking, riding, fishing, birdwatching, boating and golf the area has many opportunities.

USEFUL INFORMATION

OPEN All Year.

CHILDREN No.

CREDIT CARDS All Taken.

LICENCE Restaurant andTable.

ACCOMMODATION 5 en suite, non en-suite rooms available, plus cottage with 2 bedrooms. Phone for more information on current accommodation.

PRICES B&B High Season: £17.50 - £27.50 p.p. Low Season: £16.50 - £25.00 p.p

RESTAURANT A la carte menu. Fine selection of meat and fish dishes, fresh local produce. House speciality, Half a Devon Duckling. Table D'hote from £12.50 p.p.

VEGETARIAN Approx. 5 dishes always available.

SMOKING Lounge only

DISABLED Level access.

PETS By special permission

GARDEN Patio.

THE OSBORNE HOTEL,
Hesketh Crescent,
Meadfoot,
Torquay, Devon TQ1 2LL

Tel: 01803 213311 Fax: 01803 296788

AA 3* 78%.2 Rosettes for Fine Cuisine. RAC Merit Awards for Hospitality and Restaurant.
ETB. 4 Crowns Highly Commended.Egon Ronay & AA Good Restaurant Guide Recommended

The Osborne is known to those who have discovered its charm and its affordable elegance as 'The Country House Hotel by the sea'. It is the centrepiece of an elegant Regency crescent, which the Torquay cognoscenti will tell you is one of the most desirable places in the town. The view from the windows is stunning across five acres of hotel gardens to the broad sweep of Torbay. Yet one is always reminded that the countryside is just a few minutes away. A perfect place in which to stay for an extended holiday or for a shorter break at any time of the year. One of the great benefits of Torquay is the mild climate which makes it as pleasant to be there in the spring, autumn and winter as it is in the height of the season.

The Osborne guests immediately feel welcome and find the friendly but efficient staff always at hand to provide an unobtrusive personal service.With 29 bedrooms it is still small enough to be able to care individually for every guest. Each of the bedrooms is ensuite and charmingly appointed, most with sea views and all individually designed with every convenience. Most double rooms have kingsize beds and a number of bedrooms have a fantastic view overlooking the bay; four suites have their own private balconies. The hotel's romantic Langtry's Restaurant overlooks the sea and it has a well deserved reputation for the excellence of its food and wines which meet the most exacting gourmet standards. The talented chef combines new, innovative dishes with tempting regional specialities. The Brasserie is delightfully informal and here you can select from a wide-ranging menu at any time of the day. It has its own comprehensive bar and serves excellent Italian coffee and Devon cream teas.

There are those who come to Torquay for reasons other than leisure and for the business person, The Osborne is ideal whether it is simply to stay whilst attending to business in the Bay or for a conference. In this field the hotel excels with comprehensive business facilities and first class professional support from the staff. Social functions, anniversaries, birthdays and weddings in particular are all enhanced in the beautiful setting of The Osborne. There are some who simply revel in doing absolutely nothing during a holiday - The Osborne is just the place for that but there are those who demand a little more activity, again The Osborne can provide indoor and outdoor swimming pools, a fully equipped health suite with gymnasium, sauna, plunge pool and solarium, snooker room, an all-weather tennis court and a putting green, - all available without leaving the hotel grounds. Other sports like sailing, riding, archery, ballooning, clay pigeon shooting, fishing, golf, - these and many others can be arranged for you.

USEFUL INFORMATION

OPEN; All year   **RESTAURANT;Superb food to gourmet standards.**
CHILDREN; Welcome   **THE BRASSERIE; Food available all day + bar**
CREDIT CARDS; All major cards (Except diners)   **VEGETARIAN; Always a choice**
LICENSED; Yes. Fine wines   **DISABLED ACCESS; Yes. Lifts**
ACCOMMODATION; 29 ensuite rooms   **GARDEN; 5 acres, heated pool.**
PETS, No
RATES:-High Season £62 B&B/£77HB pppn . Low Season £41 B&B/£55 HB pppn.
Surcharges:- £5 pppn Seaview Room. £15 pppn Seaview Suite. Children 5+£18 All Year.

SUITE DREAMS COUNTRY HOTEL
Steep Hill
Maidencombe
Torquay
Devon TQ1 4TS

Tel. (01803) 313900
Fax (01803) 313841

AA 4 Qs Selected,
ETB 2 Crowns Highly Commended

Suite Dreams is a purpose-built, luxurious country hotel, set in breathtakingly lovely surroundings overlooking the South Devon coast, just outside Torquay.

The emphasis is very much on comfort, spaciousness and relaxation at this beautifully furnished and laid out hotel, where every effort is made to ensure that your stay is memorable and enjoyable. The hotel and its environment are secluded and very tranquil.

The suites are all roomy, elegant and tasteful, each containing a wide screen remote control television, a refrigerator, direct dial telephone, concealed ironing equipment, hairdryer and tea and coffee making facilities. Double and twin rooms are available, and can accommodate extra beds for children if required. Comfort is assured at all times of the year by controllable central heating. Each suite has magnificent views from its windows, either of the sea or the surrounding countryside. Three of them open directly onto the large sun terrace, set in beautiful gardens.

The resident proprietors at Suite Dreams are Ken and Lorraine James, both born and bred Devonians, who promise a friendly, helpful atmosphere, desiring to create a home from home for all their guests. The keyword, they say, is luxury.

Suite Dreams provides a wide-ranging breakfast menu in its prices. Evening meals are run in conjunction with the Thatched Tavern next door, where customers can enjoy an extensive choice of poultry, fish and meat dishes, vegetarian meals and a full selection of beers, wines and spirits.

The hotel, with its spirit of peace and comfort, is an ideal place from which to explore the endless delights of South Devon. Maidencombe Beach, quiet, safe and intimate, excellent for children, is just a short walk from the hotel, while the bright lights, shops and entertainment of Torquay are nearby. Further afield you can easily encompass the historic towns of Totnes and Dartmouth, the ancient city of Exeter and the magnificent scenery of the Dartmoor National Park.

USEFUL INFORMATION

OPEN All Year.
CHILDREN Welcome, but no special facilities.
CREDIT CARDS Mastercard, Visa, Delta, Eurocard, American Express.
LICENCE No.
RESTAURANT Breakfast only; see above.
VEGETARIAN see above.
SMOKING Permitted, but not in dining area.
DISABLED No special access.
PETS Welcome by prior arrangement.
GARDEN Patio for relaxing and sunbathing.
ACCOMMODATION 12 en suite rooms, double and twin.
PRICES High Season: £20-£30, Low Season £17.50-£25. Children £10.

SOUTHSANDS HOTEL
Alta Vista Road
Paignton
Devon
TQ4 6BZ

Tel. (01803) 557231
Fax (01803) 529947

AA 1 Star,
ETB 3 Crowns Commended,
Les Routiers

Overlooking the lovely expanse of Goodrington Sands and tree-shaded Youngs Park, south-facing and with spectacular coastal views, the South Sands is one of the most comfortable, friendly and well-situated family hotels in Torbay. Although only a few minutes' walk from Paignton town centre, it is away from the noise and makes an ideal place for a relaxing break, with something for all ages and interests.

The hotel, of local red sandstone, was originally built at the turn of the century, as a summer retreat for a canon of Exeter Cathedral. It is now owned and run by the Cahill family. Tony and Cecile Cahill bring a wide range of skills and experience to the South Sands, having been wine merchants, farmers and proprietors of a rest home. Tony is also an ex-Merchant Navy radio officer, and Cecile is a former language teacher. Their two sons work at the hotel when home from university, and Tony's parents are also involved. Many of the staff during the summer are French students, often friends and relatives of previous staff. The family atmosphere is strong.

The bright, sunny rooms, all en suite, are centrally heated and well equipped with colour televisions, teamaking facilities, telephones and baby listening service. Most of them have superb views of the sea. The popular Lounge Bar gives the same feeling of spaciousness and warmth.

One of the most enjoyable rooms to be in is the South Sands' Restaurant, overlooking the sea, where guests can partake of a substantial breakfast and an outstanding choice of quality, well-prepared English and continental meals made from fresh local produce. An extensive Wine List includes a good choice of French, German and Australian wines.

Entertainment is a regular feature at the hotel during the season, and guests can take to the woodblock dance floor. Special events like free weekly wine tastings and barbecues take place throughout the summer. The South Sands is an excellent venue for parties, celebrations and anniversaries; the Cahills will take care of everything, including the transport if necessary, leaving you free to enjoy the fun.

USEFUL INFORMATION

OPEN March to Oct, Christmas & New Year.
CHILDREN All ages welcome. Baby listening in all rooms.
CREDIT CARDS Mastercard, Visa.
LICENCE Full Restricted.
ACCOMMODATION 19 en suite rooms.
PRICES High Season: £220 half board weekly; Low Season: £170. Children half price, 2nd child Free.

RESTAURANT English and Continental cooked to a high standard. Fresh produce.
VEGETARIAN Approx. 7 dishes to choose
SMOKING Permitted.
DISABLED Level access from car park. All public rooms on ground floor.
PETS Welcome.
GARDEN Magnificent display of fuschias and hanging baskets. Lawn area for eating & drinking.

GLENSIDE
Ringmoor Road
Shaldon
Devon TQ14 0EP
Tel. (01626) 872448
ETB 3 Crowns Commended.

Glenside is a small, cottage-style hotel in the pleasant village of Shaldon. It occupies a beautiful site on the southern bank of the Teign estuary opposite Teignmouth, with unsurpassed views over the water. It is just a 10 minute, level walk to the beach, and the regular passenger ferry across to Teignmouth. The hotel was originally built in about 1820 as a private residence. During the 1930s it was a school, and amongst its unusual features are gently sloping doors and floors. In the garden there is a Judas tree. The Glenside's proprietors are Keith and Tricia Underwood, who have a high reputation for providing friendly, personal service, good, home-cooked meals and 'extras' such as a welcoming pot of tea in the garden or lounge on arrival, and their own maps giving details of local walks. There is a choice of single, double, twin or family rooms, and all bedrooms have colour television and tea/coffee making facilities. The lounge is comfortable, and the hotel has a well-stocked bar. Shaldon is a peaceful, friendly, old fashioned little place, within easy reach of quiet beaches and unspoilt coastal scenery, but the livelier resorts of Teignmouth, Dawlish and Torbay are a short distance away, as are the inland towns of South Devon and the romantic expanse of Dartmoor.

USEFUL INFORMATION

OPEN All Year.
CHILDREN Welcome over 3 years.
CREDIT CARDS Not taken.
LICENCE Residential
ACCOMMODATION 9 bedrooms, 8 en suite.
PRICES High Season: £22, Low Season: £19.50.
Children £10. Prices include breakfast.

RESTAURANT Traditional, home-cooked meals.
Dinner £13.
VEGETARIAN By request.
SMOKING Restricted to some areas.
DISABLED Some access.
PETS Welcome.
GARDEN Yes. Facilities for eating & drinking.

THE TOBY JUG INN
Bickington
Newton Abbot
Devon TQ12 6JZ
Tel. (01626) 821278

Just off the A38 main road from Exeter to Plymouth, the attractive village of Bickington has as its focal point this genuinely traditional Devon pub. At the Toby Jug Inn, dating from the sixteenth century, a very warm welcome is provided by the colourful landlady, Christine Matthews, together with her bubbly chef Vicky, bar-maid Doreen and their team of friendly waitresses. These ebullient ladies create, between them, a varied and highly atmospheric village inn, with generous food, wines, well-kept ales and a cast of friendly characters in both bars. In the busy Stable Bar, decorated with echoes of the agricultural past, the spirit is lively and local. The quieter Lounge Bar contains a fine collection of Toby Jugs. Separate from both, the restaurant serves a wide selection of home-cooked meals, ranging from traditional English to world cuisine, to tempt the palate. Those wishing for snacks or simpler bar meals will find that there is always an extensive specials board. In fine weather the beer garden provides a colourful and relaxing environment in which to enjoy excellent food and drink. The Toby Jug Inn is ideally situated between Dartmoor and the rest of South Devon, within reach of all its myriad attractions.

USEFUL INFORMATION

OPEN 11am - 2.30pm & 6 - 11pm.
Sunday: 12 -2.30pm & 7 - 10.30pm.
CHILDREN Welcome in non-smoking
dining room.
CREDIT CARDS No.
LICENCE Full.

VEGETARIAN At least 10 dishes available.
SMOKING Non-smoking areas, inc. dining room.
DISABLED No special facilities.
PETS Dogs welcome in bar.
GARDEN Flowered beer garden, many pets.

RESTAURANT Generous servings of traditional and world cuisine.
BAR FOOD Extensive choice from boards; snacks and children's meals available.

OLD RYDON INN
Rydon Road,
Kingsteignton, Newton Abbot
Devon TQ12 3QG
Tel: 01626 54626
Fax: 01626 56980

This fascinating Grade II listed former farmhouse is a totally unexpected find in the middle of a housing estate just off the busy Teignmouth/Kingsteignton road. You take the first turning right into Longford Lane and Rydon Road is at the bottom of the hill on your right. The Old Rydon Inn is now known far and wide as one of the most exciting inns in Devon and renowned too for the excellence of its food. The restaurant takes up the oldest part of the building and has original elm screens and a table with a well underneath. The cosy pub, in what was the stable, has seating upstairs in the old cider apple loft, a most unusual conservatory with grape vines above and flowering tropical plants, and a large sheltered walled garden. Altogether a delightful place to visit The Old Rydon has been owned and personally run by Hermann and Miranda Hruby since 1978 and it is their constant interest in food which has kept the menu abreast of the times without losing sight of all the traditional favourites that will always stay high on the popularity list. Whether you eat in the restaurant or just have a bar meal, the choice is extensive and always freshly cooked.The Pot roasted Gressingham Duck with a parsnip and coriander puree served on a ginger, honey and orange sauce served garnished with grilled Cumberland sausage is memorable. Steaks from the charcoal grill can be topped with sauces or other exciting things or you can have them served plain with sauteed flat cap mushrooms, garlic butter and straw potatoes. From the Blackboard Menu you might choose Grilled mussels, buttered clams or flat cap mushrooms in garlic butter as a starter and keeping to the food of the sea, follow it with Fisherman's Pie with Brixham cod, prawns, mushrooms, leaf spinach and leeks in a fresh cream and white wine sauce topped with potato, cheese and herb breadcrumbs served with salads.

USEFUL INFORMATION

OPEN; All Year Pub:11-2.30pm & 6-11pm	**RESTAURANT; Superb, innovative menu**
Sun:12-3pm & 7-10.30pm	**BAR FOOD; Wide range. Blackboard**
Rest: 7pm-midnight (Supper Licence)	**VEGETARIAN; Catered for**
CHILDREN; Welcome	**SMOKING; Not in restaurant**
CREDIT CARDS; All major cards	**DISABLED ; Steps everywhere**
LICENCED; Yes + Supper Licence	**PETS; No**
PRICES; For Food:- Bar: £3/£10 pp. Restaurant: £11/£20 pp.	

THE CHASERS ARMS
Stoke-in-Teignhead,
Newton Abbot, Devon TQ12 4QS
Tel: 01626 873670

This thatched 16th century old Devon Long House stands in 2 acres of landscaped grounds and well tended attractive gardens in a strictly rural setting yet in close proximity with all the major routes. Inside it is full of the olde worlde atmosphere with an abundance of beams, low ceilings and gleaming copper and brass. In the colder months the large inglenook fireplace throws out a wonderful heat from the burning logs and that tantalising smell that always comes with wood burning. The inn is in total harmony with the pretty village of Stoke-in-Teignhead with its thatched cottages and fine 13th century church. From here you are within easy reach of the village of Shaldon on the Teign Estuary with its old fashioned shops and Victorian Shopping Day on Wednesdays. The model village at Babbacombe is another favourite place for visitors and would make an ideal outing after a good lunch at the Chasers Arms. The menu will tempt even the most difficult palate. You can choose from the menu which proclaims a whole range of interesting starters including Salmon Gazpacho and home-made Chicken Liver and Brandy Pate with a cumberland sauce and melba toast. Pot Roast Guinea Fowl with a rich burgundy and mushroom gravy or Pork Normandy - loin pork steak cooked with fresh stock, calvados and apples and topped with a cordon of fresh cream are just two of the dishes for main courses. The Blackboard will tell you about the home-cooked Daily Specials which always includes fresh fish. The Light Bite Menu has something for anyone who only wants a snack and there are always Vegetarian meals. The comprehensive wine list will produce something to complement whatever you choose to eat. Derek and Carol Ross and their long serving, dedicated staff all have a sense of humour and a great desire to please - which they do admirably.

USEFUL INFORMATION

OPEN; . All year, from Morning Coffee onwards
CHILDREN; Welcome
CREDIT CARDS; All except Amex/Diners
LICENSED; Yes
GARDEN; Yes. 2 large patio areas for eating

RESTAURANT; Tiered areas including Non-smoking area. Good food
BAR FOOD; Excellent choice
VEGETARIAN; Always a choice
DISABLED ACCESS; Wide level entrance

OAKFIELD
Chudleigh
Devon TQ13 0DD
Tel. (01626) 852194
Fax (01626) 852194 (office hours)

A mile from the attractive old wool town of Chudleigh, Oakfield is a large and elegant Victorian country house, where bed and breakfast accommodation is offered in an atmosphere of peace and tranquility. The house, which has been tastefully modernised to provide all necessary facilities, yet without losing its period charm, stands in twenty acres of formal landscaped gardens, orchards and paddocks. It is a member of the prestigious Wolsey Lodges, the group of privately owned homes noted for providing the highest quality hospitality.

Oakfield is the home of Peter and Patricia Johnson-King, who make a point of treating all their guests as friends. The emphasis is on comfort, relaxation and good food. The house is beautifully furnished with antiques, and all bedrooms have en suite bathrooms. Guests are given free use of the Drawing Room, Billiard Room and the heated swimming pool.

At the right time of year you may find an old fashioned English gymkhana or a garden fete taking place in the grounds, and riding, walking, fishing and golf can all be enjoyed from Oakfield. There are also many good restaurants and attractions close by. It is an ideal centre for exploring the westcountry.

USEFUL INFORMATION

OPEN Easter to October.
CHILDREN 12 and over.
CREDIT CARDS No.
LICENCE No.
ACCOMMODATION 3 double en suite rooms.
PRICES £30 per person per night. £35 one night only.

VEGETARIAN Breakfast by arrangement.
SMOKING Non-smoking house.
PETS No.
GARDEN Extensive.

VIRGINIA COTTAGE
Brook Lane
Shaldon
Near Teignmouth
Devon TQ14 0HL
Tel. and Fax (01626) 872634

Virginia Cottage is a beautiful, whitewashed 17th century grade 2 listed house, set in its own secluded garden just a few minutes from the centre of the pleasant riverside village of Shaldon. Its proprietors, Jennifer and Michael Britton, who have long experience of the hotel business, offer excellent Bed and Breakfast accommodation in this peaceful house, which has many attractive features. Of particular interest is the elaborately carved front door and decorated porch timbers from South Africa.The three bedrooms are all very pretty and comfortable, with tea making facilities and views over the partly walled garden, which has a stream running through it. Breakfast is served in the attractive, bay-windowed dining room, and there is also a sitting room with a large inglenook fireplace.Finding Virginia Cottage is not difficult. Shaldon is opposite the popular resort of Teignmouth, which is easily reached from the A380 road from Exeter to Torbay, turning off onto the B3192 when signposted. From Teignmouth, take the bridge over the Teign to Shaldon and turn sharp right at the signpost for Combeinteignhead. Brook Lane is the third lane on the left, and Virginia Cottage is on the right. There is ample car parking space in the grounds. Shaldon is full of interesting shops, pubs and restaurants, and is easily placed for exploring the numerous attractions of the South Devon coast and Dartmoor National Park.

USEFUL INFORMATION

OPEN March to December
CHILDREN over 12 welcome.
CREDIT CARDS No.
LICENCE No.
ACCOMMODATION 1 twin and 1 dble
room, both en suite. 1 twin with privatebathroom. RATES: £22 pppn all year

VEGETARIAN Breakfast provided on request.
SMOKING No.
DISABLED No special access or facilities.
PETS No.
GARDEN 1 acre.

WALTON HOUSE
Plantation Terrace
Dawlish
Devon EX7 9DR
Tel. (01626) 862760
AA 4 Q Selected, 'Which?' Recommended.

Central, but quietly situated in the stylish seaside town of Dawlish, Walton House offers Bed and Breakfast in the dignified and comfortable surroundings of a Grade 2 listed Georgian building. The house was built in 1819 to a design by John Nash, and it's previous owners have included colourful characters like the Victorian sea captain and inventor George Peacock, and Dr F.W.Cann, who provided Dawlish with its first hospital. It is now the family home of John and Doreen Newton, who aim to make your stay as pleasant as possible. Both are qualified in Hotel and Guest House Management, and always offer personal service and attention. Each of the 6 bedrooms has its own individual decor and is immaculately kept. All are en suite, and have colour TV, tea making facilities, alarm clock radio, hair drier, shoe cleaning facilities and central heating. One contains a four poster bed. Breakfast is served in a cosy and intimate dining room. There is ample private parking within the grounds. Walton House is only a few minutes' walk to the attractions of Dawlish: the beach, the town centre shops, the brook with its famous black swans and the railway station. Exeter, Dartmoor, Torbay, Teignmouth and Totnes are all within half an hour's drive.

USEFUL INFORMATION

OPEN All Year except Christmas.	**RESTAURANT** B&B only. Hearty breakfast.
CHILDREN No	**VEGETARIAN** Catered for.
CREDIT CARDS No.	**SMOKING** Permitted.
LICENCE No.	**DISABLED** No special facilities.
ACCOMMODATION 6 en suite bedrooms.	**PETS** Guide dogs only.
PRICES B&B High Season from £17;	**GARDEN** Yes.
Low Season from £16.	

DEANE THATCH ACCOMMODATION
Stoke-in-Teignhead
Near Torquay
Devon TQ12 4QU
Tel. and Fax + 44(0) 1626 873724
email: D-thatch@cpages.co.uk
Internet: http://www.wctb.co.uk/deane.htm.
ETB 2 Crowns

Deane Thatch offers Bed and Breakfast accommodation in a beautiful thatched, cob Devon cottage and its adjacent linhay, in a peaceful, secluded rural setting. It enjoys uninterrupted views of the countryside, and is only half a mile from the coast between the resorts of Torquay and Teignmouth. Its atmosphere is one of total tranquility. Spring water is supplied from the cottage's own traditional well. Accommodation consists of a double bed-sitting room on the first floor of the cottage, overlooking the garden. Next to the cottage is the thatched and cob linhay - the Devon word for barn, the original use - which sleeps two to four people. Both are en suite and contain colour televisions, tea and coffee making facilities and as much space as you need. Your hostess at Deane Thatch is Mrs Rozamund Wilkinson, who trained as an artist before settling here with her husband Michael, a dental surgeon. She is very interested in dressage, and keeps her own horse. Mrs Wilkinson provides a good, traditional English or continental breakfast from a varied menu, using fresh local ingredients. Deane Thatch is easily found, being just two miles from Teignmouth along the B3199 to Torquay. Turn right at the mounted B&B sign, and you will find the cottage alone in the country, set peacefully amidst the fields. The myriad attractions of the South Devon coast, countryside and Dartmoor National Park can be enjoyed from this beautiful holiday base.

USEFUL INFORMATION

OPEN All Year	**VEGETARIAN** Breakfast if requested.
CHILDREN Welcome.	**SMOKING** No.
CREDIT CARDS No.	**DISABLED** No special facilities.
LICENCE No.	**PETS** By arrangement.
ACCOMMODATION Large double room in cottage and accommodation for up to 4 in adjacent linhay. En suite.	**GARDEN** Large garden for cottage, small secluded one for linhay with barbecue.
	PRICES From £16, young children reduced rate.

ASHFORD COTTAGE
137 Exeter Road
Dawlish
Devon EX7 0AN

Tel. (01626) 863569

Ashford Cottage is an individually designed, bright, spacious 1950s house, centrally situated on the A379 in Dawlish. Its owners, John and Ann Comber, offer Bed and Breakfast accommodation in these pleasant and convenient surroundings, and their success is demonstrated by the numbers who return to them year after year.

All the rooms at Ashford Cottage have large picture windows, are tastefully furnished and create a relaxing atmosphere. The Combers are keen gardeners, and their garden is available to guests, with seats and tables provided both on the patio at the front and the landscaped garden at the back.   The accommodation is very flexible, as the four bedrooms can be made up as various combinations of single, twin and double rooms.

All have colour televisions, tea and coffee making facilities, hot and cold water and central heating. Guests have their own front door keys, to enable them to come and go as they please. A full, large English breakfast is served, with vegetarians or those on special diets catered for by request.   Ashford Cottage is within easy reach of Devon's main attractions. A safe beach is only 400 yards away, and nearby is a large new leisure complex. Dawlish Warren, with its wildlife, is not far away and excellent fishing is available. John is himself an enthusiastic angler, and will be happy to advise.

USEFUL INFORMATION

OPEN All Year.
CHILDREN Welcome.
CREDIT CARDS No.
LICENCE None, but guests welcome
to bring their own drinks.
ACCOMMODATION 3 dbles and 1 single,
or 2 doubles, 1 twin and single or 1 Family, 2 doubles and 1 single.
PRICES B&B £13.50 per person, children half price. £1 supplement in high season for
one night booking.

RESTAURANT No. Breakfast only.
VEGETARIAN Breakfast by arrangement.
SMOKING Permitted.
DISABLED No special facilities. Steps.
PETS No.
GARDEN Yes, available for guests.

THE CROFT
Cockwood Harbour
Starcross
Near Exeter
Devon EX6 8QY

Tel. (01626) 890282
Fax (01626 891768

ETB 2 Crown Approved,
Selected by Brittany Ferries.

The Croft is a delightful Bed and Breakfast Guest House in its own acre of secluded garden, overlooking picturesque Cockwood Harbour at Starcross, on the Exe estuary. It is the nearest guest house to the unique Nature Reserve at Dawlish Warren, and is ideally situated for exploring the South Devon countryside, the coast and Dartmoor.

Its proprietors, Ian Stewart and David Allsopp, worked for twenty years on cruise ships, and the house is furnished with interesting souvenirs and pictures from their travels around the world. The atmosphere is informal and relaxed, with guests given their own keys, enabling them to come and go as they please. Two of South Devon's finest pub/restaurants are only a couple of minutes' walk away, and a meal discount card is available for both.

The spacious, well-appointed rooms all have hot and cold water, central heating, razor points, beverage making facilities and a 6 channel TV, including 2 satellite channels. There is a comfortable lounge and residents' bar, drinks and snacks are also available most afternoons and evenings, and sandwiches for picnics or homeward journeys can be made to order. A full, hearty English breakfast is served in the dining room, and a vegetarian breakfast is available on request.

The Croft is approximately one mile from Starcross on the A379 Dawlish road. There is safe, off the road parking for cars and boats. For those keen on fishing, boating, golf, walking, birdwatching or even trainspotting, there is something here to appeal to you. One mile from Powderham Castle, home of the Earl and Countess of Devon, well worth a visit.

USEFUL INFORMATION

OPEN All Year (except Christmas
CHILDREN Welcome.
CREDIT CARDS No.
LICENCE Residential.
ACCOMMODATION 9 well-appointed rooms
6 with shower/WC.
PRICES High Season: £15-£19/person;
Low Season: £14-£19. Children under 7 years £7.50.

RESTAURANT Breakfast only. Full English
breakfast served.
VEGETARIAN Breakfast available.
SMOKING Permitted.
DISABLED No special facilities.
PETS Well-behaved pets welcome.
GARDEN 1 acre, lawn and flower garden.

PENPARK
Bickington
Newton Abbot
Devon TQ12 6LH
Tel. (01626) 821314 Fax (01626) 821101

Penpark is a delightful country house within the Dartmoor National Park, in easy reach of the A38 and two miles from the old-world small town of Ashburton. It is set on a hilltop with superb views of rural Devon in every direction and is approached by a long tarmac drive. There are over five acres of secluded and beautifully laid out formal and woodland gardens, and there is a hard, all-weather tennis court. The house was built in 1928 and designed by the famous architect Clough Williams Ellis, creator of Portmeiron in Wales. Any improvements have kept faithfully to his design and are in keeping with the period. The rooms are well-proportioned and have been beautifully decorated and furnished to create a perfect blend of elegance, style and comfort.   Penpark is the much-loved home of Michael and Madeleine Gregson, who run the house on their own and look after the gardens themselves. They greatly enjoy sharing their lovely home with their guests and making them feel welcome and relaxed.   The Gregsons have three bedrooms available, all with either private bathroom or shower, hot drink facilities and colour television. They provide a continental or full English breakfast. Their aim is to provide a luxurious but homely atmosphere, which they succeed in doing very well.

USEFUL INFORMATION

OPEN All year.
CHILDREN Welcome.
under 2, free.
CREDIT CARDS No.
LICENCE No.
VEGETARIAN Can be catered for.
SMOKING Non smoking house.
DISABLED No special facilities.
PETS No pets.
GARDEN 5 acres.
ACCOMMODATION 1 twin/double room, 1 double, 1 single. All with private bathroom or shower. 1 with balcony.
PRICES £23.50 for 1 night only, otherwise £21. Children under 12 half price; under 2 Free.

MAGGIE AT PARK LANE
4/5 Park Lane
Torquay
Devon TQ1 2AV
Tel. (01803) 200755

Situated in Park Lane, a pleasant pedestrian Mews off Torquay's harbourside Strand, Maggie at Park Lane is a highly atmospheric restaurant occupying part of a converted warehouse. Many original features and different levels create a welcoming, intimate space in which to enjoy good food and drink. The restaurant adjoins the famous Hole in the Wall Inn, once said to have been the haunt of smugglers.   The proprietor and chef, Maggie Matthews, is renowned for her innovative menus using superb local produce. This includes steaks, pork, lamb, poultry and duckling, as well as fresh fish and shellfish, together with an excellent range of vegetarian dishes. All are served with fresh vegetables. At lunchtime you can enjoy a very reasonably priced selection of snack meals, or a three-course special for £8.95. In the evening there is an a la carte menu or a three-course daily special menu, which is great value at £17.95. A well varied wine list, with regular bin-end bargains, enhances the meal.   This enjoyable restaurant, with its friendly staff, is now nationally known, and is widely recognised for its seafood in particular. Maggie at Park Lane continues to live up to its enviable reputation for good food and professional service.

USEFUL INFORMATION

OPEN Lunchtime: From 12pm,
Tues to Sat from 7pm.
CHILDREN Welcome.
CREDIT CARDS Access, Visa, Barclaycard,
American Express.
LICENCE Full.
RESTAURANT Varied international cuisine.
3 course specials.
VEGETARIAN 6 dishes, specials daily.
SMOKING Permitted.
DISABLED Level entrance.

BURLEY'S RESTAURANT
43 Babbacombe Downs Road
Torquay
Devon TQ1 3LN
Tel. (01803) 316661 Fax (01803) 328023

Burley's is a successful and highly-acclaimed restaurant, with wonderful views over Babbacombe Downs and Babbacombe Bay, situated in one of Torquay's most atmospheric and peaceful neighbourhoods.　The restaurant occupies the ground floor of a Victorian hotel, and has a large bar. Here clients can enjoy a pre-dinner drink, before settling into the spacious but intimate restaurant, which is tastefully furnished and has a large picture window through which the expanse of the bay can be seen.　The youthful proprietors are Danny and Adele Burley, who opened on 14th February 1995, and have built up an enthusiastic following from near and far; it is not unusual for guests to come from Plymouth or Bristol for the evening. Danny, the chef, is a local man who trained in Torquay and worked in many hotels and restaurants before taking the opportunity to open his own establishment. Adele's caring, friendly front of house manner ensures a relaxed environment for enjoying good food.　Danny's ambitious menu includes imaginatively prepared seafood dishes, steaks and mouthwatering desserts. There is an extensive wine list, and special luncheon menus are offered for events such as Christmas, New Year, Valentine's Day and Mothering Sunday.　Car parking is available behind the restaurant.

USEFUL INFORMATION
OPEN Wednesdays to Saturdays at 7.00pm. Will open other days for parties of 8 or more. Open all year, except for approx. 3 weeks' holiday, usually in January.
CHILDREN Welcome. Special menu with prior notice.
LICENCE Restaurant.

RESTAURANT Hot/cold starters from £3.00, Main courses from around £10, desserts £4.25.
VEGETARIAN 3 starters, 1 main course always available, others by prior notice.
SMOKING Allowed in bar, but not in restaurant.
DISABLED Ground floor, but step into toilet.
CREDIT CARDS Matercard, Visa.

FLYNN'S BISTRO
14 Parkhill Road
Torquay
Devon TQ1 2AL
Tel. (01803) 213936

Flynn's Bistro is a highly-acclaimed international restaurant, specialising in provincial French cooking, which is owned and run by Robin and Jeanne Flynn. The restaurant is situated close to Torquay's Mediterranean-like harbourside area, and is within walking distance of the Marina, as well as most of Torquay's major hotels.　It seats over 50 people, and during the summer you can dine outside in a delightful courtyard.　Robin Flynn, chef and proprietor, has been in the catering business locally since the 1970s. He is well known for his dishes featuring local seafood, and for producing superb steaks and other meat dishes, with a good selection of fresh vegetables. These are supplemented by an ever-changing menu of blackboard specialities, and there is always a good choice for vegetarians. Flynn's is world-renowned for its traditional French style Moules Mariniere!　The excellence of the food is echoed by the sophisticated wine list, which contains a wide range of French and 'New World' wines.　The atmosphere at Flynn's, although spacious, is friendly and intimate, and it is no surprise to learn that people return to dine here again and again. The restaurant is only open in the evenings, and quickly fills up, so it is a good idea to book your table in advance.

USEFUL INFORMATION
OPEN All Year. Every day 6.30pm until late, Monday to Saturday. Closed Sunday.
CHILDREN Well-behaved children welcome.
CREDIT CARDS Access, Mastercard, Visa, Switch.
LICENCE Restaurant and Supper Licence.

RESTAURANT International cuisine. Fresh local seafood, prime steaks.
VEGETARIAN Always choice of at least 4
DISABLED Level entrance.
GARDEN Patio/courtyard for dining outside in the summer

PRICES Average cost of 3 course meal with bottle of house wine £16.50 per person.

Chapter Two

CHAPTER THREE

Through The South Hams

"How fine it is to enter some old town, walled and turreted, just at the approach of nightfall... and after enquiring for the best entertainment that the place affords, to "take one's ease at one's inn."
William Hazlitt

CHAPTER THREE

THROUGH THE SOUTH HAMS

The **SOUTH HAMS** is the name given to the southernmost part of Devon which, on the map, curves prominently down into the English Channel. 'Hams' may derive from an Anglo-Saxon word meaning 'homesteads', or it could come from a similar word denoting 'land surrounded by water', which certainly fits the geography of the area. Traditionally the South Hams were bounded by the rivers Dart and Plym, but the current local government District covers a slightly different area. For our purposes, it is useful to describe it as being everywhere between Dartmoor at the top and the sea at the bottom, with the conurbations of Torbay and Plymouth making natural breaks on each side.

You will find it a fertile land: a wide, expansive plateau interrupted by deep river valleys and estuaries. Geologically, the area is made up largely of slates, shales and other volcanic rocks, rather dark and coarse when used in buildings, but giving the structures of both town and country a look of having grown out of the landscape. The towns are small and compact, with the green horizon always clearly visible, even from their centres. They are characterised by slate-hung and pastel-washed houses, steep, narrow streets and valerian-covered grey walls. Each is still the natural focus for its surrounding farms and villages.

The people of the rural South Hams have, for centuries, made their living from the sea and the land, and this long and close connection with such basic activities as farming and fishing can perhaps still be felt in the generally balanced, civilised pace of life in its human-scaled communities, although of course comparatively few people today actually work in these occupations.

Its coast can be challenging, as you will read, and there are some dark stories told concerning it, but if there is one word which generally describes the atmosphere of the South Hams it is probably 'security'. The ancient, tamed landscape of orchards and small fields, the sunken lanes, solid farmhouses and quiet villages, backed by rounded hills and winding rivers, all induce a satisfying sense of coming home, even in people who have never been here before. In the hilly old towns, with their rooftops sloping down towards the water, and their old-fashioned family-run shops, visitors can feel that, if they were to stay, they could finally learn to live long, fulfilling lives.

It is not surprising, then, that so many who visit the South Hams come back here to retire, or decide to leave the pressure of life in cities in order to become rooted in this gentle environment. The area has more than its share of professional artists, writers and craftspeople, some of them famous, as well as healers, therapists and others exploring 'alternative' ways of living.

All this gives life in the South Hams a cultural and social diversity which is unusual for a rural area. The towns and villages, with their mixed populations of indigenous locals and new residents, generally have more going on in the evenings than you might expect in such small places. Pubs, restaurants and wine bars throughout the area, especially in the towns, are regular venues for live music of all kinds, though a preference for jazz is noticeable, ranging from ultra-modern to the most old-fashioned 'trad.' Those who want brighter lights and greater excitement will find that the larger towns and cities of South Devon, and beyond, are within easy reach.

An excellent way of introducing yourself to the landscapes, ecology and traditional culture of the South Hams is to attend some of the imaginative COAST AND COUNTRYSIDE EVENTS organised by the South Hams Environment Service (01803 861140). Guided walks, visits, practical activities, seasonal celebrations, storytelling sessions and recycling workshops are held regularly at locations throughout the District, enjoyed by large numbers of visitors and locals, and the current programme can be easily picked up, free, at TICs, shops, pubs and many other venues. Coming from the Torbay or Exeter directions, by road or rail, the first place in the South Hams the visitor reaches is **TOTNES** (Tourist Information 01803 863168), on the banks of the River Dart. This enjoyable town epitomises everything that has been said above about the atmosphere of the South Hams, past and present.

Totnes is a particularly good place to spend time in if you are interested in history, because although nothing very dramatic has ever happened here, it encapsulates many periods in its streets and buildings, and is often used to illustrate the different stages in the growth of an English town. Its memory seems to travel back easily through the centuries, and there are a number of unique sites to visit. It is also an excellent base for exploring the rest of the area.

Sean O'Casey, the great Irish playwright, lived in Totnes for 17 years, and thought it looked like a little old lady drowsing in an orchard of ageing apple trees, but one of the best descriptions of the town was written by the Devon topographer Thomas Westcote, in about 1630. He called it 'This city-like town...with pleasant soil, fruitful country and healthful air.' All these points are equally true today.

Totnes is enshrined in medieval legend as the landing place of Brutus of Troy, mythical founder of the British race. Half way up the main street, on the right, you can see the stone he is supposed to have first set foot on in 1170BC, when he claimed the Island of Albion, then uninhabited except by a few giants, for himself and his descendants. Totnes people have added the detail that he went on to say:

Here I stand and here I rest
And this town here shall be called Totnes.

Fantasy aside, Totnes was actually established early in the 10th century AD as a royal fortified borough, to defend this area from Viking invasion. The name means 'the fort or lookout on the nose or ridge of land', and today, eleven centuries later, you can easily imagine the Saxon walled town, covering the hilltop high above the river. Two medieval entrances, the East Gate and the smaller North Gate, can be seen, although the archways are not the original structures.

After the Norman conquest TOTNES CASTLE (01803 864406) was built, which is now in the hands of English Heritage and is a textbook example of a Norman 'motte and bailey' castle. Totnes broke free of its walls during the Middle Ages and the long main street stretching down towards the river came into existence. Until the 20th century the town was little more than this.

The greatest days of Totnes came in the Tudor period, when the town was one of the wealthiest in England thanks to the cloth industry and the export of Dartmoor tin. Its rich merchants traded throughout the known world and were involved in the opening up of the 'New World' by the famous Elizabethan explorers.

Many substantial houses from this time remain in the main street, and some of their elaborately carved ceilings can be glimpsed in the rooms above the shops. These, especially the older ones, are long, narrow and cavelike, seeming to go back forever along the ancient plots between the street and the defences.

To celebrate this age of prosperity, and perhaps in the hope of reviving some of it, a group of local people decided, in 1970, to dress up every TUESDAY during the summer as citizens of ELIZABETHAN TOTNES. Today fewer people in shops and pubs seem to do this, but the ELIZABETHAN CHARITY MARKET, outside the CIVIC HALL, continues, along with several CRAFT MARKETS around the town.

On arriving in Totnes, it is a good idea to visit the newly opened TOWN MILL (no telephone number). This is near the bottom of the town next to the large supermarket, and is a restored working mill and local interpretation centre. Its displays will set the scene for your exploration of the old town and its buildings, one of the most important of which is at 70 Fore Street, a beautifully preserved merchant's house dating from around 1575, and now TOTNES ELIZABETHAN MUSEUM (01803 863821). It contains a room dedicated to Charles Babbage, the 19th century mathematician and inventor who is increasingly recognised as a pioneer of the computer. Although he was not actually born in Totnes, Babbage's family had lived here for generations, and he was sent to the local grammar school, so the town has as fair a claim to him as anywhere. Another famous Totnesian, who is celebrated by an obelisk at the bottom of the hill, was William John Wills, one of the first men to cross the Australian continent from south to north in the ill-fated Burke and Wills Expedition of 1860/61.

Along with the Museum and the castle, the GUILDHALL (01803 862147) should be visited. The seat of the town's government since 1553, this was created from buildings belonging to the medieval priory, founded in 1088. As well as being the home of the town council, it has also been a court and town gaol, and has a powerful sense of past ages. Yet another historically interesting place to see is the DEVONSHIRE COLLECTION OF PERIOD COSTUME (no telephone number), a small but special museum at BOGAN HOUSE, 43 High Street.

GUIDED WALKS around Totnes, with the author of this book, covering its history, buildings, ghosts or a combination to suit your interests, can be arranged for groups of five or more (01803 862024).

Old as Totnes may be, it carries the weight of its history lightly, and looks forward as well as back. Today the town is a creative and socially diverse community, with a well-earned reputation for all kinds of specialist services and products, notably complementary therapies, antiquarian books, hand-made shoes, exotic gifts and musical instruments, while the shops and galleries in the main street offer a refreshingly individual range of merchandise, certainly as wonderful as anything brought back by the Elizabethan adventurers.

For characteristic Totnes shops, try PEDLAR'S PACK BOOKS, TICKLEMORE CHEESE SHOP, GREEN SHOES, BISHOPSTON TRADING and GREEN LIFE, but many more could be singled out. One of my favourite town centre locations for either coffee or a drink is RUMOUR WINE BAR. There is a relaxed, mellow but energetic spirit in the air as you walk up and down the streets, where buskers play anything from Mozart to Irish whistle tunes, and visitors jostle with the busy townsfolk.

The creative and 'alternative' side of Totnes is best experienced at the FRIDAY MARKET below the Civic Hall, which is always a lively, slightly bohemian, colourful scene. Study the posters in shops and pubs for an idea of the range of activities, conventional as well as 'alternative', that are always going on in and around this lively town.

Excellent sports and fitness facilities, including a swimming pool, can be found at TOTNES PAVILION (01803 862992) in the BOROUGH PARK, open to visitors as well as locals. FISHING is available in the Dart; you need a licence to fish above the bridge, but anyone can try their luck downstream. If you like WALKING, the town is surrounded, as are all South Hams communities, by a rich network of ancient GREEN LANES, taking you quickly into the depths of the countryside. From Totnes in every direction the beautiful South Devon landscape stretches away, full of visitor attractions and places of interest. A good way of experiencing some of these without the car is by taking a MINIBUS TOUR to the moors or the coast, with short walks and a commentary (01803 866917).

A mile from the town, on the way to the pretty village of **ASHPRINGTON**, is BOWDEN HOUSE (01803 863664), a Queen Anne mansion on a much older site, which houses the BRITISH PHOTOGRAPHIC MUSEUM and, apparently, several active ghosts.   At Ashprington, a beautifully unified village in grey and white, is AVENUE COTTAGE, in a fold in the hills above the Dart, the GARDEN of which can be visited by appointment (01803 732769).

Next to the Cottage is the SHARPHAM ESTATE (01803 732203), based around a fine 18th century mansion overlooking the river. The house, which contains a marble spiral staircase, is now home to a College specialising in Buddhist studies (01803 732542), and in the grounds is a very successful VINEYARD, which makes three varieties of white wine. Cheese is also made here, and there are woodland walks to enjoy.

If you are travelling by road from Totnes to Dartmouth or Kingsbridge, along the A381, you pass through, or near, many attractive villages, including **HARBERTON**, which, with its medieval church and the whitewashed pub and cottages surrounding it, epitomises the smaller South Hams communities. **HARBERTONFORD** was once a busy mill village, and now boasts a pleasant riverside area. Behind the church you will find FINE PINE (01803 732465), selling country furniture, pottery and fabrics.

HALWELL, a few miles further on, is a small, dark village by the side of the road, with a pub and church. Two Iron Age hillforts overlook the village, one of which was probaby refortified during the reign of Alfred the Great, to be replaced later by the fortified town of Totnes. Neither is accessible to the public.

North west of Totnes is **DARTINGTON**, a large, spread-out village at the heart of which is DARTINGTON HALL. Originally built in the 14th century by John Holland, half-brother to King Richard the Second, the Hall has, for over seventy years, been the focus for a wide-ranging attempt to revitalise rural life. In 1925 when Leonard Elmhirst, a Yorkshire gentleman, and his rich American wife, Dorothy, bought the estate, it was sadly run down, but their combination of money and vision turned it into a bewildering and sometimes quite radical 'experiment in regeneration'. The Elmhirsts started a progressive school, introduced scientific methods of farming and forestry, began craft-based businesses and patronised the arts on an impressive scale.

Today, the DARTINGTON HALL TRUST continues to work in many different fields, though it is no longer regarded as particularly controversial. The school has gone, but the College of Arts continues, and the area of the Great Hall functions as an ARTS and CONFERENCE venue throughout the year: programmes listing courses, concerts, plays, films and exhibitions can be picked up easily in shops and pubs (box office for Dartington Arts: 01803 863073; courses and conferences: 01803 866051). Dartington is the home of two special annual events, the INTERNATIONAL SUMMER SCHOOL, formerly called the Dartington Summer School of Music, and the WAYS WITH WORDS LITERATURE FESTIVAL, both of which are firmly established in the cultural calendar.

Down the hill from the Hall, SCHUMACHER COLLEGE (01803 865934), named after the influential author of *Small is Beautiful*, explores green and holistic ways of living with the planet. Some talks are open to the public.

Surrounding Dartington Hall is one of the finest 20th century GARDENS in England, which visitors are welcome to walk around. Nearby is HIGH CROSS HOUSE (01803 864114), a modernist building from the 1930s. Newly opened as a museum, it contains artworks collected by the Elmhirsts, and is best described as a 'miniature St Ives Tate.' At Shinner's Bridge, on the main road from Totnes, can be found the CIDER PRESS CENTRE (01803 864171), a complex of high quality craft and gift shops, restaurants and a garden centre.

A pleasant way of reaching Dartington from Totnes is by way of the CYCLE PATH, which can be picked up in the Borough Park.

Passing the Dartington Hall estate, running along by the river Dart, you will see - and hear - the SOUTH DEVON RAILWAY (01364 642338), formerly very well-known under its previous name of the 'Dart Valley Railway'. Originally opened in 1872 as the Totnes to Ashburton Branch, it was a much-loved country line which, like so many others, was closed in the early 1960s. The stretch from Buckfastleigh to Ashburton was lost to the A38 main road, but a group of enthusiasts bought the rest and reopened it in 1969 as a tourist attraction, using steam locomotives in the style of the old Great Western Railway.

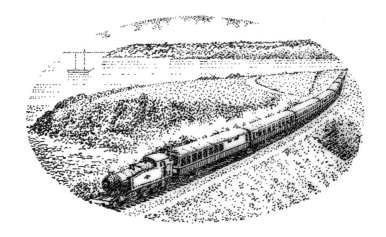

You reach it now by crossing the river on a footbridge just beyond Totnes main line station. The trains run throughout the summer from here to Buckfastleigh, mainly in sight of the river, and pass through the delightful station of **STAVERTON**, which has been used in countless films and television programmes. Staverton, just up the road from its station, is a typically peaceful Devon village, and nearby is KINGSTON HOUSE (01803 762235), now recognised as one of the most important smaller 18th century mansions in England, with a unique staircase and a restored GARDEN occasionally open to the public. Kingston also offers high class accommodation (see its advertisement at the end of this chapter).

Beyond Staverton, the rolling countryside between Totnes and Newton Abbot contains many other villages, without any prominent visitor attractions but all with their medieval churches, ancient farmhouses and, not the least of their delights, individual pubs. **LITTLEHEMPSTON, BROADHEMPSTON, LANDSCOVE, TORBRYAN** and **IPPLEPEN** are each worth a journey through the high-hedged, winding lanes, which are themselves a feature of this area and a challenge to drivers.

Ipplepen, a large village with mainly 20th century houses, features prominently in the novel *Daniel Martin* by John Fowles, who spent part of his childhood here. The church has a striking medieval tower which looks as if it is about to take off, so streamlined and engineered is its form, while inside on the screen appears, unexpectedly, the pagan sybil, alongside the more predictable apostles and saints.

Torbryan church, nestling securely in a fold in the hills, near the atmospheric CHURCH HOUSE INN, is worth experiencing as well. Between Ipplepen and Torbryan is a pleasant little area of open land called ORLEY COMMON (the locals call it 'Teddy Moor'), where wild orchids can be found.

BUCKFAST and BUCKFASTLEIGH, at the end of the railway line, are covered in the chapter on Dartmoor.

Going eastwards from Totnes, through the genteel suburbs of BRIDGETOWN on the opposite side of the Dart, you come to **BERRY POMEROY**, another classic English village grouped around its church and safely enfolded by the hills. A mile or so away, hidden by dense woods, is BERRY POMEROY CASTLE (01803 866618), one of the most romantic ruins to be found anywhere. Looked after now by English Heritage, it has only ever been owned by two families, the Pomeroys, who received the estate after the Norman conquest, and the Seymours, the family of the Duke of Somerset, who still possesses it. Berry Pomeroy Castle is reputed to be one of the most haunted castles in England and is rich in legend, though its recorded history seems undramatic.

The ultimate excursion from Totnes, however, must be the hour and a half BOAT TRIP DOWN THE DART. From Steamer Quay, on the Bridgetown side, you can take a pleasure cruiser, belonging to one of two companies, any day from Easter to October, the times varying with the tide (ring 01803 834488 or 01803 832109, or pick up a timetable at the TIC).

The River Dart journey has been fulsomely celebrated since the first steamers plied up and down during the 19th century, when the Victorians called the river the 'English Rhine.' It is still an unforgettable experience, as you move gently along, passing high tree-covered hills, quiet creeks, waterside boathouses, a hilltop ruined cottage, a wrecked paddle steamer and several distinguished mansions. The first of these is Sharpham, home to the vineyard.

Further on the boat passes the tiny hamlet of DUNCANNON, and the entrance to BOW CREEK, leading to the quiet, luxurious village of **TUCKENHAY**, which for many years was a busy industrial centre with a paper mill, now converted into flats. Lower down is **STOKE GABRIEL**, once famous for its orchards and salmon fishery, and still known for its huge yew tree in the churchyard and its atmospheric pubs. Near SANDRIDGE was born one of the less well known Elizabethan seamen, John Davis, who gave his name to the Davis Straits off Labrador and possibly discovered the Falkland Islands. He was less of a pirate than Drake, Raleigh and Frobisher, and more of a genuinely scientific explorer, who wrote learned treatises on navigation which were in use for centuries.

The next village along is **DITTISHAM**, exclusive and beautiful, climbing a long hill from the river to the church. Once known for its plum orchards and the fresh cockles picked up from the river, it now has a FRUIT FARM where you can pick your own soft fruit and buy home-made fruit liqueur and sloe gin (01803 712452). Opposite Dittisham is GREENWAY HOUSE, hidden in the trees. In an earlier house on this site was born Sir Humphrey Gilbert, another Elizabethan explorer who in 1583 claimed Newfoundland as England's first colony, and who was half-brother to Sir Walter Raleigh. The present Greenway House was the summer home, from 1938 to her death in 1976, of Dame Agatha Christie.

Finally the boat reaches **DARTMOUTH** (Tourist Information 01803 834224), famous as a port in British and world history. It is a lovely old white and grey town, bright against the green wooded heights. Full of narrow streets, long hills and seemingly endless flights of steps going up and down, it provides memorable views of the river or harbour mouth from almost every point. Although it is situated well inside this beautifully secure natural haven, the town is pervaded by an exhilaratingly salty air.

Dartmouth has always appealed to the imagination, and many have sought to express its charm. The way the houses rise above each other was pleasingly likened to 'galley pots hanging in an apothecary's shop' by the Rev. John Prince, a 17th century Devon author. An Italian spy, working for the Spanish government a century earlier, reported that the town was not walled, as 'the mountains serve as walls.'

Dartmouth has been the scene of constant comings and goings since the entire Second European Crusade left here for the Holy Land in 1147. In medieval times the mariners from the town were widely known for their daring adventurousness and an individualism which verged on piracy, while during the 16th century the famous Devon 'seadogs' were as at home here as in Plymouth, but now there is a decidedly genteel atmosphere to the place. It is not difficult to imagine its wilder days, though, as you wander around its streets, redolent as they are of past ages.

DARTMOUTH CASTLE (01803 833588), which sits right at the harbour entrance, next to ST PETROX CHURCH, with the smaller castle of KINGSWEAR opposite, was the first in England to be designed specifically for artillery. Dartmouth Castle is owned by English Heritage and open to the public, but its neighbour is still in private hands. The walk out to the castle is always a pleasant one, and the area beyond provides a variety of cliff paths, leading through the trees down to secluded little beaches.

Back in the town, make time to visit another fortress, BEARSCORE CASTLE (no charge) at the end of photogenic BAYARDS COVE, which you will probably recognise as the scene of many films and television dramas.

Seek out, as well, DARTMOUTH MUSEUM (01803 832923) specialising in maritime history. It occupies a merchant's house dating from 1640 which stands in the Butterwalk, an arcaded area similar to that of Totnes. Nearby is the NEWCOMEN ENGINE HOUSE (01803 834224), celebrating the Dartmouth-born blacksmith and engineer Thomas Newcomen, whose invention of a working steam engine in 1712 predated that of James Watt by many years. A late 18th century engine is housed here.

Dartmouth has many interesting shops, pubs, galleries and restaurants, some of them quite tucked away in its backstreets and alleyways. The town is understandably popular with artists and craftspeople, the best known probably being SIMON DREW, whose gallery can be found in Foss Street. His surreal drawings based on puns and verbal jokes decorate many a card or sweatshirt. Also in Foss Street is ART WORKS, and other outlets for high quality arts and crafts include the DENMAN GALLERY, JOHN GILLO'S, GIDDY KIPPER and FACETS.

Along the riverfront you can hire boats for cruising or fishing, or take a ferry across to the village of Kingswear opposite, where the trains of the PAIGNTON AND DARTMOUTH STEAM RAILWAY (01803 555872) can be boarded for Paignton. This beautiful line, which, like the Totnes to Buckfastleigh one, is operated according to Great Western practice, runs along by the river and through the woods before turning inland for the 'English Riviera'. A particularly enjoyable excursion, if you have the time, would be to take a 'ROUND ROBIN', consisting of a train ride and a river trip, with a bus providing the link between Totnes and Paignton. You can do the three stages of the journey - river, railway and bus - in whichever order suits you. Ask at TICs or one of the kiosks by the river.

KINGSWEAR itself is pleasant to walk around, and has some lovely views of the harbour mouth and the wooded hills, but is almost entirely residential, with only the most basic shops. Only three miles away, however, is COLETON FISHACRE GARDEN (01803 752466), owned by the National Trust. Sloping gently to the sea, the garden, created in the early years of the century for Lady D'Oyly Carte, contains rare trees and shrubs usually only found in conservatories, and is a magical place of secret paths, glades and streams.

High on the cliffs nearby at FROWARD POINT is a structure you may have seen in the distance from many places around Dartmouth, and not known what to make of. It is an 80 foot high octagonal tower, completely hollow, and with no obvious purpose. In fact it is a DAYMARK, a sort of lighthouse but without a light, which was built by the Dart Harbour Authority in 1864.

Returning to the Dartmouth side of the river, you get excellent views of its most dominant building, the long, red-brick pile of the BRITANNIA ROYAL NAVAL COLLEGE, opened in 1905 by King Edward VII. Most male members of the Royal Family have received training here since then. It is not normally open to the public.

The greatest event in the town's calendar is the annual ROYAL REGATTA in August, which involves several days of celebration and events of all kinds, in addition to the regatta itself. Other events to look out for are DARTMOUTH CARNIVAL in June and DARTMOUTH TOWN WEEK in July. Outdoor events and entertainments in Dartmouth tend to happen in or around the ornate Edwardian BANDSTAND in MAYOR'S AVENUE GARDENS, adjacent to the riverfront.

Throughout the year you can enjoy the facilities of the DARTMOUTH GOLF AND COUNTRY CLUB (01803 421686), a short distance out of the town on the Totnes road, and nearby is the 60 acre WOODLAND LEISURE PARK (01803 712598), ideal for restless youngsters, which has everything from wildlife to fast food. A short journey from here, through the deep lanes, is the attractive old village of **BLACKAWTON**, with a church and a couple of pubs which are worth seeking out. Should you be within striking distance of Blackawton in early May, you can experience one of the more bizarre local traditions, the annual WORM CHARMING COMPETITION. The aim is to entice the greatest number of worms out of a specific area of ground, and competition is intense.

The coast road from Dartmouth to Kingsbridge, the A379, is spectacularly beautiful and historically resonant. Passing through **STOKE FLEMING**, another pleasant village with whitewashed cottages and friendly pubs, you find yourself suddenly high above the sea. This unforgettable road then follows the hills up and down, and seems to wind around almost in a manner reminiscent of a hairpin mountain road. After a while you come to the idyllic cove of **BLACKPOOL SANDS**. It is usual to point out that a beach less like its northern namesake is impossible to imagine.

A gently curving shingle beach, overlooked by pine-covered cliffs, it has more than a hint of the Mediterranean. Blackpool is privately owned, and so peaceful that you can hardly imagine anything disturbing it, but the whole of this coastline has deep associations with warfare. During the 14th century a French army landed here, but was successfully repulsed by the locals. A special Te Deum was sung in Westminster Abbey to give thanks for this victory, in which stalwart peasants defeated the flower of French knighthood. The French returned in the following year and burnt Dartmouth to the ground, but this is not recorded in the English chronicles.

After the beach you pass the small village of **STRETE**, before descending steeply to **SLAPTON SANDS**. Here, for about two and a half miles, you are travelling straight along a narrow bed of shingle which runs between the sea on one side and the remarkable freshwater lake of SLAPTON LEY, now a nature reserve, on the other. The Ley is always abundant with wildlife and a haven for birdwatchers, 233 different bird species having been recorded here. A third of the way along the road, a right turn will bring you to the village of **SLAPTON**, which is famous for its pub and its ruined tower, once belonging to a medieval college of priests. The great Plymouth adventurer Sir John Hawkins had a country retreat somewhere near here, though all trace of it has gone. The story is told that when Lady Hawkins attended Slapton church, footmen had to go before her unrolling a red carpet.

Like most of the older settlements along the coast, Slapton is slightly inland, safely protected and just out of sight of the sea. It was only, perhaps, in the 15th or 16th centuries, that some fishing communities were placed right on the beach, as are the next two or three we shall come to. Out of the way of authority, literally beyond the view of both church and manor house, these seaside villages tended to draw the rebellious and desperate as well as the hardworking, and have always had an individualistic, anarchic feel to them. This quality can still be noticed in those which are not entirely taken over by second homes. On the Cornish and North Devon coasts it is even more marked.

The SLAPTON LEY FIELD STUDIES CENTRE (01548 580466) holds courses and carries out important environmental research (for information about FISHING in the Ley, ring 01548 580685).

As you sweep down to the straight run along by the sands, on the left is the STRETE GATE PICNIC AREA AND WOODLAND WALK next to the car park. Interpretation panels help you to understand the ecology of the area and the specially designed walk offers spectacular views.

At the far end of the sands, where the road suddenly leaves the shore to go inland towards Kingsbridge, is **TORCROSS**, a small village sitting vulnerably on the shingle (just how vulnerable it can be is demonstrated by the huge boulders of Dartmoor granite, brought here to help protect the houses after the rough winters of 1978 and 1979). In fine weather it is a good place in which to linger, enjoying the beach or the Ley. There is a spacious pub, a cafe, and it is sometimes possible to buy fresh crab from the cottage doors. But for many, especially for visitors from across the Atlantic, it is a place of pilgrimage and inevitable sadness.

On the beach can be found an OBELISK, erected in 1954 by the United States government, which expresses gratitude to the local people who, during the dark days of World War Two, evacuated their homes in this peaceful corner of the South Hams in order for the Normandy Landings to be rehearsed.

The entire populations of the villages of Blackawton, Chillington, East Allington, Sherford, Slapton, Stokenham, Strete and Torcross were told, in November 1943, that they had six weeks in which to leave their houses and farms, taking with them everything that could be moved, including the crops in the ground. Three thousand people left an area of thirty thousand acres for six months, so that the American forces could practice for the invasion of France, using live ammunition, in an environment which was chosen because it strongly resembled the Cotentin Peninsula. When you remember the time of year and the fact that everything had to be done in the strictest secrecy, the logistics of the whole operation are all the more remarkable and moving.

The local people had to give up a lot, which they did uncomplainingly, but at least they were not required to give their lives. The servicemen were not so fortunate. As the rehearsals were necessarily so realistic, there were bound to be casualties. For decades, rumour and folklore suggested that large numbers of Americans had been killed during the exercises, and hurriedly buried in unmarked fields. In fact, many hundreds died, but now, after years of silence, they have a memorial, and their sacrifice is officially acknowledged. Their monument is a SHERMAN TANK, raised from the seabed in 1984 and placed beside the road at Torcross, a strange reminder of conflict and death on a bright summer day, when visitors mill around eating icecreams and stroll along the beach, while swans move serenely on the ley.

A short walk from the village is the TORCROSS VIEWPOINT AND BUTTERFLY CONSERVATION AREA, a place of great beauty and peace which was donated to South Hams District Council in 1990.

The main road runs inland from Torcross towards Kingsbridge, passing through **STOKENHAM**, **CHILLINGTON**, **FROGMORE** and **EAST** and **WEST CHARLETON**, all of which are worthy of some attention if you are a 'collector' of villages. Their houses and farms are wholly typical of South Devon vernacular architecture, as natural to the landscape as the trees and contours themselves. They also have excellent village pubs.

Alternatively, by taking a series of narrow lanes, you can go more deeply into the most southern tip of the South Hams, to the tiny village of **BEESANDS** and the ghost village of **HALLSANDS**. Beesands, a once thriving fishing community beside a mile-long shingle beach, is not as active as it used to be, when almost the whole community made its living from the sea, but it is a delightful spot in the summer. The great boulders, here as at Torcross, are reminders, though, that occasional storms can severely batter these exposed settlements. At one time, the locals in these villages trained Newfoundland dogs to bring the boats onto the beach: the dogs would swim out with a rope to help winch them ashore.

In good weather you can walk along the cliff path to the haunted ruins of Hallsands. This powerful place, as the years go by, becomes more difficult to visualise as it would have been in the late 19th century, when the village had about a hundred and fifty residents. It was a busy and close-knit little place, but it was doomed from 1897 when, against the advice of the locals, who understood their surroundings, gravel from the seabed started being taken away. It was needed to build extensions to Devonport Dockyard, and the government allowed contractors to remove many thousands of tons of shingle, thus destroying the beach which acted as a protective cushion for the village.

In the autumnal storms of 1900 this lack of wisdom was revealed when the sea wall and several houses were destroyed. After much wrangling the dredging was stopped, but the damage by now had been done. In 1917 the inevitable happened and over the 26th and 27th January, most of the village was lost. Some houses were swept away completely, the others made uninhabitable. By the end only one stood undamaged.

Hallsands today is not entirely a ruin; some new buildings exist and the beach is popular, but the remains of the original settlement stand as a powerful reminder of the folly of tampering with the environment.

Stories are still told, and plays performed, about the three Trout sisters, who stubbornly refused to leave after the disaster of 1917, and instead ran a hotel here. Ella Trout received the OBE after rescuing a young man who was in difficulties while fishing.

Not far along the coast, in a dramatic position on the rocks, is the lighthouse of START POINT. The name derives from Old English 'steort', meaning a tail. Looking back from here at the wide expanse of Start Bay and the country stretching away from the shore, you can receive an unforgettable impression of the lovely South Hams, to be recalled with pleasure when your holiday is long over. The lighthouse is no longer manned, and so unfortunately cannot now be visited.

The stretch of coastline between Start Point and the mouth of the Kingsbridge Estuary, with its exposed rocks, brown and purple against the bright blue of sea and sky, and the yellow of the gorse, is one of the most satisfying to walk. After a few miles PRAWLE POINT is reached. This is the most southerly point in Devon and, if you exclude the Lizard Peninsula in Cornwall - something which would please many Cornish people - the most southerly point in England. This jagged coastal area contrasts quite remarkably with the generally soft contours of the inland South Hams, but just past the Point is a secluded little beach. The next few names along the coast all, for some reason, pertain to pork: we have GAMMON HEAD, HAM STONE and PIGS NOSE.

If you are not walking the path, Prawle Point can be reached by road from Stokenham by way of the interesting little villages of **CHIVELSTONE** and **EAST PRAWLE**. The former has the only church in England dedicated to St Sylvester, an obscure Spanish bishop, and its pulpit is carved from a single piece of oak.

Hundreds of shipwrecks have occurred along this coast, placid as it may seem on a summer afternoon. The stories of many were recorded in ballad form and sung in the pubs and around winter firesides. One such was the tale of the *Gossamer*, a full-rigged vessel from Liverpool which came to grief here in December 1868. A sad detail is that the captain's young wife of only two weeks was aboard; it is believed he tried to save her by lashing her to a spar, but they died together with the rest of the crew, and their bodies were laid out at Chivelstone church. Meanwhile, the locals, to whom a wreck was fair game, helped themselves to the cargo, and a newspaper reporter tartly commented 'The inhabitants of Prawle, Salcombe, Torcross and adjacent villages around will not need to purchase any drapery goods for a very long time.'

Returning to the main road from Torcross, the waters of the KINGSBRIDGE ESTUARY are soon encountered, and the old town of **KINGSBRIDGE** (Tourist Information 01548 853195) appears up ahead. It often describes itself as the 'Capital' of the South Hams, although this has never been true in any administrative sense. It is better to see it, like Totnes, as the traditional centre for its surrounding villages and farms. Like Totnes, it occupies a hilltop site above a tidal estuary, and may have been founded at about the same time by the Saxon kingdom of Wessex, to be another fortified borough against Viking attacks.

From the once busy quays, the main street of Kingsbridge rises steeply towards the church, and many attractive passages and alleyways lead off on both sides which are worth exploring. The most enjoyable leads from Mill Street to Western Backway, and is aptly known as 'Squeezebelly Passage'. The town is especially rich in pubs and Noncomformist Churches, establishments which are not always comfortable together, but they seem to coexist peacefully enough here.

Although they are physically so similar, the town feels more 'ordinary' than Totnes; instead of being assailed by the smells of joss-sticks and the sounds of drumming, with shops selling crystals and ethnic clothing, you will find old-fashioned family businesses and tradesmen selling fresh fish and vegetables almost straight onto the pavement (although if you want New Age therapy and face painting, no doubt there is someone offering it not too far away: these things are hardly 'alternative' in the South Hams any more, but part of the mainstream culture). For a true taste of the South Hams look for SALCOMBE SMOKIES in Fore Street, where smoked mackerel fillets, prepared in the traditional way, can be bought. Altogether, the little town feels a good place in which to be, on a bright day, with the estuary shining below, and the people moving busily between the shops. At the TOWN HALL, which doubles as a THEATRE and CINEMA, you will often find a coffee morning or jumble sale in progress.

The small, dark local slates give the buildings of Kingsbridge a homogeneity, and although there are no really outstanding architectural features, the cumulative effect of the place is very pleasant. Occupying the old 17th century grammar school is the COOKWORTHY MUSEUM (01548 853235). This is named after the Kingsbridge-born Quaker and chemist William Cookworthy, who, in the 18th century, first discovered how to use 'China clay' or kaolin for the production of porcelain. The museum contains a wealth of objects and displays covering all aspects of local history, with special emphasis on the traditional rural life of the South Hams.

The nearby Parish Church is usually singled out for the epitaph, on a slab outside the door, to Robert Phillips, who died in 1798. He was a cooper (maker of barrels) by trade, who also collected simples, or herbs, for medicinal purposes, and offered himself as a 'whipping boy': he would accept other peoples' punishments at a penny a time. His memorial reads:

Here lie I at the chancel door,
Here lie I because I'm poor,
The further in the more you pay,
Here lie I as warm as they.

One traditional taste of the area which is lost for ever is of a drink they used to brew in Kingsbridge called 'white ale' which was unique to this part of the South Hams. Over the years, writers of guide books have copied and mis-copied information from each other about this, and as there is probably no one left alive who ever drank the stuff, it is now difficult to discover the truth. It seems to have had a 'secret' ingredient, known only to one family, which contained egg yolk, and gave the beer a milky appearance.

Running almost parallel to the main street of Kingsbridge is DODBROOKE, which joins it near the quay and then goes off at an angle. Now an integral part of the town, it was for centuries a separate borough. Dodbrooke was the birthplace of the 18th century writer and satirist John Wolcot, who wrote political verses under the name of 'Peter Pindar', and was notorious for his rudeness about King George the Third. He had a sensitive side to his nature, though, and retained a deep love of his home town. Another famous resident of Kingsbridge was the early 19th century naturalist Colonel John Montague, who gave his name to Montague's Harrier.

Kingsbridge has a lively community life, with numerous groups and organisations. THE QUAY is often a busy place, where you may a catch a fete, craft market, band concert or any number of activities going on. KINGSBRIDGE FAIR WEEK takes place in July, and the AGRICULTURAL SHOW in September. The KINGSBRIDGE SPORTS CENTRE (01548 857100), adjacent to the Quay, has a wide range of facilities which visitors are welcome to use.

At the nearby village of **LODDISWELL**, a compact, hilltop community, can be found LODDISWELL RINGS, also known as BLACKDOWN RINGS. This is an Iron Age hillfort, like many in this area, but it is unusual in that it can be visited - most are on private farmland - and in that it seems to have had a Norman motte and bailey castle, of which there is no historical record, built within it.

Also near Loddiswell is HAZELWOOD HOUSE (01548 821232), the lovely and deeply peaceful venue for a wide-ranging and creative programme of ARTISTIC EVENTS, WORKSHOPS and CONCERTS. Their current programme can easily be found in shops and tourist centres anywhere in South Devon. Near Malborough, between Kingsbridge and Salcombe, is YARDE MEDIEVAL FARMHOUSE (01548 842367), a most remarkable building.

As with Totnes and Dartmouth, everyone who visits Kingsbridge should arrive or leave by water at least once. The estuary, winding away below the town, draws you down to it, and demands to be explored. It equals any of the other south coast estuaries of Devon and Cornwall in its beauty, but unlike them it is not the final stage of a river which began miles away as a fast moorland stream; this is all there is. It is an estuary without a river, and it starts here beneath the trees, beside the car parks and lamp posts of the town. In Kingsbridge you call it the Kingsbridge Estuary, while in Salcombe you call it the Salcombe Estuary, although map-makers have decided on the former.

During the summer months a RIVER CRUISE, times depending on the tide, can be taken down to Salcombe, the famous port and yachting haven (for timetable ring 01548 853607 or pick one up at the TIC).

The Kingsbridge estuary seems more open than that of the Dart. It is without the constant wooded hills, and many more creeks veer off to either side, so that the journey is more like travelling along the centre of a lake than down a river. The effect, as you move gently along, with the bright colours of water and rounded hills on every side, is almost hypnotic.

SALCOMBE (Tourist Information 01548 843927) is the most southerly town in England (if, as before, we exclude Cornwall), and is famous for its almost Mediterranean climate, although maybe this has sometimes been exaggerated. But even if Salcombe is not quite the sub-tropical paradise which is often suggested, it is beautifully warm and mild, and this enables oranges, lemons and other unusual plants to be grown here.

Artists have, for many decades, found the clarity of light and intensity of colour an inspiration. The water really can be as blue as it looks in the postcards, and the little town, white and grey against the green, climbing the hillside, with its narrow streets and flights of steps, and the ever-changing but peaceful movement along the waterfront, all add up to make Salcombe a place in which to relax and linger. It is as appealing in winter as in summer, and there is always something going on.

The SALCOMBE MARITIME AND LOCAL HISTORY MUSEUM (no telephone number) graphically tells the story of the town, which at one time entertained shipping from far-flung ports, from Europe and beyond. During the 1860s about a hundred vessels traded regularly from Salcombe, especially in fruit from the Azores. Ship building, fishing and smuggling have all been part of the port's colourful and exciting history, gentle as it may seem today. Down by the water stand the ruins of SALCOMBE CASTLE or FORT CHARLES, built as one of the many Tudor coastal defences, and the last Royalist stronghold in Devon to submit during the English Civil War.

SALCOMBE FESTIVAL takes place in June, while in August there are two REGATTAS,one run by the town and one by the yacht club. Salcombe has facilities for all watersports, diving and swimming. The ISLAND CRUISING CLUB (01548 843481) caters for all ages and gives courses in sailing at all levels. For COARSE FISHING contact (01548 856891) and for GAME FISHING (01548 852401).

Salcombe also has an abundance of interesting shops, pubs and cafes. For individual gifts and local crafts, try A-B GALLERY, JOHN'S JEWELS and TUDOR AMETHYST. Local artists exhibit at the atmospheric LOFT STUDIOS.

The town has several literary associations. The 19th century Dartington-born essayist and historian James Anthony Froude is not much read these days, but he had an inspiring prose style, and did much to make the Devon seadogs of the 16th century into heroes of the Victorian Empire. Froude spent his last years at a house called Woodcot, where he was visited by Tennyson and other luminaries. Tennyson was possibly inspired, whilst here, to write his poem 'Crossing the Bar', although as that poem is about the Isle of Wight, authorities disagree on the matter, and every book says something different. In fact, there seems no reason why he should not have been moved to write a poem about one place whilst actually being in another. Paul Gallico lived in Salcombe during the 1940s, and wrote *The Snow Goose* here, which of course is set in the East Anglian marshes.

High on the cliffs above the mouth of the estuary, reached by seemingly endless tree-lined roads, is OVERBECKS, at SHARPITOR (01548 842893), now owned by the National Trust. The Edwardian house is a fascinatingly individualistic museum, with everything from a 19th century 'jukebox' to a secret room for children, and its many ghosts are well documented.

The GARDENS (01548 843238), with wonderful coastal views, contain a wealth of rare plants from the time when the whole world was regarded as a gigantic garden centre by 19th and early 20th century collectors. You can see here a prize magnolia, Japanese banana palms and a maidenhair tree from China, amongst much else. Around the mouth of the estuary, on both sides, are many beautiful beaches. On the Salcombe side are NORTH SANDS and SOUTH SANDS, the former closer to the town and with more facilities.

On the opposite side, the beach of **EAST PORTLEMOUTH**, is also particularly popular. Regular ferries cross to it over the water, and this is the best way to approach it, as the roads are narrow and winding. It is worth observing here that all along the south coast of Devon and Cornwall the major settlements are on the west banks of their respective river mouths, with much smaller places on the east, although the smaller villages may sometimes be older.

On the Salcombe side of the estuary mouth is BOLT HEAD, and the walk along the cliffs to the next headland, BOLT TAIL, makes a spectacular journey through coastal scenery unmatched anywhere in Britain. All of the land here is owned by the National Trust, and thus, let us hope, safe for ever. In every direction around Salcombe are endless possibilities for walking, whether you want dramatic cliff scenery or quiet rural fieldscapes and sunken lanes, the latter popularly believed, with good reason, to be old smugglers' routes.

If you are feeling less energetic you can go by road through the villages of **MALBOROUGH**, which holds an enjoyable MUSIC FESTIVAL in August, and **GALMPTON** (not to be confused, as even some guide books confuse them, with the Galmpton at Torbay between Paignton and Brixham) to **HOPE COVE**, comprising the twin communities of INNER and OUTER HOPE. Pretty thatched cob cottages, two beaches, a past in which fishing and smuggling are inextricably linked, and a sheltered position on a dramatic and rocky shore, make this a romantic place, to which many dream of retiring.

Like all places along this coast, Hope Cove can present a different side of itself in winter, when storms and gales howl outside the squat cottages and it is easy to remember the hundreds of ships which have gone down in these waters. Hope Cove also has the distinction of being the only place on the Devon coast that really did see the wreck of a vessel belonging to the Spanish Armada.

The authors of Victorian guide books were fond of the fanciful notion that the dark-haired, dark-eyed inhabitants of the South West coastal villages are descended from shipwrecked Spanish sailors left over from the Armada (a few writers even today seem to believe this, or pretend to). A moment's thought would have told them how improbable it is that any surviving Spaniards, coming ashore in Devon or Cornwall, would have quietly settled down with local girls and contributed their dark good looks to the gene pool (this distinctive Westcountry strain is actually of Iberian origin, but goes back a lot more than 400 years, being the native, pre-Celtic stock). In any case, the tragedy of the Armada did not take place in the South West. In the summer of 1588 the Armada, in an imposing crescent-shaped formation, sailed confidently up the English Channel, intending to join forces with a Spanish army at Dunkirk. They would then cross over and invade England in Kent. Unfortunately, Drake and his fireships defeated them before they could do this, and the stricken fleet spent the autumn sailing round Britain in order to regain the Atlantic and finally reach home. It was on the wild coasts of Scotland and Ireland, not the South West, that so many of them were destroyed.

One of them did end its life here, though. The hospital ship *St Peter the Great*, after rounding Ireland, was blown wildly off course and foundered at Hope Cove in October. The locals, predictably enough, took all they could of the money and plate, but the ship's supply of drugs was too spoilt by damp to be of any use. The hundred and forty survivors were imprisoned.

Such tragedy all seems a long way off, on a bright day, from the village of whitewashed cottages and modern bungalows, with their civilised inhabitants, that you can visit now. If you happen to be here at the end of August, all such memories disappear and you think only of the idyllic nature of the place, as the village holds its own festival, the HOPE COVE WEEKEND.

The four towns of Totnes, Dartmouth, Kingsbridge and Salcombe, with their surrounding settlements, have received most attention in this chapter because they contain so many attractions and things to do, as well as being ideal centres from which to see the rest of the South Hams. The western part of the area, however, is equally as beautiful, and its quiet beaches, coastal paths and inland countryside, dotted with ancient villages and hamlets, can be endlessly rewarding if your tastes are for quieter exploration. The traditional red South Devon cattle can be seen in the fields, as well as the more ubiquitous Friesians, and the sense of being rooted in an ancient landscape becomes stronger all the time, as you let the area work its magic. Allow plenty of time and let the lanes take you where they will.

Between the mouth of the Kingsbridge Estuary and Plymouth, three smaller South Hams rivers enter the sea, the AVON, ERME and YEALM. Lacking major harbours and ports at their mouths they are often overlooked, but walkers, sailors and fishermen who have discovered their beauties know how special they are. The Avon's estuary finishes at **BANTHAM**, which has a beautifully long, sandy beach, and is just beyond the popular little resort of **THURLESTONE**.

The beach here is reputed to be one of the safest in the country, and the village, with pretty, flower-bedecked cottages, is a pleasure to walk around. THURLESTONE GOLF CLUB (01548 560405) is justly popular, and THURLESTONE ROCK, out in the sea, looks like nothing so much as a trunkless pair of legs.

Returning inland for a while, the main A379 road from Kingsbridge to Modbury passes through the village of **AVETON GIFFORD**. Many pages have been wasted, and many more pub discussions left undecided, on how the name is pronounced, whether 'Aveton' should be 'Awton' or 'Gifford' rendered as 'Jifford.' Although my father went to school here, I have no fixed opinion on the matter. It has a graceful medieval bridge and a fine church which has been rebuilt after being directly hit by a bomb in 1943.

You come upon the little town of **MODBURY** (Tourist Information 01548 830159) suddenly, with little warning. It appears unexpectedly out of the countryside, the road plunging down into its heart, which occupies a dip where all its streets meet, and these are hilly, as you have by now come to expect in the South Hams.

Modbury grew up in Saxon times, and though it is unusual in not being on a river, it is typical of the area. Many describe it as a smaller version of Totnes, but it is not easy to see why they do this. It actually has a clear identity of its own, nestling between the coast and the moors, but with, admittedly, a family resemblance to its South Hams neighbours. The Reverend John Prince called it a 'sweet and pleasant market town' - both words had rather more force in his day than now - and the description still fits.

It has, now, a well-heeled atmosphere, and a surprising number of the old merchants' houses in the main street are now fascinating shops selling antiques, crafts and handmade furniture. Look out for FOURTEEN A BROAD ST and YE LITTLE SHOPPE. Lovers of second hand bookshops will be able to spend a happy half hour or so at LAMB'S TALES.

Although a small place, with no fringe of housing or industrial development around it, the feel of the town is quite definitely urban, and the story its buildings tell is of past prosperity and present loving care. It was always a substantial marketing centre for the countryside, and during the 17th and 18th centuries made a lot of money from the wool trade.

Captain Thomas Savery, who helped Newcomen of Dartmouth to patent his steam engine in the early 18th century, was born at a farm near Modbury. He also seems to have invented something very like a paddle steamer, but the Navy wasn't interested. Catherine Champernowne, mother of Sir Walter Raleigh and, by another husband, Sir Humphrey Gilbert, two of Devon's most complicated heroes of the Elizabethan age, was also born here, and is buried in the churchyard. The church monuments were quite horribly mutilated during a Civil War skirmish, and it is without its original screen.

MODBURY HISTORY SOCIETY organises GUIDED WALKS around the town on a regular basis during the summer; times can be obtained from the TIC.

Devon is not, on the whole, a profoundly musical county, but Modbury has always had a thread of music running through its life. The church has a fine peel of bells, which may have sensitised the people over the years to this particular art. Sir Arthur Champernowne, lord of the manor in the early 16th century, had a choir of singing boys, in which he took much pleasure. They were so good that they were ordered to London to sing for Henry the Eighth. The king failed to pay Sir Arthur's expenses for the journey, however, and when, years later, Elizabeth I demanded a return performance, the old man complained that the cost would cripple him. 'I'll cripple you even more' retorted the queen, and increased his tax demand.

During the early 19th century the town enjoyed, for its size, a remarkably sophisticated cultural and intellectual life, and even the labouring classes formed a band amongst themselves, a reminder that it was not only in the industrial parts of Britain that this happened. More recently, Modbury has been well-known in westcountry folk music circles as the home town of Bill 'Pop' Hingston, a traditional singer who inspired and encouraged many currently active performers.

Travelling back towards the coast, the villages of **BIGBURY** and **RINGMORE** deserve a visit, before you go on to Bigbury on Sea and Burgh Island. Bigbury was used during the late 1970s for the filming of the popular television serialisation of R.F.Delderfield's *A Horseman Riding By*, and the pub at Ringmore is called 'The Journey's End' after the World War One play by R.C.Sherriff, who finished the script whilst staying here in the late 1920s. The Elmhirsts of Dartington paid for its first performance, as it was felt to be so controversial that no manager would initially put it on. Near the village the unspoilt beach at AYRMER COVE is very popular with those who have discovered it. The slates of the cliffs here are a remarkable feature, and can shine like a mirror when the sun is on them. There is a GOLF CLUB (01548 810557) at Bigbury, and worth seeking out is AVON OYSTERS (01548 810876), where fresh oysters and other shellfish can be bought.

BIGBURY ON SEA is a modern village for Devon, developed in the early years of the 20th century as a health resort by Plymouth doctors, who sent their patients here to recuperate. They were joined by the healthy, who built chalets and bungalows. Its lovely expanse of sand makes it a popular holiday destination, while **BURGH ISLAND** (it is pronounced 'Burr') adds a feeling of piratical romance. During the Elizabetan period this small island really was the headquarters of a pirate and smuggler, Tom Crocker. At low tide you can walk across the sands to the island, which has a pub and a 1930s hotel, where Agatha Christie set her story *And Then There Were None*, but when the tide comes in it is completely cut off. The famous 'Sea Tractor', based, it is said, on a World War Two American landing craft, plies to and fro. **KINGSTON**, a few miles further on and just inland from the coast, is a self-contained little village, once a centre for cider making. Not very far to the west is the mouth of the Erme, but most of the land around the estuary is privately owned and not easily accessible, which means that it is at least safe from overdevelopment. The beach of **MOTHECOMBE**, private and not always open, is much loved by those who use it.

Rejoining the main road out of Modbury you come to FLETE, originally an Elizabethan mansion rebuilt in 1876 in Gothic and Tudor style, once the home of the Mildmay family. The GARDENS (01752 830308) cover 5 acres, and overlook the Erme Valley. T.E.Lawrence ('Lawrence of Arabia') helped to design the water garden, an unexpected activity for this complex character, in an area not usually associated with him. Ring first to check whether the gardens and/or the house are open. The nearby village of **HOLBETON** has a REAL ALE BREWERY, one of many which have sprung up in the last two decades, thanks to the consumer pressure for good beer, which welcomes visitors (01752 830302). The brewery is next door to the Mildmay Colours Inn, where you can sample the product.

Next along the road, the village of **YEALMPTON** (pronounced 'Yampton') is reached. Here is a lovely old house, now a restaurant, known as MOTHER HUBBARD'S COTTAGE. The famous nursery rhyme was written in 1804 by Sarah Martin at nearby KITLEY MANOR. The Kitley estate once boasted the only quarry of green marble in England, some of which was used for the staircase at the Natural History Museum in London. KITLEY CAVES (01752 880885) are open to the public, and there are some very enjoyable WOODLAND WALKS and a PICNIC AREA on the estate.

Near Yealmpton is the well-known NATIONAL SHIRE HORSE CENTRE (01752 880268). Three times a day you can see a parade of these magnificent horses, and there are many facilities to keep young and old happily occupied for hours. Special events and rallies are held throughout the year; in July alone there is a JAGUAR CAR RALLEY and a WESTERN WEEK.

The village's AGRICULTURAL SHOW, also in July, is an important traditional South Hams event, and not to be missed. If you want to hear the genuine local accent, and mix with the farming people who actually maintain this lovely environment, spend the day wandering around the cattle pens and the beer tent.

From Yealmpton it is natural to follow the Yealm towards the coast again. It is the only one of the three smaller South Hams rivers to have the usual twin settlements near its mouth, in the manner of places like Dartmouth and Salcombe. In fact, **NEWTON FERRERS** and **NOSS MAYO** - no one knows how the latter got its name - do seem like smaller, quieter versions of these towns, with their white houses and wooded hillsides. Both villages, combined for local government purposes as 'NEWTON AND NOSS', are very popular with the yachting fraternity, and beautiful walks can be taken in the country around them. Newton Ferrers churchyard is noted for its abundant covering of cyclamen during the late summer and autumn.

The last place along the South Hams coast before Plymouth is **WEMBURY**, a large, scattered residential village, with excellent walks, a prominent church right on the edge of the cliff, and a beach sheltered between jagged rocks. The MARINE VISITOR CENTRE (01752 862538) allows you to view rare underwater wildlife, and is very restful. Off Wembury is the Great Mew Stone, once inhabited but now the home only of seabirds.

To finish this more or less circular tour of the South Hams, join the A38 main road leading out of Plymouth. This skirts the edge of Dartmoor on the left, with the rich plateau of the district laid out on the right.

At **IVYBRIDGE** (Tourist Information 01752 897035) you see a town which combines the familiar slate-hung, whitewashed building styles of the South Hams settlements with a hint of the harder, granite moorland patterns. Now an expanding urban centre, Ivybridge was, until about 50 years ago, a village, which developed along the main road from Plymouth to Exeter during the Middle Ages. It wasn't even a parish in its own right until late in the 19th century, but since the Second World War the town has made up for this slow development by becoming, it is said, one of the fastest growing towns in Europe, doubling in population every decade. In the car park between the two bridges is a piece of recently restored mill machinery, which, to me, looks remarkably like a modern sculpture of a snail. Is it fanciful to see this as a symbol of the town's slow but steady growth?

The original BRIDGE over the Erme which gave the town its name can still be seen, no longer coated in ivy, but looking very picturesque with the surrounding foliage and the rocks of the river below. Countless artists, including Turner, have recorded the view.

Not far from the bridge is an attractive 19th century PAPER MILL, which, remarkably, is still a working mill and not a visitor centre! You can walk from near here for some distance by the Erme in the woods, and onto the lower slopes of the moor. The Town Council owns and looks after PITHILL AND LONGTIMBER WOODS as a beautiful nature reserve, which is entered by passing beneath an impressive railway viaduct, one of many on Brunel's main line through Devon and Cornwall. The **TWO MOORS WAY**, an epic walk across Dartmoor, mid Devon and Exmoor, begins and ends at Ivybridge, coming off the moor at nearby Stowford.

Ivybridge has many pleasant shops, and pubs which are real 'locals', where the farmers from round about take hours over their cider and their games of euchre.

It has an excellent sports and fitness facility in the SOUTH DARTMOOR LEISURE CENTRE (01752 896999). It is worth wandering around the place to gain an idea of what a Devon town is like which has not become predominantly a tourist centre. It may lack the obvious charms of Salcombe and Dartmouth, but Ivybridge is a real community, looking forward quite optimistically to the 21st century with a relatively youthful population. Seek out the shops and cafes in the recently created GLANVILLE'S SHOPPING CENTRE, where you can sit and look out over the Erme in its rocky bed, and watch the ducks and muscovies as you drink your coffee. A mile or so out of the town, on the main road towards Plymouth, the ENDSLEIGH GARDEN CENTRE (01752 898989) is justifiably one of the busiest and most popular in the westcountry.

Ivybridge grew up at a point where four older parishes met. All are worth visiting, and it is interesting to compare the two moorland ones with the two that are classically South Hams. **CORNWOOD**, an ancient parish near the moor, has some pleasant stone buildings, and on the way to it from Ivybridge is FARDEL, a medieval manor house once owned by the father of Sir Walter Raleigh. Tradition has it that the great man buried some treasure near here on his last journey from Plymouth to London, just before his arrest at Ashburton. A stone inscribed with Celtic script was found here in the last century and is now in the British Museum. The GARDEN of Fardel is sometimes open to the public (01752 892353), but check before going. **HARFORD**, a mysterious little village on the edge of the moors, is much closer to the town, and an enjoyable walk from Ivybridge. LUKESLAND GARDENS (01752 893390) are also worth a visit.

South of the town are the attractive communities of **ERMINGTON**, with its famous crooked spire and friendly pubs, and **UGBOROUGH**, with a large village square and prominent church. Ermington church has some well-known carving of animals, birds and vegetation, made by Violet Pinwill, whose father became vicar of Ermington in 1880. Violet and her sisters decided to learn the art of carving to save the expense of restoring the church woodwork. Eventually they set themselves up in business, and Violet's distinctive work can be seen in many Westcountry churches.

Another woman from the parish who should be remembered is the novelist M.P.Willcocks, who was born at a nearby farm in 1869 and went on to be a pioneer of the radical feminist novel. Now totally forgotten, her books unread, she deserves at least a modest place in the history of English fiction. Many of her novels are set in South Devon, and give an interesting picture of its life at the turn of the century.

If you are passing Ivybridge on the A38, it is dominated by WESTERN BEACON, almost the most southerly point of Dartmoor. This view is echoed a few miles on by the setting of **SOUTH BRENT**, a large village which similarly sits beneath BRENT HILL. Near the main road is WRANGATON GOLF CLUB (01364 73229).

At South Brent you can turn off for Totnes again, or continue on towards the next chapter, which begins at Buckfastleigh. Just between South Brent and Buckfastleigh, however, is the small church and scattered village of **DEAN PRIOR**, sadly cut in two by the road, where during the 17th century the poet Robert Herrick was vicar. In the lanes and fields round about you can still find the flowers he celebrated so memorably.

Here also is to be found PENNYWELL (01364 642023), a very popular farm and wildlife centre where you really can get close to the animals. Children can enjoy collecting eggs, feeding the pigs, bottle-feeding the lambs and riding on ponies and donkeys. There is always plenty going on, so allow lots of time.

BOLT HEAD HOTEL
South Sands
Salcombe
Devon TQ8 8LL

Tel (01548) 843751
Fax (01548) 843060

AA 3 stars, RAC 3 stars

The Bolt Head Hotel must have one of the most magnificent situations of any hotel in England. In fact, the quality of the light, and the mildness and warmth of the climate, can make you wonder whether you are in England at all!

The famous old port and yachting haven of Salcombe is known throughout the world, for its beauty and the uniqueness of its position: it is the most southerly place in England apart from the far south west of Cornwall. Oranges and lemons have been known to grow outdoors here, and at the Bolt Head, which was built of wood in 1901, to a Norwegian design, you can be forgiven for thinking you are on the continent, although it is not the fjords that come to mind so much as the Mediterranean coast.

The luxuriousness of the surrounding country, with the mouth of the Salcombe estuary right below the hotel, is reflected in the Bolt Head's facilities. The light and sunny lounge with huge windows overlooking the old town, the harbour and the haven mouth, the sunny terrace, the heated outdoor swimming pool and the pine-furnished bedrooms, decorated in Laura Ashley style, not to mention the well-stocked bar, all contribute to a deliciously expansive atmosphere of relaxed good living.

You will never tire of the views which the hotel affords of the Salcombe estuary, which really is as blue as the pictures show it. The constant, graceful coming and going of yachts and fishing boats is both relaxing and stimulating. But if you are feeling active, you can step from the hotel grounds onto many delightful coastal paths. The Bolt Head is adjacent to the National Trust estate of Sharpitor, a beautifully unspoilt stretch of clifftop landscape, and nearby is the house and estate of Overbecks, with its tropical gardens. The lovely old town of Salcombe itself, and many unspoilt sandy beaches, are at your feet, and the whole of the lush South Hams surrounds you, with its beautiful villages, historic market towns and rich countryside which stretches from the coast to the romantic hills of Dartmoor.

The Bolt Head restaurant serves French and English cuisine, with an excellent 4 course Table d'Hote dinner. Freshly caught fish, lobster and crab from the local trawlers are a speciality, along with local farm produce and English cheeses, washed down by wines from all over the world.

USEFUL INFORMATION

OPEN March to Mid-November.
CHILDREN Welcome.
CREDIT CARDS Visa, Mastercard, Access, Diner's Club, Amex, Switch.
LICENCE Full.
ACCOMMODATION 28 en suite rooms with remote-controlled colour TV, phone and tea coffee facilities.

RESTAURANT English and French cuisine.
BAR FOOD Cold buffet lunches etc.
VEGETARIAN Always 1 dish available.
SMOKING Permitted.
DISABLED No special access.
PETS Welcome.
GARDEN Terrace and garden with and magnificent views.

PRICES High Season: from £85, Low Season from £64. Children sharing with 2 adults free.

THE VICTORIA HOTEL,
27-29 Victoria Road,
Dartmouth, Devon TQ6 9RT

Tel: 01803 832572
Fax: 01803 835815

ETB Three Crowns
Highly Commended.

Situated on level ground in the centre of Dartmouth, one of the most fascinating towns in South Devon, The Victoria Hotel built in the 1880's is a most comfortable establishment in which to stay. From here you are ideally based to explore not only the town but the beautiful River Dart which will take you up to the old town of Totnes and to Kingsbbridge and in between show you some of the delightful hidden villages such as Dittisham. Cross the river to Kingswear and you are within easy distance of Torbay with all its holiday attractions and superb beaches. Dartmouth itself abounds with history.

Within the elegant walls of The Victoria there are 10 luxurious en suite rooms, one of which has a fourposter complete with antique furniture and sumptuous drapes. Every room has its own character and is individually furnished and equipped with modern comforts such as colour TV, a generously supplied hostess tray, direct dial telephone and for those who require it, fax facilities are available at the reception desk. The candlelit restaurant is charming, relaxing and has the right ambience for those wanting to enjoy a delicious meal. There is a Table d'Hote and A la Carte Menu, both offer imaginative and beautifully presented dishes. All the meat is organic and you can taste the difference. Fish is caught locally, the vegetables are fresh and served al dente. Local game in season is another popular item on the menu. Great thought has been given to the selection of wines in order to produce the best and most interesting wines at affordable prices.

The hotel is owned and run by Annie Glanfield, who before she came here was involved in feature film production. The demands of that role in which the need for meticulous attention to detail was paramount, has spilled over into the way she and her very able staff care for visitors. They have enthusiasm, energy and clearly and rightly, are very proud of this small, friendly, elegant hotel.

USEFUL INFORMATION

OPEN; All year, all day	**RESTAURANT; Intimate, candlelit**
CHILDREN; No	**BAR MEALS; Home-cooked pies, fish etc**
CREDIT CARDS; Visa/Mastercard	**VEGETARIAN; Yes. Vegan by arrangement**
LICENSED; Full	**DISABLED ACCESS; No special facilities**
ACCOMMODATION;10 luxurious rooms ensuite.	**PETS; By arrangement**

RATES:- All year from £30 to £45 pppn B&B. Short breaks :Winter Season, apply for details.

FINGALS
at Old Coombe,
Dittisham, Nr Dartmouth
Devon TQ6 0JA

For much the same reason as Richard Johnston bought the remote, crumbling old farmhouse that became Fingals so today people come here to dine and stay. The reason is simple; it is away from everything and everybody and allows one to live the simple life but with the opportunity to enjoy this sociable place without formalities. It is wonderfully easy going (nobody minds if you sleep in, have breakfast at ten o'clock or don't dress for dinner). Surnames are rapidly discarded but standards never slip and the comfort of the modern day is there for you. Here you will meet interesting people, be cossetted in the nicest way and fed on the most delectable food.

Dinner is served at one long table in mellow surroundings with oak beams, wood panelling, antique carpets and open fires. You will find dishes on the menu that you love but thought had gone forever. If you wish for a more private dinner then a smaller panelled dining room is available but most people relish the lively conversation that is encouraged by good food and wine to match. The pretty bedrooms are enchanting and very individual with romantic French beds, oak chests and luxurious bathrooms; the sheets are crisp white cotton and the room service is faultless and maybe when you come down to breakfast you will decide to indulge yourself with bacon and egg 'al fresco' on the terrace in front of the beautiful Queen Anne facade. Fingals also has a self-catering barn with two small bedrooms; ideal for families who want to be independent but still enjoy the facilities of the hotel.

From Fingals one can find a host of exciting or peaceful places to be. Sometimes you may decide not to leave the sun drenched garden perhaps playing a game of croquet or tennis. The fabulous blue mosaic heated swimming pool is there for your use and you can enjoy the sauna and jacuzzi inside the conservatory which has an open roof in summer or maybe if the weather is not kind retreat indoors to while away the hours in the library/snooker room. The hauntingly beautiful River Dart with its ever changing moods is there for you to explore. From Dittisham Quay you can set off by passenger craft to explore the historic towns of Dartmouth and Totnes. Fingals has its own fleet of wooden boats which Richard describes as aged and temperamental but cater for all speeds from full on to full stop! Fingals is truly a place of pure magic.

USEFUL INFORMATION

OPEN; Easter until New Year   **DINING ROOM; Superb food, wonderful**
CHILDREN; Welcome   **atmosphere.**
CREDIT CARDS; All major cards   **VEGETARIAN; Upon request**
LICENSED; Yes   **DISABLED ACCESS; No special facilities**
ACCOMMODATION;10 ensuite rooms   PETS; No
GARDEN; Yes, heated swimming pool, sauna, jacuzz under cover, retractable roof in summer
RATES:- High Season,from £80/£135. Low Season,from £60/ £125. Single occupancy less£20.
Children under four free.Over four sharing with parents £15 pn. All prices per room.

THURLESTONE HOTEL
Thurlestone
Near Kingsbridge
Devon TQ7 3NN

Tel. (01548) 560382 Fax (01548) 561069

AA 4 Stars & Rosette for Food, RAC 4 Stars (both 71%) , ETB 5 Crowns.

The Thurlestone Hotel has a special tradition of caring service and personal hospitality. It was founded just over a century ago, in 1896, and has been continuously owned and run by the Grose family ever since. They are rightly proud of the reputation they have built up for the distinguished character of their hotel, which includes the 16th century village inn, and is set in matchless surroundings on the beautiful South Devon coast.

Brothers Graham and David Grose are fortunate in their staff, most of whom have been with them for many years. Every effort is made to ensure that you enjoy a quality of service which combines old fashioned courtesy, and attention to detail, with contemporary facilities and the best informal style of the 1990s.

The hotel is set in 20 acres of its own land, overlooking the lovely expanse of Bigbury Bay. The grounds include tropical gardens, a 9 hole golf course, tennis and badminton courts and an outdoor as well as an indoor swimming pool. Other leisure facilities include squash courts, a gymnasium, solarium, sauna and snooker table. Hairdressing and beauty salon services are available.

The bedrooms at the hotel are luxurious, with every kind of service and comfort, but the most important characteristic is individuality of design and decor. The unique ambience of Thurlestone, nurtured by its generations of owners, is carefully preserved and enhanced. All rooms have remote control colour television, direct dial telephones, bath robes, trouser press and freshly cut flowers.

The hotel has won many awards for its international cuisine, complemented by a wide-ranging and knowledgeably chosen wine list. The Margaret Amelia Restaurant, named after Graham and David Grose's great grandmother, serves an extensive 5 course Table d'hote dinner, changing daily and using the best local produce. A wide range of light lunches can be enjoyed in the cocktail bar. Vegetarians, and those on special diets, are always catered for.

Thurlestone provides excellent conference facilities for meetings of up to 120 participants, with secretarial support, audio-visual equipment and everything else you will need for a stylish and well-run event, whether a launch, a large corporate gathering or small board meeting. The hotel is three and a half hours from London or Birmingham. The nearest airports are at Plymouth and Exeter, and the nearest railway station is at Totnes.

USEFUL INFORMATION

OPEN All Year.
CHILDREN Welcome. Baby-sitting and listening service. Club during school holidays.
CREDIT CARDS All major cards except Diner's Club.
LICENCE Full.
ACCOMMODATION 65 en suite bedrooms, inc. 19 de luxe & 3 suites.
PRICES Inc. Dinner, B&B High Season £82. Low Season £44. Ring for further details.

RESTAURANT Table d'hote menu £24.
BAR FOOD Lunches
VEGETARIAN Choice available.
SMOKING Non-smoking areas.
DISABLED Level entrance.
PETS Welcome arrangement.
GARDEN Extensive grounds, including golf course, tennis courts and tropical gardens.

COPPA DOLLA INN
Broadhempston
Near Totnes
Devon TQ9 6BD

Tel. (01803) 812455

Broadhempston is a large, close-knit village in the heart of the rolling countryside between Totnes and Newton Abbot, about mid-way between Dartmoor and the coast at Torbay. It has all the classic ingredients of the English village: an ancient church, wisteria-covered cottages, working farms and winding streets. A bewildering number of country roads, no less than nine, lead in and out of the village. Along one of its quiet lanes is to be found the Coppa Dolla.

The inn's name is not, as you might fear, some modern transatlantic invention. It derives from the Old English 'coppede ealdre', the 'coppiced elder', referring to the first Anglo Saxon settlement, and in fact a local farm still bears the name as well. The building, dating from around 1746, makes a lovely, characterful inn where you are assured of a warm welcome, gourmet cooking, well-kept ales, log fires and luxurious accommodation. Everything is in keeping with the old-fashioned atmosphere of a village inn, with no fruit machines or jukebox.

The Coppa Dolla has been, since 1990, the home of Bob and Sue Burke, who took early retirement from management careers in electronics in order to build up the inn's reputation. Sue's culinary skills and Bob's 'Irish welcome', together with the attentiveness and friendliness of their staff, ensure a memorable visit.

From the comfortable bar and dining area, six steps take you up to the Old Barn Restaurant with its snug bar. The extensive menu features a wide range of classical and traditional dishes, using the best local produce including, extraordinary as it may sound, ostrich. There is also an imaginative selection of bar meals. The specially selected wine list contains 32 wines from all over the world, and Real Ales available include Draught Bass, Wadworth's '6X', Dartmoor Local and Marston's Pedigree.

The inn's two en suite apartments each contain a bathroom with bath and electric shower, a bedroom (1 double, 1 twin) and a lounge with colour television and tea/coffee making facilities. There are wonderful views across the village to Dartmoor on the skyline.

Bob and Sue Burke aim to provide 'traditional country inn hospitality, friendly atmosphere and value for money.' Come and see for yourself how well they succeed.

USEFUL INFORMATION

OPEN Winter: 11.30am - 3pm and 6.30 - 11pm. Summer: 11.30am - 3pm and 6 - 11pm.

RESTAURANT A la carte menu features classical and traditional cooking. In season, fish from Brixham and local game. Late supper restaurant licence to Midnight.

CHILDREN Welcome.   Main course £5.95 - £13.95.

CREDIT CARDS Access, Visa, Mastercard, Switch, Eurocard.

BAR FOOD Varied home-cooked meals and snacks.

LICENCE Full and Restaurant.

ACCOMMODATION 2 suites, with bedroom (1 twin, 1 double), lounge and bathroom.

PRICES High Season: £23.50, Child £12.50. Low Season: £21.50, Child £10.

VEGETARIAN 6 choices of main course.

DISABLED Welcome, but not easy access.

PETS Well-behaved dogs welcome.

GARDEN Lovely open garden with views of the moors.

THE CRICKET INN
Beesands
Near Kingsbridge
Devon TQ7 2EN

Tel. and Fax (01548) 580215

The Cricket Inn is a highly atmospheric seaside village pub, which also provides Bed and Breakfast accommodation. Situated right by the beach, in heart of the tiny South Hams fishing community of Beesands, it has unique views of the lovely and dramatic Start Bay. The South Devon Coastal Path runs directly beside it, and you only have to step across the village street to be on the shingle.

Rob and Tina Kerswell, the proprietors, and their daughter Mandy, offer a warm and friendly welcome to their inn, where both the restaurant and the accommodation have been recently refurbished to provide every comfort in an unforgettable setting. All bedrooms have magnificent views over the sea, are centrally heated and are equipped with televisions and tea and coffee making facilities. There is a well-equipped Family Room, with toys and books for the children when they are resting from the beach.

In the restaurant, comfortable and spacious, with sea-blue walls and large windows, you can enjoy a full English breakfast, as well as lunch, afternoon cream teas and evening meals. The Cricket Inn prides itself on its home-cooked meals, using fresh local produce, including, of course, fish and crab whenever possible. All cooking is done on the premises by Tina, and the menu changes frequently. Vegetarian dishes are always available. The wine list is also an extensive one.

The Cricket is famous for being a real Devon village pub, to which people come from far and wide to enjoy the ambience. In the bar you can enjoy two real ales - Draught Bass and Wadsworth's '6X' - and the friendly, down-to-earth atmosphere. The pub is the centre of this small community, with its mixed population of locals and newcomers, and caters successfully for everybody's tastes.

Beesands is beautifully secluded from twentieth century sights and sounds, but is within easy reach of the busy towns of Dartmouth and Kingsbridge. You can walk along the Coastal Path to visit the sad, powerful ruined village of Hallsands, or, a couple of miles in the other direction, the expanse of Slapton Sands, with the freshwater nature reserve of Slapton Ley and its poignant memories of World War Two. Or you can relax on the spacious beach of Beesands itself, with, of course, frequent strolls up to the Cricket for refreshment!

USEFUL INFORMATION

OPEN Summer: All Day; Winter: 11.30am - 2.30pm and 7 - 11pm.
CHILDREN Allowed in Family Room and Dining Room. Toys & books available.
CREDIT CARDS Visa, Access, Mastercard.
LICENCE Full and Supper.
ACCOMMODATION 3 bedrooms, 2 double and 1 twin. All en suite
PRICES High Season: £22.50 per night; Low Season £15. Children under 12 half price.

RESTAURANT Home-cooked, seasonal local produce. Fresh fish and crab in season.
BAR FOOD As above.
VEGETARIAN 2 dishes available at all times. Others with prior notice.
SMOKING Permitted.
DISABLED Easy level access.
PETS Dogs on leads allowed; not in dining room
GARDEN Sitting area and Beach just outside.

SPRINGFIELD HOUSE
Tuckenhay
Totnes
Devon TQ9 7EQ

Tel (01803) 732225
Fax (01803) 732834

Standing in six acres of gardens and fields, where peacocks and donkeys stroll at their leisure, Springfield is a two hundred and thirty year old country house, centrally placed in the lovely hamlet of Tuckenhay, just outside Totnes.

The village is a secluded one, hidden in the depths of the South Devon countryside on the banks of the Dart's largest tributary, Bow Creek. This beautiful creek is formed by the coming together of two small rivers, the Harbourne and the Wash, and the village can be easily reached by boat at high tide. Its present ambience belies the fact that Tuckenhay was once a thriving industrial port, with quarries, limekilns and a paper mill, but now all is quiet and the atmosphere is totally rural. Two famous old inns stand beside the water, and the many attractions of Totnes and the Dart Valley are only minutes away.

Springfield House is owned and run by Viv Whybrow, who came here after a career in advertising and the theatre. She is ably assisted by Royston, who helps serve breakfast and looks after the animals, while the gardens are tended by Alison. Together they create a gentle, family atmosphere which pervades the house and its grounds.

Springfield is not without romance, in the shape of a tunnel leading from the cellars towards the village quay, which may once have been used by smugglers, and there is a friendly resident ghost, a young woman who has often been seen at the top of the house, always in pink and with beautiful dark hair. It is thought that she was kept hidden in this part of the house after she became pregnant whilst in an embarassingly unwedded state!

Accommodation is provided in the form of two very large en suite double rooms, with one smaller double room and a twin-bedded room. There is also a family suite, comprising a large double room and a twin-bedded room with adjoining shower room. There is a sauna, a jacuzzi and a comfortable sitting room.

Outside, the grounds of Springfield contain a charming old-fashioned walled garden and a large heated swimming pool. When the weather permits, you can enjoy breakfast in the garden, looking out over the creek to the lovely, enfolding wooded hills of the valley, whilst planning how to spend your day, or you can be served breakfast in your room at whatever time you wish. There are eight regular breakfast menus for you to choose from.

Springfield's guests come back again and again. Recently Sir Clement Freud stayed, and reccommended the house in his column in *The Times*.

USEFUL INFORMATION

OPEN All year

CHILDREN Over 12 or by prior arrangement

CREDIT CARDS No

LICENCE No

ACCOMMODATION 2 large en suite double rooms, 1 smaller double and 1 twin. Family suite.

VEGETARIAN Special 'Good Health' breakfast.

SMOKING Allowed

DISABLED No special access

PETS By arrangement

PRICES £30 per person per night, all year round. Children over 12 full price, younger according to age and accomodation.

THE HUNGRY HORSE
Old Road
Harbertonford
Totnes
Devon TQ9 7TA

Tel. (01803) 732441
Fax (01803) 732780

Centrally placed in the village of Harbertonford, just three miles out of Totnes on the Kingsbridge road, the Hungry Horse is a delightful restaurant with Bed and Breakfast accommodation. The attractive old stone building was converted out of five farmworkers' cottages about twenty five years ago, and is believed to be at least two hundred and fifty years old. It sits in a sunny, sheltered spot beside the River Harbourne, and two garden tables enable you to sit and watch the river as it passes through the village and under its ancient stone bridge.

For the last year and a half the Hungry Horse has been the home of John and Caroline Tipper, who before settling here worked on luxury chartered yachts in the Mediterranean and Caribbean, John as captain and Caroline as cook and crew. Caroline, now chef at the Hungry Horse, still specialises in local seafood and shellfish, as well as prime local meats.

Accommodation consists of three double bedrooms, newly completed with pine furnishings and woodwork, and all with showers and toilets. The rooms also have colour televisions and tea and coffee making facilities. Pets are welcome, provided guests supply their bedding. Guests receive a complimentary carafe of wine and after-dinner coffee if they are dining.

The Hungry Horse restaurant is open every evening from Tuesday to Saturday, summer and winter. It is also open for Sunday lunches throughout the year.

Harbertonford is an interesting roadside village, once a mill-village, in the heart of the South Hams, with many houses and cottages built of the local slate. The lovely old towns of Totnes, Dartmouth and Kingsbridge, with all their surrounding attractions, are a short drive from the Hungry Horse's doorstep. Golf is available nearby at the Dartmouth Golf and Country Club, while for those who like to walk through characteristic countryside, the lush South Devon lanes and footpaths are minutes away from the village centre.

USEFUL INFORMATION

OPEN All year.

CHILDREN Welcome.

CREDIT CARDS Visa, Mastercard, Switch, Access.

LICENCE Restaurant.

ACCOMMODATION 3 en suite double rooms. Family room has additional single bed.

VEGETARIAN Always 2 different dishes available, more if requested in advance.

SMOKING Non smoking areas.

DISABLED Access with assistance.

GARDEN Yes, tables by river.

PRICES High Season: £25 per person per night; Low Season: £22. Children: under 2 free; 3-8 £5; 8-12 £8.

RESTAURANT International menu, specialising in local seafood and shellfish, plus prime cuts of meat. Open Tuesday to Saturday evenings all year. Sunday lunches all year.

ROYAL SEVEN STARS HOTEL
The Plains
Totnes,Devon TQ9 5DD

Tel (01803) 862125
Fax (01803) 867925

AA 2 stars, RAC 2 stars,
ETB 3 crowns

Centrally placed at the heart of the ancient town of Totnes, within easy reach of its many attractions, the Royal Seven Stars is a charming old English coaching inn, with all the associations and atmosphere that you would expect in such a place. Its imposing Regency facade suggests the coaching days of the early 19th century, when you could leave here at midday and be in London exactly twenty five hours later. But, like most of the buildings in this historic town, the hotel is older than it looks from the outside. It actually dates from 1660, since when it has been the town's major inn and an important focus for the community. There is also evidence that an earlier medieval hostelry called the Seven Stars stood here.

A famous guest was Daniel Defoe, author of *Robinson Crusoe*, who stayed here in 1723 whilst researching his *Tour Through the Whole Island of Great Britain*.

Entering the hotel, you find yourself in a spacious hall, bright with pot plants, which was once an open courtyard where horses' hooves rang on the cobbles. A flight of stairs leads up to a gracious ballroom, dating from 1840, where events of all kinds - wedding receptions, civic functions, dances, concerts and parties - take place. Most recently, the Totnes Jazz Collective has provided sophisticated modern jazz here every month.

In the comfortable Saddle Room bar, where visitors and Totnes residents enjoy the traditional atmosphere and sample a wide range of beers, wines and spirits, you can sink into a luxurious sense of the continuity over the centuries provided by an inn such as this in a historic town. This continuity is exemplified by the uninterrupted proprietorship, for over thirty years, of general manager Ken Stone, who came here in 1963. His deputy, Richard Baron, has been here for more than twenty years, and many members of staff have long service records, including head cook Julie Bull, members of the Yeo family and some of the receptionists - one, Eve Smith, still comes in despite having retired! All staff work together as a team to create a friendly and somewhat informal atmosphere for holiday-makers, business travellers and those taking a weekend break. The Brutus Room restaurant - named after the legendary founder of Britain, said to have landed in Totnes - offers breakfast, lunch and a substantial dinner, including fresh seafood, steaks, beefsteaks and poultry. A wide range of bar food is also available from the Carriage Room buffet.

USEFUL INFORMATION

OPEN All year round. Bar open all day.   **RESTAURANT** Wide range always available.
CHILDREN All ages catered for,   **BAR FOOD.** All the usual favourites.
High chairs etc available.   **VEGETARIAN** Assortment available.
CREDIT CARDS. All major cards.   **SMOKING** permitted, except food areas.
LICENCE Full.   **WHEELCHAIR ACCESS** grd.flr.
ACCOMMODATION 18 bedrooms, 12 en suite;   **PETS** Welcome
direct-dial telephones, TV,Hostess tray.   **GARDEN** No
PRICES Weekend breaks: double or twin room, £80 per person Friday to Sunday (2 days);
Daily: room and breakfast, from £27-£33. Weekly rates on request.

THE OLD FORGE AT TOTNES
Seymour Place
Totnes
Devon TQ9 5AY

Tel. (01803) 862174

AA 4 Qs, Specially Selected, ETB 2 Crowns, Highly Commended,
South Hams Tourism Best Hotel 1996, Green Merit Award for Environment

This charming and atmospheric Bed and Breakfast Hotel is situated a few minutes' walk from the centre of historic Totnes. The fine stone building was lovingly converted from a 600 year old forge, wheelwright's workshop, coach houses and stables by its owner, Jeannie Allnutt, and her late husband, who bought the property in 1985. For centuries it was the forge for the nearby Berry Pomeroy Castle estate. The smithy workshop reopened at Easter 1997 and the ring of the hammer on the anvil can be heard most days as the new blacksmith carries on the old tradition. Next door the Old Forge Pottery Studio turns out a great variety of earthenware.

The Old Forge is now reputed to offer the best accommodation in the Totnes area. 10 pretty, colour-themed rooms, all en suite, provide a comfortable and memorable stay for business travellers or holidaymakers. Each room has colour television, direct-dial telephones and beverage tray. The ground floor rooms and 'cottage suite' are ideal for elderly or partially disabled visitors or families with young children. Each room has numerous 'extras' to make it a real home from home.

Breakfast is served in a Tudor-style dining room. There is a wide choice available, with vegetarians, and those on special diets, being well catered for. Traditional Devonshire Cream Teas and daytime snacks are served in season. There are no evening meals served at the Old Forge, but Totnes and the surrounding villages are well supplied with inns and restaurants to suit every taste, and Jeannie's knowledge of them, and the area's other attractions, is always available to her guests.

A coach arch through the building gives access to a delightful walled garden. The Old Forge is an environmentally friendly zone where everything - especially the garden - has been created to be as aesthetically pleasing as possible. The owner is very conscientious about recycling and other green issues, but without compromising the very high standards. The latest addition to the hotel's provisions for guests' comfort is the conservatory-style leisure lounge with the luxury of a whirlpool spa (jacuzzi).

The Old Forge has its own safe car parking. The town of Totnes, with its Elizabethan buildings and Norman Castle, is on the doorstep, while all the delights of the South Hams, Dartmoor and Torbay are just a short journey away.

USEFUL INFORMATION

OPEN All Year
CHILDREN Welcome.
CREDIT CARDS Visa, Mastercard, Eurocard.
LICENCE Residential.
ACCOMMODATION 10 en suite rooms including ground floor rooms.
PETS In cars only.
PRICES Double: £35 - 44 Single: £25 - £33,

RESTAURANT B&B only. Cream teas and daytime snacks in summer season.
VEGETARIAN well catered for.
SMOKING No smoking indoors.
DISABLED Level entrance, 'cottage suite' and 2 rooms on ground floor.
GARDEN Secluded and sunny.

KINGSTON HOUSE
Staverton
Totnes
Devon TQ9 6AR

Tel. (01803) 762235 Fax (01803) 762444

ETB 3 Crowns, Highly Commended;
5 Keys, Highly Commended

Situated in the beautiful, secluded Devon countryside, just 4 miles from the lovely old town of Totnes, Kingston House is one of the finest surviving examples of early 18th century domestic architecture in England.

The mansion was built for John Rowe, a wealthy Totnes wool merchant and a gentleman farmer, and was completed by 1735. In its perfect proportions, simple elegance and graciousness of design it provides a rare experience of a real English Country House. Kingston's special charm, however, is that it is also, compared with larger houses, unusually intimate and home-like. Two outstanding features of Kingston are the marquetry staircase, probably the best example in Britain, if not in Europe, and the only surviving early 18th century painted china closet known in England.

The house, with its surrounding formal gardens and estate, are now owned by Michael and Elizabeth Corfield and their son, Piers, who have lovingly restored Kingston to its original beauty. They provide for their guests accommodation, fine cooking and carefully chosen wines of the highest quality, all in matchless period surroundings.

From the moment of your arrival in the marble Entrance Hall you will find Kingston a very peaceful, relaxing and romantic experience. Whether enjoying a pre-dinner drink in the panelled Drawing Room or a stroll in the formal rose or court gardens, the atmosphere is gentle and welcoming. A delicious candlelit dinner in the Dining Room which overlooks the walled garden (where much of the fruit and vegetables served are grown), with log fires in colder weather, complete a perfect evening.

The three suites on the first floor combine period style with discreet modern comfort and convenience. The Green Room, dominated by its four poster bed, is decorated in the style of 1830. The Red Suite is mainly 18th century in feel, whilst the Blue Suite remains much as it would have appeared in 1735. Each has its own unique historic features that ensure a richly enjoyable experience.

Surrounding the cobbled courtyard, the self-catering Cottages provide warm and cosy accommodation and facilities of the highest order. Whatever time of year you come to the Kingston estate, you will enjoy peace and comfort in a place resonant with history.

USEFUL INFORMATION

OPEN All Year.
CHILDREN Only in the cottages.
CREDIT CARDS All major cards.
LICENCE Full.
ACCOMMODATION 3 period suites in house, and 9 cottages accommodating up to 36.
PRICES Blue Suite £115, Green Room £100, Red Suite £105. Please telephone for cottage rates.

RESTAURANT Classic English haute cuisine in keeping with period of house. Fresh local produce.
VEGETARIAN catered for. Prior notice required.
SMOKING Non smoking areas.
DISABLED No special facilities.
PETS No.
GARDEN 5 acres, undergoing period of restoration. Occasionally open to public.

'THE OLD SHIP INN,'
Noss Mayo,
Plymouth, Devon PL8 2EW

Tel: 01752 872387

The Old Ship Inn must be one of the most popular and well known inns in South Devon. Situated as it is only a few miles from Plymouth and not much further away from the entrancing South Hams which includes Dartmouth, Salcombe and Kingsbridge as well as some truly beautiful villages, it draws its clientele from quite a large area. Built in the 16th century it sits at the head of the River Yealm in a delightful rural setting with the water lapping almost at its door. In fact the unwary have been known to leave their cars parked at low tide only to find the water rising fast around the vehicles! You can reach the Old Ship both by road and water, the latter making the hostelry particularly popular with the sailing fraternity who frequent it in large numbers. Best described as a typical traditional old inn with beamed ceilings, large exposed fire, comfortable furniture, warm and friendly, it is definitely a place that once having visited you would surely return.

Val and Norman Doddridge are your hosts and they have worked very hard over the years to build up such a good reputation not only for the well kept ales and the tremendous atmosphere but also because they provide a menu which tempts the palate. The no-smoking restaurant has 50 covers with nice polished tables and mats, gleaming cutlery and sparkling glass and here you will find a delicious choice of English country fare cooked by either Norman or Val who are both accomplished cooks. Everything is fresh including local fish, pork, lamb and game and all the produce such as garden vegetables. The menu is wide ranging and includes dishes for vegetarians as well as some exciting pasta concoctions. An interesting and well chosen wine list including wines from around the world complements the meal. In the bar you can also have food, again with a wide choice which may be as simple as a freshly cut and generously filled sandwich.

On warm days there can be nothing nicer than having a drink on the patio overlooking the water and the boats. Do not leave out this extra special inn on your travels.

USEFUL INFORMATION

OPEN; 11-3pm & 6-11pm	**RESTAURANT; English country fare.**
CHILDREN; Welcome	**Fresh fish, meat, game and vegetables**
CREDIT CARDS; Master/Visa/Switch	**BAR FOOD; Wide range**
LICENSED; Full On	**VEGETARIAN; Always a choice**
PETS; Yes, on leads	**DISABLED ACCESS; 2 steps. No special toilets**

THE MOORLAND INN
Wotter
Shaugh Prior
Plymouth
Devon PL7 5HP

Tel. (01752) 839228

The Moorland Inn is a spacious, family-run hotel on the southern slopes of the Dartmoor National Park, seven hundred feet above sea level. It is in the large parish of Shaugh Prior, in the beautiful Plym Valley, and enjoys superb views of the surrounding countryside, taking in Plymouth Sound and the Cornish hills beyond. Set in approximately an acre and a half of grounds, the hotel is in the heart of ideal walking and pony trekking country, as well as being within easy reach of golf courses, historic houses, gardens and the maritime city of Plymouth, which is only seven miles away.

The hotel is now the home of Marilyn and Paul Codlin and family, all of whom work at the inn. The Codlins, originally from the Midlands, are in the process of developing and improving all the facilities, including disabled access.

The Moorland Inn possesses eighteen en suite bedrooms, four of them with balconies, including two family rooms and a honeymoon suite. There is a Functions Room which can accommodate up to a hundred and twenty people, a bar and a separate restaurant and carvery, all enjoying wonderful views.

In the hotel restaurant the Codlins' chef prepares an impressive range of food, specialising in steaks, fresh fish and home-cooked hams. All meals, in both restaurant and bar, are made from local produce, and the variety is such as to appeal to all tastes and pockets. Vegetarians are well catered for, and the Sunday roast is a must. The wine list is extensive, and, in the bar, real ale enthusiasts will find a constantly changing supply.

The Moorland Inn, surrounded as it is by such lovely and diverse country, is an ideal base for discovering the delights of South West Devon, Plymouth and the Plym Valley. Beauty spots like the Burrator Reservoir and Bickleigh Bridge are close by, and old-world villages such as Meavy and Cornwood. Famous sites like Buckland Abbey, the unique experience of Morwellham Quay, the historic town of Tavistock and the whole of the western moor are easily reached. A slightly longer excursion can take you to the delights of the eastern moor and attractions such as Buckfast Abbey, the South Devon Railway, the River Dart Country Park, as well as the South Hams coast.

USEFUL INFORMATION

OPEN All year
CHILDREN Welcome.
Reduction if share parents' room.
CREDIT CARDS Master, Euro,
Switch, Delta, Visa,
LICENCE Full.
ACCOMODATION 18 en suite bedrooms, inc. 2 family
PETS Not in letting rooms. rooms and honeymoon suite.
GARDEN Yes. Seating area.
RESTAURANT Wide range of dishes using local produce, plus carvery Friday, Saturday and Sunday.

BAR FOOD Extensive menu,
plus blackboard specials and snacks.

VEGETARIAN 6 dishes to choose from.
SMOKING In bar, but not restaurant.
DISABLED Access.

PRICES From £20 per person per night.

DURANT ARMS
Ashprington
Totnes
Devon TQ9 7UP

(01803) 732240

Egon Ronay 1995

Conveniently situated in the centre of the picturesque South Hams village of Ashprington, the Durant Arms is a charming 18th century inn offering luxurious bed and breakfast accommodation.

Ashprington is 3 miles from Totnes, and within easy reach of both Torbay and Dartmoor as well as all the attractions of the Dart Valley and the rest of the South Hams countryside. Much of the village was formerly part of the Sharpham Estate, hence the unity of its appearance. The Durant was originally the estate manager's house, and takes its name from one of the families which once owned it. Sharpham House, a short distance away up a narrow lane, is now home to a prizewinning vineyard and creamery. The gardens of nearby Avenue Cottage, open on Tuesdays and Saturdays, 11am to 5pm, from April to September, are worth a visit.

The inn fits easily into this unspoilt, gentle environment. It has recently been taken over by Eileen and Graham Ellis, who moved here from the midlands, where they lived in a village near Stratford Upon Avon. They have placed the emphasis firmly on food and accommodation, and earned themselves a fine reputation for both, whilst still providing a comfortable village inn atmosphere. There is a lounge bar with an open log fire and two beautifully furnished restaurant lounges, where you are invited to relax and enjoy old fashioned care and hospitality. The bar sells two Real Ales, Flowers Original and Wadworth's '6X', and the wine list is long and sophisticated.

The menu is extensive, ranging from bar food to full evening meals prepared by local chef Will Stear. Whether you want a candlelit dinner for two or a party for up to 30 guests, the Durant can ensure that it is a memorable occasion. The Ellises go out of their way to give a warm, personal welcome and find out the needs of their customers.

Accommodation consists of two beautiful en suite rooms in the inn itself, while at the back is a newly restored self-catering cottage created out of a barn, which can sleep three to four people. There is a small, intimate and colourful garden, with benches where you can sit in fine weather and enjoy the ambience of this special village inn.

USEFUL INFORMATION

OPEN Mon to Sat 11.30am - 2.30pm and 6.30 - 11pm. Sunday 12-2.30pm and 7-10.30pm.
CHILDREN Welcome.
CREDIT CARDS Switch, Visa, Delta, Mastercard, Access
LICENCE Full.
ACCOMMODATION 1 double and 1 twin-bedded room, both en suite. Cottage sleeping 3 to 4 in grounds.
PRICES Rooms £20 per person per night, cottage £25. Children under 12, sharing, half price.

RESTAURANT Extensive, varied menu using seasonal produce. All main course dishes home made.
BAR FOOD As Above.
VEGETARIAN 3 or 4 always available.
SMOKING Non-smoking areas.
DISABLED Access.
PETS welcome.
GARDEN Small garden with seating.

COOMBE FARM MANOR HOUSE
Coombe Farm
Kingsbridge
Devon TQ7 4AB

Tel. (01548) 852038

Coombe Farm occupies a quiet valley just a mile from the old-fashioned South Devon estuary town of Kingsbridge. It is a family-run farm offering bed and breakfast accommodation, but it also provides a couple of unexpected extras - art and fishing!

Jonathan and Beni Robinson have created a truly unique atmosphere at their beautiful sixteenth century manor house, which, though so peacefully secluded, is very easily found, being close to the main road from Kingsbridge to Loddiswell. The Robinsons' guests can enjoy the ambience of a real working farm, and, if they wish, can join Beni and other local artists in a newly established stone-built painting studio, occupying what was once a barn. All are welcome to put paint to paper, whether experienced artists or absolute beginners. Alternatively, you can relax beside one of the three well-stocked lakes of the Coombe Water Fishery and try your hand for carp, bream, roach or tench. The fishery, open daily to non-residents, with rods available for hire, is acknowledged to be one of the westcountry's finest, and there is ample parking.

The accommodation at Coombe Farm consists of three large, elegantly furnished, en suite double or twin-bedded rooms, each with a colour television and facilities for making hot drinks. Guests enjoy a relaxed breakfast in the Robinsons' family dining room, around a comfortable oak table, all adding to the old-world farmhouse atmosphere. Fresh local produce is used, and vegetarians can be catered for.

With the charm of its setting and its fishing and artistic activities, you may be tempted never to leave Coombe Farm, but when you are ready to explore the surrounding countryside you will find a wealth of attractions on the doorstep. The pleasant old hilltop town of Kingsbridge, with its slate buildings and small family-run shops and pubs, repays exploring, and during the summer you can take a boat trip down the estuary to Salcombe. The small town of Modbury, surprisingly rich in craft and antique shops, is worth seeking out, while the cultural and artistic ambience is even stronger in Totnes, less than a dozen miles away. If you want to get away from towns for a while, even such individual towns as these, the dramatic South Hams coastline, with its tiny villages and sandy beaches, is easily accessible, but a short journey inland will bring you to another world entirely: the southern slopes of Dartmoor, best approached at Ivybridge. All this, and much more, can be experienced with Coombe Farm providing a perfect base for your holiday.

USEFUL INFORMATION

OPEN All year, except Christmas.
CHILDREN Over 12 preferred.
CREDIT CARDS No.
LICENCE No.
ACCOMMODATION 3 en-suite rooms
RATES; from £20 pppn B&B

SMOKING Not permitted in the house.
DISABLED No special facilities.
PETS No.
GARDEN yes

GABRIEL COURT HOTEL
Stoke Gabriel
Near Totnes
Devon TQ9 6SF

Tel. (01803) 782206
Fax. (01803) 782333

AA 3 Stars, RAC 3 Stars

Gabriel Court overlooks the beautiful Dart-side village of Stoke Gabriel, long famous for its salmon fishing, its orchards and the ancient yew tree in its churchyard. The hotel is an old manor house which was, for many centuries, the home of the Churchward family, the local squires. It was rebuilt in the 1860s, and since 1928 has fulfilled its present function, widely known as one of the most comfortable, friendly and peaceful hotels in the area.

The house is set in nearly three acres of Elizabethan-style gardens, with box hedges, terraces, clipped yew arches and magnolia trees, surrounded by high walls. Facing south, it is sunny and sheltered, with a heated outdoor swimming pool and lawn tennis court.

Gabriel Court is owned by the Beacom family, the resident proprietors, who assure you of a warm welcome. There are nineteen bedrooms, all en suite. Eight of them occupy an extension which was formerly a hay loft, converted in the 1960s, and one self-contained suite stands on its own in the grounds. All the rooms are fully equipped with colour televisions, radios, hair dryers, direct dial telephones and beverage trays.There are three lounges, with log fires in the winter, conference facilities, a residents' bar and a well-stocked wine cellar.

The hotel has always enjoyed a reputation for perfectly cooked English food. Fruit and vegetables in season are from the garden, salmon and sea trout from the Dart, other fish landed at nearby Brixham; venison and game from Devon estates and poultry and eggs from neighbouring farms.

Stoke Gabriel is easily reached from Paignton or Totnes. Guests arriving by train are advised to disembark at Totnes, where they can be met on request. The village itself repays attention, with its views of the river, cobbled pathways, old inns and quiet churchyard. The Elizabethan explorer John Davies, discoverer of the Falkland Islands and seeker after the fabled North West Passage, was born in the parish, and the magnificent yew tree which shades the church was already centuries old when he worshipped here. Another famous name from Stoke Gabriel is that of George Jackson Churchward (1857-1933), the Great Western Railway locomotive designer, who was the son of a local farmer.

USEFUL INFORMATION

OPEN All year.

CHILDREN Welcome. Cots and high chairs, baby listening service.

CREDIT CARDS Visa, Access, Mastercard, Diner's Club.

LICENCE Restaurant and Residents'.

ACCOMMODATION 17 double rooms, 2 singles, all en suite.

RESTAURANT Best traditional English fare.

VEGETARIAN Available on request.

SMOKING Allowed.

DISABLED No special facilities.

PETS Dogs welcome.

GARDEN nearly 3 acres with heated pool and tennis court.

PRICES Double or twin £74 per night for 2 people.

THE WATERMANS ARMS
Bow Bridge, Ashprington,
Totnes, Devon TQ9 7EG

Tel/Fax: 01803 732214

ETB Highly Commended 3 Crowns,
RAC 2 Star and
AA 5Q Premier Selected accolades.

It is hard to believe today when one looks around this entrancing inn that it has had such a turbulent history! It was once a smithy and then a brewery changing yet again during the Napoleonic Wars when it became a prison. As a hostelry it was known as a haunt for the feared Press Gangs. Now you are welcomed into a warm, atmospheric inn complete with sturdy old beams, roaring open log fires and everywhere fascinating bric a brac with not a hint of the past turbulence.

The Watermans Arms is situated on the bank of the River Harbourne, at the head of Bow Creek. It is one of the most beautiful riverside settings anywhere and yet it is only two miles from the ancient borough of Totnes and within easy distance of Torbay, the enchanting South Hams and th awesome majesty of Dartmoor. It is almost equidistant from Plymouth and from Exeter with its magnificent cathedral. People come to The Watermans for a variety of reasons, all of them good. The bars are always busy with people who live locally and with the many visitors who have discovered the charm and hospitality. Other people come to enjoy the excellent cuisine which is traditional, home-made, generous in portions and sensible in price. Many people come to the inn to stay in one of the fifteen attractively furnished ensuite guest rooms, 3 of which are twin bedded, 2 family rooms and one bedroom with a fourposter. All the rooms have colour television and well supplied beverage trays.

Returning to the subject of food the 'Special Seafood Platter' consisting of delicious Brixham Crab, Prawns, Fresh Salmon, Smoked Salmon and Smoked Trout accompanied by a freshly prepared garden salad is one of the specialities of the inn Everyday the Blackboards spell out the tasty Daily Specials, Children have special dishes, the Steaks are mouthwatering and the home-made desserts delectable. For those only wanting a quick snack there are freshly made sandwiches and The Waterman's Special Baguettes as well as Ploughmans and Jacket Potatoes. You will find the staff helpful, friendly and quietly efficient.

USEFUL INFORMATION

OPEN; All year 11-3pm & 6-11pm	**RESTAURANT; Traditional home-made fare**
Sun:12-3pm & 7-10.30pm	**BAR FOOD; Wide range. Good value**
CHILDREN; Welcome	**VEGETARIAN; Several dishes**
CREDIT CARDS; All major cards	**PETS; Permitted**
ACCOMMODATION; 15 ensuite rooms	**DISABLED ACCESS;Yes**

SHORT BREAKS; Jan,Feb,Mar, Nov (Sun-Thurs)
Min 3 nights. 3 day Xmas Break. 2 day New Year Break
RATES:- H/Season £70 per room. Low Season £46 per room. Single £36. Child £10.
Seasonal special offers and Stay with no accommodation charge:- Details on request.

FOLLATON FARMHOUSE
Plymouth Road
Totnes
Devon TQ9 5NA

Tel. (01803) 865441

In a peaceful setting on the edge of the historic town of Totnes, Follaton Farmhouse is an elegant former Georgian farmhouse offering high quality bed and breakfast accommodation, with evening meals by arrangement. The farmhouse has been sensitively restored and tastefully furnished to give you a memorable and relaxing stay. The house, which is deceptively large, with an impressive curved open stairway, and gardens with the tranquil sounds of running water and birdsong, create a very special atmosphere.

Follaton Farmhouse is now the home of Barbara and Bill Meller, who are careful to provide the little extras which make all the difference. Their house has retained many features from its past as the farmhouse of a wealthy estate. The integral dairy, with its original slate bed tables and flagstone floor, and the kitchen which has an open fireplace and is furnished with iron, brass and copper antiques, all evoke past ages in an atmosphere of welcome and comfort.

This is especially true of the lounge, where you can relax after your day exploring the attractions of South Devon, or before and after dinner. The three individually decorated en suite bedrooms are beautifully furnished, each in a distinctive style, and offer a luxurious standard of facilities, including colour televisions and tea and coffee trays. Both double and twin-bedded rooms are available.

The gardens at Follaton Farmhouse are very enjoyable, with a spring which flows into a small trout pond and gushes into a trough in the courtyard at the rear of the house. There is a forty by twenty foot swimming pool which guests are welcome to use during the summer.

Totnes, the centre of which is just a mile from the house, is one of the most interesting and attractive towns in Devon, especially for those with a taste for history and the arts. It is surrounded by a wealth of places to visit, including castles, gardens, historic houses and peaceful villages, and excellent walks can be taken in every direction around the town.

To find Follaton Farmhouse from the centre of Totnes, take the Plymouth Road (signposted to Avonwick). After half a mile look for a sign on the left saying 'Follaton House'. Continue along the road and take the second turning on the left into a private driveway to the farmhouse. Guests can be met from Totnes railway station.

USEFUL INFORMATION

OPEN All year.
CHILDREN No.
CREDIT CARDS No.
LICENCE No, but guests are welcome
to bring their own drinks.
PRICES From £24 per person per night.

VEGETARIAN by request.
SMOKING Non-smoking house.
PETS No.
GARDEN Yes.
ACCOMMODATION 3 en suite bedrooms.

TREBLES COTTAGE HOTEL
Kingston
Near Kingsbridge
Devon TQ7 4PT

Tel. and Fax (01548) 810268
Mobile (0589) 769991

AA 4 Qs, RAC Acclaimed.

Trebles Cottage Hotel is beautifully set in tranquil South Hams countryside at the top end of a valley, in the small village of Kingston. The house itself dates from 1801. Kingston, reached along winding lanes, is pleasantly remote and still in touch with its past as a cider making community. Full directions are given when you book. However, tucked away as it is, the towns and attractions of South Devon are easily reached, and Trebles makes an excellent base for exploring the entire area. The South West Way coastal path is just a mile away, along a path from the hotel garden.

Trebles is owned by Georgiana (Georgie for short!) and David Kinder, who have been in the hospitality business for ten years. Together they take special care to ensure that visitors have a memorable time. They enjoy travelling themselves, and one of their particular pleasures is meeting people from places they have visited.

As well as four en suite rooms the hotel facilities include a residents' lounge and cocktail bar, with patio adjoining. The menu gives a sophisticated choice of English dishes, using fresh local produce and featuring Devon specialities such as Salcombe Smokies. The wine list contains a good selection, including Chablis, Mouton Cadet and Chateau de neuf de Pape.

USEFUL INFORMATION

OPEN All year
CHILDREN 12+
CREDIT CARDS Visa, Access, Mastercard, American Express. A surcharge of 4% is added if cards are used.
LICENCE Restaurant and Residential.
ACCOMMODATION 4 en suite bedrooms.

VEGETARIAN Catered for.
SMOKING Not allowed in some rooms.
DISABLED No special facilities.
PETS Dogs by prior arrangement. £1.75 per night.
GARDEN Yes.

PRICES High Season: B&B from £27 per night, Dinner, B& B from £81 for 2 nights.
Low Season: B&B from £25, Dinner,B&B from £77.

THE ANCHOR INN
Lutterburn Street
Ugborough
South Devon PL21 0NG

Tel. and Fax (01752) 892283

The Anchor Inn is a delightfully traditional Devon hostelry, of medieval origins, adjacent to Ugborough's large village square. It is especially well known for its food, having an imaginative a la carte restaurant menu and a good range of bar meals. The inn also provides comfortable Bed and Breakfast accommodation.

All meals at the Anchor are prepared by the inn's owner, Mrs Sheelagh Jeffreys, who takes pride in buying the freshest local ingredients according to their season and availability; this is reflected especially in the fish and game dishes. Vegetarians are also well catered for, and everything is cooked to order.

The inn is tastefully decorated throughout to combine the traditional ambience of the village inn with an atmosphere conducive to the enjoyment of good food and drink. The bar, which is across the entrance hall from the restaurant, serves a fine selection of locally and nationally brewed real ales, and here you can meet with locals and visitors before settling down in the restaurant for a carefully prepared candlelit dinner.

The accommodation at the Anchor comprises a choice of single, double, twin and family rooms, all en suite, with TV and tea and coffee making facilities.

Ugborough is a very attractive village in the South Hams, between Plymouth and Torbay, with the lower slopes of Dartmoor only a couple of miles away at Ivybridge.

USEFUL INFORMATION

OPEN Weekdays 11am - 3pm and 5 - 11pm. Saturday 11am - 11pm. Sunday 12 - 3pm and 7 - 10.30pm.
CHILDREN Welcome (subject to licencing laws).
CREDIT CARDS Visa and cheque cards.
LICENCE Full.
ACCOMMODATION 5 en suite chalets.
PRICES Double from £40 B&B.
PETS Dogs welcome in bar. Not in accommodation.

RESTAURANT Extensive a la carte menu. Fresh local produce according to season. Main courses from approx. £10.
BAR FOOD Wide choice of pizzas, ploughmans, burgers, spaghettis, fish etc. From approx. £3.
VEGETARIAN Always a good choice of dishes.
SMOKING Permitted, not encouraged in dining areas.
DISABLED Level access.
GARDEN Small.

VENN FARM
Ugborough
Ivybridge
Devon PL21 0PE

Tel. (01364) 73240

3 Crowns Commended

Venn is a working, family-run South Devon farm, offering comfortable country house accommodation, and traditional farmhouse cooking. Situated in peaceful countryside near the ancient village of Ugborough, the house is approximately two hundred years old and is surrounded by a large wild-flower garden with a stream running through it, a gypsy caravan and a private patio with picnic table. The Garden Cottage, next to the house, provides two twin rooms with private showers and toilets, and has been specially converted from a stone-built piggery.

The resident proprietors of Venn Farm are Pat and Paul Stephens, who as well as creating a warm, home-from-home atmosphere, are busy working farmers. Children are encouraged to take an active interest in the running of the farm wherever possible.

In the house there are two comfortable sitting rooms for the use of residents, with colour televisions. Meals are taken in the guests' dining room, and consist of substantial farmhouse fare, with plenty of fresh vegetables and lovely puddings. 'Carve your own roasts' are a popular feature.

Venn Farm is near the pleasant village of Ugborough, with two lively pubs, and the thriving new town of Ivybridge, the gateway to Southern Dartmoor. Golf, pony trekking and walking can be enjoyed almost on the doorstep.

USEFUL INFORMATION

OPEN January to November.
CHILDREN Welcome.
CREDIT CARDS No.
LICENCE No.
ACCOMMODATION 2 ensuite family rooms;
2 twin rooms in cottage with private showers.
PRICES £20 B&B per person per night.
Special rates for children. Please check prices when booking.

VEGETARIAN no.
SMOKING Permitted.
DISABLED 2 ground floor beds,
suitable for partially disabled.
PETS By arrangement.
GARDEN Half acre of gardens.

LOWER GRIMSTONLEIGH
East Allington
Kingsbridge
Devon TQ9 7QH

Tel. (01548) 521258 Fax (01548) 521329

At the end of a lane, deep in the peaceful South Hams countryside, but only three miles from the old town of Kingsbridge, Lower Grimstonleigh is an unforgettable experience. It is an ancient Devon farm, mentioned in the Domesday Book, and the house is a mellow stone building in a beautiful courtyard, which has been used for the filming of a Victorian farmyard scene. The house is set in its own twelve acres of meadows, orchards and gardens.

Lower Grimstonleigh is the home of Mrs Joy Jones, who is widely travelled and lived in Hong Kong for five years. Now settled in this lovely environment she provides bed and breakfast accommodation and keeps horses, donkeys and Dexter cattle, all of which are shown at local agricultural shows. Her superb English breakfast uses free range eggs and fresh fruit from the farm, as well as other local produce.

The accommodation at Lower Grimstonleigh consists of three comfortable double bedrooms, two of them en suite and one with a private bathroom. The farm is an ideal base for exploring the beautiful South Hams, with the coastal path and many National Trust properties nearby. Walks in woods, fields and bridlepaths are literally on the doorstep.

USEFUL INFORMATION
OPEN All year.
CHILDREN No.
CREDIT CARDS No.
LICENCE No.
ACCOMMODATION 3 double rooms.
DISABLED No special facilities.
PETS no.
GARDENS Extensive and pretty courtyards.

PRICES Between £27 and £32 per night.

BURTON FARM
Galmpton
Kingsbridge
Devon TQ7 3EY
Tel. and Fax (01548) 561210
ETB 2 Crowns, Highly Commended

Burton is a working South Hams farm one mile from the fishing village of Hope Cove and just three miles from Salcombe. It was once the property of the Duke of Devonshire, and has since passed through various hands, but is now owned by Mrs Anne Rossiter. She has extensively and lovingly restored the house, while outside the farm is expertly run by David, a traditional farmer who combines the wisdom of age-old husbandry with modern technology. Guests are, where possible, invited to watch work on the farm, which possesses a herd of dairy cows and two pedigree flocks of sheep. Anne uses the farm's free-range eggs and home-grown produce in her kitchen, and local specialities such as Devonshire clotted cream are featured in her menus. There are nine centrally heated bedrooms, five of them with en suite bathrooms. There is a choice of family, double, twin or single rooms, and self-catering accommodation is also available. Burton Farm is fully licensed, with a world-wide selection of over forty red and white wines, as well as beers and ciders.   Burton Farm is within very easy reach of the South Devon coast and the beautiful South Hams countryside, with all its attractions, is literally outside the door.

USEFUL INFORMATION
OPEN All year except Christmas.
CHILDREN Welcome. Under 5, 50% discount; under 10, 25% discount
CREDIT CARDS Barclaycard, Visa, Access, Switch, Delta
LICENCE Full.
VEGETARIAN Catered for.
SMOKING Not permitted
DISABLED Level entrance.
PETS Permitted, but not in house. Dogs by prior arrangement.
GARDEN Yes - enjoy it!

ACCOMMODATION 9 rooms, 5 en suite.
PRICES From £21-23 per person per night, reduced by £2 on subsequent night.
RESTAURANT Traditional farmhouse cooking, using home-grown produce wherever possible. 4 course dinner inc. coffee etc £10.50.

GREY'S DINING ROOM
96 High Street
Totnes
Devon TQ9 5SN
Tel. and Fax (01803) 866369
Tea Council's Prestigious Top Tea Place of the Year 1996
Awards of Excellence 1993, 1994, 1995
Egon Ronay Recommended

At the top of Totnes High Street, in the attractive area known as the Narrows, the award winning Grey's Dining Room is everything that you expect a traditional tea shop to be. The well-maintained Georgian house, which at the turn of the century was the premises of a tea dealer and grocer, and has since been a sweet shop, antique shop and outlet for motor spares, is ideally suited for enjoying tea and light meals in a tasteful and intimate environment.   The heavily carved Victorian cake display cabinet greets you as you enter, and the doorway is flanked by two magnificent Boston ferns. The saucer collection on the beams and about the walls has started many an avid collector on a new track. Original wood panelling, antique furniture and carefully chosen pictures, as well as the gleaming silver of the jugs, trays and teapots, all add up to make taking tea at Grey's a highly memorable experience.   Grey's is owned and run by Gary Dowland and David Winstone, with their staff Jenny Goss and Theresa Barnes. In only six years of being here, they have gained a national reputation for the care and quality of their service. You can enjoy more than 40 types of tea or fruit infusions, home-made cakes, scones, pies and gateaux, with clotted cream and jams.   After wandering around Totnes, with all its historic sites and interesting shops, Grey's is the ideal place to stop for refreshment.

USEFUL INFORMATION

OPEN All Year. Closed Wednesdays.
Mon - Thurs 10am - 5pm.
Fri 9.30am - 5pm.
Sat 10am - 5pm. **Sun** 2 - 5pm.
CHILDREN Welcome on a lead!
CREDIT CARDS Not Taken.
LICENCE None.

RESTAURANT Specialist tea shop serving light meals. Omelettes, sandwiches (open and closed), salads, soup etc.
Home-made cakes, scones, fruit pies.
VEGETARIAN Catered for.
SMOKING No.
DISABLED One step down into premises.

TUNLEY FARM
Loddiswell
Near Kingsbridge
Devon TQ7 4ED
Tel. (01548) 550279

Tunley is a working South Hams farm nestling in a quiet valley, half a mile from the village of Loddiswell and four miles from Kingsbridge. It is the home of the Harvey family, who offer bed and breakfast accommodation and enjoy welcoming guests to their spacious, centuries-old Devon farmhouse.   A local historian believes Tunley to have existed in 1558, although it is officially listed as dating from 1608. The 1851 census records the house as having fifteen occupants, including six servants and a governess. Now it has just five, Paul and Joy Harvey and their three young daughters, and there is plenty of room for their guests in this comfortable and atmospheric building, with its pretty garden and busy dairy farm.   The accommodation consists of a large family suite, which comprises two bedrooms and an en suite bathroom. Joy provides lots of little 'extras' to enhance the pleasure of staying: a coffee/tea tray with biscuits, special teas, chocolate, fresh flowers and fruit, shower creme, bath foam etc. As the Harveys have a young family, children are especially well looked after and provided for.   Breakfast at Tunley is a real farmhouse experience, with a wide choice: fresh fruit, yoghurt, a full English breakfast and Joy's home-made preserves, local honey and the farm's own eggs.

USEFUL INFORMATION

OPEN Easter to October.
CHILDREN Welcome. Cot/high chair available. Baby sitting by arrangement.
CREDIT CARDS No.
LICENCE No.

VEGETARIAN Breakfast by arrangement.
SMOKING Non-smoking house.
PETS No.
GARDEN Guests welcome to use the garden.
Swing, sand pit and trampoline for the children.

ACCOMMODATION Family suite of 2 bedrooms with en suite bathroom.

PRICES £17.50 per person per night. Children: discount according to age.

WOODPARK
Diptford
Near Totnes
Devon TQ9 7NL

Tel. and Fax (01548) 821636

Woodpark is a beautifully converted 18th century threshing barn, surrounded by 18 acres of secluded grounds. Here the Palmer family provide luxurious Bed and Breakfast accommodation in unforgettable rural surroundings.

Woodpark is about 6 miles from Totnes, set in the lovely Avon Valley, in a designated Area of Outstanding Natural Beauty. It is approached along a short drive, and round about are its own fields, with many delightful footpaths and bridleways leading to the river, with its stone bridges and woodland. Being in the heart of the South Hams countryside, it is ideal for exploring the area, within easy reach of Dartmouth, Kingsbridge, Salcombe and the southern slopes of Dartmoor. The nearest beach is at Bigbury Bay, 15 minutes away.

Accommodation consists of two en suite bedrooms, furnished to a high standard, with colour television and tea and coffee making facilities. Breakfast is a particular feature of Woodpark hospitality, with a large choice of local organic produce, eaten in the spacious, sunny beamed kitchen, bright with fresh flowers and plants.

Everything at Woodpark epitomises the kind of quality of life which is possible in the beautiful South Hams.

USEFUL INFORMATION

OPEN Easter to October.
CHILDREN Welcome.
CREDIT CARDS No.
LICENCE No.
ACCOMMODATION 2 en suite rooms.
PRICES £30 - £35 per person. Children half price.

SMOKING not in bedrooms.
DISABLED No special facilities.
PETS No.
GARDEN Barn surrounded by its own land.

HATCHLANDS FARM
Bluepost
Avonwick
Near Totnes
Devon TQ9 7LR

Tel. and Fax (01364) 72224

Hatchlands is a two hundred and seventy five acre working South Devon dairy, beef and arable farm, deep in the lovely South Hams countryside. Luxurious bed and breakfast accommodation is provided in the farmhouse by Mrs Sheree Palmer and her husband, Fred, who own and run the farm. Hatchlands offers an unusually generous share of beauty, peace and tranquility, and is ideally placed for exploring the area, with its superb walking country and many attractions.

Visitors are welcome to take an interest in the working of the farm. In the house, filled with lovely mahogany furnishings, guests are welcome to use the lounge, which has a wood-burning fire in the centre of the room, as well as SKY television. There is also a sunlounge, with a snooker table and magnificent views over the garden and surrounding countryside. The landscaped garden is large, and features a twenty foot pond with a waterfall. The pond is home to koi carp and golden orf.

Breakfast is a special event at Hatchlands. A four course meal is available, with fruit juice, a wide choice of cereals, a cooked breakfast of your choice and toast with jam, marmalade or honey. Those on special diets are well catered for.

USEFUL INFORMATION

OPEN All year
CHILDREN Welcome.
CREDIT CARDS No.
LICENCE No.
ACCOMMODATION 2 en suite bedrooms, one with 4 poster bed.
Sky colour TV, tea/coffee facilities, alarm etc.

VEGETARIAN Breakfast available.
SMOKING Allowed in bedrooms.
DISABLED No special access.
PETS Welcome.
GARDEN Large, with barbecue, outdoor chairs and tables and pond.

PRICES High season: £18.50 per person per night; Low season £15.50. Children half price. Winter 3 night breaks £11 (£3 supplement for single person).

STOWFORD HOUSE
Harford, Ivybridge
Devon PL21 0JD
Tel: 01752 698088 Fax: 01752 895040

On the edge of Ivybridge and within the Dartmoor National Park, Stowford House is just 100 metres from the start of the Two Moors Way. With the beautiful sandy beaches of the South Hams and Ivybridge with its comprehensively equipped Leisure Centre including indoor and outdoor pools within a few minutes and historic Exeter and Plymouth easily reached, this must be an ideal house for anyone to stay in who wants a relaxed, informal atmosphere and will enjoy their hosts, Jeremy and Gisella Kneen who are both Vets. This welcoming couple moved into what was then a house in disrepair some four years ago. They have worked hard to make it a comfortable, happy home for themselves and their four children. They will tell you the garden still needs much attention but when you feel the warmth of the welcome around you such trivial things are not worth bothering about! Jeremy is a keen golfer and does Stage Rallying whilst Gisella and son Thomas have a horse each. They will tell you all about the fascinating history of Stowford which is the Georgian part of what once was a Tudor Manor House.

The accommodation comprises of one family room with a comfortable double bed and bunk beds for the children. It is ensuite and has a large air bath. The room is also equipped with a television and a generously supplied hostess tray. Breakfast is a cheerful meal, freshly cooked to your choice. No evening meals but Gisella will happily send you off in the right direction to one of the many eateries nearby.

USEFUL INFORMATION

OPEN;All Year	**DINING ROOM; Excellent breakfast**
CHILDREN; Welcome	**VEGETARIANS; Catered for upon request**
CREDIT CARDS; None taken	**DISABLED ACCESS; No**
LICENCED; No	**PETS; No**

ACCOMMODATION; Family room en-suite..
RATES:- £27.50. Children according to age.

COOMBE HOUSE
North Huish
South Brent
Devon
TQ10 9NJ
Tel. and Fax (01548) 821277

Deep in the South Hams countryside, surrounded by woods, rolling hills and fields, Coombe House is a graceful Georgian home, formerly a farmhouse, in a designated Area of Outstanding Natural Beauty. Its owners, John and Faith Scharenguivel, offer Bed and Breakfast accommodation and four Self Catering Cottages in a matchlessly beautiful, peaceful environment.   The house is reached by a winding Devon lane following the valley, and is set in its own four acres of land. Two streams and a small lake attract an abundance of wildlife, and the stone cottages, sensitively converted from barns set around a courtyard, provide an ideal country retreat.   Each of the cottages is fully equipped with everything you could need for a relaxed stay, including comfortable furnishings, fitted kitchens and colour TV. There is a communal laundry and payphone. Cots and bed linen are provided, and high chairs can be supplied by arrangement.   Coombe House, its gardens and adjacent countryside are so tranquil that you will find it difficult to tear yourself away, but when you do, the whole of South Devon, Dartmoor and the coast are at your doorstep. It therefore makes an ideal base for touring the area.   North Huish is reached from Avonwick, on the B3210 road from Totnes, or from the A38 at South Brent.

USEFUL INFORMATION

OPEN All Year.	**DISABLED No special access or facilities.**
CHILDREN Welcome.	**PETS No.**
CREDIT CARDS No.	**GARDEN 4 acres of garden and grounds.**
LICENCE No.	**ACCOMMODATION B&B: 2 double en suite bedrooms.**

Self Catering: 4 stonebuilt cottages sleeping 4 or more.
PRICES B&B: High Season £25,
Low Season £20. Self Catering from £150 to£325 per week, plus electricity (50p meter).

DIDWORTHY HOUSE
Didworthy
South Brent
Devon TQ10 9EF
Tel. (01364) 72655

Didworthy House is a large Victorian country house, standing in its own 2 acres of grounds which slope gently towards the River Avon, on the southern edge of Dartmoor. Its owners, Sam and Bente Billcliff, provide Bed and Breakfast accommodation and Self Catering Holiday Lets. Bente is Danish, and between them they can communicate fluently in Danish, German, French and some Spanish.   The house dates from 1840, but the north wing is even older. It is built in a quadrangle around a small inner courtyard, and has a large Victorian-style conservatory on the south side. Beautiful views of surrounding fields and woods can be seen in every direction, and the open moor is a ten minute walk away.   The Self Catering accommodation is in three wings of the house, each with its own entrance. All are fully equipped for the number of people they can accommodate, and are centrally heated. For additional cosiness they have wood burning stoves - logs are free! There are shared, metered, laundry facilities and a payphone.   Didworthy is a mile and three quarters through narrow Devon lanes from the village of South Brent, which is just off the A38 between Exeter and Plymouth. It is ideal for exploring both Dartmoor and the South Hams, and not far from the more extrovert pleasures of Torbay.

USEFUL INFORMATION

OPEN All Year.
CHILDREN Welcome - 2 cots and high chair available.
CREDIT CARDS No.
LICENCE No.
ACCOMMODATION In 3 wings, sleeping 6, 5 and 2/4 respectively.

DISABLED No special facilities.
PETS 1 well-behaved dog per property.
GARDEN 2 acres, open to guests, with large outdoor swimming pool, heated May to September.

PRICES B&B: £19.50 per person per night. Self Catering: Weekly rates variable, £140 - £415 per property. Short breaks (3 days) £95 - £305. Includes all heating, lighting, bed linen etc.

ASKEW COTTAGE
Ashprington, Totnes,
Devon TQ9 7UP
Tel/Fax: 01803 732417
Mobile 0374 113865

Pretty, idyllic villages abound in Devon but Ashprington must come high on the list of best loved.Close to Totnes, the second oldest borough in England, it is an ideal base from which to explore the majesty and splendour of Dartmoor, the soft Devon countryside and the glorious beaches. Ashprington has everything including a fine old church dating back to the 12th century and a splendid 18th century pub which has excellent food.
Sheena Lumley owns Askew Cottage and it is here she welcomes you into her attractive home the origins of which can be traced back to the 16th century and is one of the oldest houses in Ashprington. The oldest room in the cottage is the dining room which is delightful with its heavy oak beams, originally used as ships timbers. Here you will have a delicious, freshly cooked breakfast or a Continental one if you prefer. A Vegetarian breakfast is also available. No evening meals but there are plenty of eateries locally including the village pub. Sheena's Guest Rooms are charmingly furnished. There is an ensuite double room on the ground floor and upstairs a twin-bedded room which, if needed, can have another bed, with a private bathroom. Sheena enjoys her guests and works hard to ensure that they are comfortable and relaxed.

USEFUL INFORMATION

OPEN; All Year. (Check in time from 3.30pm)
CHILDREN; Welcome
CREDIT CARDS; None taken
ACCOMMODATION; 1dbl 1 tw both ensuite
RATES; High season £20.00 pppn B&B.

DINING ROOM; Super breakfast
VEGETARIAN; Catered for
DISABLED ACCESS; Ground floor room
GARDEN; Yes with chairs

Babies free otherwise 1/3 off * Single in High Season£ 22.00
Low Season £20.00 pppn B&B Single occupancy £25.00

CROWN YEALM
Bridgend Hill
Newton Ferrers
Plymouth
Devon PL8 1AW

Tel. (01752) 872365

Crown Yealm is a large house, dramatically situated upon the wooded hillside above the beautiful Yealm estuary, offering friendly Bed and Breakfast accommodation with unsurpassed views. Its glorious south facing location and proximity to the twin waterside villages of Newton Ferrers and Noss Mayo have ensured that countless guests have returned to this beautiful place year after year.

Crown Yealm is run by Mrs J.D.Johnson, whose family home it has been since 1943. She has three spacious, comfortable bedrooms, each overlooking the garden down to the water's edge, and containing comfortable beds, television and tea and coffee making facilities. There is a double room, a double with an extra single bed suitable for families, and a twin bedded room. An excellent breakfast is provided.

A short creekside walk from the house will bring you to the lovely village of Newton Ferrers, with its picturesque and always busy harbour, three inns, a post office and a useful selection of shops. The village is an ideal base for those who enjoy yachting, fishing, walking or birdwatching, whilst the varied attractions of Plymouth, the South Hams coast and the southern slopes of Dartmoor National Park are within easy reach.

Written confirmation for bookings is requested, with a 50% deposit. Arrival reception operates from 4pm to 10pm.

USEFUL INFORMATION

OPEN All Year.
CHILDREN Welcome.
CREDIT CARDS No.
LICENCE No.
ACCOMMODATION 3 bedrooms, 1 family sized.
RESTAURANT Breakfast only.
VEGETARIAN Breakfast by arrangement.
SMOKING Restricted
DISABLED No special facilities.
PETS By arrangement.
GARDEN Yes.
PRICES From £17.50 per night. Family of 2 adults & child £40.

THE MILL AT AVONWICK
Avonwick
South Brent
Devon TQ10 9ED

Tel. (01364) 72488

The Mill at Avonwick is an imaginatively designed pub/restaurant, based on a restored 17th century grain mill, complete with water wheel, which was later a farmhouse. It is situated in 5 acres of beautiful grounds in rural South Devon, complete with a lake, peaceful and relaxing, but also within minutes of the A38 dual carriageway at South Brent. It is a mere 6 miles from Totnes, and only a 25 minute drive from Exeter or 15 minutes from Plymouth. The lower slopes of Dartmoor National Park can be seen just the other side of the road.

The spacious building contains a large, self-contained function room, recently refurbished and ideal for all kinds of corporate meetings, presentations or wedding receptions. Outside there is a large garden and a fully-equipped play area for the children. The Mill also has ample car parking.

The restaurant serves an extensive a la carte menu, specialising in good, freshly cooked, traditional English fare, such as steaks and seafood dishes, with soups and other starters. Vegetarians are well catered for. In the bar a wide-ranging menu of lighter snacks and bar meals can be enjoyed, while Real Ale enthusiasts will find a good pint of Draught Bass.

Its great ease of access and unique ambience make The Mill at Avonwick an ideal place for either an intimate meal with friends, a family celebration or a business meeting.

USEFUL INFORMATION

OPEN Every day except Christmas Day.
CHILDREN Welcome - children's menu.
PETS: Welcome in 3 units. £8.50/week
ACCOMMODATION 2 double and
1 twin room in farmhouse,
and 7 self-cateringproperties converted
from farm buildings
PRICES B&B £16 - £19.50 per night, Self-catering from £85 to £338 per week,
depending on unit and time of year

RESTAURANT A la carte menu. Good English
dishes: steaks, fish dishes.
GARDEN Pleasant, flat main garden and
other areas for sitting and eating.
BAR FOOD Extensive menu, home cooked.
VEGETARAIN 4 - 6 dishes.
WHEELCHAIR ACCESS.

Chapter Four

CHAPTER FOUR

Around Dartmoor

"A good, honest, wholesome, hungry breakfast"
Izaak Walton

CHAPTER FOUR

AROUND DARTMOOR

T he centre of Devon is dominated by the great granite mass of Dartmoor, a high, windy, ancient tract of country, like an island above the cultivated lowlands. For many people it is the ultimate Westcountry landscape.

Everyone probably has some mental image of the moor, which can be seen on the skyline from much of Devon: the towering granite outcrops, weathered into often disturbing shapes, the heather-covered hills, the little half-wild ponies, the relics of Bronze Age humanity, the tragi-comic story of the group of farmers who attended Widecombe Fair on a borrowed horse, the grim walls of the prison... Dartmoor means vastly different things to different people, but nearly everybody attests to its powerful, haunting atmosphere, which can become nothing less than an addiction.

Devon is generally such a soft, fertile place that it can be a shock to see the bleak northern wastes of the moor and to realise that you are actually right in the heart of the county, but the two landscapes are inseparably connected. Without the empty, rain-sodden heights of the moor, where most of Devon's rivers originate, there would be no gentle lowlands; the environments are inextricably linked, 'two but not two'. You experience this unity of diverse elements very strongly in those places where you can see and partake of both the open moor and the tamed, well-ordered landscape below.

To be more precise, Dartmoor is a granite plateau, formed about 400 million years ago, rising roughly to between 1,000 and 2,000 feet above sea level. On this plateau are hundreds of bare outcrops of rock called tors, some of them famous landmarks like Hay Tor and Hound Tor, others barely noticeable amongst the surrounding boulders. There are also two main areas of blanket bog, around Cranmere Pool and Fox Tor Mire, in which great rivers like the Dart, the Teign, the Taw and the Tavy start life as tiny streams.

Two busy roads traverse the moor, the B3357 from Tavistock to Ashburton, and the B3212 from Yelverton to Moretonhampstead. You can do either journey in about half an hour, but this fact gives no idea of the real extent of the moor, for which you must stop and get out of the car, when the vastness of the place will suddenly hit you. The open moor is a place of thin soil and little shelter, yet for thousands of years people have lived here, and it is littered, to a greater extent than anywhere else in Europe, with Bronze Age huts, stone circles, standing stones, and ancient field systems. There are also extensive remains of the tin mining industry which once, at the end of the Middle Ages and the early 16th century, supplied most of the continent's tin.

It is a powerful place, seemingly cut off from the rest of the world, strangely silent and empty. Despite being in Devon, which is always less mysterious than Cornwall (even at its wildest, Dartmoor never feels as if it could be across the Tamar), there is a strong sense of ancient magic, and the land is alive with ghosts and legends, weird stories and unusual experiences.

To be somewhere away from roads on the high moor on a breathless summer day, while lizards sun themselves on the rocks and ravens sit watching on the tors, with hardly a sound from any direction, can be a life-enhancing or unsettling experience, according to your temperament, but it is unlikely to be an indifferent one. It is this stillness, at the heart of the county, which draws Devon people from the towns and cities here at weekends and bank holidays in such numbers. The thought of these empty, windswept spaces sustains them in their days filled with computer screens and office politics, and the lone figure that you spy, in the distance, walking over the hills, is more likely to be from Paignton, Plymouth or Exeter than further afield.

The moor has other, gentler terrains. Where the rivers come off the high plateau there are deep tree-filled gorges, and these became the first beauty spots when romantic tourists began to discover the moor in the 19th century. For many visitors today, the most typical Dartmoor experience is not of the granite and heather-clad hills, but of a walk through the rich green of oak and sycamore woods next to a rocky river bed, followed by tea in a low, pleasantly old fashioned, wooden cafe and souvenir shop, beside a time-worn, grey stone bridge.

Much of the land has been enclosed, and many ancient hill farms dot the landscape. The traditional dwelling for the hill farmer was the Devon Longhouse, where the animals lived at one end and the family at the other. Many fine examples of these houses, dating from no later than the 14th or 15th centuries, still exist, and some are lived in by families who have been on the moor for generations.

Dartmoor is an ancient 'Forest', meaning not a wooded area but a royal hunting ground. Although disafforested centuries ago, the name still appears on maps. It is also, of course, one of the 11 NATIONAL PARKS in England and Wales (Scotland doesn't have any), a name which needs some explanation.

A National Park in Britain is not a 'park' in the sense of being a controlled, carefully landscaped environment, nor is it 'national' in the sense of being state-owned. All the term means is that the moor has been designated by Parliament as a place in need of special protection for its scenic and environmental qualities. National Park status does not effect the usual rights of landowners, and every acre of the moor, including the traditional common land, is owned by somebody.

Important Dartmoor landowners include the Duchy of Cornwall (nothing to do with the County of Cornwall - see chapter 6), the Forestry Commission and the National Trust. The Ministry of Defence leases a large area of the northern moor for military training. The moor is used by farmers, industrialists and the water business for purposes that are often not easily compatible with the desires of holiday makers and preservationists.

Although it has become fashionable in recent years to talk and write about Dartmoor as a 'wilderness', often 'Britain's last wilderness', it is actually, compared with real wildernesses elsewhere in the world, nothing of the sort. It has, for over 4,000 years, been a place where human beings have lived and worked and exploited the land as fully as they were able. They have mined, quarried and farmed, enclosed and built. People continue to live and work here, and are anxious for their voices to be heard, more often than they have been in the past, when decisions are taken about the area's future. There is, for instance, increasing criticism, from residents, of the ideology behind the National Park Authority's activities, who see it as putting abstractions about 'landscape value' before the needs of local people. The locals are likewise often condescendingly criticised for their supposed greed and lack of sensitivity towards the beauty they live in.

Thus, far from being a place in which to escape the complexities of the late 20th century, unwitting visitors to Dartmoor can find it a hot-bed of passionate and very contemporary debate about the nature of community, the right relationship between people and their environment, the desirability or otherwise of roads and industry, and the role of planning. All these issues are far from simple.

However, there is no need to fear that any of this will stop you enjoying a peaceful or uplifting time on Dartmoor, though it is good that the discussions are happening, and the more who join in the better. Meanwhile, the visitor is welcomed on the moor, and everything is done to make the landscape, together with its ecology and history, comprehensible. Visitors, likewise, are asked to respect those whose living depends on the moor. There is, after all, plenty of it, and there should be room for everybody.

The famous beauty spots are well supplied with tourist facilities, while those who seek solitude can easily get away from the popular visitor centres to the healing loneliness of tor and stream. **THE DARTMOOR NATIONAL PARK** covers 368 square miles. This area includes whole towns and villages and a great deal of farmland and forest, as well as open moorland. The Authority employs 9

RANGERS who are there to provide information and advice, and to help ensure that the Authority's aim, of preserving and enhancing the special qualities of the moor, are carried out. Each Ranger has a specific area of moor to cover. They can be contacted during office hours, from Monday to Friday, on (01626 832093), and at weekends on (01822 890414). You will see them out in their vehicles, patrolling their areas, at all hours.

The Authority also has a series of VISITOR INFORMATION CENTRES and VILLAGE INFORMATION POINTS, the latter often in shops or post offices (locations of each will be given when we get there). The HIGH MOORLAND VISITOR CENTRE at Princetown (01822 890414) is open throughout the year, and its modern, well-made displays cover the geology, history, industrial archaeology and cultural legacy of the moor in great detail.

Maps and books on every aspect of Dartmoor are also readily available. Dartmoor must be the most written about of all the National Parks, as a glance in the local section of any bookshop, tourist office or newsagent in South Devon will confirm. Writing about Dartmoor has become such a veritable industry that there can be barely a facet of its past or present which has not been described again and again.

This vast range of books includes masterpieces of topographical, historical and descriptive writing, but it inevitably includes a great deal that is of dubious quality and is best ignored.

Serious readers and students of the region, which tends to mean anyone who has ever fallen for the special energy of the place, will want to look for the great 19th and 20th century Dartmoor books by William Crossing, Hansford Worth, Samuel Rowe, Sabine Baring Gould, E.W.Martin, Vian Smith and Brian Carter. Most of these are well known and can be found fairly easily through second hand shops, or in recent reprints. Between them they provide almost everything that is known, or has been thought, about most aspects of the place, although it will never be enough for the truly addicted. The books of Beatrice Chase, a rather eccentric and, later, a sad lady, who lived at Widecombe for many years, are highly thought of by some, and copies are easily picked up. Numerous other publications exist: walking guides, collections of legends and ghost stories, photographs old and new, studies of past industries and archaeological guides to the antiquities. There is no shortage of material.

Surprisingly, though, most of this writing is non-fiction. Dartmoor does not have a great or well-known imaginative literature. No one has done for it what William Wordsworth, Emily Bronte, George Crabbe or Thomas Hardy did for their regions, or immortalised the moor so that their name is forever linked to it, their presence hovering over it like a guardian spirit. The most famous

Dartmoor novel, Conan Doyle's Sherlock Holmes adventure *The Hound of the Baskervilles*, while an exciting enough yarn, is highly inaccurate and misleading in its descriptions of the moor's terrain, and even the time of year is inconsistently presented.

But, for those who like to search the second hand bookshops and charity shops for little-known regional fiction, there are some authors and works that can usefully be mentioned. Eden Phillpotts, an immensely prolific novelist in the early years of the 20th century, set a number of readable soap-opera type stories on the moor, with realistic use of local names and places, and loving depictions of the speech and philosophy of Devon people. The most popular of these is *Widecombe Fair* (1913). The Plympton-born Anglo-Irish writer L.A.G.Strong, in *Dewar Rides* (1929), gave a harsher view of moorland life, as did John Trevena, a reclusive and little-known author, in *Heather* (1908) and *Granite* (1909). During the 1950s and 60s Vian Smith, a respected South Devon journalist, who produced a masterly topographical 'Portrait' of Dartmoor, also wrote several beautiful but clear-eyed novels of its life, past and present, amongst them being *Question Mark* (1956), *Genesis Down* (1962) and *The First Thunder* (1966). Most recently, and much more easily available, resident playwright and novelist Jane Beeson has dealt with contemporary issues affecting Dartmoor life in *Scarhill* (1995).

All these books can contribute to your imaginative appreciation of this distinctive landscape, and help you to understand the influence of the land on the people living on it.

For more immediate purposes, you can pick up, at information centres around the moor and throughout Devon, specialist leaflets, brochures and the annual publication from the Authority, 'THE DARTMOOR VISITOR'. This is in newspaper format and contains the latest information on the moor and its facilities, with advice on how best to enjoy it safely and harmlessly. 'THE DART', a free community magazine produced every two months and found in shops and libraries around South Devon, has thoughtful and often challenging articles on current Dartmoor life, and has made the powerful National Park Authority decidedly defensive at times.

If you are intending to explore Dartmoor at all seriously you also need a good MAP and the ability to read it. The one to go for is the ORDNANCE SURVEY 'OUTDOOR LEISURE' sheet 28, which gives two and a half inches to the mile.

This chapter is not really designed, though, for the serious long-distance walker or explorer of the high moors. In it I can only hope to give a generalised, road-bound tour of the main attractions of the area, beginning in the south eastern corner at Buckfastleigh and finishing around Princetown and Postbridge in the north west (Ivybridge and the southern boundary having been covered in chapter 3, and the Tavistock and Plympton area coming next in chapter 5).

More space must be given in this book to the towns and villages around the edge of Dartmoor, with occasional forays towards the centre, than to the tors and ancient monuments that lie miles from the roads. Those who wish to learn more about the interior of the moor will, as has been made clear, have no trouble in finding plenty of information. Even so, it is well to remember a few points about moorland walking, because the temptation to stop and get out of the car, or to wander off over the hills, away from the crowds at the Viewing Place and the ice-cream van, is sometimes irresistible.

If you are going to go for a walk on the open moors, however short, it is always best to plan the route carefully first. Estimate how long it will take, and let somebody know where you are going and what time you expect to be back. Leave a note on the inside of your car windscreen as well. Have your map and compass, a torch and a whistle. Take something to eat and drink. Dress sensibly and comfortably, and carry spare clothes; if you get lost, your survival could depend on keeping warm and dry. All authorities agree that the most important single necessity for serious walkers is a decent pair of boots, so if you are spending money on your walking, don't stint on this particular item. There are many shops where you can buy clothes and equipment from people who know what they are selling: THE MOORLAND RAMBLER in Exeter and THE DARTMOOR EQUIPMENT AND CLOTHING CENTRE in Okehampton are amongst the best. Keep a close check on weather reports, and don't be afraid to abandon your idea of a walk if the forecast sounds uncertain.

All this advice will probably seem extremely pedantic, not to mention risibly 'mother hen-like', on a bright, sunny day on safe and gentle Dartmoor, when you decide to spontaneously go for a stroll across the hills wearing Tee-shirt, shorts and sandals, but the simple point is that unprepared moor walking is dangerous. Thick and damp mist can come down out of a cloudless sky in minutes, making you completely disorientated and unable to see, literally, an inch in front of your face. You can be sunbathing one moment and shivering uncontrollably the next. Heavy rain really does have a habit of appearing out of the blue, and there is nowhere on the open moor to run to for shelter. The novelty of all these predicaments very quickly wears off.

If you do get lost on Dartmoor, or are overtaken by bad weather, try to find a stream - be careful it hasn't become a mountain torrent - and follow it downwards. Eventually it will bring you to a road or house. To help people find you, blow six short blasts on your whistle every minute, or give six flashes of your torch.

Even better, of course, is not to get lost. There are many GUIDED WALKS and ORGANISED EXPEDITIONS onto the moor always available, and if you are at all unfamiliar with hill walking you are strongly advised to join one of them. At any information centre you can find details of other interesting OUTDOOR EVENTS, TALKS and ACTIVITIES organised by the Park Authority which will give you a safe and comfortable experience of this remarkable environment. PONY TREKKING is also well organised and easily available.

A few more points before we begin our circuit of the moor. These are all BYE-LAWS of the National Park:

Leave the animals alone. The ponies, sheep and cattle on the moor all belong to someone, and he or she is likely to know more about them and their welfare than you do. Keep your dog under close control. It is actually illegal to feed the ponies, however tempting it might be. If you find a sick or injured animal, contact the DARTMOOR LIVESTOCK PROTECTION SOCIETY through any Information Centre (a long list of telephone numbers is also in the 'Dartmoor Visitor.').

Remember that it is illegal to drive more than 15 meters onto the moor.

Do not light fires.

Do not block water courses.

Do not climb walls or fences.

Do not leave litter.

Overnight camping of vehicles, caravans or large tents is not allowed.

The last thing to be particularly aware of, of course, is the army's use of the northern moor for training purposes. There are three firing ranges between Okehampton and the B3357, the boundaries of which are marked by red and white posts. Firing times are announced in local newspapers and at information centres, police stations and other public places around the moor, or ring the following numbers for details: (01803 559782), (01392 70164), (01752 501478) or (01837 52939). When within this area, don't touch any bits of metal you might find lying around.

Our brief tour around the edge of Dartmoor now begins safely down in the lowlands, at the interesting, but often neglected, little town of **BUCKFASTLEIGH** (National Park Information Point: THE FRUIT BASKET).

Buckfastleigh was, until the mid 20th century, one of Devon's most industrial towns. It began in the early Middle Ages as a centre for the woollen industry, and its people have always, until quite recently, made their livings from spinning, weaving, quarrying, mining and leather tanning. Photographs of the town in the 1900s make it look like a mill village in Yorkshire or Lancashire, and the Reverend Sabine Baring Gould, in one of his guides to Devon, called it 'ruffling, modern, manufacturing' in contrast to 'old-world Ashburton', a couple of miles away.

Buckfastleigh's long, narrow streets and mill workers' cottages have often struck visitors as dull and uninteresting, but it is quite proud of its 'ruffling' history, and is a lively, close-knit community. It is true that most of the Dartmoor border towns do have a harder, less immediately appealing, appearance than those of the South Hams, with their colour-washed and slate-hung buildings, but this simply reflects the more difficult lives that people around the moor have always had to endure. In the town are a number of interesting shops, including several ART and CRAFT STUDIOS, and the pubs and cafes are enjoyable, down-to-earth local meeting places.

The town was once well-known as a horse racing centre, and on the main road between here and Dean Prior, mentioned in the last chapter, you will see a relic of this, a substantial grandstand in the middle of a field, quietly rotting away.

Buckfastleigh's Parish Church, of Holy Trinity, sits mysteriously alone on a high limestone hill outside the town, reached by 196 steps. In 1992 the church was largely destroyed by arson, but a small section of it has been rebuilt, and it is still consecrated. In the churchyard is the striking 'pent-house tomb' of the Cabell family, 17th century owners of nearby Brook Manor. Legend has it that one of them, Sir Richard Cabell, was particularly wicked, and an iron grille was placed in the side of the tomb to stop his ghost from escaping.

An equally persistent legend has it that Sir Arthur Conan Doyle, staying with a friend in the area, was inspired by the stories of Squire Cabell to write *The Hound of the Baskervilles* , but research doesn't really support this (people will go on repeating it, though). Whether the stories are true or not, the churchyard is a powerful and haunted place.

The limestone hill on which the church stands is riddled with caves, in which nationally important finds of prehistoric animal bones have been made: elephants, rhinos, hippos, bears, cave lions, wolves and bison were all roaming the banks of the Dart 100,000 years ago. The WILLIAM PENGELLY CAVE STUDIES TRUST (01364 643096) owns the caves, and carries out serious scientific research in and around them. Excellent GUIDED TOURS are held on WEDNESDAY AFTERNOONS during LATE JULY and AUGUST only.

Buckfastleigh is usually overshadowed by the neighbouring village of **BUCKFAST** and by the well known attractions to be found at the SOUTH DEVON RAILWAY terminus.

Many guide books say nothing about the town except that it is near them, but as I hope I have suggested, it is worth looking around before or after joining the throngs of visitors at these rightly popular centres.

The Railway between Buckfastleigh and Totnes has already been covered in chapter 3, but at the STATION (01364 642338) are a number of things to see and do whilst waiting for the train. There is a RAILWAY MUSEUM, a large SHOP, CAFES and a PICNIC AREA as well as the nostalgic ambience of the station and the heartwarming excitement of the steam trains themselves.

On the same site, the BUCKFAST BUTTERFLY FARM AND DARTMOOR OTTER SANCTUARY (01364 642916) is a delight to visit, with tropical plants and brightly coloured butterflies and moths flitting about. The otters can be viewed above ground and under water. There are GIFTS and REFRESHMENTS.

A short walk or drive from the railway, around the hill on which Buckfastleigh church stands, is one of the most famous and best loved places in Devon: BUCKFAST ABBEY (01364 642519).

There has been a monastic establishment here, in this peaceful corner by the River Dart, for over a thousand years. The original Abbey was founded during the reign of King Canute, and lasted until the Dissolution of the Monasteries under Henry the Eighth. During that time the monks changed their order; from being black-robed Benedictines, who tended to be quite involved with worldly affairs, they chose to become white-robed Cistercians, who were stricter and more remote from life. They kept flocks of sheep, and it has been said that the monks of Buckfast laid the foundation for Devon's great prosperity from wool in later centuries.

After the destruction of the monasteries, Buckfast fell into ruin; there is a well-known painting by Turner, making it look very picturesque. Later a house was built on the site. Then, at the end of the 19th century, a group of exiled French Benedictines bought the house and conceived the vision of rebuilding the Abbey. This they succeeded in doing, over a period of about thirty years. The monks literally built the great church themselves, with usually no more than four working at a time, shaping and laying every stone.

This resurgence of an ancient monastic community has fired the imaginations of visitors, and Buckfast claims to be the South West's most popular attraction. It is certainly well-endowed with things to experience, from the dignity of the church itself, with its soaring roof and modern stained glass, where services are held daily, to the brightness of the GRANGE RESTAURANT and the well-stocked BOOKSHOP and GIFTSHOP. Buckfast's world-famous products, the powerful tonic wine and the honey, can be bought, and the history of the Abbey is told in a well-designed exhibition. The whole site, busy and crowded as it can be, is always somehow peaceful and respectful.

A couple of miles from Buckfast, above the Dart, are HEMBURY WOODS, owned by the National Trust (no charge). Woodland walks and an Iron Age hillfort make it an atmospheric place to explore.

The old road from Buckfastleigh to its neighbouring town of **ASHBURTON** (National Park Information Point: THE TOWN HALL) runs parallel to the A38. Although only three miles apart, they are very different, if not as different as Baring Gould found them a century ago. He discovered Ashburton, compared with 'ruffling' Buckfastleigh, to be 'as if preserved in pot-pourri.' It remains a good example of an old English country town, with a collection of individual shops and an active and varied population.

Ashburton has a number of attractive, slate-hung houses, and its streets and buildings give an air of comfortable prosperity such as you find more in the lowland towns of South Devon than on Dartmoor. It was one of the four STANNARY TOWNS of the moor, where the tin mined on the open hills was brought to be weighed and stamped before it was sold on (the others were Chagford, Tavistock and Plympton). In the early 16th century it did the most business of all the Stannary Towns, and this is reflected in its houses, though the real money was made by the merchants of Totnes who shipped the tin away.

In addition to the Parish Church, of cool grey stone and shaded by mature trees, there are a couple of interesting buildings to see before looking for refreshment in one or other of the town's old fashioned tea shops or pubs. ASHBURTON MUSEUM (01364 653278) in West Street is a typical, traditional small town museum, in the sense that any can ever be 'typical.' These little museums really feel, and this is meant most respectfully, like the town's mental and physical attic, full of the conscious and, often, the subconscious memories of the place. Here, in Ashburton, these memories include bottles, posters, geology, tools and clothing. Less expectedly, you can find a collection of American Indian artefacts, presented by a local benefactor. The Museum is not always open, so check for times.

Not far away is a very atmospheric building, ST LAWRENCE CHAPEL (no telephone number). You will have seen its tower and spire, rising above the roofs, and assumed it to be another church. It was actually at one time part of a palace belonging to the Bishop of Exeter, and then for many centuries it was the home of Ashburton Grammar School. Distinguished Old Boys have included such different figures as William Wills, the Totnes-born Australian explorer; William Gifford, the very reactionary early 19th century editor and critic, who is now remembered only for the way the essayist Hazlitt abused him; and, a man as far, politically, from Gifford as anyone could get: Richard Carlile, the revolutionary fighter for press freedom.

ASHBURTON CARNIVAL takes place in June, and a varied FESTIVAL of arts events, workshops and entertainments of all kinds is held in September. In mid July a very old traditional custom is performed: the ANNUAL BREAD WEIGHING AND ALE TASTING CEREMONY. The town's official ale taster and bread weigher, elected every year, go around to all the bakeries and pubs, as they have since the Middle Ages, to check that no one is giving short measure or adulterating their products.

Ashburton is an interesting place for CRAFTS and ANTIQUES. Look for PRESENCE, POM STANLEY, SILVER LION JEWELLERY and COUNTRY GARDEN. The DARTMOOR BOOKSHOP has a good stock of second hand and antiquarian books.

From Ashburton you can easily reach some of the most popular and accessible visitor spots on the moor.

At NEWBRIDGE on the way to HOLNE is a major INFORMATION CENTRE (01364 631303), with CAR PARK and TOILETS beside the Dart. Nearby is the RIVER DART COUNTRY PARK (01364 652511), based around a Victorian estate, which has fun and activities for the whole family, including a bathing lake, adventure playground, picnic meadows and all the necessary facilities for a safe and enjoyable day out.

HOLNE (National Park Information Point: THE POST OFFICE) is an attractive village of old, whitewashed cottages, with a church where Charles Kingsley's father was curate (the author was born here, but the family left when he was quite young), and a well-known pub, THE CHURCH HOUSE (probably the most popular Devon pub name). On HOLNE MOOR is a small reservoir, VENFORD, around which a pleasant walk can be taken.

From the village you can travel on across Holne Moor towards **HEXWORTHY**, a small hamlet with an interesting bridge, and JOLLY LANE COT, which was the last house on Dartmoor to be built in a day. The story of it is this.

Two young farm servants, Tom and Sally Satterly, built the house, with some help from their friends, on Midsummer's Day in 1832, while the local farmers were at Holne Fair; the traditional right was that if you could build a house on common land in one day and have a fire burning before nightfall, no one could evict you. The farmers disapproved of the custom, as it naturally caused unrest amongst the labouring classes, but Tom and Sally succeeded, and stayed here for the rest of their lives (another storey was added to the house later, after the right had been established and the work could be done properly).

When the Reverend Sabine Baring Gould was collecting Devon folk songs in the 1880s and 90s, Sally Satterly was one of the people he came to. Unfortunately, she would only sing the songs while she went about her daily tasks, so the learned gentleman, notebook in hand, had to rush after her as she fed the chickens and cleaned the copper. She died at a ripe old age in 1901, and the local men thought it an honour to carry her coffin over the moor to Widecombe.

Not far from Hexworthy is DARTMEET, one of the best-loved places on the moor. Here the two streams of the West and East Dart come together to form Devon's loveliest river. There is a large CAR PARK, GIFT SHOP and RESTAURANT, and you will always find lots of people enjoying the atmosphere. Some excellent and safe walks can be started from here.

Returning towards Ashburton, **POUNDSGATE** is a popular hamlet of interesting cottages, with the ancient and attractive TAVISTOCK INN. Legend has it that the Devil stopped here at least once, probably on his way to Widecombe, where he was collecting a wayward soul. A tall, dark stranger, he paid for his drink in gold, but after he had gone the landlady found that the money in her hand had turned into dried leaves.

Near here is one of the most photographed places in Devon, the thatched village of **BUCKLAND IN THE MOOR**, famed for its peaceful appearance, shaded by trees, and for its Oedipal church tower, which has on the clock face, instead of numerals, the words 'My Dear Mother.' On the hills above you can find the TEN COMMANDMENTS carved into two rocks, although they are becoming harder to read.

Also at Buckland is THE ROUND HOUSE CRAFT CENTRE (01364 653234), a beautifully designed complex of craft studios, a shop, a cafe and a restaurant, where amongst much else you can get an excellent Sunday lunch.

The most famous Dartmoor village of them all, of course, is **WIDECOMBE IN THE MOOR** (National Park Information Points: SEXTONS COTTAGE, NATIONAL TRUST SHOP). As with Cockington,everyone has an image in his or her head of this gentle grey and white place, with its old houses and village green. It lies deep in a fertile valley, surrounded by trees and cultivated fields and, just beyond, the enfolding hills of the high moorland, with the tower of its magnificent church - known as 'the Cathedral in the Moor' - rising above. To visit Devon without making the journey across the moors to Widecombe would be unthinkable.

Like Cockington, it doesn't disappoint. You can spend many contented hours wandering around the streets of Widecombe and down the lanes leading out of the village, enjoying the spaciousness of the green and the worn solidity of the granite, looking at the church, visiting its many gift shops and enjoying food and drink at its two very different but equally good pubs, THE OLD INN and THE RUGGLESTONE (see their advertisements at the end of this chapter). THE CHURCH HOUSE, dating from the 16th century and formerly the village school, is now owned by the National Trust and contains an information centre and shop.

The church, of St Pancras, is a beautiful example of a late medieval Devon church, being mainly late 15th and early 16th century. Its most dramatic moment came when it was struck by lightning during the afternoon service on 21st October 1638, and four people were killed and over 60 injured. The schoolmaster recorded it all in some verses in the north aisle.

Later, local folklore explained this incident with the story that the Devil had come to the village in order to carry off to Hell a ne'er-do-well called Jan Reynolds, who had previously sold his soul in return for worldly pleasures. The day Satan arrived for his payment, Jan had gone to church with a pack of cards in his pocket, to while away the sermon, and as the Devil was hauling him off, he dropped the four aces. Their shapes can just be made out in the form of stone enclosures on the Ace Fields near Postbridge. It was while he was on his way to collect Jan that the Devil stopped for a drink at the Tavistock Inn, Poundsgate.

Widecombe's name has gone around the world, mainly, of course, because of the song, collected and published by Sabine Baring Gould, which tells the story of the group of men who borrow a friend's grey mare to visit Widecombe Fair. Not surprisingly, because of the weight of carrying eight burly men, she fails on the return trip, and dies; the last we hear of her is the sound of her ghost, bones rattling, crossing the moor at night. With its rollicking tune and hearty chorus, the song is still enjoyable, and has become a sort of unofficial Devonshire national anthem. The bands of the Devonshire Regiment used to play it as a march.

Beyond the level of tragic farce, the song and its imagery definitely strike a deep chord. The words probably refer, in a confused, almost-forgotten way, to an ancient ritual, of pre-Christian origin, in which groups of men would go around the countryside, one of them disguised in a white sheet and carrying a horse's head. They would beg to be admitted to houses, and perform songs and mumming plays to those who let them in, whilst indulging in all sorts of 'horse-play' as well, especially with those who were less welcoming. The white horse's head could have been quite terrifying if encountered in the dark, a reminder that the term 'nightmare' derives from deep-rooted and ancient fears.

Today, you cannot get away from Tom Pearce, Uncle Tom Cobley and the rest; they appear everywhere in Widecombe, and why not? Their story, and its iconography, have become as much a part of the scene as the church tower itself. Attempts are sometimes made to locate the names of the characters on gravestones in surrounding parishes, and it is often said that they came from Spreyton, north of the moor, but the evidence is vague and contradictory.

The FAIR takes place on the SECOND TUESDAY of SEPTEMBER. Prepare for a busy, crowded, tumultuous but also a genuinely Devonian event, with plenty of local accents in evidence.

The long hills out of Widecombe make you reflect that you are fortunate in not being on, or even being, a grey mare. Near here are three of the best known TORS on the moor, each a popular place to stop at.

HAYTOR, near Bovey Tracey, is an impressive mass of rock, and one of the great landmarks of South Devon, pivotal to the consciousness of people throughout the area. You can climb it fairly easily for magnificent views across to Torbay and the South Hams. The 15 mile footpath THE TEMPLER WAY, linking the granite quarries of Haytor with Teignmouth, starts here. Part of it follows the line of the HAYTOR GRANITE TRAMWAY, a remarkable engineering achievement built in the early 19th century by George Templer, of Stover, to transport granite for use in such London buildings as the British Museum, the National Gallery and the London Bridge which is now in America. Even the points of the tramway are of stone. It then follows the STOVER CANAL, built by George's father James Templer, until this joins the Teign between Newton Abbot and Kingsteignton.

At SADDLE TOR there is a CAR PARK and VIEWING POINT, and at nearby HAYTOR VALE can be found a TOURIST INFORMATION CENTRE (01364 661520). The villages of **HAYTOR VALE**, **ILSINGTON** and **LIVERTON** are pleasant, working Devon communities. The Jacobean dramatist John Ford, whose works, which include *'Tis Pity She's a Whore*, indicate a dark, rather sombre temperament, was born in Ilsington, and is traditionally believed to have come back to die here.

HOUND TOR, north of Widecombe, is the most mysterious of the great tors, and its weird, brooding shape has been used in many films, including, appropriately, a version of *The Hound of the Baskervilles*. Below the tor is a DESERTED MEDIEVAL VILLAGE, the remains of longhouses, with barns and places for corn. It was abandoned in the 14th century, and is looked after by both English Heritage and the National Trust (no charge for admission).

Not far from here, by the side of the road towards the Warren House Inn, is JAY'S GRAVE, just in front of a gateway on the left. Kitty Jay, it is commonly believed, was a workhouse girl who was apprenticed at a nearby farm in the 18th century. She was seduced; she became pregnant; the young man suddenly didn't want to know, so she did the only thing open to her: she hanged herself in a barn. As a suicide, she was buried here, in unconsecrated ground.

The grave was discovered and restored in the last century, and the Widecombe writer Beatrice Chase began the tradition of leaving flowers on it. Now many walkers and visitors do the same, and it is said that fresh flowers are always to be found here; some books have even suggested that there is something supernatural about this, but there was nothing at all supernatural about the plastic ones I found in 1990. The sad, but not uncommon, story of Kitty Jay has, in the 20th century, moved people to write poems, plays and at least one novel.

MANATON is another pleasing village, with a green and an atmospheric church, which has a mutilated cross outside it. The novelist and playwright John Galsworthy had a house in Manaton for many years, and much of his work was done here. His family origins were Devonian, and he greatly enjoyed living in the land of his ancestors. He was popular in the village, and became president of the local cricket club - the MCC! Nearby is BOWERMAN'S NOSE, one of the most famous Dartmoor images. The shape of this huge granite stack has been compared with Easter Island statues, various human figures, and - with a certain loss of dignity - the cartoon character Andy Capp. At one time, when romantic antiquarians saw the hand of the druids all over Dartmoor, it was assumed to be by them, but it is in fact a natural formation.

On the road from Manaton to Bovey Tracey you come to the much-loved BECKY FALLS (01647 221259). This is a very well looked after 50 acre site, privately owned, featuring a magnificent 70 foot waterfall on the Becka Brook. With its huge rocks and deep pools, and dense woodland all around, Becky Falls is a good place to be at any time. People of all ages can be seen walking about the paths and steps, or crossing the water on the flatter of the stones, and generally enjoying the exhilaration of the falls with the peace of the surrounding country. There is a LICENCED RESTAURANT and TEA ROOM, an ICE CREAM PARLOUR and an excellent GIFT SHOP.

BOVEY TRACEY (Tourist Information 01626 832047) is a peaceful little town, with characteristic old houses and cottages. It takes its name from the river Bovey and from the Tracey family, who owned the manor during the middle ages. The church has a good 14th century tower. The town is best known for its convenient position as a place from which to explore the moor, rather than for any great historic attractions of its own, but recently a number of interesting places have opened here which are worth visiting.

Foremost amongst these is the RIVERSIDE MILL CRAFT CENTRE (01626 832223) of the Devon Guild of Craftsmen. One of the most prestigious craft organisations in the country, the Devon Guild purchased this 19th century mill building in the late 1980s to create a permanent display case for its members' work. There are now spacious exhibition rooms with windows looking out over the river, showing ceramics, textiles, woodwork, jewellery, prints and furniture by some of the finest makers in the country. There is also a SHOP, RESTAURANT and a courtyard where you can sit and absorb the atmosphere of quality and care which has made the centre such a success. A visit to the mill is always stimulating, a reminder of the myriad ways in which the Devon landscape can inspire, directly and indirectly, the creation of beautiful and imaginative work in all media. The work of Blandine Anderson, Debby Mason, John Mullin and Fran and Frank Benatt appeals to me especially, but we will all have our own favourites.

Between Bovey Tracey and Newton Abbot lies one of the flattest areas of Devon (and one of the straightest roads) - a great contrast with the usual landscape. The land was once the bed of a prehistoric lake. Beneath the ground are large deposits of clay, so it is not surprising that pottery has always been made here.

Just outside Bovey is to be found THE CARDEW TEAPOTTERY (01626 834441) where some of the world's most collectable teapots can be seen being produced, as well as ceramic statues and other objects. The emphasis is on tea, though, and almost everything you can think of pertaining to tea is available in the shop. There is also, needless to say, a TEAROOM with outside tables. Next to the pottery is the fascinating HOUSE OF MARBLES and TEIGN VALLEY GLASS (01626 835358). Here you can watch glass being blown, visit a free museum of marbles, toys, glass and pottery, and buy all manner of beautiful things in the shop. There is a LICENCED RESTAURANT.

Also near Bovey Tracey is PARKE (01626 832093), an estate of over 200 acres in the Bovey Valley, owned by the National Trust. This features a series of lovely woodland walks and riverside strolls, and a privately owned RARE BREEDS FARM, with trails and exhibitions of farming history. There are also NATIONAL PARK and NATIONAL TRUST INFORMATION CENTRES. The house, built in 1828, is the National Park Headquarters, and is not open to the public.

More WOODLAND can be found at YARNER, run by the Nature Conservancy Council, with walks and birdwatching areas. TRENDLEBEARE DOWN is a good area of open heathland.

From Bovey you can follow the valley of the River Teign, skirting the very edge of the moor's hinterland, to the interesting villages of **HENNOCK**, **CHRISTOW** (National Park Information Point: THE POST OFFICE), **DUNSFORD** and **DODDISCOMBSLEIGH**. All are interesting to see, and off the beaten tourist tracks, with beautiful old farm houses, cottages and genuinely local pubs hidden away along their endless lanes. The three HENNOCK RESERVOIRS, Kennick, Totiford and Trenchford, are very good for FISHING and are popular picnic places. This area is beautifully evoked by Tim Pears, whose father was vicar of Christow, in his much-acclaimed first novel *At the Place of Fallen Leaves* (1993).

However, we shall now follow the main A382 road from Bovey to Moretonhampstead and the northern moor, veering off occasionally to see something of interest.

A few miles out of the town it is worth turning off to the left for **LUSTLEIGH**, a beautiful village of thatched cottages and narrow lanes in which you can easily become pleasantly lost. LUSTLEIGH CLEAVE is a steep ravine above the Bovey. During the 19th century Cecil Torr, squire of the small manor of WREYLAND, spent his time noting down a vast miscellany of local history, folklore, customs and gossip, liberally sprinkled with learned allusions and scholarly tags. The result, *Small Talk at Wreyland*, is an English country classic. An earlier, less fortunate scholar of Lustleigh, was the Reverend William Davy, who spent nearly 50 years printing, by hand, a whole system of divinity, which he finally gave to an ungrateful world in 26 volumes.

The LUSTLEIGH MAY FAIR is a lusty, traditional event, in which they crown the young May Queen in an orchard, sitting on a stone that looks positively sacrificial. The road from Bovey to Moreton is narrow and winding, and requires careful driving.

MORETONHAMPSTEAD (Community Information Point: THE SQUARE, 01647 440043) is quite an austere looking little town at first sight, with several narrow streets meeting in the centre, and little of obvious architectural interest, except the spacious, 15th century granite church, and a much-photographed row of 17th century ALMSHOUSES. However, the town is actually a fascinating little place, and is worth stopping for. The white and grey houses quickly grow on you, and it has a wealth of small, local, individual shops and businesses, with a good smattering of outlets for ARTS and CRAFTS. Many different kinds of people can be seen about the streets, obviously coexisting quite happily.

The town's best-known son was George Parker Bidder (1806-78), the 'calculating boy' who, despite his lack of formal education, was able to do the most complex mathematical operations in his head. His father, seeing the possibilities of profit in this, took him around the country as a performing prodigy. He later became a leading engineer, working on railways, telegraphy and the construction of the London docks.

Until 1903, the wonder of Moretonhampstead was a huge, ancient elm tree at the end of Cross Street. So strong were its branches that platforms used to be built onto them for festive events, and dancers and musicians would regularly perform amongst the leaves. In 1807 a group of French officers, prisoners of war at Princetown gaol, played here for the delight of the townspeople.

Amongst the interesting shops and galleries is MEARSDON MANOR GALLERIES, selling jewellery, copper, furniture, ceramics, carvings, prints and paintings, while more pottery is available from CROSS TREE POTTERY and WILL LANGWORTHY. For Fine Arts look for STUDIO EVE. The town also has many friendly cafes and pubs, and its annual events include the CARNIVAL in August.

A little outside the town, CRANBROOK CASTLE is the remains of an Iron Age fort overlooking the Teign, and can be visited with no charge, while the neighbouring village of **NORTH BOVEY** is well known as an unspoilt Dartmoor community, sometimes described as one of the loveliest English villages, with thatched cottages and a famous old pub. On the road to Princetown is the MINIATURE PONY CENTRE (01647 432400), where a wealth of small animals can be seen. Children can spend many happy hours with the ponies and other animals, and the centre has all the usual visitor facilities.

CHAGFORD (National Park Information Point: OLD FORGE TEA ROOMS) is another pleasantly individual and socially diverse small town (I have heard both Moreton and Chagford described, in Totnes, as 'the alternative Totnes', but neither seems to be as full of therapists and self-proclaimed healers as this label suggests). Both are, certainly, popular with people seeking a more natural, creative and satisfying way of life in a rural setting, as well as having a core of families who have been around for generations. This social mixture is in itself creative and stimulating, and both towns benefit from it.

In Chagford, one of the original stannary towns of the moor, as well as a market town, there are several pleasant old buildings to see, including the octagonal MARKET HOUSE in the Square, and the famous THREE CROWNS INN, in the porch of which the Cornish cavalier poet Sidney Godolphin was killed during the Civil War. Other literary connections are with Charles Kingsley, who had the idea for *The Water Babies* whilst staying here, and Evelyn Waugh, who worked on *Brideshead Revisited* in the town.

Many houses of the 16th, 17th and 18th centuries line the streets, and are worth examining. THE CIDER PRESS MUSEUM is a unique collection of Devon cider making equipment, while within BOWDEN'S clothes shop there is the BOWDEN MUSEUM, a collection of 1930s items loaned by local residents.

Chagford is well served by pubs, cafes and family run businesses. Don't forget to look out for THE COURTYARD (see their advertisement at the end of the chapter), an imaginative venture in wholefoods and ethical business.

Just outside the town, one of the most beautiful places to visit in this corner of Dartmoor is THE MYTHIC GARDEN at STONE LANE GARDENS (01647 231311), where works by leading contemporary sculptors and designers, inspired by folklore, myth and nature, are displayed in a lovely and atmospheric 6 acre garden and woodland. Please ring to check opening times.

Near Chagford is the small village of **GIDLEIGH**, which has a 16th century church and a tiny private castle, now a restaurant. According to some, the MARINER'S WAY passes through here. This is a route which is supposed to have been taken by sailors travelling between the ports of North and South Devon, specifically Bideford and Dartmouth, but it is frankly difficult to see why they would have needed their own private 'way', or why it often takes the longest and most difficult path between the two coasts - unless the seamen wanted a complete change of scene for as long as possible.

The main road from Moretonhampstead to Yelverton crosses the heart of the moor, where it joins the main road from Tavistock to Ashburton at Two Bridges. We shall finish the chapter by coming to this point from Princetown, but there are a couple of places within striking distance of Chagford and Moreton that can be mentioned here.

GRIMSPOUND is a fine example of a Bronze Age settlement, consisting of 4 acres enclosed by a boundary wall, with 24 hut circles, with evidence of doors and fireplaces.

Just beyond Chagford is the popular visitor spot of FERNWORTHY RESERVOIR, which supplies water for Newton Abbot and Torquay. The Forestry Commission have created attractive WOODLAND WALKS and PICNIC AREAS, and there is ample car parking. When the reservoir was made it involved the drowning of a clapper bridge, which sometimes reappears, mysteriously, when the water is low.

Returning through Chagford to the main A382, we come to **DREWSTEIGNTON** (National Park Information Point: THE POST OFFICE). This is another lively and varied community, and the village is very attractive, with old cottages and a well-proportioned church. Nearby is FINGLE BRIDGE, a beautiful riverside spot with a 16th century bridge, walks through the woods and the famous ANGLER'S REST INN (see advertisement). The wooded gorge of the Teign at this point is one of the loveliest and most popular places around Dartmoor. Also near Drewsteignton is SPINSTER'S ROCK, the best known Neolithic dolmen or cromlech on Dartmoor. Consisting of a huge capstone resting on top of three others, it was traditionally said to have been erected by three spinsters one Sunday morning before breakfast.

CASTLE DROGO (01647 433306) is a most remarkable building. Built between 1910 and 1930 by Sir Edwin Lutyens, and generally agreed to be one of his greatest works, it is a solid, stately granite house, and is usually described as the 'last castle to be built in England'. The castle is surrounded by very beautiful GARDENS, and gives an unforgettable impression of strength and elemental power, standing hundreds of feet above the river and the grounds. Lutyens was commissioned to build it by Julius Drewe of the Home and Colonial Stores, who fancied that he was descended from the Norman knight who held Drewsteignton after the conquest. The Castle is now a National Trust property, and there are a RESTAURANT and SHOPS.

North of Drewsteignton we pass on to **SOUTH ZEAL**, with a 16th century church and an old inn, which was originally the home of the Oxenham family. One of them, John Oxenham, sailed with Drake; he was with the great explorer in Panama, when Drake saw the Pacific Ocean for the first time and vowed to sail an English ship into it. The family is said to be haunted by a white bird, which appears shortly before a death, and many stories have been told since the 17th century of its turning up, on cue, to hover dramatically above the sickbed.

The attractive roadside village of **STICKLEPATH** is best known for the FINCH FOUNDRY MUSEUM OF WATER POWER (01837 840046), an early

19th century forge where agricultural tools are made in the traditional way. It is owned by the National Trust, and gives a vivid impression of Dartmoor's busy industrial past. There are also craft demonstrations, a shop, picnic area, walks and a cycle trail. The centre is worth lingering at for the wealth of information that can be found here.

BELSTONE is a small settlement on the edge of the open moor, and a good place for walkers to head for. The IRISHMAN'S WALL on the common is a seemingly purposeless piece of wall, all that remains of an attempt to establish a farm or 'newtake' out of the moor.

OKEHAMPTON (Tourist Information 01837 53020) is quite a large, busy town, right at the topmost edge of the moor, and a good starting-off point for exploring both this and the vast area of Devon which still remains to the north. It is now gratefully bypassed by the A30.

The town has had, over the years, a fairly bad press. Most writers of guide books have been quite amazingly rude about the place, and before them, travellers were noting in their diaries their distaste for it. One of the most readable sociological studies ever made of a small town and its rural hinterland, E.W.Martin's *The Shearers and the Shorn*, chose Okehampton as the subject, and is less than flattering. Yet despite all this, it is actually a very good town in which to find yourself, an honest, working Devon community with a wide variety of shops, pubs and facilities. It also has one of the most romantic ruined castles in Devon, an excellent museum and a lively cultural life.

Okehampton is one of the oldest towns in Devon, one of only five urban areas mentioned in the Domesday Book, although that doesn't necessarily mean there weren't others. It was founded by Baldwin, the Norman Sheriff of the county, who built his castle here soon after the conquest. The CASTLE itself, owned by English Heritage (01837 52844), is beautifully sited above the River Okement, with lovely woodland walks and picnic areas all around. There is plenty to see amongst the ruins, which date mainly from the 13th century, and the castle is complete with a ghost. It is that of Lady Howard of Tavistock, who drives here at night in a coach made from the bones of her four husbands, each of whom she is believed to have murdered. Once here, she plucks a blade of grass, and drives back. When she has succeeded in mowing the castle grounds she will be allowed to rest. In some versions the lady is accompanied by a black dog which does the plucking; in others she herself takes the form of a black dog.

The castle was owned by the Courtenay family for many centuries, until one of them, the Marquis of Exeter, fell out with Henry the Eighth and was beheaded; after this the castle was dismantled.

In the town, the award-winning MUSEUM OF DARTMOOR LIFE (01837 52295) is an excellent introduction to the traditional life and culture of the area, with changing exhibitions, craft displays, shop and tea room. It is housed in an old mill building with a working water wheel. The NATIONAL PARK INFORMATION CENTRE is also here, in an attractive courtyard where there are other interesting shops and studios. The TWO MUSEUMS WALK, which starts from this point, is a good way of introducing yourself to the moor from Okehampton, and will take you to the Finch Foundry at Sticklepath. It is actually a section of the TARKA TRAIL, of which more in chapter 9.

Okehampton has a wealth of shops, from modern supermarkets to old fashioned family-run businesses. From the main street you can easily find the MARKET HALL and RED LION YARD, where there is often something interesting going on, especially on SATURDAYS when the traditional market is held.

The town has the only CINEMA in this corner of Devon, and CONCERTS, PLAYS and WORKSHOPS are regularly presented in the COMMUNITY COLLEGE and elsewhere. For information on what is happening, look in the TIC or read the notices in shop windows. SIMMONS PARK has sports and recreational facilities, including a heated SWIMMING POOL, while GOLF can be found at OKEHAMPTON GOLF CLUB (01837 52113) and at ASHBURY GOLF COURSE (01837 55453), 4 miles from the town.

From Okehampton you can quickly be on the moor, but remember that this is the area used by the army for training, so check that firing is not taking place. The six mile military road loops around to within a mile or so of CRANMERE POOL, a place which has attained an extraordinary reputation, even a mystique. For countless people, a walk to Cranmere Pool is a pilgrimage, the ultimate Dartmoor excursion. When you get there, you are likely to wonder why; there is no 'pool', just a marshy depression in the ground, with the great northern bog, progenitor of many rivers, including the Dart, Teign, Tavy and Okement, all around. It can be a bleak spot, and is not always easy to find, even with the road so near. Don't try to get to it in bad weather or without a map and compass.

Much of Cranmere's special aura no doubt comes from the fact that it is the home of the first DARTMOOR LETTER BOX. This was originally a bottle, placed here in 1854 by James Perrott of Chagford, a Victorian guide who took the genteel visitors to inspect the beauty spots and antiquities of the moor. The idea was simply to give them somewhere to leave their calling cards, but later, when postcards were introduced, people would leave one addressed to themselves, to be collected and posted by the next visitor. The fun lay in seeing how long it took for anyone to send it. Now, there are hundreds of Dartmoor letterboxes, hidden under mounds, in quarries, behind tors and under stones. Each has a visitors' book and a distinctive stamp. People who like collecting things tramp the moor in all weathers solely to write their names in the books and use the stamps. Cranmere Pool has a well-known ghost, an ex mayor of Okehampton called Benjie or Binjie Gayer, who was, after his death, condemned to empty the pool with a sieve.

HIGH WILLHAYS and YES TOR are, at 2039ft and 2028ft respectively, the highest points on the moor. Both are well within the firing area. More accessible by far is MELDON RESERVOIR, 3 miles south of the town, which provides TROUT FISHING, an OBSERVATION AREA and PICNIC PLACES. **SOURTON** is a small village with a 15th century church and a pub, called The Highwayman, which has been made to resemble a stagecoach. It is hard to appreciate that during the 10th century **LYDFORD** (National Park Information Point: THE POST OFFICE) was one of the four burhs, or fortified towns, of Devon, along with Exeter, Totnes and Barnstaple. It seems such a small and insignificant place now, but at that time it was a royal stronghold and administrative centre, with a mint, which all royal towns had. It was designed to protect west Devon both from the Vikings and from the troublesome Cornish (troublesome to the Saxon kings, anyway). LYDFORD CASTLE, a 12th century tower, with the nearby remains of the Norman fort and the street plan of the Saxon town, are all worth exploring. The castle, now owned by English Heritage, was notorious as the tinners' prison. During the late Middle Ages the tin-miners of Dartmoor were a powerful and strongly organised force, with their own jealously guarded rights and privileges. In the early 16th century they took on Parliament itself, when they imprisoned Richard Strode, MP for Plympton, who had objected to the tin workings silting up the rivers of South Devon. He was thrown into Lydford Castle where, tradition had it, they punished first and judged later. Eventually, after paying a fine, he was released, and put a Bill through Parliament to reduce the powers of the tinners. Many descriptions exist of the horrible conditions in Lydford gaol.

LYDFORD GORGE (01822 820320), owned by the National Trust, is one of the great sites of Dartmoor. Beautiful woodland walks through this steep sided ravine take you to the 90 foot White Lady Waterfall and the dramatic Devil's Cauldron. The whole area is rich in wildlife. Be careful at all times, as the paths are steep, rocky and slippery, but the the scenery is stunning. The gorge is about a mile and a half long.

A few miles west of Lydford, away from the moorland ambience but not really so far from it, **LEWTRENCHARD** has one of the most interesting and totally individual churches, dedicated to St Peter, that you will see anywhere. It owes its distinctive decor, much of it collected from all over Europe, to the most remarkable man ever to have lived at LEWTRENCHARD MANOR HOUSE, a man who has already appeared a number of times in this chapter and now deserves the foreground for a moment: the Reverend Sabine Baring Gould.

One of the most extraordinarily versatile of all Devonians, Baring Gould packed into his ninety years enough work and experience for several lifetimes. He was 'Squarson' - both squire and parson - of Lewtrenchard, as well as novelist, antiquary, hymn writer ('Onward, Christian Soldiers' is one of his), traveller and father of fifteen children. His books, over a hundred and fifty of them, range from theology to folklore and history to hagiography. Of all this, little is read today, but he still has a following, and his own story will always fascinate.

Baring Gould was born in Exeter in 1834. He spent much of his childhood travelling in Europe with his parents in genteel poverty, and had little formal schooling; nevertheless he ended up speaking nine languages. Although the eldest son, destined to inherit the estate, he was determined to enter the church, hence his dual role when he came into possession of Lewtrenchard. Before this he served as a curate in industrial Yorkshire, where he married an illiterate mill girl. His turning of her into a 'lady' may have inspired Shaw's *Pygmalion*. He then spent several years at a parish in the Essex marshes, until coming home to Devon.

His books include several highly entertaining, chatty and opinionated topographical guides to Devon, Dartmoor and Cornwall which, though not always entirely accurate, have provided good stories, and sometimes rather dubious 'facts', for generations of guide book writers ever since (though few acknowledge him as a source).

Apart from his work as rector of his beloved parish, Baring Gould thought that the most important thing he ever did was to rescue the traditional songs and ballads of the westcountry from oblivion. For several years at the end of the 19th century he travelled tirelessly through Devon and east Cornwall, noting down the words and tunes from hedge-cutters, stonebreakers, labourers and tanners, plying them with cider to overcome their inhibitions. At a time when social boundaries were rigid, he crossed them in the belief that these old singers had something of value which ought to be preserved.

That he was right is borne out by my own experience as a member of a group which, since 1994, has been performing the songs and tunes, together with background material on the singers and readings from Baring Gould's writings, to audiences - usually not audiences of 'folk enthusiasts' - throughout the region. The positive response of present day listeners to the old songs and stories is ample proof of their power to move and inspire.

Baring Gould's old home is now a hotel - see its advertisement at the end of the chapter. He, together with other past topographical commentators on the Westcountry, will continue to occasionally be called upon, to illuminate other places in this book.

Nearby, not far from LEWDOWN, is ROADFORD LAKE, a large reservoir completed in 1989. The area all around the lake has been carefully landscaped and designed to make the negative effects of the reservoir as minimal as possible, and the place today should appeal to visitors interested in wildlife and archaeology (a lost village lies beneath the water). Roadford also provides facilities for FISHING, BOATING, WATERSPORTS and WALKING. There are PICNIC AREAS, INFORMATION POINTS and many EVENTS and ACTIVITIES are organised at different times of the year. For more information on what can be enjoyed here, call (01837 871565).

Returning towards the moor, BRENT TOR CHURCH at **NORTH BRENTOR** is one of the great landmarks of Dartmoor. The granite outcrop with the tiny church, dedicated as almost all hilltop churches are, to St Michael, is a natural place of pilgrimage. The views from the churchyard are magnificent, and the Norman church, restored in the 19th century, is worth looking at for its own sake. If you are a seeker after ley-lines and strange energies in the landscape, you will know that this is said to be amongst the most powerful sites in that mysterious system.

The twin villages of **MARY TAVY** and **PETER TAVY** near the open moor, and useful bases for walkers, have a rich industrial past. Near the former is WHEAL BETSY ENGINE HOUSE, the remains of a copper mine, which resembles the tin mine buildings in the far west of Cornwall ('wheal' is a Cornish word for mine). It is restored as a tribute to all Dartmoor miners.

Tavistock, an attractive and important old town, is covered in the next chapter, but we shall end this one by following the main road from there to Princetown, Two Bridges and Postbridge.

The grim little settlement of **PRINCETOWN** (Tourist Information 01822 890414) is one of the most visited places on Dartmoor, mainly of course because of its prison. Something in human nature makes people stop and stare at this heavy, brooding building, and buy postcards of it, not to mention mugs with 'Property of HM Prison, Dartmoor' inscribed on them. The prison began in 1806 to house French and American prisoners of war, and closed in 1815. It came back into use in 1850 as a criminal prison, which it remains to this day.

The village of Princetown was founded in the late 18th century by Sir Thomas Tyrwhitt, an employee of the future George the Fourth whilst the latter was Prince Regent, Prince of Wales and Duke of Cornwall, a title which meant the ownership of much of Dartmoor. Coming into contact with the moor through his work, Tyrwhitt conceived the vision of turning the wastes into prosperous farmland and centres of population. He devoted his life to this obsession, and created Princetown, named after his patron, to be the capital of the new civilised Dartmoor. Little remains of his attempt, but the place has a certain sombre appeal, and a look around the HIGH DARTMOOR VISITOR CENTRE (01822 890414) is, as mentioned earlier, an excellent way of making yourself aquainted with the topography, ecology, history, and culture of the moor. There are GIFT SHOPS, CAFES and PUBS, and several enjoyable walks can be taken from the town.

South West of Princetown is FOX TOR MIRE, one of the two great blanket bogs of Dartmoor, and the 'Great Grimpen Mire' of Conan Doyle's *The Hound of the Baskervilles*. Although perhaps not quite as deadly as the book suggests, it is dangerous, so don't go too near it.

At TWO BRIDGES the two main Dartmoor roads meet, and there are some picturesque bridges and a famous Hotel. From here you can follow a well-defined path to WISTMAN'S WOOD. This remarkable and atmospheric place is one of the three primeval oak woods on the moor, the other two being Black Tor Beare and Piles Copse. As you approach the wood, you gradually come under the spell of the small, twisted oak trees and the huge boulders between which they grow. It is an eerie, disquieting place, like a forest in a story by Tolkien; the stunted yet healthy trees, the rocks, the lichen and the moss, and the fact that there are said to be a lot of snakes there, all add up to a heightened sense of mystery and other-worldliness. It is not surprising that legend makes Wistman's Wood a haunt of the wisht or death hounds, which hunt the moor, sometimes led by the devil.

Also near Two Bridges and within an easy walk, is CROCKERN TOR, once the meeting place of the powerful tinners' parliament. Whether they really sat here on boulders and held long meetings, or repaired for business to a nearby building after just holding a brief ceremony in the open air, is unclear, but tradition paints them gathering at the tor, and they are known to have met from the Middle Ages down to the 18th century.

The tiny hamlet of **POSTBRIDGE** (National Park Information Centre 01822 880272) is almost in the centre of Dartmoor, and is a good place from which to walk in every direction. Its famous and well-preserved CLAPPER BRIDGE, the best known on the moor, features in thousands of photographs. These bridges, with their flat granite slabs balanced on piers, are mainly Medieval, although they appear older, and were designed for the packhorse traffic which was all there was until the 19th century.

THE WARREN HOUSE INN, two miles away on the main road, is a good place in which to end our Dartmoor chapter: there is nothing except Dartmoor for miles in every direction, and the pub is said to be the third highest in England, at 1400 feet. On a bright day you can sit with your drink outside and marvel at the view, and when the wind blows cold you can go inside, where there is a fire which is said to have been burning continuously for over two hundred years (a friend of mine says he was here one night when some gypsies attempted to put it out, but let's not spoil the story).

GIDLEIGH PARK
Chagford
Devon TQ13 8HH

Tel. (01647) 432367 or 432225
Fax (01647) 432574

email gidleighpark@gidleigh.co.uk

AA 3 red stars, Michelin 3 red turrets.
Numerous other accolades (see below).

One of the most highly acclaimed hotels in Britain, Gidleigh Park stands in forty five acres of garden and woodland within the boundaries of the Dartmoor National Park. Although only two miles from the ancient stannary town of Chagford, it feels comfortably remote, being a mile and a half from the nearest road. The North Teign river flows through the grounds.

Gidleigh Park was built in 1929 by an Australian shipping magnate on the foundations of a sixteenth century manor house. Its extraordinary transformation into such a successful hotel began in 1977 when it was discovered and bought by Paul and Kay Henderson, an American couple with no previous experience of running a hotel. They had, however, travelled widely, and knew the sort of establishment they enjoyed eating and staying in. Their vision was to create such a place of their own, and they have certainly achieved this. Kay, who taught herself to cook, is the only American woman to have been given a star in a Michelin Guide!

The accolades received by the hotel are remarkable. It was Egon Ronay's Hotel of the Year in 1990, and was the first British winner of Winecellar of the Year in 1982. In the AA guide it is one of the nineteen highest rated restaurants in Britain, and won The Times Hotel Restaurant of the Year Award in 1989. The Good Hotel Guide has given Gidleigh Park two Cesar Awards, and the American Travel and Leisure Magazine voted it the 'most romantic country hotel in the UK.' The list goes on, frequently singling the hotel out as one of the finest in Britain, or even in Europe.

The Hendersons are extremely fortunate in their youthful staff, whom they describe as 'absolutely the best at their jobs in Britain.' The head chef is Michael Caines, from Exeter, who has worked with top French chefs Raymond Blanc, Bernard Loiseau and Joel Robuchon. He prepares a highly sophisticated international menu which changes each day, using seasonal local produce. The Gidleigh Park Manager is Catherine Endacott, a local girl from Chagford who started washing dishes here as a teenager in 1982 and has worked full time since 1989. Deputy Manager is Australian Steve Edwards. They create an atmosphere which is friendly, enthusiastic and efficient.

Gidleigh Park has fourteen en suite bedrooms, individually furnished by Kay Henderson. Recreation facilities include croquet courts, a tennis court, bowling green and beautiful gardens.

USEFUL INFORMATION

OPEN All year.

CHILDREN Welcome.

CREDIT CARDS All major cards accepted.

LICENCE Restaurant and Residential.

ACCOMMODATION 14 en suite bedrooms, and 2 bedroom cottage in grounds.

PRICES Range between £260 and £390 per day, including dinner, breakfast, service and VAT.

RESTAURANT International menu, changes daily. Seasonal local produce.

VEGETARIAN Dishes available.

SMOKING No smoking in restaurant.

WHEELCHAIR access grd.flr.

PETS Welcome.

GARDEN Extensive garden with walks.

LEWTRENCHARD MANOR,
Lewdown, Nr Okehampton,
Devon EX20 4PN

Tel: 01566 783256
Fax: 01566 783332

AA2 Red Stars AA 2 Rosettes

People who have stayed in this delightfully ornate and unique Manor house will tell you that not only was it enjoyable it also felt like a privilege. There is something very special about Lewtrenchard Manor, a feeling that envelops you the moment you walk into the large welcoming hall with its huge open fireplace, comfortable armchairs, fine panelling and a profusion of fresh flowers. James and Sue Murray, the owners, have worked extremely hard since they came back to these shores to bring the house back to its former splendour, the results of their labours is evident everywhere.

There was a house here when the Doomsday book was written in 1088 but the present house was built in the 17th century as the home of the Baring Gould family. Sabine Baring Gould (1834-1924) wrote many books and hymns including 'Onward Christian Soldiers' and you will see that the bedrooms are named after melodies to his hymns. This extraordinary man was a great traveller and he brought back from his travels all sorts of wonderful artefacts which are to be seen about the house. He died here in 1924 after 40 years in residence and left behind the legacy of this beautiful house and wonderful gardens. Every room in the house has some special characteristic. The panelled non-smoking dining room looks wonderful at night and encourages any one to enjoy a delicious meal and savour the fine selection of wines from the cellar. The bedrooms are charmingly and luxuriously furnished with beautiful drapes and decor. Every room is ensuite and has a direct dial telephone and colour television.

Open to non-residents one can come here to dine or have perhaps only a bar snack and a drink or maybe afternoon tea. For those who stay it really is like staying with friends in a very special country house. There is much to see and do during your visit. Croquet, Clay Pigeon Shooting and Fishing are to be had in the grounds. An energetic walk along the floor of Lydford Gorge, Lanhydrock House set in 450 acres, Castle Drogo designed by Sir Edwin Lutyens, Buckland Abbey the home of Sir Francis Drake or Cotehele a medieval house with gardens that run down to the edge of the Tamar are just a few of the attractions.

USEFUL INFORMATION

OPEN; All year	**DINING ROOM; Beautiful panelled room**
CHILDREN; Over 8 years	**With wonderful food**
CREDIT CARDS; All major cards	**BAR FOOD; Sandwiches, soups, cheese plates**
LICENSED; Full	**VEGETARIAN; Catered for**
ACCOMMODATION; All ensuite 1 suite	**DISABLED ACCESS; Yes. Toilet**
PETS; Dogs by arrangement	**GARDEN; Beautiful grounds. Clay Pigeon Shooting, Croquet, Fishing**

RATES:- All Year, Single room £80/£95. Dble. Room £105/£145 pppn B&B.

BLACKALLER HOTEL AND RESTAURANT
North Bovey
Moretonhampstead
Devon TQ13 8QY

Tel. and Fax (01647) 440322

Internet LHp://www.intellect.Net.Com./
West/Country/hotels/Devon/BlackallerLTM

AA 1 Star & Rosette.

The Blackaller Hotel and Restaurant is delightfully situated, much-acclaimed and refreshingly individual. On the eastern edge of the Dartmoor National Park, its gardens slope down to the River Bovey and the beautiful hamlet of North Bovey is close by. The attractive old market towns of Moretonhampstead and Chagford are a few minutes' drive away.

The hotel is a converted seventeenth century woollen mill, complete with flagstone floors and inglenook fireplaces, and is tastefully furnished with carefully chosen chairs and pine tables. The name is the local one for the Black alder, which grows along the river banks, and the bedrooms are named after some of the birds which can be watched in this rich environment, such as the Buzzard and the Dipper. The atmospheric building and lovely natural surroundings combine to create an unforgettable place at which to dine or stay.

The Blackaller is owned and run by Hazel Phillips and her partner Peter Hunt, who work carefully to create a relaxed, informal and peaceful ambience, with some unique features. They own a flock of Jacob sheep and use the wool to spin garments which can be purchased in the hotel. They are also keen birdwatchers and beekeepers: home-made honey is always on the breakfast table. They have earned places in the Good Hotel Guide, the Good Food Guide and the 'Which?' Hotel Guide, as well as being highly praised for their friendlness and service by Paddy Burt in her famous *Daily Telegraph* hotel feature, 'Room Service.'

There are five attractive bedrooms at the Blackaller, a residents' bar, dining room and conference facilities for up to twenty non-resident guests. The restaurant is open to non-residents, and the food, cooked by Hazel using fresh local produce, is creative and varied. All ingredients come from Devon, including Jacobs lamb and fish from Brixham or the local rivers. Interesting westcountry cheeses are also featured. A small but carefully selected wine list enhances the menu.

Surrounded by woods and moorland, the Blackaller is ideal for walkers and naturalists, and fishing, golf and riding can be found nearby. The whole of Dartmoor is easily reached, as are the South Devon coast, Torbay and Exeter. Visitors to the Blackaller come back again and again to enjoy the unusual peace and naturalness of the hotel, and once you have experienced you will know why.

USEFUL INFORMATION

OPEN March to end of December.

CHILDREN Welcome - meals and babysitting.

CREDIT CARDS Not taken.

LICENCE Hotel and Restaurant.

ACCOMMODATION 4 double/twin rooms, all en suite. 1 single with own bathroom.

PRICES High season: £36 per person; Low season £34. Children under 11 half price.

RESTAURANT Candlelit with log fires. Creative English menu.

VEGETARIAN A choice of 2 at each course.

SMOKING Permitted.

DISABLED No special access.

PETS Well-behaved dogs welcome.

GARDEN Yes.

THE MANOR HOUSE HOTEL AND GOLF COURSE
Moretonhampstead
Devon TQ13 8RE

Tel. (01647) 440355
Fax (01647) 440961

AA & RAC 4 Stars.

   Standing in 270 acres of spectacular parkland on the eastern edge of the Dartmoor National Park, The Manor House Hotel provides sumptious, traditional service combined with all the expected modern facilities. It overlooks a beautiful unspoilt, wooded valley and the tiny village of North Bovey, but is within easy reach of the A38 main road, and is only 20 minutes' drive from Exeter. There is ample car parking and landing facilities for helicopters.
   Owned by the prestigious Principal Hotels Group, the impressive honey-coloured mansion was built, in 1907, by the 2nd Viscount Hambleden, on land originally bought by his father, the bookseller William Henry Smith (W.H.Smith and Son). In its matchless surroundings, which include a championship 18 hole golf course, the hotel provides the perfect, civilised retreat for either holiday, conference or business purposes. Many indoor and outdoor activities can be arranged for you in this beautiful rural environment.
   Inside, the spacious halls are panelled in oak, with large open fires in the Oak Bar and the Lounge. The Hambleden Restaurant looks out over the south terrace and the beautiful gardens, where seating is provided in fine weather. Everything contributes to an atmosphere of serenity and smoothly run service in which to work or relax.
   All bedrooms have tea and coffee making facilities, trouser press, hair dryer and satellite television. Room service is available.
   The restaurant serves a wide range of traditional English and continental food - steaks, roasts, fish and seafood dishes etc - using fresh local produce. A la carte and Table d'hote menus are available, as are special menus for children. A range of bar meals is served in the lounge throughout the day. The hotel has a wide range of wines and beers to choose from.
   Golf at the Manor House is a challenge to professional and amateur players alike, and is played on one of Britain's loveliest courses. Other activities to be enjoyed here include hard court tennis, croquet, snooker and fishing on the rivers Teign and Bovey. The hotel can also arrange for you to experience abseiling, horse riding, sailing, pistol and air rifle shooting and a 'Dartmoor safari', archery and many other pursuits. Whatever your needs, the Manor House Hotel provides it with efficiency, courtesy and panache.

USEFUL INFORMATION

OPEN All Year, including Christmas and New Year package
CHILDREN Welcome. Special menu.
CREDIT CARDS Visa, Access, Diner's Club, American Express, Switch.
LICENCE Full.
ACCOMMODATION 90 bedrooms, comprising singles, doubles, twins and suites. Room service.
PRICES Dinner, B&B: High Season £65, Low Season £55. Children £9.50 if sharing room.

RESTAURANT Table d'Hote £18.95. Large range of traditional English dishes with fine and extensive wine list.
BAR FOOD From 11.30am - 5.30pm.
VEGETARIAN 3 or 4 dishes available.
SMOKING permitted but not in restaurant.
DISABLED Ramp. Bars, restaurant and bed-rooms accessible from ground floor.
PETS Welcome. Small charge.
GARDEN 270 acre park with golf course.

THE EDGEMOOR HOTEL
Haytor Road
Lowerdown Cross
Bovey Tracey
Devon TQ13 9LE

Tel (01626) 832466 Fax (01626) 834760

AA 3 stars, RAC 3 stars,
ETB 4 crowns, Highly Commended

The Edgemoor is a delightful Country House standing in two acres of its own grounds, in a peacefully wooded setting just outside the small town of Bovey Tracey. As the name suggests, it is right on the boundary of the Dartmoor National Park and is a romantically styled late nineteenth century house built from the local granite covered in a rich coating of wisteria, ivy and Virginia creeper, backed by mature woodland. Originally built as the Bovey Tracey Grammar School, it has been a hotel since 1920, and has undergone extensive refurbishment and decoration.

The hotel has been owned for the last six years by Pat and Rod Day, who, with their well-trained and friendly staff, warmly welcome you to this relaxed and luxurious haven of peace and quiet. The Edgemoor has seventeen en suite bedrooms, with some Four-Posters, all of which have colour televisions, hair dryers, direct dial telephones, tea and coffee making facilities and other complimentary accessories. The newly-completed Woodland Wing offers five ground-floor rooms, linked to the main Hotel, each having its own patio, and one, 'Merrivale', has some adaptations for disabled visitors.

The Edgemoor's candlelit restaurant serves modern English and French dishes using local produce, and has been awarded 2 prestigious AA Rosettes for its food. A wide-ranging wine list complements the good food. There is a Bar with traditional beams and log fire, where simpler meals are served at Lunchtimes and Evenings. Before or after your meal you can relax in the comfortable lounge with its vaulted ceiling and minstrels' gallery, together with log fires in the chillier months.

Outside, the Edgemoor's garden, with its sweeping lawn, provides an ideal place to wander or sit. Just beyond are all the attractions of Dartmoor for the walker, naturalist or visitor to historic sites. The 'Templer Way', a disused granite tramway constructed to take stone from Haytor to the port of Teignmouth, runs past, and the famous landmark of Haytor Rocks is just two miles away. Fishing, golf, shooting and riding can all be found in the area. Becky Falls, Widecombe in the Moor, the old town of Bovey Tracey, with its Craft Centre and House of Marbles, Castle Drogo and the attractive village of Lustleigh are within easy reach, while only a few minutes away is the main A38 road which can take you to Exeter or Plymouth.

USEFUL INFORMATION

OPEN All year.
CHILDREN Welcome, but not in restaurant in evening under 8 years. Special High Tea menu
CREDIT CARDS All taken.
LICENCE Restaurant and Residential.
ACCOMMODATION 17 luxurious en suite bedrooms.
PRICES B&B High Season: £44.50, Children £3.95
Low Season: £37.50. Children as before.
2 Day Breaks HS:£55.00, LS: £47.50

RESTAURANT Modern English and French menu. 3 course dinner £18.50.
BAR FOOD Varied menu, 7 days a week.
VEGETARIAN Always 5 or 6 dishes.
SMOKING Some non-smoking areas, including restaurant.
DISABLED Limited facilities.
PETS Dogs with well-behaved owners
GARDEN Extensive.

PRINCE HALL HOTEL
Two Bridges
Dartmoor
Devon PL20 6SA

Tel. (01822) 890403
Fax (01822) 890676

The Prince Hall Hotel is an intimate, friendly, privately-run hotel situated in the very heart of the Dartmoor National Park. It is a substantial two hundred year old mansion which occupies the site of one of Dartmoor's earliest tenement farms, first mentioned in 1443. The foundations and cellars of the original house lie beneath the present one, which was built for Mr Justice Buller, later Sir Francis Buller, who at 32 was the youngest ever British High Court Judge and the first to send convicts to Australia. More recent owners were Lord and Lady Astor. The house has always been closely involved in the history of Dartmoor, and is still part of the Duchy of Cornwall; the Duke - HRH Prince Charles - is the landlord! It is thought that Sir Arthur Conan Doyle stayed here whilst seeking inspiration for his famous novel *The Hound of the Baskervilles*.

The early farmers chose the site well, as Prince Hall enjoys a secure, sheltered south-facing position, with beautiful moorland views in every direction. You reach it along a tree-lined drive, and find the house surrounded by six acres of grounds, with open moorland beyond. The West Dart river flows just below.

Prince Hall was bought in 1995 by Adam and Carrie Southwell, who had been in the catering business at home and abroad for over ten years before finding it. They now 'eat, drink and sleep the hotel.' Their aim is to provide comfort and hospitality in tranquil surroundings, and they run the hotel to a high standard, but with an informal, relaxed manner.

Prince Hall has nine bedrooms, four de luxe and five standard, all of them en suite. Two have four-poster beds, and all are decorated and furnished to a high standard, while most provide magnificent moorland views. The bedrooms are comfortable but spacious, and contain colour televisions, direct-dial telephones and refreshment trays.

The lounge continues the theme of old-fashioned comfort, with an open fire in winter and access to the terrace in summer. The bar provides more cosiness, with another real fire and shelves of good reading matter. Both these rooms have their original internal shutters, ideal for shutting out the weather when necessary.

The dining room, with exposed stone walls and full wine racks is a pleasure to sit in and enjoy a wide range of French and English cuisine, made with the best local produce including fresh trout and salmon from the River Dart.

USEFUL INFORMATION

OPEN All year, but closed for 4-6 weeks in January-February.
CHILDREN Welcome, but no special facilities.
CREDIT CARDS Visa, Access, American Express, Diner's Club, JCB.
LICENCE Restaurant and Residents'.
ACCOMMODATION 9 en suite bedrooms, 2 with four-poster beds.
PRICES From £52.50 per person per night, inc. Dinner, B&B. Children under 8 sharing parents' room half price.

RESTAURANT Quality French and English food. Non-residents £22 per head.
VEGETARIAN Available by request only.
SMOKING Non-smoking areas.
DISABLED Level access to bar, dining room and sitting room only.
PETS Dogs welcome at no extra charge.
GARDEN 6 acres. Small terrace with tables and chairs.

THE CHURCH HOUSE INN
Holne, Ashburton,
Devon

Tel: 01364 631208

Egon Ronay Recommended.
ETB. Three Crowns Commended.

The 14th-century Church House Inn to be found in the centre of the small village of Holne is everything one could wish for in a country inn. It has a stream running past and is right on the edge of Dartmoor National Park; ideal for walking, fishing and many other pastimes. The Grade II listed inn built in 1329 was probably a resting place for visiting clergy to the nearby church. Its hospitable traditions much in evidence in those far off days has continued through the centuries and was never in better hands than those of Wendy Bevan who runs it personally with the aid of a friendly, welcoming and efficient staff. Everything about The Church House has a charm and warmth that has been built up over the years. There are low ceilings, beams and furniture in keeping with the age of the pub. Coming here for a drink is always a pleasure but one should always try and take time to eat either in the Kingsley Room, a small, intimate restaurant with 24 covers, or in the lively bar. The food is both excellent and interesting, a mixture of English and Continental cuisine including such dishes as Venison in red wine, Dartmoor Rabbit or Pork in Orange Sauce.

6 pretty bedrooms, 4 of which are ensuite and all centrally heated, have television and a hostess tray. The Church House is such a happy place that anyone staying here must enjoy it and find it a relaxing and moreish experience!

USEFUL INFORMATION

OPEN; All year. 11.30-3pm & 6.30-11pm
CHILDREN; Welcome
CREDIT CARDS; Visa/Master/Euro
LICENSED; Full On
ACCOMMODATION; 6 rooms, 4 ensuite
GARDEN; Yes. Fairweather patio for eating & drinking
RATES:- All Year, £19.50 to £25. Pppn B&B.

RESTAURANT; Delicious English & Continental cuisine
BAR FOOD; Wide selection
VEGETARIAN; Always a choice
DISABLED ACCESS; Level entrance

POLTIMORE
Ramsley
South Zeal
Okehampton
Devon EX20 2PD

Tel (01837) 840209

AA 3 Qs, ETB 3 crowns.

Five miles from Okehampton, and just outside the moorland village of South Zeal, Poltimore is a charming, family-run thatched guest house, surrounded by beautiful gardens and within the bounds of the Dartmoor National Park. Originally three cottages, the house took its present form when it was enlarged during the 1880s, to make a home for the 'mine captain' of Ramsley Copper Mine, the remains of which can be seen nearby.

Inside, the oak panelling, solid beams, deepset windows and granite fireplace combine to give a feeling of old-fashioned comfort and peaceful security. Most rooms have views out over the garden or across the moor, with the magnificence of Cawsand Beacon dominating the scene nearby. The bedrooms are individually decorated and furnished, while retaining their original character. Outside you can walk directly onto the moor, or sit and relax in the well-kept cottage garden, perhaps enjoying a morning coffee or a traditional Devonshire Cream Tea.

Poltimore's seven bedrooms are all centrally heated and equipped with comfortable seating, colour televisions and tea-making facilities. In the lounge, with beams and inglenook fireplace, you can sink into the old-world atmosphere while you plan your activities, using a large selection of local books, maps and tourist information.

The dining room is intimate and cosy, with its dark old panelling, and there is a wide range of traditional English dishes. An extensive wine list is also on offer, and in the residents' bar, with its large moorstone fireplace, you may enjoy a selection of spirits, canned beers or soft drinks.

If you wish to explore northern Dartmoor by walking or riding, Poltimore is an ideal base. It is also convenient for fishing, golf and for exploring the surrounding country. The villages of South Zeal, Sticklepath, South Tawton and Belstone are all within easy reach. At Sticklepath is the Finch Foundry, a water-powered working museum, and a little way to the south, at Drewsteignton, is Castle Drogo. The solid market town of Okehampton, with its ruined castle, is a few minutes away. Travelling further afield in every direction will bring you to some of Devon's most famous attractions. Poltimore is about equally distant from Torbay, Plymouth and Bideford - what could be better than using it as a base for touring the county?

USEFUL INFORMATION

OPEN All Year.
CHILDREN Over 8 years welcome.
CREDIT CARDS Visa, Access, Amex.
LICENCE Residential.
ACCOMMODATION 5 double rooms, 4 en suite. 2 singles.
RATES:- From £19 to £25.pppn. B&B. Children half price.
GARDEN Large and secluded.

RESTAURANT Residents only. Home cooked English meals with local specials.
BAR FOOD As above. Traditional bar meals.
VEGETARIAN Plenty of choice.
SMOKING Not in dining room.
DISABLED Not easy access for really disabled
PETS By prior arrangement.

ILSINGTON COUNTRY HOTEL
Ilsington
Newton Abbot
Devon TQ13 9RR

Tel. (01364) 661452
Fax (01364) 661307

RAC 3 Stars,
ETB 4 Crowns - Highly Commended

Spectacularly situated on the edge of the Dartmoor National Park, with beautiful views of the Devon countryside in every direction, Ilsington Country Hotel provides luxurious comfort and discreet personal service in a spacious and welcoming environment.

The elegant white building sits in its own carefully tended grounds, and is beautifully designed and furnished to give you a relaxing and enjoyable experience. Staying here feels less like being in a hotel than being the house guest of particularly generous and caring hosts. The owners, Howard and Karen Astbury, and their friendly staff, do everything possible to cater for the individual needs and requirements of their guests.

The Hotel has 25 comfortable and charmingly furnished en suite bedrooms, with English toiletries and full facilities. The lounge and bar area, with an old fashioned conservatory and open fire, decorated with paintings of local views around the walls, provides an ideal space in which to sit and relax before or after dinner; winter or summer it is totally restful.

Relaxing as the Hotel is, it is also the perfect venue for those who wish to be active. It has Health and Fitness facilities second to none; an indoor swimming pool, a fully equipped gym, steam room, solarium and sauna. Fitness Assessments and individually designed exercise programmes are available, as are Reflexology treatments by a qualified practitioner. People living within easy reach of the Hotel are able to join the Health Club and use the facilities as often as they like; guests from further afield can take short term membership.

For those who crave outdoor activity, the great walking and riding opportunities of Dartmoor are literally outside the door of the Hotel. Golf and fishing are available nearby, and the South Devon coast with all its leisure opportunities is only a few miles away.

After a day of strenuous activity, to dine in the intimate restaurant, which serves an excellent 4 course Table d'hote dinner, is a delight. The wine list is carefully chosen to complement the food, and special gala dinner menus, and Christmas and New Year menus, are worth checking out.

Whatever your tastes, you will find the Ilsington Country Hotel one of the most satisfying you have ever stayed at.

USEFUL INFORMATION

OPEN All Year.
CHILDREN Welcome.
CREDIT CARDS Access, Visa, Diner's Club, Amex, Switch, Barclaycard.
LICENCE Full. **SMOKING** Permitted in lounge bar
DISABLED Welcome but no special facilities.
PRICES B&B £57 per person per night;
Dinner B&B £75.

RESTAURANT Table d'hote menu. French and English cuisine. 4 Course dinner.
BAR FOOD Good daily selection of meals.
VEGETARIAN always available.
ACCOMMODATION 25 en suite

PETS Welcome.
GARDEN Yes, with lovely views.

THE OLD INN
Widecombe-in-the-Moor
Newton Abbot
Devon TQ13 7TA

Tel. (01364) 621207
Fax (01364) 621407

The Dartmoor village of Widecombe is one of the most famous destinations in Devon and Cornwall. Even before visiting the place, almost everyone has a clear mental picture of the village, which nestles in a valley below the Dartmoor hills, dominated by its impressive church tower. When you do finally find yourself there, amongst the throng of visitors, you will find it is not a disappointment. Widecombe is justly celebrated, and nobody can say that its popularity has spoilt it. The beauty and character are as enduring as the granite itself.

At the heart of the village, in the shadow of the hundred and twenty foot high church tower, is the fourteenth century Old Inn. A large but cosy and intimate hostelry, it has five separate seating areas, each named after a character from the world-famous Widecombe Fair song. There are log fires, beams, subdued lighting and a feeling of comfort and welcome. For parties and celebrations of all kinds, there are two large dining rooms available. In fine weather you can find your way outside to the beautifully secluded sun terrace and beer garden, which has its own pond and a tiny brook running through it.

The Old Inn has two resident ghosts. One, known as Harry, is thought to have been a regular who was murdered on the premises. Mid-afternoon is the time to encounter him, and he ignores changes which have been made to the building since his lifetime. Those who have seen him say that he looks solid enough, until he disappears through a wall where there was once a door. The other ghost is of a young girl who is heard sobbing in one of the upstairs rooms. Some believe that possibly she is Kitty Jay, whose grave is a well-known landmark near Hound Tor, but the usual story does not connect this unfortunate girl with Widecombe.

Haunted as it may be, there is nothing but a friendly atmosphere at the Old Inn, which is always pleasantly busy with locals as well as visitors. The owners, Alan and Susie Bout, their general manager, Derek Peters, and the chef, Neil Elliott, all work together to ensure that your experience of the inn will be relaxing and enjoyable. For those wishing to eat, the menu is large and varied, with speciality dishes, children's portions and plenty for the vegetarian. An extensive wine list is balanced by traditional Devon cider and the unique Widecombe Wallop Bitter.

A place as special as Widecombe deserves somewhere special to eat and drink, and this the Old Inn definitely provides.

USEFUL INFORMATION

OPEN Summer: 11am - 2.30/3pm; 6.30 - 11pm. Saturdays 6 - 11pm. Sundays 12pm - 2.30; 7 - 10.30pm. Winter: open an hour later in evening, half an hour later on Saturdays.
RESTAURANT excellent food.
Dining area

VEGETARIAN At least 5 meals available.
SMOKING Allowed.
DISABLED Access through car park entrance; one stair
CHILDREN Family Room and Family Best location on the Moor for families.

WARREN HOUSE INN,
Postbridge, Yelverton,
Devon PL20 6TA

Tel: 01822 880208

The Warren House Inn is England's third highest pub and was originally built to service the surrounding tin mines. It stands isolated high on Dartmoor, with breathtaking views of unspoilt high moorland which holds a bewitching beauty whatever the season. Until you actually stand outside the pub and see for yourself, you cannot possibly understand just how wonderful and awe inspiring it is. There is nothing better in warmer weather than sitting outside to eat and drink and just soaking in the beauty. As you may imagine in such an isolated spot the spectre of a ghost has to be there and the Warren House is no different. A previous landlord shot himself in 1929 but has no intention of leaving his hostelry! No mains electricity means that the pub is powered by a generator, the water is spring fed and the fire has not been out for 150 years, something you will notice immediately as you enter the inn. It was kept in originally to keep the inn warm and dry for the tin miners who worked the local mines and lived in the valley below. In those days the fire was kept in with peat, today it is logs but the tradition remains the same; to ensure travellers feel welcome.

Inside the inn you will find a friendly atmosphere and the old world beamed bar a busy place but never too busy to ensure you are cared for. Peter and Janet Parsons are the landlords and they have built themselves a fine reputation for hospitality, well kept beers and good, home-cooked food. The menu is wide ranging with everything from a sandwich, toasted if you wish, to a 16oz T Bone steak and in between delicious dishes such as Warreners Pie - a home-made rabbit pie made to the inn's own recipe or a Steak and Ale Pie with tender pieces of steak cooked in the 'Bishops Tipple' - one of the house ales. There are fish and chicken dishes, a selection of vegetarian fare, a children's menu and some excellent desserts including a wonderful luxury chocolate sponge pudding with hot chocolate sauce.

USEFUL INFORMATION

OPEN; Summer: from Easter 10am-11pm   **RESTAURANT; Now being constructed**
CHILDREN; Welcome   **BAR FOOD; Excellent choice**
CREDIT CARDS; None taken   **VEGETARIAN; Several dishes daily**
LICENSED; Full On   **DISABLED ACCESS; Limited**
GARDEN; Large area for eating & drinking

GREAT LEIGH FARM
Doddiscombsleigh
Near Exeter
Devon EX6 7RF

Tel. (01647) 253008
Fax (01647) 252058

Great Leigh Farm and Guest House is set in a hundred and sixty nine acres of rich Devon farmland on the edge of the Dartmoor National Park, betwen Doddiscombsleigh and Lower Ashton. Guests are encouraged to explore the farm, which has been given the status of an Environmentally Sensitive Area. It is home to a wide variety of flora and fauna, and a specially designed and maintained footpath has been laid out to run around the property, offering magnificent views over the Teign Valley and surrounding area.

The farmhouse is over two hundred years old, with open fireplaces and original beams in the dining room and guests' lounge. In the courtyard, substantial barns, built of the local red stone, remain from the days when the farm was part of the estate of Lord Haldon.

In the heart of beautiful countryside, with excellent walking country all around, and close to the many attractions of Dartmoor and South Devon, Great Leigh Farm is an ideal quiet retreat at which to base yourself for your holiday.

The farm is owned and run by Maria Cochrane and her sister Angela Edwards with her husband Colin. Maria returned to Britain in 1993 after spending seven years in Australia, where she practised as a dentist and co-owned a very popular restaurant. Angela and Colin and their young children came here, after living and working in Greece, to fulfil Angela's dream of running a guest house. Now they work together to make Great Leigh a special and relaxing environment, which they do with great success. The critic and jazz singer George Melly has written: 'It's a magic place and very welcoming.'

The five bedrooms are extremely comfortable, and facilities include colour television and tea and coffee making machines. Each room has a bath and power shower. For guests' relaxation there is a snooker room with a full-sized snooker table, and the Teign Valley Golf Club is nearby.

Food at Great Leigh is generally agreed to be superb. Evening dinner is taken in the atmospheric dining room, and the menu is full and wide-ranging. Special dietary requirements can be catered for. Fresh local produce is used and a memorable meal is guaranteed.

USEFUL INFORMATION

OPEN All Year (except Christmas & New Year). **VEGETARIAN** Can be catered for.
CHILDREN Over 14 years only. **SMOKING** Permitted, but not in dining room.
CREDIT CARDS Access, Visa, Mastercard. **DISABLED** Not very good for wheelchairs,
LICENCE No, but guests are invited to bring but twin room is on ground floor.
their own wines - no corkage charge **PETS** Welcome.
ACCOMMODATION 4 double rooms & 1 twin, **GARDEN** no garden as such, but 169 acres
en suite. of all farmland.
PRICES B&B sharing double room High Season: £30 per night;
Low Season: £25. Single room supplement £10 per night.

DARTBRIDGE INN
Totnes Road
Buckfastleigh
Devon TQ11 0JR

Tel. (01364) 642214
Fax (01364) 643977

AA 4 Qs, ETB 3 Crowns,
Highly Commended

One of the best known - and most photographed - inns in the westcountry, the Dartbridge is only four hundred yards from the A38 main road. You find it on the left, almost immediately after the turn-off for Totnes. A mile from the interesting old woollen town of Buckfastleigh, it is almost on the bank of the River Dart, and within minutes of two famous attractions, Buckfast Abbey and the South Devon Railway. Its distinctive timbered appearance and magnificent floral displays, backed by mature trees, make this long roadside inn a natural stopping place on your journey into South Devon, whether you are stopping just for a traditional afternoon cream tea, or making it the base for your whole holiday.

Inside you will find real fires, oak panelling, soft lighting, a comfortable, relaxed atmosphere, luxurious furnishings, good beers and an extensive menu to be enjoyed. As well as a full a la carte menu, daily boards advertise an extensive range of dishes, including Guinea Fowl, Pheasant and Turkey. Hot snacks can be served out on the terrace, where the bright displays of flowers have won the Dartbridge Inn many awards.

A Free House, the Dartbridge is owned by Ray Evans, and managed by Mr and Mrs Thomas, whose aim is to create an atmosphere combining charm and luxury with the traditional appeal of the English inn. Eleven en suite bedrooms provide superb accommodation, and a functions room is available for special occasions which seats up to a hundred guests.

Almost literally outside the door of the inn is the famous steam railway running throughout the summer between Buckfastleigh and Totnes, and the Buckfast Butterfly Farm and Dartmoor Otter Sanctuary can be found alongside it. Other family attractions only minutes away include the Pennywell Farm and Wildlife Centre and the River Dart Country Park. For quieter enjoyment there is the world famous Abbey of Buckfast just around the corner. The mysterious wilderness country of Dartmoor is nearby in one direction, while the lovely South Hams area starts almost at once in the other, as the road to Totnes and the rest of the South Hams follows the river valley and the railway line to the east. For a complete contrast, the lively resorts of Torquay and Paignton, 'the English Riviera', are only a few miles further on. Few inns are better-placed to be central to all these delights than the Dartbridge.

USEFUL INFORMATION

OPEN Summer: 10.30am - 2.30pm . and 6.00 - 11.00pm Winter: 11.00am - 2.30pm and 6.30 - 11.00pm.
CHILDREN Welcome. served throughout the inn.
LICENCE Full.
ACCOMMODATION 11 en suite bedrooms with colour TV, tea/coffee making facilities.
PRICES High Season: £29.50 per person per night; Low Season: £25.00. Children £10 - £20.

RESTAURANT No separate restaurant area; full a la carte menu and specials served throughout the inn.
VEGETARIAN Approx. 6 dishes daily.
SMOKING Permitted.
DISABLED Ramp available.
PETS Not allowed.
GARDEN Terrace and play area.

CLEAVELANDS ST. MARY
Lustleigh
Newton Abbot
Devon TQ13 9SH

Tel and Fax (01647) 277349

AA 4 Qs.

Cleavelands is a country guest house, kept by Val and Vivyan Bates, which dates mainly from the Victorian period. It is beautifully situated, on the slopes overlooking the eastern Dartmoor village of Lustleigh. The house has stunning views of the surrounding countryside and stands in an attractive two acre garden.

You find it by leaving the A38 main road at the Bovey Tracey turn-off. After bypassing the town and going towards Moretonhampstead, turn left for Lustleigh. Going straight through the village and around the church, you take the road to the left opposite the dairy and post office. After half a mile you reach a T-junction; turn right. The entrance to Cleavelands is 500 yards along, on the left.

Inside, the house is comfortable and full of character, with a grand piano and log fire in the sitting room, and a library well-stocked with books, maps and games. Each bedroom is linked to its own bathroom, and the double or family room on the ground floor has its own separate entrance, making it ideal for those with well-behaved dogs. The garden has magnificent views, where one can sit and enjoy, or perhaps partake of a game of croquet on the lawn.

A good, traditional English breakfast is provided, but you can have a continental or vegetarian one if you wish, and a packed lunch, as well as an evening meal, can be arranged. The Bateses aim to supply fresh, organic food, locally produced.

From Cleavelands a rich and beautiful area of Devon is on your doorstep. You can walk straight from the garden onto a bridlepath which links you to a network of footpaths leading to the famous Lustleigh Cleave, or to the woods of Yarner. The Bovey Valley abounds in lovely and varied walking country, while within easy reach are the high moors, many beautiful villages, and the rivers, golf courses, castles, historic houses and cultural venues of South Devon. The small town of Bovey Tracey is home to the Devon Guild of Craftsmen, and throughout the area are galleries and studios selling quality handmade arts and crafts - it all goes very well with the homelike, personal service and quality of life to be experienced at Cleavelands, with its smell of burning logs and sense of tranquil security.

USEFUL INFORMATION

OPEN All year.
CHILDREN Welcome.
CREDIT CARDS Not at present.
ACCOMMODATION 2 double rooms, 1 twin.
All rooms en suite with colour TV, tea/coffee making facilities. 1 double/family room downstairs with own access.
VEGETARIAN Meals by arrangement.
SMOKING Not allowed.
DISABLED Entrances not really wide enough.
PETS Well-behaved dogs welcome.
GARDEN Extensive.
PRICES B & B from £20 per night, children according to age and requirements. Evening meal by arrangement from £6.

BEL ALP HOUSE HOTEL
Haytor
Near Bovey Tracey
Newton Abbot
Devon TQ13 9XX

Tel. (01364) 661217
Fax (01364) 661292

AA 3 Stars

Bel Alp, standing 900 feet above sea level on the eastern edge of the Dartmoor National Park, is an elegant Edwardian mansion in its own peaceful, south-facing grounds, enjoying spectacular views over much of South Devon. Once the home of the millionairess Dame Violet Wills, it is now a beautiful family run hotel, full of interesting architectural features. It is tastefully decorated and furnished to create an unforgettably atmospheric setting for your holiday, and has been described as one of the region's finest small hotels.

Since October, 1996, Bel Alp has been owned and run by Jack and Mary Twist and their daughter, Rachael, who have built on the reputation the hotel has long enjoyed.

The house is spacious yet intimate, with a fine oak staircase, a 1920s stained glass window at the foot of the stairs and large bay windows in most of the rooms through which you can enjoy the magnificent surrounding countryside, stretching between the moors and the sea, 20 miles away. There is a well-stocked lounge bar for the use of guests, a relaxing drawing room and a beautifully laid out restaurant. Here the family serve their well-cooked, traditional meals, complemented by an extensive wine list. Carefully chosen furnishings, antiques, paintings and houseplants enhance the atmosphere, with real fires adding a touch of luxury in colder weather.

The garden at Bel Alp makes a perfect setting for the hotel, with its dramatically terraced lawns, rock garden and surrounding shrubs and mature trees. There is a croquet lawn, or you can walk effortlessly out of the grounds towards the village of Haytor Vale or, alternatively, onto the open moor. Excellent walking country is literally on the doorstep, while golf, fishing and riding can be found nearby in the area. The myriad attractions of South Devon, with historic towns, castles, houses, coast and countryside, are literally spread out below the hotel.

To find Bel Alp from the A38 main Exeter to Plymouth road, turn off onto the A382 for Bovey Tracey. From there, follow the B3387 signposted for Haytor and Widecombe, and go straight over the crossroads. After a mile and a half you come to a cattle grid, which indicates the beginning of the open moor. After 500 yards turn left into the hotel drive, crossing another cattle grid. Bel Alp House is 400 yards along the drive.

USEFUL INFORMATION

OPEN February to November.
CHILDREN welcome.
CREDIT CARDS Amex, Diner's Club, Visa, Switch.
LICENCE Residential & Restaurant.
ACCOMMODATION 8 en suite bedrooms.
PRICES From £60 per person per night.
GARDEN Extensive, with terraced lawns, rock garden and shrubbery.

RESTAURANT Good, fresh home-cooked food.
BAR FOOD No.
VEGETARIAN Choice of meals available.
SMOKING Permitted in some areas.
DISABLED 2 ground floor bedrooms, one with wide door. Ramp.
PETS Welcome by arrangement.

WOODLEY HOUSE
Caseley
Lustleigh
Newton Abbot
Devon TQ13 9TN
Tel. (01647) 277214

Hilary Roberts, highly-acclaimed for her previous establishment at Willmead Farm on the edge of Dartmoor, has recently moved to this peaceful, well-appointed house in the same parish. Woodley House, offering bed and breakfast accommodation, is surrounded by beautiful gardens and has magnificent views of the Wray Valley. Here she has quickly added to her former success of winning the Dartmoor 'Warmest Welcome' Award, and attracted the praise of visitors and guide books from all over the world.

Hilary is a convivial hostess, and her breakfasts are widely renowned. During the summer these can be served on the patio. You can enjoy a full Devon grill, home-cooked smoked ham with fresh herbs from the garden, a variety of cheeses, farm eggs, kippers and smoked haddock, together with cereals, fresh fruit and Hilary's twelve home-made preserves.

At Woodley House there is just one bedroom and sitting room, fully en suite and with all conveniences. The uninterrupted views of the surrounding countryside of hills, fields and woods are almost worth staying for alone, while the morning and evening sun shines straight through the four leaded light windows.

Ideally situated near the attractive village of Lustleigh, Woodley House is convenient for exploring both Dartmoor and the South Devon coast.

USEFUL INFORMATION

OPEN All Year.
CHILDREN Over 10 years welcome.
CREDIT CARDS No.
LICENCE No.
ACCOMMODATION 1 en suite bedroom and sitting room, colour TV, tea/coffee making etc.
VEGETARIAN Breakfast on request.
SMOKING Non-smoking house.
DISABLED Not suitable.
PETS No.
GARDEN Delightful, with lawn, shrubs, views down Wray valley. Magnificent views.
PRICES £22.50 per person per night. No reduction for children.

PARFORD WELL
Sandy Park
Chagford
Devon TQ13 8JW
Tel. (01647) 433353

Surrounded by its own walled garden, which covers a third of an acre, and within the boundaries of the Dartmoor National Park, Parford Well is a rare, comfortable, bed and breakfast country house. Situated in the hamlet of Sandy Park, it is just a mile and a half from the historic Dartmoor town of Chagford, with the open moor and the Teign Valley almost on the doorstep, but the A30 main road is only five minutes' drive away. Beautiful countryside is all around, and Castle Drogo can be glimpsed from the garden. Parford Well is the home of Tim Daniel, who was formerly the joint owner of one of London's first 'Town House' Hotels, but gave it up to return to his native Devon. He now runs the house as a one man operation. Parford Well has three bedrooms: one double with private bathroom, one double en suite and one twin en suite. There is also a guests' drawing room. Tim provides a full English breakfast using local produce. This cosy, intimate country house is an ideal base from which you can explore the Dartmoor National Park and the adjacent areas of South and Mid Devon. Golf, riding, fishing and good walking are all easily available nearby.

USEFUL INFORMATION
OPEN All year.
CREDIT CARDS No.
LICENCE No.
ACCOMMODATION 3 bedrooms, 2 en suite.
PRICES £21 per person B & B.
VEGETARIAN Breakfast can be arranged.
SMOKING Non-smoking areas.
DISABLED No special facilities.
PETS Welcome.
GARDEN Yes.

BUDLEIGH FARM
Moretonhampstead
Newton Abbot
Devon TQ13 8SB

Tel. (01647) 440835
Fax (01647) 440436

Internet: http://members.aol.com/farmleigh/
email: farmleigh@aol.com

ETB 1 Crown Commended
2-3 Keys Commended.

Budleigh Farm is a beautiful thatched farmhouse on the eastern, drier, edge of the Dartmoor National Park, in the sheltered Wray Valley half a mile from the interesting little town of Moretonhampstead. Its owners, Arthur and Judith Harvey, offer comfortable Bed and Breakfast accommodation in the house, and have seven atmospheric self-catering properties in the grounds, converted from granite barns. These can also be used for Bed and Breakfast, giving en suite B & B facilities. In addition, there is a small camp site on two levels, tucked away in the lee of a hill.

Amenities for recreation at the farm include a large, outdoor heated swimming pool, a barbecue, archery, target shooting, table tennis and darts. Farm Walks are also available, and within easy reach are opportunities for golf, riding, walking, nature watching and fishing. Budleigh Farm has ample safe parking, and makes a perfect base for exploring in every direction. From here you can comfortably travel to the north and south Devon coasts, Exeter and east Devon, while the whole of Dartmoor is at your feet.

Moretonhampstead is a lively and varied community, with plenty of small shops, friendly pubs and interesting galleries. Many artists and craftspeople have settled here, gaining inspiration from the beauty of the surrounding moors and woodlands.

USEFUL INFORMATION

OPEN All Year.　　　　　　　　　**SMOKING** Permitted.
CHILDREN Welcome.　　　　　　　**DISABLED** Ground level access to 3 units
CREDIT CARDS No.　　　　　　　　**PETS** Welcome in 3 units. £8.50 per week
LICENCE No.　　　　　　　　　　　**GARDEN** Pleasant, flat main garden and
ACCOMMODATION 2 double and 1 twin room　　　　other areas for sitting and eating.
in farmhouse, and 7 self-catering properties converted from farm buildings.
PRICES B&B £16 - £19.50 per night. Self-catering from £85 to £338 per week, depending on
unit and time of year.

CHAPPLE FARM
Chapple Road
Bovey Tracey
Devon TQ13 9JX

Tel. (01626) 832284

Chapple is a working Devon farm, dating partly from the 14th century, kept by Mrs Raphaela Allerfeldt, who offers bed and breakfast accommodation in an unforgettable setting. The house lies in a peaceful valley on the eastern edge of the Dartmoor National Park, surrounded by its own pasture and woodland. The pleasant Dartmoor town of Bovey Tracey, with its famous craft centre, is a mile and a half away.

Although, like most Devon farms, it is of medieval origin, Chapple is mainly Georgian in style, but the date 1656 carved into the large inglenook fireplace indicates its continuity with earlier occupation. The story is that the date was put there by an ecstatic couple on their wedding night, to commemorate their great happiness!

Chapple Farm has three bedrooms: a family room, comprising two connecting double rooms, a double bedroom with shared bathroom and a twin room with bathroom.

This is a perfect base for the eastern moor, while being within a short journey from the attractions of South Devon and Torbay. Walking, riding, golf, fishing and other activities are available nearby, and the many historic sites and beauty spots of the Bovey Tracey area can all be visited whilst you are here.

USEFUL INFORMATION

OPEN All year.
CHILDREN Welcome.
CREDIT CARDS No.
LICENCE No.
DISABLED No special facilities.
SMOKING In limited areas.
PETS No.
GARDEN Yes.
ACCOMMODATION 3 bedrooms, inc. family room, 1 double and 1 twin.
PRICES B & B from £18.00 per night. Children £12.50.

THE OLD FORGE
Holne
Near Ashburton
Devon TQ13 7SJ

Tel. (01364) 631351

'Moor than a Tea Room'

The Old Forge, at the heart of the picturesque village of Holne, on Dartmoor, is, as it says, 'moor than a tea room.'

It is a unique and most enjoyable restaurant, providing breakfasts, lunches, cream teas and cakes, as well as a selection of gifts and postcards, in the fascinating surroundings of a former working forge. The low building, in the shadow of Holne's famous church, associated with Charles Kingsley, is complete with the original beams, and the bellows and anvil are still in situ.
The Forge is run by its proprietors, Anne & Mike Baker, and their assistant Lynn. They have built up an excellent reputation for their range and quality of meals, and their skill at making Devon's most noted delicacy has earned them two Devonair Radio 'Gold Ribbon' Cream Tea awards.

Amongst the fare to be enjoyed at the Old Forge are a full English All-Day Breakfast, home-made Soup of the Day, Cottage Pie, Fish Pie, Vegetable Lasagne, Indian Curries, Bakes, Jacket Potatoes, Pasties, Chips, Omelettes, Salads, Quiches, Cakes, Puddings, Ice Cream and of course the special Cream Tea with home-made scones, local clotted cream and strawberry jam.
On Fridays during the summer there is a special Late Night Opening, to which customers are invited to bring their own wine and enjoy a meal in beautiful surroundings.

USEFUL INFORMATION

**OPEN Easter to end of September,
7 days a week, 10.30am - 5.30pm
Late night Friday, July - Sept.
October: 1pm-5pm Tuesday to Sunday
CHILDREN Welcome - special meals.
CREDIT CARDS No
LICENCE None, but bring your own wine
GARDEN Spacious seating area outside.**

**RESTAURANT Seating for 40 inside, 34
outside. 3 High chairs, 1 tall chair for
toddlers
Good tasty and plentiful food.
VEGETARIAN 3/4 dishes
DISABLED Tables can accommodate most
wheel chairs. Free corkage.
Large car park**

SHYREHILL
Grange Road
Buckfast
Devon TQ11 0EH

Tel. (01364) 642819

Shyrehill is an attractive Country House, offering Bed and Breakfast accommodation, situated on the edge of the Dartmoor National Park, and only a 5 minute walk from the famous Buckfast Abbey. It stands in its own acre of gardens and enjoys lovely views of Dartmoor and the National Trust-owned Hembury Woods.

The house was built in 1921 by a generous benefactress of the Abbey, whose gifts to it include the beautiful corona which hangs over the high altar.

Shyrehill is now the home of Julia and Brian Cross, who manage the house and garden on their own and work to create a relaxing and friendly atmosphere for their guests. Brian is a retired architect who enjoys gardening and restoring furniture, while Julia is a former domestic science teacher and very involved with the local community. They have been in Devon for 12 years, and have 4 children.

Their accommodation comprises 3 rooms, all en suite: a double, twin and single. There is a guests' sitting room with television. A full traditional English breakfast is provided, complete with home-made preserves.

As well as the Abbey at Buckfast, Shyrehill is ideally placed for the Butterfly Farm and Steam Railway to Totnes, the attractive town of Ashburton and the whole of Dartmoor and the South Devon coast.

USEFUL INFORMATION

OPEN All Year.   **SMOKING** No.
CHILDREN No.   **DISABLED** No rooms on ground floor.
CREDIT CARDS Not taken.   **PETS** No.
LICENCE No.   **GARDEN** Yes.
ACCOMMODATION En suite double, twin and single room.
PRICES £20 per night.

THE OLD COFFEE HOUSE
27-29 West Street
Ashburton
Devon TQ13 7DT

Tel. (01634) 652539

The Old Coffee House, a charming restaurant and tea room with bed and breakfast accommodation, is beautifully situated in the historic Dartmoor Stannary town of Ashburton. It stands on a corner next to the fifteenth century Parish Church of St Andrew, and was originally two cottages, where the masons stayed whilst working on the church. It was expanded upwards and outwards in the early Victorian period to make it the atmospheric, comfortable place it remains today. It is a Grade 2 listed building.

The Old Coffee House is owned by Mike and Annabel Bridge, who took it over in 1988 after twenty years of, respectively, running an engineering business and teaching. They now share the running of it and the cooking, Mike doing the vegetables and main courses while Annabel creates the sweets and cakes. They always use fresh local vegetables, and the meat is also local, naturally reared and additive free. The meals are described as 'traditional and exotic', and vegetarians are well catered for.

The Bridges' accommodation consists of a very comfortable suite containing one double room with adjacent bathroom and lounge, well supplied with colour televisions, books, local information and games.

Ashburton itself is a fascinating old town, within easy reach of the moors and numerous attractions.

USEFUL INFORMATION

OPEN All year. Restaurant: 10.00am - 5.00pm Tue to Sat,12.30 - 5.00pm Sun. Close 2.00pm weekdays November to Easter.
CHILDREN Well-behaved children welcome.
CREDIT CARDS No
LICENCE Table.
ACCOMMODATION 1 double bed room with adjacent bathroom.

RESTAURANT Fresh, local home-made food.
VEGETARIAN Normally 4 dishes available.
SMOKING Non-smoking throughout.
DISABLED Easy access to restaurant.
PETS No.
GARDEN Outside tables in summer.
PRICES £35 for suite with 2 people sharing; £25 single. 10% discount for 7 nights or more.

THE COPPER KETTLE
Station Road
Bovey Tracey
Devon TQ13 9AS
Tel. (01626) 832243

In the pleasant old town of Bovey Tracey, known as the 'gateway to the moor', can be found the Copper Kettle, a delightfully olde worldy, warmly welcoming tea room which also provides bed and breakfast accommodation. The entrance to Dartmoor National Park is just a hundred yards away, and superb park and river walks are literally within walking distance.

The Copper Kettle is the home of Sylvia and Paul Brown, who have both had interesting and varied careers, and who greatly enjoy meeting all sorts of people. In their tea room they serve delicious lunches, including Sunday roasts, cream teas and snacks, while, for those staying with them in the comfortable bedrooms, there are substantial breakfasts to look forward to. Outside there is an ample car park and a beautiful garden with a stream running through it, where in warm weather you can sit and enjoy your tea.

The Copper Kettle is extremely easy to find, being situated by the roundabout on the way into Bovey Tracey.

USEFUL INFORMATION

OPEN All year
CHILDREN Welcome
CREDIT CARDS No.
LICENCE Restaurant.
ACCOMMODATION 3 en suite double bedrooms with colour TV, tea/coffee etc.
PRICES From £17.00 per person per night. Children negotiable when booking,

RESTAURANT Good quality lunches, cream teas, sandwiches.
VEGETARIAN Salads, omelettes.
SMOKING Permitted.
DISABLED Level entrance.
PETS By arrangement.
GARDEN Yes. Facilities for eating and drinking, and children's play area.

NEW COTT FARM
Poundsgate
Newton Abbot
Devon TQ13 7PD
Tel. (01364) 631421 Fax (01364) 631338
ETB 2 Crowns.

One mile from the interesting Dartmoor village of Poundsgate, and just five miles from the main A38 road from Exeter to Plymouth, New Cott offers spacious and comfortable Bed and Breakfast accommodation on a working Devon farm. New Cott is a 130 acre cattle and sheep farm run by Margaret and Terry Phipps, who both come from farming families. Margaret has also been in the B&B trade for over thirty years. They provide excellent and caring service in their attractive modern bungalow surrounded by a large and well-kept garden, a short distance away from the farmyard. Both have a deep love and knowledge of the countryside, and have won the Bronze Otter Award for conservation in Devon. There are two double rooms, one family room and one twin, all en suite and on ground floor level. Each room has a personal flavour, with many little 'extras': tea, coffee and chocolate making facilities etc. Guests have use of a large dining room and lounge with television, and a comfortable Victorian-style conservatory. Breakfast always includes a choice of at least six cereals and fruit juice, while those who wish to have an evening meal will find dinner at New Cott Farm an excellent experience.

USEFUL INFORMATION

OPEN All Year.
CHILDREN Well behaved children over 5 welcome
CREDIT CARDS Not taken.
LICENCE None, but wine etc can be bought in.
ACCOMMODATION 4 en suite bedrooms on ground floor overlooking garden.
PETS No.
PRICES B&B from £17. Dinner £10. Rates for children on application.

RESTAURANT 3 course dinner, traditional farmhouse fare. Special diets
VEGETARIAN On request.
SMOKING No.
DISABLED Easy access. ETB c
Category 3.
GARDEN Large and peaceful with picnic area

LOWER JURSTON
Chagford
Devon TQ13 8EQ

Tel. (01647) 433443

Two and a half miles from the moorland town of Chagford, Lower Jurston is one of the last remaining examples of an unspoilt medieval Dartmoor farmstead. Dating in part from the late 15th century, it is a lovely thatched Devon longhouse and is a Grade 2 listed building. The house contains two circular stone staircases, ancient oak beams, inglenooks and some of the best granite features of any building on the moor. Outside there is a traditional farmyard with barns and stables, and a beautifully secluded walled garden. The whole place is mellow, warm, comfortable and deeply welcoming, and makes the ideal centre for exploring the surrounding area.

Mrs Valerie Evans, and her husband Martin, provide luxurious bed and breakfast accommodation at Lower Jurston which will make your stay a peaceful and memorable experience. The three bedrooms are either en suite or with private bathrooms, and the whole ambience of the farmhouse, with log fires burning in cold weather, naturally induces a completely satisfying sense of well-being, with an awareness of the generations who have lived here over the centuries. A full English breakfast is provided.

Lower Jurston is on the edge of the open moor, and is within easy reach of golf, riding, fishing, tennis and excellent walking country.

USEFUL INFORMATION

OPEN All Year (except Christmas).   **VEGETARIAN** Breakfast available.
CHILDREN No   **DISABLED** No special facilities.
CREDIT CARDS No.   **PETS** No.
LICENCE No.   **GARDEN** Pretty, south-facing walled garden.
ACCOMMODATION 1 double en suite room,
1 twin room with private bathroom, 1 single with shared bathroom.
PRICES B&B From £20.

LANTERN'S INN
Knowle Hill
Holne
Near Ashburton
Devon TQ13 7QY

Tel. (01364) 652697
Fax (01364) 654325

Lantern's is a large English Country Inn on the edge of the Dartmoor National Park. Like many such establishments, it is full of character and enjoys a high reputation for its food, ale and accommodation. But it is also a Dartmoor Inn with a difference.

What makes it unique is that Lantern's is also famous as a Live Music Venue featuring international artistes. Musicians who have performed here include Dave Berry, Hazel O'Connor and Labi Sifri, to name but a few.

It owes its success to its proprietor, Barry Blackman, who has run pubs for over 30 years, including jazz pubs, a wine bar and cocktail bar. He is ably assisted by his lady cook and numerous capable and experienced bar staff.

Lantern's has 12 comfortable en suite rooms with television, telephones and beverage facilities. The food is good, English traditional fare, complemented by an excellent selection of wines. The bar specialises in Real Ales, with always a choice of four available.

Because Lantern's regularly features such 'big names' and consequently becomes very busy, it is always a good idea to telephone first, to discuss your requirements and to find out what might be happening. Lantern's is always happy to cater for your particular needs and is a very friendly, as well as busy, establishment.

USEFUL INFORMATION

OPEN All Year. 11am - 2.30pm and 6pm until Late.
CHILDREN Welcome.
CREDIT CARDS No.
LICENCE Full and Night Club licences.
ACCOMMODATION 12 en suite rooms, many with marvellous views.
PRICES B&B £22.50 single, £40 double. Children approx. £10. Group bookings negotiable (eg sports groups).

RESTAURANT Traditional English good home cooking. Fresh local produce.

BAR FOOD Bar restaurant. 70 covers. Carvery in summer.
VEGETARIAN Choice of 15. Vegan if required.
SMOKING permitted.
DISABLED Level entrance.
PETS Welcome at owners' discretion.
GARDEN Outside area for eating and sitting.

OLD INN RESTAURANT
2 The Square
Drewsteignton
Devon EX6 6QR

Tel. (01647) 281276

Drewsteignton is a pretty village on the edge of Dartmoor, and inside the bounds of the National Park. It is famous for the nearby attractions of Fingle Bridge and Castle Drogo, the twentieth century 'castle' designed by Lutyens, which is less than a mile away. In the village square, almost within the shadow of Drewsteignton's ancient church tower, is the Old Inn Restaurant.

Formerly an 18th century inn, this is now a comfortable licensed restaurant with accommodation, owned and run by Margaret and Edward Butcher F.H.C.I.M.A.

The emphasis at the restaurant is on good English food. All meals are prepared to order, and only fresh produce is used. A typical three-course dinner will have soup or smoked salmon pate as a starter, followed by a main course of Dover sole, Lemon sole fillets, steak, lamb chops or a chicken dish. An exquisite dessert finishes the meal. Bread, soups and preserves are all home made, and an interesting wine list supplements the menu.

Accommodation is provided in three rooms: one en suite double, one double and a twin room. All have tea/coffee making facilities and colour television. A residents' lounge and cocktail bar are also available. Rates include full English breakfast and the morning newspaper of your choice.

USEFUL INFORMATION

OPEN February to December.
CHILDREN From 10 years
CREDIT CARDS American Express, Visa, Access
LICENCE Restaurant.
ACCOMMODATION 2 double bedded rooms,1 of them en suite. 1 twin bedded room.
PRICES B&B £22.50. Children 10-14 £15 pppn..

RESTAURANT Traditional English menu. 3 course Table d'hote Dinner £18.50.
VEGETARIAN To order.
DISABLED Access to restaurant only.
PETS Dogs by arrangement.
GARDEN None.

RUGGLESTONE INN
Widecombe-in-the-Moor
Newton Abbot
Devon TQ13 7TF

Tel. (01364) 621327
Fax (01364) 621224

Egon Ronay Recommended

A short walk down one of the lanes leading from the centre of Widecombe will bring you to one of the most enjoyable and unique pubs to be found anywhere. The Rugglestone shows you what a Dartmoor village inn was like before the days of fruit machines, fake beams and horse brasses. Standing beside the road, with a stream flowing through the garden and the huge, 22 foot long granite logan stone, which gives the pub its name, resting on the nearby common. It is a traditional stone building, with little outward sign of being an inn, yet it is often busy and is justly famous.

Here you can find the authentic, unspoilt pub atmosphere, with real ale straight from the barrel, local farm cider, good wine and varied home-made food. Roaring log fires greet you in cold weather. You will also hear the real Dartmoor accent, as well as voices from all over the world: the Rugglestone is one of those places whose fame has spread largely through word of mouth, although it is rightly beginning to be acclaimed in guide books and publications.

The Rugglestone's proprietors are Lorrie and Moira Ensor, who will give you a warm welcome. Children are welcome in the large garden.

USEFUL INFORMATION

OPEN Mon to Fri 11.30am - 2.30pm and 7pm (6pm in Summer) -11pm
Saturday 11.30am -3pm and 6pm (5pm in Summer) - 11pm.
Sunday 12 - 3pm and 7 (6 in summer) - 10.30pm.
CHILDREN Under 14 not allowed in bar.
CREDIT CARDS Not taken.
LICENCE Full.

BAR FOOD Traditional country fare using local produce wherever possible.
VEGETARIAN Always something available.
SMOKING Permitted.
DISABLED Level access.
PETS Welcome.
GARDEN Large, with stream and shelter for children.

RING O 'BELLS
44 The Square
Chagford
Devon TQ13 8AH

Tel. (01647) 432466

In the heart of the interesting old Dartmoor town of Chagford, the Ring O'Bells is a charming traditional 16th century inn, offering friendly and informal service.

With an attractive wood panelled bar, open fireplace and low ceilings downstairs, it is everybody's idea of a historic inn, and the walls are decorated with photographs of local scenes and characters, past and present. Parts of the building were once used as a holding prison for miscreants on their way to Okehampton Assizes, and in the event of an unusual death, the Coroner's Court was held here. The front upper rooms were also used for meetings of the Dartmoor tin-mining body, the Stannary Court. The Ring O'Bells is an ideal place in which to absorb a sense of Chagford's colourful life over the centuries, and things have been known to go bump in the night! Outside there is a delightful walled garden, providing a sun-trap for eating and drinking in the summer.

The Ring O'Bells offers a wide range of food and drink for residents and non-residents alike. Breakfast time is flexible. In the small dining room you can enjoy a variety of dishes using fresh local produce, and bar snacks are also available.

Chagford is a fascinating little town, with friendly, family run shops selling everything imaginable. It makes an ideal centre for walking, riding, fishing and exploring Dartmoor.

USEFUL INFORMATION

OPEN All Year, Every Day
CHILDREN No.
CREDIT CARDS Visa, Access, Switch, Delta, Mastercard.
LICENCE Full.
ACCOMMODATION 4 bedrooms, 2 en suite. All with Colour TV, hand basins, tea/coffee facilities.
PRICES £18.50 to £25.00
GARDEN Secluded, walled and lawned.

RESTAURANT interesting and varied menu, changing daily. Fresh meat, fish and local produce.
BAR FOOD Varied choice always available.
VEGETARIAN Always catered for.
SMOKING Non-smoking first floor.
DISABLED No special access.
PETS Well behaved dogs by arrangement.

RING OF BELLS INN
North Bovey,
Devon TQ13 8RB

Tel: 01647 440375
Fax: 01647 440218

email Ring of Bells Inn
@ compuserve. com

North Bovey, with its ancient cross, pump and commemorative Oaks on the village green, is one of the best villages on Dartmoor and makes a wonderful base from which to explore and enjoy all the facilities on offer. Horse Riding, Fishing, Walking, Bird-Watching, Cycling and Golf are just a few of the many activities available.

At the heart of the village is the Ring of Bells Inn, the epitome of what a country inn should be. It is a 13th century thatched inn with an excellent dining room and three delightful letting rooms, built originally as a lodging house for the Stonemasons who came into the village to build the church. It would have been a hospitable place then and through the centuries, but none more so than today in the competent and friendly hands of Tony and Brenda Rix. Their blend of informality with sheer professionalism is what makes the Ring of Bells such a popular place.

No one comes here without feeling part of the inn, no one leaves without the desire to return whether they have just called in for a drink, a snack, a meal or decided to stay in one of the pretty bedrooms, all of which are ensuite and two have fourposters. Each room has tea and coffee making facilities and catering for families is not a problem as there is a single bed always available in each room and a cot can be supplied on request. The Ring of Bells is a Freehouse and the food is delicious and great value. There are imaginative bar meals and a full a la carte dining room renowned for local fish, game and vegetarian meals.

USEFUL INFORMATION

OPEN; All year	**DINING ROOM; A la Carte. Delicious food**
CHILDREN; Welcome. Cot available	**BAR MEALS; Imaginative, sensible prices**
CREDIT CARDS; All major cards	**VEGETARIAN; Always a choice**
LICENSED; Full On	**DISABLED ACCESS; Yes. Not accommodation**
ACCOMMODATION; 3 ensuite rooms	**GARDEN; Yes**
Four posters.	**RATES: High season from £25/£30 pppn B&B**
	Low season from £15/£20 pppn B&B
	Children 5-12 yrs £5 all year
	Special Breaks - Details on request

HIGHER WEDDICOTT FARM
Chagford
Devon TQ13 8EH

Tel. (01647) 433246

Higher Weddicott is set amidst rolling Devon hills in the heart of Dartmoor National Park, a mile from the historic stannary town of Chagford. It is a 70 acre working farm where Farmhouse Bed and Breakfast Accommodation is provided in comfortable, homelike surroundings.

The farm is the home of David and Sue Rogers. David is a born and bred Dartmoor farmer, who keeps South Devon beef cattle, sheep, pork and poultry in the traditional way, as well as growing heather and conifers. Sue, from Yorkshire, is trained in catering and cooking. She is helped in the three hundred year old farmhouse by Kathryn, a friend and neighbour. The atmosphere they create is relaxing, peaceful and friendly; guests leave feeling they have known the farm all their lives, and they recommend others to come and experience the deep tranquility of this totally genuine experience.

There are two en suite bedrooms, one King sized and one double, and a single room. Guests share the cosy living rooms, complete with open fires, and are welcome to use the garden; Sue wishes people to feel completely at home, to come and go as they please and use the place as their own. She is good at providing little extras to make everyone feel special.

Breakfast is traditional and generous, enough to see Dartmoor walkers through the day, and there is plenty for the health-conscious as well.

Higher Weddicott is what many dream of when they see the words 'Dartmoor farmhouse.' In this case, the reality definitely comes up to standard!

USEFUL INFORMATION

OPEN All Year.
CHILDREN Welcome.
CREDIT CARDS Not taken.
LICENCE No.
ACCOMMODATION 3 rooms, 2 en suite.
PRICES £17 per person per night; £19 for
1 night only. Children under 7 half price.

RESTAURANT Breakfast only. Good traditional
home-cooked food.
VEGETARIAN Catered for on request.
DISABLED No special facilities.
SMOKING No.
PETS No.
GARDEN Large and tranquil.

THE DARTMOOR INN,
Merrivale Bridge,
Yelverton,
Devon PL20 6ST

Tel: 01822 890340

This attractive 17th century inn is set in a valley at Merrivale Bridge right in the heart of Dartmoor and surrounded by stunning scenery looking over moorland and the Walkham Valley towards Plymouth. You will find it on the B3357 Tavistock to Princetown road and it is no wonder that it is almost a showstopper in the sense that many people cannot resisting taking photographs of it. Inside it is warm and welcoming with wonderful beamed ceilings, a large open fireplace with chimney breasts built of local granite stone. The furnishing with cushioned seating is comfortable and invites one to relax and enjoy what the pub has to offer. People from all sorts of walks of life, local and visitors, come here to enjoy the friendly atmosphere and the hospitality. Dartmoor always attracts walkers and horseriders and somewhere in the inn you will always find them exchanging stories and experiences.

Apart from the bar which permanently stocks Merrivale Real Ales, Draught Bass and Guest Ales as well as some 20 various country wines, there is a Dining Room seating 50 which also doubles as a function room. Paul Grist has been the landlord for the last ten years and he understands what his customers like whether it is drink or food. The menu is wide ranging, freshly cooked and offers a full A La Carte Bar and Evening Menu. If you would like to stay here there are 4 well appointed double rooms two of which are ensuite and the other two share a bathroom with shower and toilet. Breakfast is an excellent meal which will more than set you up for a day on the moor or exploring further before you come back to enjoy the fun and banter in the bar in the evening.

USEFUL INFORMATION

OPEN; Winter:- Mon-Sat 11-3pm & 6-11pm   DINING ROOM; Good a la carte menu
Sun: 12 noon-3pm and 7-10.30pm   BAR FOOD; Wide range. Good value
Summer:- 11am to 11pm.   WHEELCHAIR ACCESS.(not rooms.)
CHILDREN; Welcome   VEGETARIAN; Variety of dishes
CREDIT CARDS; All major cards except Amex
LICENSED; Full On   GARDEN; Yes. Enclosed paddock for horses
ACCOMMODATION; 4 dbl. 2 ensuite   or campers
PETS; Yes
RATES:- All Year :- from £45 pppn.Share bathroom. En-suite £48 all pppn B&B.

THE COURTYARD
76 The Square
Chagford
Devon TQ13 8AE
Tel. (01647) 432571

The Courtyard, near the centre of the interesting old town of Chagford, is a successful, cooperatively run community business. It comprises a Cafe and an outlet for organic produce, wholefoods, local crafts and books on 'green' issues. It grew out of a popular composting scheme and has wide support throughout the town.

The Courtyard is jointly managed by Alice Scott, Sarah Williams and Jo Hodges of the Proper Job Cooperative. The good, resonant Devon expression - 'proper job' being a local term of approval - also neatly encapsulates the ethical business ideals of the members.

You reach The Courtyard through an iron gateway set in a whitewashed wall decorated with floral designs. In fine weather, people sit outside enjoying refreshments from the cafe, which, with the shop, is right ahead. The whole place serves as a lively community meeting place, where locals share news and ideas, and occasionally music is provided.

A wide choice of organic/fair traded teas and coffees is available, with home-made cakes and biscuits made principally from organic ingredients. There are also vegetarian lunches, salads and soups using local organic produce.

THE ANGLERS REST
Fingle Bridge
Drewsteignton
Exeter
Devon EX6 6PW
Tel. (01647) 281287

Set in the heart of the romantically wooded Fingle Gorge, next to the famous Fingle Bridge over the River Teign, is The Angler's Rest. This lovely inn is the oldest tourist business on Dartmoor, and has been serving Devonshire Cream Teas longer than anywhere else. It has been in the hands of the Price family for four generations, and celebrates its centenary in 1997.

A low, welcoming building with riverside terraced gardens, the Angler's Rest provides a warm, old fashioned, comfortable atmosphere, with log fires in the winter and plenty of angling pictures, memorabilia, antique fishing tackle and record fish. Superb views of the river can be seen through the windows.

Jon and Christine Price are proud of their Poachers Bar, which seats 80, and serves a selection of local ales, local farm cider and a wide selection of wines. The Restaurant seats 110. The emphasis is on good, traditional English meals, using seasonal local produce, including, for example, home made game pies, poached salmon salad, steak and kidney pie, pan fried fresh fish. Lighter snacks are also available. Local farm cheeses are a speciality, and the Sunday Roasts are very popular. Devonshire cream teas delight the visitor, just as they did the Victorian fishermen and walkers who discovered the spot a century ago.

The Anglers Rest is ideally suited for walking, birdwatching, fishing or just idling in this idyllic corner of Dartmoor.

USEFUL INFORMATION

OPEN Summer: 11am - 11pm.
Winter: 11am - 2.30pm.
CHILDREN No facilities.
CREDIT CARDS Visa, Mastercard.
LICENCE Full.
ACCOMMODATION No.
BAR FOOD Local farm cheeses a speciality.
VEGETARIAN 5 to 6 choices daily.
SMOKING Permitted.
DISABLED Level premises, easy access.
PETS Dogs welcome.
GARDEN Well furnished riverside terraces.
RESTAURANT Traditional English cooking, local produce including fish and game. Blackboard of daily specials.

GRENDON
Drewsteignton
Exeter
Devon EX6 6RE

Tel. and Fax (01647) 231486

One mile from the A30 dual carriageway at Whiddon Down, Grendon is a traditional Devon farmhouse of medieval origin surrounded by beautiful countryside, where Bed and Breakfast accommodation, with dinner by arrangement, are provided in a relaxed, flexible family atmosphere.

The thatched house contains many fascinating original features. These include, in the cosy sitting room, a large inglenook fireplace, with the beam above it supported on one side by a huge piece of granite and on the other by an intact bread oven. A screen dating from approximately 1450 is at one end of the room, and the window seat is of home-grown oak.

Grendon is the home of the Robinson family, who work the farm and offer a warm welcome. The accommodation is very comfortable, and guests are invited to use the south-facing, recently enlarged garden, where tea can be served in fine weather. There is also a hard tennis court (this requires non-marking shoes and your own racquets and balls).

No one leaves the table hungry at Grendon. Guests choosing to enjoy an evening meal are offered an impressive selection of home or locally produced meats and game, vegetables, bread, cakes and preserves. Individual dietary requirements can be catered for, and children can be fed earlier if necessary.

Grendon is ideally placed for exploring Dartmoor, Mid and South Devon.

USEFUL INFORMATION

OPEN All Year, except Christmas Day.
CHILDREN All ages welcome. Babysitting available.
CREDIT CARDS Not taken.
LICENCE None, but guests welcome to bring their own wine.
ACCOMMODATION 1 double room, 1 twin and 1 single. Private shared bathroom.
PRICES £17 - £19 per night, reduced if staying over 3 nights. Children reduced according to age and requirements.

RESTAURANT Dinner by arrangement. Local meat and game, home grown vegetables, home made bread, preserves etc.
VEGETARIAN Catered for with prior warning.
SMOKING No smoking please.
DISABLED Difficult for wheelchairs.
PETS No.
GARDEN Large. Tables and chairs for guests.

HUNTS TOR
Drewsteignton
Devon EX6 6QW

Tel. (01647) 281228

Hunts Tor is a highly acclaimed hotel and restaurant situated in the pleasant village of Drewsteignton, within the boundaries of the Dartmoor National Park and close to the beautiful Teign Valley. Castle Drogo and Fingle Gorge are not far away, and the village itself, with its ancient church and attractive houses, is a vibrant and youthful community which is worth getting to know.

The spacious white house is largely Victorian, but, like so many houses in Devon, it is older than its external appearance suggests, having a 17th century core. Inside, the furnishings are complemented by imaginative Art Nouveau and Art Deco themes.

Hunts Tor is owned and run by Sue and Chris Harrison, who have won recognition both for their accommodation and food. They appear in the Good Hotel Guide, and are considered the Best Small Restaurant in Devon in the 1997 Good Food Guide. They also have a 'Red M' from the Michelin guide. The food in the restaurant - for which it is essential to book 24 hours in advance - is a rich and varied blend of French and English dishes.

The hotel has three double bedrooms, all en suite, each with its own private sitting area. There are two dining rooms and a shared sitting room. Hunts Tor is an excellent base for exploring the eastern area of Dartmoor and the lovely valley of the Teign.

USEFUL INFORMATION

OPEN March to end of October.
CHILDREN Older children welcome.
CREDIT CARDS Not taken
LICENCE Restaurant.
ACCOMMODATION 3 en suite double rooms.
PRICES Double £60 - £70, Single from £40.
Dinner £20 - £23.

RESTAURANT English and French cuisine.
VEGETARIAN Catered for as required.
SMOKING Allowed in most areas.
DISABLED No special facilities.
PETS Welcome.
GARDEN None.

WHITEMOOR FARM
Doddiscombsleigh
Near Exeter
Devon EX6 7PU

Tel. (01647) 252423

ETB 1 Crown.

Whitemoor Farm is a lovely 16th century thatched farmhouse, standing in its own gardens and farmland, in Devon's beautiful, and relatively unknown, Haldon Hills, between Exeter and the Teign Valley. The farm is half a mile outside the village of Doddiscombsleigh, 3 miles from the A38 main road. Doddiscombsleigh is noted for its famous inn and historic church, where some unique stained glass can be seen. Although only seven miles from the city of Exeter, it is deep in the country. Both Dartmoor and the sea are within easy reach.

The farm's owner, Mrs Barbara Lacey, provides bed and breakfast accommodation in this relaxing, rural environment, from which there are unforgettable views over the surrounding countryside. The farm has its own well, with at least 13 feet of water, and in the garden is an old cider press, dated 1666. There is also a solar heated swimming pool, which guests are welcome to use.

Whitemoor farm has full central heating and is cosy with log fires in the winter. All bedrooms have wash basins. Tea and coffee making facilities are in the corridor, with a bathroom and toilet nearby.

Forested Haldon Hill rises to 750 feet above the farm, with woodland walks and the eye-catching Lawrence Castle or Haldon Belvedere. From here, the whole of South Devon is literally at your feet.

USEFUL INFORMATION

OPEN All Year.   **DISABLED** No special facilities.
CHILDREN Welcome.   **PETS** Welcome.
CREDIT CARDS Not taken.   **GARDEN** Large.
LICENCE None.   **ACCOMMODATION** 4 bedrooms: 1 double, 1 twin and 2 singles.
PRICES £17 - £17.50 per person per night. Children according to age.

MIDDLE LEAT
Holne
Ashburton
Devon TQ13 7SJ

Tel. (01364) 631413

Centrally situated in the beautiful and historic Dartmoor village of Holne, Middle Leat offers comfortable Bed and Breakfast family accommodation in a spacious modern bungalow, which enjoys wonderful views of the surrounding countryside.

Its owners, Philip and Anne Torr, offer a warm welcome to their home, where they breed more than a dozen varieties of hens and ducks, as well as their own Dartmoor ponies. The large, 3 acre garden provides space for both quiet reflection and family enjoyment, with play areas for children and seating for guests outside the bedroom.

The accommodation consists of one big room which can sleep up to 5 people, with bathroom and full facilities.

Breakfast is a speciality at Middle Leat, Mrs Torr providing a substantial English meal which includes free range eggs from her own hens. Vegetarians receive just as much care and attention as meat eaters.

Holne is a highly attractive village on the edge of the open moor, with a famous pub and a church where Charles Kingsley's father was vicar - the novelist was born here. Attractions as diverse as the River Dart Country Park, Buckfast Abbey and the steam trains of the Primrose Line are on the doorstep.

USEFUL INFORMATION

OPEN All Year (except Christmas).
CHILDREN Welcome.
CREDIT CARDS Not taken.
LICENCE No.
ACCOMMODATION Lge family room, sleeps 2 - 5, with large private bathroom.
PRICES £17.50 per night. Reduction for weekly bookings. Children according to age.

RESTAURANT Very full English breakfast.
VEGETARIAN Full vegetarian breakfast can be provided.
SMOKING Not in house.
DISABLED Bungalow with a few steps to room.
PETS By arrangement.
GARDEN With seating for guests, swing, slide etc.

STOWFORD GRANGE FARM
Stowford,
Okehampton, Devon EX20 4BZ

Tel: 01566 783298

Stowford Grange Farm is just three miles away from the majesty and mystery of Dartmoor and a quarter of a mile off the old A30 making it an ideal place in which to stay whilst you explore all the interesting and historical places within easy reach including Lydford Gorge and the old stannary town of Tavistock. Stowford is a small rural place with an old church, private fishing ponds and a good, traditional inn just a quarter of a mile away. Stowford Grange Farm is interesting in its own right. It is a listed building and has an unusual tower and granite features. Mrs Vigers looks after the guests whilst her sons look after the farm. It is a friendly, welcoming house where informality is the order of the day. No one stands on ceremony and all Mrs Vigers wants you to do is to feel at home and enjoy your stay.

The farmhouse has 3 double rooms and a family room, none of them are ensuite but there are 2 bathrooms with wash basins and toilets as well as a separate toilet with a wash basin. Centrally heated throughout, the bedrooms are well furnished and the beds comfortable. Downstairs there is a cosy lounge with television, a dining room, sun lounge and outside a delightful garden. A real farmhouse breakfast awaits you every morning, everything is freshly cooked and you have a choice. In the evening Mrs Vigers shows you what a good cook she is providing an excellent traditional meal, usually a roast joint or chicken with fresh vegetables. Her soups served with fresh bread rolls are all home-made and so too are the puddings.

USEFUL INFORMATION

OPEN; All year	**DINING ROOM; Good traditional fare**
CHILDREN; Welcome	**VEGETARIAN; Catered for on request**
CREDIT CARDS; None taken	**DISABLED ACCESS: Not suitable**
LICENSED; No. Bring your own	**PETS; No**
ACCOMMODATION;3dbl 1 fm not ensuite	**GARDEN;Yes**
RATES:- All Year, from £17. Pppn B&B.	

MOOR FARM
Dunsford
Exeter
Devon EX6 7DP

Tel. (01647) 24292

ETB Listed
and Commended

Moor Farm, set in beautiful rolling countryside in the heart of Devon, offers farmhouse Bed and Breakfast in comfortable and peaceful surroundings. Although only two and a half miles from the A30, one of the two main roads through Devon, it is beyond the sound of traffic and enfolded by the hills, with the thatched village of Dunsford, once famous for its cider orchards, a mile and a half away. Moor Farm has three orchards growing tradional cider apples.

The Devon longhouse, with cob walls and oak dining room furniture, is the home of Joyce and Geoff Dicker, whose family have worked the farm for three generations. Guests have their own wing of the house, which makes it an ideal place for families, and children of all ages are catered for. Tea and coffee making facilities are available in the bedrooms, and guests have use of the large dining room/lounge with colour television

All guests are welcomed with tea and cake on arrival. A full cooked breakfast is provided, with fresh grapefruit and home-made jam. Porridge is available on cold mornings. Afternoon tea can be served in the garden by arrangement.

Moor Farm is ideally placed for exploring the many attractions of South Devon, with the Dartmoor National Park on the doorstep and the resorts of the coast only a few miles away. Three golf clubs - Manor, Teign Valley and Fingle Glen - are close by.

USEFUL INFORMATION

OPEN March to November
CHILDREN Welcome, any age. Cot available.
CREDIT CARDS No.
LICENCE No.
ACCOMMODATION 1 family and 1 dble room.
PRICES High Season: £15 per night.
Low Season: £14. Children according to age.

VEGETARIAN Welcome.
SMOKING Non-smoking house.
DISABLED No special access.
PETS No.
GARDEN Yes. Afternoon teas in garden by arrangement.

THE ROYAL OAK INN
Bridge Street,
Dunsford, Devon EX6 7OA

Tel: 01647 252256

West Country Tourist
Board Approved.

Situated within Dartmoor National Park, this delightful village pub with accommodation should be a must on every visitor's list of good pubs in this part of Devon. Standing in the lovely Teign Valley, Dunsford is an exceptionally pretty village with a plethora of cob and thatched cottages and houses. People come here for all sorts of reasons. The Teign valley is superb for birdwatchers, you can fish on the River Teign, Botanists and lovers of flora and fauna delight in the woods which are probably at their most beautiful in spring when the river banks are covered firstly with daffodils and then bluebells. Apart from some wonderful walks there are many other activities including horseriding. Dartmoor is within easy reach, not far away are some superb beaches and the historic cathedral city of Exeter provides a great day out as well as the many National Trust properties in the vicinity.

Essentially a village inn, owned by Mark and Judy Harrison, it is a great place to be. The Harrison's have managed to create a great rapport between locals who have lived in Dunsford forever and those from all sorts of walks of life who have made the village their home. Between them they, in turn, make visitors welcome. The beer is good, the food is excellent including a very good Sunday Roast and a Fish and Chip night on Tuesdays, There is a non-smoking dining room and a Games Room. Built 300 years ago, the inn was destroyed by fire 120 years ago and all that remains of the former inn is the old cob barn which has been converted into 5 charming ensuite bedrooms furnished in a pretty cottage style. In the inn there are 2 family rooms sharing a bathroom. As well as a welcome from the Harrisons' and their family you will meet 'Bill' the goat who keeps an eye on the garden and 'Birdy' the Guinea Fowl who supervises the car park!

USEFUL INFORMATION

OPEN;12-2.30pm & 6.30-11pm Sun7-10.30pm   DINING ROOM; Delicious home-cooked
Mon:7-11pm BAR FOOD; Wide range, good value   CHILDREN; Welcome
VEGETARIAN; Daily choice   CREDIT CARDS;All major cards except Amex/Diners
DISABLED ACCESS; 2 rooms grd/fl.   LICENSED; Full On
ACCOMMODATION; 5 ensuite in Cob Barn   GARDEN; Yes. Ideal for children
2 rooms in inn (Family)   PETS;Welcome
RATES:-All Year.from Single £22.50/£27.50.pppnB&B.Dble.from £20/£22.50.pppnB&B.
Children sharing with parents under 10 years £5.pn. Special seasonal rates: Details on request.

THE BRIDFORD INN,
Bridford, Exeter,
Devon EX6 7HT

Tel: 01647 252436

Bridford is an attractive small village set above the Teign Valley in the Dartmoor National Park. The surrounding countryside is glorious and a walker's paradise. The reservoirs of Kennick, Tottiford and Trenchford are closeby. The Bridford Inn is the sort of hostelry that one seeks out and having once visited determines to return.

The premises were originally a group of 17th century cottages which were converted into an inn some thirty years ago. The conversion was skillfully done and the result is very pleasing. The original granite walls and massive granite fireplace were retained and you will notice the beams in the main Bar which arc from oak left over from the building of the replica Mayflower. Certainly an historical mishmash but the result is a welcoming, warm, friendly inn enjoyed by everyone who comes here.

There is no separate restaurant but table service is available in the cosy bar with its large, crackling log fire. The food cooked by Maureen Munday, whilst her husband Patrick and son Nick look after the bars, is good simple fare beautifully cooked and presented. There are always Daily Specials which might be a Fish Bake containing salmon, peppered smoked mackerel and prawns, served with a salad or the vegetables of the day or maybe Pork Loin Steaks grilled and served with Apple and Calvados Sauce.

There are delicious starters including Baked Avocado, Mushrooms and Tomatoes in Garlic Butter. Several dishes for vegetarians are also included. The portions are more than generous and the price is definitely right! If you want something less than a full meal you will find a whole range of interesting sandwiches, Ploughmans as well as the old favourites, a locally made pastie or sausage egg and chips. Everything is cooked to order so please do state when ordering if you are in a hurry.

USEFUL INFORMATION

OPEN; All year

CHILDREN; Welcome.

CREDIT CARDS; None taken

LICENSED; Full Licence

RESTAURANT; Not applicable

BAR FOOD; Excellent choice, home-cooked

VEGETARIAN; Always a choice

DISABLED ACCESS;No special facilities

FAIRWAY LODGE GUEST HOUSE,
Thorndon Cross,
Near Okehampton, Devon EX20

Tel/Fax: 0837 52827

AA QQQ Recommended.

A finalist in the AA 'Landlady of the Year' in 1996, Daphne Burgoine is the lively owner with her husband Andy, of Fairway Lodge. They came to Devon to start their business, and in order to get the sort of house they wanted, they built the stone farmhouse themselves over a period of three years specifically with facilities for the disabled and Bed and Breakfast in mind.. Now this comfortable home is a very welcoming place for all those who come to stay. The house is set in an acre of garden and 10 acres of pasture with miniature Shetland ponies which the Burgoines breed, free range Chickens and Aberdeen Angus Cattle.

There are 3 well appointed ensuite bedrooms all with outstanding views as well as a self catering unit specially designed for the disabled. Cooking and wine making are two of the main interests of this enterprising couple and everyone enjoys the excellent meals in which seasonal organic vegetables and fruit play a large part. Daphne and Andy share their home-made wines after dinner with their guests in the lounge where good conversation and much laughter is the order of the evening. It is a very happy house and you have only to read the visitors book to know that most people cannot wait to come and stay again.

USEFUL INFORMATION

OPEN; All year
CHILDREN; Welcome
CREDIT CARDS; None taken
LICENSED; No
ACCOMMODATION; 3 ensuite rooms
PETS:- No.

DINING ROOM; Home-cooked food
Using seasonal organic vegetables & fruit
VEGETARIAN; Upon request
DISABLED ACCESS; Yes.
GARDEN; Yes + 10 acres pasture
RATES:- Family room £58.50. Double/Twin £36.00.
Single £19.50.all B&B. All Year.

Chapter Five

CHAPTER FIVE

Plymouth, The Tamar Valley & South East Cornwall

"There is no love sincerer than a love of food"
G.B.Shaw

CHAPTER FIVE

PLYMOUTH, THE TAMAR VALLEY AND SOUTH EAST CORNWALL

Some tidy-minded purists may object to the fact that this chapter contains parts of both Devon and Cornwall, rather than insisting on keeping the counties defiantly separate.

Whilst I have much sympathy with the view that their strong awareness of possessing different identities ought to be respected whenever possible, it does make sense to describe the two sides of the Tamar estuary together, as a coherent region.

As you will see, it was once, on both sides, a thriving industrial area, with mines for copper, tin, lead and arsenic, all of which were transported down the river from once busy ports like Calstock and Morwellham, now nestling in rural peace. It is also a fact of history that Plymouth has always drawn talent and energy from its Cornish hinterland as much as from its Devonian, and the distinctive Plymothian accent is a rich and strange blending together of the speech heard in both counties. The character of the countryside on the west bank of the river, and along the relatively short section of the south Cornish coast which we shall explore here, is not, on the whole, too strikingly different from what we have experienced so far in South Devon. Geography, after all, doesn't immediately follow county boundaries, even those as definite as the one we're dealing with here.

This is in no way to deny that this area of East Cornwall has many of the special qualities of 'Cornishness' which make the county unlike anywhere else in Britain, and which do begin to appear as soon as you cross the river. Looe is, actually, as unmistakeably Cornish as Plympton is recognisably Devonian.

But chapters must be divided up somehow, and this section of Cornwall seems to relate sufficiently to its neighbouring land to be embraced by the same overview. A general introduction to Cornwall will therefore come in chapter 6, when we enter the more uncompromisingly Cornish landscape and atmosphere by way of Launceston which, with its old gateways and hilltop castle, is a border town if ever there was one.

PLYMOUTH (Tourist Information 01752 264849) has long been one of Britain's great maritime cities, and though that aspect of its life is now rather painfully changing, it is inevitably the place's connections with the sea, and with famous voyages, that first come to mind when you hear the name, which has been given to over 40 other towns and cities around the world.

Plymouth is also, with 244,000 inhabitants, by far the largest urban area in Devon and Cornwall. Its seemingly endless suburbs cover, in military-like rows, the hills and valleys around its two estuaries, which flow from the north and east. These are the strangely named Cattewater, the estuary of the Plym, and the equally strangely named Hamoaze, the combined estuaries of the Tamar and Tavy. They flow into and mingle in the magnificent PLYMOUTH SOUND, the view of which, from the HOE, is surely one of the seminal sights of England. Although the city endured great damage during the Second World War and much of it is modern, there are many things to see and do, and it has a number of historic sites which still retain a sense of past ages.

Plymouth is easily reached by AIR (for information telephone British Airways on 01345 222111) as well as by road and rail. BRITANNY FERRIES operates sea services from ROSCOFF and SANTANDER (01752 221321). Developing from an original settlement around SUTTON HARBOUR during the Middle Ages, Plymouth blossomed during the 16th century as the home port of the great Elizabethan explorers, and as one of the country's main naval bases during the long fight against Spain.

Since then Plymouth, and the later town of DEVONPORT alongside it (originally possessing the unsubtle name of 'Dock'), has played an essential part in the history of Britain. Throughout the 17th, 18th and 19th centuries the various surrounding villages and hamlets of the area, possessing names which often strike visitors as rather odd, like Mutley, Eggbuckland, Ernesettle, Laira and Swilly, gradually coalesced into the 'Three Towns' of **PLYMOUTH**, **STONEHOUSE** and **DEVONPORT**, and though they had, for years, been one continuous urban spread, they only joined together politically to become a city in the early 20th century.

Famous names associated with Plymouth include, amongst the seafarers like Sir John Hawkins and his family, the antarctic explorer Captain Scott, and the writers Hawker of Morwenstow, L.A.G.Strong and J.C.Squire. Thomas Hardy's first wife, Emma Lavinia Gifford, was born in Plymouth, and after her death he wrote a series of heartbroken, heartbreaking poems in her memory, three of which are set here.   Plymouth has also been the home of a surprising number of distinguished artists, although some of these properly belong to neighbouring Plympton: Benjamin Haydon, Sir Joshua Reynolds, William Payne (remembered more for his shade of grey than for his pictures), Alfred Wallis, who is forever associated with St Ives but was actually born here, and Cecil Collins. Today this strong tradition of painters is represented by Beryl Cook and Robert Lenkiewicz who, though not natives, have become very much part of the scene.

Two leading 20th century politicians, Michael Foot and David Owen, were Plymouth born, and the first woman to take her seat in the House of Commons, Nancy Astor, was a long-serving member for the city. If your imagination is inspired by the thought of the people who have been associated with a place, and walked its streets and buildings, then Plymouth will have plenty of ghosts for you.

The postwar CITY CENTRE is based on a grid pattern of wide, mainly traffic-free streets, which some find inspiringly open and expansive, and others find confusing and exposed. Whichever view you agree with, you will find the thoroughfares clean, well cared for and imaginatively landscaped, with a series of attractive GARDENS running down through the middle, which are worth a second glance for the trouble that has been taken over them.

There are very few buildings left from before 1941, when almost everything was flattened, but the odd one or two can be seen, such as the red-brick former WESTERN MORNING NEWS building, now home to several shops, including WATERSTONES (the new WESTERN MORNING NEWS building, a huge, prestigious design by Nicholas Grimshaw and looking, as it is meant to do, rather like a ship, is worth seeing as well; it's some way out of town, though, at Derriford). Plymothians who remember the city as it was before the blitz will tell you that it was very densely packed compared with now. Fortunately, there are not too many tower blocks.

The COUNCIL HOUSE, next to the 14 storey 1960s CIVIC CENTRE, has displays of the city plate, regalia and pictures. GUIDED TOURS are available by appointment. The GUILDHALL, opposite, and open to visitors when not in use, contains stained glass windows showing scenes from the city's past. Check at the TIC for more details about seeing these buildings.

The most historic church of the city, ST ANDREW'S, is a little to the east of the Guildhall. Mainly 15th century and rebuilt after the blitz, it has many monuments and a window by John Piper and Patrick Reyntiens. It was here that the people of Plymouth received the news that Sir Francis Drake had returned from his long voyage around the world; within minutes the church was empty and everyone had rushed down to the harbour. The hearts (one book I have says the entrails) of two famous non-Devonian seadogs, Sir Martin Frobisher and Admiral Blake, are buried here.

CHARLES CHURCH, now in the centre of a roundabout near the BUS STATION, was left in ruins as a memorial to the thousands of Plymouth people who died during the Second World War.

All visitors to Plymouth will naturally make their way to THE HOE, a high, wide, green promenade overlooking the SOUND. We may no longer stand here, as our grandparents did, and swell up with personal and patriotic pride at the thought of the Empire, but the near-religious feeling of being at the very heart and fountain-head of Britain's greatness was at one time very real to all classes, and you can still pick up something of it as you look out from this resonant spot. The place seems crowded with relics and memories. This is where Drake played, and insisted on finishing, his game of bowls before going out to meet the Armada, and here he is, looking out to sea past his island (this statue is actually a copy of the one in his home town of Tavistock).

The tall WAR MEMORIAL reminds us that Plymouth has been intimately connected with the armed services for hundreds of years, and you could, in the past, virtually rely on finding most of the British Navy here (probably in UNION STREET, which had more bars and drinking clubs than any street in England; it is quieter now, by all accounts, but is still the place in Plymouth for NIGHT CLUBS, DISCOS, CASINOS etc).

Today, the Hoe is a pleasant place to stroll or sit, as indeed it has been for generations, and very often it is where you will find a FETE, FAIR or event of some kind being held.

On the Hoe you will also find SMEATON'S TOWER (01752 600608), one of the many Eddystone Lighthouses (the present one can sometimes be spotted from the Hoe). It was built by John Smeaton to be the fourth lighthouse on the notorious Eddystone Rock in 1789, and brought here in 1884.

Just below the lighthouse is the extraordinary PLYMOUTH DOME (01752 600608), which describes itself as 'Britain's most up-to-date visitor centre'. Using the most recent technological aids, it introduces you to the story of the city in the most vivid ways, using lights, sounds and amazing gadgetry to reproduce the reality of life aboard the 'Mayflower', the Elizabethan town, a luxury liner and the besieged Plymouth of the Civil War, amongst much else. There is also a CAFE and GIFT SHOP.

At the Dome you can buy tickets for a GUIDED TOUR of the massive, stone-built fortress, still in military use, which spreads away on your left: the ROYAL CITADEL (01752 775841/266496), basically dating from the late 17th century. Next to this is another great attraction, the AQUARIUM (01752 222772).

If you follow the road down past the Citadel, you eventually come to the most individual quarter of Plymouth, that 'village within the city' known as THE BARBICAN.

Squeezed between the Hoe and Sutton Harbour, this is a highly enjoyable concentration of narrow old streets, lanes, passages and warehouses, with a wealth of historic buildings which, miraculously, escaped the bombing. The Barbican is a stimulating, slightly bohemian area, with a creative and colourful population. This is the part of Plymouth where the ART GALLERIES, CRAFT SHOPS, ETHNIC RESTAURANTS, EXOTIC CLOTHING SHOPS and ANTIQUE CENTRES are to be found, as well as an imaginative little THEATRE and a range of lively PUBS. If, like all such areas, it is a touch self-conscious, the close proximity of the harbour and fish market prevents it from becoming too precious. At night, indeed, it is sometimes decidedly raw.

The Barbican is a 16th century suburb of Plymouth. It consists of several parallel streets running away from the harbour, linked by narrow little lanes. It ends suddenly, and you find yourself, rather disconcertingly, back with the busy roads and uninspired buildings of the modern city. Whilst you are in the Barbican area, however, you will find plenty to enjoy.

There are art, craft, antique and gift shops as packed with treasures as an ancient sea chest. A recent arrival is a shop in the old fish market selling the well-known DARTINGTON GLASS from Torrington (see chapter 9). You can buy bread from the oldest bakery in England, JACKA'S, which has been here for four centuries. There are excellent places to eat, including some real old fashioned fish and chip shops, and the unique CAP'N JASPER'S, where you can purchase tea, coffee or burgers and indulge in them in the open air next to the harbour.

The Barbican is full of ghosts and echoes. Drake and Hawkins had houses here, and planned their voyages in these streets; the Pilgrim Fathers left from the

MAYFLOWER STEPS by the waterside; four of the six Tolpuddle Martyrs, after they were pardoned and returned from Australia, landed here and immediately went for a drink in THE DOLPHIN. If you visit that splendid pub today, where the beer is served straight from barrels on top of the bar, you will not find it hard to connect in your imagination with what it was like 150 years ago. For countless sailors, fishermen, emigrants, exiles and adventurers, these few streets below the Hoe have been the beginning and end of England.

The ELIZABETHAN HOUSE (01752 264878) in New Street is a beautifully restored dwelling such as any merchant or sea captain would have lived in, complete with furnishings of the time. It also has a National Trust Shop. The BLACK FRIARS DISTILLARY (01752 667062) is the original home of PLYMOUTH GIN, which has been made here for over 200 years. GUIDED TOURS of the premises are available.

Away from the Barbican and back towards the city centre are THE MERCHANT'S HOUSE (01752 264878), a Jacobean town house full of fascinating objects relating to the city's past, and the oldest building in Plymouth, THE PRYSTEN HOUSE (01752 661414), a 15th century priest's dwelling, where there are exhibitions of embroidery and a herb garden.

North of the centre is the CITY MUSEUM AND ART GALLERY (01752 264878). Here there is a large and varied collection, as you would expect in such a museum, including geological specimens, natural history, ceramics, silver and fine art, much of it of national and international importance. There are also many changing exhibitions.

Some distance further north is another reminder of Plymouth's long connection with warfare: CROWNHILL FORT (01752 79375), a Victorian barracks, one of many established around the city, where you can explore underground tunnels, secret passages, gun emplacements and regimental exhibitions. There is a RESTAURANT and free parking.

An excellent way of learning about Plymouth and its surroundings is to take a BOAT TRIP to see the Naval Dockyard or along the Tamar. Cruises also go as far as the Yealm estuary. They can last several hours, so plan carefully. For information on what is available, call (01752 822797 or 822105).

TOURS of the ROYAL WILLIAM VICTUALLING YARD, currently undergoing large-scale restoration and development, can be arranged by contacting (01752 775841). For an OPEN TOPPED BUS TOUR of the main sites of the city, call (01789 294466).

Whilst in DEVONPORT look for the old TOWN HALL (now a library) and the Egyptian-style ODDFELLOWS HALL, both by the local architect John Foulson. In the PARK at MOUNT WISE is a memorial to Scott of the Antarctic.

Plymouth does increasingly well for arts and entertainments. It has recently aquired a university, formed out of previously separate institutions, and this will no doubt influence the cultural life of the city, although the lack of a single campus perhaps makes it harder than it could be.

PLYMOUTH ARTS CENTRE (01752 660060) was one of the first of its kind in the country, and, though small and intimate, puts on a wide and important range of exhibitions, films and events. There is a good shop selling cards and books, and an inexpensive restaurant. The BARBICAN THEATRE (01752 267131) is a pleasant venue for imaginative contemporary performance, and has many good activities for children.

For bigger and more mainstream events, the THEATRE ROYAL (01752 267222) is one of the best modern theatres in Britain. Its smaller companion, THE DRUM THEATRE (same number), is ideal for quieter and more reflective plays and performances. WARLEIGH HOUSE (Box Office: 01752779432), just outside the city at TAMERTON FOLIOT, also presents concerts and arts events in an atmospheric setting.

Back in the heart of the town, PLYMOUTH PAVILIONS (01752 229922) combines a space for concerts and shows of all kinds with sports and recreational facilities, including the latest in water slides and wave machines. The MAYFLOWER LEISURE CENTRE (01752 564564) is good for sport of every variety, while pools can be found at CENTRAL PARK (01752 560436) and CROWNHILL (01752 778355).

Those wanting WATERSPORTS should try QUEEN ANNE'S BATTERY MARINA (01752 671142).

The PLYMOUTH SKI CENTRE (01752 600220) is the biggest dry ski slope in the Westcountry, and caters for absolute beginners as well as the experienced.

GOLF can be had at STADDON HEIGHTS GOLF CLUB (01752 401998) and at ELFORDSLEIGH HOTEL GOLF CLUB (01752 336428).

Spectator sports are also well catered for: PLYMOUTH ARGYLE FC performs league SOCCER, and PLYMOUTH ALBION plays league RUGBY UNION.

Enjoyable and civilised as Plymouth can be, compared with some cities, most visitors will, nevertheless, eventually want to move out into the surrounding country, where there are a number of famous and worthwhile attractions within easy reach.

Three and a half miles east of the city, above the Cattewater and hidden by trees, is SALTRAM HOUSE (01752 336546).

Owned by the National Trust, this is often described as the most impressive house in Devon. Certainly it is more of a classic 'stately home' than most in the county. It dates mainly from the time of George the Second, when it was owned by the Parker family, and is set in a beautifully landscaped park. It has been used many times as a film and television setting, most recently for the award winning film version of *Sense and Sensibility*. There is much original furniture and decor, including two rooms by Robert Adam, original Chinese wallpaper, Axminster carpets especially woven for the house, a bed by Chippendale and paintings by Sir Joshua Reynolds of nearby Plympton, who was a regular visitor (on one occasion he brought Dr Samuel Johnson). In the GARDEN can be seen an ORANGERY and several FOLLIES. In the CHAPEL there is now a GALLERY selling works by local artists, and there is a well-stocked SHOP and LICENSED RESTAURANT. Saltram is justly popular, and is well worth visiting.

The neighbouring town of **PLYMPTON** (Tourist Information 01752 266030/1) is, at first sight, an incomprehensible mass of new roads, housing estates, industrial buildings and big stores, but if you take the trouble to look around you can find, underneath all this, a historic town with some delightful corners.

It is actually based on two Medieval settlements, both probably older than Plymouth itself. **PLYMPTON ST MARY**, a large village which spread along the main road, is now the main shopping street and focus of the town's life. Some distance away was the little borough of **PLYMPTON ST MAURICE** or **PLYMPTON ERLE**, nestling below in the valley, centred around its Norman CASTLE which is now surrounded by a park.

If you climb to the top of this (there is no charge), which is like a tiny version of the castle in Totnes, and look down, you can see the narrow, winding streets, grey rooftops and rising hills of a typical little South Devon town; it could be another Modbury or Ashburton, hidden away in the heart of the fast, new suburban sprawl which is contemporary Plympton. If you can no longer smell the dung in the streets and feel that the place has been forgotten by time, as the Devon historian W.G.Hoskins said of it in the 1950s, you can still appreciate what he was getting at. There are some arcaded houses, reminding you of the Butterwalks in Totnes and Dartmouth, and a 17th century slate-hung GUILDHALL.

Plympton GRAMMAR SCHOOL, built in about 1664, numbers amongst its old boys a remarkable group of painters who, if no longer exactly household names, are permanent figures in the history of English art: Haydon, Northcote and Eastlake. The town's most famous character, however, is still a household name and one of the greatest portrait painters the country has produced. Sir Joshua Reynolds was the son of the schoolmaster, and always retained a love of the town where he was born in 1723. Becoming mayor of Plympton meant more to him than most of the other honours bestowed on him. Unfortunately, the house he was born in was demolished in the 19th century.

The church at Plympton St Mary, with a granite tower and monuments to the Strode family, is rather more interesting than the one down the road at Plympton St Maurice. It was originally connected to Plympton Priory, the second most important medieval monastery in Devon (after Tavistock Abbey).

At **SPARKWELL** is the well-known DARTMOOR WILDLIFE PARK (01752 837209) where, in a site spreading over 30 acres, you can see the biggest collection of big cats in the South West, plus bears, eagles, owls and many other wonderful beasts and birds. Falconry displays are given daily, and the park has a LICENSED RESTAURANT, PICNIC AREA and ADVENTURE PLAYGROUND.

Plympton was one of the four Dartmoor Stannary Towns, where the tin was brought for weighing and assaying, and the moor is not very far away, but this edge of it has become quite heavily industrialised - particularly for china clay extraction - and does not always seem very accessible. A good way of reaching the moor and bypassing the industry is to take a walk or a cycle along the PLYM VALLEY CYCLE TRACK, which starts at LAIRA on the way into Plymouth and mainly follows the line of an old railway towards Tavistock, finishing at Clearbrook. For details of the route, ask at the TIC.

Don't be put off by the presence of the china clay workings, which anyway have a certain visual appeal, because the area of the Plym Valley actually includes some of the most popular visitor spots of the moor.

SHAUGH PRIOR is an interesting village with a number of hut circles and enclosures nearby. SHAUGH BRIDGE, in the beautifully wooded BICKLEIGH VALE, is one of the most attractive riverside spots around the moor. The rivers Plym and Meavy join together here, and there is plentiful car parking and WOODLAND WALKS in land owned mainly by the National Trust.

DEWERSTONE TOR, above the woods, can be reached quite easily, and THE DEWERSTONE itself towers dramatically above. This has long been a popular place for artists and poets. CADOVER BRIDGE, on the Plym, a little to the east, is another well known place for a picnic and a gentle walk.

Following the River Meavy from Shaugh Bridge onto the moor, you can reach an area of very attractive villages, each worth stopping the car for and exploring. These include **MEAVY**, with its ancient oak tree and a pub by the green, **WALKHAMPTON** and **SHEEPSTOR**, which has in the churchyard a monument to Sir James Brooke, the 'Rajah Brooke of Sarawak'. This obscure Dartmoor spot always seems a strange place in which to be reminded of the Indian Empire. Sheepstor takes its name from the huge tor behind the village, where there is a cave known as the 'Pixie's House.' I have seen it stated in print that Sheepstor is the only village in England with no sparrows, and while I certainly don't remember seeing any when I went there, it seems a dubious fact to be so confident about. This area features in L.A.G.Strong's powerful novel *Dewar Rides* (1929).

BURRATOR RESERVOIR is the largest of the many around Dartmoor, and serves the water needs of Plymouth. It was completed in two stages, in 1898 and 1928, and covers 150 acres. It has been landscaped and there are lengthy WOODLAND WALKS, abundant CAR PARKING and excellent VIEWING PLACES. At weekends the people of the city come here for fresh air and inspiration.

Deep in a lane between Sheepstor and **DOUSLAND** can be seen some folly-like arches. These were constructed out of doorways belonging to farms that were drowned during the making of the lake. Surrounded by the ferns and branches of an archetypal Devon lane, they look very strange and atmospheric.

CLEARBROOK has a delightful inn called 'The Skylark', and when I first visited it I heard a skylark rhapsodising far above in the clear air. This is also a justly popular weekend venue, and you can sit with your drink on the bank opposite the pub and enjoy the sight of many people, of all ages and backgrounds, relaxing in the sun.

Part of DRAKE'S LEAT, a small canal originally constructed in the 16th century to take water to Plymouth, when the great man was mayor of the port, runs nearby.

From here it is a journey of minutes to **YELVERTON** (National Park Information Point: THE POST OFFICE), which is on the main A386 road out of Plymouth towards Tavistock. Yelverton looks like a bit of seaside town planted on the edge of the moors, with its great white buildings and wide green lending it a bracing, expansive air.

The YELVERTON PAPERWEIGHT CENTRE (01822 854250) houses the largest collection of antique and modern glass peperweights in Europe, as well as selling a variety of weights and local paintings.

To the left is **BUCKLAND MONACHORUM** which has two great attractions not to be missed.

BUCKLAND ABBEY (01822 853607), now cared for by the National Trust in partnership with Plymouth City Council, is a strong, peaceful, grey-stoned building, above the valley of the River Tavy and surrounded by trees and parkland.

Buckland was founded as a Cistercian Abbey in 1278. After the Dissolution of the Monasteries it became the home, in succession, of two of the greatest Devon heroes of the Elizabethan age: Sir Richard Grenville of the 'Revenge' and Sir Francis Drake. It was probably Grenville who converted the monks' old church into his Great Hall. Usually, when monastic property was taken over by upwardly mobile gentry, they left the most overtly religious parts of the buildings to fall into ruin, and used the more practical sections to live in.

Not Grenville; he was, like most of the Devon landowners and merchants of the day, fiercely Protestant, and would most likely have enjoyed the sense of sacrilege involved in turning a monkish church into a secular home. Buckland is almost unique amongst the ex-monastic great houses of England in this feature. The Hall contains beautiful plasterwork, and the kitchen has an open hearth and period cooking utensils.

The Abbey presents the visitor with a great deal to see and much to enjoy, so allow yourself plenty of time. There is an INTRODUCTORY VIDEO, aswell as EXHIBITIONS, FURNISHED ROOMS, CRAFT DISPLAYS by local potters and other makers, well-laid out WALKS and a HERB GARDEN.

The most famous artefact at Buckland, of course, is DRAKE'S DRUM. Many people are somewhat surprised to discover that this actually is a drum, of the sort which would have accompanied a 16th century sea captain on his voyages. There is no actual evidence that it was a possession of Drake's, but no evidence either that it wasn't. The legend that the drum will be heard, beating, whenever England is in danger, to summons Drake from wherever he is to come and save his country, is not so very old, but everybody now knows it. In fact, it probably owes more to literary sources than to genuine folklore, but there have certainly been instances of mysterious beatings on a drum being heard, especially during the two World Wars, which for want of a better explanation have been attributed to the great relic.

At Buckland there are also displays of original letters, pictures and banners from Drake's time.

Buckland Monachorum's other great attraction is THE GARDEN HOUSE (01822 854769), which has what is often described as one the most beautiful of all the beautiful gardens in the south west. Covering 8 acres, it includes a romantic terraced garden set around a ruined 16th century vicarage, a quarry garden, glades, meadows and walks, all rich in colour and variety. The overall effect is one of intimacy and informality, yet the design is clearly very well thought out, and it has its formal elements where these are appropriate.

LIGHT LUNCHES and CREAM TEAS are served in the Georgian house, but most of this is not open to the public. The garden itself is not open all the year, so please telephone before visiting.

HORRABRIDGE (National Park Information Point: THE PAPER SHOP) is a village few people have been polite about; the old bus conductors' version of the name, 'Horror-bridge', sums up the typical reaction to its modern commuter houses and busy road. Like all places, though, it feels different if you get to know it and imagine its life from the inside, and the area around the pub and the old bridge itself is quite attractive. There are good WOODLAND WALKS to be had in the surrounding country.

TAVISTOCK (Tourist Information 01822 612938) is the largest and most important town on the western side of Dartmoor, and has, for centuries, been a marketing, industrial, trading and cultural centre for this corner of Devon. It was one of the four Dartmoor Stannary Towns, and has an air of old-fashioned dignity, combined with present prosperity, which is very attractive. Its narrow streets and numerous lanes and side passages provide a sense of intimacy and continuity with the past. Much of the town is built of a distinctive grey-green volcanic slate called 'Hurdwick', more commonly found far away in the Lake District, which gives the buildings what has been called a lovely 'underwater' effect.

In its thousand or so years of existence, Tavistock has been dominated until recently by two great landlords: the Medieval Benedictine Abbey, which was the largest and richest in England west of Glastonbury, and, later, the Russell family, who became the Earls and Dukes of Bedford.

Tavistock Abbey was founded in 974, by Ordulf, Earl of Devon, who was half-brother to King Edgar, and the town probably grew up around this establishment. Throughout the Middle Ages the Abbey increased steadily in wealth and influence, owning land in many parts of the county. Just before the Dissolution it had what was probably the first printing press in Devon.

Little enough of all this survives today. There is an L-shaped fragment of wall, next to the 14th century Parish Church, which is all that remains of the great Abbey Church. Records show that this edifice was not much shorter than Exeter Cathedral. The COURT GATE in Bedford Square was the main entrance to the Abbey, and 'BETSY GRIMBAL'S TOWER', in Plymouth Road, was the GREAT WESTERN GATE. Its local name is probably a corruption of 'The Blessed Grimwald', an obscure saint of the 9th century. Ghost stories are told of this atmospheric ruin, and it is from here that Lady Howard sets out on her nightly journey to Okehampton Castle, in the coach fashioned from her husbands' bones, as described in the last chapter. The only other physical relic of the monastery is the ABBEY CHAPEL, formerly the monks' refectory or dining hall.

The Russells took over the lands formerly owned by the Abbey, and for several hundred years their influence on both the life and the physical appearance of the town was immense. The 7th Duke, who inherited the title in 1839, was especially concerned with the social and moral welfare of the people, and was responsible for building the beautiful rows of model workmens' cottages which are such a feature of the town. His statue is in the Guildhall car park.

Tavistock has not always been the genteel, civilised town which you can see today. In past times it has had a decidedly wild atmosphere. During the Middle Ages, it was a centre for the tin mining industry, and later the cloth trade. Another period of prosperity came at the end of the 18th century when seams of copper were discovered, and for a few years Tavistock became a booming mining town, as people flocked to work in this and other flourishing industries. Arsenic and iron ore were also mined here.   A four mile canal was designed by a young local man called John Taylor, linking the town to the small port on the Tamar called

Morwellham (of which more in a minute). This was used to transport the copper ore. In the mid 19th century much of the world's copper was extracted from this area around the Tavy and the Tamar, with no fewer than 156 active mines in the vicinity of the town. By the end of the century, however, the boom was over, and from being a roaring, dirty industrial centre, Tavistock, thanks to the Russell influence, again became a comfortable market town. Baring Gould in 1905 described it succinctly as 'clean', and it remains so today.

The town's history is brought to life at TAVISTOCK MUSEUM (no telephone number - ask at the TIC for opening times) in Drake Road.

Sir Francis Drake is, of course, Tavistock's most famous son. He was born at a farm called Crowndale about a mile south of the town in 1542. The farm itself has now vanished, and Drake spent most of his childhood outside Devon, learning his sea-craft whilst living around the Thames and Medway. He returned to his native land as a young man to join his cousin, John Hawkins, who was working out of the expanding port of Plymouth.

In his exploits and his character, Drake represents the essence of his age, the outward-going, visionary England of Elizabethan, freshly confident in its power, its Protestant religion, its developing language and its ability to take on the hegemony of Catholic Europe. He must have been a charismatic figure to have inspired men to leave their hearths and their fields to sail with him, and to have become such an archetypal popular hero, of whom apocryphal stories and legends abound.

It is in the nature of genuine folk heroes to be constantly recreated to suit the times, and if in our cynical age we are more prepared than the Victorians to acknowledge the fact that Drake was a bit of a pirate, this doesn't stop us retaining our affection for him; in fact his most recent biographer, in the early 1990s, saw him as epitomising the spirit of Thatcherite free enterprise. However he is viewed, the charisma remains. The statue of Drake, by Boehm, at the end of Plymouth Road was erected in 1883, at the height of the British Empire which he and his fellow Devonian adventurers sowed the seeds for. The one on Plymouth Hoe is a copy of this.

Tavistock was the birthplace of an attractive minor poet of the 17th century, William Browne, whose work influenced Milton and is worth looking at for its own sake. During the 19th century it was also the home of an interesting lady novelist, one of those Victorian writers who are known to posterity as 'Mrs' somebody or other; in this case 'Mrs Bray', wife of the town's vicar. She wrote a number of historical novels using local settings, and compiled a collection of Devon customs and superstitions which is still useful to folklorists. Described by her contemporaries as pretty, excitable and highly strung, she was once accused of trying to steal the Bayeux Tapestry, but it was all a misunderstanding.

You will obtain a very good impression of the comfortable life that can be lived in and around Tavistock today from the novels of a contemporary Devon writer, Marcia Willett, whose characters tend to be well-heeled and have a background in the armed services. They occupy cottages, manor houses and vicarages in the villages surrounding Tavistock and on the edge of the moor, and are always meeting for coffee at the Bedford Hotel or running into each other whilst shopping at Creber's. Those who know the lifestyle depicted tell me she has got it completely right, and they cannot visit the town without the feeling of having strayed into a Marcia Willett story.

The BEDFORD HOTEL is the leading establishment of the town; CREBER'S is an excellent delicatessan. Other shops worth looking for include a number of outlets for crafts, arts, gifts and quality foods.

BRIGID FOLEY'S beautifully made embroidered sweaters and shirts can be found at her shop in Paddon's Row, not far from THE MIRROR DESIGN STUDIO, selling glassware and gifts of all kinds. Other characteristic Tavistock shops, indicating the good life that can be lived here, are NATURAL NOMADS, THE SPIRAL STAIRCASE, MAYFLOWER GALLERIES, THE WINE CENTRE and COUNTRY CHEESES. THE VILLAGE SHOPPING ARCADE is a delightful collection of small shops selling jewellery, pottery, hand-made jumpers and much else. A diversity of PUBS and RESTAURANTS gives you somewhere to enjoy in the evenings, whatever your tastes.

As is fitting for an ancient market town, Tavistock holds a weekly PANNIER MARKET every FRIDAY, as well as various collectors' markets and special events (for information telephone 01822 611003). It is a lively community, with plenty of traditional celebrations and events throughout the year. TAVISTOCK CARNIVAL happens in July, while the famous GOOSE FAIR ('Tavistock Goosey Fair') is in October. Just before Christmas there is a DICKENSIAN EVENING with late night shopping and street entertainment.

For the arts, the town has a new purpose-built venue, THE WHARF (01822 611166), where CONCERTS, FILMS, DRAMA and all kinds of events take place seven days a week. It also has a RESTAURANT and BAR.

MEADOWLANDS POOL (01822 617774) has everything for the swimmer, while TENNIS and BOWLS can be found in the park in Plymouth Road. Three golf clubs are nearby: TAVISTOCK GOLF CLUB (01822 612344), HURDWICK GOLF CLUB (01822 612746) and YELVERTON GOLF CLUB (01822 852824). WALKING, CYCLING, RIDING and FISHING can all be enjoyed in the surrounding countryside.

Tavistock is not situated, 'like the boss of a shield, in the middle of the huge circle of Dartmoor', as Conan Doyle put it, memorably but quite inaccurately, in his Sherlock Holmes story 'Silver Blaze'. Even so, the moor is not far away, and the town makes an ideal base for anyone wishing to explore it. The main B3357 road to Ashburton, via Two Bridges, takes you quickly to the centre of the moor, while Lydford, Okehampton and the northern moor are equally accessible. In fact, Tavistock probably makes one of the best centres for touring the moor, as well as for venturing into the eastern part of Cornwall. Like the towns of the South Hams, it is big enough to be interesting to stay in for its own sake, but small enough not to keep you for too long from the lovely country surrounding it. Also like them, it is a good place to come back to in the evening; a town which it is easy to feel at home in.

A few miles north of Tavistock, towards Launceston and the next chapter, is the village of **MILTON ABBOT**, near which is the famous GARDEN of ENDSLEIGH. Now a hotel, the house was built in 'cottage orne' style for the Duke of Bedford. The much-acclaimed GARDENS are sometimes opened to the public (not to be confused with the garden centre near Ivybridge - see chapter 3).

The old river port of **MORWELLHAM**, four miles west of Tavistock, is a remarkable place by any standards. Deep in the wooded, secretive countryside of the Tamar Valley, seemingly miles from anywhere, its story is of spectacular rise and fall followed by rebirth as a major educational and recreational attraction.

Morwellham began in the Middle Ages as part of the extensive estates of the Abbey of Tavistock. It flourished in the 19th century when the copperdeposits of the region were discovered and exploited. The Devon Great Consols Mine was the largest in Europe, and for a few years most of the copper for the Victorian empire, together with lead, silver and arsenic, came from this area around the two rivers, the Tamar and the Tavy. Morwellham became the busiest inland port in Devon after Exeter. Schooners, paddle steamers and barges came and went, while hundreds of people worked in the mines and on the quays, and on the tramway linking them.

But by the end of the century it was all over. The mine closed in 1901 and the once thriving port went back to sleep, forgotten and disregarded, literally a backwater, until 1970. It was then that the Dartington Amenity Research Trust, an offshoot of the Dartington Hall Trust near Totnes, began to restore the port and its surrounding landscapes with the idea of creating an open-air museum, a relatively new concept at that time.

Now, after more than twenty five years of work, MORWELLHAM QUAY (01822 833808), run by the Morwellham and Tamar Valley Trust, provides a fascinating day out for all ages (at least four to six hours are recommended to see it all). There are INTRODUCTORY SHOWS, MUSEUM DISPLAYS, STORYTELLING SESSIONS and VIDEOS which set the scene in an imaginative and accurate way.

You can then walk the quays and examine the village school, forge, houses and workshops as they would have been in the 1860s, with costumed inhabitants going about their daily business. You can also ride on a tramway and go into a genuine copper mine, marvel at a huge water wheel, and explore the sailing ship, 'The Garlandstone', which rests by the quay. A VICTORIAN FARMYARD gives the opportunity to meet the animals and take a CARRIAGE RIDE pulled by a Shire horse. There is also a HYDRO-ELECTRIC STATION. In addition, the site has SHOPS, a seasonal PUB and RESTAURANT, and RIVERSIDE WALKS.

A new development, for which you will need a separate entrance ticket, is the TAMAR VALLEY WILDLIFE RESERVE, a 200 acre site with specially designed trails, birdwatching hides and beautiful views. It deserves a day to itself; trying to cover it in a visit to Morwellham is unfair to both.

Before crossing the Tamar, it is worth taking some time, if you like quiet, out of the way places, to explore the two villages in the peninsula of land between the Tamar and the Tavy, **BERE FERRERS** and **BERE ALSTON**. The 'bere' in both names refers to the fact that when the Anglo Saxons first penetrated this far the whole area was heavily wooded, as indeed in places it still is. With its peaceful valleys and winding lanes, and just the occasional relic of the industrial past, it is hard to imagine the area as it was in the 19th century when the lead, copper, silver and arsenic were being frantically extracted from beneath the ground.

From Tavistock the most direct way into Cornwall is by crossing the Tamar on the A390 at **GUNNISLAKE**. Even here, where the river has narrowed considerably, it feels like the crossing of a real border. Gunnislake has a 16th century seven-arched bridge, and plentiful remains of mining. It was the scene of a skirmish during the Civil War.

Rather prettier is the next village along as we follow the banks of the Tamar southwards, **CALSTOCK**. Here there is an impressive railway viaduct, a hilltop church and the pleasantly sad air of a once busy port, now partly silted up.

Near Calstock, at **ST ANN'S CHAPEL**, is the TAMAR VALLEY DONKEY PARK (01822 834072), where most of the resident donkeys have been rescued from ill-treatment. There are donkey and cart rides, goats, rabbits and a children's play area. A mile from Calstock by footpath, but six miles by road, is one of the finest of the 'great' houses in Cornwall, and one of the best preserved Medieval manor houses anywhere: COTEHELE HOUSE (01579 351346).

It was owned for nearly 600 years by the Edgecumbe family, and is now in the hands of the National Trust. Secluded and deeply peaceful, it is surrounded by beautiful GARDENS, which are worth a visit for their own sake. Inside the house there are tapestries, armour, paintings and, in the chapel, a 15th century clock, which may be the oldest clock in the country still in its original position. Also in the house are a National Trust SHOP and a LICENSED RESTAURANT.

The adjacent estate is large and full of interest. As well as the gardens there are a Medieval DOVECOTE, ESTATE WORKSHOPS and MILL completewith WATERWHEEL. Walking in the extensive WOODLANDS, you can find a small, serene chapel, and if you continue by the river you will come to COTEHELE QUAY. Here, against the wall, is the last Tamar sailing barge, built in 1899. 'Shamrock' is now restored to her original glory, and is able to give occasional trips on the river. There is also a NATIONAL MARITIME MUSEUM OUTSTATION (01579 50830), which has displays covering the river's shipping past.

Following the Tamar southwards, through the rich countryside visible on both banks, there is no other major settlement until we get to **SALTASH**, opposite Plymouth, to which it was linked for centuries by a ferry. The town is now reached by the magnificent TAMAR SUSPENSION BRIDGE, opened in 1962. Next to it is one of Brunel's masterpieces, his ROYAL ALBERT RAILWAY BRIDGE of 1859. Both are a joy to cross the river on, but if you use the road bridge you miss the town of Saltash, as a tunnel takes you beneath it, and straight into the Cornish countryside stretching away behind, which I suppose adds to the feeling of entering a foreign country. Saltash is worth a look, though, before moving west.

It is very steep, with some attractive houses, an interesting church and MARY NEWMAN'S COTTAGE (01752 822211). This 15th century house is believed to have been the childhood home of Sir Francis Drake's first wife. Inside is period furniture on loan from the Victoria and Albert Museum, and outside are some fine trees and a HERB GARDEN with views of the river and bridges.

Five miles north of Saltash is the well-known and much-acclaimed ST MELLION HOTEL, GOLF AND COUNTRY CLUB - see their advertisement at the end of this chapter.

Just outside the town is a well-preserved little Medieval motte and bailey castle, like a miniature version of the ones at Launceston and Totnes. TREMATON CASTLE is privately owned and never open to the public, but you can get a good view of it from the train as it passes the village of **FORDER**, and it can be viewed from **ST STEPHENS**, Saltash.

Continuing round to the mouth of the Tamar, the next settlement is **TORPOINT**. Unlike Saltash, the town is still linked to Plymouth by car ferry. It is mainly a suburb of the city, and has, perhaps, little of interest in itself, but nearby are some attractive villages and a couple of important houses.

The first of these is ANTONY (01752 812191), now owned by the National Trust.

Antony House is an elegant mansion, in silver-grey Pentewan stone, built in the early 18th century. It is on the site of an older dwelling of the Carew family, who have been here since the 15th century. In the entrance hall can be seen a portrait of one of the most interesting of them, the Richard Carew who published, in 1602, one of the first, and best, county topographical studies, his *Survey of Cornwall.* Everyone who has written about the county has, in a sense, been following him. The house is beautifully furnished, with paintings, tapestries, embroideries and family documents.

The GARDENS, overlooking the River Lynher, which joins the Tamar estuary between Saltash and Torpoint, contain the national collection of day lilies, a yew pavilion, Indian carvings and a Burmese temple bell, brought back from the Far East by a member of the family. Also in the gardens is a BATH POND HOUSE dating from 1789, but this can be seen by arrangement only. ANTONY WOODLAND GARDEN AND NATURAL WOODS (01752 812364) is a landscaped park, created with help from Humphrey Repton, with lovely views over the river. It contains 50 acres of woodland and as much cultivated garden, with camellias, rhododendrons, azaleas and many other plants and shrubs.

A few miles along the Lynher is **ST GERMANS**, which has a well-known church, created from a Medieval priory which was itself on the site of a Saxon cathedral. Before Exeter became the diocesan capital for both counties, in the 11th century, the church in Cornwall was administered from here. There is a beautiful Norman doorway and a fine east window. A misericord illustrates the warning tale of the monk Dando, who hunted on a Sunday and regretted it for ever afterwards (some say his ghost haunts the area). PORT ELIOT HOUSE is not open to the public, but many will remember the open air arts festivals that were held in the grounds during the early 1980s, under the title 'ELEPHANT FAIR'.

Near St Germans is CATCHFRENCH MANOR (01503 240759), home to a Trust running Christian retreats. The GARDENS, also designed by Repton and in the process of restoration, are sometimes open; please ring for details.

Returning to Torpoint and turning south, MOUNT EDGCUMBE HOUSE AND COUNTRY PARK (01752 822236), overlooking Plymouth Sound, can be reached (from Plymouth you take the CREMYLL PASSENGER FERRY).

The house was built by Sir Richard Edgcumbe of Cotehele in 1553, who decided to move the family seat to this more impressive site with its views of Plymouth and the Sound. It was gutted by a bomb in 1941. Rebuilt after the war and furnished in 18th century style, it and its magnificent surroundings are owned and run jointly by Cornwall County Council and Plymouth City Council.

What began as a 16th century deer park around the house has developed into one of the most spectacular series of gardens in Britain. There are FORMAL GARDENS in French, Italian and English style, a Victorian 'Earl's Garden' and the collection of the International Camellia Society. The PARK has wonderful WALKS with views of the Sound and across to Plymouth, and as you wander around you will perhaps get a glimpse of the deer who live here.

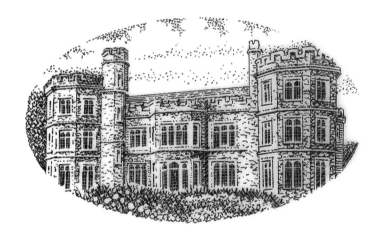

The granite GARDEN BATTERY, built in the 1860s, is one of a whole series of forts erected all around Plymouth, on both sides of the Sound, at a time when a French invasion was feared. The Crownhill fort which we visited earlier in the chapter is one of these, and several more were placed all around the area of the RAME HEAD PENINSULA, which is the most southerly point on the Cornish side of the Sound. Others, though not accessible to the public, can be seen from various angles, and their names alone insist on their being listed: Cawsand Battery, Fort Picklecombe, Fort Tregantle and Polhawn Battery.

The two villages of **CAWSAND** and **KINGSAND** sit on the shore towards the end of the peninsula, opposite PLYMOUTH BREAKWATER. Two miles from the Hoe, this long, narrow 'island' was constructed in the 19th century to protect theSound from storms and make it a safer haven for shipping. The breakwater is a mile long and is made from four and a half million tons of local limestone. About 10 miles south of here is the EDDYSTONE LIGHTHOUSE.

Cawsand and Kingsand are both popular with sailors and with those who like fairly quiet, pretty coastal villages with sandy beaches and an air of having been overlooked by the more obtrusive of 20th century developments. The were both at one time notorious for their smuggling, and before the breakwater was built Kingsand was a deep water port. Good WALKING and FISHING can be enjoyed from them.West of Rame Head, the exposed four-mile expanse of WHITSAND BAY was once the graveyard of many fine ships. The tiny villages of **PORTWRINKLE, DOWNDERRY**, **SEATON** (not to be confused with the Seaton in East Devon) and **MILLENDREATH** cling to the yellowish cliffs and the inhabitants haul their boats onto their beaches, as they have for generations. For places that do not seem particularly well known, they are often surprisingly full of visitors. At Portwrinkle is the WHITSAND BAY HOTEL, GOLF AND COUNTRY CLUB (01503 230276).

The first major place we come to along the South Cornish coast, however, is **LOOE** (Tourist Information 01503 262072).

The two little Looe rivers meet in a narrow estuary before joining the sea, and on both sides of this are the twin towns of **EAST** and **WEST LOOE**. The eastern settlement is bigger and more lively, but both are equally old, and at one time they both sent two members to Parliament, as all boroughs did. They are linked by a graceful BRIDGE built in the 1850s, replacing one built in the 15th century which had 15 arches and a chapel on it. From the bridge you can admire the natural site of the town and the two communities which comprise it.

Both are built tightly against the steep sides of the estuary, and are full of character. The white and grey of the houses and the brightness of the gardens behind them, lining the deep valley, makes a relaxing sight, and the towns are justly very popular with visitors of all ages. Their buildings are attractive and sometimes unusual; In West Looe, for instance, the little quayside church of St Nicholas who, amongst much else, was the patron of seamen, is worth a look.

Looe began as a centre for fishing, but grew in the 19th century as a busy industrial port for the inland mining areas. This is now long over, and fishing is again an important activity, along with tourism. SHARK FISHING is a speciality of Looe, and for those who wish to partake in the sport, boats can be hired and information given on the QUAY.

As is the case with all harbour towns, it is quite possible to idle away many hours doing, apparently, nothing but watch the tide come in and out, and the rocking of the boats on the water. This is fine, but should you wish to be more active there is plenty to do and see.

The SOUTH EAST CORNWALL DISCOVERY CENTRE (01503 262777) provides an excellent introduction to the history, culture and environmental distinctiveness of the area through video presentation and exhibitions. There is also a SHOP and INFORMATION POINT.

The OLD GUILDHALL MUSEUM (01503 263709), a 16th century building in East Looe, contains pictures, objects and exhibitions relating to the town's development, and the LIVING FROM THE SEA exhibition at the BULLER QUAY FISH MARKET (no telephone number) graphically shows you all you could want to know about the area's fishing history. There is also an AQUARIUM.

Not far from the town, the LANREATH FARM AND FOLK MUSEUM (01503 220321) contains a vast amount of material on the traditional lives of the people. Domestic items, farm machinery, tools and mill equipment all invoke the work and culture of past centuries, but there is also a collection of telephones and related objects. CRAFT DISPLAYS are given here.

Also at Lanreath, PORFELL ANIMAL LAND at Trecangate (01503 220211) is a gentle place where visitors can see a selection of deer, wallabies, goats and other animals in a natural setting. WOODLAND WALKS, a CHILDREN'S PLAY AREA and PONDs are also featured.

At the MONKEY SANCTUARY (01503262532) rare Amazonian Woolly Monkeys have been bred and kept successfully for over 30 years. They are given the freedom of their own territory in both the house and its gardens, and can be seen living as they would in their natural environment.

Looe has its expected share of GIFT SHOPS, GALLERIES, PUBS and RESTAURANTS. There are BEACHES, separated from the harbour entrance by the unique BANJO PIER (if you want to know why it is called this, just look at its shape). GOLF can be enjoyed at LOOE BIN DOWN GOLF CLUB (01503 240239), and the area is ideal for WALKERS. KILMINORTH WOODS, on the west bank, provides 100 acres of oak woodland walks rich in wildlife.

For FISHING in the estuary, permits are available from LOOE PET SUPPLIES, and COARSE FISHING can be found at SHILLIMILL LAKES, LANREATH (01503 220886). BOAT TRIPS around the estuary and out to LOOE ISLAND, outside the mouth, can be taken from the QUAY. The island is quite a spectacular piece of rock, a mile round and 150 feet high. A highly enjoyable scenic railway line runs from Looe to the inland maket town of Liskeard.

This chapter ends with one of the most famous and photogenic villages in Cornwall, familiar from a million postcards and those much maligned chocolate boxes: **POLPERRO**.

Clinging to the high, steep sides of a narrow valley, with its tightly packed white and grey cottages, backed by the deep green of oak woods, rising above the little harbour, it has an instant appeal (and anyway, if a picture of somewhere like Polperro on a chocolate box leaves people feeling uplifted, and reminds them of a holiday by the sea, what is so superior about reacting cynically?). Cars are now banned, and visitors can enjoy the narrow streets and well-kept old houses without danger.

Until the 19th century, the people earned their livelihood from the twin activities of fishing and smuggling, and many hiding places and secret entrances are said to be still found in some of the houses. Buildings to look out for include the HOUSE ON PROPS, the OLD WATCH HOUSE and the 16th century COACH HOUSE.

The village is understandably popular with artists. The EAST CORNWALL SOCIETY OF ARTISTS has a GALLERY in a converted chapel, and local paintings, crafts and gifts can be easily found.

LAND OF LEGEND AND MODEL VILLAGE (no telephone number) has small-scale displays of old Cornwall and a miniature railway. Wander about the steep old streets or linger by the harbour wall, watching the boats and the people, and let the spell of the place work on you.

THE HORN OF PLENTY
Gulworthy
Tavistock
Devon PL19 8JD

Tel and Fax (01822) 832528

AA Hotel of the Year 1995

'A Restaurant With Rooms'
   Winner of many accolades and awards, the Horn of Plenty is a very special country house hotel - or 'restaurant with rooms' - set in unsurpassed landscape between the rivers Tamar and Tavy and enfolded by the foothills of Dartmoor.
   It is surrounded by gardens and orchards covering four acres, which in spring and early summer are enriched by the brilliant colours of azaleas, rhododendrons and camellias, and has spectacular views of the Tamar Valley and across into Cornwall, where Bodmin Moor sits brooding on the skyline.
   The house is nearly two hundred years old, being built originally by the Duke of Bedford, Marquis of Tavistock, the most important local landowner, and it has the deeply satisfying atmosphere which develops in a much-loved house, lived in by successive generations and rooted in its surrounding countryside. It is tastefully furnished and decorated throughout to give a feeling of warmth, comfort and peaceful security, with log fires in winter and fresh flowers at all times.
   The Horn of Plenty has earned its proprietors, Elaine and Ian Gatehouse, a plethora of good reviews and awards since 1991. Critics are especially impressed by the food and the imaginative, careful way it is prepared and served. The restaurant has been given three rosettes by the AA and a star by Egon Ronay for the excellence of its cooking, including a special award for outstanding desserts. The style of cuisine is modern and international.
   The restaurant seats up to fifty guests and is open seven days a week, but there is no lunch served on Monday. The Music Room, seating up to fifteen people, is available for private dinner parties or small business meetings.
   There are seven en suite double bedrooms at the Horn of Plenty, with balconies overlooking the walled garden and distant countryside.
   The Horn of Plenty is a perfect base for exploring the richly beautiful and historic countryside of the Tamar Valley and the western side of Dartmoor. The comfortable old town of Tavistock is only a few miles away, and golf, walking, riding, fishing, canoeing and sailing can all be enjoyed within easy distance. The historic city of Plymouth and the open wilds of the moor are equally almost on the doorstep, and both Devon and Cornwall can be covered from here. Or you can just stay in the garden and recharge your batteries in this deeply peaceful and relaxing environment.

USEFUL INFORMATION

OPEN All Year except Xmas & Boxing Day.
CHILDREN Welcome over 13; no facilities.
CREDIT CARDS Mastercard, Access, Visa, Amex.
LICENCE Restaurant.
ACCOMMODATION 7 en suite double rooms.
PRICES Low Season: £83 - £93, single £63 - £73;
High Season: £88 - £98, single £68 - £78.

RESTAURANT Open daily, but not Monday lunchtime. Modern international cuisine.
VEGETARIAN 2 or 3 to choose from.
SMOKING Not in restaurant.
DISABLED Level access.
PETS Well behaved dogs welcome.
GARDEN Extensive and beautiful, 4 acres.

ST MELLION HOTEL, GOLF AND COUNTRY CLUB
St Mellion
Near Saltash
Cornwall PL12 6SD

Tel. (01579) 351351
Fax (01579) 350537

e mail: Stay@St-Mellion.co.uk

AA 3 Stars & 2 Rosettes for Restaurant,
RAC 3 Stars, ETB 3 Crowns

St Mellion is one of the leading golf and leisure resorts in the UK.

It offers 2 18-hole golf courses - including one designed by Jack Nicklaus - a new, much sought after Sport, Health and Leisure Club, 2 restaurants, bars and a choice of accommodation. All this is set in magnificent Cornish countryside in a designated Area of Outstanding Natural Beauty. The story of St Mellion is one of extraordinary vision and success. The Bond family have been farming in the Tamar valley for over 250 years. In 1972, brothers Martin and Hermon Bond, who were farming a 40 acre holding with their parents, decided to diversify, inspired by their love of sport. They determined to create a premier International Golf Championship Club, and this is exactly what they have achieved - and they have expanded the farm to 1,200 acres as well! In addition to the 2 golf courses, St Mellion has brand new health and fitness amenities opened in 1997, including a 25 metre swimming pool, family leisure pool, sauna, spa bath, steam room, aromatherapy massage and beauty rooms, tennis, badminton and squash courts, aerobic studio, cardio-vascular gymnasium, snooker room and solarium. Country pursuits such as cycling, horse riding and guided walks to local places of historic and environmental interest are also available. The Hotel offers 3 star en suite accommodation and the 32 luxury Fairway Lodges have earned many awards. In addition there are 4 function rooms catering for meetings and conferences from 10 to 150 people.

St Mellion has 2 restaurants, one serving an excellent choice of main and 3 course meals, complemented by a wide-ranging wine list, which has won 2 AA Rosettes for cuisine. Upstairs is the attractive Garden Room Brasserie, where lighter meals, teas and coffees are served all day long. Lounge and Club bars are available to residents and members. The staff at St Mellion are friendly, professional and helpful, making the whole experience of visiting the club a relaxing and enjoyable one. Martin and Hermon Bond are understandably and justifiably proud of what they have created in this beautiful landscape, where everyone can enjoy first class golf and leisure activities in well-kept and magical surroundings.

USEFUL INFORMATION

OPEN All Year, 365 days.
CHILDREN Welcome. Creche, club, babysitting.
CREDIT CARDS Yes.
LICENCE Residential.
ACCOMMODATION 24 hotel rooms: 8 double, 16 twin, plus 32 luxury 1-4bedroom Fairway suites. All en suite.
PRICES From £31 per person per night, including full Westcountry breakfast. STAY FREE ACCOMMODATION AVAILABLE

RESTAURANT: award winning Restaurant overlooking 18th green. 3 course meal £22.50. Garden Room Brasserie serves tea, coffee, Snacks & main meals. Lounge & Club bars.
VEGETARIAN Always approx. 5 dishes.
SMOKING Non-smoking areas.
DISABLED Ramp to Garden Room.
PETS No.

TALLAND BAY HOTEL
Talland by Looe,
Cornwall PL13 2JB

Tel: 01503 272667 Fax: 01503 272940

AA/RAC XXX 4 Crowns Highly Commended.
One Rosette. 1996 GHG Caeser Award.

Talland Bay Hotel is set some 150 feet above sea level in a quiet, rural location on the coast mid-way between the bustling little seafaring towns of West Looe and Polperro. It is in a particularly spectacular and beautiful setting and one's first impression is of a lovely old house, mellow with age that has withstood the wear and tear of time for over four hundred years. It did not become a hotel until the late 1940's and it has never been better than in the loving and capable hands of Barry and Annie Rosier who have enhanced an already wonderful house, making it more delightful for the guests who come here, some regularly and some for the first time who are quite determined to return. It is that sort of place; welcoming, relaxed, informal, superbly run and with a staff who are as thoughtful and caring as the owners.

From the moment you step over the threshold the contented atmosphere is apparent, the light Reception Hall leads to the pretty, comfortably furnished, Drawing Room with its open fireplace for colder days. Each of the nineteen bedrooms has a private bathroom ensuite, some have four posters, a single room has a private garden and sea view. In fact the views over the glistening blue sea, from most of the rooms are stunning. Every room is individually decorated and has charming drapes and bed covers as well as a telephone, television, radio and hair drier amongst many nice touches. In the panelled dining room where an attractive collection of plates is on show, and a log fire burns cheerfully to enhance the candlelit tables laid with gleaming silver and glass, you will dine on menus offering the very best of regional produce, in particular fresh fish and other seafood from Looe, including locally caught lobsters, crabs and scallops, but also West Country cheeses and tender Cornish lamb, all complemented by over one hundred personally selected fine wines from around the world At lunch time snacks and light meals are served informally in the bar on on the terrace. Afternoon teas with home-made scones and lashings of Cornish clotted cream are memorable. Many people come to Talland Bay just for the view and to relax in the hotels two acres of carefully tended sub-tropical gardens. There is a croquet lawn and a putting green. Talland Bay Hotel surely has to be in the top echelon of Cornish hotels.

USEFUL INFORMATION

OPEN; February - January   **DINING ROOM;** Superb regional produce
CHILDREN; Welcome   **VEGETARIAN ;** Catered for
CREDIT CARDS; All major cards   **DISABLED:** No Wheelchair access.
LICENSED; Yes. Residential   **PETS;** By arrangement - small charge
ACCOMMODATION; 19 ensuite rooms   **GARDEN;** Wonderful 2 acres, sub-tropical,
Non-smoking dining room & 1 lounge   Croquet, putting
RATES:- High Season, from £69 D/B&B.   Low Season,from £59 D/B&B.
Rates include afternoon tea and morning news paper
Special promotion and Break packages:- Details on request..

PLYMOUTH HOE MOAT HOUSE
Armada Way
Plymouth
Devon PL1 2HJ

Tel. (01752) 639988
Fax (01752) 673816

RAC 4 Stars, AA 4 Stars,
ETB 5 Crowns.

The impressive Plymouth Hoe Moat House towers over the heart of the historic maritime city. From its rooms and public areas you are given breathtaking, panoramic views over the Hoe, the Sound and the city in every direction. The hotel's highly acclaimed restaurant, leisure facilities, range of bedrooms and suites, and its friendly service, all make a stay at the Moat House a memorable, relaxing experience.

Each of the 209 en suite bedrooms is luxuriously appointed, with colour teletext television, direct dial telephone, trouser press, hairdryer and tea and coffee making facilities. There is 24 hour room service, and a wide choice of room types available, from comfortable lower floor rooms to international class and the highest quality suites.

The famous Blue Riband Restaurant is known as one of the finest places to dine in the South West, specialising in fresh seafood, brought each day from where it is landed at the city's historic Barbican. An impressive variety of meals is available, with a good choice of a la carte and Table d'hote dishes.

If you feel like a drink, you can choose between the intimate atmosphere of the Sports Bar, which has a choice of wines, beers and spirits from all over the world, or the Terrace Bar, high up at the top of the building, where you can enjoy cocktails with stunning views of the surrounding city and the world-famous Pymouth Hoe and Sound.

The Moat House provides a vast range of services and activities for children, and everyone can enjoy the sports and leisure facilities of the Club Moativation, which include a heated indoor swimming pool, a sauna, sunbed, steam room and gym. Outside activities including golf, pony trekking, moorland walks, water sports and visits to the area's major tourist attractions can be arranged for you.

For business meetings, conferences and banquets the hotel can provide room for up to 500 people.

Whatever your requirements, the friendly, helpful and well-trained staff will do their best to satisfy them.

USEFUL INFORMATION

OPEN All Year.

CHILDREN Welcome.

CREDIT CARDS Visa, Mastercard, Switch, Delta, Diner's Club, American Express.

LICENCE Full.

ACCOMMODATION 209 en suite rooms.

PRICES From £99. Suites £125. Ring for more details, special breaks etc.

RESTAURANT Table d'hote £18.95. A la carte.

BAR FOOD Wide variety of meals available.

VEGETARIAN Good choice daily.

SMOKING Non-smoking areas.

DISABLED 2 toilets and some ramps.

PETS No.

GARDEN No.

JUBILEE INN
Pelynt
Near Looe
Cornwall PL13 2JZ

Tel (01503) 220312
Fax (01503) 220920

AA 2 stars RAC 2 stars
ETB 3 crowns

The village of Pelynt is conveniently situated just two miles from the South Cornish coast, between the popular resorts of Looe and Polperro. Its inn, the Jubilee, dates from the 16th century. This atmospheric old inn changed its name from The Axe in 1887, to mark Queen Victoria's fiftieth year on the throne, and many reminders of the queen have been included in the decor.

The Jubilee's low-beamed ceilings, open hearths and antique prints on the walls create the classic charm of a traditional inn, with roaring fires in the winter and fresh flowers everywhere in the summer. But it also has individual features which help to make it unique. One of these is the special spiral staircase, designed by the well known westcountry artist Stuart Armfield, whose distinctive and delicate paintings can also be seen on the walls.

The owners, Tim and Judith Williams, have been at the Jubilee now for thirty years. Their chef, Peter Catnach, and second chef, Mark Puckey, join with them in their committment to providing the best possible service in this historic inn. Their aim is to be 'casual but comfortable, relaxed yet efficient.' There are three bars, a restaurant, a residents' lounge and, outside, a large beer garden with childrens' play area.

In the bars, popular with locals and visitors alike, you can sample two traditionally made real ales: Draught Bass and the local brew, Trelawney's Pride, which was launched at the Jubilee in November 1995, after being blessed by the Bishop of Truro in Pelynt Parish Church.

The restaurant offers an impressive a la carte menu, specialising, as might be imagined, in freshly caught fish and seafood from the Looe fishing boats. The Sunday lunch is also highly regarded by visitors and locals. The Jubilee's wine list is extensive, and the bar food menu is an attractive mixture of traditional home-made fare with something a little more adventurous. For vegetarians there is always a good selection of dishes.

Pelynt is a good base for exploring east Cornwall. The inn is within easy reach of the coast, with its delights of boating, sailing, fishing and bathing, of the rugged mysterious beauty of Bodmin moor, and of several National Trust properties - Antony House, Cotehele and Lanhydrock. You can set off to explore the coastal paths and swim from secluded beaches, returning to the Jubilee and to a welcome that already feels like home.

USEFUL INFORMATION

OPEN All Year. **Bar: Mon to Fri 11am -3pm & 6-11pm; Sat 11am -11pm; Sun 12-10.30pm.**
CHILDREN Welcome.
CREDIT CARDS Visa, Access, Master, Switch.
LICENCE Full. SMOKING Allowed.
ACCOMMODATION 9 en suite rooms, 1 family room.
PRICES Double £56; DBB £84. Children half price, under 3 yrs free.

RESTAURANT a la carte menu. Seafood a speciality.
BAR FOOD Extensive range, home made.
VEGETARIAN Always 6 dishes available.
DISABLED No special facilities.
PETS Welcome.
GARDEN Large beer garden & play area.

TREVANION HOTEL
Hannafore
West Looe
Cornwall PL13 2DE

Tel. (01503) 262003
Fax (01503) 265408

email: 106165.1261@Compserve.Com
Internet: http://www.purcom.org/Trev

ETB 3 crowns

Beautifully situated in West Looe, overlooking the famous harbour, the Trevanion Hotel is a tastefully restored Victorian gentleman's house. Its owners, Paul and Jenny French, extend a warm welcome, and you will soon feel at home in their elegant rooms. The emphasis at the Trevanion is on discreet, personal service and attention to detail, ensuring that your stay is a comfortable and memorable experience.

Each bedroom has its own private facilities, television and coffee bar. There is a cosy television lounge and residents' bar, while the sun lounge, dining room and patio enjoy unsurpassed views over East Looe Bay and the south Cornish coastline. Everything adds up to create a spacious and relaxing atmosphere.

The hotel is noted for the quality of its food. All meals at the Trevanion are home cooked by Jenny French using fresh local produce. The menu is very flexible, and something vegetarian is always available.

The Trevanion Hotel is just a few minutes' walk from Hannafore Beach, and a short ferry ride from the busy and popular town of East Looe. One of Cornwall's most interesting ports, Looe has a wealth of interesting things to see, and there is much for all ages to do. Walking in the surrounding countryside is especially enjoyable, and ask about the Trevanion's Inclusive Short Break Walking Holidays, which cover the finest section of the Cornwall Coastal Path.

Fishing and sailing are also easily available in the area, and there are opportunities for golf nearby. Many historic houses and gardens are within a comfortable drive. In fact, whatever way of spending your holiday appeals to you, the Trevanion makes an ideal base, as its growing number of friends and regular guests will testify.

Anyone wishing for more information on the Hotel and the many attractions of its surrounding area is welcome to call the Trevanion on the Internet, at the site given above.

USEFUL INFORMATION

OPEN All Year.
CHILDREN Welcome.
CREDIT CARDS Access, Visa, Master,
LICENCE Residential.
ACCOMMODATION 12 en suite bedrooms.
PRICES B&B from £22 to £27 daily, £131 to £161 weekly. With evening meal from £32 to £37 daily, £193 to £223 weekly

RESTAURANT Residents only. Good home-cooked English meals, flexible menu.
SMOKING Permitted, but not in dining area.
DISABLED No special facilities.
PETS By prior arrangement.
GARDEN No, but terrace with plants and lovely views.
VEGETARIAN; Always dishes available.

FORTE POSTHOUSE PLYMOUTH
Cliff Road
The Hoe
Plymouth
Devon PL1 3DL

Tel. (01752) 662828
Fax (01752) 660974

AA 3 Stars

Ideally situated in the heart of Plymouth, with spectacular views across Plymouth Sound embracing the Breakwater, Drake's Island and Mount Edgecumbe, the Forte Posthouse is one of the city's leading hotels.

It provides comfortable facilities for all your needs, whether you are on business or taking a holiday, and offers luxurious surroundings, a high quality of food and drink, excellent service and many little 'extras'. These range from secretarial services, including word processing, faxing and copying, to Sky Sport in the bar.

Forte Posthouse possess over 90 hotels throughout the UK and Ireland, so they have plenty of experience and expertise when it comes to looking after their customers. But they also manage to make each place personal and individual, so that once you are inside, you forget about big chains and think only of the careful attention you receive and the relaxed, friendly atmosphere. As well as travellers and holidaymakers, you will see local, Plymouth people using the bar and restaurants; reputedly the Forte Posthouse has for many years made the best coffee in the city.

Each bedroom contains a well-stocked mini bar, tea and coffee making facilities and an interactive television. The restaurants, informal but smart and well-run, offer everything from Table d'hote meals to light snacks, international cuisine to fish and chips, while the vegetarian choice is one of the biggest anywhere. The hotel also offers meeting and conference facilities, including 3 rooms taking 100 people.

There is an outdoor heated swimming pool available from May to September, and all you have to do is step outside the hotel to be within easy walking distance of Plymouth's many attractions. These include the award-winning Plymouth Dome heritage centre, the atmospheric Barbican, the famous Hoe, and nearby golf clubs, parks and the spacious shopping centre. Or you can take a boat trip on the Tamar. From Pymouth it is a short drive to the fascinating Morwellham Quay near Tavistock, the Dartmoor National Park and the beautiful countryside of the South Hams.

The Forte Posthouse is one mile from the Plymouth railway station and three miles from the airport.

USEFUL INFORMATION

OPEN All Year.   **RESTAURANT** A la carte and Table d'hote menus.
CHILDREN Welcome.   **BAR FOOD** Available all day until 10.30pm.
CREDIT CARDS all major cards taken. **VEGETARIAN** Large menu always available.
LICENCE Full   **SMOKING** Some non-smoking rooms & areas.
ACCOMMODATION 106 rooms, all en suite.   **DISABLED** No special facilities.
PRICES From £69 per person per night. **PETS** Welcome.   **GARDEN** No.

THE HOLLAND INN MOTEL & RESTAURANT
Hatt, Saltash,
Cornwall PL12 6PJ

Tel: 01752 844044
Fax: 01752 849701

If you had ever met Kevin Almond who owns the Holland Inn you would soon realise that this talented man has a knack for running successful establishments. In addition to the Holland Inn he also has the WINDY RIDGE EATING HOUSE at Trerulefoot, which has grown from the time when it was just a stopping place for lorry drivers, into a good, inexpensive restaurant, where the food is plentiful and it is ideal for families. The Holland Inn, once a coaching inn, is equally good, if a little more sophisticated. You will find it in rural surroundings on the Callington Road. It is beautifully run and well known for the excellence of its food. The Non-Smoking Restaurant is pleasantly informal, the service excellent and the A La Carte menu is extensive. For example you choose from 11 starters which may include a Prawn Cocktail or Savoury Mushrooms. Then you have the choice of the Carving Table where hot roast joints are carved for you by the chef who then encourages you to help yourself to as many freshly cooked seasonal vegetables as you wish. Grills are cooked to order with steaks done exactly as you wish. For those who enjoy the traditional Fish and Chips or Scampi, you will not find better anywhere. There are salads, a number of side dishes and a special Vegetarian Menu. Desserts or Cheese and Biscuits round the meal off perfectly. For youngsters 12 and under there is a Rumbletums Menu. The wine list is well chosen from wines of the world. If you prefer it, you may eat in the Lounge where the food is just as good. There is also a Coffee Menu which is tempting.

Staying here is both good value and comfortable. Furthermore The Holland Inn is wonderfully situated for exploring either Devon or Cornwall. Good beaches are within easy reach, there are attractive villages, National Trust properties, some wonderful gardens and many other places to visit. The Holland Inn is close to many great golf courses and only 5 minutes away from the Championship Course at St Mellion in one direction and the testing and enjoyable Parkland Course at the China Fleet Club in the other. The accommodation, all in ensuite chalets, is kept immaculately and comfortably furnished, particularly good for families who incidentally have a nice non-smoking Family Room in the inn..

USEFUL INFORMATION

OPEN: All Year.	**RESTAURANT; Good value, varied menu.**
CHILDREN; Welcome	**GARDEN; Yes. Outside seating**
CREDIT CARDS; All major.	**BAR FOOD; Wide selection**
LICENSED; Full on.	**VEGETARIAN; Yes.**
ACCOMMODATION; 16 en-suite chalets	**WHEELCHAIR ACCESS; Yes.**

RATES:- All Year Single from £25 pppn B&B. Dble/Twin from £20 pppn.
SPECIAL BREAKS AVAILABLE ALWAYS:- Apply for details.

THE SNOOTY FOX
Morval, Near Looe,
Cornwall PL13 1PR

Tel/Fax: 01503 240233

One of the busiest and largest Freehouses in Cornwall, The Snooty Fox has become well known for its atmosphere, its hospitality and the warmth of the greeting from the owners Chris and Penny Barnes. Sometimes one finds with large establishments who have intensely busy times in the season, that the staff get so wrapt up in the necessity to work hard and fast that they forget to treat the customer as a person but this is not so here. Whatever time of the year you visit you will find a personal welcome. Since Chris and Penny took the pub over they have spent time and money refurbishing it to make it the sort of place they themselves like to visit. There is a flat access to both front and rear entrances, the Bar areas where Chris's lovingly tended Real Ales are much appreciated, have been made hospitable places to be and the large comfortable Restaurant is very inviting. The whole of the Snooty Fox is centrally heated but cheerful log fires create a nice atmosphere on colder days.

The Restaurant which seats 70 is non-smoking and has superb views across Looe Valley to the sea. Here you will be offered over 50 choices at any time and always with much local produce and fresh, locally grown fruit and vegetables which are delivered daily. On Sunday at lunchtime a traditional Roast Carvery is on offer and very popular it has proved to be. Children under 14 are not allowed in the Lounge Bar. Many people have discovered that booking the self-contained Function Room for special occasions provides them with an excellent venue for wedding receptions, private parties and sometimes business. It has its own bar and stage and can take anything from 25-120 persons. The catering is excellent and Chris, Penny and their staff will do everything in their power to make the occasion memorable.

Staying at the Snooty Fox is very comfortable. There are eight ensuite rooms including one single, a family suite with 4 beds and one 4 poster. Some rooms have views across the valley to the sea. They are all furnished in a modern style and have colour TV, Tea and Coffee facilities. Morval is ideally situated for anyone wanting to explore this part of Cornwall.

USEFUL INFORMATION

OPEN;Mon-Sat 11.30-3pm & 6-11pm
Sun: 12-3pm & 7-10.30pm
CHILDREN; Welcome
CREDIT CARDS; Master/Visa
LICENSED; Full On
ACCOMMODATION; 8 en-suite rooms
PETS; No
RATES; B&B from £60 per double room.

RESTAURANT; Good food
Sensible prices
BAR FOOD; Wide range
VEGETARIAN; Always a choice
DISABLED ACCESS; Yes
GARDEN; 3 acres at head of valley
Large car park

THE CARPENTERS ARMS,
Lower Metherell,
Nr. Callington, Cornwall PL17 8BJ

Tel/Fax: 01579 350242

The Tamar Valley is designated as an area of outstanding natural beauty and in its midst is the sleepy village of Lower Metherell. The focal point of this little village is the 15th century Carpenters Arms, as popular with local people as it is with visitors who seek it out because of its welcoming atmosphere and the certain knowledge that they will be well fed and if they are staying will find the accommodation comfortable and well appointed.

Don Mills is the landlord and he prides himself on running a friendly inn in a relaxed and informal manner that belies how efficient he and his staff are. Everything seems to hum along on oiled wheels however busy it is. The pub has three double letting rooms which have just been made ensuite and are charmingly furnished with four poster beds, television, hostess tray, complimentary chocolates and sherry. The pretty restaurant with its pink and blue table cloths gracing tables laid with shining cutlery and sparkling glass, seats 43 and has an excellent a la carte menu whilst in the bar at lunchtime one can have a basket meal or choose from the comprehensive Blackboard Menu. A first class full English Breakfast is served every morning.

The Carpenters Arms makes an excellent base from which to seek out many of Cornwall's great attractions. The Tamar Valley Railway Line has a 50 minute ride from Gunnislake to the city of Plymouth passing through the Tamar Valley. Cotehele, belonging to the National Trust is one of the oldest houses and gardens in Cornwall and stands on the banks of the River Tamar. Morwellham Quay is the only place in the world where you can go by train into a real, ancient copper mine. There are wonderful walks, beaches within easy distance, fascinating fishing villages and so much more.

USEFUL INFORMATION

OPEN; All year except Xmas.	**RESTAURANT; Good a la Carte menu**
CHILDREN; Welcome	**BAR FOOD; Basket meals lunchtime only**
CREDIT CARDS; None	**Comprehensive Blackboard menu**
LICENSED; Full On	**VEGETARIAN; Always a choice**
ACCOMMODATION; 3dbl	**DISABLED ACCESS; Not suitable**
PETS; Public Bar & Patio. Not bedrooms	**GARDEN; Patio. Eating & Sitting area**

RATES:- Double from £27.50. Double room single occupancy £40 pppn B&B.

CALLISHAM FARM
Meavy
Near Yelverton
Devon PL20 6PS

Tel. and Fax (01822) 853901

Callisham is an atmospheric stone-built farmhouse, offering bed and breakfast accommodation, nestling in the Meavy valley within the Dartmoor National Park. It is half a mile from Meavy village, and although Plymouth is only a twenty minute car journey away in one direction, and Tavistock about the same distance in another, the setting is idyllically rural. Built on the site of the fifteenth century manor house, Callisham is everybody's image of a traditional Devon farm, with flagstone floors, beamed ceilings and inglenook fireplaces. The Lovaton Brook flows through the meadows next to the house.

Callisham is a family home, run by Mrs Esme Wills, who trained in all aspects of hotel management, with help from her husband Brian, who was a chef before taking up farming eleven years ago. Their daughters Jaime and Leanne also lend a hand when needed.

A real English breakfast is provided, fresh and tasty, with large quantities if required. Vegetarian, vegan and other special diets can be catered for on request.

Callisham Farm is ideal for those wishing to explore the western edge of the moor. Excellent walking country surrounds it, and the popular beauty spot of Burrator Reservoir, with paths leading directly onto the moor, is just half a mile away.

USEFUL INFORMATION

OPEN All year.
CHILDREN Welcome.
CREDIT CARDS No.
LICENCE No.
ACCOMMODATION 2 en suite family rooms,
can be let as doubles; 1 other double room with bathroom nearby.
PRICES £17.50 per person per night. Children under 12 from £3 to £6.

VEGETARIAN Breakfast on request.
SMOKING No.
PETS By arrangement.
GARDEN Large with table and chairs.

THE BRASSERIE,
Ocean Quay,
Richmond Walk,
Plymouth PL1 4LS

Tel: 01752 500008

Looking at The Brasserie from outside one could not imagine the number of well known people who have eaten and enjoyed both the meal, the wine and the hospitality. Sir Robin Knox-Johnston visits regularly, many of the local media personalities find this slightly out of the way eaterie ideal. Here they can relax and be themselves. You will find The Brasserie at the entrance to the Mayflower Marina where yachts of all shapes, colours and sizes are moored alongside the pontoons. For this reason a large proportion of the clientele is the yachting fraternity but Plymouth business people come here to have a quiet meal at lunchtime, perhaps to get away from the office but more often than not to entertain clients. The decor is interesting. In the bar there is much to remind one of matters nautical and the remarkable draping in the restaurant makes one believe that one is dining in a marquee but with all the comfort of an elegant establishment. The tables are attractively laid with pristine tablecloths, shining cutlery and sparkling glass and always a small vase of flowers. On a fine day the patio has the air of the continent with happy chatter as people sip their drinks and savour the beautifully cooked food. One of the most entertaining times to come here is at lunchtime on a Sunday, a strictly informal affair, but not to be missed.If one had to succinctly sum up The Brasserie one would say that it has a strong French feeling with the additional bonus of being part of a flourishing Marina.Chris and Eileen Hadlington are your hosts and aided by their excellent staff they achieve something very special here.

USEFUL INFORMATION

OPEN;All year 11-3pm & 7-11pm 7 days in Summer
Winter: Closed Sun. Mon.Tues nights
CHILDREN; Welcome
CREDIT CARDS; Visa/Master/Switch
LICENSED; Full + Childrens licence
PETS; Yes on leads

RESTAURANT;Brasserie style
Specialising in Fish and Seafood
BAR FOOD; Light meals
VEGETARIAN; Catered for
DISABLED ACCESS; One step.Toilets
GARDEN; Patio area

KINGFISHER COTTAGE
Mount Tavy Road
Tavistock
Devon PL19 9JB

Tel. (01822) 613801

ETB 2 Crowns,
Commended.

Kingfisher Cottage, situated in a peaceful conservation area by the River Tavy, just two minutes from the busy centre of the major Dartmoor town of Tavistock, is a newly built character cottage offering comfortable Bed and Breakfast accommodation.

It was built in 1989 of local stone and Dartmoor granite by its owner-occupiers, George and Maureen Toland, and specially designed for the convenience of their guests, whilst blending in beautifully with the distinctive style of the older houses in the town. George, a builder by trade, is also a keen gardener, and provides all the flowers for the hanging baskets, which recently won him an award, shared by a neighbour, for the best display in Tavistock. Kingfisher Cottage has ample parking.

Inside the cottage, Maureen ensures that guests enjoy the best possible facilities and catering. Her three bedrooms, one en suite, one double and one twin, take up to six people, all have colour television and tea and coffee making facilities. Breakfast is a full, traditional English meal, using fresh local farm eggs and bacon and sausages made by a local butcher, Paul Howells, on his own premises.

Tavistock is a fascinating old town, and the surrounding area is rich in beauty, with many interesting places to visit, including Buckland Abbey, the Garden House and Morwellham Quay. The whole of Dartmoor National Park, with its myriad attractions, is on the doorstep.

USEFUL INFORMATION

OPEN All Year.
CHILDREN Welcome - cots available.
CREDIT CARDS Not taken.
LICENCE No.
ACCOMMODATION 3 rooms: double, twin and en suite. All with colour TV and hot drink facilities.
PRICES From £15 per night. Children sharing with 2 adults, £9. Cots £2.

SMOKING Non smoking house.
DISABLED No special facilities.
PETS Small dogs by arrangement.
GARDEN Runs down to river. Breakfast on patio in summer.

GABBER FARM,
Down Thomas,
Plymouth, Devon PL9 0AW

Tel/Fax: 01752 862269

ETB Two
Crowns
Commended

If you enjoy the friendly, informal hospitality of a farmhouse then Gabber Farm is the place for you. It is situated in an area of outstanding natural beauty, close to good beaches and only a short bus ride into the historic city of Plymouth with its superb Plymouth Hoe and harbour, probably one of the finest in the world, certainly one of the most stunning. From Gabber Farm you can go for wonderful walks on the farm itself, explore the coastal paths, hire bikes in the village if you prefer not to be on shank's pony. Dartmoor is no distance away and just up the coast there is Dartmouth, Salcombe, Kingsbridge and the ancient town of Totnes, as well as a host of delightful villages and National Trust properties all begging to be explored.

Margaret MacBean is your hostess, and this caring, cheerful lady is always delighted to welcome her guests and make them feel at home in the farmhouse which is 13th century in parts. The house is wonderfully atmospheric with its low ceilings, big fireplaces and a sense of the past mixing happily with the present. There are five well furnished bedrooms, two of which are ensuite. Each room is centrally heated and has a beverage tray. Families are especially welcome. Breakfast is a wonderful farmhouse meal which will set you up for the day and at night the optional evening meal is a three course affair with traditional dishes and superb home-made soups.

USEFUL INFORMATION

OPEN; All year   **DINING ROOM; Good farmhouse breakfast**
CHILDREN; Welcome   **And home-cooked 3 course evening meal**
CREDIT CARDS; None taken   **VEGETARIAN; Catered for**
LICENSED; No   **DISABLED ACCESS;Not suitable**
ACCOMMODATION; 5 rooms, 2 ensuite   **GARDEN; Yes. Working farm**
RATES:- High Season,£16/£18 pppn.B&B. Weekly Rate, £100/£110.pp.B&B.
Low Season, £24/£26 pppn D.B&B Weekly Rate, £150/£160 pp.D.B&B.
Children, Under 2 yrs free/.up to 10 yrs Half price. 10/13 yrs. 75% of Adult Price.
Special rates for Senior Citizens :- Details on request.

CHAPTER SIX

Mid & South Cornwall : From Callington To Truro

Chapter Six

"The whole terra firma, or body of the land, makes this part of the isle of Britain seem to be one solid rock, as if it were formed by Nature to resist the otherwise irresistible power of the ocean."
Daniel Defoe

CHAPTER SIX

MID AND SOUTH CORNWALL FROM LAUNCESTON TO TRURO

U nless you are approaching Cornwall from the far north west of Devon, you enter the county over the River Tamar, which divides it almost totally from the rest of Britain. The crossing is, of course, experienced most spectacularly at Plymouth, whether you are making it by ferry, railway bridge or road bridge. Despite the similarity of the terrain on both sides, the scale of the crossing alone makes it feel as if you really are leaving England for another country.

Even if you are only coming into Cornwall between Tavistock and Launceston, where the river is spanned by a modest road bridge, the sense of entering a new land is strong, emphasised by the bilingual road signs which use both the English 'Cornwall' and the Cornish 'Kernow.'

Cornwall is undoubtedly 'different'. People often struggle to define just where the difference lies, but it is definitely more than a mere romantic cliche. Most would agree that there is something mysterious, elemental, deeply resonant and haunting, about this near-island, a long, tapering granite peninsula right at the end of Britain. The usual lists of attributes, containing ingredients such as unspoilt sandy beaches, steep, whitewashed fishing villages, melancholy ruins of mine buildings, cream teas and pasties, do little to convey this special atmosphere. Cornwall is much too powerful a place to be described by words like 'quaint' and 'picturesque.'

The comparison with Devon is especially striking. It was stated in the Introduction that the two counties tend to appeal to different temperaments; people who feel at home in one probably don't connect quite so strongly with the other. As someone who has lived in both counties put it to me, 'in Devon you're protected, in Cornwall you're not.' She meant, I think, much more than just the greater shelter from the wind afforded by the Devon combes.

Everything is harder and more exposed in Cornwall, from the underlying rocks to the quality of the light and the accents of the indigenous people. There is something about the starker, uncompromising nature of the landscape, and the relentless presence of the elements in Cornwall, which can make you feel peculiarly vulnerable. Here, it may seem, you are being encouraged to confront the basics of life, within yourself as much as in the environment. Some people find this energy of the county deeply invigorating, and certainly it has given power and vision to a great many artists and writers, just as it once fired the Celtic saints and missionaries.

On a more fundamental level, the people of Cornwall have always had to make a difficult living from this hard land, which they have done by subsistence farming, fishing the surrounding seas and digging beneath the ground for minerals. Engineers and inventors have always been amongst the county's 'great men', the best known probably being Richard Trevithick and Sir Humphrey Davey.

When it became impossible to live adequately at home, from about the mid 19th century, many thousands of Cornish people took these skills, especially mining, all over the world, so that it used to be said that wherever there was a hole in the ground, a Cornishman, or 'cousin Jack', would be found at the bottom of it. This great 'Cornish diaspora' has meant that there are still whole communities in the USA, South Africa and Australia of people whose origins lie in this haunted land, and whose ancestors probably left Britain without having ever set foot in England.

Throughout the last hundred years, while it has been discovered by increasing numbers of visitors and settlers, Cornwall has simultaneously become actively aware of its nature as an ancient Celtic country in its own right, one which, during the 'Dark Ages', was never quite absorbed into what became Saxon England (the Anglo Saxons originally referred to the land as 'West Wales'). It has a language, 'Kernewek', closely related to Welsh and Breton, which has been revived with extraordinary success, and which you can now learn at evening classes in most Cornish towns, and even take examinations in. It is as much like the language spoken in Britain before the Romans arrived as anything now can be.

The Cornish Gorsedd, which has met in various placesevery year since 1928, is a gathering of Cornish bards, modelled on the rather older Welsh bardic tradition. Members of the Gorsedd are men and women who have, in some way, contributed to the cultural life of the county or shown proficiency in its language. Some distinguished 'foreigners', like the composer Malcolm Arnold, are bards, together with Cornish-born scholars and poets. An American friend of mine, of Cornish origin, has a bardic name, 'Lef an Dhvrysow', which means 'The Voice of the Exiles.'

There are also a number of Old Cornwall Societies who study and keep alive the history and traditions of the county.

Cornwall enjoys, altogether, a cultural life of great energy and distinctiveness. Its ancient festivals and calendar customs, though inevitably a trifle self-conscious these days, are remarkably enduring, and anyone who has seen the effect of the Padstow May Day celebrations, on both its watchers and participants, will know that it generates deep magic still (and it is certainly less self-conscious than it would be in Surrey).

The county seems to be a more naturally musical one than Devon, at least as far as communal music making is concerned, with a rich choral tradition, especially of male voices (Cornish choirs specialise in basses, just as Welsh ones are famous for tenors). Brass bands flourish, as they always tend to do, in the more industrial areas, and the best of them - St Austell, St Denis, Camborne, Redruth, Mount Charles, Bodmin - are as good as any you will hear anywhere outside Yorkshire. Both traditions have produced performers, conductors and composers whose talent has earned them wider recognition beyond the county and both, especially in their emphasis on unity, and the social mission of music to edify and uplift, perhaps owe something to the energy of Methodism, which caught on very strongly here and is still a powerful element in Cornish life.

Cornwall's contribution to the visual arts in the last hundred years is of international significance, and will be dealt with when we reach the Penwith peninsula in chapter 7.

The Cornish sense of Celtic identity also manifests itself in a Nationalist movement committed - by entirely peaceful, democratic means, it must be stressed - to some degree of political separation from England, but you get the feeling that this is motivated by pride more than by anger. Two parties, the Cornish Nationalists and Mebyon Kernow ('Sons of Cornwall') regularly contest local and national elections.

Standing on the wild northern or western coast you can experience this Celtic element of Cornwall, its affinity with Wales and Ireland, very powerfully, with the ancient rocks and the remains of prehistoric activity all around you. But Cornwall, as the most southerly situated of the Celtic lands around Britain, is different from the others in the warmth and clarity of its climate, so that along with the Celtic crosses, holy wells, bards and stories of saints and heroes, you get sub-tropical plants in sunlit valleys and a purity of light that seems nothing less than Iberian or Greek. It can all be very disconcerting, but immensely stimulating as well.

Nevertheless, strange, elemental Celtic kingdom as it may be, Cornwall on another level is, and has been for a long time now, an English county, like Hertfordshire and Essex, with a county council responsible for prosaic things like roads and social services. Its ordinary buildings and landscapes, of town and country, are, as many have pointed out, often very prosaic indeed. Perhaps part of the peculiar atmosphere of the place comes not so much from the absence of this side of its life, as from the coexistence of it with the other, romantic side, and the consequent tension between them.

It is quite likely that some heads may have been shaken on reading the above statement that Cornwall is a 'county'.

Since the end of the last century there has been a tendency amongst journalists and writers of guide books, and even those responsible for official tourist publications, to refer to Cornwall as 'the Duchy' when what they actually mean is 'the county'. This has become so widespread that many, including people who should know better, use the words 'Duchy' and 'county' as if they covered exactly the same geographical and administrative area. Some are even under the impression that, being a Duchy, Cornwall cannot therefore be a county at all, as if the terms are mutually exclusive.

In fact, the 'Duchy of Cornwall' and the county you have just entered are completey different entities. The 'Duchy' simply means all the land owned by HRH Prince Charles, Prince of Wales, in his capacity as Duke of Cornwall.

The title was created in 1336 by Edward the Third, who gave it to his son, Edward the Black Prince, and since then it has been one of the offices traditionally held by the sovereign's eldest son, reverting to the crown when there hasn't been one. The Duchy's land is spread over 22 counties, and consists of 129,000 acres, only 20,578 of which are actually in Cornwall itself.

That the confusion exists in the first place is, in a way, indicative of the 'otherness' of Cornwall. No one, after all, would expect the lands owned by the Duke of Devonshire, who lives at Chatsworth in Derbyshire, to literally correspond to the county of Devon, and no one would dream of suggesting it. Yet here it has stuck, and has become another way of demonstrating Cornwall's distinctiveness. It is incorrect, though, however often it occurs, and this will be one of the few books you will read which doesn't perpetuate the error.

A very good means of seeing the county by way of a short, intense journey is to cross it by train. The main line from Plymouth to Penzance takes only a couple of hours to traverse, but is one of Britain's great train rides, and gives an unforgettable experience of many of the different landscapes to be found in Cornwall.

The first section, from the Tamar to Lostwithiel, skirting Bodmin Moor, is across deep valleys, steep sided and tree-filled. The countryside, although fertile, is immediately perceived as more challenging than that of Devon, without the rounded gentleness of contour. Travelling into Cornwall has often struck people as being like an inner, as much as an outer journey; the experience of moving into the landscape, going deep inside it, can be singularly like a symbolic voyage into the self. That some of the ancient inhabitants of the peninsula, with their close relationship with their surroundings, viewed it like this, is quite probable, and certainly it has effected many artists and writers in this way.

Past Lostwithiel, you reach the industrial region around St Austell, an area of white clay tips, chimneys, small fields and grey villages. The industrial ambience may be familiar to those who know Wales, the Midlands and North, but the colour of the waste tips gives it a typically Cornish sense of 'differentness'. Passing through Truro, surprisingly genteel, with its dominating Victorian gothic cathedral and safely enfolding hills - like a last reminder of England - you soon encounter the tortured mining landscape of Redruth and Camborne.

Finally you arrive at the magical Penwith peninsula, with its famous light and the almost abstract shapes of rock and headland against sea and sky. No one can fail to be moved as the train approaches Penzance, the last major town in Britain, facing the Atlantic across the low shore with St Michael's Mount on the left looking like a mystic island out of Arthurian legend. Beyond, you realise, is the lost land of Lyonesse, strange murmurs in the sunset, vague memories of meetings and partings... can any other train journey in Britain in the 1990s possibly be looked at in this highly romantic way with any degree of credibility? In Cornwall it still works, it is a valid response to the landscape.

You do not have to travel far into Cornwall to notice that the names of places become increasingly un-English, literally, because in the far west the people spoke their own language until at least the 18th century (various individuals are claimed as 'the last Cornish speaker'). In east Cornwall, the local accent is quite similar to that of west Devon, and the place-names have Saxon elements, but as you go further down, the accent is quite different. This is because the people never spoke an English dialect, and when they did finally start speaking English they learnt the 'educated' version rather than a regional one. It is worth listening to the locals to hear how the names of places are pronounced, as it is not always clear from the spelling. People will appreciate your taking the trouble.

While a detailed introduction to the Cornish tongue is clearly outside the scope of this guide, an explanation of a few of the most common elements in the place-names might be useful: TRE (farm), PORTH (cove), POL (pool), PEN (end), NAN (valley), HAYLE (river). A vast number of places are also, of course, named after the CELTIC SAINTS of the 'Dark Ages', many of them Welsh, Irish or Breton, who established Christianity in the Westcountry long before the famous mission of St Augustine to convert the English which we all learnt about at school.

Cornwall has a number of beautiful GARDENS, some interesting HOUSES and CASTLES and many unusual MUSEUMS and 'HERITAGE' sites. Its coastal towns and villages are world-famous, while its inland towns, although not so immediately appealing, are all strongly individual.

The Celts have never been, on the whole, natural town dwellers, and most urban areas in Cornwall, except the fishing ports hanging on the cliffs, look planted rather than natural growths; their well-defined limits and prominent municipal buildings have an air of something imposed from outside. This is something which you don't feel, for instance, when regarding the towns of South Devon, but the visitor who is familiar with Wales or Ireland will recognise the look. As a 'foreigner' (though not entirely; I had a Cornish grandmother, which gives me at least a quarter of the nationality), I shall not presume to try and say, necessarily, what the character of each place is, but you will find that every town and village is remarkably different from the one next to it.

Here, more than anywhere, it is impossible to offer a mile-by-mile route around the county. The Cornish roads and landscape just weren't designed for that. Instead, each major place will be described, followed by its surrounding attractions in a way which I hope makes some kind of sense.

If you enter the county from north or west Devon by way of **LAUNCESTON** (pronounced 'Lanson' or 'Larnson'; Tourist Information 01566 772321) you get a very vivid sense of arriving at a place guarding a border. The old town on the hilltop, the only walled town in Cornwall, with castle and gateway, feels as if it is still on the frontier.

Launceston was once the county town, and the county assizes were held here until Bodmin took over that function in the 19th century; some judges would not, it was said, venture any further than here into this strange and disquieting county.

LAUNCESTON CASTLE (01566 772365), owned by English Heritage, was built after the Norman conquest by Robert de Mortain, half-brother to William the Conqueror. It was probably rebuilt and added to during the 13th century. It was always a grim stronghold, where prisoners were being incarcerated as late as the 17th century; George Fox, founder of the Quakers, was thrown into gaol here in 1656. During the Civil War, Cornwall was staunchly Royalist (and Devon almost entirely Parliamentarian) and the castle held out for the king until taken by Sir Thomas Fairfax in 1646.

In the town, the SOUTH GATE survives, now with an ART GALLERY above it. The streets are steep and narrow, with many interesting old houses along them, and individual small-town shops.

The LAWRENCE HOUSE MUSEUM (01566 773277) is a pleasant Georgian town house built by Humphrey Lawrence, a lawyer, in 1753. The collection includes charters, relics of the Napoleonic Wars, local objects and a display in memory of Philip Gidley King, who founded Launceston in Tasmania.

Launceston Parish Church, of St Mary Magdalene, has a strong granite tower and some striking external carvings, dating from 1542 when they were put here at the request of Sir Henry Trecarrel, after the deaths of both his wife and son. Trecarrel's house, of the same name (01566 82286), near the village of LEZANT, is sometimes opened by appointment, but ring first. The story of Sir Henry is told in a well known poem by one of Cornwall's foremost living writers, the poet Charles Causley, whose home town this is.

A popular attraction is the LAUNCESTON STEAM RAILWAY (01566 775665), on which Victorian steam locomotives operate on a narrow (2 foot) gauge along the course of the old North Cornwall Railway. It winds through the Kensey Valley to New Mills. At the Launceston end there is a MUSEUM, SHOP, PICNIC AREAS and CAFE.

The TAMAR OTTER PARK AND WILD WOOD (01566 85646) at **NORTH PETHERWIN** is a delightful place where you can see otters, deer, waterfowl,peacocks, pheasants and owls in natural surroundings. There are WOODLAND WALKS, a TEA ROOM and SHOP.

TREDIDON TRAILS (01566 86463) offers a series a specially designed trails in an attractive valley setting, challenging all ages. A rather more extrovert attraction is the TRETHORNE LEISURE FARM (01566 86324), where a great many activities are available for children, and there is a GOLF CLUB and LICENCED RESTAURANT for the parents.

Launceston itself also has a GOLF CLUB (01566 773442), and the town has an excellent LEISURE CENTRE (01556 772551) with an INDOOR POOL, SQUASH COURTS, GYM, SOLARIUM and FITNESS SUITE.

STOKE CLIMSLAND is a small village in rolling country with a restored church of the 15th century and an agricultural college based on what was once the Duchy of Cornwall Home Farm.

Nearby is the little market town of **CALLINGTON**, half way between Tavistock and Liskeard. Once a mining centre, and possibly associated with a stronghold of King Arthur, whoever he really was, it is a quiet place with few obvious attractions. Baring Gould in 1900 wondered whether it had a future, but it is surely enough for a place to be a quiet little town, with genuinely local pubs and shops serving the surrounding community. The church, of St Mary, has a fine tower with a peal of bells that has got itself into at least one popular folk song.

DUPUTH WELL, a mile away on the A388, is an ancient holy well with an almost complete well house built over it in the 15th century. It is cared for by English Heritage, and can be visited at any reasonable time. Traditionally its waters were a cure for whooping cough.

From KIT HILL, on the Tavistock road, you can see, on a clear day, Dartmoor, Plymouth Sound, Bodmin Moor and the clay tips around St Austell. NATURE TRAILS have been laid out, and it is wise to use them, as this area is riddled with old mine shafts and holes.

Moving westward, **LISKEARD** (pronounced 'Liskard' with the emphasis on the last syllable) is a lively little hill-town with a long history. It was one of Cornwall's Medieval boroughs, and one of its four Stannary Towns, where the tin was assayed (like the four around Dartmoor); the others were Lostwithiel, Truro and Helston. There was a castle, or at least a fortified place, near the site of the present church.

Liskeard was described by one writer in the 1970s as Cornwall's most 'progressive' town, but my impression is that it epitomises the nature and values of slightly old-fashioned, small town life. It still serves as a marketing centre for the surrounding area. It has narrow streets and some pleasant buildings of the 18th and 19th centuries, including the PASSMORE EDWARDS LIBRARY and WEBB'S HOTEL. An earlier building is the slate-hung STUART HOUSE where Charles the First stayed whilst campaigning here during the Civil War.

The town is dominated by the second largest church in Cornwall (after the one in Bodmin), St Martin's, mainly 15th century but with a tower rebuilt as recently as 1902.

LISKEARD TOWN MUSEUM (01579 342233) in West Street is a typical local history museum of relics and exhibitions, vividly showing the development of the place. The GUILDHALL dates from the 19th century, and is Italian in style, with a tall clock tower. On the site of the MARKET HALL is PIPE WELL, a Medieval water supply with four spouts. It has never dried up, even in the fiercest drought.

Liskeard has an enjoyable variety of SHOPS and PUBSwhere you can get a strong sense of the community. At MERLIN GLASS (01579 342399) you can see glass-making demonstrations and buy the finished product.

The town also has a LEISURE AND SPORTS CENTRE at LUX PARK (01579 342544), and the nearby STERTS ARTS AND ENVIRONMENTAL CENTRE (01579 362382) puts on dance, music and dramatic events. Around and about Liskeard are a great many attractions of all kinds, to appeal to all tastes.

One of the most original is PAUL CORIN'S MAGNIFICENT MUSIC MACHINES (01579 343108), a splendid collection of fairground organs, a wurlitzer, player pianos and other such instruments. You can reach it very pleasantly from the town by way of the railway line towards Looe.

At LYNHER VALLEY DAIRY (01579 62244), Netherton Farm, Upton Cross, you can see the process of making cheese, including Cornish yarg, a vegetarian cheese covered with nettle leaves. Lynher is a working dairy farm with NATURE TRAILS and a PICNIC AREA.

DOBWALLS FAMILY ADVENTURE PARK (01579 320578) has a huge adventure playground and miniature American steam locomotives pulling trains through an American landscape. There is much more for younger visitors to enjoy. LOCAL CRAFTS are also exhibited here.

Quieter pleasure can be obtained from the Forestry Commission's HERODSFOOT FOREST, a couple of miles south of the town, with WOODLAND WALKS, DEER and CABIN ACCOMMODATION.

At **CARNGLAZE**, just off the Liskeard to Bodmin road, there are SLATE QUARRIES dating from the Middle Ages, from which much of the slate which adorns many of the buildings in this part of Cornwall was obtained. GUIDED TOURS are available from April to October (01579 320251). As in South Devon, the slate-hung buildings give a very characteristic quality to the South Cornish communities.

BODMIN (Tourist Information 01208 76616) is quite a large town which yet retains a sense of intimacy. It is narrow and hilly, with a long main street, and though it lacks, maybe, any outstanding buildings and features, except the church, it is a good place to walk around.

Bodmin became the county town of Cornwall in the 1830s, replacing Launceston. It still is, although the County Council headquarters is at Truro, which is also the Cathedral City, but unless you are particularly fascinated by the minutiae of local government there is no need to bother too much about all this. Nowhere really serves Cornwall as a regional capital in the way Exeter does for Devon.

If you arrive by train you disembark some way out of the town at Bodmin Parkway Station, formerly Bodmin Road, which is one of the most totally rural stations it is possible to find on a main line. Enfolded by high hills, it feels like a minor halt on a small branch line. At a station like this, so remote and yet with such a major name as Bodmin's on it, you realise how far you are from London, even England.

Bodmin has the largest church in the county, dedicated to the 6th century Celtic saint whose name crops up all over the South West, St Petroc. The present building was originally Norman, but was largely rebuilt by the people of the town in the 15th century. The font and stained glass windows are worth seeing.

The town had an important priory, traditionally founded by Petroc, whose bones were kept here, until the Dissolution of the Monasteries, and though there is little trace of this today, the MUSEUM (01208 74159) occupies the site of a Friary. Inside, the museum has a large and comprehensive collection covering Bodmin's long history as a major focus of the county's life.

Another museum in Bodmin is that of the county regiment, the DUKE OF CORNWALL'S LIGHT INFANTRY, situated in the keep of the VICTORIA BARRACKS (01208 72810). Paintings, uniforms and relics tell the story.

The former BODMIN GAOL (01208 76292) can also now be visited. Dungeons, cells, stocks and pillory are all here, and after you have looked around there is a SHOP, CAFE and BAR.

Prominent for miles around, and virtually surrounded by the town, the BEACON HILL NATURE RESERVE is a peaceful place, dominated by a 144 foot high granite column in memory of a local hero, Sir Walter Raleigh Gilbert, whose name suggests that his ancestry was Devonian rather than Cornish, who died shortly after the Indian Mutiny.

Bodmin is a lively social, commercial and cultural centre for this area of Cornwall, with a great deal always going on. It is well served for leisure facilities, with the CORNWALL INDOOR TENNIS AND SPORTS CENTRE (01208 75715) and the LEISURE CENTRE, with a POOL, SOLARIUM and SQUASH COURTS (01208 72210). BODMIN HERITAGE DAY takes place in JULY.

The town makes a good base for exploring the middle parts of the county. For WALKERS and CYCLISTS there is the lovely CAMEL TRAIL which follows the River Camel westwards to WADEBRIDGE and PADSTOW and northwards to WENFORDBRIDGE. Bicycles can be hired: (01208 72557).

The area is rich in nature reserves and historic places to visit. BRENEY COMMON NATURE RESERVE, run by the Cornwall Wildlife Trust, is a site covering 180 acres, with heath, marshland and a series of pools left by the tin streaming of past centuries. Also owned by the Trust is RED MOOR NATURE RESERVE, a mile or so off the main road to Lostwithiel. This also has bogland, heath and pools. Both are beautifully laid out and maintained.

Craft lovers will find many outlets in the area. At the PENCARROW GALLERY, WASHAWAY (01208 841465), part of a lovely Georgian house set in 50 acres of GARDEN and WOODLAND, exhibitions are put on by the CORNWALL CRAFTS ASSOCIATION, and at nearby WENFORD is the CARDEW POTTERY AND MUSEUM (01208 851038).

LANHYDROCK (01208 73320), a nearby National Trust property, is sometimes described as the finest house in Cornwall. Overlooking the lovely River Fowey, surrounded by magnificent GARDENS and PARKLAND covering 450 acres, it is certainly a beautiful and atmospheric place.

The house was originally built in the 17th century by Sir Richard Robartes, a leading Truro merchant. Most of the mansion was destroyed in a fire in the 1880s, and was rebuilt in late Victorian style, incorporating what was left. The Gatehouse and North Wing are original. Altogether, 49 rooms are open to the public, and there are the usual National Trust facilities: RESTAURANT, SHOP, GARDEN SALES etc.

LOSTWITHIEL (Tourist Information 01208 872207) is a very pleasant, if unspectacular, little town lying around a gentle valley on the River Fowey, which is rather like a smaller version of the Dart. It was once a Stannary Town, and the seat of the Duchy (not the county) administration. It is the lowest bridging point on the river, which is crossed by way of a fine 15th century bridge. The 14th century spire of St Bartholomew's Church towers 110 feet above the rooftops.

The town has some attractive buildings of the 18th century, including the GRAMMAR SCHOOL. There is a small MUSEUM (01208 872207) in what was originally the CORN MARKET, a GUILDHALL and a few remains of the STANNARY COURT.

Lostwithiel is not a town on the major tourist routes, so its SHOPS and PUBS are geared towards the local trade rather than the visitor. If you like small places off the beaten track, quietly getting on with their lives, you may well wish to linger here.

The dramatic remains of RESTORMEL CASTLE (01208 872687), cared for by English Heritage, are just outside Lostwithiel. This is a very well preservedNorman motte and bailey castle, rebuilt in stone in the 13th century. It stands firmly on its mound surrounded by a moat, now dry, but the walls have fallen away from around the entrance, giving, somehow, a sense of imminent movement. During excavations in the moat, two skeletons were found, holding on to each other as they drowned, in some unknown tragedy of long ago. The famous warrior Prince Edward, the Black Prince, after he became Duke of Cornwall, is known to have visited the castle in the 14th century. It was besieged during the Civil War.

LOSTWITHIEL GOLF AND COUNTRY CLUB (01208 873550) is overlooked by the castle, and enjoys lovely views of the estuary.

At the mouth of this beautiful little river is the historic town of **FOWEY** (pronounced, like the river, as 'Foy'; Tourist Informatrion 01726 833616).

This lovely old place, with its secure natural haven guarded by castles, is very reminiscent of Dartmouth, with which it had, in the Middle Ages, great rivalry. It is the 'Troy Town' in the once-famous stories by 'Q' - Sir Athur Quiller Couch - and the little grey town described so lovingly by the Sea Rat in the 'Wayfarers All' chapter of *The Wind in the Willows*. It is a delightfully restful place, with its boat-rocking harbour, steep, winding streets, old houses and flower-covered walls. Popular as a YACHTING centre, it is still a working port, with ships coming to and fro carrying the china clay from the inland towns. However, the over-riding feeling is one of peacefulness.

So relaxed is Fowey, in fact, that it is difficult to appreciate its past importance as a naval centre. During the long Medieval wars with France the men of Fowey played a part out of all proportion to the town's size and remoteness. Even wilder than the men of Dartmouth, they sent 47 ships to the seige of Calais in 1346, nearly twice as many as London. They continued baiting and pillaging the French after Edward the Fourth achieved peace in 1475.

The church of St Finbarrus reflects the warlike history of Fowey. The original Norman church was destroyed by pirates, and the replacement was burnt by the French in 1456. The present one is noted for its high wagon roof.

There is an interesting MUSEUM (01726 832712) which is full of objects and displays illustrating the local history, emphasising the town's maritime importance and its literary associations. GUIDED WALKS around the old town are given on TUESDAYS from June to September (01726 833616).

About a mile from the centre of the town is TRISTAN'S STONE, a very old monolith with a Dark Age inscription on it. This is generally believed to be the tombstone of the historical Tristan or Tristram, who in the Middle Ages was transformed into the hero of one of the world's great love stories. It was originally situated near CASTLE DORE, an Iron Age hillfort a few miles upriver near **GOLANT**, which, tradition has it, was King Mark's castle. Standing here, it all seems a long way from Wagner.

BOAT TRIPS on the river are available from the Quay, and regular FERRIES will take you across the water to the little settlements of **POLRUAN** and **BODINNICK**, where there are boatyards and some excellent riverside and woodland WALKS. LANTEGLOS CHURCH is worth a look, as is POLRUAN CASTLE. This is the better preserved of the two harbour-mouth castles, which are looked after by English Heritage. Originally a great chain was stretched between here and ST KATHERINE'S CASTLE on the Fowey side, until the men of Dartmouth came and stole it, in order to stretch it between their own two castles.

At Bodinnick is a house called FERRYSIDE (not open to the public) where Daphne du Maurier lived from 1926. We are definitely in du Maurier country here, as just a little to the west of the harbour mouth, towards Gribbin Head, is MENABILLY, which was theinspiration for 'Manderley' in *Rebecca*. It is not open to the public either, but a way-marked CIRCULAR WALK from the nearby village of **POLKERRIS** takes you around the outside of the estate.

GRIBBIN HEAD is the easternmost point of ST AUSTELL BAY.

Moving inland now we shall approach St Austell by way of **ST BLAZEY**, where is to be found the MID CORNWALL GALLERY (01726 812131), a major outlet for CRAFTS and FINE ARTS.

ST AUSTELL (Tourist Information 01726 76333) is now the centre of the Cornish CHINA CLAY industry. It is mainly a large, modern town, with suburban housing estates, shops and industrial buildings which might be anywhere, but the sight of an old engine house on the skyline reminds you that this is a former tin and copper mining town. There are some older parts, however, with a more distinctive character, and the Parish Church has a good tower and the TOWN HALL is attractive. There is also an impressive railway viaduct.

ST AUSTELL BREWERY (01726 66022) is a successful small brewery which owns a chain of pubs and hotels around Cornwall. GUIDED TOURS of the brewery are often available, with, of course, samples of the ale at the end of the tour.

A.L.Rowse, the distinguised historian, poet and Shakespearian scholar was born near St Austell at **TREGONISSEY** in 1903, and a most unexpected literary association is the one between George Bernard Shaw and St Austell railway station; he finished his notorious attack on the medical profession, The Doctor's Dilemma, whilst waiting here for a train.

A mile to the south is **CHARLESTOWN**, a planned, model 18th century port which has featured many times in films and television programmes. The SHIPWRECK AND HERITAGE CENTRE (01726 69897) graphically tells the story of the port and the adjacent coastline, which has seen the ends of many fine ships. The centre claims to have a greater collection of shipwrecked material than anywhere else.

Nearby, at **CARLYON BAY**, is the CORNWALL COLISEUM (01726 814004), one of the largest concert and entertainment venues in the South West peninsula, where shows of all kinds happen throughout the year. Also at Carlyon Bay is CORNISH LEISURE WORLD.

For sport and recreation, St Austell has the POLKYTH LEISURE CENTRE (01726 61585) with sports facilities, pool, sauna, bar and restaurant. There are two golf clubs, ST AUSTELL GOLF CLUB (01726 74756) and CARLYON BAY HOTEL GOLF COURSE (01726 814250).

The town is surrounded by beautiful WALKS, and near BLACK HEAD, the western end of ST AUSTELL BAY, can be found the Cornwall Wildlife Trust's ROPEHAM CLIFF NATURE RESERVE, two miles of beautiful coastal woodland. A mile to the north is a particularly beautiful Holy Well at Menacuddle.

North and west of St Austell you are in the strange, rather compelling china clay country, which to me is one of the most fascinating areas of Cornwall. It is a landscape of semi-moorland, with gorse bushes growing profusely around the edges of the small fields, with their Cornish 'hedges', which are actually walls. There are squat, grey villages of low houses and chapels, stretches of white road, overgrown industrial buildings and, dominating it all, the unique white lunar mountains of the clay tips, brightly coloured pools and beautiful stones adding their impact to the glare. This is the landscape invoked in the intense, passionate and rather mystical work of the blind and deaf poet Jack Clemo, who has spent his life here.

The tiny, dusty villages have intriguing, poetic names: **STENALEES, ST DENIS, FOXHOLE, INDIAN QUEENS, BUGLE, NANPEAN**. It is, for me, an intensely musical landscape, the music being made by that unique institution, the British brass band. The sound of the medium is warm, full-bodied, and slightly nostalgic, and seems to match the scene perfectly. Indeed, you will probably not be in this area long before hearing it, because at least three of these places have bands today, and all of them did at one time. If you are within reach of the little village of BUGLE on the third Saturday of JUNE, you can judge for yourself the appropriateness of the music to the environment, by experiencing the famous OPEN AIR BRASS BAND CONTEST. This draws bands from all over the county and beyond. It is a unique event, and is as much a part of the culture of Cornwall as the May celebrations in Helston and Padstow.

Between Bugle and St Austell is the WHEAL MARTYN CHINA CLAY MUSEUM (01726 850362) which celebrates and interprets the industry which has created this landscape, past and present. Exhibitions, videos, a china clay trail and views of the present workings vividly tell the story. There is also a nature trail.

Just to the north of this strange area is the impressive ROCHE ROCK, a 60 foot high granite outcrop, with a ruined Medieval CHAPEL, dedicated to St Michael, clinging to its side.

A few miles south of St Austell, towards Mevagissey, is one of Cornwall's newest attractions, but one which has inspired millions.

THE LOST GARDENS OF HELIGAN (01726 844157), at Pentewan, have only been opened a few years, after lying, forgotten, beneath trees and undergrowth, for most of this century. They are already the most visited gardens in Britain, but somehow their magical atmosphere makes every visitor feel a personal relationship with the place; going to Heligan really is like returning to an old friend. There is no other garden quite like it, with its giant rhododendrons, Elizabethan mound, Italian garden, walled fruit and vegetable plots and greenhouses, all being restored as they would have been for the Victorian estate. Then there is the sub-tropical paradise of giant tree ferns and bamboos known as 'the jungle.' A day at Heligan is not to be missed.

The CORNWALL SPRING FLOWER FESTIVAL takes place here in APRIL.

From the walk down to 'the jungle' you get a very good view of the pretty little town of **MEVAGISSEY**, the archetypal steep, narrow-streeted, Cornish fishing settlement. Beautiful to look at, relaxing to wander round, it is a centre for FISHING and SAILING, and is understandably popular with artists and craftspeople. Amongst them is PHILIP GARDENER, whose POTTERY, selling his skilfully made stoneware, can be visited.

Mevagissey has a FOLK MUSEUM (01726 843568) with exhibits showing the domestic and working life of the community in times past. It also has an AQUARIUM (01726 843305) and THE WORLD OF MODEL RAILWAYS (01726842457).

Nearby is the POLMASSICK VINEYARD (01726 842239), where you can enjoy a GUIDED TOUR of the vineyard, look around the GARDEN and, inevitably, sample the products of the vineyard.

At **GORRAN HAVEN**, a tiny, once-important fishing port, there are fine, uninvaded beaches, good walking country and Iron Age fortifications. Colin Wilson, that most prolific author and thinker, has lived here very productively for 30 years, after leaving London to escape the notoriety of being an 'Angry Young Man.'

Moving inland again, at PROBUS is the award-winning 20 acre TREWITHEN GARDENS (01726 882764/883647). Laid out early in the 20th century, the gardens contain magnificent rhododendrons, camellias, magnolias and other shrubs and trees. There are woodland walks and a children's play area. Nearby are the PROBUS DEMONSTRATION GARDENS (01726 882597), started by the Cornwall County Council in the 1970s to encourage and inspire local horticulture. It describes itself as 'a place to get ideas'.

TRURO (Tourist Information 01873 74555) is, like Wells, one of those lovely English (sorry Cornwall, British) anomalies: a cathedral city and countyadministrative centre which is only the size of a small town. Surprisingly urbane, with its Georgian houses rising around the valley, like a memory of Bath, it is actually quite English in style, and can feel a long way from the Celtic land of Kernow.

Dominating the city is the late Victorian CATHEDRAL, dedicated to the Virgin Mary.

The diocese of Exeter, as mentioned earlier, included both Devon and Cornwall from the 11th century onwards, but in 1877 Cornwall again became a separate see, as it had been long ago when it was run from St Germans. Truro was chosen as the seat of the new diocese, and the first bishop was Edward White Benson, father of the literary Bensons (E.F., R.H. and A.T.) and later Archbishop of Canterbury. The cathedral, of Cornish granite, was started in 1880 and finished in 1910: the first English cathedral to be built since St Paul's. Its three pointed steeples are landmarks from a long way off; the central one is 250 feet high, and, as it happens, 250 miles from London.

John Wolcot, alias 'Peter Pindar', the satirical poet (see the section on Kingsbridge in chapter 3), practised as a doctor in Truro for several years, when the town had a social and intellectual life of some sophistication. In an earlier century the Elizabethan composer Giles Farnaby was born near here, though his ancestry was English rather than Cornish.

THE ROYAL CORNWALL MUSEUM AND ART GALLERY (01872 72205) contains important and extensive collections covering the history and archaeology of the county, as well as art works and ceramics relating to it. Travelling and seasonal exhibitions are also featured.

The TRURO THREE SPIRES FESTIVAL, with MUSICAL, THEATRICAL, DANCE, LITERARY and VISUAL ARTS events, is held every July.

The city has a wide range, for its size, of PUBS, HOTELS and RESTAURANTS, with many interesting SHOPS and GALLERIES.

BOAT TRIPS can be taken down the RIVER FAL from Truro - for times, ask at the TIC.

Near Truro, at **FEOCK**, which Pevsner thought looked more like a Devon village than a Cornish one, are the much-acclaimed TRELISSICK GARDENS (01872 865808), owned by the National Trust. Rare shrubs and trees, parkland and woods, as well as riverside walks with views down to Falmouth, make them a special and memorable experience. There is an ART AND CRAFT GALLERY at the HOME FARM COURTYARD where shows are put on by the CORNWALL CRAFTS ASSOCIATION.

Further down towards the sea, on a tidal creek of the Percuil River, which flows into the broad expanse of the CARRICK ROADS and thence into FALMOUTH BAY, is that much-loved and exquisite little place, **ST JUST IN ROSELAND**. It nestles in deep woods, and is a perfect sun trap. There is a tiny 13th century church in a churchyard filled with sub-tropical plants and religious texts. The water comes right up to the churchyard.

Opposite Falmouth, **ST MAWES** has one of Cornwall's finest CASTLES (English Heritage, 01326 270526), sitting opposite Falmouth, built by Henry the Eighth as part of his coastal defence system. It has three great circular bastions with gun emplacements, but this warlike pose is belied today by the beautiful GARDENS which surround it. In the vicinity of St Mawes there are some excellent WALKS. The village is popular with sailing and fishing people.

Chapter Six

ALVERTON MANOR,
Tregolls Road,
Truro, Cornwall TR1 1XQ

Tel: 01872 276633
Fax: 01872 222989

AA 3Star 2 Rosettes
RAC 3 Star ETB.
Four Crowns Highly Commended

Set on a hillside amidst 6 acres of private gardens, Alverton Manor is one of the finest hotels in Cornwall and an hotel of which the cathedral city of Truro is proud. Ten years ago the manor was the home of nuns, the Sisters of the Epiphany and 150 years ago the Bishop of Truro lived here but apart from the ghosts who contentedly haunt the house, and for the chapel which is now used for conferences and functions including Marriage Ceremonies, all signs of its religious past has disappeared and instead of austerity one now has the most luxurious comfort throughout the hotel. There are thirty four individually designed bedrooms, all ensuite and four of which are suites. There are lifts to the first floor and ground floor rooms are available. The public rooms are stunning. The 60 cover, non-smoking Terrace Restaurant with its soft colour scheme has tables perfectly laid with Irish linen, shining silver cutlery and sparkling glass. The food, in the modern English style, prepared by talented chefs has a well deserved reputation and the service is friendly, efficient and non obtrusive.

Conferences, seminars, special occasions and especially weddings which can be performed in one of two places in the hotel, are run perfectly, by a staff who are dedicated to ensuring that everything goes smoothly. For conferences all the relevant equipment is available.

Throughout the year there are Special Breaks available from a Champagne Weekend to a Garden Break which includes a trip to Tresco on the Isles of Scilly. Alverton Manor also offers you a chance to stay in the idyllic St Martins Hotel on the Island of St.Martins. Truro itself deserves exploration and you will find some wonderful gardens within easy reach as well as good beaches.

USEFUL INFORMATION

OPEN; All year **RESTAURANT; Modern English menu**
CHILDREN; Welcome
CREDIT CARDS; All major cards **BAR FOOD; Sandwiches available**
LICENSED; Full On **VEGETARIAN; Catered for**
ACCOMMODATION; 34 ensuite inc 4 suites **GARDEN; 6 acres**
Wheelchair access to parts of the hotel. **PETS; by arrangement.**
RATES:- Single Room from £63. Dble./Twin Room £99/£109. Suite from £130
and include a morning newspaper. All rates are for B&B, inclusive of VAT,

THE NARE HOTEL
Carne Beach, Veryan,
Nr. Truro, Cornwall TR2 5PF

Tel: 01872 501279
Fax: 01872 501856

RAC 4 Star + merit awards
AA 4 star 74%

Few hotels have a better position than The Nare Hotel at Carne Beach, Gerrans Bay with its wonderful views. The hotel is a long, low attractive building which looks as though it is contented with its situation. It has the virtue of not only being on a beach but close to many others and to the coastal path for those who enjoy walking. People come here to enjoy the relaxed, friendly atmosphere and appreciate the informality that exists - something that only comes about when a hotel is extremely well run. The Nare is frequently described as 'the country house by the sea'.

Within the hotel the emphasis is on comfort. All 38 bedrooms are ensuite with 30 doubles, 6 singles and 2 suites. Many of the rooms have sea views and some have balconies; all have direct dial telephones, television, a hostess tray with fresh milk, hairdryers and some have trouser presses. Every room always has fresh fruit and flowers and if the weather is a little chilly you will find a hotwater bottle! The elegant restaurant which has a reputation locally for its excellent cuisine, has arched windows and stunning views. Every table is immaculately laid with linen cloths and napkins, high quality glassware and sparkling cutlery. The imaginative chefs produce superb English cuisine including some Cornish specialities as well as mouth-watering pastry, and the well chosen wine list with its world wide choice complements the food perfectly.

In the 5 acre garden which is beautifully maintained, you can stroll, enjoy a drink or perhaps swim in the pool, which is heated from mid-May to mid-September, or play tennis on the all weather court. There is also an indoor heated pool, a childrens play area and a paddling pool.

With a Sauna, Hydro Therapy Spa, Beauty Clinic and a Gym, the Nare Hotel provides just about everything for its guests.

USEFUL INFORMATION

OPEN;All year except 3rd Jan-1st Feb.
CHILDREN; Welcome (Over 7 in rest)
CREDIT CARDS; Mastercard/Visa
LICENSED; Residential & Restaurant
ACCOMMODATION; 38 ensuite rooms
PETS; Rooms only except guide dog

RESTAURANT; Superb English cuisine
BAR FOOD; Not applicable
VEGETARIAN: A dish every day
DISABLED ACCESS; Ground floor rooms
GARDEN; 5 acres. Swimming pool.
Play area

TARIFF:- Single room £53 to £115 B&B. Double room £106 to £200 B&B.
Suite £263 to £420 B&B. All prices include morning and afternoon tea. VAT is inclusive.

THE CORMORANT HOTEL & RIVERSIDE RESTAURANT
Golant, Fowey,
Cornwall PL23 1LL

Tel/Fax: 01726 833426

Two AA Rosettes.
ETB Four Crown Commended.
AA/RAC Two Star.

Wonderfully situated beside and above the River Fowey, The Cormorant has stunning views over the whole Estuary and onto the National Trust timbered slopes beyond. At low tide Herons can be seen feeding in the shallows. An idyllic setting for any holiday or short break. This is a family owned and run hotel with George and Estelle Elworthy at the helm, Estelle's mother Carla Keen helps her run the front of the house and John Keen, a talented chef, who has been awarded 2AA Rosettes provides the delicious meals for which the hotel and its restaurant is renowned. The family have the right approach to hotel keeping interlacing an informal and friendly atmosphere with the abilities of the professional. People come to The Cormorant knowing they will be well looked after and tend to repeat their visits with a certain amount of regularity. Families are especially welcome here.

There is no question that the views dominate the hotel and frequently the conversation especially if guests are visiting for the first time but no matter how stunning the scenery one must never underestimate the attractive decor in the rooms both public and bedroom. There are seven doubles and 4 twin bedrooms, all ensuite and all have been individually decorated in different styles. There are romantic honeymoon rooms amongst them. Every room has colour TV, a hostess tray and a direct dial telephone and all have full length windows overlooking the estuary. Downstairs the large lounge with its deep, comfy armchairs and sofas has a log fire, and in the bar the cheerful chatter in the evening draws guests in to meet friends and to greet newcomers. The Restaurant will delight everyone both with its decor and choice of imaginative, beautifully cooked and presented fare. The well chosen wines come from around the world. To complete the picture of this nice hotel, there is an indoor swimming pool, with magnificent views over the estuary, which has a motorised roof that can be retracted in the summer months. It is a hotel that richly deserves its 2 Star AA/RAC, ETB's 4 Crowns Commended and 2 AA Rosettes.

USEFUL INFORMATION

OPEN; All year except 2 weeks in January
CHILDREN;Welcome
CREDIT CARDS;Master/Visa/Amex/JCB
LICENSED; Residential
ACCOMMODATION; 11 ensuite bedrooms
PETS; Yes. Small charge
RATES:- All Year, High Season £84.pppn B&B.

RESTAURANT; Award winning chef
who produces imaginative menus
VEGETARIAN; Upon request
NO WHEELCHAIR ACCESS.
GARDEN; Yes + indoor swimming pool
with motorised roof for summer
Low Season £70 pppn B&B

LAMPEN MILL
St Neot
Liskeard
Cornwall PL14 6BP

Tel. (01579) 321119
Fax (01579) 348055

Lampen Mill, a recently-restored mill dating from 1740, complete with water wheel, is a unique and comfortable Guest House, nestling in complete seclusion in the lovely Cornish countryside. It is situated in an Area of Outstanding Natural Beauty and close to Bodmin Moor, yet is also within easy access of both the A30 and A38 main roads. This makes it an ideal base for anyone touring both Cornwall and Devon.

The mill is the home of Heather and Chris Pearce and their two children, Ben and Laura. Heather ensures that guests are given a warm and friendly welcome, while Chris, a local man with a wealth of knowledge of the area, is always happy to advise on places to go and things to do. He is a professional builder, and lovingly restored and converted the mill himself, which was totally derelict when the family bought it. The rich beauty of Columbian Pine is evident in the heavily beamed ceiling, the strong doors and the unique spiral staircase which is a special feature of the house. A large fireplace of granite and local stone houses the woodburning stove, while an underfloor heating system ensures warmth and comfort at all times.

Lampen Mill offers Bed and Breakfast with a choice of Evening Meals by arrangement. There are three bedrooms: one large family double with en suite shower, a good sized double with en suite shower, and a twin with en suite bathroom. They all have restful views over the surrounding countryside, tea and coffee making facilities and colour television. Guests have their own private dining area and lounge, and are welcome to relax in the conservatory or stroll in the extensive garden. In fine weather it is good to sit by the large ponds, enjoying a cream tea and watching for the resident kingfishers, as well as herons, wagtails, dippers and Canada geese. The mill is a haven for wildlife of all kinds.

Guests who wish to take an evening meal are offered two choices. There is a three course a la carte menu, for example: prawns in marie rose sauce and Mexican salsa salad, chicken pie with saute potatoes and choice of vegetable, fresh fruit pavlova and clotted cream. Alternatively you could have a simpler family style dinner, consisting perhaps of lasagne with broccoli and crusty bread followed by apple crumble and clotted cream.

Lampen Mill is surrounded by places of interest, including the nearby village of St Neot, steeped in Cornwall's mining history, the famous Lost Gardens of Heligan and the wild and mysterious Bodmin Moor. Whatever brings you to this lovely area, the Pearces look forward to meeting you and welcoming you to their beautiful home.

USEFUL INFORMATION

OPEN All Year.
CHILDREN All ages welcome. Cot provided.
CREDIT CARDS No.
LICENCE No, but please bring your own.
ACCOMMODATION 3 en suite bedrooms.
PRICES B&B £20 - £22 per person.

RESTAURANT Evening meal: choice of a la carte for £15 or family style for £10.
VEGETARIAN If required.
SMOKING No.
DISABLED No special facilities.
PETS No.
GARDEN Large.

FOWEY HOTEL,
Fowey,
Cornwall PL23 1HX

Tel:01726 832551
Fax:01726 832125

Walking into the Fowey Hotel is liking going back over a hundred years to the Victorian era. It is gracious, dignified and beautifully appointed with the service that our ancestors would have expected in which the guests comfort comes first.. It stands in one acre of luscious gardens complete with a Tea Garden and faces the glory of the Fowey estuary with its ever changing moods and busy marine life. Fowey has always been popular with the yachting fraternity and particularly well known to the afficionados of Daphne Du Maurier who lived nearby and used this part of Cornwal for the setting of many of her books. In fact the hotel took a major part in the very successful Daphne du Maurier Festival held in May 1997. Many famous people have stayed here since it first opened its doors in 1882 and during World War I it became a convalescent home for wounded soldiers. Its role in World War II was slightly different - it was taken over by the Americans who used it for their Naval Amphibious Forces.

Within the hotel the needs of the modern traveller have been carefully attended to. The 28 bedrooms all facing the sea, are ensuite and have television, direct dial telephones and a hostess tray. Some of the rooms are termed 'superior' and have additional touches such as jacuzzis. The furnishings throughout the hotel are attractive and colour co-ordinated. The bar is a cheerful meeting place for locals and visitors throughout the day and the 60 cover restaurant is sumptuous It has always had a name for good food but now it has been completely refurbished and is a delight to dine in. Whilst one is studying the menu or waiting for the arrival of the food, there is an opportunity to look out over the estuary - therapeutic after a busy day and certainly an aid to the digestion! . There is a wonderful family atmosphere about the Fowey Hotel which is why so many people return again and again having discovered its virtues.

USEFUL INFORMATION

OPEN;All year

RESTAURANT; English/French cuisine

CHILDREN; Welcome

BAR FOOD; A selection of hot & cold dish

CREDIT CARDS; Visa/Master/Switch

VEGETARIAN;Always available

Delta/Amex

DISABLED ACCESS;Welcome.. Lifts

LICENSED; Full On

GARDEN; Yes. Eating & Drinking. Tea Garden

ACCOMMODATION; 28 ensuite rooms   PETS; Yes. 3.00 per day

RATES;- High Season from £67/ £73 pppn. Low Season from £53/£59.pppn.

Prices include Full English breakfast and Dinner. Spring Breaks :- Prices on request.

PORTH AVALLEN HOTEL
Sea Road,
Carlyon Bay, St Austell,
Cornwall PL25 3SG

Tel:- 01726 812802.
Fax:- 01726 817097.

AA Three Stars.
Egon Ronay Recommended,
Les Routiers.

Carlyon Bay is one of Cornwall's greatest beauty spots and has the added benefit of being centrally situated for visiting all of Cornwall's attractions. It is on the coastal path and ideal for country walks.The Porth Avallen Hotel in Sea Road is just a few minutes away from the bay with its one mile stretch of beach and beach attractions. It is only a short walk from the fascinating 200 year old harbour at Charlestown - a harbour so small that one watches in awe as ships enter and leave.Here too you will find the romantic tall ships moored.The Lost Gardens of Heligan and many other beautiful gardens and National Trust Properties are within easy reach as well as some excellent golf courses.

The Hotel was once a family home but judicious additions have extended it into an elegant comfortable place to stay, without taking away the atmosphere of a welcoming home. The oak panelled lounge and staircase are impressive and every room is charmingly decorated, light and airy. People from all walks of life enjoy staying at Porth Avallen. Visitors include such famous names as Prunella Scales, Richard Wilson and Tony Blackburn. The 24 ensuite bedrooms are well equipped with colour television, hostess trays and many other tasteful touches. Three rooms have fourposters - wonderful for honeymoons or a romantic weekend. Both the restaurant and the bar are inviting and the cuisine is delicious. Choose either from the Table d'hote which changes daily or from the excellent A La Carte menu which includes many varied dishes served with local fresh vegetables. In addition the Porth Avallen has facilities for conferences for up to 70 people and can cater for banquets or buffets for up to 80 people. The beautiful setting is ideal for wedding receptions. Mary and Neil Perrett are the owners whose professionalism shines through and they have an efficient, caring, long serving staff to ensure that everyone enjoys the Porth Avallen. When you realise that 90% of the guests are revisiting or have come on the recommendation of other satisfied customers, one does not need to emphasise how highly regarded this hotel is.

USEFUL INFORMATION

OPEN; 1st Jan-26th December

RESTAURANT; Table d'hote and A La Carte. Open to non-residents

CREDIT CARDS;Visa/Master/Amex/JCB/Switch/Delta.
LICENSED; Residential & Restaurant
ACCOMMODATION; 24 ensuite bedrooms
GARDEN; Delightful. For sitting, eating, drinking

NO WHEELCHAIR ACCESS.
PETS; No
VEGETARIAN, Catered for.

RATES:- High Season,from £44 pppn B&B. Double or Twin. £61.50 Single occupancy.
Low Season,from £38 pppn B&B. Double or Twin. £52.50 Single occupancy.

SHARKSFIN HOTEL,
The Quay,
Mevagissey, Cornwall PL26 6QU

Tel:- 01726 843241
Fax:- 01726 842552.

ETB. Three Crowns.
AA Two Star.
Les Routiers (Casserole Award)

One sometimes comes across something different in the world of the hotelier and restaurateur and this is the case with the very interesting Sharksfin Hotel on the Quay at Mevagissey. It is a former eighteenth-century Pilchard warehouse and factory and to add to the fascination it still contains many original features. Today it has been tastefully converted into an 11 bedroom Hotel and Waterside Restaurant which dominates the waterfront. Mevagissey at the foot of the beautiful Pentewan valley and still with a working harbour, is described as 'The real Cornwall' with some justification. It is full of the atmosphere of the past with its winding streets, pretty cottages and added to this is the Sharksfin right on the Quay.

Family run by June Winter and her kin, it is a welcoming establishment where the evidence of total professionalism is very strong and yet it makes one feel relaxed and contented. June and her staff work very hard to ensure your stay is a happy and memorable one. The hotel has 11 prettily furnished bedrooms, eight of which are ensuite and the other three have showers. Every room has colour TV and tea/coffee making facilities, direct dial telephones, and six rooms have stunning harbour views. It is wonderful to wake up in the morning to the sounds of the sea and fishermen at work. Breakfast is a sumptuous affair with a lot of choices and always freshly cooked. In the Restaurant dinner is always memorable and offers both Table d'Hote and an A La Carte menu. Fresh fish and seafood is always available brought in locally from the harbour or closeby. Mevagissey Crab and Lobster comes directly from the fishing boat Danielle Louise, Chargrilled Monkfish, Salmon En-Croute, Scallops, Mussels and Oysters from the Helford River and other delicious fish appear regularly on the menu but for those who prefer meat or poultry there is an equally good choice of beautifully presented dishes. Open to non-residents, the Restaurant should always be included in a visit to Mevagissey.

The area around Mevagissey entices everyone to explore. There are picturesque villages, stately homes and above all locally the Lost Gardens of Heligan, the largest garden restoration project in Europe, which has to be seen to be believed.

USEFUL INFORMATION

OPEN ; February - December
CHILDREN; Welcome
CREDIT CARDS; All major cards
LICENSED; Yes
ACCOMMODATION; 11 ensuite rooms
PETS;Small dogs, small charge

RESTAURANT; Wonderful food especially
Fish and seafood caught locally
BAR MEALS; Bar snacks available
VEGETARIAN; Catered for
DISABLED ACCESS; No special facilities
SHORT BREAKS; Special terms

RATES; All Seasons, Single Rooms from £32 pppn B&B.Double Rooms from £32 pppn B&B
 Double Rooms with harbour views, from £35 pppn B&B.

HOTEL NEBULA
27 Higher Lux Street,
Liskeard,
Cornwall
PL14 3JU

Tel: 01579 343989

Higher Lux Street is a hill which leads to and from the centre of the small, market town of Liskeard. Half way up the hill is the Hotel Nebula which was built between three and four hundred years ago and to the uninitiated might look like a private house, once inside you will realise that it goes back a long way and has both space and charm. The old beams have been retained in the Bar where you may also have coffee and when the hotel was being refurbished a quantity of hand made bricks were found which now grace the bar and the back of the fireplace. Liskeard is full of interest, in Stuart House Charles I is presumed to have stayed and it is also said that Oliver Cromwell stayed in the Hotel Nebula. That probably accounts for the ghost which has been seen by a member of the family!

William and Daphne Rogers own and run the hotel with the help of a friendly staff whose aim it is to make your stay pleasureable. They are a mine of information on where to go and what to see in Cornwall which is very helpful especially to people visiting Cornwall for the first time. Within a short drive there are some excellent beaches, the delightful Looe and Polperro and many other enchanting villages. National Trust properties abound and the historic naval city of Plymouth is a mere seventeen miles away. Comfortably furnished, the hotel has a mixture of double, single and family rooms all of which have bathrooms with either shower or bath. Most rooms have colour television and all have tea and coffee making facilities. Food is always important and probably more so at holiday times when you have the opportunity to relax over meals. Breakfast at Hotel Nebula is a relaxed meal with a delicious, freshly cooked full English Breakfast offering several choices and always including as much toast and preserves as you can eat as well as freshly brewed coffee and piping hot tea. A Continental breakfast is available for those who prefer a lighter meal. Traditional English home-cooking in the evenings with a choice of starters including a very good home-
made soup with fresh crusty bread followed by a Roast of the day and a delectable sweet. The prices are reasonable and there is a special rate for people staying three nights or more.

USEFUL INFORMATION

OPEN; January-December. All day	**DINING ROOM; Good traditional English fare**
CHILDREN; Welcome	**BAR MEALS; Sandwiches to order**
CREDIT CARDS; Visa, M/card,Amex.	**VEGETARIAN; Catered for**
LICENSED; Full On with provision	**NO WHEELCHAIR ACCESS.**
PETS; Yes £10 per week	**GARDEN; No**
ACCOMMODATION;6 ensuite rooms	**RATES:- Single £25. Dble £47. Room rates.**
Special seasonal prices:- Details on request.	

THE OLD RECTORY COUNTRY HOUSE HOTEL,
 St Keyne,
Liskeard,
Cornwall
PL14 4RL

Tel: 01579 342617

One AA Rosette for good food.
ETB. Three Crowns Commended.

Comfort in beautiful surroundings is how one would describe this delightful Country House Hotel set in its own peaceful three acres of grounds surrounded by farmland and with beautiful views of the countryside. The house was built in the early 1800's and is now a family run hotel owned by Pat and John Minifie. The first thing that strikes one upon arrival is the homely, friendly, warm atmosphere. It combines the gracious charm of bygone days, cheery log fires on cooler evenings, with modern amenities such as central heating. It is clearly a much loved house and considerable loving care has gone into the furnishing which is of the highest standard and carefully chosen to complement the original architecture. Panelled doors, a black marble fireplace, a handsome staircase with barley-twist balysters, and velvet sofa's, are just a taste of the elegance which greets you.

The eight ensuite bedrooms are charming and have extremely comfortable beds. Two have fourposters to make an occasion special. All the rooms have colour television and well supplied beverage trays. For anyone not wanting to climb stairs or perhaps disabled there is an ensuite ground floor bedroom. The Old Rectory is not suitable for children under twelve years. You may bring a well behaved pet by prior arrangement. The food at The Old Rectory lives up to the standard that one expects in this gracious house. In the morning you will come down to a delicious full English breakfast offering a choice and you dine from an a la carte menu which includes traditional fine English cooking and the adventure of Continental cuisine. The chef is both talented and imaginative. Everything is home prepared, and the selection of table wines has been carefully chosen to complement the food.

St Keyne is situated off the little-used B3254, five miles from the picturesque fishing village of Looe, and three miles from the market town of Liskeard. The hotel offers an excellent centre for touring, boating, golf, sailing, tennis or fishing, and convenient to bowling and putting greens, riding stables and other activities.

USEFUL INFORMATION

OPEN;All year except Christmas
CHILDREN; 12 years & over
CREDIT CARDS; All major cards
LICENSED; Full On
ACCOMMODATION; 8 ensuite rooms
PETS; By arrangement. 2.00 per night

DINING ROOM; Delicious home-cooked fare
BAR FOOD; Not applicable
VEGETARIAN; Catered for
DISABLED ACCESS; Ground floor room
GARDEN; 3 acres

RATES:- High Season £30/ £35 pppn.B&B. Low Season £25 / £27.50 pppn B&B.
Special seasonal rates and Stay free accommodation :- Details on request.

THE WHITE HORSE INN
14 Newport Square,
Launceston,
Cornwall
PL15 8EL

Tel: 01566 772084
Fax: 01566 772090

This famous old inn in the centre of Launceston, the historical capital and gateway to Cornwall, is known to have one of the best restaurants in the area and a bar menu, second to none. Something of which Nick and Sharon, the licensees are justly proud. They have good reason to be proud of this friendly inn in every department. The busy bars hum with the contented chatter of the locals and the many visitors who find its welcoming atmosphere very pleasing. The ale is well kept and the famous brand lagers always popular so it is no wonder that there is never a lack of trade.

Nick and Sharon have been here 19 years and in that time have acquired many friends, not surprisingly because it is in their nature to be outgoing. Their staff have also been with them a long time and are well known to the regulars which adds to the banter in the bars especially the Public Bar complete with two Pool tables and the best Juke Box in Cornwall. Nick is the chef and he cooks daily some superb dishes for which he is well known. He always makes a point of coming out of the kitchen to meet his customers and make sure they are enjoying their meal. The Lounge Bar Diner is very comfortable with a non-smoking area for lunch time diners. The Restaurant is most attractive and relaxing - just the right ambience in which to enjoy Nick's dishes.

For anyone wanting to stay in a happy, unpretentious environment at reasonable prices you would not do better than to book in here. There are four comfortable bedrooms, not ensuite but there are two bathrooms and plenty of hot water. You will find TV in all the rooms and for just fifteen pounds per person you have a full English breakfast as well. Launceston is an excellent centre for touring and The White Horse Inn will add to the enjoyment of your holiday.

USEFUL INFORMATION

OPEN; Mon-Sat 11am-11pm Sun: 12-10.30pm
CHILDREN;Welcome
CREDIT CARDS; Visa/Mastercard
LICENSED; Full On
ACCOMMODATION; 4 rooms, not ensuite
RATES:- All Year, £15 pppn B&B.

RESTAURANT; Home-cooked fare
BAR FOOD; Board choice
VEGETARIAN; Catered for
DISABLED ACCESS; Yes. Not rooms
GARDEN; Yes. Eating out in summer

PEREGRINE HALL
Lostwithiel,
Cornwall
PL22 0HT

Tel/Fax: 01208 873461

Built in 1864 in Gothic style by George Edmund Street, architect of the Law Courts in London, its purpose was a nunnery and a home for wayward women - history does not relate what success rate the nuns had! Today Peregrine Hall has a vastly different role. The main house has four rooms dedicated to bed and breakfast and the chapel and west wing have been converted into 8 holiday cottages which are exceptionally good value and mainly suited for couples. There is a solar heated swimming pool and the long broad terrace in front of the house looks out over 10 acres of gardens and paddocks. You will be very comfortable in the holiday cottages and warmly welcomed into the main house by the owners, Barry and Jo Nicolle. The four bedrooms are all ensuite and highly individual. One room has a 5ft canopied bed with a sitting area as well as a dressing room, two rooms have fourposters and the twin bedded room like the others has Television and a generously supplied beverage tray. A delicious full English breakfast is served every morning either in the dining room or if the weather is good, the conservatory.

If for no other reason you should come to Peregrine Hall for the stunning views from many of the rooms and the terrace. From April to October given that the soft Cornish rain holds off, the hills and valleys are an arresting sight. The cool bright light of early morning sparks and flashes through the trees; because the house is south facing, the sun warms the old flags throughout the day and in the evening it is time to sit out and watch the scene before you gradually soften in golden light - the sheep and lambs turn almost a pinkish colour reflecting the peachy pink clouds; the sense of peace is timeless and disturbed only by rooks and smaller birds hurrying late to their nests, and occasionally an early owl. As the sun finally goes down over the western aspect and the majesty of Restormel Castle, the lights of the small town of Lostwithiel far below are a friendly reminder that 'civilisation' is not far away. Turn away from looking west and look across the valley in front of you, lift up your eyes to the glorious beauty of the night sky - it is breathtaking.

Lostwithiel is an excellent centre for anyone wanting to explore the magic of this part of Cornwall. Within six miles is Lanhydrock House and Gardens, Bodmin Steam Railway, Restormel Castle, Fowey and the South Coast. Many other National Trust properties, Padstow and Newquay and family attractions are within easy reach.

USEFUL INFORMATION

OPEN;2nd Jan-22 December   DINING ROOM; Delicious English breakfast
CHILDREN; Welcome   VEGETARIAN; Catered for
CREDIT CARDS; None taken   DISABLED ACCESS; No facilities
LICENSED; No   PETS: In cottages but not in house
ACCOMMODATION; 4 rooms ensuite   GARDEN; 10 acres gardens & grounds
8 self-catering cottages .... Long weekend/short breaks 10% discount B&B
RATES:- High Season £25 to £30 pppn B&B. Low season £20 to £25 pppn B&B.
Special Rates:- Seasonal offers, details on request.

CLAWFORD VINEYARD
Clawton, Holsworthy,
Devon Ex22 6PN

Tel: 01409 254177

ETB Two Crowns.
AA Three Q Recommended.

This is a quite remarkable place. Not only is it a successful vineyard with cider and apple orchards, it also provides 14 acres of coarse carp fishing in its lakes. There are woods, recreational spaces, superb walking countryside and ideal for cycling . It is a bird watcher's paradise with a wide diversity of birds including Kingfishers, Barn Owls, Skylarks and Buzzards. For golf enthusiasts there are a wide range of excellent courses within easy reach. If you stay here you will be entertained almost without leaving the grounds. If you want to explore further afield the golden sands at Bude and the wonderful surfing beach at Widemouth Bay are less than a 15 minute car ride.Merlin's Cave and the legendary King Arthur's Castle at Tintagel - 20 minutes. The former capital of Cornwall, Launceston, 15 minutes, Okehampton, the gateway to Dartmoor - 20 minutes. The setting for the film Long John Silver's Treasure Island at beautiful Clovelly - 30 minutes. Bodmin Moor is just 20 minutes away, and within a 45 minute drive are Exeter, Plymouth, Newquay, Barnstaple, Bideford and Westward Ho! Holsworthy with its two-day Markets (the largest in Devon) is just 10 minutes down the road.

Clayford has eight spacious bedrooms some in the new Visitors Centre, all ensuite and with wonderful views of the fishing lakes, the vineyards, orchards, gardens and the beautiful Devon countryside.. One room has a fourposter and all the double rooms have 6ft beds. The large Residents Lounge has a 28" Colour TV and a wood burning stove for colder days. There is a friendly Public Bar, a Games Room with Pool and Darts, a Snug area and a shop. Fishing tackle and bait is sold in the shop as well as some fishing tackle items, mainly hooks, fishing lines and that sort of thing. A substantial traditional English Breakfast is served in the conservatory and an evening meal is available on request. Smoking is restricted to the Games Room only.

USEFUL INFORMATION

OPEN; All year	**RESTAURANT; Substantial English breakfast**
CHILDREN; If well behaved	**Evening meal upon request**
CREDIT CARDS; None taken	**VEGETARIAN; Upon request**
LICENSED; Yes	**DISABLED ACCESS; Yes + toilets**
ACCOMMODATION; 8 ensuite rooms	**GARDEN; 78 acres**
PETS; No	

RATES:- All Year, from £17 pppn B&B. Single Supp.£4. Children under 12 £12.

THE THATCHED COTTAGE
COUNTRY HOTEL & RESTAURANT
Sprytown, Lifton,
West Devon PL16 0AY

Tel: 01566 784224
Fax: 01566 784334

AA Rosette/Two Stars for food/service.
RAC Highly acclaimed.

This is one of the most delightful establishments in Devon. The Thatched Cottage dates back to the 16th century. Right on the edge of Dartmoor it is set in beautifully landscaped gardens complete with ponds and a family of geese who call it home! If ever one wanted to find a place that would remove the stress of modern living, this is it. You have only to step outside, preferably taking your gin and tonic with you, and look around you; the views are breathtaking and everything is peaceful. It is not surprising to know that there is a resident ghost Godfrey, who sits in the lounge and mischieviously plays with the lights - you can even smell his pipe smoke. He has been there a long time and obviously has no wish to move on!

The 16th century part of the Thatched Cottage is the Restaurant, Lounge and Bar whilst the five pretty bedrooms, all ensuite, are to be found in the converted stable block, just a few yards away. Each bedroom has wonderful views and is furnished in a country cottagey style. Each is individually designed and appointed with everything one could wish for including a hostess tray, hair dryer, a mini bar, direct dial telephone, iron and ironing board. The house and the accommodation are furnished with some fine antiques which enhance the old worlde charm.

Lunching or dining here is to be recommended. At lunchtime there is a simple menu with four starters including a delicious Crunchie Prawn Salad and the Entrees offer a very good home-made Steak and Kidney pie or you may opt for a Double Decker Sandwich with unusual fillings such as Curried Chicken or Smoked Halibut. Old fashioned puddings like Fruits of the Forest Roly Poly served with either custard, ice cream or clotted cream, appear regularly on the menu. Dinner is a sumptuous feast with five starters which may include Goose pate with Blackberry Jelly followed by Rack of Lamb stuffed with white Hogs Pudding and a Honey and Rosemary Sauce. There is also a Weight Watchers Menu which makes dieting a pleasure. Vegetarians also have their own menu which has been prepared with flair and imagination. The excellent wine list has wines from around the world and boasts some 50 different wines. The Thatched Cottage richly deserves its AA Rosette and 2 stars for food and service. The latter is in keeping with the standard of the hotel.

USEFUL INFORMATION

OPEN; All year
CHILDREN; 12 years and over
CREDIT CARDS; Master/Visa/Amex/DeltaBAR
LICENSED; Restaurant & Residential
ACCOMMODATION; 5 ensuite rooms
PETS;Yes, Dogs.

RESTAURANT; Beautifully cooked and
presented International fare
FOOD; Good choice daily
VEGETARIAN; Imaginative menu
DISABLED ACCESS; Yes + toilets
GARDENS;Yes, landscaped & views

RATES:- Single from £38.50/£49.50. Double from £77/ £99 per night. All Year.

THE OLD FERRY INN
Bodinnick-By-Fowey,
Cornwall
PL23 1LX

Tel: 01726 870237 F
ax: 01726 870116

The River Fowey is without doubt one of the most beautiful in Cornwall and set in a hamlet close to the car and passenger ferry which takes visitors across the river from Bodinnick to Fowey itself, is the delightful 16th-century Old Ferry Inn which has been offering hospitality to travellers throughout the centuries and never has it been better than it is today in the competent and friendly hands of Royce and Patti Smith. Even if the inn was not such a brilliantly run and welcoming place in which to stay, the stunning views of the Fowey Estuary from the lounge and from most of the bedrooms would be worth a visit for that alone. The building is fascinating, it is set into the hillside, giving irregular features throughout on different levels, one room has the actual rockface as part of the wall.

Royce and Patti describe The Old Ferry Inn as friendly, unpretentious and relaxed which is fair but in reality it is much more. There is something very special about it. The beer is well kept, the food beautifully cooked and presented is traditional in its content and ensures that there is something for everyone whatever their tastes. You may choose from the A La Carte menu in the intimate Restaurant or indulge in a tempting Bar meal which offers tasty Specials every day. The prices are excellent value for money and the wine list has a good choice at sensible prices. In the bars which are full of wonderful old photographs and nautical bric-a-brac you will find a genuine Cornish welcome and at night you will sleep in comfortable beds in prettily furnished mostly ensuite rooms, including one with a fourposter, before coming down to a splendid full English breakfast.

There is so much to do and see in this particularly beautiful part of Cornwall. From the Old Ferry Inn you are close to the start of the famous Hall walk where Charles Ist nearly lost his life from an assassins bullet. The enchanting small harbour at Charlestown is very near and if you enjoy gardens the Lost Gardens of Heligan are near Mevagissey and the Victorian Lanhydrock House with its formal gardens is also easily reached. Wheal Martin near St Austell has a fascinating China Clay Museum.

USEFUL INFORMATION

OPEN;All year. All day
CHILDREN; Welcome
CREDIT CARDS; Most major cards
LICENSED; Full On
ACCOMMODATION;Mainly ensuite rooms
CAR PARKING; Available

RESTAURANT; A La Carte beautifully
 cooked and presented
BAR MEALS; Excellent value
VEGETARIAN; Catered for
PETS; Welcome
DISABLED ACCESS; Not advisable

RATES:- All Year, from £20/£30. Single supp.£10. Children sharing £10.(all pppn B&B).
20% Discount on rooms Nov-March excluding Xmas, New Year & Easter

THE SHIP INN
Portloe,
Truro,
Cornwall
TR2 5RA

Tel: 01872 501356

It would be hard to find a more unspoilt village than Portloe which, apart from its tiny fishing harbour has only an hotel, a Post Office which is also Tearooms and The Ship Inn. To come here is to step back into the past and from here it is easy to set forth to explore this particularly beautiful part of South Cornwall with its sandy beaches, spectacular cliff walks and farmland, picturesque villages and historic churches.

You will find that Lewis and Jane Snowdon, the landlords, jealously guard The Ship and ensure that it remains a proper 'local' with two darts teams and a pool team in winter. It is a warm, friendly and welcoming hostelry where the locals are very happy to encourage visitors to join in their conversations and pastimes. Parts of the building date from the 17th century with low beamed ceilings and tiny windows and the other part dates from the beginning of this century but with most of its original woodwork and panelling it blends in complete harmony with its older counterpart. Log fires burn in the Bar and the Dining Room most of the year emitting that wonderful burning wood smell. Jane is a renowned cook and her delicious and exciting food is eagerly anticipated. You will find all the staff anxious to make sure you enjoy your stay. They all have good local knowledge which is a great asset when planning your days. The Snowdon's have a People Carrier and they are happy to ferry walkers around the Roseland to take the best advantage of the wonderful walks. They will also deliver luggage and meet trains. There are 4 guest rooms. The twin and a smaller double have ensuite showers and toilets and the larger double a fourposter and an ensuite bathroom. The rooms are attractively furnished in a cosy cottage style with some antiques and patchwork quilts, and all have TV, tea/coffee facilities, hairdryers and nice extra touches like bubble bath. There is also a luxury cottage, fully equipped, sleeping six.

The large garden, part of which is set aside for families, has an old tractor which children love. Children are very welcome at The Ship Inn and so too are pets - well behaved please.

USEFUL INFORMATION

OPEN; All year. Winter: 11.30-2.30 & 6.30-11pm weekdays
Sun: 12-3pm & 7-10.30pm Summer 11-11pm weekdays
Sun: 12-10.30pm (Whitsun to Mid-Sept)
BAR FOOD; Traditional fare abd board specials.
DINING ROOM:- Superb freshy cooked county fare.   CHILDREN; Welcome
VEGETARIAN; Always available.   CREDIT CARDS; Master/Visa
DISABLED ACCESS;Limited   LICENSED; Full On
GARDEN; Yes. Play area ACCOMMODATION; 3 ensuite rooms. One single private facilites.
PETS; Welcome   RATES:- All Year £18 pppn. (Speical Rates available on request)..
STAY FREE ACCOMMODATION AVAILABLE

THE PLUME OF FEATHERS,
Mitchell,
Nr Truro,
Cornwall

Tel/Fax:01872 510387

John Wesley preached in this former 16th century coaching inn situated in the centre of the village of Mitchell adjacent to the A30. One wonders what he thought about the beer being a strict teetotaller but one can be quite sure that his listeners would have been longing for a pint at the end of his long sermons! It is also said the pub is haunted by a young lady but not whether she had anything to do with Wesley. The Plume of Feathers can lay claim to all sorts of historical connections including Poldark and Sir Francis Drake. Even today there is a well in the bar complete with a bucket! In fact we have it on good authority that visitors may find themselves joined by other long-time guests over lunch - legend has it that this is one of many of the region's older eating places which are favourite haunts of ghosts.

Whatever the veracity of the legend, it is without doubt true to say that this is a friendly, welcoming hostelry in which Stuart Wilkie and his staff will do everything in their power to ensure your visit is memorable. Low ceilings, oak beams and warmth add to the ambience. The 60 cover, non-smoking restaurant has a great reputation for food which is always prepared from fresh local produce wherever possible and top quality produce. The menu is very varied and offers something for everyone . Everything is home-cooked freshly to order. You will find the steaks exceptionally good but the standard remains very high whatever you choose. The Bar menu is also wide ranging and varied with some of the best home-cooked ham you will find anywhere.

The Plume of Feathers has 9 acres of garden and grounds which are always enjoyed by customers in the warmer weather either for drinking or for having a meal. In point of fact the grounds are so large you can take a walk before lunch to work up an appetite! Stuart Wilkie is new to the pub but he has already made his mark and it will be interesting to see all the improvements he has planned.

USEFUL INFORMATION

OPEN; All year 11-3pm & 6-11pm
CHILDREN; Welcome. Play area
CREDIT CARDS; Not at present
LICENSED; Full On
PETS; No

RESTAURANT; Good traditional fare
BAR FOOD; Wide range. Sensible prices
VEGETARIAN; Varied selection
NO WHEELCHAIR ACCESS.
GARDEN; 9 acres. Play area

BROOMERS,
14 Marine Parade,
St Mawes,
Cornwall
TR2 5DW

Tel/Fax: 01326 270440

400 yards away from St Mawes Castle built in the 16th century is the delightful small and intimate restaurant Broomers. It stands right by the water's edge with beautiful views across the sailing waters of St Mawes Bay and St Anthony's Head - a view that is constantly changing throughout the year. It might be an old building and retain its wonderful olde worlde atmosphere but the style is modern and it is a Bistro type operation. It delights people not only because of the excellence of its food but also because when you go there you immediately feel relaxed and very welcome. Broomers opens every day from mid-March until early January but during the winter months the owners, Keith and Emily Jo Ives open for private parties, functions and special theme evenings.

Open all day, it is a pleasure to have morning coffee there. Broomers Breakfasts are served from 10.30-11.45 . At lunchtime from 12 noon until 2.30pm there is an excellent choice of dishes for a light lunch including Scallops Mornay - locally caught scallops simmered in a cheese and white wine sauce, served with a salad garnish and new potatoes or maybe a light, fluffy omelette or a Ploughmans with freshly baked bread. Lunchtime Desserts tempt many customers who adore the Chocolate Fudge Cake or the Red Cherry Pie both with lashings of clotted cream. Afternoon Tea is another popular occasion with several choices including the traditional Cornish Cream Tea and a selection of wickedly tempting cakes and gateaux. Busy as Broomers is all day it settles down more restfully in the evening for candlelit suppers. Homemade Crab Bisque is frequently on the menu with several other delicious Starters. Main Courses are too numerous to mention but if you enjoy locally caught fresh fish you will be in your element. Roast Duck, Broomers Chicken Canton, Medallions of Pork Loin just to mention a few dishes to illustrate the range available. Followed of course by some delectable desserts. All day long Broomers also have a Pizza Takeaway where Pizzas are freshly prepared and cooked to order. There is something for everyone in point of fact including a children's menu and Broomers is certainly not to be missed.

USEFUL INFORMATION

OPEN; All Year. Restricted Nov-Feb   **RESTAURANT; Bistro style. Delicious food**
CHILDREN; Welcome   **TAKEAWAY; Yes. Freshly made Pizzas**
CREDIT CARDS; Yes. 3% surcharge   **VEGETARIAN; Always a choice**
LICENSED; Yes   **DISABLED ACCESS; Yes**
PETS; Yes   **GARDEN; Courtyard rear of restaurant**
BABY CHANGING FACILITIES; Yes

THE SHIP INN,
Lerryn,
Lostwithiel,
Cornwall
PL22 0PT
Tel: 01208 872374
ETB. Commended.
AA/RAC Listed.

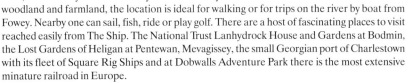

The Ship Inn got its name because until the end of the second World War, ships used to sail up the River Lerryn to collect lime from the kilns in the village. Nowadays the old port has gone and the river is far more occupied by those who sail for pleasure. For example the River Lerryn Yacht Squadron hold two events on the river at the Summer and Winter Solstice. You will find this charming hostelry close to the banks of the river, tucked away in a small valley. Surrounded by National Trust woodland and farmland, the location is ideal for walking or for trips on the river by boat from Fowey. Nearby one can sail, fish, ride or play golf. There are a host of fascinating places to visit reached easily from The Ship. The National Trust Lanhydrock House and Gardens at Bodmin, the Lost Gardens of Heligan at Pentewan, Mevagissey, the small Georgian port of Charlestown with its fleet of Square Rig Ships and at Dobwalls Adventure Park there is the most extensive miniature railroad in Europe.

Part of the Inn was once a slaughter house and butcher's shop. The oldest part of the building with its original flagstone slate floor and cozy log fire is known to have been a pub in the early 17th century. The whole atmosphere of the inn is welcoming and delightful, relaxed and friendly. There are four ensuite bedrooms all with double beds, bath and shower and furnished in soft shades of pink with co-ordinated bedlinen and curtains. Each room has colour TV with remote control, radio alarm clocks and tea/coffee making facilities. Apart from its hospitable bars the inn is known for the excellence of its home-made English fare cooked by Mandy Packer who with her husband Howard, are the landlords. Mandy has a wonderfully light touch with pastry and her pies are renowned. Try the Exmoor Lamb Pie, the Somerset Pork Pie, the Leek and Potato Pie or the Savoury Pumpkin Pie amongst many and you will yearn for more. The whole menu is carefully thought out and the choice varied. The food which also includes fresh fish is available in the 53 seater restaurant or the bar. On Sundays there is a Carvery at lunchtime with plenty of vegetable options.

The Ship Inn offers 3 night breaks and 6 night breaks at amazingly low prices. It is as much fun staying in The Ship in winter or out of season as it is in the height of the summer.

USEFUL INFORMATION

OPEN; All year. 11.30-3pm & 6-11pm   **RESTAURANT;English fare,**
CHILDREN; Welcome   home-cooked style. Pies a speciality
CREDIT CARDS; All major cards   **BAR FOOD; Wide range, sensible prices**
LICENSED; Full On   **VEGETARIAN; 6-12 dishes available**
ACCOMMODATION; 4 ensuite rooms   **WHEELCHAIR ACCESS.**
GARDEN; Yes with tables & Play equipment   **PETS permitted.**
RATES:- All year, £22.50 pppn B&B. Children £10 pppn B&B.
Short Breaks :-Details on request. Stay Free(no charge for accommodation) Details on request.

THE IDLE ROCKS HOTEL
St Mawes,
Cornwall TR2 5AN

Tel: 01326 270771
Fax: 01326 270062

ETB Four Crowns Highly Commended.
Two AA Rosettes for food and service.

This enchanting hotel sits, as its name implies, right on the rocks in the beautiful village of St Mawes looking out at the sparkling ocean. Looking at its elegant persona today it is diffcult to imagine a time when it was a boathouse and then a bakery! The size of the hotel with just twelve bedrooms means that it has a splendidly personal atmosphere where there is always time to care for the needs of the guests. Every member of staff is dedicated to the task of ensuring that guests have a thoroughly relaxed and enjoyable stay. The hotel has recently been refurbished throughout and the result is stunning. There is a pleasing mix of antique and old furniture throughout producing a feeling of elegance and stability. The 12 bedrooms are beautfully appointed and all ensuite. Each is individually designed and has direct dial telephone, television, hairdryers and a beverage tray. After a restful nights sleep you will come down to enjoy a splendid breakfast with many choices; a meal to set you up for the day whether you are going to spend it delighting in the beauty of St Mawes or more energetically, perhaps sailing, walking, swimming or taking a look at one of the glorious gardens that are not too far distant. You will return in the evening to enjoy a drink in the friendly Cocktail bar, much used by local people, before going into the non-smoking restaurant to dine on a menu full of imaginative dishes, some English and some Continental. The restaurant is open to non-residents and it is quite usual to find as many local people dining as there are people staying in the Idle Rocks. There is either an a la carte menu or table d'hote and either will provide you with a memorable meal. The wine list has bottles chosen from around the world and quite a number of half bottles giving you the opportunity of trying one or two unfamiliar wines perhaps.

The Idle Rocks will give you a wonderful holiday or break at anytime of the year and one you will treasure for a long time.

USEFUL INFORMATION

OPEN; All year. Bar: 11am-11pm   RESTAURANT; Local crab & other
CHILDREN; Welcome   Seafood a speciality
CREDIT CARDS;Visa/Master   BAR FOOD; Not applicable
LICENSED; Full On   VEGETARIAN; Yes + special diets
ACCOMMODATION; 12 ensuite rooms   DISABLED ACCESS; Yes + toilets
GARDEN; Terrace garden   PETS; Yes, by arrangement
RATES; B&B: low season £51 - £72 pppn, high season £67 - £77 pppn
DBB: low season £63 - £84 pppn high season £79 - £89 pppn
Special promotions available throughout year : Details on application

CLIMSON FARM
Stoke Climsland
Callington
Cornwall
PL17 8NB

Tel (01579) 370709

Climson is an ancient Cornish farmhouse, formerly owned by the Duchy, and now the home of Diane and Peter Willsteed. It sits, surrounded by rolling countryside, at the head of a secluded combe in the Tamar Valley, inside a designated Area of Outstanding Natural Beauty. The house is a grade 2 listed building, and is believed to date in part from the period of the Domesday Book, in which the name 'Climson' appears. Surrounded by its own gardens, it is within comfortable driving distance of both north and south coasts, local National Trust properties, footpaths, golf courses and the many attractions of East Cornwall and the Tamar Valley.

Diane Willsteed's love of gardening and cooking ensure that the environment and catering at Climson are of a high standard. Meals contain home-grown and seasonal local ingredients, including, for example, such delicacies as Cornish peppered mackerel, local new potatoes and fresh herbs.

Climson has three large double bedrooms, all en suite, and a guest lounge with television, video games and music facilities. Breakfast is served in a large, south-facing conservatory which features an open well. In the winter you can enjoy cosy log fires, while during the summer the large garden is available for outdoor dining and recreation.

USEFUL INFORMATION

OPEN All year.
CHILDREN Welcome.
LICENCE None, but you are welcome to bring your own drinks.
ACCOMMODATION Three large double en suite bedrooms.
children half price if two are sharing.
Single person in a double room £20.

VEGETARIAN Can be catered for.
SMOKING Smokers welcome/
DISABLED No special facilities, but level access.
PETS Welcome - bring your own horse!
GARDEN 1 acre
RESTAURANT Best of local seasonal produce, cooked with flair.

THE TAWNY OWL RESTAURANT
19 North Street
Lostwithiel
Cornwall
PL22 0EF

Tel. and Fax (01208) 872045

The Tawny Owl restaurant is situated in the historic stannary town of Lostwithiel. Easily accessable from the A390, the restaurant has it's own car park adjacent to the community centre. Owned and run by David and Shirley Mason, and supported by an attentive and helpful staff, guests are sure to feel welcome and relaxed.

The decor displays a fine example of early cornish stone walls and log fire, and is tastefully modernised with soft furnishing and mahogany woodwork and tables.

The food is traditional English with some ethnic dishes, fresh fish, fresh vegetables, home-made dishes; including duck, guinea fowl and chicken dishes, our chef's specialities. And of course the famous Tawny Owl Home-made Sweets which are all made on the premises. The emphasis on fresh produce is what makes this restaurant popular with locals and visitors alike.

The bar offers a wide selection of draught and bottled beers and lagers, also an excellent wine menu featuring an award winning local chardonnay to compliment your meal. With full A La Carte served lunchtime and evening, plus blackboard specials and lunch snack menu diners are sure to find a meal to suit all tastes.

Lostwithiel has much to offer the visitor seeking the real Cornwall, The Tawny Owl has much to offer the discerning diner. You won't be disappointed by either.

USEFUL INFORMATION

OPEN 10am until after lunch, 6pm until late. Open all day at peak times. Closed Mondays except Bank Holidays. Sunday lunchtimes.
CHILDREN Welcome. Special menu.
CREDIT CARDS All major cards accepted.
LICENCE Table
ACCOMMODATION None
DISABLED Level access
GARDEN Area for outside sitting and eating

RESTAURANT Traditional English food with some ethnic. Fresh seasonal ingredients. Good stock of wines, draught and bottled beers and lagers.
VEGETARIAN Yes
SMOKING Yes - non smoking area
PETS Outside only

THE HARRIS ARMS,
Portgate,
Nr Lifton,
Devon
EX20 4PZ

Tel/Fax: 01566 783331

This old 16th century inn set on the edge of Dartmoor with panoramic views of Brentor Church and the moor was once part of the estate of Hayne Manor which belonged to the Harris family hence its name. Hayne Manor is in the pretty village of Stowford close by with its lovely thatched cottages and one of the finest 15th century churches in the South West. It is one of those relaxed, friendly establishments where everyone is welcome and is sure of a friendly greeting from Graham and Miriam Short, the landlords and from the locals who frequent the bar and relish the well kept ale frequently including Guest Beers. It is a real pub and furnished comfortably in keeping with its age.

Graham is the chef and he produces good wholesome food which comes to the table well cooked and well presented. The food is traditional and as well as the menu there is a Daily Specials board with a wide choice of tasty dishes providing something for everyone. Special theme evenings are one of the specialities of The Harris Arms. There is a rip roaring Burns Night for example complete with a Scottish Pipe Band and both Haggis and Neaps on the menu. These evenings are great fun and well supported. The main Bar and Dining Room are both available for eating and in the dining room smoking is definitely discouraged. In the summer the large Beer Garden is a favourite place and looks across to Dartmoor.

USEFUL INFORMATION

OPEN; 11-3pm & 6.30-11pm
CHILDREN; Welcome
CREDIT CARDS; All major cards
LICENSED; Full On with Supper Licence
GARDEN; Yes. Beer Garden

DINING ROOM; Good, wholesome fare
BAR MEALS; Daily Specials. Good menu
VEGETARIAN; Always available.
DISABLED ACCESS; No special facilities

KEA HOUSE RESTAURANT,
69 Fore Street,
Tregony,
Truro,
Cornwall
TR2 5RW

Tel: 01872 530642

Tregony is the gateway to the Roseland Peninsula, one of the prettiest unspoilt areas of South Cornwall. There are beautiful beaches, miles of country and coastal walks, pretty villages, National Trust properties, St Mawes Castle, St Just-in-Roseland church, the Lost Gardens of Heligan and Trelissick Gardens and much more. From the 12th-15th century Tregony was a busy port but is now unnavigable and just a pretty village in which Kea House Restaurant plays an important role. At one time it was one of 13 pubs in the village!

Personally run by the Proprietors Ann and Alex Nixon, Kea House has a tremendous reputation way beyond the confines of the village. Ann and Alex who are both trained chefs, set very high standards in everything they do. This is apparent immediately when you see how attractively and immaculately the restaurant is laid out. With only 30 covers it is intimate, the white linen tablecloths have sage green slip covers, the stainless steel cutlery gleams and the pink ravel porcelain crockery together with the candles and fresh flowers on the table make a perfect picture.

The superb food includes Local Fresh Fish and Seafood in season as well as many other tempting dishes and the wines have been carefully selected to complement the food. For lovers of Scottish Malt Whiskies there is a special collection. A popular place, it is always advisable to make a reservation for Evening Meals and in the winter months it is essential..

USEFUL INFORMATION

OPEN; All year except November   **RESTAURANT; Superb food. Local fish**
Easter-Sept Mon-Sat from 7pm   **Seafood. English & Scottish fare**
CHILDREN; Welcome   **VEGETARIAN; Advance notice please.**
CREDIT CARDS; All major cards   **DISABLED ACCESS; All Ground Floor.**
LICENSED; Yes. Restaurant   **PETS; No**
Winter months Tues-Sat from 7pm

POLHILSA FARM
Nr Kelly Bray,
Callington,
Cornwall
PL17 8PP

Tel/Fax: 01579 370784

Tourist Board
Registered.

This 300 year old farmhouse is situated beside the lake in the Duchy Parish of Stoke Climsland which has many Royal links. When you are within its quiet tranquil acres where wildlife is in abundance as are birds in their natural habitat surrounding the farmhouse, it is hard to believe that it is only one mile from the main road. The house is even supplied with its own natural Spring water.

The farm has been in the hands of the Barriball family since 1918 and is family run until this day. Margaret Barriball and her daughter Kay look after the guests whilst Margaret's husband Phillip farms. It is a wonderful place for a stress free holiday and is well placed for anyone wanting to explore Dartmoor and Bodmin Moor and it is not far from the sea either on the south or the north coast.

The farm is warm and comfortable, with a lovely welcoming atmosphere. There are four guest rooms, not ensuite but the bathroom is for guest use only. All the rooms have generously stocked hostess trays and TV is available on request. The Guest Lounge has TV and Satellite TV. Much fun is had on some evenings with a Barbecue by the Lakeside.

No evening meals are served but there are many eateries within easy reach. You will come down in the mornings however to a wonderful farmhouse breakfast, freshly cooked and generous enough to keep you going all day!

USEFUL INFORMATION

OPEN; February-November   **DINING ROOM; Excellent breakfast only**
CHILDREN; Welcome   **VEGETARIAN; By arrangement**
CREDIT CARDS; None taken   **DISABLED ACCESS; No facilities**
LICENSED; No   **GARDEN; Yes. BBQ. Seating.**
ACCOMMODATION; 1 fam, 1dbl, 1 tw 1sgl   PETS; Yes
RATES:- High Season, £15 pppn B&B. Low Season, £12.50.pppn B&B.
Children £8.50/£7.50. Seasonal respectively.

SPA HOTEL
Polkirt Hill,
Mevagissey,
Cornwall
PL26 6UY
Tel: 01726 842244

ETB Three Crowns.
AA QQQ.

Smoking is only allowed in the Bar in this friendly, comfortable hotel situated at the end of a private road with ample parking space. The Spa Hotel has a large garden with a 9 hole putting green and from it you can look across the valley to Portmellon and the sea and to Chaple Point. The views are stunning and whet your appetite for the many walks you can take in this spectacular part of Cornwall. The Spa is only 7 minutes walk from Mevagissey, one of the quaintest and most picturesque fishing villages in Cornwall. Close by are Gorran Haven, Dodman Point and the golden Pentewan sands. A ten minutes drive will take you to the enchanting Lost Gardens of Heligan.

Valerie and Trevor Hounslow are your hosts and together with the aid of a small staff they take care of the many guests who have discovered them and return regularly and the newcomers who rapidly become friends. There are eleven comfortably furnished en suite bedrooms consisting of 4 family rooms, 5 doubles and 2 twin-bedded. All the bedrooms have TV and tea/coffee making facilities, are strictly non-smoking and 3 have direct access to the Patio. The Bar is the focal point at night when people return from their day out.

Here you can enjoy a drink, chat to new found friends and make plans for the following day or play a game of Pool or Darts. The Television Lounge is a restful place and the pretty dining room puts one in the right mood every morning when you come down to a great breakfast with several choices. Traditional home-cooked fare is served every evening.

USEFUL INFORMATION

OPEN; March to October
CHILDREN; Welcome
CREDIT CARDS; Accepted
ACCOMMODATION; 11 ensuite rooms
PETS; Yes. Minimal charge

DINING ROOM; Good home-cooked fare
VEGETARIAN; Catered for
DISABLED ACCESS; Yes. Ground floor room
GARDEN; Yes with 9 hole putting green

RATES:- High Season, D/B&B £35 pppn. Per room B&B £25. Low Season, D/B&B £31 pppn. Per room B&B £21. Children 11/14 yrs. H/P. Under 11 by arrangement.

HAWKINS ARMS
Fore Street,
Probus,
Cornwall
TR2 4JL

Tel: 01726 882208

This sturdy hostelry which has served travellers for centuries stands in the heart of the pretty village of Probus and right next to the ancient church of Saint Probus and Grace, famed for its collection of the skull's of saints and for having the tallest bell tower in the county. Probus is also the home of the County Demonstration Gardens which provides a service to the numerous great gardens of Cornwall that are within easy reach of the village and welcome visitors.

The pub took its name from the infamous Sir Christopher Hawkins, a mean and unpopular local landowner which seems strange for such a welcoming establishment in which you can be sure of good ale and excellent food. The pub stands on the old coaching road to London, with the stagecoach mounting steps still forming part of the cobbled frontage of today.

There is an attractive garden with a children's play area extending down to meet the old Parish Rectory. Derek and Joan Wills are the landlords and together with their young staff who are both well trained, attentive and polite, they provide a genuine welcome to visitors which is endorsed by the locals who soon make sure that one feels at home. The Hawkins Arms has three guest bedrooms all with hot and cold water, television and tea/coffee facilities.

USEFUL INFORMATION

OPEN:-12-2.30pm.&5-11pm.	**BAR FOOD; Traditional & Seafood specialities**
CREDIT CARDS; All major cards.	**VEGETARIAN; Catered for**
LICENSED; Full On	**DISABLED ACCESS; Yes. Toilet facilities**
ACCOMMODATION;2dbl 1 tw not ensuite	**GARDEN; Yes. Children's Play area**
PETS;Yes	**RATES:- All Year £17.pppn B&B.**

THE WHEEL INN,
Tresillian,
Truro,
Cornwall
TR2 4BA

Tel: 01872 520293

Thatched buildings always have a special charm and this is personified by the 14th-century Wheel Inn at Tresillian, a small village 3 miles from the Cathedral City of Truro. Although it is on the main road into Truro it still has a quiet rural charm especially when one looks at the tidal Tresillian River flowing peacefully along at the back of the inn just beyond the car park. It has served travellers for centuries and was used by General Fairfax as his Headquarters in the Civil War as long ago as 1646 and it was here that the Peace Treaty with the Royalists was signed.

The Wheel Inn is a true village pub with its back firmly turned on fruit machines, dart boards and Juke Boxes, here you will only find quiet background music and plenty of conversation. The atmosphere is friendly, welcoming and congenial. Because of its age the ceilings are low and there are several small nooks and crannies which give a delightful air of intimacy.

David and Jacqui Hulson have been mine hosts here for fifteen years and have made many friends both locally and with the many visitors who return once having discovered what fun the pub is and how good Jacqui's home-made fare is. The menu is traditional and every day there are Blackboard Specials at lunchtime including a delicious home-made steak and kidney pie. There are always dishes for Vegetarians and either small portions or a special Children's Menu.Sunday Lunch is always popular and it is advisable to book.

USEFUL INFORMATION

OPEN; All Year. (Normal licencing hours)
CHILDREN; Welcome to eat
CREDIT CARDS; Yes
LICENSED; Full On
GARDEN; Yes   PETS; No

RESTAURANT; Very Popular for Food
BAR FOOD; Wide range, home-cooked
VEGETARIAN; Daily choice
DISABLED ACCESS; Difficult

KERRYANNA COUNTRY HOUSE,
Treleaven Farm,
Mevagissey,
Cornwall
PL26 6RZ

Tel/Fax: 01726 843558

ETB Three Crowns
Commended.
AA Four Q Selected.

Kerryanna is built on the remains of an ornamental garden which once belonged to the original farmhouse. It was once owned by the Tremayne Estate, now world famous as the Lost Gardens of Heligan, and contains some of the rare plants found at Heligan. It is a truly beautiful place situated at the head of the valley overlooking the fishing village of Mevagissey. Surrounded by farmland, with beautiful gardens, a superb outdoor swimming pool and leisure facilities which include an 18 hole putting green, Kerryanna is quite the best place in which to stay and enjoy a totally relaxed holiday. Once a dairy farm with some 100 cows, now, due to a change in farming policy the milking cows were sold and a livery yard for horses takes their place together with beautiful barn conversions for self-catering holidays with 3 delightful units sleeping from 2-6 people.

Percy and Linda Hennah have been at Treleaven for over 30 years, opening their home to guests in 1971 and from that moment on welcoming visitors who have become friends and newcomers who leave as friends. It is that sort of friendly, happy house. The food is delicious and everything is home-made by Linda. Local fresh vegetables and fish, home-made soups, tender, succulent roasts and tasty casseroles plus mouth-watering desserts with lashings of Cornish Cream, make every meal eagerly awaited. Kerryanna is licensed. The bedrooms are all ensuite and charmingly decorated. 2 have romantic lace canopies over the beds. Each room has colour TV and a hospitality tray. There are 3 lounges, one very cosy with an open fire, one with stunning views across the countryside, the village and glimpses of the sea. The third is a plant filled conservatory where you can have a quiet drink.

USEFUL INFORMATION

OPEN; Easter to October	**DINING ROOM; Excellent home-cooked fare**
CHILDREN; Welcome	**VEGETARIAN; Catered for**
CREDIT CARDS: None taken	**DISABLED ACCESS; Not accessible**
LICENSED; Residential	**PETS; Not permitted**
ACCOMMODATION;Ensuite rooms	**GARDEN; 1 acre. Swimming Pool. Putting**
3 self-catering barn conversions	

RATES:- High Season,£23.50. Low Season £20. Single Supp.£5.Children from £10.
All rates are for pppn B&B.

THE NEW INN
Veryan,
Truro,
Cornwall
TR2 5QA

Tel/Fax: 01872 501362

The villages in the Roseland district of Cornwall all have a particular charm, enjoy a mild climate and many have sandy beaches which are safe for bathing. Add this to the beautiful countryside which provides excellent walking and the chance to go horseriding, and you have a very good reason for coming to this exceptionally beautiful part of Cornwall. Veryan is just such a village and has the added benefit of having a genuine, friendly old hostelry,

The New Inn. Once two cottages built in the 16th century it is full of atmosphere. Two inglenook fireplaces have been attractively converted and are now cheerful open fires and one bread oven has been preserved. Jack and Penny Gayton the owners are welcoming, interesting people. Jack is a retired naval officer who after retirement searched for wrecks in the Isles of Scilly and with his team found HMS Association which sank in 1707 and Hollandia which sank with a cargo of silver in 1743.

Penny is a noted cook and produces some super food. You will see the menu offers a range of tasty dishes at lunchtime, crisp, fresh baguettes as well as Ploughman's Lunches, Jacket Potatoes, Sandwiches, Toasted Sandwiches and a choice of home-made Pizzas which are extremely popular. In the evening the menu is a little more sophisticated although the Pizzas still remain a favourite option.

There are nine starters including Baked Snails. The Main Courses excite the palate with Pheasant and Chestnuts with Red Plums, Wing of Skate, Salmon Supreme amongst the varied dishes. Everything is freshly cooked to order so please do be a little patient - the result is definitely worth the wait! 4 Guest rooms are spacious and well appointed with Colour TV, Tea/Coffee facilities, hairdryers etc. None of them are en suite but in this happy establishment the loss is not felt.

USEFUL INFORMATION

OPEN; 11.30-3pm & 6.30-11pm
Sundays: 12-3pm & 7-10.30pm
CHILDREN; Welcome
CREDIT CARDS; Visa/Master/Euro
LICENSED; Full On.Good wine list
ACCOMMODATION;1dbl, 1tw, 2 sgl
RATES; B&B from £15.50 pppn All Year

BAR FOOD; Exciting home-cooked fare
Including Pizzas. Lunch & Evening
VEGETARIAN; Catered for
DISABLED ACCESS; In Bar
PETS; By arrangement
GARDEN; Beer Garden

THE BUGLE INN,
57 Fore Street,
Bugle, St Austell,
Cornwall
PL26 8PB

Bugle is right in the centre of the China Clay Area of Cornwall, 2 miles from the historic Roche Rock with its incredible views spanning Cornwall. It is on the main A391 road between Bodmin and Austell, not difficult to find but you will be intrigued by the scenery around you. Much has now been landscaped by English China Clay but there is still much that is ghostly white with large craters and quarries. It is here that the cameras have been active for many Sci-Fi films. It does not take much imagination to understand why.

The Bugle Inn dates back to 1840 and is a Grade II Listed Building and once a coaching inn incorporating stables, a history of which can be found around the walls of the inn providing a great talking point for visitors. The landlord will set you on the quest of trying to find the water mark above sea level in the granite walls whilst you are waiting for your meal! The food is traditional pub fare with Daily Specials high on the list of popularity. There is a good Sunday Roast lunch and teas, coffee and Cream Teas are served all day. There is no restaurant but the very comfortable bar area with its open coal fire burning on chillier days, makes a pleasant place in which to enjoy the food. In the season it does help the landlords Simon and Pam Rodger if you book your meal in advance.

USEFUL INFORMATION

OPEN; All day every day 11am-11pm
CHILDREN; Under supervision
CREDIT CARDS; None taken
LICENSED; Full On
PETS; On a lead

RESTAURANT; Not applicable
BAR FOOD; Good traditional fare
Specials. Sunday Roasts
VEGETARIAN; Always available
DISABLED ACCESS; Yes

THE VICTORY INN
Victory Hill,
St Mawes, Cornwall
TR2 5DQ
Tel: 01326 270324

Victory Hill in St Mawes is close to the harbour and it can be seen clearly from the 18th century Victory Inn. Built in 1740 as three cottages supposedly occupied by pirates, it is a true, traditional pub with a cosy atmosphere, beamed ceilings and lots of photographs of working boats adorning the walls. Much of the contented air of The Victory stems from the landlords, Bridget and Phillip Savage who are friendly, welcoming people who love their work and delight in making sure their customers are well cared for. St Mawes is stunningly beautiful and a wonderful place to stay for a holiday. To enjoy this, the simple hospitality offered by the Victory is ideal for those who do not want anything more than a relaxed stay in an informal atmosphere. The inn has two double guest bedrooms, one furnished in a modern style and the other very traditional. The small, non-smoking restaurant has 21 covers and there is an eating area in the bar. The food is all home-cooked using fresh produce. Seafood dishes, exotic curries and steaks are all firm favourites with people but there are many more dishes to choose from. Vegetarians will always find at least two dishes on the menu every day.

USEFUL INFORMATION

OPEN; 11am-11pm Sundays 12-11pm
CHILDREN; Welcome
CREDIT CARDS; Visa/Master
LICENSED; Full On
ACCOMMODATION; 2dbl
GARDEN; Patio garden
RATES:- £20 pppn. All Year.

RESTAURANT; Good traditional fare
Fresh produce. Non-smoking
BAR FOOD; Good selection
VEGETARIAN; Always a choice
DISABLED ACCESS; One step
PETS; Yes

TREGONY HOUSE
15 Fore Street
Tregony
Cornwall
TR2 5RW

Tel: 01872 530642

Tregony, frequently referred to as the Gateway to 'The Roseland Peninsula' lies between Truro and St Austell. It is a thriving village with quite a bit of history attached to it including the famous Town Clock erected in the 18th century and still a commanding feature of the village.It is a very convenient situation for anyone who wants to explore virtually all of Cornwall or stay closer to home and enjoy the many beautiful gardens, beaches and coastal walks within easy reach.

In the main street is Tregony House, a Grade II Listed building which is the home of Andrew and Catherine Webb who welcome guests from February to November. They are hospitable people who do everything in their power to ensure that guests have an enjoyable and memorable stay. The house has an air of well being as well as a relaxing atmosphere. There are five bedrooms in all, an en suite double,a twin and a single sharing a bathroom and at the rear a double ensuite. On a separate staircase there is another twin room with a private bathroom. They are all charmingly furnished and have radios and a hostess tray. The lovely 17th century beamed dining room is where you will be served a delicious breakfast cooked to your order and at night, after a busy day exploring, you will return to dine there for a perfectly cooked four course dinner.Pleasant classical and easy listening music plays in the background whilst you are eating - something that is greatly enjoyed by guests,

USEFUL INFORMATION

OPEN; February- November
CHILDREN; Over 7 years
CREDIT CARDS; Visa/Mastercard
LICENSED; Restaurant & Residential
ACCOMMODATION; 5 rooms mainly ensuite

DINING ROOM; Delicious home-cooked fare
VEGETARIAN; Prior notice please
DISABLED ACCESS; Not suitable
GARDEN; Yes
PETS; No

QUITHER MILL
Nr Chillaton,
Tavistock,
Devon

Tel: 01822 860160

This is a fascinating, listed house built in the 18th century as a water mill. Even today you will see the wheel of the mill adorning the front of the house. Quither Mill stands in eight acres of beautifully maintained gardens and paddocks in which it is a sheer pleasure to stroll, breathing in the clean, fresh air and filling your eyes with the stunning views of Dartmoor. Everything about the house pleases. There is a contented, relaxed air about Quither Mill which wraps itself around guests making them feel cared for. Your hosts, Jill and David Wright had an hotel in Wales before they came here but they will tell you that looking after a smaller number of people is far more fulfilling. They have made the house beautiful, with some fine antique furniture, elegant drapes and a soft welcoming decor and somehow it is not only elegant but essentially a home at the same time.

There are two comfortable and well appointed double rooms and another twin room in 'Owl Cottage'. You will be cossetted and supremely well fed on delicious meals which are a mixture of English and French cuisine accompanied by a good selection of wines from around the world.

Quither Mill makes an excellent base for exploring Dartmoor and many other great places closeby.

USEFUL INFORMATION

OPEN; All year - Closed occasionally
CHILDREN; 5 years & over
CREDIT CARDS; Visa/Mastercard
LICENSED; Yes
ACCOMMODATION; 2dbl 1tw
PETS;By prior arrangement
RATES:- £30 pppn. Single occupancy £10 surcharge. All Year.

DINING ROOM; Delicious food
VEGETARIAN; Prior notice required
W/CHAIR ACCESS; Ground floor room
  plus toilet
GARDEN; 8 acres garden & paddocks

CHAPTER SEVEN

West & South West Cornwall and The Scillies

Chapter Seven

"Even the rarest delicacies of all the lands and seas will taste insipid without salt."
Nichiren Daishonin

CHAPTER SEVEN

WEST AND SOUTH WEST CORNWALL AND THE SCILLIES

West of Truro, Cornwall divides into the two dramatic peninsulas with which Britain comes to an end.   The **LIZARD PENINSULA** is the most southerly part of the whole island, and is a wide, rather bald plateau of ancient palaeozoic rocks, notably the distinctively coloured Serpentine, dark, greenish and shiny (you can buy pieces of it, shaped and polished, in local craft workshops), which gave the area its name.

Beyond the Lizard, stretching out to the west, is the unique, granite **PENWITH PENINSULA**, unlike anywhere else for its light and openness to sea and sky, where everything literally comes to its conclusion at the famous fluted cliffs, familiar to us all even if we have never actually seen them, of LAND'S END. After Land's End are those magical islands, far out in the Atlantic, which we only really have space to briefly mention in this book, **THE SCILLIES**.

We begin, however, on the west bank of that broad waterway, the Carrick Roads, opposite St Mawes, at **FALMOUTH** (Tourist Information 01326 312300).

This is a large, important town with a beautiful setting. It is not as old as most places along the South West coast, and is not particularly full of historic buildings or associations. But Falmouth has a proud maritime tradition and is still a working port, with facilities for large ocean-going ships, as well as a centre for SAILING, FISHING and WATERSPORTS.

The town was developed in the 16th century by the Killigrew family, and prospered at the expense of both Penryn and Truro, the original ports further upriver, much to their annoyance. It was the first headquarters of the Post Office Packet Service, from 1688 to 1852, when it was replaced by Southampton.

PENDENNIS CASTLE (English Heritage, 01326 316594), twin to St Mawes, guards the harbour, and is worth a wander round to admire the strength of its mass and its position.

Falmouth has a strong connection with the ARTS, with a respected Art College and many GALLERIES. The presence of the college and its students does help to give the place a more youthful, active atmosphere than many coastal towns. The most prestigious gallery is the FALMOUTH ART GALLERY (01326 313863) where permanent and travelling exhibitions of old and new work can be seen.

FALMOUTH ARTS CENTRE (01326 212300) puts on a wide ranging programme of events all through the year, and things also happen at the PRINCESS PAVILION AND GYLLYNGDUNE GARDENS (01326 211222).

There are a number of beautiful GARDENS in the area, taking advantage of the sheltered, sunny nature of the setting. The three following are the best known.

GLENDURGAN (01326 250906) is a National Trust garden in a valley, and features fine trees, rare plants and a water garden, as well as a recently restored laurel MAZE from 1833.

PENJERRICK (01872 870105) is another magical collection of jungle plants, tree ferns, ponds and a fairly wild garden.

TREBAH (01326 250448), the famous 26 acre garden in a ravine overlooking the Helford River, also has hundred year old tree ferns, waterfalls, ponds with koi carp, and a special Hydrangia collection. There is a play area for children.

For sport, Falmouth has a GOLF CLUB (01326 311262) and a PITCH AND PUTT (01326 317311). The SHIPS AND CASTLES LEISURE POOL (01326 212129) provides fun and games, and at WINDSPORT INTERNATIONAL (01326 376191) there are facilities and tuition for SAILING, CANOEING, WATERSKIING and WINDSURFING.

Just over the water from Falmouth, **FLUSHING** is a pleasant little village with steep, narrow streets and a number of attractive old houses. It owes its name and style to the presence in the 17th century of some Dutch seamen who settled here.

Moving south into the Lizard Peninsula, the beautiful HELFORD RIVER is passed, with its myriad creeks and inlets. Amongst them is the original FRENCHMAN'S CREEK of Daphne du Maurier's novel, peaceful and idyllic, as are so many of the coves and inlets around the Lizard.

At the tidal head of the river is **GWEEK**, a small village popular with artists. Here can be found the NATIONAL SEAL SANCTUARY (01326 221361), where rescued seals and sealions are given care and a safe home. There are wonderful WALKS and a CAFE, and plenty of opportunity to relate to the animals.

The LIZARD PENINSULA is, despite the delightful coves and creeks, a bare, rather treeless expanse of land. If walking around the edges, be careful of the Serpentine rock which, lovely as it is to look at, is quite slippery. It is always best to keep to the well-defined paths and routes.

The main town of the Lizard area is **HELSTON** (Tourist Information 01326 565431). This is the 'quaint old Cornish town' of the 'Floral Dance' song, written in 1911 by Katie Moss to celebrate the traditional floral or 'FURRY' DANCE, which takes place every year, always on MAY 8th. Helston was a Stannary Town, a function recalled by the name of Coinagehall Street. It received its borough charter in 1201.

Helston is a good looking old town, with a long street from which you can see the countryside, and a stream running down the side. It contains plenty of Georgian buildings, and feels prosperous and confident in both its past and present.

The May festival for which Helston is world famous is a more gentrified affair than the May Day celebration in Padstow, which happens a week earlier (see chapter 8), but it is pagan enough, and certainly well worth catching. It is a genuine folk tradition which, you feel, the people of the town would perform anyway, whether anyone else came to watch it or not.

To the lilting dance tune, which sounds like, and probably is, an 18th century hornpipe, played with hypnotic regularity by the town's brass band, couples in their best clothes dance through the streets, and sometimes in and out of the houses, to give thanks for the coming of summer. There are several dances throughout the day; the most formal, led by the mayor, with the men in top hats and tails, is at Mid day. It is all very colourful, joyful and gracious, and it is hard to see in it the 'vulgar' and 'uncouth' junketings which shocked the odd Victorian traveller who ventured this far to see it.

Earlier in the morning, the young people of the town perform an entertaining MUMMING PLAY, and this feels more ancient than the present form of the dance.

In the MARKET PLACE can be found the HELSTON FOLK MUSEUM which has a collection demonstrating the traditional social and working life of the area, and material on Helston's two great men. The first of these was Bob Fitzsimmons, born here in 1863, who emigrated to the USA and became the only Englishman to win the World Heavyweight Boxing title. He was also the only man ever to win world titles in Light, Middle and Heavy weights. The cottage where he was born is near the top of Coinagehall St. The other man celebrated at the Museum is Henry Trengrouse, 19th century inventor of ship to shore rocket life-saving apparatus.

HELSTON LEISURE CENTRE (01326 563320) has a POOL, FITNESS SUITE and SQUASH COURTS, and there is a GOLF CLUB (01326 572518). Nearby are two major attractions, both owing their existence and popularity to television programmes.

FLAMBARDS VILLAGE THEME PARK (01326 564093) offers all-weather family fun and entertainment to suit all tastes, with RIDES, EXHIBITIONS and prizewinning GARDENS.

A little to the north of the town is POLDARK MINE (01326 653166). The site covers three acres, and contains a complete 18th century village based on the setting of Winston Graham's bestselling Poldark novels which were so successfully serialised in the 1970s. There is a TIN MINE with a working BEAM ENGINE, MUSEUM, SHOPS, CINEMA and RESTAURANT.

The ROYAL NAVAL AIR STATION at **CULDROSE**, the largest military helicopter base in Europe, with the FLEET AIR ARM MUSEUM and SHOP, is sometimes open to the public - information is available from the TIC.

A reminder of the long human connection with this ancient land is HELLIGYE FOGU at **TRELOWARREN**, where Iron Age underground passages looked after by English Heritage can be visited at any reasonable time (no charge).

Returning to the 20th century, and possibly the 21st, the BRITISH TELECOM GOONHILLY SATELLITE EARTH STATION (01326 221333), on the bare expanse of GOONHILLY DOWNS, offers GUIDED TOURS of the site, permanent EXHIBITIONS and a new HIGH TECH VISITORS' CENTRE. There is also, slightly incongruously but a good thing anyway, a WILDLIFE AREA, and CHILDREN'S PLAY AREA and a LICENSED CAFE.

As we approach the southernmost place in Britain, at LIZARD POINT, there are some very attractive little villages tucked away on the eastern side of the peninsula. At **RUAN MINOR** can be found KENNARD POTTERY (01326 290592); **CADGWITH** is a beautiful thatched fishing village in a small cove and at **CANDEWEDNACK** is a church built from the unique green-black Serpentine rock.

LIZARD POINT itself is owned by the National Trust. The lighthouse gives a beam visible for 20 miles. To the west is the LIZARD NATIONAL NATURE RESERVE and the village of **MULLION** with its famous COVE. The nearby MULLION GOLF CLUB (01326 240685) is, of course, the most southerly in the country.

Above POLDHU COVE is POLDHU POINT, where Marconi in 1901 sent the first transatlantic radio message. A MEMORIAL marks the spot.

Moving around the peninsula, we reach the pleasant little fishing town of PORTHLEVEN, which is still a working port.

PRAA SANDS (pronounced 'Pray') are a popular beach, a mile long. PRAA SANDS GOLF CLUB is nearby (01736 763445).

A little to the north west is GODOLPHIN HOUSE (01736 762409), ancestral home of the distinguished old Cornish family (one of them, the Cavalier poet Sidney Godolphin, got killed during the Civil War at the Three Crowns in Chagford, as recorded in (chapter 4). It is a 16th century house, extended in the 17th.

The ancient custom is for the Reeve of the Manor of Lambourne to call at the house every Candlemas Day (February 2nd) and make the following statement: 'Here come I to demand my lord's dues, eight groats and a penny in money, a loaf, a cheese and a collar of brawn, and a jack of the best beer in the house.'

MARAZION is one the oldest chartered towns in Cornwall. It sits at the eastern end of MOUNT'S BAY, overlooking the sea and the extraordinarily romantic island of **ST MICHAEL'S MOUNT**, which can be reached on foot at low tide and by FERRY when the tide is in. Marazion has some nice old buildings, a MUSEUM, a MARKET HALL with an interesting clock, and BEACHES. It is also a centre for WINDSURFING.

ST MICHAEL'S MOUNT is looked after by the National Trust. Originally it had an 11th century Benedictine chapel on it. The present CASTLE (01736 710507) dates from the 14th century. It contains beautifully decorated rooms with lots of interesting objects and pictures.

A few miles inland from Marazion, CHYSAUSTER IRON AGE VILLAGE (01736 618890), protected by English Heritage, contains the stone remains of houses, workshops and enclosures in use over 2,000 years ago.

The next town around the Bay, **PENZANCE** (Tourist Information 01736 62207), is, as stated before, the last major town in Britain. Somehow it feels like it, as it slopes gently down towards the waterfront. The name means 'HOLY HEADLAND', from the Cornish 'pen', meaning headland, and 'sans', holy. Its position on the mysterious, powerful Penwith Peninsula does give it a strong sense of the numinous, and the town is quite 'alternative'; there are many people here who concern themselves with healing, mysticism and the peculiar qualities of the landscape. It is good for ARTS, CRAFTS, WHOLEFOODS, ALTERNATIVE THERAPY, ANTIQUES and BOOKS. Penzance is also, however, quite down to earth. It has a varied and creative population, comprising what seems to be a good mixture of locals and 'foreigners'. This makes it a varied and lively town to spend time in.

During the 13th century Penzance was a tiny fishing community, with Marazion being the main market and fishing centre, but by the end of the 16th century it was an important enough base to make the Spanish feel it was worth attacking, which they did, burning it and its neighbours, Newlyn and Mousehole, to the ground in 1595.

The main street, MARKET JEW STREET, which probably derives from the Cornish 'marchasdiow' - the street of two markets - has a raised pavement on one side. There are some pleasant old parts to the town, with cobbles and good views out over Mounts Bay. Its PUBS are suitably individual.

Sir Humphrey Davy, chemist and inventor of the miner's safety lamp, was born here in 1778, and there is a statue of him. Maria Branwell, mother of the Bronte sisters, was also from Penzance, and some like to think that a vital part of their genius came this this Cornish background. The main museum in Penzance is the PENLEE HOUSE ART GALLERY AND MUSEUM (01736 62207) which contains important collections of local history and archaeology and a great deal of art from the NEWLYN SCHOOL of the late 19th and early 20th centuries.

The CORNWALL GEOLOGICAL MUSEUM (01736 332400) is a brand new interpretation of the county's geology, with fossil displays, using the latest presentation methods.

There is also in Penzance the world's first lighthouse museum (01736 60077) in the TRINITY HOUSE NATIONAL LIGHTHOUSE CENTRE.

One of the most extraordinary buildings in Cornwall is THE EGPTIAN HOUSE, designed by the early 19th century Plymouth architect John Foulson. It now houses the NATIONAL TRUST SHOP.

PENLEE MEMORIAL PARK, laid out in memory of those who died in the Second World War, with sub-tropical GARDENS, a CHILDREN'S PLAY AREA and an OPEN AIR THEATRE, where performances are given during the summer.

The MORRAB GARDENS are also rich in sun-loving plants, and summer CONCERTS of all kinds are given in the traditional BANDSTAND.

The ACORN CENTRE (01736 65520) is another venue for MUSIC, DRAMA and DANCE. The GOLOWAN FESTIVAL in late JULY features MUSICAL and THEATRICAL events, and FIREWORKS.

One of the area's most enjoyable GARDENS is TRENGWAINTON at Treanor, a couple of miles north west of the town, which is cared for by the National Trust. FISHING, YACHTING and SURFING can all be partaken in here, and the surrounding country provides spectacular WALKING.

From Penzance you can also SAIL to the lovely **ISLES OF SCILLY** (Tourist Information 01720 422536), of which it is only possible to make a brief mention here, although a whole book would barely do full justice to them.

Twenty eight miles south west of Land's End, this group of granite islands is different from all those around Britain. The sense of space, the light, the intensity of colour, the flowers, the ancient monuments,the brilliantly white beaches and the extraordinarily calm placidity of the sea between them - at some of the time, anyway - all add up to make them unique and very special.

There are over a hundred islands altogether, but only five are inhabited: **ST MARY'S, TRESCO, BRYHER, ST MARTIN'S** and **ST AGNES**. About 2,000 people live and work on them.

St Mary's is the biggest and the main administrative centre, with year-round transport links to the mainland. Tresco, the next in size, has the world-famous ABBEY GARDENS, which really are a sub-tropical paradise.

Early chroniclers refer to an 'Island of Scilly', and it is clear that there was once more land beneath the shallow seas between them. Lying between the islands and Land's End, it is said, there is the lost country of Lyonesse. Such romanticism is easy to understand in this lovely environment.

By sea, you can get to Tresco very enjoyably from Penzance on the *Scillonian III*, a journey of about four hours. Or you can FLY to ST Mary's from Land's End, Newquay, Plymouth or Exeter. For more information, ring (0345 10 55 55).

At right angles to Penzance, and only about a twenty minute walk along the front, is the famous old fishing town of **NEWLYN**. This is now one of the busiest fishing ports in England, and feels very much a working town. Those who know of it only through its associations with art, and are expecting another St Ives, will be surprised at how unlike that town it is.

The connection with art came in the late 19th century, and the 'Newlyn School', centred around Stanhope Forbes, became a major force in British painting. The artists who came here were attracted by the visual qualities of the sea and the Penwith landscape, and the brightness of the light, but their particular desire, inspired by the similar schools of painting in Brittany, was to paint the lives and activities of 'ordinary people', and Cornish fisherfolk fitted what they were after. Forbes wrote of the 'lodestone of artistic metal' in Newlyn, the effects of which were felt in Paris and Antwerp. His colleague, Henry Scott Tuke, made sensitive pictures of ships and many fine studies of naked boys and youths, carefully draped about the rocks. The 'school' continued to draw important artists here into the 1920s and 1930s, including Dame Laura Knight.

There is an excellent ART GALLERY (01736 63715) in Newlyn, showing contemporary work of all kinds, on the way into the town from Penzance, with a good bookshop covering the art of Cornwall in general. Despite this, however, Newlyn is not, any more, an 'arty' town in the way that many others in Cornwall are. For works of the Newlyn School itself you need to go to the Penlee House Museum in Penzance.

The NEWLYN FISH FESTIVAL in August celebrates the real source of the local economy.

Travelling on around the coast towards Land's End, we come to the beautiful old village of **MOUSEHOLE** (pronounced 'Mowzel'), still a focus for fishing and a lovely place for a holiday. In December, TOM BAWCOCK'S EVE is movingly celebrated on the 23rd, with a torchlight procession around the harbour, and music. This commemorates the traditional story of the fisherman Tom Bawcock who, with his faithful cat, saved the village from starvation, as beautifully retold in the bestselling children's book by Antonia Barber and Nicola Bayley,*The Mousehole Cat.*.

Nearby, the BIRD HOSPITAL is a heartwarming place, with a shop selling local ARTS and CRAFTS.

Passing **LAMORNA** with its celebrated COVE, we reach the unique cliff theatre of MINACK (01736 810694). What more magical place could there be in which to watch any dramatic performance, on a summer evening, than here, with the incomparable backdrop of Mount's Bay behind the Greek-style theatre? There are productions here throughout the season. Bring something warm to put on.

The landscape around Lamorna is, for many thousands of people, resonant with memories of the 'Minack Chronicles', that much-loved series of books in which the late Derek Tangye, a descendant of the 19th century Cornish industrial family, described the fulfilled life he created, together with his wife Jeannie and their family of cats, donkeys and other creatures, on a clifftop smallholding, growing flowers and writing books. Another literary inhabitant of this area is David Cornwell, alias John le Carre.

The whole of the Penwith Peninsula is ancient granite, and is riddled with Neolithic, Bronze Age and Iron Age monuments. Stone circles, standing stones, ancient dwellings and field systems vie with old mine buildings from more recent ages in looking as if they were shaped by the weather.

Amongst the best known monuments are THE MERRY MAIDENS STONE CIRCLE and the MEN AN TOL stone with the famous hole in it, which children were once passed through as a protection from rickets. Its ancient magic is invoked, amusingly but rather improbably, it must be said, in the Cornish-born author D.M.Thomas's novel *Birthstone*.

There is no space here to cover the many archaeological, and perhaps mystical, sites of West Penwith, but detailed leaflets and books describing walks to, and speculations about, the many monuments around the area can be picked up locally in bookshops. If this haunted landscape appeals to you, will not need encouragement to linger and study its antiquities in detail.

So, moving around, we reach **LAND'S END**, right at the end of the country, and of the A30. This seems to be a place that everyone has to get to, at least once, just for the sake of doing so. The great red-brown, heavily fractured cliffs and castle-like outcrops 200 feet above the sea do have a powerful sense of finality, and few can fail to be impressed, standing here, at the far end of what William Blake called 'Albion's ancient, druid, rocky shore', and considering that no land except the Scillies separates this point from America.

For those who like to play at places like this, there is the LANDS END THEME PARK (01736 871220), where all kinds of experiences are available, using the latest gadgetry. CRAFTS, EXHIBITS and ANIMALS are also to be enjoyed. But if you would rather wander about and sit or stand in quiet contemplation, there is plenty of room to do that as well.

Moving inland, the first place you come to is the little granite mining town of **ST JUST IN PENWITH**, surrounded by ancient and not so ancient monuments, including some classically poignant engine houses of deserted tin mines, especially the one at BOTALLACK. This is one of the most powerful images of Cornwall, and if you respond to this landscape, you can spend happy days based around St Just. It has several GALLERIES.

At **PENDEEN** on the north coast is the famous LANYON QUOIT, a Neolithic chambered tomb, with three upright stones capped by a huge flat slab. Also here is the GEEVOR TIN MINE MUSEUM AND HERITAGE CENTRE (01736 788662). Cornwall's industrial past is vividly brought to life by experienced guides, and the tour includes a brief visit underground. There is a shop selling CRAFTS and BOOKS.

ZENNOR epitomises the most mysterious elements of this country. A tiny granite village, surrounded by granite walls and granite cliffs, it is impossible to imagine in being anywhere else. The granite church has beautiful carvings, including the famous one of the ZENNOR MERMAID, who haunts PENDOUR COVE. The story is that she fell in love with the singing of a local choristor, Michael Trewhella, and succeeded in enticing him away with her. He was never seen again, but his voice was sometimes heard in the evening light by the people of the village.

The privately owned WAYSIDE FOLK MUSEUM (01736 796945) at Zennor covers every aspect of life in this locality from earliest times.

On a hilltop behind the village the naturalist W.H.Hudson used to sit and watch the birds. He wrote an excellent book on the natural history of the Land's End area, and his friend, the artist Arnold Forster, had the words 'W.H.Hudson Often Came Here' carved into a huge seat-like boulder.

D.H.Lawrence lived here for a while during the First World War, with his German wife Frieda, but did not enjoy it very much. The locals thought he was a spy, he was laughed at by a young farmer he fancied, and the whole experience made him decidedly paranoid.

ST IVES (Tourist Information 01736 796297) is one of the most remarkable places in Cornwall, or indeed anywhere. For anyone who appreciates 20th century art, especially of the abstract, modernist, internationalist variety, the profound role that this little Cornish town has played in its history is extraordinary.

Once a busy pilchard fishing and mining town, its famous light (which is actually quite ultra-violet) began to attract painters to the place in the late 19th century, Sickert and Whistler amongst them. But it was in the early and mid 20th century that St Ives became one of the world's most important centres of contemporary art, acting as a magnet for numerous painters and sculptors, and influencing countless others who never actually came.

The visitor to St Ives who is at all aware of any of the work of the best known artists who have lived here, Hepworth, Nicholson, Wallis, will find that she or he is seeing the place through the eyes of those artists. The almost abstract shapes of the hills and rocks and headlands might have been fashioned by Barbara Hepworth. The forms and colours of rooftops and harbour activity from above recall Ben Nicholson, and the confusion of streets and alleyways, seemingly going off in all directions at once, were clearly laid out by Alfred Wallis. The work of these artists, and others, has determined the way we see the town, which is surely a tribute to the fruitful meeting of people and place which happened here.

Other leading artistic figures associated with St Ives during the century include Wilhelmina Barns-Graham, Patrick Heron, Sven Berlin, Terry Frost and the locally born Peter Lanyon, the only leading abstract painter to actually be indigenous to the town. The potter Bernard Leach is also inseparably connected with St Ives; his memorial for the poor Plymouth-born seaman who turned to painting after his wife died, Alfred Wallis, can be seen near the church (I must admit to sometimes wondering how it is that, though the educated classes eagerly took Wallis up, and learnt from his vision, they still allowed him to end up, and die, in the workhouse, which surely they had the resources to prevent; social boundaries are clearly a deeply-rooted thing).

To acknowledge and celebrate the importance of the town in 20th century art, the TATE GALLERY ST IVES (01736 796226) was opened in 1993, in a singularly beautiful building designed by Eldred Evans and David Shalev, on the site of the old gasworks. This is the perfect setting to appreciate both the art itslf and the unique environment which has nurtured it. It is a gallery of international importance, and a joy to visit.

The BARBARA HEPWORTH MUSEUM (01736 796226), also run by the Tate, shows this remarkable artist's work in her own house and garden. It is inspiring yet profoundly peaceful, a tribute to a sculptor of rare integrity and vision.

There are plenty more art galleries, studios and outlets for both fine arts and CRAFTS in St Ives. Amongst them are the PENWITH GALLERY (01736 795579), the ST IVES SOCIETY OF ARTISTS (01736 795582), the LEACH POTTERY (01736 796398) and the SLOOP MARKET, full of CRAFT workshops and studios. There are dozens of others; one I found enjoyable was the CAT GALLERY, where all the artefacts relate to felines.

At MUSEUM WHEAL DREAM (01736 896005), you can see a very diverse museum of art objects, household items and much else.

St Ives has not only inspired the visual arts. Virginia Woolf spent childhood holidays here, and though her novel *To the Lighthouse* is ostensibly set in Scotland, many descriptions obviously fit the local scenery. Some critics are of the opinion that the local qualities of light and colour are strongly featured in the music of the Cornish composer George Lloyd, who was born here in 1913. His very traditional, late romantic works are enjoying popularity after decades of neglect. St Ives holds an important ARTS FESTIVAL in SEPTEMBER, but the place feels creative and festive at all times.

Altogether, St Ives is a marvellous place to wander around, whether or not you are drawn here because of the art. Its winding streets, hills, beaches and harbour are full of life and people, and its range of shops and pubs would satisfy anyone. For younger visitors, a short journey inland towards Hayle to LELANT, brings you to MERLIN'S MAGIC LAND AMUSEMENT PARK (01736 752885).

Above St Ives is KNILL'S STEEPLE, a 50 foot high triangular granite monument placed here at the request of John Knill, a customs collector in the town in the late 18th century. He intended to be buried in it, but died in London in 1811 and was interred there. In his will he left a legacy for the following ceremony, which he instigated in 1801, to take place every five years, on July 25th.

The mayor of the town, the vicar, a customs officer and three trustees have to walk, in procession, from the Guildhall to the steeple, where, accompanied by a fiddle player, ten little girls in white and two widows dance around it, presumably until everyone is satisfied.

It all sounds rather horrible, though I must admit to not having seen the ceremony in the flesh, so cannot say what atmosphere it has today. I once saw a film of it, made in the 1920s, with the children looking terrified and the two very aged women, dressed in traditional widows' weeds, barely able to move their old limbs. It sent shivers down my back, in a way which no genuine folk tradition would. But maybe I am wrong about it all. The 'Knillian' next happens in 2001, so you can go along and judge for yourself.

HAYLE, a long village beside the estuary, is a decayed industrial centre. It has a certain sombre appeal, especially if looked down upon from its viaduct, and helps to link the strange, magical and creative land we have been in for most of this chapter with the area in which we shall finish. Perversely or not, this is the very down-to-earth area around the industrial towns of **CAMBORNE** and **REDRUTH**.

Although so different in character from such places as Mousehole and St Ives, they are equally Cornish, and the landscape around them, ravaged by mining and industry, has its own stark fascination.

The two places are now more or less one continuous growth along the A3047, and make up the largest urban area in Cornwall. Of the two towns, both of which fiercely maintain their own identity, Camborne is the bigger and older, while Redruth possibly is more visually interesting.

They have long been places associated with MINING, ENGINEERING and EARTH SCIENCES. Many important inventors have been nurtured here. The most famous, of course, is Richard Trevithick, inventor of the first steam locomotive, who was born in 1771 at **ILLOGAN** by Camborne. There is a statue of him in front of the LIBRARY and MUSEUM. The well-known song, 'Going up Camborne Hill, Coming Down', is commonly believed to refer to his first machine.

Trevithick's COTTAGE, run by the Trevithick Trust, is open on WEDNESDAYS, and they also run CORNISH ENGINES (01209 216657) where you can see an impressive display of mining history and machinery.

CAMBORNE MUSEUM (01209 713544) contains items of local interest and, unexpectedly, some Egyptian and Aztec objects.

The world famous CAMBORNE SCHOOL OF MINES possesses a small MUSEUM (01209 714866), with the emphasis on rocks and minerals, but it also displays changing exhibitions of work by local ARTISTS and CRAFTSPEOPLE.

Between Camborne and Redruth is the dramatic granite ridge of CARN BREA, with three summits and often weirdly shaped rocks. Ancient fortifications are here, as well as a miniature CASTLE, now a RESTAURANT, and, in the centre, a tall monument built in 1836 to Francis Bassett, Lord de Dunstanville, known as 'the miner's friend.' Excellent views can be obtained here over the towns and beyond, to the St Ives coast and Penwith.

In Redruth a Scotsman, William Murdoch, was the first person in the world to light his house with gas, in 1792. Benjamin Luxon the singer was born here.

At CORNISH GOLDSMITHS, at TOLGUS MILL (01209 218198) you can see craftspeople at work and marvel at the largest collection of jewellery in the South West.

Not far from Redruth is **ST DAY**, a pleasant little town in the middle of the mining country. Nearby is the famous GWENNAP PIT, a circular bowl with grass terraces, where John Wesley turned the Cornish people dramatically on to Methodism in the 18th century. Services are still held here, and not far away at **CARHARRACK** is the MUSEUM OF CORNISH METHODISM (01209 212104), recording the important role the church has played in the county's life.

Chapter Seven

BUDOCK-VEAN
Golf and Country House Hotel,
Helford River,
Mawnan Smith, Falmouth,
Cornwall TR11 5LG

Tel:01326 250288
Fax: 01326 250892
Reservations: 01326 250230

AA Three Star & Rosette RAC Three Star
Hospitality & 4 Crown Highly recommended

Budock Vean is the sort of place one dreams about finding and so rarely does. Imagine a country house hotel set in some of the most spectacular scenery in southern Britain, an hotel combining the style, elegance and discreet service of a bygone age with all the comfort and amenities of today. The hotel stands in sixty five acres of gardens and parkland with a private foreshore to the tranquil Helford River stirring up romantic memories of Daphne du Maurier and her famous book 'Frenchman's Creek' which is here for you to explore. The hotel is situated in a designated area of outstanding natural beauty from where you can explore some of Britain's most dramatic coastline, including the wild grandeur of Kynance and the Lizard Point. There is the Seal Sanctuary at Gweek, heritage sites, and many magnificent gardens and properties of the National Trust. For the energetic there are many activities including watersports, horseriding, yachting, boating, fishing and much more within easy reach and above all there is the idyllic and challenging parkland golf course which provides a nine or eighteen-hole layout, courses which play exceptionally well all the year round. The 65 acres of parkland form the perfect backdrop for this outstanding hotel. In Spring and Summer the gardens are in majestic full bloom and in Autumn, the trees lining the walkways down to the creek are magnificent, displaying the rich and varied hues of this golden season.

The Hotel is furnished with three comfortable lounges and a well stocked cocktail bar and lounge. Everywhere has the elegance of days gone by especially brought to mind in the large sun-lounge which reminds one of 'colonial' days. The beautifully appointed ensuite bedrooms, some of which have sitting rooms and the majority stunning views over the hotel's Golf Course and sub-tropical gardens towards the river. The award winning Hotel restaurant is renowned for the standard of its food and service and naturally with a thriving fishing industry on its doorstep, local Seafood is an obvious speciality, with lobsters and Helford oysters featuring on the menu. Finally there are three charming self-contained cottages in the hotel grounds, just a few steps from the hotel entrance; stay here and you are entitled to all the amenities this wonderful hotel has to offer.

USEFUL INFORMATION

OPEN;9th February 1998-2nd January 1999
CHILDREN; Welcome
CREDIT CARDS; All major cards except Amex
LICENSED; Full On. Fine wines
ACCOMMODATION; Suites & ensuite rooms
GARDEN; 65 acres . 9 & 18 hole Golf Course.
Tennis Courts, Swimming Pool
TARIFF; D/B&B High Season £63 - £79 pppn, Low Season £43 -£69 pppn

RESTAURANT; Award winning. Seafood
 a speciality
BAR FOOD; Good choice. High standard
VEGETARIAN; Always a choice
DISABLED ACCESS; Not suitable
PETS; Yes £5 per night

THE PANDORA INN,
Restronguet Creek,
Mylor Bridge, Falmouth,
Cornwall TR11 5ST

Tel/Fax: 01326 372678

In the brochure written for The Pandora Inn, everything is said about this famous old inn where Helen Hough is mine host. Taking extracts from this for this piece will give you an insight into what a wonderful place it is and how strongly Helen Hough feels the responsibility in keeping it as it should be for future generations.It is an enchanting place with flagstone floors, low beamed ceilings, gleaming brasswork and memorabilia that catch your eye at every turn. Parts of the building date back to the 13th century when there was a farm on the site; the Restronguet Estate Accounts for 1468 state that the rent was eight shillings and fourpence a year! It has had many names over the centuries including The Passage House and the The Ship until finally it was named The Pandora after a ship that was sent to capture the mutineers of Captain Bligh's Bounty, in Tahiti. The ship floundered on a remote part of the Barrier Reef with the loss of many of the crew and mutineers. The Captain, Captain Edwards, was court martialed and on his return he retired to Cornwall where he is reputed to have bought the inn.

Today you will find a wonderful old world atmosphere, a very friendly staff and excellence at every turn. There are three bars where the ale is well kept and the food terrific with an accent on local produce cooked to order and served indoors or out, weather permitting. Mussels, crab, prawns and mackerel generally feature on the menu since most visitors wish to take advantage of the local seafood. Tasty club sandwiches and home-made treacle tart with clotted cream are perennial favourites. The Andrew Miller Restaurant which is open in the evening, except on Sunday evenings in winter, is upstairs and away from the atmosphere of the traditional inn. Here you can relax and enjoy the delicious food by candlelight. The menu changes frequently and there is always something new and exciting to tempt you.

You can reach The Pandora by sea or land. Whichever way you arrive you will be delighted that you did come and for sure you will come back again and certainly tell all your friends about this unique, enchanting hostelry.

USEFUL INFORMATION

OPEN; All year. 11-11pm (10.30pm Sundays)
CHILDREN; Welcome
CREDIT CARDS; All major cards
LICENSED; Full On
ACCOMMODATION; Not applicable
GARDEN; Yes for eating in summer.
140' Floating pontoon

RESTAURANT; Superb food. Seafood
and fish a speciality
 BAR FOOD; Wide choice
VEGETARIAN; Catered for
DISABLED ACCESS;Yes.Level entrance
PETS; On lead

PENMERE GUEST HOUSE
10 Rosehill
Mylor Bridge
Falmouth
Cornwall
TR11 5LZ

Tel: 01326 374470
Fax: 01326 378828

ETB 2 CrownsCommended
AAQQQQ selected

Mylor Bridge has for long been a great holiday centre. It is a delightful creekside village on the Fal Estuary ideally situated for both the holiday and the business visitor. Within walking distance is the local pub and only a few minutes drive away is the world famous Pandora Inn at Restronguet Creek. The safe waters of the Fal provide perfect conditions for the watersport enthusiasts. The historical port of Falmouth with its Marinas, beaches and nearby mysterious inlets and coves, is a mere three miles away. The rugged cliffs and sandy beaches of the North Coast are only ten miles; and the Cathedral City of Truro with its fine shops and cobbled streets is just nine miles distant. For those who enjoy visiting gardens there are two stunning National Trust Gardens at Glendurgan, Mawnan Smith and Trelissick at Feock, 4 miles south of Truro.

Penmere Guest House, owned by Richard and Sally Cuckson, is in the centre of Mylor Bridge and provides a perfect base for a holiday in this area. Recently refurbished, it is one of those happy houses, with a delightfully relaxed atmosphere inviting one to unwind and enjoy all that it has to offer. There are 4 en-suite bedrooms; 3 with shower rooms & WC and 1 with a bathroom & WC. Two more bedrooms share a bathroom and both have hand washbasins. One of these is a family room with a double bed and a single bed and the other is a twin bedded room. All the rooms have a colour TV and tea/coffee making facilities.

A perfectly cooked, full English breakfast is served every morning in the spacious breakfast room and adjoining this room is a comfortable sitting room for the use of guests.

USEFUL INFORMATION

OPEN: 15 January - 15 December   **BREAKFAST ROOM: Delicious, freshly**
CHILDREN: Welcome   **cooked to order**
CREDIT CARDS: None taken   **VEGETARIAN: Upon request**
LICENSED: No   **DISABLED ACCESS: No facilities**
ACCOMMODATION: 4 en-suite, 1 tw, 1 fam   **PETS: No**
RATES: £22 - £26 pppn, Children under 2; £5 per day, Children 2 -12; £11 - £13 sharing parents room

THE TOP HOUSE.
The Lizard,
Nr Helston,
Cornwall TR12 7NQ

Tel: 01326 290974
Fax: 01326 290313

Originally a farmhouse, then a coaching inn, and after that a two star hotel, The Top House is now the village pub to the delight of all who go there. It has been a licensed hostelry one way and another for 200 years and for the last 45 years the Greenslade family have been mine hosts. The present incumbents are Peter and Anne Greenslade whose cheerful personalities and total professionalism make this one of the nicest hostelries in Cornwall. Amongst the many people who are drawn to the Top House are art lovers who come to enjoy the food and drink but also come to see the exhibitions in the bar of local arts and crafts. Apart from original paintings always on show, The Top House exhibits its own collection of artefacts, water colours, antique prints of local scenes and a miniature bottle collection. Peter has a wide ranging knowledge of local lifeboats, shipwrecks and The Lizard in general and is never averse to talking about them.

Extensive hot and cold meals are served at lunchtime and in the evenings throughout the year. Good traditional fare is on the menu and there is something for everyone including a Children's Menu and a choice for Vegetarians. In the winter there is a roaring log fire which acts as a magnet and in the summer the pub's small garden delights those who enjoy a drink in the open. The Lizard is the most southerly mainland village in the British Isles, less than a mile from the spectacular grandeur of the unspoilt Cornish coast. Surrounded by the sea on three sides, it is a wonderful place to be.

With a large car park, it makes sense to use The Top House as a 'stopover' while you enjoy a walk along the coastal footpath before returning to the pub to enjoy to the full its welcome and hospitality.

USEFUL INFORMATION

OPEN; Mid-May- end Oct 11am-11pm   **RESTAURANT; Not applicable**
CHILDREN; Welcome   **BAR FOOD; Wide choice .**
CREDIT CARDS; Visa/Master/Switch/Amex **VEGETARIAN; Always 3 dishes**
LICENSED; Full On   **DISABLED ACCESS; Difficult**
GARDEN; Yes. Eating & drinking in summer **PETS; Yes**

PENKERRIS,
Penwinnick Road,
St Agnes, Cornwall TR5 0PA
Tel/Fax: 01872 552262

2 Crown approved Les Routiers,
AA,QQ.
RAC Listed Cornwall TB.

This lovely Edwardian residence built by the famous Cornish Architect, Sylvanus Trevail, stands in its own grounds. Penkerris is just on the edge of the unspoilt village of St Agnes with fields on one side, yet on the other, shops, restaurants, (including a Meadery) and several fine old Pubs of character. As one walks up to the house one is aware of how prettily it has aged with mellow stone covered with deeply coloured creeper. Inside the house is elegantly but comfortably furnished and feels more like staying with friends in a country house rather than in a small hotel. The owner, Dorothy Gill-Carey is responsible for this warm welcoming atmosphere. She runs the house immaculately with the help of her small, friendly and competent staff who all want above all things to ensure you enjoy your stay.

There are family rooms, twin rooms, double rooms - en suite if required. In addition there are two bathrooms and a big shower room. There is also an attractive bed-sitting room. Every room has a wash basin, colour television, tea making facilities, electric heaters and shaver points. Guests are welcome to use their bedrooms during the day to rest, eat snacks and make hot drinks. The food, cooked by Dorothy, is delicious whether it is the sumptuous breakfast, a snack lunch, a cream tea or dinner at the end of the day. Dorothy describes her cooking as offering 'real food' and this is absolutely true. She uses fresh local produce including vegetables and fish, traditional roasts, home-made fruit tarts and for a complete change curries and pasta dishes.

Just along the road from Penkerris is St Agnes Leisure Park - a theme park featuring Cornwall in Miniature, Fairyland, Dinosaurs etc and Pressingoll Barns where fudge, candles and pottery are made. There are three beaches at St Agnes - all with magnificent surf. The cliff walks in the area are absolutely magnificent and the whole area is steeped in the history of Cornwall's tin and copper mining era.

USEFUL INFORMATION

OPEN; All year   DINING ROOM; Excellent home-cooked fayre
CHILDREN; Welcome   BAR FOOD; Not applicable
CREDIT CARDS;All major cards   VEGETARIAN; Upon request
LICENSED; Table & Residential   DISABLED ACCESS; Not really suitable
ACCOMMODATION; fam,dbl, tw rooms   GARDEN; Yes, croquet, badminton
PETS; Yes
RATES:- High Season £20 pppn B&B. Low Season £15 pppn B&B.

THE FOX AND HOUNDS
Comford, Gwennap,
Nr Lanner, Redruth,
Cornwall TR16 6AX

Tel: 01209 820251

The Fox and Hounds, a traditional old fashioned pub, has a superb rural location amid farmlands on the A393. It dates from 1742 and is full of character with genuine beams, exposed stone walls, very low ceilings, a 'drop down fireplace' which is still used and is supposedly haunted although history does not relate by whom! Two walls have exciting murals depicting the area centuries ago which is always a talking point for visitors. The outside garden provides a lot of interest especially to those who are interested in wildlife. There is a spring fed pond, well stocked with plants and you will frequently see moorhens, ducks and cootes as well as many other birds.

Mike and Sue Swiss have been the landlords here for some time and have built themselves an enviable reputation for the sincere welcome they give to everyone who crosses the threshold of the pub. Their friendly staff are equally happy to look after you and chat if you feel so inclined. Whilst Mike looks after the bar and the beer, Sue with the aid of a chef cooks food with flair and imagination. The menu is a la carte or table d'hote plus a carvery, and served in the attractive restaurant which has polished tables and pretty tablecloths always adorned with fresh flowers. Every day there are special dishes in addition to the varied menus. You may find yourselves enjoying a perfectly cooked steak or simply have a freshly cut sandwich in the bar. The prices are very acceptable and it is no wonder that so many people make a beeline here for the food. Whilst the wine list is not vast, it is varied and has some 30 wines from all over the world. Many people come here to enjoy a drink and take advantage of the picnic area in the garden from which they can watch all the wildlife activity. The Fox and Hounds appears in the Camra Good Beer Guide and in the Good Pub Guide both confirming the standard of the hostelry.

USEFUL INFORMATION

OPEN;All year. 11.30-3pm & 6-11
Sat & Sun: Open all day
CHILDREN: Welcome
CREDIT CARDS; All major cards inc Amex
LICENSED; Full On
GARDEN; Yes & Picnic area

RESTAURANT; Imaginative cooking
With a la carte & table d'hote menu
BAR FOOD; Wide range. Home-cooked
VEGETARIAN; Always 6 dishes
DISABLED ACCESS; Yes. 3 steps
PETS; Bar only if necessary

ST AGNES HOTEL
Churchtown, St Agnes,
Cornwall TR5 0QP

Tel:01872 552307
Fax: 01872

This unspoilt village has attracted film makers galore and in particular recently the TV series Wycliffe. The author Winston Graham made the village a model for his Poldark books and the filming was done here. It is a delightful place, once noted for mining. The remains of the Blue Hills mine and Wheal Coates are still to be seen. There are superb beaches, coastal walks and stunning scenery, in fact all the ingredients for a perfect Cornish holiday and there is no better place from which to enjoy that holiday than the St Agnes Hotel in Churchtown. Known as the 'Aggie' by the locals it is the friendliest of places with an interesting history. It has grown over the years and today what was the old pub is now the dining area and the new bar on the left was once a Gent's Outfitters. The whole village, like the hotel, has a sense of stability and continuance, for example in the 1800's the local doctor was William Whitworth and since then there has always been a Whitworth in practice.

The hotel has 6 ensuite guest rooms, all charmingly decorated and with pretty drapes and wall coverings. Each room has colour TV and a generously supplied hostess tray. Downstairs the large bar is almost a home from home for locals who welcome visitors happily into their midst. Here there is a well-planned eating area where you can enjoy a great Cornish breakfast if you are staying and wholesome healthy food both at lunchtime and in the evening. There are Specials every day, a Children's menu and one of the specialities of 'Aggies' is Mexican dishes. The excellent range of wines includes some very good house wine at sensible prices. In the summer one can sit out at the front or the back savouring a drink or eating some well cooked and presented fare. Janet and Tony Savage are the welcoming licencees and they are ably supported by their daughter Louise who is the cook and a competent, friendly staff.

USEFUL INFORMATION

OPEN; All year Winter 11-3pm & 6-11pm   RESTAURANT; Good wholesome fare
Open all day Sat & Sun. May-Sept open all day every day
CHILDREN; To eat but not stay   BAR FOOD; Wide range, home-cooked
CREDIT CARDS: All major cards   VEGETARIAN; Several dishes
LICENSED; Full On   PETS; Permitted
ACCOMMODATION; 6 ensuite rooms   DISABLED ACCESS; No facilities
GARDEN; Yes, back & front for sitting & eating
RATES:- High Season, £30. Low Season £25. Rates are pppn B&B.

THE KINGS HEAD INN
Fore Street,
Chacewater, Truro,
Cornwall, TR4 8LN

Tel/Fax: 01872 560652

Cornwall has many good pubs but few, if any, can boast the extraordinary and fascinating mineral collection from local mines which is on view in the bar together with a host of pictures showing mining history. Chacewater was very much the heart of mining so it is not surprising that such a collection should be found here. There are many good reasons for visiting this friendly hostelry but the mineral collection certainly makes it different and demands a visit.

You will find the Kings Head in the heart of the village which lies halfway between Truro and Redruth. It is within easy reach of King Harry Ferry and on the main Plymouth, St Austell, Truro, Penzance bus route and very close to the Mineral Tramways and Poldice Valley Walks.

Dave and Sue Blackborow have been the landlords here since 1990 and have definitely made their mark. They are popular with the locals who come to enjoy the well kept Guest Beers, the fun and the banter at the bar. Visitors are extended the same cordial welcome. Sue is an award winning chef and her food is much sought after. She provides a simple menu of tried and trusted favourites from simple sausage egg and chips to a perfectly cooked steak which will melt in your mouth. You have a choice of omelettes, salads, first class mixed grills and fresh fish caught locally. For the Vegetarian there are always several dishes. Sunday roasts are very popular and booking is advised. The Kings Head has good parking facilities and a large garden set well back from the road. Children are welcome at lunchtimes but not after 9pm for young children

USEFUL INFORMATION

OPEN; 11.30-2.30pm & 5-11pm   RESTAURANT; Not applicable
CHILDREN; Welcome until 9pm   BAR FOOD; Good choice, traditional fare
CREDIT CARDS;Visa/Master/Delta/Switch   VEGETARIAN; Several choices
LICENSED; Full On   DISABLED ACCESS;No special facilities
PETS;Dogs on leads   GARDEN; Large and safe

THE OLD INN
Ludgvan
Nr. Penzance.
Cornwall TR 20 8 EG.

Tel 01736 740419

The Old Inn is an old country pub close to the main A30 in the farming village of Ludgvan not far from Penzance. This village has two interesting features, the ancient old church and the Old Inn. This old coaching inn is unique in that it's stables are still in use. Years ago the inn had a small holding in which all the fresh vegetables were grown. Sadly this is not so today as the small holding had to make way for a car park. Splendid views of the historic St. Michaels Mount can be seen through the lounge window; even more interesting, in the inn itself is a mural which was painted by a local artist, Margaret Ryan, depicting Ludgvan, Lower Quarter in the year 1883.

It really is a nice old pub where visitors and locals mix easily and natter about the weather and local affairs, whilst drinking well kept beers and ales. It is attractively furnished and has a warm atmosphere. Tom Wheatley is mine host who keeps a first class cellar and is a real ale perfectionist. The food is traditional with an appetizing choice of favourite dishes, including genuine steak and kidney pie made from locally reared stock, the Sunday Roast is outstanding value and of such quality that it can not be beaten in Cornwall. For those whom may wish something a little lighter there are bar snacks, ploughmans, sandwiches and much more besides. The board specials are extensive and there is a wide variety of puddings available. The Old Inn has three letting rooms, comfortably furnished but not en-suite, however each room has private facilities. The village is well situated for local walks and as a focal point to explore this exciting part of the Duchy.

USEFUL INFORMATION.

Open; All Year.   **BAR FOOD, Traditional & good value.**
CHILDREN; Family room.   **VEGETARIAN; Dishes always available.**
CREDIT CARDS; Not taken.   **WHEELCHAIR ACCESS; Yes**
ACCOMMODATION; 3 rooms.   **GARDEN; Yes, with swings etc.**
RATES:- All Year £15/£18 pppn B&B.   **(Children by arrangement).**

THE WELLINGTON HOTEL,
Market Square,
St Just-in-Penwith,
Nr. Penzance, Cornwall TR19 7HD

Tel:01736 787319
Fax: 01736 787906

AA Three Star.
ETB Three Crowns.

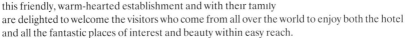

Many people will tell you that St Just-in-Penwith, the historic mining and coastal town is considered by many to be the last of the 'real' Cornwall, and really a delightful place to visit, situated on the spectacular, scenic B3306 coastal road from Land's End to St Ives. You will find no better place to stay, drink or eat, than Wellington Hotel named after the Iron Duke just afte Battle of Waterloo. Rod and Jenny Gray are the owner this friendly, warm-hearted establishment and with their family are delighted to welcome the visitors who come from all over the world to enjoy both the hotel and all the fantastic places of interest and beauty within easy reach.

Loving and tender care went into the modernisation and refurbishment of the Wellington in recent years and the result is modern comforts but the retention of all the old, splendid features of the building. Hotel it may be, and a very successful one, but neither Rod or Jenny ever forget that it is also the local inn where regulars congregate to enjoy their beer and chat over matters pertinent to the village. They are a friendly lot and more than willing to include visitors in their deliberations! The food at The Wellington is noted for its quality and excellence. There is a wide choice right across the board with a traditional Sunday Lunch and in Bar Food The Wellington has Prize winning Ploughman Lunches as well as fresh crab and local fish. There is a Children's Choice Menu which is frequently the choice of people with small appetites. Vegetarians are catered for and although the wine list is small it does have some good wines. The accommodation includes standard or ensuite facilities. There is a honeymoon suite and family rooms, capable of being linked together to provide a larger suite. Every room has TV, a Beverage Tray, Trouser Press and Hair Dryer. The hotel is open all the year round and in winter is particularly warm and cosy - just the place for an off season break.

USEFUL INFORMATION

OPEN; All year. 10.30am-11pm
CHILDREN; Welcome. Childrens Room
CREDIT CARDS; All major cards
LICENSED; Full On
ACCOMMODATION; Standard & ensuite rooms
GARDEN; Yes. Children's Play Area
PETS; Yes. Must have own bedding
RATES:- All year £20 and £25 pppn. B&B.

RESTAURANT; Noted for its food
BAR FOOD; Excellent. Prize winning
Ploughman Lunches
VEGETARIAN; Always a choice
DISABLED ACCESS; Yes. 3 ground
Floor rooms & toilet facilities

THE QUEENS HOTEL,
Promenade,
Penzance, Cornwall TR18 4HG

Tel: 01736 362371
Fax: 01736 350033

3Star AA
RAC 4 Crown Commended

This elegant hotel in an unique setting on the sea front promenade of the old market town of Penzance was built in 1854 to coincide with the completion of Brunel's Great Western Railway Line from Paddington to Penzance. It has always been the place to stay in Penzance for several reasons, not the least being the majestic views which sweep across Mounts Bay from Newlyn to St Michael's Mount and the Lizard Peninsula. Another reason is because it is ideally placed for those who want to explore the myths and legends, the Celtic Stone Circles, the coastal footpath which runs from St Ives to Penzance, the beautiful sandy beaches and also the Newlyn Oriel and the Tate Art Gallery in St Ives. You can play golf, go pony trekking, surfing and wind surfing as well as many other sporting activities.

Within this beautifully appointed and comfortable hotel, now owned by three local people, you will be cosseted in the nicest possible way, fed on superb food in the gracious 100 cover restaurant with a meal that is complemented by the finest wines. The chefs are talented, dedicated people who delight in ensuring that every meal is perfect and that there is something to suit everyone's palate. There are bar meals, simple snacks, afternoon teas, in fact everything you wish for. The 70 bedrooms are immaculately appointed and all ensuite. 30 have sea views and recently 23 rooms have been completely refurbished and are called 'superior' rooms. Throughout the building there are some fine antiques and some equally good paintings - not as many as there were at one time when the then owners bought any number of paintings of the Newlyn School which resulted in a famous sale in 1984 by Phillips of London. One thing that highlights the success of The Queens is the contentment of the staff who love their jobs and many have been in them for over a quarter of a century. This in itself is recommendation enough for one of the premier hotels in Cornwall.

USEFUL INFORMATION

OPEN; All Year
RESTAURANT; Non-smoking. Superb food
CHILDREN; Welcome
BAR FOOD; Buffet lunch served daily
CREDIT CARDS; All major cards
VEGETARIAN; Catered for
LICENSED; Full On
DISABLED ACCESS; Yes. 7 steps. Toilets
ACCOMMODATION; 70 ensuite rooms
GARDEN; No
PETS; Yes £6 a night
Winter / Summer Breaks and all year Mini Breaks:- Details available on request.
RATES:- High Season, from £38 pppn B&B. Low Season, from £32 pppn. B&B.

STRATHALLAN
Monument Road,
Helston, Cornwall TR13 8HF

Tel/Fax: 01326 573683

3 Crown Commended (ETB)

This comfortable Guest House is small enough with seven ensuite rooms to retain the pleasant feeling of a home from home. Owned and run by the owners Mike and Rosemary Wadley with the help of local staff, who are not only as meticulous as their employers in the running of the house, but also have a wonderful rapport with the guests. The whole house has this friendly, happy atmosphere and one wonders if it was just the same when it was built in the middle of the 19th century; a time when buildings were both elegant and gracious and the rooms always spacious. Strathallan stands in its own grounds with pretty gardens in which to sit or stroll. It is on the edge of Helston, famous throughout the world for its annual 'Furry Dance' when people dance through the streets and in and out of houses. Helston is well situated for anyone wanting to discover some wonderful beaches, go deeper into Cornwall to Lands End or seek out some of the very pretty coves and villages. There are any number of attractions and gardens nearby to visit including Flambards, an Air and Period Theme Park, Trebah Gardens at Mawnan Smith, an old Cornish (Listed) Garden which adjoins Glendurgan a National Trust Garden on the Helford River. The Royal Naval Air Station at Culdrose, part of Helston has an excellent public viewing area. Goonhilly Down Earth Satellite station nearby has an excellent Visitors Centre.

Within Strathallan the bedrooms are all prettily decorated and furnished with delightful colour co-ordinated drapes and bed covers. Each room has a beverage tray, colour television and other nice touches. There is a comfortable lounge and an attractive, non-smoking dining room in which you will be given a delicious breakfast, cooked to your choice or a simpler continental one. Vegetarians are catered for. In the evening one can enjoy a home-cooked meal with lots of fresh vegetables and tempting desserts but you must order it in advance. If you decide to eat out there are all sorts of interesting eateries within a 15 minute drive and the well known Blue Anchor Public House - home of 'Spingo' Real Ale is a 3 minute walk into town.

Strathallan is licensed and so you can look forward to a drink in the evenings when you return after a day out and there are honesty mini-bars in each room.. The garden is delightful and a restful place to be for a quiet time at the end of the day. Whatever you decide you will find your whole stay here is relaxed and just what is needed to recharge your batteries for the stress of modern day life.

USEFUL INFORMATION

OPEN; All year	**DINING ROOM; Excellent wholesome food**
CHILDREN; No	**Dinner by arrangement. Non-smoking**
CREDIT CARDS; Amex	**VEGETARIAN; Upon request**
LICENSED; Yes. Mini-bars in rooms	**NO WHEELCHAIR ACCESS.**
ACCOMMODATION; 7 ensuite rooms	**PETS; No.**
GARDEN; YES.	**RATES:- Double £38 per room. Single £27. All Year.**

AN MORDROS HOTEL
Peverell Terrace,
Porthleven, Cornwall Tr13 9DZ

Tel/Fax:01326 562236

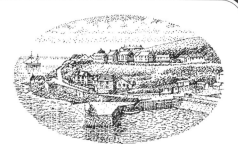

Porthleven is situated in the middle of the Mounts Bay Coastline and regarded as England's most southerly port. A 465ft long granite pier extends seawards and prominently nearby is the old 70ft high clock tower which has for long been a landmark. On the otherside of the slipway is the famous Ship Inn, arguably the oldest building in the village. Porthleven is one of the very few unspoilt, traditional fishing villages left and has a wealth of history. It is especially famous or perhaps it should be infamous, for its smuggling and wrecking history, very prevalent in the 18th and 19th centuries.

In the midst of Porthleven is the friendly and very comfortable An Mordros Hotel owned and run by a lively Italian lady, Maria Kelynack and her daughter Sandy. They are both gregarious and love nothing better than socialising with their guests. There are 8 comfortable bedrooms, four of which are ensuite and complete with television and a hostess tray. The food is plentiful and excellent. Maria cooks a substantial breakfast, offers bar snacks and packed lunches and in the evening cooks a sumptuous four course meal. Everything is home-made and not to be forgotten are the delectable Cream Teas!

An Modros is the catalyst from which one can book accommodation in three well appointed houses closeby. **Anchor Cottage** owned by Peter and Margaret Ingham has 1 double and 1 twin letting rooms both with sea views. An excellent breakfast is served and light snacks and cream teas are available if you wish. One of the benefits of staying here is that you can have breakfast whenever you wish; your hosts are totally flexible. **Mounts Bay Villa** is self-catering and sleeps 8. It has a fully fitted modern kitchen and is well furnished. It is 60 yards from the sea on a cliff-top position with wonderful views over the bay. **Tripolitania** also self-catering, is an architect designed modern house. Sleeps 8, has a fitted and well equipped kitchen. The bathroom has an exceptionally large bath. Open tread stairs lead to a huge lounge furnished with cane and pine furniture. Superb views over the Bay. Both these houses have 4 keys status from the Tourist Board.

USEFUL INFORMATION

OPEN; All year
CHILDREN; Welcome
CREDIT CARDS; All Major Cards
LICENSED; An Modros, yes
AN MODROS: Great food
ANCHOR COTTAGE: Breakfast only
GARDEN; Yes
DISABLED ACCESS; Not suitable
ACCOMMODATION; An Modros: 8 rooms 4 ensuite (Rate; H/S £17/25.L/S £15/20 PPPN)
Anchor Cottage: 2 double rooms(Rate; £15 PPPN All Year)
Mounts Bay Villa: Sleeps 8 (Rate; H/S £733 p.w.L/.S£186/364 p.w.)
Tripolitania: Sleeps 8 (H.S. £475 p.w. L/S £150/350 p.w.)

THE DRIFTWOOD SPARS HOTEL
Trevaunance Cove,
St Agnes, Cornwall TR5 0RT
Tel/Fax: 01872 552428 or 553323

ETB Three Crowns Commended.
Egon Ronay, Good Pub/
Beers guides Recommended.

Built in the 17th century of slate, granite and enormous ships spars from which the hotel now takes its name, the building has in its time been a mine warehouse and sail loft before being lovingly converted into its present form of a fine hotel and friendly public house in which Jill and Gordon Treleaven are your hosts. The Driftwood Spars previous history shows around every corner with the huge rough hewn beams, small lead light windows and granite fireplaces, there is even a wreckers tunnel running behind the bar which can be glimpsed through a porthole in the Tween Decks Bar. There are 9 en suite bedrooms, some with wonderful sea views and one with a delightful half tester Victorian bed. Each room has colour TV, telephone, hostess tray and hair dryer. It is a happy place to stay at any time of the year.

Just a stones throw from one of the country's finest surfing beaches, where the remains of the lost harbour of St Agnes can be seen at low tide, the Driftwood Spars is popular with locals and tourists alike offering three cosy bars including one for games where children are very welcome. Regularly featured in the Campaign for Real Ales National Guides and entered every year in the Cornish Guide the Driftwood is noted for the quality of real ale available with 6 hand pulled ales including a weekly guest beer always on tap and in addition the Lower Deck Bar boasts a collection of over 100 malt whiskies from home and abroad.

Open all day throughout the year, live music is a popular feature, with both local and nationally known bands performing on Friday and Saturday nights from 10pm until midnight. Whether you are just passing through mid-Cornwall or looking for somewhere special, do visit the Driftwood Spars, the large car park offers convenience for the road user or the coastal footpath across the cliffs passes the front door

USEFUL INFORMATION

OPEN; All day, (Midnight Fri & Sat).	**RESTAURANT; English fare**
CHILDREN; Welcome	**BAR FOOD; Wide choice, Board specials**
CREDIT CARDS; All major cards	
LICENSED; Full On	**VEGETARIAN; Always a choice**
ACCOMMODATION 9 en suite rooms	**NO WHEELCHAIR ACCESS.**
PETS; Permitted 1.50per night	**GARDEN; Beer Garden**

RATES:- High Season £29 pppn B&B. Low Season £27 pppn B&B., Single Supp. £11.

THE TOBY JUG,
1,Park Avenue,
St Ives, Cornwall TR26 2 DW
Tel: 01736 794250
Tourist Board Inspected.

You will certainly never come across another Guest House quite like The Toby Jug. It has a charm all of its own and takes your interest the moment you cross the threshold. It lives up to its name; there are Toby Jugs of all sizes and colours everywhere - you even pour your tea from one! It is quite delightful. Run by a qualified chef Bill Stirling and his wife Margaret this family guest house is in an ideal position. It is only minutes away from the picturesque harbour, the main shopping centre and many beaches. Open all year, the house is warm and comfortable and just the place for a holiday or short break at any season. Christmas menus are available for anyone who would like to come here at the festive season.Many people enjoy St Ives out of season more than when it is at its busiest in the summer. It is the most picturesque resort in Cornwall with its ever changing combination of magnificent coastal views with narrow cobbled streets which wind their way between quaint fishermen's cottages. There is so much for holidaymakers to do and see with fascinating shops, craft markets, museums, galleries including the famous Tate Gallery and a host of Cornish inns. Within easy distance of The Toby Jug you can fish, go surfing, play tennis, golf or squash, bathe, take a boat out, go horse riding and trekking.

There are no ensuite bedrooms but every room is charmingly furnished, the beds are king size, the linen fresh and crisp, with continental quilts, towels are changed daily and the bed linen twice weekly.. Each room has colour TV and tea and coffee making facilities and the majority have sea views. The house is centrally heated throughout. Breakfast is a delicious meal with a choice of several dishes and eggs cooked whichever way you like them. In addition to the traditional breakfast there are also grilled kippers and smoked haddock. The evening meal is home cooked and something guests look foward to.

USEFUL INFORMATION

OPEN;Jan-Dec	**DINING ROOM; Traditional English Breakfast**
CHILDREN; Welcome	**Home-cooked evening meal**
CREDIT CARDS: None taken	**VEGETARIAN; Upon request**
LICENSED; No	**DISABLED ACCESS;Yes. No special facilities**
ACCOMMODATION; Sleeps 20 maximum	**PETS; No**

RATES:- All Year, £14 pppn B&B.Children half price.
Special seasonal break price available:- Details on request.

CORNISH RANGE,
6 Chapel Street,
Mousehole, Cornwall
TR19 6SB

Tel:01736 731488
Fax: 01736 732255

Once the centre of the busy Pilchard Fishing Industry, Mousehole has largely shed its scales and devotes itself almost entirely to the enjoyment of tourists who come here to revel in the quaint village, pronounced 'Muzzle' incidentally, with its narrow winding streets. It still has a harbour used mainly by small local fishermen, the larger trawlers use the facilities of neighbouring Newlyn.

Cornish Range is an exciting restaurant housed in an old building which was once a Pilchard Press and has had many different occupants but none more suitable than its present purpose owned and run by Sue Perry , her partner Richard who you will find looking after customers in the evenings, together with a talented chef.

The menu covers a wide range of dishes from traditional English to more exotic food from the Continent. Prepared with care, using local produce and ingredients wherever possible, you can be sure of a truly memorable meal. There are always vegetarian options and vegans can be catered for with notice.The atmosphere is restful and intimate, just the place to be after a days exploration in this fascinating part of Cornwall which has so much to offer.

USEFUL INFORMATION

OPEN; Easter-October Mon-Sat 7pm
Nov-Easter: Thurs/Fri/Sat 7pm
+ 12 noon Sunday
CHILDREN; Welcome
CREDIT CARDS; All major cards
LICENSED; Yes. Restaurant

RESTAURANT; Super food
beautifully cooked & presented

VEGETARIAN; Catered for
DISABLED ACCESS; Yes
PETS; Not permitted

THE OLD SUCCESS INN
Sennen Cove,
Nr Lands End, Cornwall
TR19 7DG

Tel: 01736 871232
Fax: 01736 871457

AA/RAC Two Star.
ETB Three
Crowns Commended.

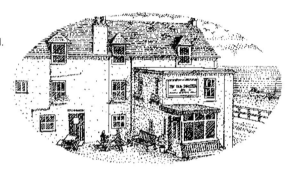

Sennen Cove calls up all the romanticism of Cornwall with its history of Pilchard fishing and smuggling. The Old Success is a 17th century Fishermen's Inn nestling in one of Cornwall's most beautiful bays with fabulous views of Cape Cornwall. It is just one mile from Lands End and has a major Blue Flag surfing beach which hosts the British Championships. Sennen Cove itself is a small unspoilt village.

The Inn richly deserves all its accolades which include ETB 3 crown commended, 2 Star AA & RAC, Le Routier, Good Pub Guide and Discover Britain Inn of the year highly commended. It has 12 delightful bedrooms, 10 of which are ensuite and include 2 four poster rooms. There are also 2 Self-Catering Holiday Apartments. The restaurant is renowned for its food especially the locally caught fish. Seafood also features although 12 hours notice is normally required for lobster. The Bar Menu covers a wide range of mainly traditional fare including the famous Cornish Pasty made in St Just by W.T Warren who have been bakers since 1860. You will see much evidence of the Lifeboat in the bars, the assistant manager and two members of staff are members of the crew. Above all The Old Success is a friendly, welcoming inn, run by professionals who make everything seem so simple!

USEFUL INFORMATION

OPEN; All year. Summer: 11-11pm
Winter: 11-2.30pm & 6-11pm
CHILDREN;Welcome
CREDIT CARDS; All major cards
LICENSED; Full On
ACCOMMODATION; 12 rooms, 10ensuite

RESTAURANT; Excellent menu with
lots of locally caught fish and seafood
BAR FOOD; Traditional fare
VEGETARIAN; Always a choice
DISABLED ACCESS; Not easy
PETS; Welcome. No charge

2 Self-Catering Holiday Apartments, Short breaks: From Nov-late Dec & Jan-Easter
RATES:- High Season, from £34. Low Season,from £25 . rates are pppn b&b
Children under 12 half price.

YARD BISTRO
Trelowarren,
Mawgan, Helston.
Cornwall TR12 6AF

Tel:- 01326 221595.

This is a very unusually situated establishment, you will find it in a courtyard, which in turn is surrounded by 1,000 acres of wooded countryside. Quite idyllic in fact. The Bistro is a cleverly and attractively converted carriage house which has retained may of the original features, including an open fire place, granite stanchions with large stable windows, overlooking the courtyard. One of the many pleasures of eating here is to be able to sit outside on a warm evening, revelling in the peace and quite, whilst savouring quite delicious food with a distinct Cornish influence.

The Bistro can seat forty in perfect comfort and there is a fascinating change of ambience between lunchtime and dinner. Perhaps it is the change from the cottage type table dressing of the lunch period to beautiful damask cloths at night, but probably one has time to relax and enjoy the atmosphere and superb food at night, which is sometimes not possible during the day. You will find displays from local artists here for sale, which always makes for an interesting discussion on one's personal choice. Occasionally there are Jazz evenings, these nights are extremely popular, it may be necessary to book, please make enquires if you are a Jazz fan. The menu is changed daily, and is always very interesting sporting a wide choice. There are blackboard choices also apart from the main menu, the Bistro specialises in using only fresh local produce, free range eggs, locally reared beef etc. In the high season it really is advisable to book in advance to be certain of a table.

USEFUL INFORMATION

OPEN; All Year. Season variations.
Usually 12 - 2pm. 7 - 12 pm.
CREDIT CARDS; Mater/Visa/Switch.
LICENCED; Fully
GARDEN; Courtyard for eating in good weather

BISTRO; Interesting fare.
VEGETARIAN; Good selection
CHILDREN, Always welcome.
WHEELCHAIR ACCESS/toilets.
PETS; No (Except G/D).

TYE ROCK HOTEL,
Loe Bar Road,
Porthleven, Nr Helston,
Cornwall TR139EW
Tel/Fax: 01326 572695

ETB. Three Crowns

Tye Rock Hotel is one of the outstanding hotels in Cornwall. Not because it is the biggest, the most upmarket or even the most elegantly furnished but because it is different, fun, comfortable, welcoming and the owners, Pat and Richard Palmer and their staff delight in pleasing their guests and providing a fund of entertaining events. You might find yourselves part of a Victorian weekend, with a definite touch of the 'Upstairs, Downstairs, syndrome. Members of the MG Owners Club meet here bringing their vintage cars with them. There are 50's weekends, Gourmet Breaks Murder Mystery Weekends, a magical Christmas Break and if you have any special theme break you would enjoy, just contact Pat and Richard and they will see if they can 'tailor' a break to suit you. Add all this to the stunning situation of Tye Rock overlooking Mount's Bay and ten minutes walk to the unspoilt fishing village of Porthleven, you can understand why the hotel is special.

There are seven en-suite, individually decorated bedrooms all with sea views. Meals are served in the elegant Victorian dining room. The well stocked cosy bar and a comfortable lounge with log fires are meeting places. There is nothing like having a drink on the terrace and watching the fabulous sunsets over Mounts Bay. The whole atmosphere is relaxed and happy. There are eight self-catering apartments which all look out across the swimming pool and the sea. They are fully equipped - the only things you need to bring are towels. They also have the benefit of all the hotel facilities including the bar and meals in the dining room.

USEFUL INFORMATION

OPEN; All year	RESTAURANT; Good home-cooked fare.
CHILDREN; Welcome	VEGETARIAN; Catered for
CREDIT CARDS;Mastercard	WHEELCHAIR ACCESS Yes
LICENSED; Residential/Restaurant	PETS £3. Per day.

ACCOMMODATION; 7 ensuite rooms, 8 Apartments
GARDEN; Yes with large, deep heated swimming pool
RATES:- Hotel en-suite rooms, from £60/68 per room per night. B&B. All year.
Apartments £155/440 All year. Special Breaks:- November to March, Details on request.

TREWORDER FARM
Ruan Minor, Nr Helston,
Cornwall TR12 7JL

Tel: 01326 290970

If you want to stay in a comfortable friendly home owned by two people, John and Barbara Rosindale, you will not do better than visit them at Treworder Farm, a few yards from the village centre. The farm has not been worked since 1980 and the Rosindale's home was a derelict barn which has been delightfully converted. It is such a peaceful, happy place. John and Barbara are both retired teachers and keen gardeners who with their dog and cat make everyone extremely welcome. The house is not furnished to any particular period but gives the impression of lived in comfort. The Lounge overlooks the courtyard to the front of the house - full of flowers in summer with an old fig tree at the entrance. The dining room has french windows leading to the garden which guests are welcome to use, and there is a gas barbecue for guests' use if they wish. Both bedrooms - one double and one twin - overlook the garden and have panoramic views. Colour Television and a generously supplied hostess tray are to be found in both rooms. In May, June and September Barbara offers the double or the twin with a private bathroom. In July and August the double and twin have a shared bathroom. Barbara makes fresh bread daily which is served at breakfast when there is always a varied choice and plenty of it. An evening meal is not provided but there is an excellent, reasonably priced restaurant in Cadgwith, ten minutes walk away. Pub meals can be found at the Cadgwith Cove Inn and there are various restaurants, hotels and pubs at The Lizard and Mullion and a little further away at St Keverne, Coverack, Helston and Helford. This is a wonderful and very beautiful part of Cornwall. The Lizard Peninsula is a naturalists delight. Spring comes early and Indian Summers are common.

USEFUL INFORMATION

OPEN; May-September
CHILDREN; Over 5 years
CREDIT CARDS; None taken
LICENSED; No
ACCOMMODATION; 1dbl 1tw
GARDEN; Yes.

DINING ROOM; Varied choice at Breakfast
Home-baked bread. No evening meal
VEGETARIAN; Upon request
DISABLED ACCESS; Not suitable
PETS; No

RATES:- All Year:- from £16 pppn B&B. Children 5 - 12 yrs sharing £8. Older full rate.

Chapter Eight

CHAPTER EIGHT

NORTH CORNWALL : FROM NEWQUAY TO BUDE

"Hospitality consists in a little fire, a little food and an immense quiet."
Emerson

CHAPTER EIGHT

NORTH CORNWALL FROM NEWQUAY TO BUDE

The North Cornish coast is a place of romance, legend, wildness and excitement. It takes the full force of the Atlantic, and has imposing and rugged cliffs, interspersed with sandy beaches, dunes and safe little harbours. It is amongst the best and most challenging surfing country (if 'country' is the word) in the world, although it is admittedly not as perfect for the sport as California and Australia.

This area is really one which needs to be explored at leisure, following the mood that takes you. Rather than darting from one major attraction to another, travel around slowly, seeking out the remote and atmospheric villages, the myriad coves, secretive beaches and poetic headlands. If you have the time and inclination, try a stretch of the SOUTH WEST COAST PATH, which here provides some of the most magnificent cliff scenery of the whole peninsula.

The NORTH CORNWALL HERITAGE COAST AND COUNTRYSIDE SERVICE produces a free guide, 'COAST LINES AND COUNTRYSIDE NEWS', providing information and advice on how to get the best out of this fascinating environment.

This area has the major seaside resort of Newquay, but generally its settlements are smaller and very individual, tending to attract people who are equally so.

Inland, as we travel north east, is the rough country of Bodmin Moor, a smaller version of Dartmoor, with its granite outcrops and lonely wastes.

We start this chapter a few miles north of Camborne-Redruth at the steep old tin-mining town of **ST AGNES**, which also had a harbour where the tin was once shipped away. The area is rich in industrial relics and beautiful cliff WALKS. Uncrowded BEACHES can also be found.

Two distinguished sons of the parish were the 18th century artist John Opie, a poor boy who was taken up by the intelligentsia and made good, and John Passmore Edwards, a Victorian newspaper proprietor who endowed many libraries and public buildings throughout Cornwall (and beyond: the library in Newton Abbot was given in memory of his mother, who came from there).

In the town are an interesting local history MUSEUM and several GALLERIES and GIFT SHOPS, including IMAGES OF CORNWALL and the SAFFRON GALLERY.

The saint after whom the town is named, St Agnes, was a wandering Celtic missionary, who unfortunately drew to herself the unwanted attentions of a rather stupid Cornish giant called Bolster. He followed her around everywhere, loudly proclaiming his infatuation. The holy lady eventually hit on a solution to the problem, though. Taking him to a hole in a rock at nearby CHAPEL PORTH, she asked him to prove his devotion by filling it up with his blood. Thinking that only the tiniest drop would be enough, the giant immediately cut himself over the hole. Unfortunately, this went right through the cliff into the sea, so the poor giant, still swearing eternal devotion, bled to death. A reddish stain can be seen on the rock to this day.

PERRANPORTH has a 3 mile BEACH and is a popular family resort. The splendidly named PERRANZABULOE FOLK MUSEUM (01872 573368) vividly recaptures the social and domestic life of past ages. There is also a model of St Piran's original oratory, which now lies beneath the shifting sands.

We are in Cornish saint country here; many of them crossed over from Wales or Ireland during the 5th and 6th centuries, in order to convert their fellow Celts to their distinctive brand of Christianity (the fact that they were often said to have floated over on millstones or similar objects is not the point).

The early Celtic church has attracted sympathy from many peope in recent years, because of its apparent ecological awareness and sense of reverence for nature, and for its unexpectedly enlightened respect, at that time, for women. The colourful stories of the Cornish saints are usually on a rather different level, but it is easy to see why the idea of these sometimes fiery, sometimes gentle missionaries, walking by the shore and on the moors, building their little cells and preaching, should appeal to us.

At Perranporth, Winston Graham wrote the first 'Poldark' novel, little knowing how successful the series would be. A very worthwhile CELTIC MUSIC FESTIVAL is held here in OCTOBER.

Inland, at **GOONHAVEN** (evocative name), is WORLD IN MINIATURE (01872 572828), which has scale models of world famous buildings like the Leaning Tower of Pisa, the Statue of Liberty and the Taj Mahal. It is set in 12 acres of landscaped grounds, and also features a cimema, an aventure dome and recreation of Tombstone, Arizona.

CRANTOCK is a pretty little village with a huge expanse of beach, and could not be more different in style from its close neighbour, the well-known holiday town of **NEWQUAY** (Tourist Information 01637 871345).

This is a large, mainly modern seaside resort, with all the expected features: long, golden BEACHES, SURFING, spacious thoroughfares, colourful and beautifully kept PARKS and GARDENS, dazzling white hotels overlooking the sands, warm sunshine and just a few memories of the original, modest fishing community which Newquay once was, before the resort developed in the 19th century. Sir David Willcocks, the conductor, was born here.

One of the older memories of Newquay is embodied by the little whitewashed HUER'S HUT on TOWAN HEAD, from which the 'huer', a man or a woman with good eyesight, a loud voice and the ability to look at the sea for long hours without losing concentration, would watch for the shoals of pilchards. When they were spotted, he or she would cry out 'Heva! heva!' and the fishing fleet would put to sea, directed by the huer to where the fish were.

Newquay today is not a place for especially subtle pleasures. Everything is geared towards fun and hedonistic relaxation by the seaside, but for those who just want to sit in a flowery park or watch the sea coming in and out, it provides more genteel corners. Amongst its more youthful attractions are an AMERICAN THEME PARK (Cowboys and Indians) (01637 88160), ANIMAL WORLD (01637 873342), an 8 acre landscaped wildlife park, the DAIRYLAND FARM WORLD (01872 510246), and LAND OF ILLUSION (01637 877531).

The LAPPA VALLEY RAILWAY (01872 510317) provides an enjoyable 2 mile journey, by narrow gauge steam train, to the site of a historic lead and silver mine, wheal Rose. There was a serious flood disaster at the mine in 1846, but now there is a theme park with a BOATING LAKE, WOODLAND PATHS and NATURE TRAIL.

For sport in Newquay there is a GOLF CLUB (01637 874354) and the BLUE LAGOON LEISURE CENTRE is the place for SWIMMING, SPORTS of all kinds and NIGHT LIFE. The town has, of course, a very wide range of HOTELS, PUBS, RESTAURANTS and GUEST HOUSES to suit all tastes. A few miles outside is a quieter, older attraction, the National Trust's TRERICE HOUSE AND GARDEN (01637 875404).

A beautifully secluded little Elizabethan Manor with a gabled facade, it has 576 panes of glass in the great hall, good fireplaces, plaster ceilings, oak and walnut furniture and clocks. A small MUSEUM devoted to the history of the humble LAWN MOWER is housed in a barn. The GARDENS are peaceful and contain rare plants, as well as an ORCHARD of old fashioned fruit trees. A delightful place.

More typically Cornish in atmosphere than Newquay and its modern amusements is the little town of **ST COLUMB MAJOR**, a narrow-streeted place of attractive buildings like the granite CORN EXCHANGE and the slate-hung Glebe House, which dates from 1638. BARCLAYS BANK, in the centre, is more ornate, with its turrets and decoration, than most branches of high street banks tend to be. The church is large for the size of the town.

It must be quite fun here at election times, because the LIBERAL and CONSERVATIVE CLUBS face each other across a narrow street.

Perhaps, though, being confrontational comes naturally in this apparently peaceful community, because the traditional Cornish game of HURLING, rather like very primitive football, is played here every SHROVE TUESDAY. The mayor throws a silver ball into the air, and two teams, Townsmen and Countrymen, compete to convey it, in whatever way they can, to the goals, which are two miles apart. The lower windows of the town are boarded up, just to be on the safe side, but it is all good fun. Another match is played on the second Saturday after the event, when everyone has recovered from the first.

St Columb Major holds an ANNUAL MUSIC FESTIVAL in JULY.   The Nobel Prize-winning novelist William Golding was born here, and returned to Cornwall late in his life. In addition to his achievements as a writer, he deserves a mention as it was he who suggested that the name of the old Greek goddess of the Earth, 'Gaia', might, with propriety, be used for the concept of the planet being a self-regulating system. This idea was developed by Golding's scientist neighbour, James Lovelock. He could, therefore, be indirectly held responsible for all the trendy talk that can be heard, especially in the more 'alternative' parts of Devon and Cornwall, on the need to have reverence for 'guyah'. (which is incorrect pronunciation, anyway; it should be 'jee-ah').

At **TREDINNICK** is the CORNISH SHIRE HORSE CENTRE (01841 540276), where visitors can see a parade of horses, inspect smithies and wheelwright's shop, displays of carts and machinery and much else. There is also a working water wheel. A special feature is the OWL SANCTUARY, where barn owls can be seen flying freely and mysteriously in a moonlit atmosphere.

WADEBRIDGE (Tourist Information 01208 813725) is a lively market town in an archetypal situation at the highest navigable point on its river. In this case the river is the Camel, which is spanned by a long Medieval bridge. This has been altered over the years for traffic, but its foundations are said to rest on bundles of wool.

The railway from Bodmin to Padstow came through here, but this is now the CAMEL TRAIL CYCLE AND FOOTPATH, an excellent means of seeing the surrounding countryside. The town's old STATION has become the JOHN BETJEMAN CENTRE, which celebrates the life of the poet and his local connections (of which more in a moment).

The name of Eddystone Road commemorates the fact that the lighthouse was designed and made here of local stone, before being shipped around to its home on the dreaded rocks south of Plymouth Sound, from the town's quay.

Wadebridge has a pleasant pedestrianised main street, with some interestingly individual shops and pubs. It gives the feeling of being quite an ordinary town, confidently getting on with its life.

It is the venue for both the prestigious ROYAL CORNWALL SHOW in JUNE, with many kinds of entertainment, show-jumping, food and drink as well as agricultural displays, and the CORNWALL FOLK FESTIVAL at the end of AUGUST. This is a very full weekend event of traditional music and performance from all over the Westcountry and beyond. WADEBRIDGE CARNIVAL is in early AUGUST. The town has a SPORTS CENTRE (01208 814980) providing all kinds of recreational facilities.

EGLOSHAYLE (from the Cornish 'Eglos' - church, 'hayle' - estuary, with no 'sh' sound), across the river, has the original mother church of the town, a fine edifice, with a good peal of bells.

At nearby **ST TUDY** Captain Bligh of the *Bounty* was brought up, though he was actually born in Plymouth.

At **ST ISSEY** is the MELLINGEY MILL WILLOW CRAFT CENTRE (01481 540604), where baskets are made in the traditional way using willows grown beside the mill, which has possibly the oldest working water wheel in Cornwall. The spacious old stone building, surrounded by the MILLPOND and WILLOW BEDS, with WOODLAND WALKS, PICNIC AREAS and SHOP and TEA ROOM, makes an ideal day out.

Five miles from Wadebridge along the Camel estuary, by way of the Trail, is the famous old port of **PADSTOW** (Tourist Information 01841 533449), on the western side of the river near its mouth.

The town has one of the best harbours on the coast, and with its narrow streets, grey-roofed and slate-hung buildings, old warehouses and quayside, with the hills rising around, it makes a good place in which to idle; which indeed, as readers who have come this far will know, is a characteristic of all old river and harbour towns, or, at least, of those that have not turned away from their original source.

It is a lively and interesting place, with a good variety of PUBS, RESTAURANTS, SHOPS and GALLERIES. The air is bracing and the light is clear, and many people over the years have found the town easy to love.

Padstow means 'Petroc-stow', Petroc's holy place, and the saint himself landed here in the 6th century and founded a monastery, where his bones were kept until the establishment was destroyed by the Vikings; they were then taken to St Petroc's church at Bodmin. Possibly the present church at Padstow is on the site of this monastery. As a port, the town flourished for many centuries, with schooners being built here in Victorian days.

The TOWN MUSEUM (01841 532574) is in MARKET PLACE, and tells the tale of the port through pictures and artefacts. There is a tribute to the famous PADSTOW LIFEBOAT, which is also of course the subject of a rousing march by Malcolm Arnold, who used to live nearby; the sound of the foghorn off TREVOSE HEAD is used to great effect. In the town there is also a SHIPWRECK MUSEUM (01841 532663).

The reason everybody has heard of Padstow, of course, is because of the traditional MAY DAY ceremony of the 'OBBY'OSS, and the celebrations that accompany it on its dance through the old streets.

No one knows what the origins or meaning of the 'oss, or the dance, are. It seems reasonable to assume that it has something to do with gratitude for the return of summer and the hope for fertility. That its roots lie far back in our collective past is clear, and whatever it is all about, it works a deep magic, with the incessant rhythmical drumming, which fills the town and brings tears to the eyes, the unforgettable tune played endlessly on accordians, and the barely comprehensible old words:

Unite and unite
And let us all unite
For summer is icumen today
And whither we are going we will all unite
In the merry morning of May

Then there are the antics of the 'oss, the strange relationship he has with the 'teaser' who dances in front of him: all of it has a profound effect on people, who find themselves laughing, crying, generally losing their inhibitions and joining in with wherever the energy of the event is taking them. This custom, you realise, is not being performed for the tourists (called, by the way, 'emmets' in Cornwall and 'grockles' in Devon); it is being performed for its own sake, because it has to be.

Padstow becomes very crowded on May Day, but it is worth experiencing. It epitomises all that makes Cornwall different from the rest of England. The town also has a FISH AND SHIPS FESTIVAL in early APRIL.

For more usual pleasures, the town makes a good centre for BATHING, SURFING, FISHING and BOATING of all kinds, and there is the TREVOSE HEAD GOLF AND COUNTRY CLUB (01841 520208).

ROCK, across the estuary from Padstow, is a well-known centre for SAILING and WATERSKIING. There are sandy beaches at low tide, and good WALKING country round about. Rock is linked to Padstow by FERRY. Wealthy people from the popular music industry have retreats here; one reason, presumably, is because it amuses them to have an address with the word 'Rock' in it.

The nearby Church at **ST ENODOC**, with a 13th century spire, lies in a hollow by the sand dunes, and very close to the ST ENODOC GOLF CLUB (01208 863216). Sir John Betjeman was buried in the churchyard in 1984. Although he is so much the poet of Home Counties suburbia, his connection with the North Cornwall landscape was strong, and he wrote about it frequently.

Towards the estuary mouth is **POLZEATH**, a peaceful place with good, expansive BEACHES. It was while he was sitting on the cliffs here, in 1919, meditating on the terrible carnage of the First World War, that another poet, Lawrence Binyon, wrote the words that are recited every year on Remembrance Day:

> *They shall grow not old*
> *As we that are left grow old*
> *Age shall not weary them*
> *Nor the years condemn*
> *At the going down of the sun*
> *And in the morning*
> *We will remember them.*

Further along the coast is **PORT ISAAC**, a steep fishing village with a small breakwater. Overlooking the village, the LONG CROSS VICTORIAN GARDENS (01208 880243) are very atmospheric with protective hedges from the wind, and beautiful views.

THE CORNWALL DONKEY AND PONY SANCTUARY (01208 84242) at **ST KEW** rescues ill-treated animals; they can be petted, groomed and enjoyed here, and there is a PLAY AREA, SHOP and CAFE.

Moving inland we must briefly skirt **BODMIN MOOR**, although it is impossible in a book of this kind to give more than a simple sketch of the area. Travelling across it on the A30 between Bodmin and Launceston, which cuts right through the middle of the moor, does give you a very good, quick, impression of what it is like.

The resemblance to Dartmoor is strong. The granite outcrops, blanket bogs, high hills, boulders, heather, together with the grazing ponies and sheep, are all familiar. There are primitive and medieval remains, and more recent mine workings and clay pits, just as there are on Dartmoor. But the western moor is different from its larger neighbour, in some hard-to-define way, and it is somehow definitely Cornish, perhaps because it does not have the typically Devonian wooded valleys around the edge, which would add a touch of softness more in keeping with that county.

Unlike Dartmoor and Exmoor, this is not a National Park, and has no comparable service of Rangers and Information Points. Bodmin Moor is probably as much loved as the larger moors are, by those who know it well, but there seems to be nothing like the compulsion to write about the place which there is for Dartmoor. Nor is there so much folklore attached to it. But Bodmin Moor does have the same tendency as Dartmoor for mists to come down out of nowhere, so if you plan to go walking over it, bear in mind the points given in chapter 4.

The main features of Bodmin Moor can be listed very simply. BROWN WILLY, the highest point, at 1375 feet, is to the north of the main road. ROUGH TOR, which is not quite so high and easier to reach, is not far off. The atmospheric DOZMARY POOL, where King Arthur's sword 'Excalibur' is supposed to lie beneath the water and which the ghost of the wicked Jan Trageagle was sentenced to empty with a perforated limpet shell, can be found near the centre of the moor, not far from where the youthful River Fowey flows southwards.

BOLVENTOR, a tiny hamlet in the heart of the wastes, but on the main road, is where the famous JAMAICA INN of Daphne du Maurier's novel is to be found. TRETHEVY QUOIT is the largest stone burial chamber in Cornwall, and the CHEESWRING is a huge granite formation reminiscent of BOWERMAN'S NOSE on Dartmoor. In addition to Dozmary Pool there are a couple of small RESERVOIRS, at COLLIFORD and SIBLYBACK, which make good bases for PICNICKING, WALKING and ANGLING.

Should you wish to explore Bodmin Moor properly on foot, and get to know its terrains in detail, a good base is **ALTARNUN**, just off the A30 towards Liskeard. This attractive village has a very interesting church and some pleasing houses. It is a refreshing place to come back to, after the wilds of the moor. Many good and safe WALKS can be taken from here.

To the north of Bodmin Moor, **CAMELFORD** (Tourist Information 01840 212954), in much the same position on the A39, is also a useful base.

A little, old-fashioned town, with bright colourwashed houses and lots of flowers, sitting peacefully between the moor and the sea, it has the NORTH CORNWALL MUSEUM AND GALLERY (01840 212954) and the BRITISH CYCLING MUSEUM (01840 212811). It also has, if you prefer to keep fit in other ways than walking in the wild, a SPORTS CENTRE AND POOL (01840 213188). Not far away is the famous DELABOLE SLATE QUARRY and the country's first commercial WIND FARM.

At nearby SLAUGHTER BRIDGE, King Arthur is said to have fought and killed his treacherous nephew, Mordred.

Returning to the coast, we cannot escape King Arthur at **TINTAGEL**, that most inspiring, rocky place where his name and memory are everywhere. This is all right if we are clear that what we are dealing with is the Arthurian story of literary tradition, of Geoffrey of Monmouth, Mallory and Tennyson, rather than what might really have happened in the Dark Ages, when a Celtic leader based in the Westcountry may have rallied the people against the Saxon incomers.

The legendary and literary Arthur was born at TINTAGEL CASTLE (English Heritage, 01840 770328), which the real leader could not have been, as it was originally a Norman Castle built by Reginald, Earl of Cornwall. Erosion has put half of it almost on an island, making it stranger and more mysterious yet. Numerous poets and musicians have responded to the spell of the place, and sought to evoke its atmosphere, including Tennyson, Swinburne, Bax and Elgar, whose Second Symphony was partly inspired by a holiday here. Also at Tintagel is the OLD POST OFFICE, owned by the National Trust, a beautiful 14th century house.

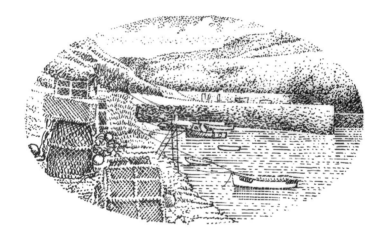

BOSCASTLE is another romantic little town inside a rocky, fjord-like natural harbour. Sir Richard Grenville of the *Revenge* built the Quay during the 16th century. The white houses and cottages and the surrounding cliffs make this a special place for a holiday. THE OLD FORGE provides National Trust INFORMATION and a SHOP, and a truly unique POTTERY produces ware with living ferns and trees on it (01840 250291). The 'castle' part of the name refers to the Norman CASTLE BOTTREAUX, which stood at the top of the hill above the community, but of which no trace remains.

BOSCASTLE VISITOR CENTRE (01840 250010) provides information about the history and ecology of the area.

Boscastle would be a good place for any kind of festivity, but the BEER FESTIVAL they hold here in APRIL sounds positively mouth-watering. THE CRYSTAL CAVE (01840 250248) is a remarkable exhibition of holography and illusion.

Near here, in the VALENCY VALLEY, is the little church of ST JULIOT, which the young Thomas Hardy, in his days as an architect, came to restore. While here he did an indifferent job on the church, but fell in love with the vicar's young sister-in-law, Emma Lavinia Gifford, whom he later married. After her death he poured out his heart in one of the greatest series of love poems in English, many of which are about this area. Readers of Hardy cannot walk these lanes and cliff paths without being continuously reminded of the poems, as well as the novel *A Pair of Blue Eyes*, which is set here.

CRACKINGTON HAVEN lies in a cleft in the 400foot high cliffs. A long, beautiful beach, excellent WALKS on the coast and inland, make it a favourite spot for many. The tiny church at neighbouring **ST GENNYS** has a rare altar tabernacle.

WIDEMOUTH BAY also has beautiful golden sands, rock pools, stunning cliff scenery and good walks. The last town on this coast before we return to Devon is **BUDE** (Tourist Information 01288 354240).

It is rather a strange place, with marvellous beaches, especially at CROOKLETS and SUMMERLEAZE, and it is a centre for SURFING, but the main parts of the town are away from the sea. Betjeman thought it the 'least rowdy' resort he had ever seen. There is plenty to do, with a VISITOR CENTRE, explaining the town and its area, and numerous SHOPS and RESTAURANTS.

The town grew mainly in the 19th century, and has a spacious, confident feeling to it. A canal was built linking it to the inland town of Holsworthy in Devon, and a stretch of this, along with some MARSHLAND, is now a NATURE RESERVE.

Bude has a GOLF CLUB (01288 352006) and a well-endowed LEISURE CENTRE (01288 353714).

Bude holds a FOLK FESTIVAL in JUNE, a CARNIVAL in AUGUST and in the same month, a popular JAZZ FESTIVAL, with the emphasis very much on the 'TRAD' variety.

Just inland is the older settlement of **STRATTON**, where an important battle took place during the Civil War. The BUDE AND STRATTON MUSEUM (no telephone number) records the local history.

KILKHAMPTON stands 600 feet above the sea. STOWE BARTON (not open to the public) is on the site of STOWE HOUSE, seat of the Grenville family, including the aggressive Sir Richard and his descendant Sir Bevil, who led the local Royalist forces during the Civil War.

A few miles north, **MORWENSTOW** is worth visiting, for its magnificent church and its churchyard filled with the remains of shipwrecked sailors, and its memories of the individual parson, Robert Stephen Hawker the poet, who lived and worked here for over 40 years in the 19th century.

Romantic, visionary, deeply committed to practising Christianity as he understood it, he worked hard to discourage his parishioners from indulging in the ancient local custom of wrecking; most unfairly, he has in some books been accused of joining in with them, and the blame for this must partly go to our old friend Baring Gould, who wrote a wholly inaccurate biography of him. Hawker's rectory has chimneys based on church towers.

Hawker introduced the HARVEST FESTIVAL as we know it today in the church calendar. This is commemorated by the 4 day HARVEST AND ARTS FESTIVAL held here in JUNE.

THE PORT GAVERNE HOTEL,
Port Isaac,
North Cornwall PL29 3SO

Tel: 01208 880244
Fax: 01208 880151

Midge Ross, the Resident Proprietor of the Port Gaverne Hotel, a 17th century inn, has made this hotel one of the best in Cornwall. She will tell you that since coming to the hotel in 1969 the hotel has had the pleasure of providing for thousands of resident guests from Great Britain and most parts of the world and has served many thousands of meals to residents and non-residents alike. The Port Gaverne has been offering hospitality to visitors since 1608 and at no time has it been better than it is today. Midge's philosophy is that only the best will do for the hotel's guests whether it is in service, comfort or food and everywhere in every department of the establishment this is upheld.

There are seventeen charming bedrooms, all of which are ensuite and every room has colour television, a hostess tray and many other nice touches adding to the comfort of guests. Some of these are family rooms. Downstairs the bar is always a busy place and it is here that you can have bar lunches or suppers in preference to the dining room if you wish. The menu in the dining room is a la carte and beautifully presented, imaginative and frequently innovative but always maintaining traditional dishes. You will always find that fresh garden produce, local beef and lamb, locally landed fish, lobster and crabs in season are all used. The carefully selected wine list offers wines from around the world, amongst which are several half bottles allowing you to sample perhaps a wine you have not tried before. To allow parents to have a peaceful dinner away from their offspring, there is a Children's early sitting. Packed lunches are available on request. The Dining Room is open to non-residents.

Wonderfully situated, from The Port Gaverne you can explore the miles of particularly spectacular coastal paths. There is a sheltered swimming cove within seconds of the front door. Golf, fishing, riding, surfing, and sailing are within easy reach. You would be hard put to find a better, more comfortable, friendly and informal hotel in Cornwall.

USEFUL INFORMATION

OPEN; Mid-February - early January
CHILDREN; Welcome
CREDIT CARDS; All major cards
LICENSED; Yes. Full On
ACCOMMODATION; 3 sgl 7dbl 5triple
6 self-catering cottages (sleep 3-6)
2 large flats (sleeps 8)

DINING ROOM; Excellent food using local
Produce, fish, vegetables, lamb & beef
BAR FOOD; Lunches & Suppers
VEGETARIAN; No
GARDEN; No
PETS; Yes £3 per night

RATES:- High Season £47.50/ £49.50 pppn B&B.Low Season £49.50/£51.50 pppnB&B

SMUGGLERS DEN INN,
Trebellan, Cubert,
Newquay, Cornwall TR8 5PY

Tel/Fax: 01637 830209

Hidden away as it is down a narrow lane with high hedges it might well be that this interesting and atmospheric inn, built 400 years ago, was the haunt of 'the gentlemen' in years gone by. Certainly this part of Cornwall was renowned for freetrading. Today apart from all the interesting bric a brac, beams and furnishing in keeping with the age of the inn the only reminder of the past is the mischievous ghost who haunts the Smugglers Den and tends to turn music on in the middle of the night, remove things that go missing for a while and then mysteriously reappear. Perhaps it is a smuggler who found himself in the pub after the door into the secret tunnel at the back of the bar closed on him, leaving him to the mercy of the Excise-Men. The tunnel reputedly leads to the beach.

Simon and Sue Hancock run this pleasant hostelry which is renowned for its friendly atmosphere and hospitality. Simon cares for the well kept beers and looks after the bars, frequented by contented locals who come for the beer and the banter and Sue is an imaginative cook who plans some very exciting menus. Mainly traditional English you can also be sure of some unusual and interesting dishes as well. Seafood is one of the specialities of the house and the steaks are superb. You can enjoy a full meal if you wish or settle for a bar snack which could be anything from a Ploughmans with crispy bread to a pasta dish. There are always dishes for vegetarians.
The Smuggler's Den does not have a restaurant but has a very comfortable dining area.

On fine days it is very pleasant to drink and eat outside in the courtyard, the patio or in the Beer garden. The area around the Smuggler's Den is wonderful. The beaches are a short drive, with the resort town of Newquay virtually on the doorstep and the cathedral city of Truro not far away.

USEFUL INFORMATION

OPEN; 11-3pm & 6-11pm Sun: Normal hours.　　**RESTAURANT; Not applicable**
CHILDREN; Welcome　　**BAR FOOD; Excellent. Good value**
CREDIT CARDS; Visa/Master/Switch　　**VEGETARIAN; Catered for**
LICENSED; Full On　　**DISABLED ACCESS; One step**
GARDEN; Courtyard. Patio. Beer Garden

WHITEHAY
Whitehay Withiel
Bodmin
Cornwall PL30 5NQ
Tel. (01208) 831237
Fax (01208) 831600

Whitehay is a beautiful L-shaped Cornish farmhouse, approximately 300 years old, completely surrounded by its own deeply peaceful grounds. Its owners, Ian and Felicity Lock, offer high quality Country House Bed and Breakfast, with Self Catering Accommodation. Some of the latter is provided in a former Mill House, complete with a working water wheel.

The ambience at Whitehay is, undoubtedly, very special. Ian, a farmer, and Felicity, an interior designer, have skilfully brought out and enhanced the loveliness of the house, built of gentle, honey-coloured stone, and its surrounding land, to create a welcoming, homely environment where you will want to relax and linger.

The grounds include 23 acres of woodland, through which the River Ruthven flows, and where the Locks' two labradors will happily take you on their favourite walks. There is an orchard where 120 different varieties of apple are grown, and all round the house and its lands are the most beautiful rural views.

All the accommodation at Whitehay, whether Self Catering or Bed and Breakfast, is to a high standard, the house and mill being as beautifully furnished inside as they look from outside. A good English breakfast is provided for B&B guests, and evening meals can be arranged if requested in advance.

Whitehay is situated almost in the middle of Cornwall, and being just 3 miles from the A30 main road through the county, it is an ideal centre for exploring both coasts and all that lies between them. From here you are within easy reach of a wide variety of attractions. These range from the gentlest - National Trust properties like Lanhydrock and Cotehele, and gardens like the famous Lost Gardens of Heligan - to the more active: the area has many golf clubs, and the traffic-free Camel Cycle Trail provides a a safe walking or cycling route from Bodmin to Wadebridge and Padstow.

However you spend your days, when you return to Whitehay in the evening you will feel, as you approach the mellow old house, set so perfectly in its surrounding gardens and woods, as if you are coming home.

USEFUL INFORMATION

OPEN All Year except Christmas & New Year.
CHILDREN Welcome over 12.
CREDIT CARDS Not taken.
LICENCE None.
ACCOMMODATION Self Catering: Mill House has 2 bedrooms, double downstairs, twin upstairs, with Wing of Main House has 3 beds upstairs, with bathroom. B&B: 2 rooms in Main House, double with en suite bathroom, twin with private bathroom
RATES:- All Year, from £35. Pppn.

RESTAURANT No, but evening dinner
by arrangement.
VEGETARIAN By arrangement.

SMOKING No.
DISABLED Level access to
downstairs room
PETS No.
GARDEN Extensive grounds.

WENN MANOR
St Wenn, Wadebridge,
Cornwall PL30 5PS

Tel: 01726 890240
Fax: 01726 890680

AA. One Rosette for good food.

The hamlet of St Wenn lies amid the rolling farm land and steep forested valleys close to the edge of Bodmin Moor that is 'undiscovered Cornwall'. With a school, a church, a W.I. hall, Wenn Manor itself and about a dozen houses, St Wenn is the model of a sleepy little rural community. Untroubled by passing traffic and subject only to the everyday events of local agriculture, it is tranquillity itself.

Wenn Manor owned by Paul and Jo Stretton-Downes has been restored to provide a panelled bar with an inglenook fireplace in which a fire burns every night, a candlelit dining room (30 covers) with two open log fires that overlooks the croquet lawn and a Garden Room for light lunches and party dinners. There are three large bedrooms with bathrooms en suite for those that may like to stay. Forty five pounds single occupancy and seventy pounds double. This includes full English breakfast. Dinner is a memorable affair with a wide choice of starters including Roquefort Stuffed Pear or Smoked Salmon and Prawn Ramekin. The main courses would tempt even the most discerning of palates with seasonal fresh fish landed daily cooked in many delicious ways. You might prefer Roast Duck with Black Cherry Sauce. The vegetables are perfectly cooked and the salads fresh and crisp. Delectable home-made puddings and a good cheese board finish the meal. You might prefer the informal Garden Room where 'Huffers' - a large Salad Bap with a variety of fillings - are available as well as a variety of light dishes, the main menu is always available. A selection of fine wine is racked in the bar for customers to peruse and choose - all sensibly priced.

The four acres of secluded gardens were designed by the Rashleigh family of Menabilly and boast what is probably Cornwall's most complete Grotto. There are regular sightings of 2 benevolent ghosts, and a cavernous 42' deep well in the bar. This really is a great place to stay or just to come and eat. Your hosts are charming, friendly and know their business well.

USEFUL INFORMATION

OPEN; All year except Sundays & Christmas	**RESTAURANT; Candlelit, delicious food**
CHILDREN; Over 14 years	**BAR MEALS; Wide range available**
CREDIT CARDS;All major cards	**VEGETARIAN; Catered for**
LICENSED; Full. Fine wines	**DISABLED ACCESS; One step.**
ACCOMMODATION;3 large ensuite rooms	**GARDEN; 4 beautiful acres**
PETS; No	**RATES:- All Year, from £45/ £70 pppn B&B.**

MAER LODGE HOTEL
Crooklets Beach
Bude
Cornwall EX23 8NG
Tel. (01288) 353306
Fax (01288) 354005
Internet: http://www.webscape.co.uk/maer_lodge_hotel
E:Mail - maerlodgehotel@btinternet.com

RAC 2 Stars, AA 2 Stars, ETB 3 Crowns Approved.
Member of Minotels of Europe, Logis of GB, Les Routiers

The Maer Lodge Hotel is situated in two acres of its own sheltered gardens, approximately half a mile from the famous holiday town of Bude, and only a 300 yard walk from the beach. Although close to the town it is away from the main road, so guests are assured of a quiet night's sleep. With its pleasant south-facing aspect and suntrap lawns, the Maer Lodge is an ideal place for a relaxing holiday.

The hotel has been in the hands of the Stanley family for nearly forty years, who have acquired a well-earned reputation for their innovative, caring service and devotion to the tourist industry in the South West. Two generations of the family are involved in the running of Maer Lodge, and they create a personal, friendly atmosphere which draws visitors back again and again. Their many skills and fields of expertise are always there to be called upon.

The hotel was originally a 17th century farm, which has been added to over the years to create a unique building which is an enjoyable blend of old and new. John Logie Baird, the inventor of television, is known to have stayed in the house during the Second World War.

Maer Lodge's 18 en suite bedrooms arc individually furnished and equipped with televisions, radios, telephones and hot drinks facilities. A hair dryer and trouser press can be provided at no extra charge. The modern dining room, light and spacious, serves an excellent choice of traditional English and some Continental dishes, prepared by the chefs. There is a comfortable lounge and a residents' bar, where a full range of drinks is available at reasonable prices.

Maer Lodge is a popular venue for golfers. Bude's fine course is only 100 yards away, and within a half-hour drive are 6 championship courses. The hotel will be happy to book tees for you, and can often offer reduced rates.

To find this special and friendly hotel, leave the A39 at Stratton and follow the Bude road for 1 mile. Turn right into the Strand and take the road to Crooklets Beach. The hotel is half way down to the right. There is ample safe car parking in the grounds.

USEFUL INFORMATION

OPEN All Year.
CHILDREN Welcome.
CREDIT CARDS All accepted.
LICENCE Restaurant, Residential and Restricted Full Licence.
ACCOMMODATION 18 en suite bedrooms.
PRICES Low Season: B&B from £26.00 per person, with Dinner £35; High Season: B&B £31, with Dinner £40. Phone for full tariff.

RESTAURANT Traditional Home Cooking at its best. Typical 5 course dinner from £8.50.
BAR FOOD Lunches and other refreshments
VEGETARIAN Choices always available, but it helps to know in advance.
SMOKING Permitted, but not in bedrooms.
DISABLED Level access; several ground flr rms.
GARDEN Yes. **PETS** Welcome.

THE EARL OF ST VINCENT
Egloshayle
Wadebridge
Cornwall
PL27 6HT

Tel. (01208) 814807
Fax (01208) 814445

The picturesque village of Egloshayle (Cornish for 'the church by the estuary') sits across the River Camel from Wadebridge, from where you get a fine view of its church tower. During the 1820s the church boasted a prizewinning team of five bellringers, all local tradesmen, who were so respected that a song was written about them. This is still sung by westcountry folk singers, and today in the churchyard you can discover the headstones of four of the five ringers.

You can also drink in the inn where they celebrated their successes, because the Earl of St Vincent in Egloshayle is the only pub in the village. Surrounded by pleasant old houses, in the heart of the community, it is a real old fashioned village local, which also offers a wide and imaginative restaurant menu.

The inn is an attractive whitewashed stone building, well-known for its colourful floral displays. It dates from the Middle Ages, when it was built to accommodate the masons and craftsmen who were engaged in the building of the church. It took its present name to commemorate Sir John Jervis, the Earl of St Vincent, who was a local MP and at one time Nelson's superior officer.

Inside, the inn is comfortably furnished to enhance the feeling of continuity with past ages, which is one of the special joys of visiting such places. Various antiques, including an interesting collection of old clocks, are a particular feature. Here you can enjoy a wide range of beers and spirits. The Earl of St Vincent is owned by St Austell Brewery, and their various Real Ales attract enthusiasts from far and wide.

The inn's licensees are Edward and Anne Connolly, who have been here for eight years, and have no plans to leave. They take pride in their restaurant, which serves a high quality selection of home-cooked meals, including fresh fish and seafood, steaks and grills. This is complemented by an international wine list. Another pleasure of the inn is that on fine days and peaceful summer evenings, customers can sit outside in the garden or at tables by the door, and enjoy the village ambience.

Altogether, with its friendly traditional atmosphere and well-prepared food, the Earl of St Vincent is one of those classic village inns that manages to 'revive the soul', just as the bell ringing of its long-vanished customers used to do.

USEFUL INFORMATION

OPEN Weekdays: 11am - 3pm & 6.30 -11pm.
Sundays: 12- 3pm & 7 - 10.30pm.
CHILDREN No facilities.
CREDIT CARDS Access, Visa, Delta, Switch.
LICENCE Full.

RESTAURANT Lunches and evening
Steaks, fish dishes, grills, roasts. Specials.
Extensive wine list. Sunday 3 course roast
lunch a speciality.
VEGETARIAN Always 2 or 3 available.

THE WELLINGTON HOTEL,
The Harbour, Boscastle,
Cornwall PL35 0AQ,

Tel: 01840 250202
Fax: 01840 250621

AA. & RAC.Two Stars.
ETB Three Crowns Recommended.

The village of Boscastle nestles at the end of a deeply wooded valley where the rivers Valency and Jordan converge before flowing onward to the sea. The river Jordan actually flows under The Wellington Hotel and keeps the barrel cellar at just the right temperature to maintain the ales in peak condition. The Elizabethan harbour has an interesting 'blow hole'. An hour before and an hour after low tide it produces the most amazing sound that can be heard clear across the harbour as it throws cascades of water high into the air.

A warm and traditional welcome awaits every visitor to the affectionately named 'The Welly'. It offers all the facilities, comforts and care to make your stay both enjoyable and memorable. Parts of the hotel are 400 years old and it is one of the oldest coaching inns in North Cornwall with a history and a heritage that the owners, Victor and Solange Tobutt, acknowledge must be preserved for future generations. Extended in 1860 the Wellington is a listed building of historical interest. As late as 1926 Boscastle was dependent on horse drawn coaches. A number of prominent people have been guests here. In 1870 or thereabouts Edward VII is believed to have been in a royal party that stayed in the hotel. Sir Henry Irving was another guest and so too was Thomas Hardy. More recently Guy Gibson VC of Dambuster's fame wrote in his book that the Wellington was one of his favourite hostelries.

The Wellington is a Freehouse and offers a variety of well kept Real ales and good food. The beamed ceilings and real log fires create a cosy and intimate atmosphere. The Long Bar is an interesting legacy from the coaching days and a haunt of locals. The Georgian restaurant is called 'La Belle Alliance' after the famous inn that gave its name to the victory hill at Waterloo. It is renowned for its high standard of both traditional English fayre and French regional cuisine. The cellar caters for the discerning palate - and pocket! The hotel has 19 bedrooms, 16 of which are ensuite and all are centrally heated and well appointed with direct dial phones. There are 10 acres of grounds with beautiful hillside woodland walks. Pets are very welcome. A hotel to be enjoyed.

USEFUL INFORMATION

OPEN; All year	**RESTAURANT; Anglo/French regional cuisine**
CHILDREN;Childrens Room	**BAR FOOD;Wide selection inc Chef's Specials**
CREDIT CARDS; Most major cards	**VEGETARIAN;Several dishes + other diets**
LICENSED; Full & Restaurant	**DISABLED ACCESS; Not accommodation**
ACCOMMODATION; 16 ensuite rooms	**GARDEN; 10 acres.**
3 not ensuite. Colour TV. D/ D Telephones	**PETS; Very welcome**

RATES:- High Season, from £18/ £30. Low Season, from £14/ £31. All pppn. B&B. Children 7/12 yrs. 25% Discount to adult rates. Special prices for seasonal breaks:- Details on request.

BOSSINEY HOUSE HOTEL
Bossiney Road
Tintagel
Cornwall
PL34 0AX
Tel. (01840) 770240
Fax (01840) 770501

RAC 2 Stars, AA 2 Stars,
ETB 3 Crowns.

Bossiney House Hotel is a welcoming, family-run hotel standing in two and a half acres of its own grounds above Bossiney and Benoath Coves. It overlooks one of the finest stretches of coastline in Great Britain, and is half a mile from the centre of romantic Tintagel, with all its wealth of legendary and creative associations.

Heather and Ian Graham are the resident partners in the hotel, and are more than ably assisted by Pat and John Cannings, Heather's parents. Other members of staff are introduced to guests, to ensure a personal and highly responsive service, in which the emphasis is on friendliness, honesty and willingness at all times. A holiday at Bossiney House can be a completely relaxing and comfortable experience.

All bedrooms are tastefully furnished, with televisions, hair dryers, tea and coffee making facilities and spectacular coast or countryside views. There are two spacious lounges, a bar, a modern and comfortable dining room and, for guests' active enjoyment, a putting course and a heated indoor swimming pool, solarium and sauna housed in an attractive Scandinavian style chalet.

Food at Bossiney is good, traditional English fare, with an excellent daily choice of dishes using fresh local produce, and with plenty for vegetarians. The wine list of 24 specially chosen wines complements the food, and is very reasonably priced. The bar is small but well stocked.

Basing your holiday at Bossiney, you are in an ideal position to explore not only the wild and beautiful coast of North Cornwall, but the south west peninsula as a whole. For walking, riding, fishing, bird watching and visiting historic houses, towns, gardens and villages, the hotel is superbly placed.

Tintagel itself, with its wonderful ruined castle, its historic post office and stories of King Arthur and Merlin, which have inspired poets and musicians for generations, is all that anyone can require in a romantic setting, with beaches, cliffs and intimate coves.

USEFUL INFORMATION

OPEN 1 Feb - 30 Nov
Hours: 8am - Midnight.
CHILDREN Welcome.
CREDIT CARDS Visa, Mastercard, Switch, Delta, Amex, Diner's Club.
LICENCE Restaurant and Residential.
ACCOMMODATION 19 double/twin bedrooms, 1 family room. 18 are en suite, 2 with private facilities.
PRICES B&B per person. High Season: £30. Low Season: £28.
Children under 5 - free, 5 - 11 - 50% 12 - 15 - 30%

RESTAURANT Table d'Hote evening meal with main course choice of meat, fish or vegetarian dish. Menu changes nightly. £12 per person.
BAR FOOD General bar meals.
VEGETARIAN Always 1 choice per meal.
SMOKING Permitted - not in dining room
DISABLED Very welcome, but regrettably no special facilities.
PETS On ground floor only.
GARDEN 2 and a half acre garden.
CAR PARK Up to 30 vehicles

THE DOWER HOUSE
Fentonluna Lane
Padstow
Cornwall PL28 8BA
Tel. (01841) 532317 Fax (01841) 532667

Featured in 'Which' Bed and Breakfast Guide.

The Dower House is situated in the Old Town of Padstow with memorable views over the slate rooftops to the beautiful Camel estuary and Bodmin Moor beyond. It is a grade ll listed building of Cornish stone and granite mullions and five brave chimneys mark the bygone age of young maidservants struggling with buckets of coal to heat this large family house. Today, the owners have decided to install Solar Heating which is a testament to their commitment to conservation. They acknowledge the interesting history in their presentation and care of the house. Originally called The Nook, the building dates from 1858 when it was built for Mary Jenny Prideaux-Brune, daughter of the Reverend Charles Prideaux. It was later occupied by Dr Henry Marley and his family of eight daughters. Dr Marley's father was a great friend of Charles Dickens and his name was made famous in A Christmas Carol as Marley's Ghost. Subsequently, several vicars lived here amongst whom the Reverend Slocombe is remembered in the Slocombe bar. Dr Sheldon bought the freehold in 1955 and his valued contribution to the health and welfare of the community is recorded in his surgery which is now the Sheldon Lounge. The house became an hotel in 1971 and the previous owner changed the name to The Dower House. The names of the bedrooms are taken from the Prideaux family and have their own unique character but they all have in common full en suite facilities, television, telephone, radio, hospitality trays and very comfortable beds. It is now owned by Paul and Patricia Brocklebank who purchased it in 1993. Paul is a retired bank manager with a vigorous interest in food which is evident in his extensive breakfast menu and his weekly barbeques. Patricia concentrates on providing the detail behind the comforts of the hotel and ensures a warm welcome for guests. Their full time assistant, Emma Rojano, has great experience in catering and all aspects of tourism and Jenny Tallis has joined the team to provide refreshment during the day on the sunny terrace or in the bar. Together they all have a common goal of quality, combined with a personal and homely approach to hospitality.

The comprehensive breakfast to suit all tastes is served in the elegant dining room where the granite mullioned windows provide a wonderful view of the ancient crenellated manor house, Prideaux Place. Paul and Patricia will happily advise you on the choice of restaurants in Padstow and the surrounding area for your evening meal. Padstow is an acient town with a fascinating history as a seafaring and religous centre. It is an ideal base for exploring the coastal paths and countryside of North Cornwall.

USEFUL INFORMATION

OPEN March to December.
CHILDREN Welcome.
CREDIT CARDS Visa, Mastercard.
LICENCE Resident, Restaurant & Function.
ACCOMMODATION 6 double rooms, one available as a single. All en suite, 5 with showers, 1 with bath.
PRICES B&B for 2 people from £47 to £74 per night, Children in own room 80% of full tariff, less if in family room. Babies under 3 yrs £5. Ring for full tariff.

RESTAURANT Breakfast, light lunches & a barbecue on Monday nights.
BAR FOOD salads and sandwiches freshly prepared.
VEGETARIAN Not specifically.
SMOKING In Bar only.
DISABLED Not really suitable.
PETS Prior arrangement, £3 pn
GARDEN Terrace and car park

SEA SPRAY HOTEL
Atlantic Terrace
Trevone Bay
Padstow
Cornwall
PL28 8RB

Tel. (01841) 520491

The Sea Spray is a small, privately owned and run hotel, offering personal service in a friendly, relaxing atmosphere. It is beautifully situated, overlooking a sandy beach between two bays, on the romantic North Cornish coast near the unspoilt old port of Padstow. Most rooms have spectacular views of the Atlantic Ocean and the North Cornwall Coast Path passes right by the hotel.

The Sea Spray is owned and run by Steve and Shirley Thomas. Steve is an ex-Royal Navy Chief Engineer and Shirley is a trained chef, as well as being a mother and grandmother. They do everything themselves, ensuring that guests are offered individual service in a home-like environment.

Each of the 7 bedrooms is centrally heated, with en suite toilet, shower and washbasin facilities. The rooms provide a combination of double and single beds. All guests are supplied with door keys, enabling them to come and go as they please.

The Snug Bar, open to residents until 11.30pm, provides a varied selection of spirits, liqueurs, beer and lager, and you can sit here and watch the sun setting over the Atlantic whilst awaiting dinner, or move into the comfortable Lounge, with large picture windows and colour television.

The Sea Spray is an ideal base for exploring the beautiful North Cornwall coast and countryside, or indeed the whole county: Land's End is only 57 miles away. Swimming, surfing, boating, sailing, waterskiing, fishing, golf, riding, birdwatching and walking are only a few of the activities which can be enjoyed from here.

Trevone Bay itself, with its two bays, one sandy and one rocky, is amongst the most lovely spots on the Cornish coast, and though popular, it is completely uncommercialised. Padstow, the famous old town with its unique 'Obby 'Oss dance every May Day, and the Camel Estuary, repay detailed investigation. Across the estuary from Padstow, amongst the sand dunes, is the ancient church of St Enodoc, where Sir John Betjeman is buried. The whole area is rich in history, legend and associations.

To find the Sea Spray, take the B3276 from Padstow, and turn off at Windmill. Follow the road through Trevone village and past the Beach Store and Car Park on the right. You will find the hotel on the left.

USEFUL INFORMATION

OPEN All Year, except our holiday.
CHILDREN Over 6 years Welcome.
CREDIT CARDS No.
LICENCE Restaurant & Residential.
ACCOMMODATION 7 en suite bedrooms.
PRICES Bed, Breakfast & Dinner from £29 for 1 night. Bed & Breakfast from £19.
Children sharing with adults half price.

RESTAURANT Dining room overlooking bay.
14 day Table d'hote main course menu.
VEGETARIAN Catered for.
SMOKING Not in dining room. Guests asked to be considerate.
DISABLED No special facilities.
PETS By arrangement.

LONDON INN,
6-8 Lanadwell Street,
Padstow, Cornwall
PL28 8AN

Tel: 01841 532554

Ian and Pauline Cortis, the landlords of this old inn are Padstonians and take a keen interest not only in their own pub but all sorts of pub activities in the neighbourhood, including Padstow's famous 'Obby Oss' on May Day and the annual Summer Carnival, which is probably why The London Inn is such a popular hostelry. They have a terrific regular following which always augurs well and tells strangers that this is the place to be. You may well have seen the pub on television when it featured in Rick Stein's 'Fruits of the Sea' on BBC2. The London, a listed building, became a hostelry in 1803 and before that it was 3 fisherman's cottages. It is a happy pub and whenever you walk into the bars you will find local people enjoying their drinks and discussing the topics of the day. One of its great virtues is that no one ever feels a stranger here for long.

The London Inn is renowned for its good food which is served seven days a week at Lunch from 12-2pm and in the evening from 7-9pm. Here you can have morning coffee or afternoon tea, lunch or dine in the intimate 22 seater restaurant which is strictly non-smoking. Fish straight from the Quay is served every day as well as seafood, there are tender steaks cooked just as you prefer, chicken in various forms and duck which is only available on the evening menu. In addition there are all sorts of Daily Specials. For those who just want a snack, the Bar menu has a whole list of freshly cut sandwiches, Ploughman's, Jacket Potatoes with a variety of fillings and many other things. Above all the food is always well cooked, well presented and sensibly priced. For those who want to stay there are 2 double bedrooms, not ensuite, but very comfortable with Colour Tv and tea/coffee facilities, and you can be sure of an excellent breakfast in the morning. Padstow is a good place for a holiday with so much going on and so many places that can be easily reached from beaches to stately homes.

USEFUL INFORMATION

OPEN; All year 11-11pm 10.30pm Sundays
CHILDREN; Welcome to eat
CREDIT CARDS: None taken
LICENSED; Full On
ACCOMMODATION; 2 dbl not ensuite
RESTAURANT; Good, interesting food
BAR FOOD; Wide range. Daily Specials
VEGETARIAN: Always a choice
DISABLED ACCESS:Yes.Stairs to rooms
PETS; Only in bar
RATES:- High Season :- £17.50 pppn B&B. Low Season £15. pppn B&B.

TRENANCE LODGE HOTEL & RESTAURANT,
Trenance Road,
Newquay, Cornwall TR7 2HW

Tel: 01637 876702
Fax: 01637 872034

Les Routiers.
ETB Three Crowns.

Staying or Dining at Trenance Lodge Hotel gives one the two sides of Newquay. Firstly it is close to the beaches of this premier Cornish Resort and so able to offer its guests easy access to all the amenities and secondly, it is situated in the older part of the town where peace and tranquillity prevail. Trenance Lodge stands in its own large, beautifully kept grounds overlooking lakes and gardens of the Trenance Valley leading to the Gannel Estuary. It is also adjacent to Trenance Heritage Cottages now charmingly restored to show the way of life in the 19th century. Add to this a heated outdoor swimming pool and the blessing of a large, safe car park; a rarity in Newquay and staying here is a wise choice. Walking along side the Gannel river is a magical experience - an opportunity to refresh ones soul soaking in the natural beauty and peace. For those who want to play golf, there are good courses closeby and endless other sporting activities.

Within this immaculately kept hotel the lounge is elegantly appointed and beautifully decorated and in keeping with the bar and the dining room, the colour scheme of soft creams and blues prevail, making the whole restful and relaxing. The bar is always a popular place for locals and guests to enjoy a drink, mull over the pleasures of the day and discuss the programme for the following day. Trenance Lodge which describes itself as a Restaurant with Accommodation is open to non-residents and has an established reputation for serving the best seafood, steaks and poultry in comfort and by a staff who are both friendly, attentive but not intrusive. The Head Chef uses his unique talents to combine the natural simplistic qualities of first class produce with sophisticated balanced intricacy, resulting in an absolute culinary delight presented to tempt even the most reserved palate. In short it is just like everything else at Trenance Lodge, first rate, and makes dining a pure pleasure. Naturally the 5 ensuite bedrooms are lovely, again with a subdued decor and well appointed with everything the modern traveller of today would expect. Perhaps what makes Trenance Lodge so very special is the warm welcome from owners Mac and Jenny. Their unpretentious friendly style makes you feel immediately relaxed and ready to take onboard the pleasures that await you here.

USEFUL INFORMATION

OPEN; January-December	**RESTAURANT; Superb food**
CHILDREN; Not suitable	**BAR FOOD; On request. Specials on blackboard**
CREDIT CARDS: All major cards	**VEGETARIAN; Always available**
LICENSED; Restaurant & residential	**DISABLED ACCESS; Yes. 2 steps**
ACCOMMODATION; 5ensuite rooms	**GARDEN; Large. Heated outdoor swimming**
SHORT BREAKS; Spring/Autumn/Winter.	**Pool, Terrace**
PETS; No	**PARKING; Ample, safe**

RATES:- All Year, Double £46/£56 per room.B&B. Single £30/£35 B&B.

TREBARWITH HOTEL
Trebarwith Crescent,
Newquay, Cornwall TR7 1BZ

Tel: 01637 872288
Fax: 01637 875431

AA/RAC Three Star.
ETB Four Crowns Commended.

The Tarrant family have owned and run the Trebarwith Hotel for over 35 years and today it is almost time for the 4th generation to take over! David Tarrant is the present incumbent, whilst the hotel is managed by Nigel and Jane Tarrant. David and his family will tell you with a wry smile that they have been in situ for so long 'they think they are getting the hang of it now'! They certainly have got the hang of it for this spacious, elegant, comfortable hotel is superbly run. Guests are important people here and cossetted in the nicest way to ensure that the holiday or the break is memorable. The Trebarwith is located right on the sea edge, occupying probably the finest position in Newquay. From the hotel gardens and terraced patios there are sea views across Newquay Bay and the Atlantic ocean. From here you can walk along the coastal footpaths, tour Cornwall by car, visit some wonderful gardens and a stately home or two. For the really energetic there is golf and fishing from the local harbour, horse riding, surfing and many other sporting activities. For those who simply enjoy the beach the hotel has private steps down to Great Western beach from the garden. Or you need never leave the confines of the hotel grounds enjoying the indoor swimming pool and the luxury indoor leisure complex with its solarium room, spa and sauna room for all the family. There is a Video Theatre so that you can enjoy a night at the movies, a large games room with full size snooker table and dances and entertainment held regularly.

The 41 bedrooms all have private bathroom suites with colour TV, hostess trays and many other touches. There are family and four poster suites available. The delightful Wedgwood Restaurant is where you will enjoy a full English Breakfast, and a multi Table D'Hote or A La Carte meal at night. Vegetarians are catered for. There is an intimate bar where a comprehensive range of cold and hot bar lunches are available. Free car parking is available in the hotel grounds - something to be valued in Newquay where parking is often difficult. This really is a splendid hotel in which to take a holiday or break. The atmosphere is warm and welcoming and it is somewhere where everyone smiles!

USEFUL INFORMATION

OPEN; Easter to November **RESTAURANT; Gourmet food**
CHILDREN; Welcome **BAR FOOD; Ample Selection**
CREDIT CARDS; All major cards **VEGETARIAN; Catered for**
LICENSED; Yes. Residential **WHEELCHAIR ACCESS; One room..**
GARDEN; Sun Terraces, Swimming Pool, Sea Vista,many extras. PETS;No,
ACCOMMDATION; 41 ensuite rooms AA, RAC 3 star 4 Crowns ETB Commended
TARIFF :- High Season, from £45.50 pppn. D/ B&B. Low Season, from £28 pppn D/B&B.
Children Free if sharing, 75% in Family Room for one child.
Special prices for Short Breaks, please request details.

THE HARVESTER,
70 Henver Road,
Newquay, Cornwall
TR7 3BN

Tel: 01637 878089

The Harvester is a friendly welcoming hostelry where Roy and Lynne Hooton are the landlords. They have exactly the right temperaments for running a pub; they are both outgoing, welcoming people who have a genuine liking for their fellow man which ensures that everyone who walks through the doors is immediately made to feel at home. This is so whether you just pop into the bar for a drink or whether you come here to stay and enjoy not only all The Harvester has to offer but the proximity to so many interesting places to visit. The nearest beach is Lusty Glaze, only a few minutes walk away and nearby at Tolcarne and Porth Beach, twelve to fifteen minutes walk. They are all superb sandy bays for which Newquay is renowned. Not far from Newquay there are some wonderful gardens and fine National Trust properties which are a pleasure to visit.

For those who enjoy the relaxed informality of a good pub rather than an hotel, The Harvester is definitely the place for you. It has become renowned for its service and comfort and with the help of the chefs and familiar faces behind the bar, they offer you either a relaxing a la carte meal in the Harvest Bar Restaurant, or a choice, from the imaginative selection of bar meals, accompanied by the fine range of award winning real ales, keg beers and lagers. All are available both at lunchtime and in the evening. Many people use the quiet atmosphere for meeting clients at lunchtime knowing they can do so without the disturbance from a juke box or pool table. There is a pleasant family room with facilities for children and there is ample free car parking on the premises.

There are eight double,comfortably furnished bedrooms. Each has tea/coffee making facilities and colour television as well as a wash basin, shaver point and central heating.

USEFUL INFORMATION

OPEN; All year. 11am-3pm & 6-11pm   RESTAURANT; Good, traditional fare
CHILDREN; Yes. Family room   BAR FOOD; Good variety, good value
CREDIT CARDS; All major cards   VEGETARIAN; Always a choice
LICENSED; Full On   NO WHEELCHAIR ACCESS.
ACCOMMODATION; 8 dbl rooms not ensuite   GARDEN; Outside terrace
PETS; Only outside   RATES:- £15 + VAT pppn. All Year.

THE BRENDON ARMS
Falcon Terrace,
Bude, Cornwall
Ex23 8SD

Tel: 01288 354542

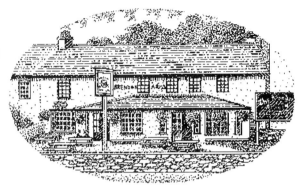

The Brendon Arms is celebrating its 125th anniversary 1872-1997 in the ownership of the Brendon family. Sophia Brendon the present licencee is the 5th generation of the family to run what is an exceptionally nice, traditional pub. A celebration cask ale called George Brendon's Best Bitter has been brewed specially for the anniversary.

The lounge bar has recently been renovated and is a comfortable place in which to enjoy a quiet drink whilst you take stock of the two large murals on the wall depicting old Bude. They are fascinating and always a talking point. The pub is full of interesting nautical memorabilia which adds character to what is already a friendly, welcoming hostelry known to be the warmest welcome in the West!

The bars are always busy with local trade but this does not mean that the welcome is any less sincere for those who are visiting Bude. In fact more often than not visitors find themselves drawn into the friendly chatter. The food to be had at lunchtime and in the evenings is traditional pub fare and The Brendon is especially well known for its Steak Pie and Chicken and Mushroom Pie. You can have a full meal or simply settle for a freshly cut sandwich or a Jacket Potato with a variety of fillings. In the warm weather the large front garden with picnic tables and garden furniture is very popular with drinkers.

For those who would like somewhere homely and comfortable stay The Brendon Arms has 8 letting rooms one of which is ensuite. They are all simply, but well furnished and have television and that boon to travellers, a well stocked beverge tray. You can be quite sure of a comfortable nights sleep and an excellent, traditional English breakfast in the mornings.

USEFUL INFORMATION

OPEN; Mon-Sat 11am-11pm Sun:12-10.30pm
CHILDREN; Welcome. Not in Public Bar
Over 10 years in lounge bar
CREDIT CARDS; Visa/Master/Switch/ Delta
LICENSED; Full On
ACCOMMODATION; 8 rooms 1 ensuite
TARIFF:- From £18 / £20 pppn. All Year.

RESTAURANT; Not applicable
BAR FOOD; Good value, traditional fare
VEGETARIAN; Catered for
WHEELCHAIR ACCESS.
GARDEN; Yes with picnic tables
PETS; Public bar only

BOTTREAUX HOUSE HOTEL AND RESTAURANT
Boscastle
North Cornwall
PL35 0BG

Tel. (01840) 250231

ETB 3 Crowns,
Commended

This attractive hotel and restaurant is centrally situated in a conservation area at the top end of the pretty and historic village of Boscastle. It offers good food and accommodation in an atmospheric setting, with magnificent views from most rooms of the surrounding rooftops, beautiful countryside and the sea.

The building occupies the site of the original manor house of the Bottreaux family, who arrived after the Norman conquest and built a castle nearby, hence the name of the village. The hotel is about 200 years old and is next door to the 16th century Napoleon Inn, used for recruitment purposes during the Napoleonic Wars.

The hotel is owned and run by Graham and Hazel Mee, who have professional backgrounds and came here a few years ago. Their aim is to create a warm, relaxed and personal atmosphere for their guests. This they do very successfully.

Bottreaux House has seven bedrooms, with combinations from family to double rooms. All are en suite with individual decor, colour television and drinks facilities. On the ground floor is a lounge with comfortable furniture and a good selection of books, TV and video. The restaurant and bar area are relaxing and intimate.

Boscastle is surrounded by beautiful coast and countryside, and many interesting attractions are within easy reached.

USEFUL INFORMATION

OPEN All Year.
CHILDREN Over 9 years welcome.
CREDIT CARDS Barclaycard, Access, Eurocard, American Express, J&B.
LICENCE Table and Guest.
ACCOMMODATION 7 en suite bedrooms.
PRICES High season: £23 per person per night; Low season: £18.

RESTAURANT Informal, offering high quality menu.
VEGETARIAN Good proportion of dishes.
SMOKING Some non-smoking areas.
DISABLED No special access or facilities.
PETS By arrangement.
GARDEN No.

HALLAGATHER FARMHOUSE
Hallagather
Crackington Haven
Bude
Cornwall EX23 0LA

Tel. (01840) 230276

ETB 2 Crowns,
Commended.

Hallagather is an atmospheric Farm Guest House providing high quality Bed and Breakfast Accommodation. The farmhouse, in its peaceful, 'wildish' garden, is a listed building, parts of which are 600 years old. It has slate flagstones, granite fireplaces and oak beams, and sits in an Area of Outstanding Natural Beauty, close to the Atlantic coast and the magnificent beach at Crackington Haven. It is an ideal base for exploring the romantic and powerful landscape of North Cornwall.

The farm is the home of Pat and Roger Anthony, who have been in the holiday business since 1959. Their son, Jonathan, does the bulk of the work on Hallagather's 184 acre livestock farm. The Anthonys enjoy meeting people, and like to create an atmosphere as casual and informal as their guests wish. There is a comfortable lounge with colour TV and log fires in cold weather. In an alcove, a fridge is supplied for guests' exclusive use. Outside there is ample parking space.

Breakfast is a special treat at Hallagather, offering substantial farmhouse food and individual attention. The menu varies with the season, but typically will include fresh fruit, a choice of cereals, cooked bacon, pork sausages, fried potatoes, eggs cooked in any style, mushrooms, toast and preserves.

USEFUL INFORMATION

OPEN All Year except December.

CHILDREN Welcome except in July & August.

CREDIT CARDS No, but Travellers and Eurocheques

DISABLED No special facilities, but downstairs room could be available.

ACCOMMODATION 1 family, 1 double & 1 large single, all en suite or with own facilities.

PRICES B&B High Season: £20; Low Season £14.50.

VEGETARIAN breakfast by arrangement.

SMOKING Not in bedrooms or dining area.

LICENCE No.

PETS By prior arrangement.

GARDEN Large, 'wildish', with lawns, apple trees, garden furniture, barbecue.

TRENANCE GUEST HOUSE
Trenance
Crackington Haven
Bude
Cornwall
EX23 0JQ

Tel. (01840) 230273

Trenance Guest House is situated in a beautiful bay on the romantic North Cornish coast. Its owners, David and Jo Beldham, offer Bed and Breakfast accommodation with optional Evening Meals.

The spacious building was formerly a farm house, and the name, in Cornish, means 'the dwelling place (tre) in the valley (nance)'. It stands beside the Heritage Coast Path, on land which is protected by the National Trust and has been designated an Area of Outstanding Natural Beauty. The house has excellent views over Crackington Haven, renowned for its safe, sandy beach and geological features. The whole area is rich in dramatic and varied landscapes and is full of historic associations with smuggling and shipwrecks. All this makes it an ideal base for exploring the wonderful South West peninsula.

All bedrooms at Trenance have full central heating and tea and coffee making facilities. There is a television lounge for the use of guests, and plentiful parking space.

A full English breakfast, or an alternative, is provided, and evening meals are available by arrangement. A typical menu might include stuffed tomatoes, fish pie with fresh vegetables, summer fruit's pie with cream or syllabub or cheese. All food is fresh and home-cooked. Afternoon cream teas or packed lunches can also be provided, and those on special diets can be catered for.

Everything at Trenance combines to ensure that you have a memorable stay.

USEFUL INFORMATION

OPEN All Year except Christmas.
CHILDREN Welcome. Cot & high chair available.
CREDIT CARDS No.
LICENCE None.
ACCOMMODATION 5 rooms, inc. single, 3 doubles and twin. 2 en suite, bathrooms and toilets nearby.
PRICES B&B from £16 per person per night. Children under 4 free if with adult, 4-12 half price if sharing. Ring for other terms.

RESTAURANT Breakfast, evening meals and packed lunches provided by arrangement. Traditional home-made and cooked food.
VEGETARIAN Varied choice.
SMOKING Non smoking policy in house, but smoking room available.
DISABLED No special facilities.
PETS No.
GARDEN 2 acres.

HENDRA COUNTRY HOUSE
St Kew Highway
Near Wadebridge
Bodmin
Cornwall
PL30 3EQ

Tel. and Fax (01208) 841343

Hendra Country House is a small, individual hotel a few miles from the dramatic North Cornish coast. It is an elegant, early 19th century manor house, latterly a farm house, set in rural tranquility, and retaining many original features. These include the huge slabs of slate in some of the floors and the large sash windows, all of which give a sense of solidity and permanence.

Hendra is the home of Eddie and Irene Jones, who have themselves converted the building. Irene's talents range from cooking to plumbing, while Eddie is a qualified accountant who is now a market gardener and smallholder; he raises the pork, lamb, eggs, vegetables and fruit which Irene uses with flair and distinction in the kitchen. Fresh fish comes from nearby Port Isaac. Irene's meals have been described as 'the real taste of Cornwall.' A carefully selected wine list complements the food perfectly.

There are five en suite bedrooms, one of them a single, all with colour television, central heating, radio alarm and tea/coffee facilities.

The surrounding country is idea for walking and cycling, bird watching and other country pursuits, while there are many historic houses and gardens in the area. Whatever your interest, you will remember your stay at Hendra

USEFUL INFORMATION

OPEN February to November and Christmas.
RESTAURANT 'A dinner party every evening.' 4 course meal £14.50 per person.
CHILDREN Welcome. Under 2 years Free.
VEGETARIAN Full menu available.
CREDIT CARDS Visa, Access, Mastercard, American Express.
DISABLED No special facilities.
PETS By prior arrangement.
LICENCE Residential.
GARDEN Large garden with seating and tables.
ACCOMMODATION 5 bedrooms, all en suite.
PRICES B&B per person. High Season: £25, Children 2 to 12, £12.50. Low Season: £20, Children £10.

THE WOOTONS COUNTRY HOTEL,
Fore Street,
Tintagel,
Cornwall PL34 0DD

Tel: 01840 770170
Fax: 01840 770978

4 Crowns E.T.B. XXAA

Situated at the entrance road to Tintagel Castle reputedly the home of 'King Arthur' and overlooking the Vale of Avalon towards the sea, The Wootons is an old Coaching House built in the 1800's. Purchased by the present owners in 1989, it has undergone a two year period in which the property was gutted and an extension built.

Everything has been done to the highest standard and the result is a relaxed and comfortable establishment in which it is a delight to stay or to call in for a drink or a meal. Special attention has been given to the needs of the modern traveller and every bedroom apart from having very comfortable beds is ensuite and has colour TV, Tea and Coffee facilities and telephones.

This family managed hotel has Paul West as Manager and his sister Jackie as Head Chef who together with their competent and friendly staff make everyone welcome. The Period Bar is well stocked and here you can have an excellent Bar meal chosen from an extensive menu or full a la carte in the restaurant. There is a Billiards Room, Pool and Darts and a charming Garden Patio; ideal for drinks on a warm day.

USEFUL INFORMATION

OPEN;All year. Food served all day	**RESTAURANT; Delicious food. Local produce**
CHILDREN; Welcome	**BAR FOOD; Excellent range. Home-cooked**
CREDIT CARDS; All major cards	**VEGETARIAN; Always a choice**
LICENSED; Full On	**DISABLED ACCESS; Not accommodation**
ACCOMMODATION;All ensuite rooms	**GARDEN; Yes & Patio PETS;No**

RATES:- High Season £35 pppn B&B. Low Season £25 pppn B&B.Children under 12 H/P.

KING ARTHUR'S CASTLE HOTEL,
Tintagel,
Cornwall PL34 0DQ

Tel: 01840 770202
Fax: 01840 770978

ETB Three Crowns.

This fantastic hotel took five years to build from 1894-99. The exterior construction represents a castle and you first see it situated high on a rugged headland from which there are panoramic and uninterrupted coastal views from Lundy Island to Trevose Head and it overlooks 'Tintagel Castle' reputedly the home of King Arthur. There is a great romantic feel about Tintagel which is heightened by staying in this stunning hotel with its fine timbers, wonderful glass windows, a magnificent staircase and a Lounge with Marble pillars. Every attractively appointed bedroom has recently been fitted with new European ensuites and have TV, Coffee and Tea facilities and a computerised telephone system.

Family run and in the same hands since 1953, King Arthur's Castle Hotel has a friendly air of well-being which makes visitors feel happy and relaxed. The Restaurant has both an A La Carte and a Table d'Hote menu with excellent choices of beautifully presented dishes on either menu. The wine list has been carefully chosen to provide wines from around the world. From Tintagel there are so many places one can visit or simply enjoy the fascination of this rugged coastline. Whatever you choose to do you will always feel contented to come back to the welcoming environment of King Arthur's Castle Hotel.

USEFUL INFORMATION

OPEN; April-October	**RESTAURANT; Open to non-residents**
CHILDREN; Welcome	**A La Carte & Table d'hote menu**
CREDIT CARDS;Master/Visa/Euro	**BAR FOOD; Not applicable**
LICENSED; Full On	**VEGETARIAN; Always a choice**
ACCOMMODATION; All ensuite	**DISABLED ACCESS; Yes. Level entrance**
PETS; No	**GARDEN; Large, open cliff land**

RATES:- £30 pppn B&B. Children under 12 years. £15.

THE MILL HOUSE INN
Trebarwith
Tintagel
Cornwall
PL34 0HD

Tel. (01840) 770200 and 770932

ETB Approved.

Beautifully situated in the dramatic and unspoilt Trebarwith Valley, a ten minute walk away from the popular surfing beach at Trebarwith Strand, the Old Mill House Inn is a highly atmospheric Cornish inn popular with locals and visitors alike.

The inn occupies a lovely stone-built 16th century corn mill, complete with slate flagstone floors and massive beams. The trout stream that used to work the mill runs through the garden, and the whole place is framed by the sycamores that grow profusely in the surrounding valley. In the summer it is a perfect sun trap.

Roy and Jenny Vickers, with their family, are the resident proprietors of this Free House, and they and their staff assure you of a warm and friendly welcome, whether it is your first visit or your hundredth.

The inn's seven cottage-style bedrooms are all centrally heated, and there is a separate children's room as well as the Bar, Lounge, Restaurant and Beer Garden.

The menus for the restaurant and bar are imaginative and wide ranging, with special children's menus and always a choice for vegetarians.

The Old Mill House Inn is just off the B3263 from Tintagel to Camelford, through Treknow village. It is ideal as a base for touring Cornwall and West Devon.

USEFUL INFORMATION

OPEN 11am-11pm all year.
CHILDREN Welcome.
CREDIT CARDS Visa, Amex
LICENCE Full, Supper and Residents'.
ACCOMMODATION 3 double en suite, 2 double with private bathroom, 1 family en suite, 1 twin en suite.
PRICES High Season: £25, Low Season £18. Children 5 - 11 half price.

RESTAURANT Extensive English and Continental menu and Wine list
BAR FOOD Range of main course or light meals.
VEGETARIAN Always something available.
SMOKING Non smoking areas.
DISABLED No special access.
PETS Permitted.
GARDEN Beer garden and patio/terrace.

OLD TREDORE HOUSE,
St Issey,
Padstow, Cornwall
PL27 7QS

Tel: 01841 540291

Padstow Area Tourist
Association Member.

Set between the tranquil villages of Little Petherick and St Issey, Old Tredore House dating from the 17th century is in a quiet rural position surrounded by its own garden and with far reaching views over the open countryside. Quiet and restful it maybe but if you are looking for a little more activity, the house is only three miles from the picturesque and unspoilt harbour town of Padstow, famed for 'Obby Horse Day' on May 1st and these days for Rick Stein, chef and broadcaster extraordinaire and his incomparable restaurant. Much of the local countryside is National Trust owned and offers a wealth of interest to the walker and the ornithologist whilst there are an abundance of leisure facilities within easy reach of the house to suit all ages. Golden sandy beaches are within a few minutes drive, or simply follow a coastal path to enjoy some of Cornwall's most spectacular scenery. The Camel Estuary is ideal for sailing, wind surfing and water skiing. Deep sea and freshwater fishing are available in the surrounding waters.

Old Tredore House was updated in the 18th and 19th century and most of the facilities created at that time still remain, such as servant bells and bell pulls, and a slate horse mounting block is set in the wall at the front of the house. Directly positioned to one corner of the garden is a Victorian Toilet House - not in use, of course, - reached by way of a red brick path. The house is charming and beautifully furnished with a mixture of antiques and other fine pieces. There are three bedrooms all ensuite and each very different. The Ground Floor double is ideal for the partially disabled. There is a spacious double or twin on the First Floor as well as a large ensuite room with a Victorian Queen Size Four Poster. Each has television and a hostess tray. Your hosts, Gill and Bob Claridge enjoy people and have the knack of making their guests feel at home immediately. Breakfast is a sumptuous feast with several choices and cooked to order. No evening meals but there are many eateries of all kinds nearby.

USEFUL INFORMATION

OPEN; 1st January-30th November   **DINING ROOM; Excellent breakfast**
CHILDREN; Welcome   **VEGETARIAN; Upon request**
CREDIT CARDS: None taken   **DISABLED ACCESS; Yes. Ground floor   room**
LICENSED; No, bring your own   **GARDEN. Yes. Sun Loungers provided**
ACCOMMODATION; 3 ensuite rooms   **PETS; Not allowed in the house**
RATES:- All Year, from £22 / £26 pppn B&B.

ANVIL GRILL
Churchtown,
Cubert,
Nr Holywell Bay,
Newquay
Cornwall
TR7 5EY

Tel: 01637 830631

The Anvil Grill is located near Holywell Bay which is separated by an extensive National Trust hinterland. It is wonderful walking countryside and the views over the sea are stunning. Just half a mile away is a Par 3 18 hole Golf Course - an ideal way to work up an appetite for a meal at the restaurant.

If you ask the owners, Bill Farrow and his wife, Geraldine, how they would describe their business they will tell you they offer the taste of good home cooking from Tummy Tempters to a Light Bite with Steaks a Speciality. Their clientele will tell you that the food is excellent, good value and with something for everyone. The Farrows have the ability to create a happy and contented atmosphere in the restaurant which is confirmed by the fact that their staff remain with them for a long time, some of them over ten years. They know their regulars and their tastes well but they are equally attentive and caring about newcomers to the Anvil Grill.

You will find the menu far reaching. Bill Farrow is the chef and he will tempt you with all sorts of interesting dishes from a farmhouse soup which is a meal in itself, to a hearty home-made Beefsteak Pie. Poached Halibut with Hollandaise sauce and garnish is a firm favourite or the tried and tested Cod and Chips.

If you are really hungry the 'Tummy Fillers' offer a wide choice from a Turkey Steak to a home-made Chicken Curry. From the Charcoal Grill you can have an Anvil Mixed Grill, a Gammon Steak, a T-Bone steak or some delicious Lamb Chops. Puds come in different guises including an unusual Brandy Junket with Cream. There are Vegetarian dishes, Daily Specials and Children's Portions. Anvil Grill is licensed and whatever you choose the price is right.

USEFUL INFORMATION

OPEN; April-October
CHILDREN; Welcome
CREDIT CARDS; All major cards
LICENSED; Yes

RESTAURANT; 60 covers. Good food
VEGETARIAN; Several choices
DISABLED ACCESS; Yes
PETS; No

THE ST MABYN INN,
St Mabyn,
Bodmin,
Cornwall
PL30 3BA

Tel: 01208 841266
Fax: 01840 212415

St Mabyn is a quiet country village where life goes on in a leisurely contented way yet it is only 4 miles from the busy market town of Wadebridge and 6 miles from Bodmin. Much of the life of the village centres on two places, the beautiful old church for one, and right next to it, The St Mabyn Inn. The latter was originally a 16th century hotel with an old Tythe Barn (currently under renovation). It is now the heart of village life with a busy local trade but made even busier by the reputation it has acquired for the excellence of its food which brings people to its tables from miles around.

Visitors soon discover its charm and its fascinating bric-a-brac which is always a talking point. It has been described as one of Cornwall's finer eating houses and that is fitting. The menu in the Restaurant is both imaginative and interesting prepared by a chef who uses fresh meats, daily fresh fish in season and as much locally grown vegetables and produce as possible. You will find also that she has a light touch with pastry and an inspired handling of Continental dishes. If you would rather have something less than a full meal, the Bar menu will appeal with its wide selection.

The St Mabyn is a Free House and always has four traditional bitters, 2 stouts, 2 lagers and cider (Scrumpy in summer).

USEFUL INFORMATION

OPEN; All year. 11.30-3pm & 6-11pm   **RESTAURANT; Excellent menu. Specials**
CHILDREN; To eat only   **at lunchtime. Unusual dishes**
CREDIT CARDS; All major cards   **BAR FOOD; Wide range**
LICENSED; Full On   **VEGETARIAN; Choice of 2/3 dishes**
PETS; No   **GARDEN; Yes. Eat outside in summer**
DISABLED ACCESS; Welcome but one step & no special facilities

KINGS ARMS,
Howells Road,
Stratton,
Nr. Bude,
Cornwall
EX23 9BX

Tel: 01288 352396

Stratton is a mile inland from Bude and very close at hand to beautiful beaches, rugged coastline, coastal path walks and breathtaking scenery and on the main road of the village is the Kings Arms, a delightful 16th-century hostelry full of character. The Bar has a beautiful slate floor with a cast iron log burner to making the whole place very cosy. There is another large cast iron fireplace in the lounge which is traditionally furnished in keeping with the charm and atmosphere of the pub. Very much aware that smoking is not popular today, there are two air filter machines which dispense with any smoke.

As one might expect in a village inn, there are many regulars who were either born here or have become 'naturalised' over the years. It is always a pleasure to listen to their cheerful chatter and feel part of village life. There is always a nice atmosphere enhanced by the fact that there is no Juke Box! Everyone is made to feel very welcome by Steve and Jayne Peake, even dogs, kept on leads, who are provided with biscuits and water. Steve is a traditional beer enthusiast and a mad keen football fan - Hereford United is his club - and so football frequently looms largely in conversation.

The food, cooked and prepared by Jayne and her Bar Meals are much appreciated. She is particularly noted for her Steak, Kidney and Ale Pie. There is an extensive menu including fish and vegetarian meals and all at acceptable prices.

USEFUL INFORMATION

OPEN; Mon-Thurs: 12-2.30 & 6.30-11pm	**RESTAURANT; Not applicable**
Fri-Sun:11-11pm Food:12-2pm & 6.30-9pm	**BAR FOOD; Mainly home-cooked**
CHILDREN; Welcome	**VEGETARIAN; Catered for**
CREDIT CARDS; None taken	**DISABLED ACCESS; With assistance**
LICENSED; Full On	

THE BUSH INN,
Morwenstow,
Nr Bude,
Cornwall
EX23 9SR

Tel: 01280 331242

Like Phoenix rising from the ashes, the friendly old pub, The Bush Inn at Morwenstow, is once again its hospitable self after a major fire. It is a thoroughly unpretentious and comfortable hostelry, the sort of inn where it is pleasant just to sit and drink whilst listening to the humorous banter of the regulars across the bar.

They are obviously happy drinking here and that atmosphere spills over right throughout the pub which is furnished with some fine old wooden settles and lots of brass and copper and unusual bric a brac which is always commented on by visitors.. Beryl Moore is the licensee and she has a great ability to make strangers feel rapidly at home. This talent comes very much to the fore during the season when visitors flock to this part of Cornwall to enjoy the magnificent beaches, the rugged coastline and the breathtaking scenery.

Bar food is only served at lunchtime and the menu provides the traditional favourites one associates with a pub. Much of it is home-made and every day there is an excellent homemade soup which with some crusty fresh bread is a meal in itself.

USEFUL INFORMATION

OPEN; 11.30-3pm & 7-11pm	**RESTAURANT; Not applicable**
Closed Mondays from Nov-April except Bank Holidays	
CHILDREN; No facilities	**BAR FOOD; Good traditional fare. Lunch only**
CREDIT CARDS; None taken	**VEGETARIAN; Upon request**
LICENSED; Full On	**DISABLED ACCESS; No facilities**
GARDEN; Tables in courtyard	**PETS; No**
Ample play area on adjoining green	**PARKING; Ample parking**

CHAPTER NINE

North Devon : From Hartland To Lynton

Chapter Nine

"He goes not out of his way that goes to a good inn."
George Herbert

CHAPTER NINE

NORTH DEVON FROM HARTLAND TO LYNTON

The area covered by this chapter is a vast one, and the method of presenting it must again be more of an overview than an exact description of any possible route around it. **NORTH DEVON** is a region that has to be explored slowly, piece by piece, following the lanes and the road signs that take your fancy, and not being surprised if they take you by the longest imaginable way to where you weren't sure you were going in the first place.

But to anyone who has arrived in North Devon, which for the purposes of this book means parts of West Devon, Torridge and North Devon Districts, this will be clear already. It is probably just possible for the visitor to 'do' the major tourist spots of South Devon - Torbay, the edge of Dartmoor, the better known parts of the South Hams - in a couple of days; but that kind of approach is impossible up here, even if you restrict yourself, as we must now, to the main towns and the coast. As you turn north from Okehampton or Exeter, with the whole area laid out before you, rich, expansive yet inward-looking, a half-hour's drive to a familiar destination can feel like a major expedition into the unknown. It is the sort of landscape you can easily spend a lifetime, or so, getting to know.

North Devon has always been rather a remote, old-fashioned, self contained part of the country. It feels, maybe, less open than South Devon, and is less obviously spectacular in its beauty, apart from along the coast, but, as was stated in Chapter 1, it is also clearly the same county. If you are one of those people who finds Cornwall a little disturbing, you can breathe freely again here, now that you are safely back over the Tamar!

North Devon grows on you, and as you journey around in this apparently endless landscape of smallish fields, hills and woods, with hidden villages, tiny hamlets, isolated farms, lonely churches and sudden arrivals in busy little towns that are, despite their size, completely urban in atmosphere, you will find yourself wondering about the lives of the people you see who have chosen to be here. The communities all seem very civilised and human-scaled, and it is clear that many people are managing to live, today, in the northern half of Devon, very contented and creative lives. Craftspeople, poets, painters and therapists coexist here with the indigenous population very amicably.

Amongst the latter, Noncomformity is strong, just as it is in Cornwall, and very often, driving through the depths of the country, without a village or a hamlet in sight, you will come upon a small roadside chapel or meeting house. The same leaning towards traditional forms of community-made entertainment is also apparent, with the smallest place having its brass band, handbell team or choir. Bell ringing is an especially strong part of the local culture, and what was said in chapter 3 about Devon not being a noticeably musical county must be qualified by the intensity with which the art of ringing is practised. There are said to be more teams, or 'bands' of ringers here than anywhere else, and competition between them has long been the matter of song and legend.

The rocks are, like those in South Devon, a complicated mixture of sandstones, slates, grits and shales.

Coming into the region from Bude, the first town the visitor reaches is **HOLSWORTHY**. This little market town in the centre of a wide farming landscape is not particularly beautiful, in fact its buildings are all remarkable for being decidedly prosaic, except the church, which is well-proportioned, if rather dark. But should you choose to spend a bit of time here, you will observe a varied, friendly community with a lot more happening than appears on the surface.

Holsworthy describes itself as a PORT, but this has nothing to do with the old Bude canal; it comes from the original meaning of the word as denoting a place where markets and trade take place, without necessarily having anything to do with water transport.

HOLSWORTHY MUSEUM (01409 253336), in the Manor Offices, has a local history collection and material on the traditional rural life and culture of the area.

The town has good SHOPS and PUBS which serve the needs of the surrounding area very well, and where you can experience the daily life of North Devon as it is lived today. There is an INDOOR POOL and SPORTS HALL, and a GOLF CLUB (01409 253177) on the road from Bude.

HOLSWORTHY AGRICULTURAL SHOW is a real North Devon event, where the local spirit is strong; it is held in MAY. They also have a VINTAGE CAR RALLEY in JUNE.

A few miles away, near the village of **BRADWORTHY**, is the GNOME RESERVE AND WILDFLOWER GARDEN (01409 241435). Here can be seen a gathering together of over a thousand garden gnomes and pixies, in a beautiful environment with 250 species of wild flowers, herbs, ferns and grasses, all labelled. A very English combination of meticulousness and whimsy.

North east of Holsworthy on the A388 is the attractive old hill-top town of **GREAT TORRINGTON** (Tourist Information 01805 624324).

Torrington (as it is always called, the 'great' is just to distinguish it from **LITTLE TORRINGTON**) is a Medieval borough and market town standing above the River Torridge. It had a castle, but nothing of this remains. The town was virtually the only one in Devon to support the king during the Civil War, and 200 people suffered as a result of this loyalty; when the Parliamentarians blew up the church, they were still inside it.

The town is probably best known today as the home of Dartington Crystal (formerly Dartington Glass), and for the lovely views it enjoys of the surrounding country and the valley of the River Torridge.

The glass factory was set up during the 1960s by the Dartington Hall Trust from South Devon. Having shown at Dartington that life in a rural community in the 20th century could be both economically viable and socially creative, the Trust wanted to see if the same combination of craft-based industry and artistic opportunity could be attempted in a huge and, at that time, fairly depressed area like North Devon. They decided on an industry that had no traditional association with the region, and brought over Swedish glassmakers to teach their skills to the locals. They also established the BEAFORD ARTS CENTRE in a small village not far away to the south east, which promoted, and promotes, arts events all over the area. It sounds a bit paternalistic, and the people were suspicious at first, but both the glass and the arts centre have been very successful, and have given a great deal to the region, commercially and culturally.

At the DARTINGTON CRYSTAL FACTORY (01805 624233) there are GUIDED TOURS, a HISTORIC GLASS CENTRE and of course a SHOP where you can buy the finished product. There is also a RESTAURANT.

The town has a MUSEUM, which tells its story and that of the surrounding countryside through a diverse collection. There are one or two old houses, some atmospheric pubs and a sense of a close-knit, confident old community getting on with its life.

A special place in Torrington is the PLOUGH ARTS CENTRE AND CINEMA, established by the Beaford Centre. An impressive range of MUSICAL and THEATRICAL events, as well as ART and CRAFT EXHIBITIONS, with a strong emphasis on community arts, is presented here to the people of North Devon at all times of the year. In December 1995 I took part in a performance here, devised by a composer friend, called 'Midwinter Ceremonies', which involved local schools, players and groups from all over the region, and the sense I had of the centre's connection with its catchment area was as moving as the piece itself. The Plough clearly plays an important role in the lives of many people. It has a BAR, CAFE and BOOKSHOP. From Torrington, beautiful WALKS can be enjoyed in every direction, and the natural setting of the old town can be appreciated.

Not far away, the Royal Horticultural Society's ROSEMOOR GARDEN (01805 624067) should not be missed. In a lovely setting, covering 40 acres, the garden contains thousands of varieties of trees and plants.

Near Torrington, the village of **FRITHELSTOCK** has the romantic ruin of a Medieval Priory next to the church. The monks got into trouble with the Bishop during the 14th century, when it came to the prelate's ears that they were worshipping an unconsecrated statue, which sounded to him more like a figure of 'unchaste Diana' than of the Blessed Virgin, in the woods. They were ordered to destroy it. A touching story of Frithelstock Priory is that of a little boy who visited the ruin with his mother and grandmother during the 1930s, and suddenly started remembering how, long ago, when he was 'an old man', he had rung the bell in a long-vanished tower. Although the place he was pointing at seemed an unlikely location for a bell tower, later excavations revealed the plan of one in exactly that spot.

Following the Torridge as it winds north westwards, we eventually arrive at the famous old town of **BIDEFORD** (Tourist Information 01237 477676), with its ancient 24 arched bridge across the water.

Charles Kingsley, in *Westward Ho!*, memorably called it the 'little white town', and though there seems today to be as much grey, brown and red in the composition as white, the description, as you contemplate the town, sitting peacefully on the banks of the wide, muddy river, still fits.

Kingsley's story, although dated and flawed by his Victorian prejudices, gives a good flavour of the town's past, and the book is as much an inescapable part of the scene here as *Lorna Doone* is on Exmoor. In it he mythologises the 16th century adventurers and seamen of Devon, especially Sir Richard Grenville, whose home port this was. In the 17th and 18th centuries the town was very prosperous, thanks to the trading links with North America, and many fine houses built by the old merchants of this time adorn the streets. It remains a thriving town, an important urban centre for its surrounding region.

Kingsley's statue is on the long Quay, where it is very pleasant to wander and watch the life of the river, and at one end is a pleasant PARK, with TENNIS and BOWLING.

The famous BRIDGE, linking the twin communities of Bideford and EAST-THE-WATER, as the part of town on the other side is called, dates from 1460, but it was renovated in 1925. The fact that each arch has a different sized span maintains a feeling of antiquity. The BURTON ART GALLERY AND MUSEUM (01237 471455) is a major show-case for fine art, craft, exhibitions and local history.

Bideford is a centre for shopping and recreation of all kinds, with good pubs, hotels and eating places. The town has a SWIMMING POOL with SAUNA, FITNESS SUITE etc (01237 471793).

NORTHAM, once a separate community but now a suburb of Bideford, was the home of the Borough brothers, two lesser known Elizabethan seadogs who journeyed far and wide. Here can be found the SKERN LODGE OUTDOOR CENTRE (01237 415992), where tuition and opportunities are given for CANOEING, SAILING, SURFING, CLIMBING, ABSEILING and much else.

APPLEDORE, at the mouth of the Torridge, is a winding, narrow-streeted little sea town, where a vivid sense of the past can be experienced. Shipbuilding has always been carried on here, and today the town's shipyard has the largest covered shipbuilding dock in Europe. Other traditional industries include salmon fishing and the collecting and preparation of a particular kind of edible seaweed or LAVER, which is worth trying. Appledore is a rare place, where the life of the river is still the life of the town.

This makes it an appropriate setting for the NORTH DEVON MARITIME MUSEUM (01237 474852), which tells its stories through videos, dioramas and models as well as paintings and other more traditional exhibits.

Anyone with a desire to try SHARK FISHING can do so from here, and the town's REGATTA in AUGUST again focuses the attention on the Torridge.

Around the headland to the west of the estuary mouth, where both the Torridge and the Taw meet the sea in the diplomatically named BARNSTAPLE OR BIDEFORD BAY, you come to **WESTWARD HO!**   This spacious resort was created from nothing by speculative Victorian developers in the 1860s, as a direct response to the popularity of Kingsley's novel. It has long sandy beaches facing the Atlantic, a 2 mile long and 20 foot high pebble ridge, large white hotels and boarding houses, and an air that Kipling would probably recognise. He was sent to the United Services College here, and used the experience in his *Stalkey and Co.*

Excellent WALKS can be taken from here, and it is a noted resort for SWIMMING and SURFING.

Ten miles westwards from Bideford you come to CLOVELLY, with its steep old street of cobbled steps dropping 400 feet down the wooded hillside, its donkeys and its white, flower-bedecked cottages.

Along with Widecombe, Cockington forge, Plymouth Hoe, Polperro, St Michael's Mount, Land's End and Tintagel, Clovelly is one of the places that you cannot really visit the Westcountry and not see, at least once in your life. Another description of the village almost seems superfluous, but, as with the others, the beauty has not been exaggerated, and unless you automatically, and determinedly, mistrust anywhere which is so popular and has been so lavishly praised, you cannot help being entranced by it. Clovelly really does look like the postcards, and you will love the place, whatever time of year you come.

Before joining the throngs of equally entranced people making their way down to the little harbour, it is worth having a session at the VISITOR CENTRE AND INFORMATION POINT (01237 431781), which presents an audio-visual show explaining the story of the village, beginning right back in 2000BC. Then you will be ready to absorb all the pleasure you can from the real thing.

On the hills above the village can be found CLOVELLY DYKES, a huge Iron Age hillfort, with earthworks coverng 20 acres.

A memorable excursion from Clovelly is a WALK along the HOBBY DRIVE, a thoroughly romantic winding, tree-sheltered, fern-bedecked cliff road that gives wonderful views over the village and the sea. It was built by Sir James Hamlyn, lord of the manor, in 1829, to give himself something interesting to do, hence the name.

The little hamlet of BUCKS MILLS, just east of Clovelly, is also very attractive. At one time every family in the village was said to have the name Braund; a dark-haired, dark-eyed clan, the predictable story was told of how they were descended from shipwrecked Spanish sailors from the Armada, for which belief see the comments on Hope Cove in chapter 3.

The nearby MILKY WAY AND NORTH DEVON BIRD OF PREY CENTRE (01237 431255) is a popular theme park with plenty to do for all ages.

HARTLAND, once said to be 'furthest from railways' in Britain, is a very small town (not, however, a village) and a huge parish, high up in the top left hand corner of Devon. Its coast is wild and rocky, and still quite Cornish in atmosphere, though it is not too fanciful to say that the town itself feels Devonian. Its church, dedicated to the Celtic St Nectan, is large and striking. The publisher John Lane, who came from near here, is buried in the churchyard.

Hartland has the well-known SMALL SCHOOL, an attempt to provide secondary education in a genuinely local, personal form as an alternative to the local children having to travel to a large school miles away. There is a working FORGE and a POTTERY.

The major coastal landmark of HARTLAND POINT rises to 350 feet, and has the most powerful LIGHTHOUSE in the British Isles. At **HARTLAND QUAY**, in an exposed position 2 miles west of the town, is a good MUSEUM (01288 331353) which covers the local history and geology, as well as having a great deal of information on the countless SHIPWRECKS which have occurred on this hard coast.

HARTLAND ABBEY (01237 441264), between the town and the Quay, is a country house based on the religious establishment dissolved in 1539. It has been owned by the same family for many generations, and possesses good displays of pictures, furniture and porcelain, while the GARDENS lead down to the beach.

HARTLAND FOREST GOLF AND LEISURE PARK (01237 431442) welcomes visitors.

In the Hartland area there are some enjoyable WOODLAND WALKS at the SUMMERWELL FOREST TRAIL, near a village with the splendid name of **WOOLFARDISWORTHY WEST**, usually shortened in both speech and writing to 'Woolsery' (there is another Woolfardisworthy in Devon, near Crediton, which is also pronounced 'Woolsery). In the parish are many ancient and remote farms, many of them continuously occupied since Saxon times.

Twelve miles north west of Hartland Point, **LUNDY ISLAND** is clearly visible at most times from along the North Devon coast. It is a substantial lump of granite, 3 miles long and half a mile wide, sitting in the Bristol Channel. On the island there is a CASTLE, a LIGHTHOUSE and a CHURCH, and the place has a wild and romantic history. It is owned by the National Trust and administered by the Landmark Trust. Regular sailings to it on the Oldenburg are made from Bideford throughout the year, and from Ilfracombe during the summer. For all you need to know about Lundy, contact the LUNDY SHORE OFFICE on the Quay at Bideford (01237 470422).

Returning to Bideford you can take the A39 for a direct run to Barnstaple, or take the slightly longer route of the B3233, passing near the estuary and going through the villages of **INSTOW** and **FREMINGTON**. The LOBSTER POT at Instow is a famous venue for all kinds of performances.

BARNSTAPLE (Tourist Information 01271 388583) is the major town of North Devon, and one of the county's most important urban centres. It functions as an administrative, commercial, cultural and educational centre for the whole region. Coming to it from Exeter, after the apparently endless road across the Mid and North Devon plain, it can, in some moods, feel like a remote outpost of urban civilisation; the sight of contemporary buildings and road junctions again is always a bit of a surprise.

Barnstaple sits on the River Taw just where this opens out into its wide, muddy estuarine stage. The BRIDGE over it dates originally from the late 13th century, but is much restored. The Taw shares a mouth with the Torridge, and there is inevitable rivalry between Barnstaple and Bideford. Daniel Defoe, who passed this way in the 1720s, reckoned that if the two towns ever joined together along the estuary they would make a city second to none in the kingdom outside London, but most of us today are glad this didn't happen.

Barnstaple is very old, but you do not get much sense of this without exploring the town in some detail. It appears a large, busy, modern place, and the developers and planners, who have made it what it is in the last 30 or so years, did not feel that they needed to be restricted by the original Medieval street pattern, so they ignored it. But Barnstaple is quite aware of its history, even if there are fewer obvious traces of it than there might be, and 'Barumites', as the indigenous inhabitants are called, are very proud of their town and its traditions.

Barnstaple is often described as the 'oldest borough in England', but whether this is actually true in any meaningful sense is doubtful. It is certainly not the oldest town, although it was one of Devon's earliest urban places, replacing the adjacent village of **PILTON** as the local Anglo Saxon fortified burh against the Vikings. What most people mean when they say it is the 'oldest borough' is that it has (or once had) the oldest borough charter, which was traditionally granted in 930, but there is no actual proof of this.

This is clearly one of those issues where fierce local pride and historical accuracy are slightly at odds. Similarly, Totnes in the South Hams claimed for some years to be the 'second oldest borough in England' (they thought Chester was the first), but this is completely untrue, as I finally persuaded them to see; by the time Totnes got its piece of parchment granting a degree of self-government, any town which could afford one was a chartered borough. Who really cares anyway, except perhaps a few pompous councillors?

Barnstaple's most famous son is the 18th century poet and wit John Gay, best known for *The Beggar's Opera*, based on popular songs and ballads. This work taps a perennial source of inspiration, as can be seen by the 20th century recreations of it by people like Brecht, Weill and Britten.

Another creative name worth mentioning is that of the composer and conductor Hubert Bath, who was born here in 1883. His music bestrides popular and more serious forms, and is romantic and tuneful; he is best remembered as a pioneer of British film music, and had his greatest hit with the theme tune "Cornish Rhapsody", written for the 1940s film *Love Story*.

The MUSEUM OF NORTH DEVON (01271 388583) is not to be missed. It houses a major collection, covering the development of the town and of the whole area, with local pottery, art, the region's literary inheritance, maritime and military history and much else.

Barnstaple made its money in past ages from the woollen trade and as a port. Although less of the old town survives than we could wish, there are some features that are worth seeking out. BUTCHER'S ROW is a Queen Anne terrace of shops, originally all, as the name suggests, for purveyors of flesh, and the GUILDHALL has some good 17th century panelling. TOURS of the building can be arranged through the TIC.

Barnstaple has a full range of SHOPS, PUBS, RESTAURANTS and CAFES. It is well served for RECREATIONAL FACILITIES, with the excellent NORTH DEVON LEISURE CENTRE (01271 73361), which has SWIMMING POOLS, FITNESS SUITES and SPORTS HALLS, and a RESTAURANT and BAR overlooking the Taw.

CONCERTS, PLAYS and other events happen at the QUEENS HALL, and the famous BARNSTAPLE FAIR, a highly traditional one, and firmly rooted in the centuries-old agricultural year, but with all kinds of contempoary additions as well, is not to be missed if you are around in SEPTEMBER.

You cannot be long in North Devon without coming across references to Henry Williamson's famous novel *Tarka the Otter*, written when the exhausted author, shattered by his experience of the Great War, was living in isolation by the River Taw and seeking to heal his life by communion with nature (or rather Nature). The acute observation of wildlife in this and other books made his name, and many of the locations of the story can be seen today.

The whole area is now marketed as the 'TARKA COUNTRY', and the TARKA TRAIL, a 31 mile CYCLE AND FOOTPATH between Barnstaple and Bideford, embracing both the Taw and the Torridge, is a wonderful way of safely exploring the countryside of North Devon. Information about it can be picked up at any TIC.

Williamson himself spent much of his long life at **GEORGEHAM**, a small village not far from Braunton. He was a complex, difficult man, whose espousal of fascism makes him hard to like, but his perception of nature and the life of North Devon have a value which will ensure that he continues to be read.

On the way to Braunton is MARWOOD HILL GARDENS (no telephone number), a beautiful 18 acre bog garden with lakes, rare trees and shrubs.

ARLINGTON COURT (01721 850296) , a major National Trust property 7 miles east of Barnstaple on the A39, is an imposing house dating from 1822 surrounded by PARKS and GARDENS. It was the home of the Chichester family and contains a fascinating collection of furniture and artefacts. Sheep and ponies wander in the park, and there are woodland walks and the usual facilities of a National Trust house.

At **LANDKEY** is the NORTH DEVON FARM PARK and 'JUNGLELAND' (01271 72103), with tropical and Mediterranean plants in natural surroundings, and fish ponds.

North west of Barnstaple, over the Taw, is **BRAUNTON** (Tourist Information 01271 816400), sometimes said to be the largest village in England (who works these things out?). It has attractive, narrow streets, an old-fashioned atmosphere and plenty of individuality. The large sandy tract of BRAUNTON BURROWS, comprising 1,000 acres of dunes, is now a Nature Reserve, and GUIDED TOURS are available over it - ask at the TIC. The village and its surrounding area can be reached safely from Barnstaple by way of the ESTUARY CYCLE TRACK.

Braunton is also famous for its GREAT FIELD, one of only two surviving examples in England of the Medieval 'strip' system, which is quite remarkable, as this system was generally replaced by enclosed fields at an earlier time in Devon than in most other parts of the country.

BRAUNTON has a small MUSEUM (no telephone number) in Church Street, and the COUNTRYSIDE CENTRE, which offers interpretation of the local landscape and ecology.

There are several interesting shops and galleries here. The ELLIOTT GALLERY (01271 812100) displays and sells all kinds of art and craft, and STUDIO CERAMICS has a good range of work.

BRAUNTON CARNIVAL is in MAY.

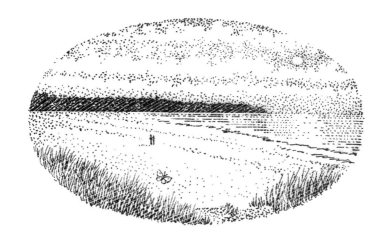

This area of North Devon is best known for its incomparable broad, sandy BEACHES facing the Atlantic, mile upon mile of them, backed by dramatic coastal scenery and cliff walks. The feeling is one of space, light, air and energy.

SAUNTON SANDS, 2 miles away from Braunton, is a very popular and spacious sandy beach by the mouth of the double estuary. It stretches for 3 miles and is ideal for BATHING,SURFING and all WATERSPORTS.

CROYDE, named after the Viking raider Crydda who landed on this coast over a thousand years ago, is a cob and thatch village with a stream running through it. There is a GEM, ROCK AND SHELL MUSEUM (01271 890409), but the main attraction is again the beautiful sandy beach, reputed to be one of the best in the country and ideal for all kinds of activity.

WOOLACOMBE and **MORTEHOE** have more miles of beach, with dunes and downs behind them. The MORTEHOE HERITAGE CENTRE (01271 870028) tells the story of this coastline and provides many activities for children.

ILFRACOMBE (Tourist Information 01271 863001) is a large, old fashioned seaside resort which developed in Victorian times. It has a beautiful harbour dominated by LANTERN HILL, with a little chapel dedicated to St Nicholas on top of it. Apart from this very photogenic, and much photographed, area around the harbour, the town is mainly 19th and 20th century and architecturally quite ordinary, but the general feel of the place is one of spaciousness, with the genteel white and green of the town contrasting well with the rocky shore, the steep cliffs and the challenging sea.

BOAT TRIPS leave from here in the summer for Lundy, Wales and along the coast.

ILFRACOMBE MUSEUM (01721 863541) is a delightful small town museum as full as a treasure chest of strange and beautiful memories. Like the one at Ashburton (chapter 4) you get the sense of being in the town's attic.

Ilfracombe has lovely safe beaches, with tunnels carved through the cliffs to reach them. For entertainment there is the PAVILLION THEATRE, and the town has CARNIVALS in AUGUST and DECEMBER, and a VICTORIAN FESTIVAL in JUNE. There is also a YOUTH ARTS FESTIVAL in JULY and a FISHING FESTIVAL in AUGUST.

Nearby a popular theme park, WATERMOUTH CASTLE (01271 867474), provides many things to see and do in and around a Victorian 'castle'.

COMBE MARTIN (Tourist Information 01271 883319) is a long village gently leading to the sea. Its mile and a half long street, with field strips stretching behind, is sometimes said to be the longest in the country. Silver and lead were mined here extensively for many centuries, and a ruined mine can be seen above the village.

There is a MOTORCYCLE MUSEUM (01271 882346) and a WILDLIFE AND DINOSAUR PARK.

We are now entering the area of the **EXMOOR NATIONAL PARK**.

The second of the Westcountry's National Parks, and the third of its moorland areas, Exmoor is different from both Dartmoor and Bodmin Moor. The underlying rock is sandstone, rather than granite, and it is on the coast. This makes it somehow more open and gentler than the others, and some say more beautiful. R.D.Blackmore, whose Exmoor novel *Lorna Doone* it is difficult to avoid up here, stated that 'the land lies softly', which puts it very well.

Only about a third of Exmoor lies in Devon. The rest is in Somerset, and so a full exploration of the moor must wait for another volume in this series, but a brief overview can be given here.

It is a region of high ridges and deep valleys. There are many BARROWS and STANDING STONES, although none as well-known as the Dartmoor antiquities.

The highest point is on WESTERN COMMON, near KINSFORD GATE, and is 1617 feet. Popular and easily accessible places on the moor include

BRENDON COMMON, the DOONE VALLEY off the Lynmouth and Porlock road, and MOLLAND COMMON.

The distinctive EXMOOR PONY, popular as a riding pony for children, is, unlike the Dartmoor, an ancient breed, a direct descendant of the original horse brought to Britain from Europe by the Celts.

The National Park's symbol is the Red Stag, and this brings us to an aspect of Exmoor life which has to be confronted: it is STAG HUNTING COUNTRY. Like it or not, the sport has a large popular following, and is an important part of the local culture. Whether this will change, which one hopes it eventually will, remains to be seen.

Exmoor is also a place with a strong FOLKSINGING tradition, and there are many pubs around the area where you can catch a good, local, unselfconscious singing session.

For more information on all aspects of the moor, contact the EXMOOR NATIONAL PARK AUTHORITY (01398 23665), or pick up information at any TIC. The authority publishes an annual 'EXMOOR VISITOR' in newspaper format, which gives details and advice covering everything you could want to know. The Park also has a RANGER SERVICE.

LYNTON and **LYNMOUTH** (National Park Information Centre 01598 752509) are a good base for exploring this land and seascape, and are very beautiful in themselves.

Lynton is a little town at the top of a 500 foot cliff, and Lynmouth an old fishing port in the river valley at the bottom. They have been linked by an enjoyable CLIFF RAILWAY since 1890. Both have spectacular views of the moor and the sea. Because of their natural setting, the growth of both places has been restricted.

There is an excellent local MUSEUM in Market Street, Lynton, illustrating the story of the to communities.

The life of both places has generally been quiet, but one terrible night in August 1952 much of Lynmouth was swept away in the famous flood disaster. The waters of the River Lyn poured through town, and 93 homes were damaged or destroyed, while no fewer than 34 people died. Little evidence of this tragedy remains today, however, and they make a delightfully restful place to visit.

Nearby, the VALLEY OF THE ROCKS is a famous sight.

SOUTH MOLTON (Tourist Information 01769 574122) is a friendly little market town in rich farming landscape. It has many shops and pubs, and a lively community life. It is a good centre for CRAFTS and ANTIQUES, but is also a real down-to-earth Devon town, with the local accent much in evidence.

Chapter Nine

HALMPSTONE MANOR HOTEL
Bishops Tawton,
Barnstaple, Devon EX32 0EA

Tel:- 01271 830321
Fax: 01271 830826

AA Red Star Hotel. AA (1990)
Award for best newcommer.
AA Two Rosette Restaurant Award.
Johansen-Excellence & Best Hotel awards.
Egon Ronay,
Good Hotel Guide & Ackerman Recommended.
' Which' Hotel of the Year.

Halmpstone Manor Hotel has a 400 year tradition of hospitality and when in 1630 John Westcote wrote in his book 'A View of Devonshire', that the hospitality he had received at Halmpstone Manor had been 'delightful' he had no idea that centuries later Jane and Charles Stanbury would be continuing the tradition and that the same description would apply. It is the most delightful place where Jane and Charles welcome you warmly. Set in the heart of rural Devonshire it is an English country house at its best in which everything conspires to make you feel relaxed, loved and cared for. The church bell tolls in the distance on a Sunday morning, the air is laden with the lovely smells of flowers, trees and shrubs and the scent of the Wisteria through an open window. In the summer the sun reaches every corner of this ultra charming and quite unique small Manor and in winter crackling log fires spread warmth and a sense of well being.

The romantic bedrooms have 4-posters, coronet beds and superb bathrooms and windows that look out onto the purple moor. Every bed has snowy white linen, the elegant drapes and wall covers and the many individual touches make the rooms a memory to be treasured. The elegant and comfortable drawing room is superbly furnished, the cosy bar somewhere to gather before a meal. The panelled, candlelit Dining Room has a special atmosphere of its own created, no doubt, by the many people who have dined here on superbly, creative cooking, relishing every mouthful and marrying it to wines from the extensive wine list. In Summer Devonshire Cream Teas in the garden are another happy memory for you to take away.

The Barnstaple area has much of interest for the visitor with wonderful beaches, a staggeringly beautiful coastline, stately homes, gardens and much more. Whatever your interest, Halmpstone Manor will provide you with a never to be forgotten break or holiday. Excellent too for small business meetings of up to ten people.

USEFUL INFORMATION

OPEN;All year except Nov & Jan	**DINING ROOM;** Creative cooking
CHILDREN; Over 12 years	**VEGETARIAN;** Needs catered for
CREDIT CARDS; Visa/Amex/Master/Diners	**DISABLED ACCESS; Unsuitable**
LICENSED; Restaurant	**PETS; Well behaved dogs**
ACCOMMODATION; 5 ensuite rooms	**GARDEN; Delightful**

SMOKING; Yes except for 2 bedrooms & dining room
RATES; All Year £50 to £58.50. pppn B&B,includes Morning and Afternoon Tea.
All rates are VAT inclusive, and include a complimentary morning newspaper.
20% Discount on rooms Nov-March excluding Xmas, New Year & Easter

THE HOOPS INN,
Horns Cross, Clovelly,

Tel: 01237 451222
Fax: 01237 451247

Two Star RAC.ETB.
3 Crowns Commended.

The Hoops Inn with wheaton-red thatched roof and massive white cob walls, is situated on the A39 between Bideford and Clovelly. This 13th.Century Inn is one of Devon's most famous, notorious as a meeting place for smugglers before it became a coaching inn. The Hoops was regularly used by Sir Richard Granville, Raleigh, Drake and Hawkins who sponsored the 1556 Bill calling for the contsruction of Hartland Quay nearby, when tobaccco and potatoes were first imported into England. The bar still has an original well in use today, the water from which was once used for the home-brewed ales for which the Inn was renowned. The proprietor Gay and her husband Donald run the Hoops helped by a small staff whom assure you of their best attention at all times.

The Inn specialises in regional fayre using the best Devonshire produce, with daily changing fresh fish and shellfish dishes complimented by a wide selection of delicious desserts served with Devon clotted cream. The extensive menu is served in both bars, and the candlelit restaurant known as The Drake Room. Complimenting the food is an excellent wine list full of interesting and varied wines from around the world.

The Hoops has 12 en-suite bedrooms, some with period furnishing including four-poster and half-tester beds. Luxurious would the best description of them and each has a T.V., hostess tray and direct dial telephone. People come from all over the world to stay here to enjoy the hospitality, the friendly atmosphere, the wonderful food and to explore the magic of this part of Devon.

USEFUL INFORMATION

OPEN; All year 11-11pm
CHILDREN; Welcome
CREDIT CARDS; All major cards
LICENSED; Full on
ACCOMMODATION; 12 ensuite rooms
SHORT BREAKS: Winter at reduced rate.

RESTAURANT; Candlelit. Superb food
BAR FOOD; English, traditional, wide range
VEGETARIAN; Always a choice
NO WHEELCHAIR ACCESS.
GARDEN; Courtyard and lawn

RATES:- All Year from £28 to £56 pppn B&B. £45 to £72 D/B&B

THE DURRANT HOUSE HOTEL
Heywood Road,
Northam, Bideford, North Devon.
EX39 3QB
Tel: 01237 472361
Fax: 01237 421709

ETB Four Crowns Highly Commended.

This stunningly beautiful hotel has to be the premier hotel in North Devon if not the county. One is left almost breathless by the sumptuousness of some of its rooms and the elegant simplicity of others. Vincent and Maria Borg bought the hotel in 1984 when it had 58 bedrooms and 2 suites now it has an additional 70 bedrooms; 30 of them being executive quality. These rooms have luxury marble bathrooms, with hair dryers, trouser presses and remote control TV's. The suites, perfectly appointed and equipped consist of bedroom, ensuite bathroom, separate shower room, colour TV in bedroom and lounge. Imagine having a 'Romantic Weekend' special break here which would give you and your partner the opportunity to enjoy a wonderful short stay. Champagne, Fresh Flowers and Chocolates with the compliments of the management are placed in your room on arrival!

The bedrooms, beautiful as they may be are only a minor part of the pleasure this hotel gives its guests. The staff have enormous pride in their hotel and with no apparent effort ensure every guests well being whether it is in the rooms, the bars, the restaurant or in any other part of the hotel You will seldom see the like of the Country Restaurant which derives its name from its ceiling beautifully painted by Philip Malpass. The panelled walls are covered with delightful paintings, a mixture of landscapes and flowers. The soft lighting enhances the charm of the finely upholstered banquette seating with its mahogany pillars above giving one the feeling of complete privacy. Other tables by the window look out over pretty scenery. The tables are laid with fine linen, sparkling glass and gleaming silver. Everything is there to make you eager to enjoy the meal which matches up to the splendour of the surroundings. The bars have the same elegance, if a little more restrained but either creates the right atmosphere in which to enjoy a drink .

Durrant House is expert at Special Functions of all kinds whether it be a Conference where they can cater for groups of 10-350 delegates and provide everything that can possibly be needed or maybe a Birthday, a wedding or a Christmas Party, all equally important and attended to with the meticulous care that is so much part of this hotel. North Devon has some of the most beautiful coastline in the British Isles, Romantic sunsets, miles of golden sands, breathtaking cliffs and quaint unspoilt fishing villages. Alternatively there is the wildness of Exmoor or a trip to Lundy Island. Whatever your choice, you will always have the happy knowledge that you will return to the exceptional Durrant House Hotel.

USEFUL INFORMATION

OPEN; All year except 2.1.98 for 2 weeks   **RESTAURANT;** Sumptuous decor & food
CHILDREN; Welcome   **BAR FOOD;** Snacks lunchtime only.
CREDIT CARDS; All major cards   **VEGETARIAN;** Yes. Vegan on request
LICENSED; Full. Fine wine list   **DISABLED ACCESS;** Yes
ACCOMMODATION; 130 ensuite   **GARDEN;** Yes. Swimming pool
RATES:- High Season, Single from £45 pppn B&B. £55. D/B&B.
Two Sharing £35 pn B&B. £45D/B&B.pn.
Low Season, Single from £40 pppn B&B. £48 D/B&B.
Two Sharing £30 pppn B&B. £38 D/B&B.
Children by arrangement. Stay free / seasonal offers; Request details.

WATERSMEET HOTEL,
Mortehoe, Nr Woolacombe,Devon
EX34 7EB

Tel: 01271 870333
Fax: 01271 870890

Two AA Rosettes.77%.
AA/RAC Three Star.
ETB. Four Crowns Highly Commended.

Watersmeet is literally only a few steps from a golden beach. As you cross the garden a white kissing gate leads to steps down to the rocks, some of the best rock pools in the world and a sandy beach below. It is such a pretty spot and so peaceful. It was built in 1907 as an Edwardian gentleman's country residence by the sea and from that special beginning the hotel, now in it's 70th year, has blossomed into one of the nicest and most welcoming havens in the South West. It is much more than just a hotel, throughout the year many events occur, there are duplicate bridge weeks in the Spring and Autumn, and Sheila Jay's painting week in April. In the hotel grounds there is lawn tennis or croquet and a heated outdoor swimming pool. This year the hotel has lost it's 1935 ballroom and in it's place a spectacular indoor swimming pool and spa have been built. This has already proved very popular with many of the guests. Open to non-residents, the hotel has an AA three star rating with a quality assessment of 77% and the restaurant has been awarded two rosettes from the AA. These two assessments alone place Watersmeet among the elite of three star hotels in the South West. The 24 bedrooms are all en-suite and offer a mix of singles, twins and doubles - Queen and King size - and most have glorious sea views. They are all individually furnished with pretty colour-co-ordinated soft furnishings. Every room has colour TV, a direct dial telephone, radio alarm and hair dryer.

After a comfortable nights sleep with no more than the lapping of the sea as it reaches the shore to disturb you, you will come down to enjoy one of the best breakfasts to be found in the county in a restaurant having panoramic sea views from Woolacombe Bay past Hartland Point to Lundy Island. Lunch is available from 12-2pm and in the evening dinner is served from 7pm. Children under the age of 8 are served a substantial high tea at 6.15pm every day. Everyone enjoys the food here with lots of fresh vegetables and locally supplied meat and fish. Watersmeet cannot be bettered for either a seaside holiday or a place just to rest quietly perhaps interspersed with a few spectacular coastal and moorland walks. The owners Brian and Pat Wheeldon and the staff, many of whom have been at the Watersmeet for many years, work hard to ensure that you are well cared for. There is so much of interest nearby including some National Trust properties, and some Nationally important bird watching sites. The Hotel has direct access to the South West coastal path, and you are only 20 minutes from the heart of Exmoor.

USEFUL INFORMATION.

OPEN; Feb.to Dec.	**RESTAURANT; Delicious food all meals.**
CREDIT CARDS; All majorcards	**VEGETARIAN; Catered for**
LICENSED; Yes Full Licence	**DISABLED ACCESS; 1 Ground floor room**
ACCOMMODATION; 24 ensuite rooms	**CHILDREN; Welcome, High Tea.**
PETS;No	**GARDEN; Yes. Swimming pool outdoor &**

Special rates for Three nights plus.Incl.Dinner.   **Indoor. Tennis, Croquet**
TARIFF:- High Season, from £80. Low Season from £58 both pppn D/B&B.
High Season,Weekly from £160. Low Season £116. D/B&B.Children according to age.

HOLMESDALE HOTEL
Bay View Road
Woolacombe
North Devon EX34 7DQ

Tel. (01271) 870335
Fax (01271) 870088

ETB 3 Crowns.

Holmesdale Hotel, overlooking Woolacombe's famous 2 mile long beach, is a friendly, family run hotel, full of character and with an excellent reputation for its food. Its Spanish owners, Carlos and Teresa Oyarzaba, are very warm and welcoming, and create a jovial, holiday atmosphere throughout the hotel, while in the Gema Restaurant Carlos shows his skills as a careful and imaginative chef.

The hotel offers 16 comfortable bedrooms, most of them en suite, with central heating, double glazing, continental quilts, tea making facilities, baby listener and radio. All rooms also have colour satellite televisions and videos. There is a special Honeymoon Suite, containing a four-poster bed and a balcony overlooking the bay.

Holmesdale also has a relaxing, intimate lounge bar serving a comprehensive range of beers, wines and spirits, which is open from 6pm to midnight. In the nearby chalet is a games room, with pool table, darts and fruit machines. The small garden behind the hotel is a perfect suntrap, while overlooking the beach is a beautiful sun terrace.

The Gema Restaurant, which is also open to non-residents, has been highly acclaimed for its superb range of English, Spanish and continental dishes. Carlos returns to Spain each year, coming back with fresh ideas and recipes with which to delight his regular clientele. As befits a seaside establishment, fish features prominently on the menus, cooked in all styles.

The Holmesdale makes a convenient and enjoyable base for exploring the dramatic coast of North Devon. Woolacombe itself is one of North Devon's most well-loved resorts, but is relatively uncommercialised, still retaining a strong Edwardian flavour. Its magnificent sandy beach, a mere 2 minute walk from the hotel, and its unspoilt downs, make it popular for swimming, surfing and just lying around on the spacious sands. A short walk away in the direction of Mortehoe, is Shell Beach, a sheltered cove which is noted for the wonderful varieties of shell which can be picked up there. The North Devon Coast Path runs beside the hotel, and inland there are attractive villages to be discovered. If you are keen on catching your own fish, the hotel can arrange trips on the Torridge and Taw estuaries.

USEFUL INFORMATION

OPEN Easter to October. Please ring for other times.

CHILDREN Welcome. Special menu.

CREDIT CARDS Visa, Access.

LICENCE Restaurant & Residential.

ACCOMMODATION 16 bedrooms, mostly en suite.

PRICES Low Season: from £160 per week,
High Season: from £222 per week. Please ring for daily rates and more details.

RESTAURANT Highly acclaimed restaurant, open to non-residents. International cordon bleu.

VEGETARIAN Catered for.

SMOKING Permitted, but not in dining room.

DISABLED No special facilities.

PETS Welcome.

GARDEN Sun trap.

BLACK HORSE INN
High Street
Great Torrington
Devon EX38 8HN

Tel. (01805) 622121

Situated in the heart of the pleasant country town of Great Torrington, the Black Horse Inn is a picturesque and atmospheric old coaching house. It dates from at least the 17th century, and is reputed to be one of the oldest pubs in North Devon.

During the Civil War, when Torrington was amongst only three towns in Devon to have any significant Royalist sympathy, the inn served for a while as the headquarters of Lord Hopton, Cavalier leader, who was defeated at the Battle of Torrington by General Fairfax in February 1646. It is now a very comfortable, charming, old-fashioned inn, complete with genuine oak beams, wooden panelling and inglenook fireplaces. It is equally popular with locals and visitors, and has featured in many guides to good beer and pubs. The Black Horse is also widely known for its food.

The owners are David and Val Sawyer, who create a friendly, welcoming atmosphere for visitors and regulars, and employ their son, Peter, as full-time chef. Both he and his mother are experienced, qualified chefs with a love of creating good food. Whether you are dining in the restaurant or simply partaking of a bar meal, the choice is wide and the quality excellent. Sunday lunch is especially popular, and it is wise to book in advance.

The Black Horse Inn provides three comfortable en suite bedrooms, each with central heating, colour television and tea and coffee making facilities.

Torrington is a friendly and attractive old town, beautifully sited on a hill above the Torridge Valley, with spectacular views over much of North Devon. A network of footpaths takes you across Torrington Commons, and not far away is the famous Tarka Trail. The town has an interesting museum, the Plough Arts Centre, which stages a range of events throughout the year, and the Dartington Crystal glass factory, of which guided tours are available. Nearby are Rosemoor Gardens, owned by the Royal Horticultural Society.

While you are exploring all these, and the many other delights in this corner of North Devon, the Black Horse makes a perfect base.

USEFUL INFORMATION

OPEN Weekdays: 11am - 3pm & 6 - 11pm. Sat:11am - 11pm. Sun: 12 - 3pm & 7 - 10.30pm.
CHILDREN Welcome.
CREDIT CARDS Visa, Access, American Express.
LICENCE Full.
ACCOMMODATION 3 en suite rooms.
PRICES B&B £16 per night single, £28 double.
RESTAURANT Good selection, generous portions.

BAR FOOD From sandwiches to steaks.
VEGETARIAN Always 4-5 dishes.
SMOKING Permitted throughout.
DISABLED Easy access to lounge and restaurant.
PETS Welcome.
GARDEN None.

SMYTHAM MANOR
Little Torrington,
Devon EX38 8PU

Tel: 01805 622110

ETB Three Crowns.

This 17th-century Manor House set in 25 acres of beautiful parkland, offers both serviced and self-catering accommodation in the heart of Devon and is so well situated that visitors can enjoy both the many sandy beaches and coastal resorts as well as the magnificent and mysterious Dartmoor and Exmoor. In addition there are stately homes to be explored as well as the fascination of watching glass blown at Dartington Glass and for those who love gardens the famous RHS Gardens at Rosemoor are just a mile away. If you want to be really active you can walk or cycle the scenic and famous Tarka Trail, fish at one of the reservoirs, rivers or trout farms within a short distance. For golf enthusiasts there are five courses, including one championship course nearby. Horse riding, surfing, windsurfing, sandsailing or straightforward sailing are also near at hand.

Smytham Manor has comfortable, well-furnished bedrooms most of which have en-suite facilities. The fully licensed restaurant is well known for the excellence of its food, together with bar snacks, Children's meals and take-aways. There is a well equipped games room with pool and table tennis. Outside there is a heated swimming pool,pitch and put course, badminton or volley ball, together with a small adventure playground. The static self-catering holiday homes are all modern amd fully serviced with shower, toilet, refridgerator and gas cooker, colour TV and free electricity and gas. All holiday homes are fully equipped with everything you need except bed linen, towels etc. Touring caravans have electric hookups, a modern purpose built toilet block with flush Wcs, hand basins, showers, shaver points, hairdrying facility and chemical disposal point. There is also a laundry and ironing room. Tents are welcome and there are several sheltered spots. Wonderful place for children and well behaved pets are welcome

USEFUL INFORMATION

OPEN; March-November
CHILDREN; Welcome
CREDIT CARDS; Master/Visa
LICENSED; Residential
ACCOMMODATION;Serviced & self-catering

RESTAURANT; Good reputation. Open to
Non-residents. Snacks. Takeaway
VEGETARIAN; Good choice
DISABLED ACCESS;Yes.1 Ground floor room
GARDEN; 25 acres

RATES:- High Season, from £17/£22. Low Season,from £16/£19. All rates are pppn B&B.
Special seasonal breaks available:- Details on request.

NORWOOD FARM HOUSE,
Hiscott, Barnstaple,
North Devon
EX31 3JS

Tel: 01271 858260

What strikes one on first entering Norwood Farmhouse is the grace and style with which it is decorated and furnished. The reason becomes apparent when one meets the owner Linda Richards who is an interior designer and decorator and who has worked on set designs for the theatre. She has a great eye for colour, design and line which combined makes this a house full of charm.

In addition there are some fine antique family pieces of furniture which just put the finishing touches on the house. The house is 17th century and has a lot of character and many interesting features.

There are three double and one twin bedroom all of which are en-suite and have colour TV and in keeping with the rest of the house are decorated in Classic English Country House style. The rooms are restful and just the place to stay for those wanting a break away from the stress of modern life. Linda enjoys cooking which is obvious from the excellent breakfast with its many choices to the evening meal which starts with a glass of sherry.

You may find the menu for the evening is Baked Quails Eggs, followed by Smoked Trout filleted and stuffed with prawns. The vegetables are fresh and cooked just to that al dente state which is delicious. For dessert, if you have room, there might be a Creme Caramel. A friendly house which has had much love bestowed upon it.

USEFUL INFORMATION

OPEN; All year except Chistmas
DINING ROOM; Good breakfast/ dinner   **CHILDREN; No**
CREDIT CARDS; No   **LICENSED; No**
DISABLED ACCESS; No   **VEGETARIAN; Catered for**
ACCOMMODATION; 3dbl 1tw ensuite   **GARDEN; Yes**
RATES:- £50 per room per night B&B All year.

TOWELL FARM,
Beaford,
North Devon EX19 8LL

Tel/Fax: 01805 603210

Beaford is a small, thriving village, well known for its Art Centre founded by the Dartington Trust. It is particularly well situated for exploring Dartmoor, Exmoor and the North Devon Coast with the beautiful Torridge River nearby and surrounded by many lovely walks including the Tarka Trail for which cycle hire is available.

On the edge of the village is Towell Farm with a Victorian farmhouse owned by Clarissa and Andrew Bass who welcome people into their home. The gardens spreading over two acres are delightful and make a fitting frame for the house. Indoors you will find all the gracious features that one expects from the Victorian era. It is comfortably furnished mainly with antiques and the whole atmosphere encourages one to relax. There is one ensuite double bedroom and a single sharing a bathroom. Both rooms have TV and a generously supplied hostess tray and in the house there is a friendly family dining room and sitting room for guests' use.

In addition there is self-contained accommodation in an attractive barn conversion with a double bedroom, bathroom and living area, furnished in a simple, comfortable style. Andrew and Clarissa both enjoy good food and wine and apart from a delicious breakfast a three or four course table d'hote dinner is available in which mainly local produce, home grown vegetables and free range eggs are used.

USEFUL INFORMATION

OPEN; January-December   **DINING ROOM; Home-cooked fare.**
CHILDREN; Over 8 years   **VEGETARIAN; Upon request**
LICENSED; No   **DISABLED ACCESS; Not suitable**
CREDIT CARDS; None taken
ACCOMMODATION; 1dbl ensuite 1sgl, Self-contained apartment in barn conversion
GARDEN; Beautiful two acres with lovely views
RATES;- from £18/22 Per person per night. All Year.

COURT HALL,
North Molton,
North Devon,
EX36 3HP

Tel: 01598 740224

Court Hall which has been in the hands of the Bampfylde family for over four hundred years and used by them as a Hunting Lodge, was partly pulled down in 1956 and rebuilt in 1985. None of the alterations have detracted from the charm of the house with its lovely old walled garden. Today it also has an extensive vegetable garden, a swimming pool and a tennis court. The house stands surrounded by Parkland with beautiful views over woods to Exmoor. Inside the house there are all sorts of splendid features including the beautifully carved black oak fire over mantle and the many family portraits.

Court Hall is the home of Charles and Sally Worthington who are a gregarious couple with many hobbies including bridge and gardening but above all they love entertaining and sharing with their guests their knowledge of wine and good food. Charles is a superb cook and chooses and presents his menus with a skill which would do credit to Raymond Blanc or the Roux brothers. Probably the nicest thing about staying at Court Hall is the relaxed atmosphere that the Worthingtons have created in which they truly want you to have a happy and memorable time.

There are two guest rooms, one with an enormous 6ft bed and bathroom and the other with 2 single beds and a bathroom with a shower over the bath. Both rooms are delightful and furnished with some beautiful antique pieces. Each room has a radio and a beverage tray. You are asked not to smoke in the house apart from the Drawing Room.

USEFUL INFORMATION

OPEN; March- end of October   **DINING ROOM; Superb food both at**
CHILDREN; Over 12 years   **Breakfast and Dinner**
CREDIT CARDS; None taken   **VEGETARIAN; With prior notice**
LICENSED; Restaurant   **DISABLED ACCESS; Not suitable**
ACCOMMODATION; 2 ensuite rooms   **GARDEN; Yes**
PETS;Yes, but not in the house   **RATES:- All Year £30 to £40 B&B pppn.**

COMBAS FARM
Putsborough, Croyde,
North Devon
EX33 1PH

Tel: 01271 890398

ETB Two Crowns Commended.
West Country TB inspected.
'Which Guide' Recommended.

Anyone who has stayed in this attractive 17th century farmhouse will tell you that one of the many things that appealed to them about Combas Farm was its tranquillity and the fact that they felt so at home there. Many visitors cut short their daily expeditions just to come back in the late afternoon and sit in the garden with a pot of tea, watching the great variety of birds, sometimes foxes or even badgers and rabbits all close to the house but most of all just 'listening' to the silence!

Gwen Adams who runs this excellent farmhouse accommodation is a lady who has very definite standards when it comes to caring for her guests. Comfort, peace and good food are her maxims. The first she has achieved by making all the rooms cosy and relaxing with soft decor and pretty drapes. The 5 bedrooms, 2 of which are ensuite and 2 with private bathrooms, have beds that would defy anyone not to sleep. There are inglenooks in the sitting room and dining room to enhance the air of well being.

Peace is inherent in the situation of Combas Farm which has a stunning outlook over completely unspoiled countryside. Food is delicious. All home-cooked using local produce and vegetables, fruit and salad that are not picked until four o'clock in the afternoon to be ready for the evening meal. The menu is imaginative and exciting with something to suit everyone. The home-made sweets will tempt the strongest willed and there is even home-made yoghurt. Finally Combas is close to so many wonderful places to visit including the beach at Woolacombe Bay which is the 7th best beach in the world. You can walk the coastal path, explore the villages, go surfing or wind surfing, play tennis and indulge in many other sports locally.

USEFUL INFORMATION

OPEN: March-December   **DINING ROOM; Excellent home-made fare**
CHILDREN; Welcome   **DISABLED; Not suitable**
CREDIT CARDS; None taken   **VEGETARIAN; Given notice**
LICENSED; No. Bring your own **PETS; Only to sleep in car. Not in house**
ACCOMMODATION; 5 rooms 4 ensuite **GARDEN; Delightful, peaceful**
SMOKING; Lounge only
RATES: High Season, £20.50 pppnB&B Dinner £9 Low Season £18 pppnB&B.Dinner £9.
Children, According to age, reductions up to 14 yrs.
Short Breaks :- Three Days less 5%. Seven Days less 10%. From normal tariff.

HUXTABLE FARM
West Buckland,
Barnstaple, Devon
EX32 0SR

Tel/Fax: 01598 760254

ETB Three Crowns Commended.
Farm Bureau/
Tarka Country Tourism Member.

In its secluded position at the end of a private lane known as 'Strawberry Lane' because of the wild strawberries in its high banks in early summer, Huxtable Farm, a medieval listed long house has to be one of the pleasantest settings for anyone wanting a restful holiday. The house dates back to 1520 and has many original features such as oak beams, screen panelling, open fireplaces with bread ovens, uneven floors and low doorways. It is the home of Antony and Jackie Payne who farm the eighty acres with the main stock sheep and also of Antony's parents Barbara and Freddie, a much travelled couple who have added the many fascinating pieces they have collected in their travels to the house.. Children love being here and are encouraged to make friends with, and feed, the lambs, tame sheep, chickens and Pygmy goats. The sheepdog 'Patch' attempts to keep all in order whilst 'Bimbo' the springer spaniel loves attention. There is much wildlife on the farm, an abundance of wildflowers, rabbits, badgers pheasants, partridge, buzzards and even deer in the early morning.

There are 6 bedrooms, 5 ensuite and one with a private bathroom, all of them with delightful names like Blue Forget-me-Not and Pink Campion; the colour of the flower denotes the colour of the decor. It is all charming and very relaxing and every room has nice additional touches to ensure your well being. Jackie loves meeting people and is an exceptionally good cook which means that every meal is eagerly awaited. At night you dine on a four course meal in the Medieval Dining room in candlelight. The delicious food is set on side-tables from which you help yourself to tender meat and a variety of freshly cooked vegetables. A complimentary glass of homemade wine adds to the pleasure of the meal. Wonderful at anytime of the year, there is so much to do. During the winter you can go for bracing walks and return to a crackling log fire. In spring the glory of the flowers and in the autumn the warm colours of the woodlands. Breathtaking sunsets, stunning scenery and a welcoming house. What more can you wish for.

USEFUL INFORMATION

OPEN; All year except Xmas 20-27th Dec inc.
CHILDREN; Welcome
CREDIT CARDS; None taken
LICENSED; No.Can bring your own
ACCOMMODATION; 5 ensuite rooms 1with private bathroom room.
PETS; No
DINING ROOM; Wonderful food in
Medieval Dining Room
VEGETARIAN; Yes but not Vegans
DISABLED ACCESS; Yes. 3 ground floor
GARDEN; Yes + separate play area
RATES:- All Year £23/£24 pppn B&B. Children £10 when sharing with parents in same room.
Short Breaks available:- Details on request.

MOLE COTTAGE
(Watertown)
Chittlehamholt,
Devon
EX37 9HF

Tel/Fax: 01769 540471

Since 1994 Pauline and Mark Donaldson have been restoring their unique 17th Century, Grade II Listed, Thatched Cottage with loving care and ensuring that the spirit of the past was not disrupted. The result is delightful and set in the magical environs of the Mole Valley, with the front gardens beside the clear waters of the River Mole. You will be given a great and very genuine welcome; the Donaldson's ethos is that this is your home and if something is not there that you need, please ask for it. Looking around their pretty, beautifully furnished bedrooms complete with hot and cold water, colour TV, tea and coffee facilities, it would be hard to imagine what you could possibly need. There are wonderful views from every window. Breakfast can be taken in your room or in the homely atmosphere of the dining room. From Mole Cottage which is strictly non-smoking, you are spoilt for choice of places to visit. Rosemoor Gardens at Great Torrington with its 40 acres of stunning gardens, The National Trust Property, Arlington Court at Barnstaple, Quince Honey Farm at South Molton are just a few of the places. Pauline and Mark run Creative Breaks in their spacious workshops where the aim is to nurture the latent skills for ceramic pottery that exist in all of us to some extent. The Courses are rewarding, highly informative and a chance to meet fascinating people.

USEFUL INFORMATION

OPEN; All year	**DINING ROOM; Great breakfast**
CHILDREN; Welcome	**VEGETARIAN; Upon request**
CREDIT CARDS; None taken	**DISABLED ACCESS; Property not suitable**
LICENSED; No	**GARDEN; Yes**

ACCOMMODATION;   1 en-suite king size bed
1 family room double & single bed + 1 single all with private bathroom
CREATIVE BREAKS on Pottery   NON-SMOKING HOUSE
RATES:- All Year, Single Room £22.50.B&B. Double Room ensuite £23.50 pppn B&B.
Family room, from £21.pppn B&B.

ASHELFORD
East Down,
Nr Barnstaple,
North Devon
EX31 4LU

Tel: 01271 850469
Fax: 01271 850862

Ashelford can rightly be described as 'off the beaten track'. It is set superbly half a mile from its nearest neighbour in 68acres with 6 acres of woodland. It abounds with wildflowers, orchids, bluebells, primroses and much more, Red Deer, Badgers and Foxes feel at home and above soar Buzzards and Skylarks. There are ponds filled by natural streams, wonderful walks, the Heritage Coast is nearby and above all there are stunning views across to Exmoor. There are many places to visit which are easily reached from here. It could not be better placed for a great holiday.

Tom and Erica McClenaghan renovated Ashelford after it had been empty for 36 years. They love living here and are very happy to welcome guests. Tom is a keen runner, Erica has her own horse and rides - between cooking. Tom was a playwright and is keenly interested in astronomy. If you are interested he will take you out on clear nights. These two have made the house a thoroughly comfortable, relaxed and beautifully furnished and decorated place in which to live. The three ensuite bedrooms are delightful, all have power showers - one with a French bath under and another with separate bath.

Every room has 4'6 beds , hostess trays, refrigerators with fresh milk, orange juice & Spring water, TVs, radios, hairdryers, electric blankets and hotwater bottles - purely for comfort! Ashelford is very special, something that is endorsed by guests. The food is wonderful and the menus frequently planned with guests for their enjoyment. Often Tom and Erica will eat with you.

USEFUL INFORMATION

OPEN; All year.   **DINING ROOM; Meals by arrangement, Superbly planned menus for your enjoyment**
CHILDREN; Block booking only   **VEGETARIAN; Catered for**
CREDIT CARDS; Visa/Delta/Master/Euro/JCB.   NO WHEELCHAIR ACCESS.
LICENSED; Yes   **PETS; Well behaved dogs**
ACCOMMODATION; 3 ensuite rooms   **GARDEN; 68 acres gardens & woodland**
RATES:- High Season £80 per room pn. B&B. Low Season £60 per room pn. B&B.

THE PARK HOUSE
South Molton,
Devon EX36 3ED

Tel: 01769 572610

Recommended:-
Which? Hotel Guide,
Good Hotel Guide,
Michelin

The setting of the Park House revealed at the top of a lime tree lined drive in a horseshoe of ancient woodland with sweeping lawns and three acres of gardens is sure to delight you. With extensive views down the Mole Valley and a 3/4 acre walled garden, it really is stunning and makes one look forward eagerly to meeting ones hosts, Mike and Anne Gornall and to seeing the interior of this much loved house of mellow stone.

The Gornalls offer a totally 'non-commercial' atmosphere with a country house ambience you might have found here sixty years ago. There are two very comfortable lounges in which to relax, one of which is for smokers. Service is courteous and unobtrusive. Unexpected delights include antiques, fine pictures, bric-a-brac, marble pillars, stone archways and a fine carved Regency staircase with domed skylight. There are seven ensuite double bedrooms, one of them has an additional bedroom or dressing room, and there is a further bedroom with an adjacent private bathroom. Some beds are King and Queen sizes and all rooms are charmingly decorated with pretty drapes and bed linen, each has a hospitality tray, colour TV, direct dial telephone, radio/alarm clocks and other nice touches.

All bedrooms are non-smoking. An excellent full English breakfast is served in the non-smoking dining room where, in the evening, you dine by candlelight at tables covered with lace, fine china and sparkling Dartington glassware. A four course dinner is served with several choices at each course, part of which changes daily. The Gornalls describe the food as 'Gourmet home-cooking with a (Robert) Carrier flavour'! It is certainly delicious and includes fresh local produce with fish, game and local cheeses. The comprehensive cellar offers you a choice of 50 different bottles from a dozen countries, all at modest price.

USEFUL INFORMATION

OPEN; Early March to late January
CHILDREN; Over 12 years
CREDIT CARDS; Visa/Mastercard
LICENSED; Restaurant/Residential
ACCOMMODATION; 3tw 4dbl all ensuite
RATES;- £50 pppn. Dinner - B&B.

RESTAURANT; Gourmet -cooking
VEGETARIAN; Variety on request
DISABLED ACCESS; Welcome
PETS; Sleep in vehicles only
GARDEN; 3 acres

DENHAM FARM AND COUNTRY HOUSE,
North Buckland,
Branton,
Devon
EX33 1HY

Tel/Fax: 01271 890297

ETB Three Crowns.
AA QQQQ.
RAC Acclaimed.

If you are an artist or revel in beautiful scenery you are going to enjoy the view from Denham Farm especially at the highest point on the farm. It is stunning. The whole area is beautiful and the house is just a short walk from Chapel Wood Bird Sanctuary and Henry Williamson's writing hut where he wrote many stories including Tarka the Otter. It is a superb rural area with greenfields, rolling hills, coastal walks, wonderful beaches for surfing and for golfers, the Saunton Championship Course.

You will find your hosts Jean and Tony Barnes real country people born in Devon and who have maintained the Devonshire accent. They have an immense knowledge of the area particularly the quaint villages and secret hideaways. They are both keen on tracing family history and Tony is a keen skittler who will arrange a competition with a local team so that you can bring your friends and have a fun game - the Games Room has a Skittle Alley, Darts, Snooker and Table Tennis.

The whole atmosphere of the house is friendly, full of humour and relaxing and it is no wonder that so many guests make repeated visits. Look around the house and you will see Jean's passion - her collection of Commemorative Plates. There are 10 ensuite rooms all beautifully appointed and the food is memorable. All home-cooked with lots of fresh vegetables, locally produced meat and lovely old fashioned desserts with clotted cream followed by local cheeses. Breakfast is equally sumptuous.

USEFUL INFORMATION

OPEN; All year except Christmas	**DINING ROOM; Superb home-cooked fare**
CHILDREN; Welcome	**VEGETARIAN; Catered for**
CREDIT CARDS; Master/Visa	**DISABLED ACCESS: No special facilities**
LICENSED; Yes	**PETS; No**
ACCOMMODATION; 10 ensuite rooms	**GARDEN; Yes with seating**

RATES :- High Season £54 per room per night. Low Season £46 per room per night.
Children, Two years and over, from £12/15 per night sharing with two adults.

THE SPINNEY COUNTRY GUEST HOUSE,
Shirwell,
Barnstaple,
Devon
EX31 4JR

Tel: 01271 850282

ETB 2 Crowns
Commended

The Spinney is surprisingly quiet and rural when one considers it is directly on the A39 leading into Barnstaple. During the evening one can hear the quiet settling down on this pretty house making sure that all its occupants have an undisturbed night's rest. The house began as a cottage about 1750 and has had several careful additions including a Victorian Conservatory complete with a flourishing vine, here one breakfasts and dines in the summer. The house is surrounded by parkland and one looks over a patchwork of fields towards the awesome magnificence of Exmoor.

The garden and lawns are attached to a small wood. Guests are very welcome to wander and enjoy the smells and sounds of the countryside.

Janet and Richard Pelling have spent some years improving their home with loving care to bring it to the very comfortable standard it has today. There are 5 bedrooms, one with a kingsize double plus a single is ensuite. Then there is a large family room with a king size bed, another king-size double, a twin and a single all of which share two bathrooms. Janet and Richard tend to share the cooking which is always imaginative. Richard is a chef by profession. Breakfast is a generous meal with several choices and in the evening there is an optional choice of a three course dinner. It is a happy house in which to stay and much to recommend it.

USEFUL INFORMATION

OPEN; All year
CHILDREN; Welcome
CREDITS CARDS; None taken
LICENSED; No. Welcome to bring your own
ACCOMMODATION; 5 rooms, 1 ensuite
RATES:- All Year from £16.50 to £19.50 B&B.
Special seasonal break rates:- Details on request.

DINING ROOM; Good home-cooking
VEGETARIAN; If pre-ordered
DISABLED ACCESS; No facilities
PETS; Yes
GARDEN; Yes + woodland

KITTIWELL HOUSE HOTEL & RESTAURANT
Croyde,
North Devon
EX33 1PG

Tel: 01271 890247
Fax: 01271 890469

AA/RAC Two Stars.

The 16th century Kittiwell House on the edge of Croyde is a thatched building of immense charm and more than a little character.Croyde itself is the perfect example of an olde worlde village complete with thatched cottages and a stream.It has a backdrop of undulating countryside and before it an expanse of glorious, sparkling sea. The hotel stands back from the road in its own grounds with a cobbled courtyard where you leave your car. What pleases one most about this hotel is the constant finding of new niches and corners, inglenook fireplaces, low doorways over which are wooden warnings 'Duck' or 'Grouse'. Log fires blaze on cool evenings, the beamed bar welcomes one for a drink before dinner and the award winning, non-smoking restaurant with its panelled walls and numerous artifacts just invites you to sit at one of the beautifully appointed tables in the certain knowledge that your meal is going to be memorable. A La Carte and Table d'hote menus are available on which you will find imaginative dishes including vegetarian created by the hotel's highly trained chefs

There are 12 well appointed ensuite bedrooms, some with four posters whilst others have French doors leading to the garden and patio. Each room has been individually decorated with pretty soft furnishings enhancing the characteristics of the rooms.The rooms are comfortably warm in winter and cool in summer. The mild Devon climate encourages one to laze in the garden or from the front door of Kittiwell one can set about many activities.Saunton Golf Club a 5 minute drive away is a Championship course. The Royal North Devon is the oldest Club on it's original site in England. It has the widest bunker in the world and a fascinating Golfing Museum. There are any number of wonderful walks along the Tarka Trail, or in Lorna Doone country, not forgetting the majesty of Exmoor. Clay Shooting, Cycling, Horse Riding or simply touring the many beautiful areas make Kittiwell an excellent base for guests

USEFUL INFORMATION

OPEN; Mid January-end December   **RESTAURANT; Superb imaginative food**
CHILDREN; Welcome   **VEGETARIAN; Cooked to order**
CREDIT CARDS; Visa/Master/Switch/JCB   **No Wheelchair Access.**
Electron/Euro   **PETS; Yes - small charge**
LICENSED; Full licence. Fine wines   **GARDEN; Yes with furniture**
ACCOMMODATION;12 ensuite rooms (4 non-smoking)
RATES:- High Season £39 pppn B&B. Low Season £35 pppn. B&B.

MASONS ARMS INN
Knowstone,
South Molton,
North Devon
EX36 4RY

Tel: 01398 341582 & 341231

Knowstone is only a small hamlet but is picturesque and largely a conservation area. It is a tranquil spot and the surrounding country is noted for riding, fishing, golf, walking and painting but most of all Knowstone is well known because of the delightful, thatched Masons Arms Inn which dates from the 13th century. It is a great place to visit, tucked away in the foothills of remote Exmoor yet only 15 minutes from the M5 (Junction 27). From the Masons Arms there is easy access to the famous North Devon coast and to historic places such as Exeter and Taunton; to Bideford and Barnstaple with their famous pannier markets; to picture-postcard villages like Dunster and Dulverton and South Molton with its wealth of antique shops.

Famous National Trust houses likes Knighthayes with its wonderful gardens, Arlington Court and Killerton are nearby as are the RHS gardens at Rosemoor and Dr Smart's renowned Marwood Hill. Competing with these beautiful places, the pretty small garden of the Masons Arms stands up well to the challenge and is very popular with customers who enjoy the beauty of the garden behind the inn and the lovely view over Exmoor.

David and Elizabeth Todd own and manage this pleasant pub and their welcoming presence makes every visit memorable. The inn is attractively furnished with an eye to elegance and comfort. The four double rooms and one single are all ensuite and furnished in a cottage-style with antique furniture. In the small, intimate restaurant with its 14-20 covers, delicious home-cooked meals are served in the evenings and at Sunday Lunch. Light meals are served in the bar both at lunchtime and in the evenings. The whole atmosphere of the Masons Arms is warm and welcoming at all seasons.

USEFUL INFORMATION

OPEN; All year from 29th Dec to 23rd Dec.
CHILDREN; Welcome
CREDIT CARDS; None taken
LICENSED; Full On
ACCOMMODATION; 4 dbl 1 sgl all ensuite
GARDEN; Delightful with fine views
RATES:- All Year £27.50 pppn B&B.

RESTAURANT; Delicious,
evening meals. Sunday Lunch
BAR FOOD; Light meals
VEGETARIAN; Catered for
WHEELCHAIR ACCESS.
PETS; Yes

CHOUGHS NEST HOTEL,
North Walk,
Lynton, North Devon
EX35 6HJ

Tel: 01598 753315

AA 1 Star. RAC 1 Star
ETB 3 Crown Commended

It would be difficult to find a more beautiful setting than the Choughs Nest Hotel which stands, high up, overlooking Lynmouth Bay as far as the Countisbury Headland and woodlands behind. The stone house was built for a Dutch millionaire one hundred and twenty years ago, 400 feet above sea level giving most rooms a breathtaking view. Throughout the traditionally furnished house there is a wonderfully relaxed atmosphere which is really down to the way that Andy and Jo Collier run the business in a professional but very informal manner. It takes no time whatsoever to feel at home and ready to enjoy a holiday in one of the most fascinating and beautiful parts of Devon.

Within the house the twelve bedrooms, all of which are ensuite, are comfortably and attractively furnished and have both television and hostess trays. Breakfast is a sumptuous feast, a forerunner to the excellent dinners that are served. Andy Collier is the chef and he has not only a talent for creating dishes but loves his work. The results are mouth-watering.

USEFUL INFORMATION

OPEN; March to November inclusive
CHILDREN;Welcome. 4 years + for dinner
CREDIT CARDS; All major cards except Amex
LICENSED; Restaurant & Residential
ACCOMMODATION; 12 ensuite rooms
RATES :- £29/32 pppn B&B £40/44 pppn D/B&B All Year.

DINING ROOM; Home-cooked fare
VEGETARIAN; A daily choice
DISABLED ACCESS; Not suitable
GARDEN; Yes. Terrace - sea vista.
PETS; No

HIGH PARK,
Bradworthy, Devon
EX22 7SH

Tel/Fax: 01409 241492

ETB Two Crowns Highly Commended.

High Park is a delightful Victorian House with many splendid original features including some truly beautiful fireplaces. It stands in 5 acres with stunning views over rolling countryside. Marilyn and Michael Cook own High Park and while Michael farms, Marilyn looks after guests and feeds them on scrumptious home cooking. They, with their daughter Keri, thoroughly enjoy people and most nights dinner is rather like dining with friends at a candlelit table. However if you prefer to dine separately individual tables are laid. If you ask Marilyn what is the speciality of the house she will probably tell you 'Candlelit suppers" where the conversation and the wine both flow readily with not a sign of the dreaded Hyacinth Bucket in sight! There are three bedrooms, each with private bathrooms, all beautifully furnished, one double room with king size bed, one twin room and a single room with french windows leading onto a balcony.

This is a very sporting household with a particular interest in Field Sports. The Cooks keep horses and are keen racing enthusiasts whether it is at Point to Points, Flat Racing or over the sticks. The house is half a mile from the village of Bradworthy which has the largest village square in Devon dating back to Saxon times. Bradworthy Common is behind High Park and is a haven for wildlife with many varieties of Butterflies and Birds, Foxes and Rabbits, Weasels and Stoats and many others. It is wonderful walking country. Fishing and golf are both readily available.

USEFUL INFORMATION

OPEN; February to December   **DINING ROOM; Scrumptious food**
CHILDREN; Welcome   **VEGETARIAN; Always available**
CREDIT CARDS; None taken   **No W/CHAIR Access**
LICENSED; No   **GARDEN; 5 acres**
ACCOMMODATION; 1 dbl, 1 twin & 1 sgl   **PETS; Yes in outside kennelling**
RATES; £17 per person per night. All Year. Children under 12 - £12

HENAFORD MANOR,
Welcombe, Bideford,
North Devon EX39 6HE

Tel: 01288 331252

Tourist Board 1 Keys Commended

Henaford Manor dates back to the Domesday Book of 1086 and its history is available for guests to read and fascinating it is. The farmhouse is set in 226 acres and is full of charm and interest. There are many traditional features with beamed ceilings, large traditional fireplaces with copper canopies and a bread oven.

It is a wonderful place to stay, quiet, relaxing and comfortable and you will be superbly cared for by Petre Josephine Tunnicliffe who owns Henaford Manor, with the help of her mother-in-law, Amy. The food is traditional farmhouse fare, home-cooked and plentiful with a wonderful breakfast and a dinner that might be a roast or one of the many delicious casseroles at which Petre excels. There are four guest rooms, beautifully appointed, 2 of which are ensuite and they all have television and a hostess tray.

From Henaford Manor you are within three miles of Devon's Atlantic coast with its golden sandy beaches, small coves and wonderful surfing. There are walks along the coastal paths and bridleways. Picturesque Clovelly is closeby with its cobbled street leading steeply down to the sea.

USEFUL INFORMATION

OPEN; All year   **DINING ROOM; Good farmhouse fare**
CHILDREN; Welcome   **VEGETARIAN; Upon request**
CREDIT CARDS; None taken   **DISABLED ACCESS; One ground floor room**
LICENSED; No. Welcome to bring your own   GARDEN; 226 acres
ACCOMMODATION; 2dbl ensuite 2twin   PETS; Yes
RATES:- All Year £20 pppn B&B. Children over 10 years. Adult rate.

CHAPTER TEN

Mid & East Devon

"A genial hearth, a hospitable board and a refined rusticity."
William Wordsworth

CHAPTER TEN

MID AND EAST DEVON, FROM HATHERLEIGH TO AXMINSTER

What was said in the last chapter about the nature of North Devon is equally applicable to the area embraced by this one, which is something of an arbitrary division anyway, containing parts of North, Mid and East Devon Districts.

Much of the region feels, when you are journeying through it, and even more when you stop and look around, to be vast and inward-looking. The visitor sees an endless landscape stretching to the horizon, a constantly changing but always recognisable patchwork of fields and hedges, with towns, villages and farms buried peacefully within it, seemingly little changed for generations. It is an area rich in ghost stories and folklore of a very traditional kind, with tales that have clearly been handed down for centuries.

As in most parts of the South West, numerous writers, artists and craftspeople live round about here, often in old farms or cottages at the end of winding lanes, which are not always well signposted. Two amongst them are the poet laureate Ted Hughes and the short story writer William Trevor. Many creative souls draw strength and inspiration from the colours of the landscape and the sense of a rootedness, which are clearly very satisfying to some temperaments.

From this area have also come, over the centuries, a number of people who have distinguished themselves in some way, in the great world outside Devon. They are not marketed at all, nor do they have "trails" and museums named after them, but they deserve a mention, to show the diversity of talent which an area like this, securely based on the ancient rhythms of small town and rural life, can nurture.

That the isolation and inwardness of the region, and the weight of tradition, can sometimes have a darker effect is illustrated by the sad story of the end of the Luxton family, who had farmed here for generations, as told in John Cornwell's best-selling book *Earth to Earth*.

This is not at all an area which is geared towards tourism in the way that many parts of the West country are. There are no theme parks, and not so many museums or big houses. Instead there are quiet, individual villages and tiny hamlets with intriguing names; to pick a few at random, you could do worse than spend time exploring **MORCHARD BISHOP, CRUWYS MORCHARD, STOCKLEIGH POMEROY, BLACK DOG, BRAMPFORD SPEKE, CHERITON FITZPANE,** or **HOLCUMBE ROGUS.** There are interesting old farms, small manor houses, unrestored Medieval churches and quiet rivers. This is a landscape for informal walking, birdwatching, fishing and wandering around country churchyards. There are, however, some fine outlets for quality CRAFTS, and there are also a number of PRIVATE GARDENS that are worth seeking out.

Here, therefore, even more than anywhere else in this book, it is impossible to suggest a logical way of touring it as a self-contained entity, and visitors tend not to do this anyway; most people are passing through here on the way to somewhere else. I shall just say something about the main towns and places of interest, starting in the area between Okehampton and Torrington, and moving gradually eastwards to cover Crediton, Tiverton and, finally, the inland towns of East Devon.

Most of what has been said applies specifically to the areas that lie now to the west of the M5 motorway. The countryside of EAST DEVON, around Honiton, Ottery and Axminster is, as readers will remember from the first chapter of the book, much softer, more open, less mysterious and without the feeling of remoteness.

We start, however, with two small towns that lie deep in the country between Dartmoor and the north coast. **HATHERLEIGH** is a gentle little place of cob buildings in narrow streets that end suddenly at the edge of the countryside. You come upon it a few miles above Okehampton, on the River Lew. It was the birthplace of one of the lesser-known Jacobean dramatists, whose work you are not likely ever to see revived at the National Theatre, but who rejoiced, however, in the rather memorable name of Jasper Mayne.

On November 5Th, BURNING TAR, BARRELS are dragged through the streets on sledges, in an ancient ceremony, the origins of which are clearly older than the Gunpowder Plot of 1605.

From nearby HATHERLEIGH MOOR, a tract of common land traditionally left to the poor of the town, there are good views of both Exmoor and Dartmoor, and the surrounding country is good for, WALKING and FISHING.

Two places here that are worth a visit are HATHERLEIGH POTTERY (01837 810624) and STOCK IN TRADE, a textile workshop where work with a strong African flavour is produced.

WINKLEIGH, to the north east, is another quietly busy little community, a focus for numerous scattered farms and hamlets. The thatched cottages around the church give it a pleasing appearance. THE SQUARE GALLERY (01837 83145) shows a diverse range of contemporary and traditional ART and CRAFT by many respected names.

The celebrated INCH'S DEVON CIDER is made here.

Not far to the East of Winkleigh is the A377 road leading from Exeter to Barnstable, passing through Crediton and many small villages. To get a real sense of the size of North and Mid Devon you only need to travel along this road, or perhaps travel by train from Exeter and enjoy the scenery in comfort: the railway line is quite close to the road for much of the journey. It has been named, rather inevitably, the TARKA LINE.

Of the many Towns and Villages beside or near to this road, **CHULMLEIGH** is quite atmospheric, a large village that, like so many in Devon, at one time almost became a town. It has a GOLF CLUB (01769 80519) and several good local hostelries where you will feel a real sense of the life as it is lived in this area. John Garland, a Medieval alchemist, philosopher and musician, who became a leading figure at the Universities of Paris and Toulouse in the 13th.Century, came from a remote farm in the parish called Garland.

At **EGGESFORD** there is a tiny station for nearby **CHAWLEIGH**, and not far away is a FOREST beside the main road with WALKS and a PICNIC AREA.

EGGESFORD GARDEN (01769 580250) is a large garden centre, with specially laid out walks and always a variety of EVENTS. At the OLD GLEBE there is a special seven acre garden at the old rectory, with lawns of distinction, rhododendrons and a bog garden. This garden is open by appointment only, so please ring before visiting (01769 580632).

A little to the west of the main road is what remains of EGGESFORD HOUSE, now a melancholy ruin. This was the birthplace of John Christie, founder of Glynbourne. During its heyday it was a major social focus, frequented by intellectuals from around the country, which is unexpected for somewhere hidden in this remote corner of Devon.

The steep, hill hugging village of **LAPFORD** has a church dedicated to Saint Thomas a Becket, whose ghost is reputed to run around the church and through the village on the night of July 9Th.

Following the main road toward Crediton, **COPPLESTONE** has an ancient CROSS, 12 feet high and decorated with scrollwork, this is worth a visit.

This whole wide region of countryside between South Molton and Crediton strikes many visitors as unusually intense, absorbing and a little haunted, and there may be a very compelling reason for this. It is likely that the ancient Dumnonians, the Celtic inhabitants of Devon and Cornwall, had a large sacred area, probably densely wooded, covering the landscape bounded today by the many villages with 'Nymet' or 'Nympton' as part of their current names. These probably derive from 'nemeton' meaning a sacred grove. In fact this suggestion seems to be authenticated by the discovery, in 1980 of a 'henge' monument in the very heart of what would have been a sacred forest (this is on private property). This may explain why some people feel a certain disquieting atmosphere when in this region, even today.

CREDITON (pronounced Kirton by the older indigenous populace; (Tourist Information Centre 01363772006), is a solid town centred around one main street, its buildings are of quite a distinctive red and yellowish brick, and there are some very old houses, however much of the town was destroyed by fire in the 18th century. It now serves as a shopping and business centre for a wide rural area, with a tradition for cultivating the best cider apples in Devon.

Crediton is on the river Creedy, the name of which Baring Gould thought probably derived from the Celtic word 'crwydr', meaning 'wandering and winding. He considered it an apt description of the course of the winding Creedy, as it wriggles about through the fat red soil, biting into its banks and gorging itself with the ruddy earth, the Creedy joins the river Exe to the south at Cowley Bridge.The parish church, of red sandstone, is a cathedral like edifice, which is appropriate for a town with an important religious history. Crediton was from 909 to 1050 the diocesan capital, when Bishop Leofric moved the 'see' to Exeter. There is today a suffragan Bishop of Crediton, the title chosen in memory of the past significance of the town.

Crediton is traditionally thought to be the birthplace of St. Boniface, or Winfrith, who in the 7Th. Century travelled widely in Northern Europe converting the heathen. A Saxon, it has been suggested that his early life in this area, resonant with the numinous energy of the Celtic grove, fired his missionary zeal to defeat paganism. Just outside of the town towards Barnstaple is DEWSMOOR ART where sculpture by Witold Kawatec can be viewed. The town has a GOLF CLUB at Hookway (01363 773025).

West of Crediton, towards Okehampton and Dartmoor, is the small village of **SPREYTON**, traditionally the home of Uncle Tom Cobley and the ill-fated group of pleasure seekers who went to Widecombe Fair (see chapter four). I am reliably informed that from the top of Speyton Church tower you can, on a clear day, see the whole of Devon and Cornwall from coast to coast and to the border with Somerset, a great experience for any devotee. Spreyton was trouble in the 17th.Century by a tiresome poltergeist or 'spectrum' as the old records name it, which was widely discussed by the learned parsons and squires of the area.

NEWTON ST CYRES, to the South towards Exeter, is a village of thatched white washed houses with a renowned pub, which also brews its own ale, THE BEER ENGINE, much resorted to by the real ale enthusiast, and the food is comparable to the excellence of the ale.

Several miles north east of Crediton, just off the A3072 toward Tiverton, is **CHERITON FITZPANE**, a sprawling village in lovely sloping country. The novelist Jean Rhys, of *Wide Sargasso Sea* fame, spent her last years living quietly in this peaceful haven and is buried in the local churchyard. A few miles on we reach **TIVERTON** (Tourist Information 01884 255827, and also, during the summer months, at Junction 27., M5., 01884 821242).

This lively old town is a major urban centre for this part of Devon. In past centuries it was one of the leading wollen centres in the West country, and therefore a veritable hive of industry. It was the home of many wealthy merchants, such as Peter Blundell, founder of the nearby public school, and John Greenway, builder of the numerous almshouses in the area, who is commemorated in the parish church. The town has an interesting architectural heritage of fine buildings, dating back to the 16th, 17th, and 18th.centuries.

As well as being an industrial centre, embracing over the years trades such as cloth manufacture, brewing and lace making, Tiverton has always been a market town for the surrounding farms and villagers. The author of Blacks Guide to Devon in 1867,who was so rude about Topsham (see chapter one) was much more enthusiastic when he visited Tiverton; 'From its position in a pastoral district of great fertility, its markets are of much importance; and a pleasant place, of a truth, it is, when the farmers and their apple-cheeked lasses crowd into the town on market day, and Devonshire butter, Devonshire cream and Devonshire poultry attract the wistful gaze'.

The town is built on a slope between the Rivers Exe and Loman, which join just below it. The main church, St. Peters, stands high above the River Exe and is an ornate 15th.Century building with a 99-foot high tower. Inside are many indications of past wealth, with elaborate carvings and memorials to the leading merchants.

The Victorian TOWN HALL dominates the west end of Fore Street, and in Gold Street there are the GREENWAY ALMSHOUSES and the National Trust's OLD BLUNDELL'S SCHOOL. These are the original school buildings as described by Blackmore in *Lorna Doon.* Bampfylde Moore Carew, younger son of a distinguished local family from nearby Bickleigh, who became a wandering 18th. Century rogue and ended up as 'King of the Beggars' was also a pupil.

Other Tivertonians to achieve fame include Richard Cosway, the miniature portrait painter and Hannah Cowley, who went to London and became a dramatist; her work affirms the traditional roles of women inrelation to their husbands, which is probably why feminists have not reclaimed her as an 'unduly neglected woman writer'. She came back and died in her home town in 1809, and is buried in the local church yard.

Endowing ALMSHOUSES for the poor was clearly a popular way for the rich merchants of the town to ensure that they would be respectfully remembered by future generations. In addition to the houses by Greenway there are two other groups, built by John Waldron and George Slee, in Welbrook Street and St. Peters Street respectively.

TIVERTON MUSEUM (01884 256295) is a large, award winning museum with very interesting collections, and what remains of Tiverton Castle (01884 253200), once a possession of the Earls of Devon, has a collection of clocks and armour.

The town has an excellent CRAFT CENTRE (01884 258430) with a large range of high quality work. There are four separate rooms for you to enjoy.

The GRAND WESTERN HORSEBOAT COMPANY (01884 253345) provide BOAT TRIPS along the GRAND WESTERN CANAL,dating from 1796 which was built to link the English and Bristol channels. In the end it did no more than connect Tiverton with Taunton. Eleven miles remain open today.

At the attractive village of **HALBERTON** the canal crosses the railway line by way of an aqueduct which instead of being the high arched, a noble feat of engineering which the word 'aqueduct' conjures up, is actually a cast iron trough. At the GRAND WESTERN CANAL COUNTRY PARK there are well laid out country walks, a shop and restaurant.

PURPLE HAYES (01884 821295), at Halberton is a garden for plantaholics, with bog plants and much, more. Pigmy goats and ducks are also in residence, and Devon cream teas are available. Please telephone before visiting.

A little to the north of Tiverton is KNIGHTSHAYES COURT (01884 254665), owned by the National Trust. The ornate Victorian house has one of the most important of the larger gardens in Devon, created in the main since by Sir John and Lady Amory. It covers almost 25 acres, with rare trees and shrubs, spring bulbs and summer borders. Not to be missed by garden lovers at any time of the year. There is a licenced restaurant and all the usual National Trust facilities.

Further north will bring you to **BAMPTON**, a small town with Georgian houses, a NORMAN CASTLE and a MUSEUM (01389 331532) which, in addition to local history, has a unique collection of early radios and gramophones. The town is renown for its traditional AUTUMN HORSE FAIR, at which Exmoor ponies are sold at auction. YERJA CERAMICS and TEXTILES in Ford road has a stunningly beautiful hand made craft work on display, created by Chris Speyer and Kath Uklejha.

Between Bampton and Tiverton is a WILDFLOWER and WILDLIFE GARDEN at Spillifords (01884 255353). Please telephone first.

Directly to the south of Tiverton, in rich archetypal Devon countryside on the Exe, is **BICKLEIGH**. This is yet another picture-postcard Devon village, featuring thatched cottages and colourful gardens, surrounded by hills rising hundreds of feet. In addition to the visual aspects of the village there are several interesting places to visit here.

BICKLEIGH CASTLE (01884 855363) is really a fortified medieval manor house with later additions, as opposed to an authentic castle, though it is has quite a massive Norman gateway. It was for many years owned by the Courtenay family, the Earls of Devon from Powderham Castle. They used it as an estate for their younger sons, to provide them with a useful role in life and somewhere to live. Later it became the home of the Carew family, one of whom was the wild Bampfylede Moore Carew, mentioned previously. 'There have always been persons who have rebelled against the restraints of culture, and have reverted to a state of savagery' intoned Baring Gould, who wrote about him in an entertaining two-volumed work called *Devonshire Characters and Srange Events.*

Bampflyde was the son of the rector of Bickleigh (it was usual for the Lord of the Manor, if he had the living in his possession, to give it to a younger brother or other relative, which explains why at this time the squire and the parson were of the same name). He was born in 1693 and educated, as we have seen ,at Blundells and became a beggar, rogue and trickster.

A master of disguises, one of his favourite ruses was to pretend to be the only survivor of any shipwreck, battle or disaster that happened to bein the news. He travelled extensively, and at one time was transported to the American colonies, where he lived amongst the Indians. He published an autobiography, which was dedicated to the novelist Henry Fielding. After a lifetime of adventures, Bampflyde died in 1978 and joined his ancestors in Bickleigh churchyard.

At the Castle you can see the chapel, armoury, guard room, Great Hall, bedrooms and some well planned gardens. There is a 'spooky' tower which provides fine views over the Exe river and the castle site. The building contains a good collections of fine furniture, some Tudor, and domestic objects, toys etc., of the era.

DEVONSHIRE'S CENTRE (01884 855419), at Bickleigh Mill, is a restored water mill. It houses an excellent CRAFT GALLERY and SHOP, where work of the highest quality can be viewed and purchased. There is also a RESTAURANT and a FISHING CENTRE.

At the GARDEN HOUSE studio (01884 855682) objects by the internationally known sculptor John Mulvey can be seen and purchased. Please telephone before visiting.

Elegant BICKLEIGH BRIDGE, over the river Exe, has a good claim to be the inspiration for Paul Simon's 'Bridge Over Troubled Waters'. The singer and songwriter is known to have been in the area during the 1960's, when performing at the Exeter Folk Club, and was grateful for the mere £10 they were able to pay him. The bridge is 16th.Century, but was rebuilt after the floods of 1809. A ghost is said to hover over the bridge on Midsummer's Eve.

Returning to Tiverton and taking the A361 eastwards, the village of **SAMPFORD PEVERELL** is just off to the right. Here, in the early 19th.Century there was another celebrated poltergeist case, which was widely reported. The house which contained the ghostly happenings has now gone, but part of it remains in a garage wall.

If you go to the M5 at junction 27, but cross over the motorway, two miles further on you will reach the village of **UFFCULME**. Here can be found one of the leading attractions Devon: COLDHARBOUR MILL (01884 840960).

There is plenty to see and do at this fully restored working woollen mill, one of the many which used to bring work and prosperity to the area. The mill is now a highly acclaimed Museum of milling. For those who prefer art to industrial history, the site also houses the Quaker inspired NEW WORLD TAPESTRY, recording the Westcountry's prominent involvement with the colonising of the Americas.

Heading south just off the M5, in the fertile valley of the River Culme, which another tributary of the Exe, you will find the market town of **CULLOMPTON** (Pronounced Collumptun by the locals).

The 120 ft. Sandstone tower of the richly endowed parish church is reminiscent of the style of towers throughout Somerset, which indeed is now not far away. Like most towns hereabouts, Cullompton's former riches were due to the wool trade. The wide High Street, lined with trees, and the narrower Fore Street, have some attractive buildings, but little is extremely old: like Crediton and many other East Devon towns, Cullompton has suffered badly from fire damageover the years. The oldest buildings are the Walronds, an early 17th century merchants house, and the Manor House, an Elizabethan dwelling enlarged in the 18th.century.

The novelist E.M.Delafield, otherwise known as Mrs Dashwood, of *Diary of a Provincial Lady* fame, was a popular resident and a magistrate in the town for many years, until her death in 1943.

A strange story concerns an old house near here, a Domesday manor which cannot be named as it is not open to the public. Early in the 20th.Century it was the home of the explorer W.J.A.Grant, after whom a cape in Antarctica is named. In 1884, whilst in Egypt, Grant was presented with a mummified hawk, said to have been found in the tomb of Tutankhamen's sister. Just before the outbreak of the Boer War, the hawk began to ooze blood. It did this again in the summer of 1914. Many reputable witnesses, including Lord Baden Powell, confirmed the phenomenon. Mr. Grant died in 1935, and the house was requisitioned in 1939 and the contents put into storage, it is not known if the hawk bled again in anticipation of WorldWar Two, but it is back in the house now. The current owner of the property keeps it in a box, made from wood taken from Cullompton church at the time of the Reformation. Regretfully there is no information on the reaction of the hawk prior to the Falklands or Gulf wars.

BRADNINCH to the south, is another former borough and woollen centre which never quite managed to become a town, and is now a peaceful village. The sloping main street, tree lined like that of Cullompton, is attractive and indicative of a prosperous past.

Returning to Cullompton, take the A373 for the major East Devon town of **HONITON** (Tourist Information 01404 43716). As with many places, the locals pronounce it differently from visitors, emphasising the 'Hon': the latter tend to make it 'Huniton'.

This is a handsome old town with a long main street. For generations travellers coming into Devon along the high road from London made Honiton the first resting place. The town is now bypassed by the A303.

Somehow it is easy to imagine the old coaching days, as you wander up and down the main thoroughfare, amongst spacious Georgian and Victorian buildings.

When the novelist and topographer Daniel Defoe rode into Devon in the 1720's, at a slightly earlier date than the coaching era, he was very impressed. He thought that the view from the road, on the stretch   from about half of a mile outside the town the slope leading into it, was the loveliest he had ever seen anywhere. It can still increase the pulse rate today as you journey towards Honiton and anticipate the whole of the Devon and Cornwall peninsula laid out ahead of you. Defoe went on the describe Honiton as a ' large and beautiful market town, very populous, and well built'.

There are not many very old buildings in the town, as no fewer than four fires devastated it during the 17th and 18th.Centuries. This makes the appearance of the main street uniform and well planned.

Honiton was also of course famous for lace making, as were many towns and villages in this area. The local Honiton lace is very fine and delicate. The art was probably introduced into East Devon by Huguenot refugees during the 16th.century, and at the ALLHALLOWS MUSEUM (01404 44966) the full story of the industry, and the general local history, is recorded.

The town has become a good centre for CRAFTS,ANTIQUES and SECOND HAND and ANTIQUARIAN BOOKS. The Honiton POTTERY and CRAFT CENTRE (01404 42106) exhibits and sells a wide variety of good work. There are also three good bookshops in the town to keep browsers happy for several hours.

Just outside of the town, near the village of **PAYHEMBURY**, is HEMBURY FORT (not to be confused with the one near Bucfastleigh; see chapter Four), a spectacular hill fort of Neolithic origin or possibly even earlier, and reused during the Iron Age. The Romans built a fortress of their own inside of it, during their advances into the kingdom of Dumnonia.

Honiton has a super GOLF COURSE (01404 42943).

Amongst the surrounding villages, **GITTISHAM** is one of the prettiest, with thatched cottages of cob and a green outside of the church. At the junction of the roads from Honiton to Sidmouth, and from Ottery to Colyton, is the

ROLLING STONE, a prehistoric monument which, according to legend, was a place of human sacrifice. At full moon the stone rolls down to the river Otter to drink, which is a common belief concerning these monuments, and to wash itself free of the human blood.

Gittisham was the birthplace, in 1760, of Joanna Southcott, the maid servant who led a perfectly ordinary life until she reached the age of 40, when she became a religious teacher, who ended up living in London with many thousands of disciples. The general view of her is that she was either a very clever charlatan, which her portrait dos not suggest, or a sadly deluded fanatic, which it does.

At **BROADHEMBURY** the vicar was once the Reverend Augustus Toplady, who wrote the hymn 'Rockof Ages'.

OTTERY ST. MARY (Tourist Information 01404 813964), to the south east of Honiton, is an interesting old town, full of thatched buildings, in rich east Devon countryside. We are now firmly back in the fertile red sandstone plain of Chapter one. The early 20th.century naturalist W.H.Hudson went so far as to say of the Ottery are that it was ' the most luxuriant in its vegetation, and perhaps the hottest in England' and certainly Ottery makes a good inland base for exploring the area. There are numerous footpaths around the town and a special HERITAGE TRAIL.

The great romantic poet Samuel Taylor Coleridge was born here, there is a small plaque on the outside wall of the church to commemorate him. Little is made of Coleridge in the town, as a whole. This is probably because his character was not considered particularly edifying by the Victorians. After all, he took drugs and esponged off his friends (quite a modern day type) and this, rather than the fact that he was one of the seminal figures in English literature, is what his 19th.Century descendants, whom became pillars of the establishment like judges and Bishops, tended to remember. It is as if Ottery still is not quite sure of him, and there is nothing like the industry that exists in the Lake District to celebrate Wordsworth, his friend and colleague.

In fact, Coleridge did not spend very much of his time in his native town, despite the fact that his family roots were deeply Devonian, and that he rather surprisingly retained his local accent throughout his life. He was born in Ottery in 1772, the youngest son of the vicar and schoolmaster, but was sent away to school at an early age and never really returned. The local environment only enters indirectly into his verse, except for an early poem in which he invokes to Otter, *Wild streamlet of the West*. As a child he spent many hours alone in the local churchyard.

Another literary connection on the town is its appearance as 'Clavering St.Mary' in Thackeray's novel *Pendennis*, and in the late middle ages James Barclay, author of the satirical work *The Ship of Fools*, was the vicar here.

The Parish Church is on an old site, but was rebuilt in the 14th.Century by Bishop Granisson, a local man, and modelled on Exeter Cathedral. It has the oldest weathercock in Europe, and is generally agreed to be one of the finest churches in Devon, full of rich craftsmanship.

In November a rather exiting and wild ceremony take place here, which is reminiscent of the custom at Hatherliegh, and seems more in keeping with the anarchic character of North Devon than this genteel place: the men and youths of the town roll blazing tar barrels through the streets; ostensibly, like Hatherleigh's, the ceremony is to celebrate the discovery of the Gunpowder Plot in 1605 and the coming of William of Orange in 1688, both victories for the Protestantism over the old faith, but the roots are clearly earlier.

CADHAY HOUSE (01404 812432) is a beautiful Tudor mansion, situate a mile from the town, where guided tours are regularly given, and LITTLE UPCOTT GARDENS (01404 822797) are worth a visit.

AXMINSTER (Tourist Information 01297 34386) is our last town in Devon. It is probably one of the most pleasant in the County, established on the 2,000 year old Roman Road, THE FOSSE WAY. Axminster is famous for carpets which were made here in the 18th.and early 19th.Centuries, and are once more manufactured. The narrow winding streets are full of Victorian buildings, but the shape of the Saxon town can still be appreciated. The Parish Church of St.Mary dominates the town landscape, and has many facets to discover. The MUSEUM in the Old Courthouse has material on all aspects of the town's history.

SHUTE BARTON (01297 34692), owned by the National Trust, is a medieval mansion with later additions, which must be seen to complete your visit to Axminster.

No guide book can contain everything there is to see, do and visit in Devon and Cornwall, but I hope I have been able help in the enjoyment of your visit, and that the places you have chosen from this Guide to eatand stay have been to your satisfaction. I will endeavour to contain more interesting places to visit and folklore to relate, when I revise this Guide in the year 2,000. If , during your visit you discover places or history that you think would assist me with the revised edition, or should you find a venue that has looked after you particularly well, I would be delighted to hear from you.

My next journey of discovery will be to the counties of Wessex. This guide will be available in the Spring of 1998.

THE FISHERMANS COT,
Bickleigh, Nr Tiverton,
Devon EX16 8RW

Tel: 01884 855289
Fax: 01884 855241

AA/Rac Two Stars.

Standing right next to the 16th century Bickleigh Bridge and with lawns that run down to the burbling River Exe as it dances its way downstream to the sea, The Fishermans Cot is a picturesque thatched country inn beloved by all who go there. It is rumoured that Simon and Garfunkel stayed here in the 70s and were inspired to write the haunting song 'Bridge Over Troubled Waters'. Be that as it may you will soon discover that one would have to be without soul not to be inspired by the whole atmosphere of this inn which is also an hotel boasting 21 ensuite rooms. Apart from being a delightful place in which to stay, it is also a favourite watering hole for the many visitors who come this way during the season and for those who prefer the quieter times in the autumn, winter and spring. In the cooler months, the bars are warm, welcoming and friendly and in the summer there can be no nicer way of having a drink or a meal than alongside the river bank. From the Fisherman's Cot it is easy to get to the historic city of Exeter with its superb cathedral and within 30-40 minutes drive you are at the coast. For those who love the majesty of the moors both Dartmoor and Exmoor are there to be explored and closeby the inn is Bickleigh Castle, steeped in history and a fascinating place to visit. Bickleigh Mill and Fish Farm is just across the bridge.

The Fisherman's Cot has always been known for the quality of its food. You will find a wide range of dishes to suit every taste with a Blackboard spelling out the Daily Specials. The Carvery is always popular and here you will be served by a chef who not only enjoys cooking but people as well and tends to entertain them while he carves! There are all sorts of dishes on offer as well as Daily Specials to be chosen from the Blackboard. You do not have to order a full meal, there are plenty of simple choices like well filled sandwiches or jacket potatoes with a variety of fillings. In winter you eat in the warmth of the bar and restaurant but in the warmer months it is totally delightful to have a meal and a drink at tables set out along the river bank. Afternoon tea is served between 3pm and 6pm. The 21 ensuite bedrooms are all attractively furnished. 4 new rooms have patios and the upstairs rooms have a splendid view of the river. Every room has colour television and a hostess tray and 11 of the rooms are strictly non-smoking. If you love fourposters, the Honeymoon Suite has a magnificent one. The staff of the Fisherman's Cot from the management down to the most junior member are friendly, helpful and their mission is to ensure every visitor enjoys coming to the inn and will want to come again.

USEFUL INFORMATION

OPEN; All year. Winter 11-3 & 6-11pm	**RESTAURANT; Excellent choice including**
Summer: Open all day	**A Carvery**
CHILDREN; Welcome	**BAR FOOD; Wide range. Good value**
CREDIT CARDS; All major card	**VEGETARIAN; Catered for**
LICENSED; Yes. Good wine list	**DISABLED ACCESS; Yes**
ACCOMMODATION; 21 ensuite rooms	**GARDEN; Down to the river bank**
(11 non-smoking)	**PETS; Not permitted**

**RATES:- All Year per room. £46 Single.£56 Twin.£66 Double. Family room £76.
Seasonal special offers:- Details on request.**

HUNTSHAM COURT,
Nr Bampton, Devon EX16 7NA

Tel: 01398 361365
Fax: 01398 361456

Egon Ronay and Good
Hotel Guide Recommended.

Everything about Huntsham Court is different from the norm and everything has an unrepeatable charm which leaves people talking about the owners Morgen and Andrea Bolwig and the house long after their departure. This in many ways is why it is one of Devon's best kept secrets. It does not advertise but acquires its guests by word of mouth from those who have been lucky enough to hear about it. What makes it special? Firstly it is a fascinating Listed Grade 2 building with unusual Gothic features that make the interior a journey back in time. Secondly it is so private that 'the Spy' Oleg Gordievski used Huntsham as his safe house when he arrived in England; pharmaceutical companies use Huntsham to discuss confidential marketing plans; novelists such as Douglas Adams, Martin Amis and musicians from EMI find Huntsham the perfect creative hideaway. Thirdly for anyone wanting to forget the world, Hunstham has to be the right place to come. It has no televisions anywhere, the closest to modern living you are likely to get is the BBC Home Service issuing from the antediluvian console radios which sit in every room! Music dominates quite a lot of life at Huntsham; every room is named after a composer and almost every room has a piano. The only concession to modernity is the plentiful hot water and warmth that permeates the house although you may find yourself bathing in an enormous Victorian bath in a ballroom sized bathroom! The furnishing of the house is charmingly eclectic. Your hosts are exciting people and one tends to feel that you are staying in a country house enjoying a weekend with them. It is blissful.

Come down for breakfast early and you will find you are probably on your own - no one minds if you do not break your fast until mid-day! Dinner is one sitting from a fixed menu arrived at by consultation and it is memorable. Five courses are served at the long Victorian table, glinting as the candlelight reflects on the sparkling wine glasses. There is no such thing as a wine list. It may well be that Mogens will take you to the cellar to have a mini wine tasting before the meal. There is plenty to do at Huntsham, you can play snooker, the piano, chess or croquet, tennis by the walled garden. There is a mini gym and a sauna to relax you before dinner. For music lovers there is a vast selection of records spanning the classics to jazz. Other outside activities nearby include shooting, fishing, golf, riding, outdoor pursuits, flying, hot air balloon flights and go carts. Huntsham cannot be appreciated fully from the written word and nothing you read here is exaggerated. Go there for yourselves and find out! Make sure you get clear directions first. It is not easy to find.

USEFUL INFORMATION

OPEN; All year   DINING ROOM; Wonderful food, no formal menu
CHILDREN; Welcome   VEGETARIAN; With notice
CREDIT CARDS; All except Diners   DISABLED ACCESS; Ground floor rooms
LICENSED; Residential   PETS; No
GARDEN; Yes. Croquet, tennis, BBQ   ACCOMMODATION; 14 ensuite rooms
RATES:- All Year, Double £110 per room pn B&B. Single £80 pn. B&B.

THE SWAN HOTEL
Station Road,
Bampton, Devon
EX16 9NG

Tel: 01398 331257

1991-1997 Les Routiers
Casserole Award

The Swan, built in 1450, is one of the oldest buildings in the small market town of Bampton on the edge of Exmoor. It was built by the Stone Masons working on the church and used by them as accommodation. There have been alterations over the centuries but in no way has its charm been destroyed. It has that warm, welcoming feeling, which comes from contented people over the centuries enjoying what it has to offer. Today Pam and Brian Dunesby are 'mine hosts' and they continue the tradition of hospitality for which The Swan is renowned. Brian is a skilled and talented chef who has been preparing meals for over 40 years, much of the time when he was serving in the RAF and cooked for everybody from the men to Royalty. His food today has a great reputation locally. You can choose from no less than 13 starters, all beautifully presented. There are a whole range of main courses from Medalions of Beef Provencal to succulent steaks with optional sauces, to Halibut Crevettes. All the dishes are served with the chefs choice of potatoes and a selection of fresh vegetables. You can eat in the attractive 34 cover restaurant where there is both a table d'hote menu and a la carte, or in the Lounge Bar which has a very good Bar menu.

There are six bedrooms, attractively furnished, two of which are ensuite and they all have television and a well supplied hostess tray. The whole atmosphere of The Swan is homely and comfortable and it makes an ideal base from which to explore Devon. Bampton itself is a delightful town. It is well known for its floral displays and has been a winner of the 'Britain in Bloom' competition. Bampton Fair is held once a year in October - a time of great revelry. From The Swan one can go horse riding, fishing, shooting and enjoy some splendid walks. Tiverton nearby has its historic castle and a fine church. Exeter is no distance and will provide anyone with a fascinating day taking in the magificent cathedral and enjoying the interesting shops tucked away in alleys off the Cathedral Close. A little further afield the North Devon Coast has some superb beaches.

USEFUL INFORMATION

OPEN; All year. 12-2pm & 7-11pm	**RESTAURANT; Imaginative Fare**
CHILDREN; Welcome	**BAR MEALS; Wide range**
CREDIT CARDS; Visa/Master/Switch/Amex	**VEGETARIAN; Always a choice**
LICENSED; Full On	**DISABLED ACCESS; Yes + toilets**
ACCOMMODATION; 6 rooms 2 ensuite	**GARDEN; No. PETS; Yes**

RATES:- £15 pppn. Children under 8 years from £7.50. per night. All Year.

THE BARLEYCORN INN
Shillingford, Nr Bampton,
Devon EX16 9AZ

Tel: 01398 331320

Shillingford is a very rural and very pretty village sitting on the edge of Exmoor known especially for its wonderful floral displays which have made it a winner of the Britain in Bloom competition. It is close to the historic old market town of Bampton which has a famous fair every October. The Barleycorn Inn is the heart of the village. Said to be about 250 years old it is reputed to have a ghost to add to the already vibrant atmosphere. Diane Beavan is the landlady and in the short time she has been here she has made quite an impression not only on the pub where she has made careful changes but on the locals who use the bar of the Barleycorn for their daily pints. The whole atmosphere is cosy and warm and described by some who have been to the inn for a meal as 'dining in the comfort of one's own front room'. The furnishings have a lot to do with it; there are old, sturdy beams, an original fireplace and some fine antiques. The decor is a pleasing mixture of magenta and gold which adds to the feel of warmth.

Diane has an excellent chef who not only cooks like a dream but has been known to serenade diners as well! In fact he is known as 'the singing chef'! He has a deft touch and both flair and imagination in the cooking and presenting of his dishes. His Chicken Supreme is absolutely delicious. It is breast of chicken stuffed with asparagus and cheese and served with a light white wine sauce. Tender sauteed fillet steak in mushroom, stilton and a cream sauce is another favourite. For the very hungry there are 32oz steaks. Enormous but tender and succulent. Every day there are Daily Specials which might be Venison casserole in season or Barnsley Lamb Chop with a light Rosemary Gravy. Whatever you choose it will be tasty. You can eat either in the bar or the restaurant.

For those who like the idea of staying a night or two in this part of Devon which is ideally situated for the North Devon Coast, Exmoor, many Stately homes and gardens, Diane has two pretty ensuite guest bedrooms with pine furniture, television and a hostess tray. The inn has attractive gardens which are just the place to enjoy a drink or a meal on a warm day.

USEFUL INFORMATION

OPEN; All year 12-3pm & 6.30-11pm	**RESTAURANT; Imaginative food**
CHILDREN; Welcome	**BAR MEALS; Substantial. Daily Specials**
CREDIT CARDS; None taken	**VEGETARIAN; Always 1 Special a day**
LICENSED; Full On	**NO WHEELCHAIR ACCESS.**
ACCOMMODATION; 2 ensuite rooms	**GARDEN;Yes. Eating & drinking in summer**
PETS; On leads. Not in restaurant	**RATES:- from £17.50 pppn B&B.**

HIGHER WESTERN RESTAURANT
Oakford, Tiverton,
Devon EX16 9JE

Tel: 01398 341210

It is unusual to find such an interesting restaurant situated on a main route. Higher Western is a charming, old world, licensed restaurant situated on the Taunton/Barnstaple Holiday Route B3227, one and a half miles west of Oakford. It is an area of outstanding beauty and a relaxing base for touring Exmoor and the North Devon coast. Owned by Colin and Christine Cook, the restaurant has achieved a well deserved reputation for excellent food, cooked to order, specialising in imaginative menus using local and their own produce, complemented by a carefully chosen wine list, mainly European with the addition of some delicious country wines. The restaurant seats 22 and one can eat in the cosy bar and lounge as well. The simple, inexpensive bar snacks and childrens meals make the Higher Western an ideal stopping place for families. In the restaurant the meals are equally sensibly priced and very generous in portions. You will always find two roasts and fish on the lunchtime menu. The home-made sweets are a very popular feature of the menu. Above all it is the friendly welcoming atmosphere that Colin and Christine have created that makes this a pleasureable place to stop.

Higher Western is an 300 year old farmhouse and still has many of its original features including oak beams, bread ovens and fireplaces. It is comfortably furnished and beautifully warm in winter when the fires burn cheerfully in the grate. Not the place to come for anyone without a car, Higher Western is not really close to anywhere in particular but very central for all of Devon and the Somerset coast as well as both Exmoor and Dartmoor. It is surrounded by open countryside with views of Exmoor from the rear and the garden. The farm to which it belonged is still working.

For those who would like to use Higher Western as a base for exploring, there are two double and one twin guest room and all are ensuite. All three bedrooms have television and a beverage tray whilst one double at the back has an amazing view of Exmoor including Dunkery Beacon which is about 20 miles away. Higher Western is welcoming, is unpretentious and more than worth a visit.

USEFUL INFORMATION

OPEN; All year. Rest: 11.45-2pm. 6.30-9pm   **RESTAURANT; Good, wholesome fare**
Closed Monday Lunch. Booking advisable   **BAR FOOD; Good value. Wide range**
CHILDREN; Welcome   **VEGETARIAN; Always a choice**
CREDIT CARDS; Visa/Mastercard   **WHEELCHAIR ACCESS No**
LICENSED; Restaurant   **GARDEN; Yes. Wonderful views**
PETS; Dogs only   **ACCOMMODATION;2dbl.1tw ensuite**
RATES:- £15 pppn. Children £3.50 per night.   **ALL Year.**
Special Low Season Breaks:- £12.50. Per night for stays of three nights or more..

ALLER BARTON FARM,
Cullompton, Devon EX15 1QQ

Tel: 01884 32275
Fax: 01884 35837

ETB Two Crowns Commended.

Just one mile from Junction 28 of the M5, Aller Barton is a working farm of some 250 acres on which you will find both Sally Cooke and her husband working. She is a very busy lady but always finds time to make sure her guests are happy and contented when they are staying at the farm. It is a quiet and peaceful place; ideal for those who want a restful time in which to recharge their batteries from the stress of modern day living. It is set in the beautiful countryside of Mid-Devon and makes a great base for those wanting to enjoy the glory of Devon. Nothing is too far away! If your preference is for the coast you will find the beaches of Exmouth, Sidmouth, Seaton, Beer and Budleigh Salterton within striking distance or a little further away the spectacular North Devon coast. Cullompton is virtually half way between the cathedral city of Exeter, steeped in history and going the other way is Taunton, the county town of Somerset and host to Somerset Cricket Team. From Aller Barton golf and fishing are closeby, there is some excellent walking country and it all makes for a great holiday.

The two guest bedrooms at Aller Barton are both ensuite and the double room can be made into a family room by adding a bed - there is plenty of room. If you would like to have television in your room it is available, there is a clock radio in both rooms and a well supplied beverage tray. If you are a smoker you are asked to restrict your smoking to the sitting/ dining room only - the latter not at meal times obviously. Having had a night's sleep disturbed only by the silence of the countryside you will come down to breakfast in the spacious dining/sitting room with its traditional oak furniture, and find that you can choose various variations on the full English breakfast. For example scrambled egg rather than fried if you wish. Everything is freshly prepared to your order. The evening meal, which is optional, is true farmhouse cooking in which Sally uses lots of local and farm produce. The large, well maintained garden is there for you to enjoy. If you are energetic you might like to make use of the tennis court. In an outside stable there is also a Games Room with a Pool table.

USEFUL INFORMATION

OPEN; All year

CHILDREN; Welcome

CREDIT CARDS; None taken

LICENSED; No

ACCOMMODATION; 1dbl. 1tw both ensuite
Can be added to dbl for a child

DINING ROOM; Good farmhouse fare

VEGETARIAN; Upon request

DISABLED ACCESS; Not suitable

GARDEN; Large. Tennis Court. Stable
Games room with snooker.

RATES:- High season £17 pppn. Low season £16 pppn.

Children :- Under 12 High Season £12. Low Season £11.

Children :- Under 6 High Season £8.50 Low Season £8.

THE OTTER INN,
Weston, Nr Honiton,
Devon EX14 0NZ

Tel/Fax 01404 42594

Pretty hamlets abound in Devon but Weston, near Honiton must surely be one of the prettiest. It is a sleepy place, nothing seems to be so important that it must be done in a rush and this gives one a great sense of tranquillity. This relaxed feeling is enhanced by a visit to the 14th century Otter Inn, which is at the heart of the hamlet. Over the centuries it has been altered but it has never lost its old world charm nor the features which make the interior so special. There is an inglenook with a spit which is used on Thursday evenings for roasts - giving the meat a particularly delicious flavour. An old bread oven is always a conversation piece and one part of the bar has bookshelves and is known as 'The Library'. Whatever table you sit at has a name that comes from its situation in the bar; it could be pulpit, mirror or big table. The whole atmosphere of the Otter Inn, in the capable hands of Mrs Wilkinson, is everything one could wish a traditional inn to be. Fine antiques, old irons and all sorts of interesting bric a brac add to the character of the inn. The Otter even has a resident ghost, 'Humphrey' who appears near the fire and stands near a pillar - obviously enjoying the company!

Whilst there is no specific restaurant or dining area, one can eat throughout the bar informally and in total comfort. The inn has four chefs led by the head chef, John Allison, who has been at the Otter for a number of years and is largely responsible for the very good reputation the inn has for its food. He is an imaginative cook and constantly creates new dishes which appear regularly on the extensive menu.Sea Bass cooked in a white wine and prawn sauce, Roast Duckling, Peking Pancakes and 'Mussels Fiji' - mussels steamed in orange, ginger, saffron and cream - are just a few of the dishes available.

The Otter gets its trade from the locals but mainly from the vast number of people who live in the Honiton area and have discovered its charm and good food and in the summer make good use of its 2 acres of garden on the banks of the River Otter. Certainly a place that should not be missed.

USEFUL INFORMATION

OPEN; All year 11-3pm & 6-11pm Sun: 12-3pm &7-11pm

CHILDREN; Welcome	**BAR FOOD; A superb range of dishes**
CREDIT CARDS; All major cards taken	**Plus a variety of snacks**
LICENSED; Full On	**VEGETARIAN; Always 3-4 choices**
PETS; Yes, on leads	**DISABLED ACCESS; Yes + toilets**
GARDEN; 2 acres on River Otter	

THE RED LION
Rookery Hill,
Oakford, Devon
EX16 9ES

Tel/Fax: 01398 351219

Oakford is a charming village situated in a delightful and often undiscovered part of Devon, four miles from Dulverton and 2 miles west of Bampton. It is surrounded by the very best of rural Devon countryside with picturesque scenery, rolling hills and peaceful lanes making it an ideal spot for a holiday especially when one can stay in The Red Lion which has been a Coaching Inn since the early 17th century and is known for its warmth and charm to its many regular visitors. It is close to the River Exe and the Bellbrook Fishery. Graham Kinson, the genial landlord of The Red Lion will gladly arrange fly fishing, shooting and riding on Exmoor if you wish. For those with sporting instincts what could be better than a day out enjoying your own particular liking and returning to The Red Lion for an excellent dinner, conversation about the day's sport and in the certain knowledge that you will have a restful nights sleep and come down to a delicious breakfast in the morning ready for the next day's fun.

The Red Lion has four comfortable, ensuite guest rooms, two doubles and two twin bedded and each well appointed with televisions. There is only one bar in the Red Lion which makes for a companionab!e atmosphere. On cooler days the large inglenook fireplace is filled with logs and sends out a splendid warmth. There is an intimate dining room seating 20-24 people and here you can eat good, traditional fare, much of it cooked using local produce especially local fish. When you are dining and enjoying wine from a small but well chosen list or sampling one of the 3 Real Ales, you may well think about the days when The Red Lion was a coaching inn catering for travellers to the towns of Barnstaple and South Molton. They would have pulled in here looking forward to the hospitality and the stabling provided for the horses. Those days may have gone but the hospitality still remains making this one of the nicest hostelries in the area.

USEFUL INFORMATION

OPEN; All year. Mon-Fri 5.30-11pm Sat/Sun usually all day
CHILDREN; Welcome
CREDIT CARDS; None taken
LICENSED; Full On
ACCOMMODATION; 2dbl 2tw all ensuite
PETS; By arrangement
RATES:- High Season £18.50. pppn. Low Season £ 15. pppn.
Special breaks available:- Apply for details.

DINING ROOM; Good traditional fare
BAR FOOD; Good range, value for money
VEGETARIAN; Always a choice
DISABLED ACCESS; Yes. Ground floor toilet but no special facilities
GARDEN; Yes. Chairs & tables Pergola opposite the pub

THE TUMBLING WEIR
HOTEL & RESTAURANT
Ottery St Mary,
Devon EX11 1AQ

Tel/Fax: 01404 812752

AA/RAC Two Stars.
ETB.Four Crowns Commended.

Jane and Barry Young have made the 17th century thatched Tumbling Weir Hotel somewhere that one really ought to visit. They are charming people and together with their very able staff they have created one of the nicest small hotels in Devon with an equally good restaurant which has a great reputation locally. Its situation is perfect for those who love exploring different places. Ottery St Mary lies in the valley of the River Otter, 12 miles from the Cathedral City of Exeter, with its many attractions, and 6 miles from the coastal resort of Sidmouth, with its cliff walks and sea views. Golfers will enjoy Nigel Mansell's splendid Golf and Country Club at Woodbury Common 3 miles away with its Championship Course. There are also Courses at Sidmouth, Honiton, Exeter and Budleigh Salterton. The Devenish Pitt Stable at nearby Farway offers riding for the whole family and Ottery is proud of its recently opened Bowling Green. The Spa also encourages you to enjoy a game of croquet in the Hotel's garden.

The 12 ensuite bedrooms have everything you require for comfort including Colour TV, Trouser Press, Hair dryer, Direct dial telephones and a generously supplied beverage tray. After a good nights sleep you come down to breakfast in the pretty restaurant with its antiques and pale pink decor. The breakfast menu is delicious and will certainly set you up for the day. Dinner is a relaxed affair with French and English Cuisine. Fresh fish and crab are a speciality of the house. As much local produce is used as possible. The Tumbling Weir is open for lunches with a menu that changes daily. During the day Bar snacks are also available. Open to non-residents, many people have discovered what a great place The Tumbling Weir is for conferences, small meetings, private functions and especially wedding receptions for up to 100 persons. Nothing is too much trouble for the Youngs and their staff and they succeed in making every event a very special occasion.

USEFUL INFORMATION

OPEN; All year except Christmas.
CHILDREN; Welcome
CREDIT CARDS;.All major cards
LICENSED; Yes
ACCOMMODATION;12 ensuite rooms
PETS; Yes. 2.50per night
RATES:-Double £29.25 pppn.B&B. Single £38.75 pppn B&B.
Speical Rates:- Low season 2 nights for the price of one, other offers details on request.

**RESTAURANT; Delicious home-
cooked fare. Open to non-residents**
BAR FOOD; Small menu
VEGETARIAN; Upon request
GARDEN; Yes. Croquet

THE KINGS ARMS INN
At Stockland,
Nr Honiton,
Devon
EX 14 9BS

Tel: 01404 881361
Fax: 01404 881732
E_Mail: kings.arms
   @virgin.net.com
Egon Ronay Recommended.

The focal point of the village of Stockland is the thatched 17th century Kings Arms Inn, an establishment that has a reputation for hospitality and good food way beyond the village.Owned and run by Heinz Kiefer, Paul Diviani and John O'Leary it is one of the most attractive hostelries for miles around. It has charm, atmosphere and everything that one wants from an inn. When you know that in the past it housed the evil Judge Jeffrys, known as 'the hanging judge' it is no wonder that it is supposedly haunted. There have been sightings of a lady in a long dress, over the years; perhaps a widow of one of Judge Jeffrys hapless victims. The whole of the inn has lots of interesting nooks and crannies including the large inglenook fireplace in the dining room complete with a Bread Oven.

The Kings Arms is always lively and has almost a cosmopolitan clientele who come for several reasons, sometimes to stay in the three, ensuite, prettily decorated bedrooms complete with television and hostess trays. Sometimes merely to enjoy the fun and chatter in the busy bars but more often than not to dine in the restaurant from an a la carte menu designed by Heinz Keifer who is an accomplished and imaginative chef with a lot of experience.The wide ranging menu may well offer you a Mediterranean-style Fish Soup followed by Supreme of Chicken Jerez and then a delectable sweet such as a Baked Alaska or maybe a choice from the excellent Cheese Board which has an emphasis on West Country cheeses. Whatever you choose it will be delicious and the accompanying wine list offers both bottles and half bottles of champagne and bottles of wine from around the world. Whilst Paul Diviani is to be found behind one of the bars, John O'Leary personally introduces each 'dish of the day' to his guests. The three men will tell you that the Kings Arms is not a particularly peaceful place to stay, it is just happy and full of people enjoying good wines, real ales (including Exmoor Ale and Otter Ale , both local and very popular!), good food and good conversation.

USEFUL INFORMATION

OPEN; All year 12-3pm & 6.30-11pm	**RESTAURANT; Imaginative food, well**
Sunday eve: 7-10.30pm	**presented**
CHILDREN; Farmers Bar for under 14	**BAR FOOD; Wide range, exciting food**
Dining room for under 12s	**VEGETARIAN; All diets catered for**
CREDIT CARDS; All major cards except Amex.	**DISABLED ACCESS; Yes + toilets**
LICENSED; Full On.Good wine list	**GARDEN; Yes & Patio**
ACCOMMODATION; 3 rooms en suite	**PETS;In bedrooms, gardens, Farmers Bar**

RATES:- Single occupancy £25 pppn. Double/Twin occupancy £40 per night. All Year.

THE OLD MILL GUEST HOUSE,
Shillingford, Nr Bampton,
Devon EX16 9BW

Tel: 01398 331064
Fax: 01398 331598

AA Four QQQQ Selected.

Apart from the comfort and relaxed atmosphere of The Old Mill Guest House what strikes one quite forcibly is the shining cleanliness everywhere. Diane Burnell prides herself, quite rightly, on the high standards achieved. You will find the house on the edge of the village of Shillingford set in pretty riverside gardens with ample parking .Its history is interesting and goes back a long way. The house was once an important water-powered corn mill. The situation could not be better for anyone who enjoys walking, riding and outdoor pursuits and for those who like National Trust properties and gardens.Horse riding is available from the premises. The North Devon coast is not too far distant.

The accommodation is arranged in three self-contained units each one having its own private entrance and sitting area, providing the maximum privacy. The House Suite sleeps four and has a large lounge. The Barn Suite is ideal for two or three people and also has a large lounge and the Patio Bedroom is a spacious room, ideal for a family and with its own sitting area. All the suites have television as well as a hostess tray, alarm clocks, hairdryers and a small library selection. There is a large, well furnished lounge with a log fire for pre-dinner drinks and for those who enjoy a little conversation over a night cap. Diane describes her evening menu as 'Bespoke Dinners' largely because she designs the meals around the wishes of her guests. There is a restaurant license and a selection of fine wines is available to compliment meals. Diane is a skilled cook with a great love for her task and the end result is delicious. Fresh produce and ingredients are bought in every day and everything is home-made in the Old Mill's kitchen. Diane uses the best traditional recipes and there is no one who does not rave about her desserts especially the old-fashioned puddings! Breakfast is sumptuous and both meals are served in the attractive dining room at tables laid with floral cloths at Breakfast and at Dinner with damask cloths, shining silver, sparkling glasses and Wedgwood bone china. You will leave the Old Mill feeling rested, cosseted and wanting to come back as soon as possible.

USEFUL INFORMATION

OPEN; All year
CHILDREN; Well behaved over 5years
CREDIT CARDS; Visa/Master/Delta/
Electron/Euro/JCB/Switch
ACCOMMODATION; 3 s/c suites
RATES:- All Year £28 -£42 pppn B&B.

DINING ROOM;Wonderful 'Bespoke'dinners
VEGETARIAN; To individual needs
W/CHAIR Access, Ground floor room
GARDEN; Yes, riverside
PETS; No SMOKING No.

LITTLE HOLWELL
Collipriest,
Tiverton,
Devon
EX16 4PT

Tel/Fax: 01884 257590

Tourist Board Approved.

Ruth Hill-King is a lady who just loves entertaining and for this reason she has opened her pretty home, some of which is 13th century and the later part 16th century, to visitors and takes especial pride in the way in which they are cared for.Little Holwell has all sorts of interesting features including a spiral staircase, fine oak beams and an inglenook. In the hallway there is wood panelling added about the 16th century. It all helps to make this house so attractive together with the soft decor and the beautiful drapes.The furniture compliments the decor and gleams with the patina of age. There are 3 guest rooms two of which are ensuite and the other shares a bathroom. Each room has comfortable beds, clock radios, hairdryers and a tea/coffee making facility. Breakfast is a sumptuous meal cooked by your hostess. Little Holwell is a strictly non-smoking house.

You will find the little hamlet of Collipriest one and a half miles south of Tiverton amid rolling hills and wooded landscape, in a charming rural position. Tiverton itself has a famous castle and a wonderful church as well as an interesting museum.

USEFUL INFORMATION

OPEN; All year except Christmas   **DINING ROOM; Breakfast only,**
CHILDREN; Welcome   **VEGETARIAN; Upon request**
CREDIT CARDS; Euro/Master/Visa   **DISABLED ACCESS; No facilities**
LICENSED; No   **GARDEN; Yes with garden furniture**
PETS; No
RATES:- £16 to £20 pppn. All Year. (Dinner by arrangement)

HORNHILL,
Exeter Hill,
Tiverton,
Devon
EX16 4PL

Tel/Fax: 01884 253352

This is a nice house which one hundred years ago was a coaching inn, providing hospitality for weary travellers. The house was built in the late 18th century and has had various additions and changes made all of which have enhanced rather than detracted from this comfortable family home. It stands in 75 acres of grassland and overlooks the lovely Exe Valley creating a wonderfully tranquil feeling in anyone who stays at Hornhill.

Barbara Pugsley owns and runs Hornhill in which she has three guest rooms, one double ensuite, one double with a fourposter bed and a private bathroom and one twin-bedded room with a private bathroom. They are all attractively furnished and have television as well as a well supplied hostess tray.. In the morning after a restful night you come down to breakfast in the dining room where you will be served a delicious, freshly cooked breakfast. It is a meal that is so good it will set you up for the day no matter what your plans are.

USEFUL INFORMATION

OPEN; All year	**DINING ROOM; First class breakfast**
CHILDREN; Over 14 years	**VEGETARIAN; Upon request**
CREDIT CARDS:None taken	**DISABLED ACCESS; No special facilities**
LICENSED; No	**GARDEN; Yes**
ACCOMMODATION; 3 ensuite rooms	**PETS; By arrangement. Sleep in car**

RATES £19.50 pppn throught the year - £2 supplement for single occupancy

AYLESBEARE INN
Aylesbeare,
Nr Exeter
Devon
EX5 2BX

Tel: 01395 232524

Garry Pell and Vanessa Arnold have not been here long but have joined together to make the Aylesbeare Inn a traditional village pub with its own skittles, darts, pool and euchre teams as well as good ale and good food. The latter is all important but they stress that they do not want the Aylesbeare to be known as merely a restaurant. It is a fine old pub, some 400 years old which was known until quite recently as the Blue Anchor. Inside it is furnished in a comfortable fashion and you will see some fascinating documents in the Lounge Bar which tell of its smuggling past. The welcome you will get is second to none whether it is from the locals who keep the bar lively, or from Vanessa and Garry.

You can eat either in the restaurant or in the bar - children under 14 are not allowed in the bar. The food is essentially good pub grub with lots of traditional dishes. The Dinner Menu has 8 starters and a main choice of fish and grills and a choice of freshly made desserts or cheese and biscuits. The Bar Menu offers a choice of Basket meals, a great home-made steak and kidney pie, Steaks, an all day Breakfast and lots of other good things as well as Ploughmans and freshly cut sandwiches.

USEFUL INFORMATION

OPEN; All Day.	**RESTAURANT; Good traditional fare**
CHILDREN;Not in bar under 14	**BAR MEALS; Wide range. Daily Specials**
	Restaurant has Childrens Licence
CREDIT CARDS; None taken	**VEGETARIAN; Catered for**
LICENSED; Full & Supper licence	**DISABLED ACCESS; Yes**
PETS; Welcome	**GARDEN; Yes. BBQ Swings. Rabbits**

LIVERMORE FARM,
Aylesbeare,
Exeter,
Devon
EX5 2DH

Tel: 01395 232351

In a wonderfully quiet and serene setting just on the edge of the village of Aylesbeare, Livermore Farm makes a perfect base for a holiday in this part of Devon. Here you are within minutes of the centre of the cathedral city of Exeter and not far from several good beaches on one side and the awesome majesty of Dartmoor on the other. Nigel Mansell's championship golf course is just two miles away at Woodbury Common and there are some excellent walks in the area. The views are quite outstanding.

Livermore Farm goes back many years, in fact parts date back to the 15th century and it has that intangible atmosphere of contentment that comes with age and when a house has been loved. There are fine old beams, an inglenook fireplace complete with bread oven. Ruth Turner is the owner of this nice establishment and she is a lady who is equally as interested in her guests as she is in her horses which you will find grazing happily in the fields around the farm. A trained caterer, Ruth once owned a restaurant and puts all this knowledge to good use in caring for her guests.

You will find breakfast is a memorable meal with several choices, freshly cooked to order. The three non-smoking guest bedrooms are all ensuite and have power showers, Each room has television, hair dryers, a beverage tray and full central heating. There is a residents lounge.

USEFUL INFORMATION

OPEN; All year   **DINING ROOM; Excellent breakfast only**
CHILDREN; Welcome   **VEGETARIAN; Upon request**
CREDIT CARDS; None taken   **DISABLED ACCESS; Not suitable**
ACCOMMODATION; 3 non-smoking ensuite rooms   **PETS;By arrangement**
RATES:- All Year £17. Pppn B&B.

CLAYPITTS FARM
East Hill,
Ottery St Mary,
Devon
EX11 1QD

Tel: 01404 814599

ETB TWO CROWNS.
AA QQQQ Selected.

Claypitts Farm is both a beautiful and a relaxing place in which to stay. It stands amidst 65 acres of land used for sheep and arable farming. The views over the fields and wooded hillside are delightful and tempt one to go for walks along the footpaths and country lanes, full of wild flowers.

The farm is just 3 miles outside the old town of Ottery St Mary renowned for its stunning church designed on the lines of Exeter Cathedral and dating back to 1257. Ottery is also famed for its annual Tar Barrel race when teams carry the flaming barrels from pub to pub, causing general mayhem but giving a great deal of fun to everyone. Ottery was also the home of the poet Samuel Taylor Coleridge. There are many attractive places to visit and some charming villages including Tipton St John, a mile and a quarter away, which has an excellent pub serving good food. The pretty, unspoiled seaside town of Sidmouth with its delightful Georgian and Regency architecture is only four and a half miles away.

Anthony and Jane Burrow have farmed Claypitts for the last 16 years and in that time have made a lot of friends from the many people who have stayed here. It is such a friendly house, warm, comfortable and happy. Every bedroom has its own individual character with beamed ceilings, stencilled wall decoration, good beds and central heating.. One room is ensuite, the other two share a bathroom and each room has hot drink facilities. The Guest Lounge is massive but very restful and here you have television and a video recorder. Breakfast is a sumptuous affair with everything freshly cooked. What a difference it makes to have newly laid eggs!

USEFUL INFORMATION

OPEN; Easter-end of November	**DINING ROOM; Excellent full Breakfast** Evening meal optional
CHILDREN; Over 3 years	**VEGETARIAN; Catered for**
CREDIT CARDS; None taken	**DISABLED ACCESS; No**
LICENSED; No	**PETS; No**
ACCOMMODATION;3 rooms. 1 ensuite	**GARDEN; Large, lovely views. Childrens** Play area. Wendy House. Garden furniture

RATES:- £20 pppn B&B Double en-suite. £18.50 pppn B&B Double/twin. Non.en-suite.
Special Rates:- Seasonal offers, details on request.

THE NEW INN
Sampford Courtenay
nr Okehampton
Devon

Tel 01837 82247

The New Inn is a true village pub situated in the heart of Sampford Courtenay. To add to its attraction it is both 16th century and thatched, in fact every visitors idea of an English Inn. It is even said to have a ghost called Ann! Mike and Rosemarie Spiers are the landlords and in the years they have been in situ they have established a great reputation for the atmosphere, the friendly welcome and above all the food. It is Rosemarie's cooking that has brought the food accolade both from locals and from visitors. She serves good home cooked food and produces delicious dishes using local produce as much as possible. You will find duck, trout, succulent steaks and many other tempting dishes on her mainly English menu.

Whenever you walk into the bar of the New Inn you will find contented regulars at the bar -always a sign that it is a well run pub. Their chatter, frequently on sporting matters, is always entertaining and certainly adds to the happy atmosphere. Not a pub to be missed.

USEFUL INFORMATION

OPEN; All year. 11-3pm & 6-11pm
CHILDREN; Welcome
CREDIT CARDS; None
LICENSED; Full On
GARDEN; Yes. Eating & Drinking in summer

RESTAURANT; Not Applicable
BAR FOOD; Recommended, Home cooked
VEGETARIAN; Options always available
DISABLED ACCESS; No Special Facilities
PETS; No

THE MERRY HARRIERS,
Westcott,
Nr Cullompton, Devon EX15 1SA

Tel/Fax: 01392 881254

It is worth coming off the M5 to discover The Merry Harriers in the hamlet of Westcott. It takes just five minutes to reach its welcoming doors. It is a pub at which the local hunt meet, presenting a colourful, truly English scene, for the visitor to witness. However whenever you come here and whatever time of year you will always find that Charlotte Harvey, the licencee and her staff will make you feel at home and take care of your needs. It is a traditional hostelry and furnished throughout in keeping with its age. You will find Bass Real Ale and a selection of lagers and bitters as well as a small but well chosen selection of wines.
There is a small restaurant with 24 covers and nicely laid tables where the a la carte menu provides some good wholesome English fare, In the Bar there is always a wide range of snacks, sandwiches, Ploughmans and some very tasty Daily Specials. No one ever leaves The Merry Harriers hungry!

USEFUL INFORMATION

OPEN; All year 11.30-2.30pm & 6-11pm
CHILDREN; Well behaved welcome
CREDIT CARDS; Visa/Master/Switch
LICENSED; Full On
GARDEN; Yes for eating & drinking

RESTAURANT; A la Carte menu
BAR FOOD; Wide range traditional fare
VEGETARIAN; Always a choice
W/CHAIR ACCESS; entrance + toilets
PETS; No

THE WHITE HART,
Colyford, Devon

Tel:01297 552358

You will find this 300 year old inn at the end of Colyford, on the main road and on the route of the famous Seaton tramway. It is an old flint building which might once have been a farmhouse and has a warm, comfortable air about it which welcomes locals and visitors with equal pleasure. It is full of nooks and crannies and it might well be that the bar once formed part of an old Inglenook. Craig and Irene Sullivan are the landlords and their genuine liking for people, means that visiting here will be memorable both for its hospitality and its food.

The 'Caruso' Restaurant is fascinating. It only has 12-14 covers and has a delightful intimacy in which to enjoy the delicious food accompanied by wine from an extensive and well chosen list from around the world with the main interest on Italian wines. The restaurant lives up to its name! There are pictures everywhere of famous old singers - all of them signed, also a fine old wind-up gramophone, in the Bar you will find the tables that were once old treadle Singer sewing machines. Theme evenings are a popular monthly feature of The White Hart. It might be Burns Night with a piper, an Australian or Italian night - with the appropriate food. On Sundays there is always live music, anything from Jazz to Irish Folk music. The Garden attracts people in fine weather and you will frequently see the game of Boules being played. The White Hart should definitely be visited.

USEFUL INFORMATION

OPEN; 11-3pm & 6.30-11pm   **RESTAURANT; cordon bleu cooking**
CHILDREN; Welcome   **BAR MEALS; Wide range**
CREDIT CARDS; Visa/Master/Euro/Delta   **VEGETARIAN; 3 choices daily**
LICENSED; Full On   **DISABLED ACCESS; Yes + toilets**
GARDEN; Yes   **PETS; Yes, on lead**

THELBRIDGE CROSS INN,
Thelbridge,
Tiverton,
Mid Devon
EX174SQ

Tel/Fax: 01884 860316

ETB Three Crowns
Highly Commended.

One of the most interesting inns in Mid-Devon, Thelbridge Cross Inn is to be found just 2 miles west of Witheridge on the B3042. It is charming and full of character. From the front of the inn there are views across to Dartmoor, while from the rear, there are views across to Exmoor. Within half a mile you can join the Two Moors' Way - ideal for a country walk. Fishing, horse-riding and golf can be arranged locally by Bill Ball who plays there and obtain cheap fees for guests.

Bill and Ria Ball are the owners. Two people who are gregarious and enjoy the cheerful banter that goes on across the bar with its beamed ceiling and blazing log fires in cooler weather. The original Lorna Doone stage coach calls at the inn from time to time, bringing up to 15 passengers to enjoy Ria's wonderful Sunday Lunch. This is a lady who is a talented cook and who, with her very able staff, produces some superb home-cooked meals. So popular are the meals at Thelbridge Cross Inn that it is advisable to book. Good value Bar food is available every day. The inn has eight delightful ensuite rooms which are all individually furnished and have television, direct dial telephones, a hostess tray and a trouser press is available on each floor.

USEFUL INFORMATION

OPEN; 11.30-3pm & 6.30-11pm
CREDIT CARDS; All major cards
LICENSED; Full On
ACCOMMODATION; 8 ensuite rooms
DISABLED ACCESS; Yes. 3 ground floor rooms
GARDEN; Yes for drinks & food in summer PETS; No
RATES:- Single Occupancy Dble.Room. £35 pn.B&B. £25. pppn B&B Double.
Special Golfing 'Packages' :- Details on application.

RESTAURANT; English & Continental
Superbly cooked and presented.
BAR FOOD; Good value Pub Grub
VEGETARIAN; Fresh dishes daily

THE ROSE AND CROWN
Rose and Crown Hill,
Sandford, Devon EX17 4NH

Tel: 01363 772056

The Rose and Crown is a village pub which has the advantage of being close enough to one or two towns making it a popular watering hole for all sorts of people. The bar almost always has a sprinkling of local people who know that Keven and Krissie Symons who own the pub keep some of the best ale for miles around. Keven is especially proud of the way in which he deals with many of the prizewinning real ales in stock. Keven produces good home cooking, many items of which are made on the premises. He lived in Canada for ten years and that is where he met his wife. They are both keen collectors. Keven has a passion for beer cans and bottles from around the world whilst Krissie collects tins, sewing machines and country memorabilia - it is all in evidence around the pub. Krissie is also excellent at organising special events which are fun and attract a lot of people to the pub. Probably the friendliness of the Rose and Crown is what makes it so pleasant. It is the sort of place where a woman on her own would feel comfortable. There is a small restaurant and a function room that is licensed for entertainment. You can play skittles in the Skittle Alley and enjoy a Barbeque in the Garden in good weather.

USEFUL INFORMATION

OPEN; All year 12-2pm 7-11pm every day   RESTAURANT; Good traditional fare
Friday open for 'Fish Friday' @5pm. Sunday 12 - 3pm. 7 -10.30 p.m.
CHILDREN; Welcome   BAR FOOD; Wide range. Good value
CREDIT CARDS; None taken   VEGETARIAN; Always a choice
LICENSED; Full On. Supper Licence   DISABLED ACCESS; Yes. Toilets
PETS; Yes. On lead. Public Bar only   GARDEN; Yes. Barbeque. Skittle Alley

STAY FREE

The following superb venues are happy to offer **STAY FREE** accommodation, subject to availability, please telephone prior to arrival. You will be requested to pay for breakfast, lunch and dinner at their normal prices.

St Mellion Golf & Country Club
St Mellion, Cornwall, PL2 65D
Tel: 01579 351351 Fax: 01579 350357

The Watermans Arms
Bow Bridge, Ashprington, Devon, TQ9 7EG
Tel: 01803 732214 Fax: 01803 732214

Danson House
Marsh Green, Exeter, Devon, EX5 2ES
Tel/Fax: 01404 823260

The Old Rectory
St Keyne, Liskeard, Cornwall, PL14 4RL
Tel/Fax: 01579 342617

The Ship Inn
Lerryn, Lostwithiel, Cornwall, PL22 0PT
Tel: 01208 872374

The Ship Inn
Portloe, Truro, Cornwall, TR2 5RA
Tel: 01872 501356

The Durrant House
HotelHeywood Road, Northan, Bideford, N.Devon EX39 3QB
Tel: 01237 472361

INDEX

Georgham	437	Lynton	440
Gidleigh	188	Manaton	184
Gittisham	479	Marazion	346
Golant	298	Malborough	128
Goonhaven	383	Marldon	77
Gorran Haven	301	Mary Tavy	194
Great Torrington	429	Meavy	250
Gweek	343	Millendreath	263
Hallsands	121	Milton Abbot	257
Halwell	112	Modbury	130
Harberton	112	Morchard Bishop	470
Harbertonford	112	Moretonhampstead	186
Hartland Quay	433	Morewellam	257
Hatherliegh	470	Morewenstow	393
Hayle	353	Morthoe	438
Helston	344	Mothecombe	132
Hennock	185	Mousehole	349
Holcumbe Rogus	470	Mullion	245
Holne	179	Nanpean	300
Holsworthy	428	Newlyn	349
Honiton	478	Newquay	349
Hope Cove	128	Newton Abbot	78
Horrabridge	253	Newton Ferrers	133
Ilfracombe	438	Newton St Cyres	473
Illogan	253	North Bovey	186
Ilsington	183	North Brentor	194
Indian Queens	301	North Petherwin	291
Ipplepen	114	Northam	431
Ivybridge	133	Noss Mayo	133
Kilkhampton	393	Okehampton	190
Kingkskerswell	78	Otterton	31
Kingsbridge	123	Ottery St Mary	480
Kingsland	263	Padstow	386
Kingsteignton	80	Paignton	71
Kingston	132	Payhembury	479
Lamorna	350	Pendeen	351
Landkey	437	Penwith	338
Lands End	350	Penzance	346
Landscove	114	Perranporth	383
Lapford	472	Peter Tavy	194
Launceston	290	Plymouth	241
Lewtrenchard	193	Plympton	249
Little Hempston	114	Plympton St Mary	249
Little Torrington	429	Plympton St Maurice	249
Liverton	183	Polkerris	296
Loddiswell	125	Polruan	296
Looe	263	Polzeath	388
Lostwithiel	296	Port Isaac	389
Lustleigh	185	Porthleven	346
Lyme Regis	24	Portwrinkle	263
Lympstone	36	Postbridge	196
Lynmouth	440	Poundsgate	180

Praa Sands	195	Stoke Gabriel	116
Princetown	195	Stokeinteignhead	87
Redruth	353	Stokenham	121
Ringmore	131	Stratton	392
Rock	388	Strete	120
Ruan Minor	245	Tavistock	253
Salcombe	126	Teignmouth	84
Salcombe Regis	29	Thurlstone	129
Saltash	259	Tintagel	390
Sampford Peverall	477	Tiverton	473
Saunton Sands	438	Topsham	36
Seaton	263	Torbryan	114
Shaldon	86	Torcross	120
Shaugh Prior	250	Torpoint	260
Sheeps Tor	250	Torquay	64
Sidbury	29	Totnes	108
Sidmouth	29	Tredinnick	358
Slapton	120	Tregonissey	299
Sourton	192	Trelowarren	345
South Brent	135	Tresco	348
South Molton	441	Truro	302
South Zeal	187	Tuckenhay	116
Sparkwell	249	Uffculme	477
Spreyton	473	Ugborough	134
St Agnes	348	Wadebridge	385
St Annes Chapel	259	Walkhampton	250
St Austell	299	Wembury	133
St Columb Major	384	West Charleton	121
St Day	355	Westward Ho!	432
St Dennis	300	Widecombe in the Moor	181
St Enodoc	388	Winkleigh	471
St Gennys	392	Woolacombe	438
St Germans	261	Woolfardsisworthy West	434
St Issey	386	Yealmpton	132
St Ives	351	Yelverton	251
St Just in Penwith	351	Zennor	351
St Just in Roseland	303		
St Kew	389		
St Marys	348		
St Mawes	303		
St Michaels Mount	346		
St Stephens	260		
St Tudy	386		
St. Agnes	348		
St. Martins	348		
Starcross	120		
Staverton	114		
Stenalees	300		
Sticklepath	187		
Stockleigh Pomeroy	470		
Stoke Climsland	292		
Stoke Fleming	119		

READERS COMMENTS

Please use this page to tell us about venues and PLACES OF INTEREST that have appealed to you especially.

We will pass on your approval where it is merited and equally report back to the venue any complaints. We hope the latter will be few and far between.

Please post to :
Kingsley Media Ltd, Freepost PY2100,
The Hoe, Plymouth, PL1 3BR

.... and expect to receive a book as a token of our appreciation!

Name of Establishment:

Address:

Comments

Your Name (Block Caps Please)

Address

READERS COMMENTS

Please use this page to tell us about venues and PLACES OF INTEREST that have appealed to you especially.

We will pass on your approval where it is merited and equally report back to the venue any complaints. We hope the latter will be few and far between.

Please post to :
Kingsley Media Ltd, Freepost PY2100,
The Hoe, Plymouth, PL1 3BR

.... and expect to receive a book as a token of our appreciation!

Name of Establishment:

Address:

Comments

Your Name (Block Caps Please)

Address

READERS COMMENTS

Please use this page to tell us about venues and PLACES OF INTEREST
that have appealed to you especially.

We will pass on your approval where it is merited and equally report back to the
venue any complaints. We hope the latter will be few and far between.

Please post to :
Kingsley Media Ltd, Freepost PY2100,
The Hoe, Plymouth, PL1 3BR

.... and expect to receive a book as a token of our appreciation!

Name of Establishment:

Address:

Comments

Your Name (Block Caps Please)

Address

KING CARD JOINING FORM

TITLE... INITIALS............................

SURNAME...

SEX   M.......................   F.......................

NATIONALITY..

AGE GROUP   18 - 30................... 31 - 49................... 50+...................

ADDRESS...

TOWN..

COUNTY..

POSTCODE...

HOW MANY HOLIDAYS DO YOU TAKE A YEAR...............................

HOW MANY OF THESE IN THE UK?...................... EUROPE...................

OTHER...

HOW MANY OF THESE ARE :

SHORT BREAKS? .... W / ENDS ....

PLEASE STATE YOUR INTERESTS:

i.e. Fishing, Golf, Antiques etc...

DO YOU NORMALLY BOOK IN ADVANCE?...

WHICH OF THESE DO YOU NORMALLY STAY IN?:

HOTEL.......................... INNS.......................... COUNTRY HOUSE...........

OTHER...

HOW DO YOU SETTLE YOUR ACCOUNT?

CREDIT CARD - CHEQUE - CASH

HOW OFTEN DO YOU EAT OUT?..

WHERE DID YOU BUY THIS BOOK?...

ARE YOU CONNECTED TO THE INTERNET?

PLEASE STATE - WEB SITE / EMAIL ADDRESS:

....

SIGNATURE...

DATE...

Please send this form to :-
Kingsley Media Ltd, Freepost PY2100, The Hoe, Plymouth, PL1 3BR